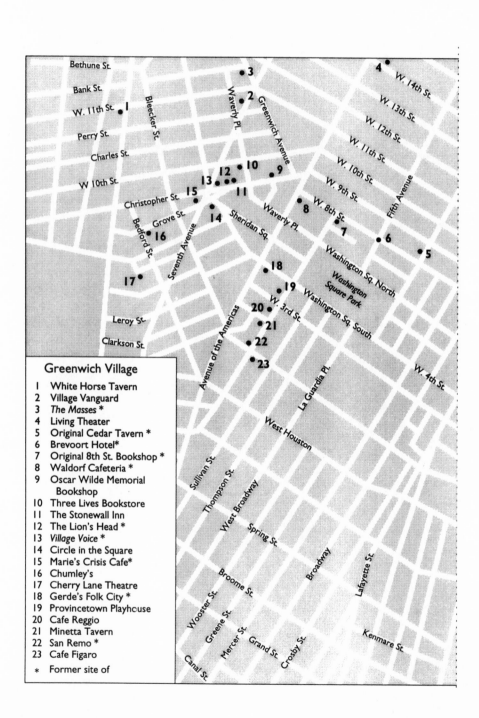

Greenwich Village

1 White Horse Tavern
2 Village Vanguard
3 *The Masses* *
4 Living Theater
5 Original Cedar Tavern *
6 Brevoort Hotel*
7 Original 8th St. Bookshop *
8 Waldorf Cafeteria *
9 Oscar Wilde Memorial
   Bookshop
10 Three Lives Bookstore
11 The Stonewall Inn
12 The Lion's Head *
13 *Village Voice* *
14 Circle in the Square
15 Marie's Crisis Cafe*
16 Chumley's
17 Cherry Lane Theatre
18 Gerde's Folk City *
19 Provincetown Playhouse
20 Cafe Reggio
21 Minetta Tavern
22 San Remo *
23 Cafe Figaro

* Former site of

Sawyers: *The Greenwich Village Reader*
3rd proof
Bill Nelson 9/19/01

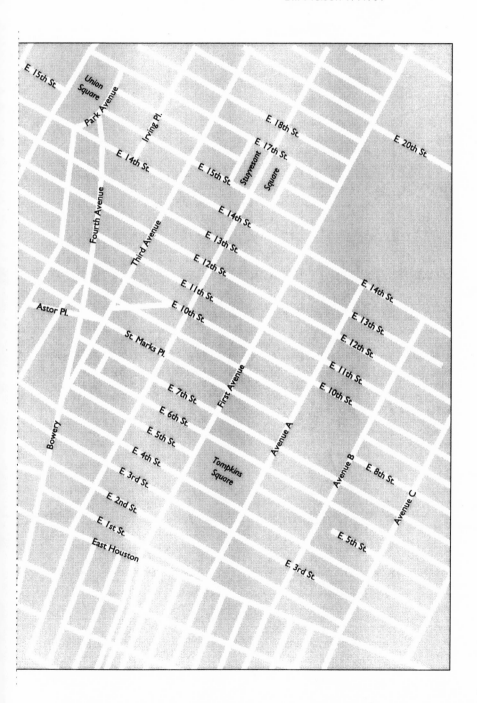

To Bill
Best,
June Skinner Sawyers

The Greenwich Village Reader

Fiction, Poetry, and Reminiscences, 1872–2002

To ELIZABETH ~
So you CAN KNOW YOUR NEIGHBORHOOD
OF THE NEXT FOUR YEARS AND SOME
OF YOUR FORMER NEIGHBORS.
                            -UNCLE SONNY
                                +
Edited by June Skinner Sawyers AUNT MAUREEN
                              -JUNE, 2017

Cooper Square Press

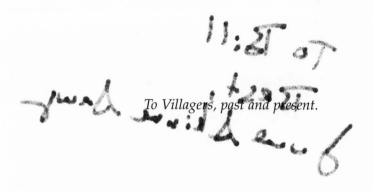

To Villagers, past and present.

Every effort has been made to seek out and obtain permissions from the copyright holders of the pieces selected for inclusion in *The Greenwich Village Reader.* Pages 723–727 constitute an extension of the copyright page.

First Cooper Square Press edition 2001

This Cooper Square Press hardcover edition of *The Greenwich Village Reader* is an original publication. It is published by arrangement with the editor.

Published by Cooper Square Press
An Imprint of the Rowman & Littlefield Publishing Group
150 Fifth Avenue, Suite 911
New York, New York 10011

Distributed by National Book Network

Library of Congress Cataloging-in-Publication Data

The Greenwich Village reader : fiction, poetry, and reminiscences, 1872–2002 / edited by June Skinner Sawyers.
    p. cm.
  Includes bibliographical references.
  ISBN 0-8154-1148-0 (alk. paper)
    1. Greenwich Village (New York, N.Y.)—Literary collections. 2. American literature—New York (State)—New York. 3. Greenwich Village (New York, N.Y.)—Biography. 4. Greenwich Village (New York, N.Y.)—History. I. Sawyers, June Skinner, 1957–

PS549.N5 G74 2001
810.8'0327471—dc21

2001034618

⊗™ The paper used in this publication meets the minimum requirements of American National Standard for Information Sciences—Permanence of Paper for Printed Library Materials, ANSI/NISO Z.39.48-1992.
Manufactured in the United States of America.

Bobby Edwards

"The Village Epic"

Way down South in Greenwich Village,
There they wear no fancy frillage,
For the ladies of the square
All wear smocks and bob their hair.
There they do not think it shocking
To wear stencils for a stocking,
That saves the laundry bills
In Washington Square.

Way down South in Greenwich Village,
Where the spinsters come for thrillage,
Where they speak of "soul relations,"
'Neath the guise of feminism,
Dodging social ostracism,
They get away with much
In Washington Square.

Bobby Edwards. "The Village Epic" from *The Little Book of Greenwich Village* by Egmont Arens (New York: Washington Square Bookshop, 1922). Public Domain.

Way down South in Greenwich Village,
Where they eat Italian swillage,
Where the fashion illustrators
Flirt with interior decorators,
There the cheap Bohemian fakirs
And the boys from Wanamaker's
Gather "atmosphere,"
In Washington Square.

Way down South in Greenwich Village,
Where the brains amount to nillage,
Where the girls are unconventional,
And the men are unintentional,
There the girls are self-supporting,
There the ladies do the courting,
The ladies buy the "eats,"
In Washington Square.

—1922

Acknowledgments

I would like to thank publisher Michael Dorr for his enthusiasm and ongoing support as well as the entire staff of Cooper Square Press, especially Michael Messina for his marketing expertise. I also wish to offer words of appreciation to my sister, Margaret Batson, for keystroking many of the selections and to researcher Megan McDowell for countless hours spent in numerous libraries.

J. S. S.

Contents

A Select Village Chronology

1600. Peter Minuit, first governor of New York, after purchasing the island of Manhattan from the Native American population, sets aside Sapokanican farm for the Dutch West India Company.

1664. The area now known as Greenwich Village is given the name of Greenwich or Grinnich by the British.

1739. First smallpox epidemic in New York turns the Village into a health resort.

1776. George Washington makes his headquarters in the Village.

1789. Potter's field established on site of what is now Washington Square.

1802. Tom Paine comes to the Village.

1807. Gov. Morris tries to "fix" the streets of the Village, but gives up.

1821. The nation's first black theater, the African Grove, opens at Mercer and Bleecker streets.

1822. Yellow fever epidemic strikes lower Manhattan, causing thousands of New Yorkers to flee to the safety of the Village.

1827. America's first black newspaper, *Freedom Journal*, is published.

1828. Washington Square parade grounds open.

1830. Stone cutters' riots near New York University.

1833. The nation's first black Roman Catholic church opens in 1833 on Sixth Avenue.

1854.   The Brevoort Hotel opens.

1855.   Charles Pfaff opens Pfaff's, a basement tavern frequented by Village bohemians, at 653 Broadway, including Walt Whitman.

1856.   The Tenth Street Studio opens, brainchild of art collector John Taylor Johnston, as a haven for artists. Among the many artists associated with the building over the years included Winslow Homer, John La Farge, Augustus Saint-Gaudens, and Alexander Calder.

1858.   The *New York Saturday Press*, reportedly America's first countercultural publication, opens.

1889.   Washington Arch, designed by Stanford White, is erected in honor of the centenary of Washington's birthday.

May 4, 1895.   Formal dedication of Washington Square Arch.

1890.   Judson Memorial Church is constructed and designed in Renaissance style by the firm of McKim, Mead, & White.

July 1907.   Gertrude Vanderbilt Whitney opens her studio at 19 MacDougal Alley (now 17½).

1911.   John Reed moves to the Village.

1911.   Triangle Shirtwaist Factory fire kills nearly 150 workers, mostly young immigrant Jewish women.

June 1913.   Headquarters of the radical publication *The Masses* moves to 91 Greenwich Avenue with Max Eastman as editor.

January 1913. Mabel Dodge inaugurates the first of her famous Wednesday evening literary gatherings, the most successful salon in American literary history.

July 1915.	Bruno Guido's Thimble Theatre opens at 10 Fifth Avenue.
July 1916.	The first Village tearoom, the Mad Hatter, opens in the basement of 150 Fourth Street.
November 3, 1916.	The Provincetown Players make their debut at 139 MacDougal Street, offering a triple bill of Eugene O'Neill's *Bound East for Cardiff* and one-acts by Floyd Dell and Louise Bryant. Only twenty-seven people attended opening night.
1916.	Charles and Albert Boni open the Washington Square Bookshop at 135 MacDougal Street.
1917.	Don Dickerman's The Pirate's Den opens at 10 Sheridan Square.
1917.	"Romany" Marie opens her first tearoom on Washington Square South.
1917.	Sinclair Lewis' *Hobohemia*, a satire of Village life, opens at the Greenwich Village Theatre.
January 1917.	Six Villagers climb to the top of Washington Square Arch to declare Greenwich Village to be the Free and Independent Republic of Washington Square.
August 1917.	The *Masses* is banned by the U.S. Post Office under the Espionage Act; the government revokes its mailing permit, which leads to its eventual demise in December of that year.
1918.	The *Masses* trials lead to hung juries; the charges are eventually dropped.
July 1919.	*The Greenwich Village Follies* staged by John Murray Anderson opens to huge success. Features the talents of Village troubadour-writer Bobby Edwards.

1919.   Prohibition takes effect.

1919.   The Liberal Club disbands.

1920.   Volstead Act passed.

1920.   Eugene O'Neill's experimental play *The Emperor Jones* opens at the Provincetown Playhouse, starring black actor Charles S. Gilpin.

1922.   *Reader's Digest* publishes its first issue from a rented basement on MacDougal Street, the future site of the Minetta Tavern.

1925.   The San Remo opens.

1926.   Chumley's opens at 86 Bedford Street by Lee Chumley.

1927.   Caffe Reggio, the first European-style coffeehouse in the Village, opens at 119 MacDougal Street.

December 14, 1929.   The Provincetown Players give their last performance.

1930.   Permanent headquarters of the New School opens on Twelfth Street. Designed by Joseph Urban in a bold International Style, it attracts some of the finest artists. Its many teachers have included Aaron Copland, Martha Graham, Bernice Abbott, Thomas Hart Benton, Claude Levi-Strauss, John Cage, and Alfred Kazin.

1930.   The Stonewall Inn opens.

November 1931.   Gertrude Vanderbilt Whitney opens the Whitney Museum, dedicated to the work of modern American artists, on Eighth Street row houses with works by Charles Demuth, Georgia O'Keeffe, Stuart Davis, and others.

1933.	*The Villager* is published.
1933.	Lee Chumley dies of a heart attack.
1934.	The Village Vanguard opens its doors.
December 1938.	Barney Josephson opens the Cafe Society, a Village supper club that is among the first clubs in the country to break the racial barrier. Among the performers he introduced to the public was a young Billie Holiday.
1952.	John Clellon Holmes' *Go*, one of the first Beat novels, is published.
1952.	Tennessee Williams' *Summer and Smoke*, starring Geraldine Page, opens at the Village's Circle in the Square theater.
May 1953.	One of the first Village artist-run coffeehouses, the Rienzi, opens at 107 MacDougal Street.
October 26, 1955.	Dan Wolf and Ed Fancher found the *Village Voice*, with financial support from Norman Mailer.
1956.	Norman Mailer withdraws from the *Village Voice*.
1957.	Jack Kerouac's *On the Road* is published.
August 1957.	Joe Gould, the quintessential Village bohemian, dies.
1958.	Jack Kerouac's *The Subterraneans* is published.
December 1958.	Caffe Cino opens, the birthplace of Off-Off Broadway.
1958.	Jack Kerouac and jazz musician David Amram participate in the first "jazz poetry reading" in New York.

1958.	New York's first "Happening" takes place at Judson Memorial Church.
1958.	The Village Gate opens.
May 3, 1960.	*The Fantasticks* premieres at the Sullivan Street Playhouse with an original cast including Jerry Orbach, Kenneth Nelson, and Rita Gardner.
March 3, 1963.	Closing of the original Cedar Tavern.
October 17, 1967.	*Hair* premieres at the Public Theater.
1967.	Joe Cino commits suicide.
1969.	Jack Kerouac dies in St. Petersburg, Florida, at the age of forty-seven.
June 28, 1969.	Stonewall Inn riots.
1970.	Three members of the militant Weather Underground accidentally blow themselves up.
1997.	Allen Ginsberg dies at the age of seventy.
1997.	William S. Burroughs dies at the age of eighty-three.
2001.	Gregory Corso dies at the age of seventy.

Introduction

"There seems to be something intangible about a genuine Bohemia. As soon as the public puts its finger on it and says 'this is the real thing,' it crumbles away."

—*Everybody's Magazine* (1905)

Greenwich Village. Few neighborhoods in the world are as littered with literary landmarks or as distinctive in everything from its charmingly chaotic streets to its unconventional residents, from bohemians and beats to punks and yuppies. So many writers, poets, and critics have lived or worked in the Village over the years that its crooked little byways and weathered brownstone buildings have become an indelible part of the American literary landscape. If it is no longer the literary capital of the United States, it still holds a permanent place in the pantheon of America's literary imagination.

Ever since its humble beginnings as a marshy terrain outside the main commercial center of New York City some 350 years ago, the Village has been located on the periphery of mainstream society. Indeed, the Village has always been different from the rest of Manhattan, a village within a village.

What exactly is Greenwich Village? Physically, that's fairly easy to answer: its boundaries run from West Fourteenth Street on the north, Broadway on the east, West Houston Street on the south, and the Hudson River on the west. Other than that, the Village defies all facile categorization, for defining the Village involves more than just identifying specific boundary lines.

In fact there have been many Villages throughout its long, complex history. But the image that sticks in most people's minds is the bohemian ideal. It is the Village of myth and imagination, of smoky coffeehouses and poetic revelry. No matter how far removed from the truth, that is the image that lingers.

Writers were not the only creative residents of the Village. Many painters and art advocates also settled here, including John Sloan, George Luks, Gertrude Vanderbilt Whitney, Robert Motherwell, and Jackson Pollock, as well as musicians Thelonious Monk, Charlie Parker, and David Amram.

In truth, though, the Village is constantly reinventing itself. Think of the various transformations the neighborhood has undergone during its singular existence. From the aristocratic Washington Square of Henry James and Edith Wharton to a working-class enclave populated by thousands of Irish, German, and Italian immigrants. Think too of the later generations of writers who came here. The pre–World War I bohemians. The post–World War II existentialists. The Beats of the 1950s. The hippies of the 1960s. The underground scene of the 1970s. The yuppies and neoconservatives of the 90s. And the Village of the present day—popular, entertaining, and, ironically, too expensive for most writers and artists to afford.

What exactly is it about this small, densely populated corner of a congested island that appeals to so many people? And why do the images linger still?

Old New York

The impressive, white-marble clad Washington Arch is the official entry into Greenwich Village. The arch that stands today replaced a temporary structure built in 1889 to commemorate the centennial of George Washington's inauguration. The noted architect Stanford White designed both the original temporary arch and its marble replacement. But there are other works, on a much less grand scale, also well worth noting. Look around and admire the Greek Revival houses, built in the 1830s, which hover around the Square, offering a soothing blend of order and harmony. Despite the illusion of stability, the Square has witnessed many changes over the years. As long ago as 1949, essayist E. B. White was lamenting the Village of old and yet he thought not all was lost:

> In Greenwich Village the light is thinning: big apartments have come in, bordering the Square, and the bars are mirrored and chromed. But there are still in the Village the lingering traces of poesy, Mexican glass, hammered brass, batik, lamps made of whisky bottles, first novels made of fresh memories—the old Village with its alleys and ratty one-room rents catering to the erratic needs of those whose hearts are young and gay.

—*Here Is New York*

The Native Americans called what is now Greenwich Village by the name of Sapokanican. Originally it was a marshy terrain that was converted into farmland by early Dutch and English settlers during the pre–Revolutionary War era. The Dutch knew it by another name—Noortwyck—until finally it developed into the little village of Greenwich, or Grin'wich, consisting of a hamlet of farms and scattered settlements located some two miles north of the center of New York: a peaceful community in the country.

In the 1780s the city of New York bought the eight-acre Washington Square Park for use as a potter's field and execution site as well as a burial ground for victims of the city's sporadic outbreaks of yellow fever and cholera. The hangman's tree stood at the northwest corner of the park.

During the summer of 1822 a particularly virulent strain of yellow fever swept New York. The inhabitants fled in a panic to the relative safety of Greenwich. Most returned after the immediate danger was over but others chose to stay. In the early years of the nineteenth century Thomas Paine, author of *Common Sense* and one of the Village's earliest literary residents, had lived there when it consisted of little more than a cluster of small wooden houses. After 1850 the community grew rapidly, however. And yet the buildings were constructed on a human scale, the glow of their warm red brick bringing a sense of intimacy to the narrow streets. And since the Village had developed before Manhattan's grid system took effect, the Village remained different from the rest of the island in both look and feel.

For most of the nineteenth century the Village was known as the American Ward. Indeed, the heyday of Old New York was during the 1840s when it was considered New York's most prestigious suburb; country living at its finest. The most elegant area of the Village was Washington Square.

Washington Square Park was dedicated in 1828. In the same year distinguished houses were built on the south side of the Square. Several years later, additional red brick row houses were erected on the north side. The opulence of the exteriors was mirrored inside as well. White marble steps would often lead to parlors boasting bronze chandeliers and Italian carved mantelpieces.

It's easy to forget that during the second half of the nineteenth century, New England served unofficially as the literary capital of America, not New York. And yet the Village in particular remained a literary presence, albeit on a smaller and subtler scale. Some of the nation's most distinguished writers were living in the Square then, including Herman Melville, who wrote *Mardi*, *Redburn*, and *White-Jacket* while living at 103 Fourth Street. Edgar Allan Poe also lived in the Village. Melville and Poe were regulars at the social evenings held at the Waverly Place house of Anne Charlotte Lynch. Some historians credit Lynch with starting the first literary salon in the United States. At the same time, the editor Evert Duyckinck hosted literary gatherings—albeit of a more academic sort—at the basement of his house on Clinton Place.

Most people though associate Washington Square with Henry James, who was born in the Village in 1843. He lived on Washington Place only six months before being taken by his parents to Europe. The family returned to New York in 1847 and young Henry spent most of his childhood years on West Fourteenth Street, where his parents entertained the literary elite of the day, including Ralph Waldo Emerson. He spent many hours at the home of his grandmother at 10 Washington Square North, which he would later recapture in his signature novel *Washington Square*. An offhead anecdote told to him by the English actress Fanny Kemble formed the basis for the battle of wits and wills that took place between the novel's protagonists, Dr. John Sloper and his daughter, Catherine.

New York's first bohemian community can probably be traced back to the 1860s when members of the city's most important literary magazine, the *Saturday Press*, congregated at Pfaff's basement tavern at 653 Broadway.

Founded in 1858 by Henry Clapp, a journalist and theater critic, the *Saturday Press* published Walt Whitman's early poetry as well as the short stories of Mark Twain and the work of William Dean Howells. More and more writers, publishers, and editors settled in the Village, attracted by the twin pleasures of cheap rents and convivial atmosphere. Twain of course would eventually become a huge celebrity, exulting in the adoring crowds that greeted him in the Village streets, as he paraded up and down Fifth Avenue in his glimmering white serge suit.

But it was Pfaff's that became the center of literary activity in the Village. The *Saturday Press* was considered America's first radical publication. Village historian Terry Miller described it as a "dim, smoke-filled cave," a gathering place of "like-minded rebels who here became America's first bohemians. It served the best coffees in town, offered rich German beers and cheeses, and had the best-stocked wine cellar." Or, in the words of Pfaff's "poet laureate" Walt Whitman:

> *the vault at Pfaffs where drinkers and laughers*
> *meet to eat and drink and carouse*
> *While on the walk immediately overhead pass the*
> *myriad feet of Broadway.*

—"The Two Vaults"

By the late nineteenth century, Italian, Irish, German, and other newly arrived immigrants began to move into the older housing stock along Bleecker and elsewhere. As the real estate values declined, more artists and writers began moving in, mostly in the western and southern sections of the Village. As further evidence of the signs of the changing times, once handsome row houses on the south side of Washington Square were subdivided into multifamily dwellings and high-rise tenements. Houses of ill repute, sweat shops, and other fly-by-night operations sprouted up, contributing to the bawdy streetlife. Artists such as George Luks and John Sloan—members of the so-called Ashcan School—depicted the changes sweeping through the Village in works like "Thompson and Bleecker Streets" (1905) and "Bleecker Street, Saturday Night" (1918).

Soon, the literary life of this new bohemian Village centered on the corner of Washington Square South and MacDougal Street.

The American Latin Quarter

"Its labyrinth of secluded courtyards, odd lanes, and low, dormered houses crumbling into disrepair led to frequent comparisons with such artistic enclaves of Paris as Montmartre, Montparnasse, and the Latin Quarter."

—*Greenwich Village: Culture and Counterculture*

The backstreets and lanes of the Village, especially around tiny Minetta Lane, had turned into a notorious slum by the turn of the century. Stephen Crane, then a young reporter hungry for a juicy story, commented on the area's moody, dimly lit streets that were surrounded by buildings of "dingy brick" and populated by menacing and unsavory characters. It all made for good ink.

This area immediately south of Washington Square—around Bleecker, Sullivan, Thompson, and MacDougal streets—was predominantly African American for most of the nineteenth century. According to Susan Edmiston and Linda D. Cirino, the first African-American newspaper, *Freedom Journal*, was published here in 1827 while the first African-American theater in the country, the African Grove, opened on Mercer Street a few years earlier, in 1821.

By the turn of the century and into the teens, the Village really consisted of two very different worlds. Coexisting within the Village proper, for example, were immigrants, working-class butchers and longshoremen, and other residents more concerned with putting a roof over their head and feeding their hungry children than pursuing lofty intellectual pursuits. They left the latter to the insatiable curiosity of the bohemian Villagers, which included a well-educated and sophisticated group of poets and writers, socialists and anarchists. The two groups lived entirely separate lives. Indeed, "ordinary" Villagers looked at these "strange Bohemians" with a mixture of suspicion and contempt. It is important to remember, though, that this vocal bohemian minority never amounted to more than a small portion of the Village's population.

Max Eastman claimed that the Village had, by this time, become "an American Bohemia or Gipsy-minded Latin Quarter." The Village of the popular imagination had now been born. Villagers always did things their own way anyway. They felt different, quite distinct from the rest of Manhattan. In January 1917, six Villagers (including painter Gertrude Dick, who referred to herself as Woe, "Because Woe is me") mounted, under the cover of darkness, the eleven winding steps to the roof of the Washington Square Arch, where they strung Chinese lanterns and balloons. They then served food and uncorked bottles of wine. Firing cap guns into the night air, they proclaimed that the Village was seceding from the Union and would now be known as the "Free and Independent Republic of Washington Square."

Notes Albert Parry, author of the seminal study of bohemia, *Garretts and Pretenders*: "The Village was a state of mind helped along by certain adverse economic conditions . . . those Bohemians were our society's marginal men and women. While waiting for the public to recognize their talents, writers, artists, dancers, actors, directors, refused to forsake their media, declined humdrum jobs and banded together in a Bohemia to make a gay virtue of their poverty."

Around 1916 or so another generation of young literary types arrived in the Village, including Hart Crane, Edmund Wilson, Matthew Josephson, and e. e. cummings. They came because the rents were still cheap, and their friends had recommended the place. New York was now the literary capital of the country and the only place for a serious writer to be.

As the new bohemians began to settle down in their new digs, they started to establish literary and artistic clubs and organizations, such as the Liberal Club. Regulars included Theodore Dreiser, Upton Sinclair, Vachel Lindsay, Lincoln Steffens, Sinclair Lewis, Sherwood Anderson, Louis Untermeyer, and Max Eastman. According to Edmiston and Cirino, the Club featured "two large parlors and a sunroom with high ceilings, fireplaces, mahogany doors and cubist and futurist art on the walls."

Little magazines flourished in the Village. *Others: An Anthology of New Verse* appeared in 1915. Edited by the imagist poet Alfred Kreymborg, it published the work of Wallace Stevens, T. S. Eliot, Maxwell Bodenheim, Marianne Moore, and William Carlos Williams, among others. Additional small magazines and journals included the *Ink Pot*, which was devoted to promoting the Village's bohemian ideals.

Probably the most important radical magazine to emerge from the Village during that time was the *Masses*. An anarchist with the unlikely name of Piet Vlag established the *Masses* in 1911. He soon left and the magazine continued with the help of its contributors, which included painter John Sloan and critic Louis Untermeyer. Through a stroke of luck, they had come into contact with Max Eastman, who then was teaching philosophy at Columbia University. They volunteered him as editor of the *Masses*. No pay was involved. Already familiar with the publication, Eastman readily accepted.

Under Eastman's helm, the *Masses* devoted its space to politics, art, literature, and dark humor. Political drawings and cartoons were specialties. It didn't take very long for the *Masses* to gain circulation, attracting the best of the New York intelligentsia. Headquartered at 91 Greenwich Avenue, the staff held fundraising costume balls at Webster Hall, which became something itself of a Village tradition. Among its contributors included John Reed, Carl Sandburg, Harry Kemp, Randolph Bourne, and William Rose Benét. Floyd Dell, another early contributor, would eventually become managing editor.

With the outbreak of World War I, the editorial content of the publication became increasingly critical of the government. Because of its antiwar stance, the authorities took action. The *Masses* shut down in 1917 when the government rescinded its mailing privileges, and since the paper's revenue derived primarily from subscriptions, the action effectively siphoned off its chief source of income. In November of that year the Department of Justice charged Eastman, Reed, and Dell on charges of conspiracy against the government as well as "interfering with enlistment." Two trials were set, in April and then in October 1918. Both resulted in hung juries.

But such controversy did not stop Eastman. He started a new magazine, called the *Liberator*. Located at 138 West Thirteenth Street, it continued to publish the *Masses* writers in addition to the work of Edna St. Vincent Millay, William Carlos Williams, e. e. cummings, John Dos Passos, and a young man with the last name of Hemingway.

Another important literary journal was the *Little Review*, founded in Chicago by a Hoosier named Margaret Anderson. In 1917 she moved the magazine from Chicago to a basement studio at 31 West Fourteenth Street. The *Little Review* was ahead of its time in many ways—it published installments of James Joyce's *Ulysses*. For this Anderson and her assistant editor—and lover—jane heap (she always spelled her name in lowercase) were convicted of obscenity and fined $100 each.

The short-lived *Seven Arts*, edited by James Oppenheim, published some of the finest writers around, including Sherwood Anderson, Eugene O'Neill, D. H. Lawrence, Robert Frost, Carl Sandburg, Amy Lowell, Stephen Vincent Benét, and John Dos Passos. Oppenheim's opposition to World War I, though, led to the withdrawal of funds by his sponsor and the magazine folded. *Bruno's Weekly* was another early Village literary magazine while the *Quill*, a Village humor magazine, was edited by the ubiquitous Bobby Edwards, a real Village character who in his spare time played the role of troubadour in Village tearooms, strumming a ukulele to his many admirers.

In the early 1920s, Kreymborg and Harold Loeb started *Broom*, which they billed as an international magazine of the arts. Loeb was also owner of the Sunrise Turn Bookshop on West Forty-fourth Street. Founded in Europe, *Broom* later moved its headquarters to

3 East Ninth Street. And yet it was the *Dial* that was considered the most important literary magazine of the 1920s. (In 1925, Marianne Moore, a longtime Village resident, became its editor). Founded in 1840 in Cambridge as an outlet for the transcendentalists, it later resurfaced under a different guise in Chicago in 1880. In 1917 it moved to New York, where it showcased the work of writers like Randolph Bourne and Van Wyck Brooks. Still another journal, the *Partisan Review*, founded in 1934, had its office slightly east of the Village although many Villagers were associated with it, such as founding editors William Phillips and Philip Rahv as well as Dwight Macdonald.

Attending literary salons continued to be an important feature of Village cultural life. Mabel Dodge ran one of the Village's most famous salons. As hostess of countless "evenings," as she referred to the gatherings, she brought together a wide cross section of the social classes. Here was a woman who not only understood the fine art of conversation, she knew how to massage it, stroke it, turning into an exquisite art form all its own. The muckraking journalist Lincoln Steffens encouraged Dodge to host these literary functions once a week. She selected the topic. Occasionally, she would invite a guest speaker.

The first literary gatherings of the Mabel Dodge salon began in January 1913. Each evening was organized around a particular theme. Topics ranged from socialism and workers rights to sexual equality to free love and the theories of Sigmund Freud. For a few years, every important writer and artist—including Jo Davidson, Carl Van Vechten, Lincoln Steffens, and Hutchins Hapgood—hankered to get an invite. Other guests included socialist Walter Lippman, Village poet Harry Kemp, Max Eastman, feminist Henrietta Rodman, Margaret Sanger, Emma Goldman, Amy Lowell, Edwin Arlington Robinson, Floyd Dell, John Sloan, Bill Haywood, and the anarchist Hippolyte Havel, among many others.

Experimental theater groups also flourished in the Village during the early years of the twentieth century. Most didn't last. One group that did make a difference consisted of John Reed, Max Eastman and his wife Ida Rauh, George Cram Cook, and Susan Glaspell.

Calling themselves the Washington Square Players, they reportedly received their name by mounting an early production in the back room of the Washington Square Bookshop on MacDougal Street.

In 1915 a brooding young man by the name of Eugene O'Neill came to the Village. He wrote seven hours a day in his cramped flat on Washington Square. In the evenings he ventured over to a shabby saloon at Sixth Avenue and Fourth Street called the Golden Swan but known popularly and perhaps more accurately as the Hell Hole. A salt of the earth type named Tom Wallace ran it. Later, O'Neill reportedly used Wallace as the model of the character Harry Hope in *The Iceman Cometh*.

Of course, the most successful experimental theater group with roots in the Village was the Provincetown Players. Founded in Provincetown, Massachusetts, during the summer of 1915, it consisted of a core of artists and intellectuals, including Washington Square Players veterans Reed, Cook, and Glaspell. So successful was their inaugural season on the Cape—they started with O'Neill's *Bound for Cardiff*—they decided to mount productions in the Village itself, in a brownstone at 139 MacDougal Street and then to a slightly bigger space at 133 MacDougal. Their mission was to produce American plays by new writers of an experimental nature. In 1920 their production of O'Neill's *The Emperor Jones* had to move to Broadway to accommodate the crowds. At that point, there was no turning back. They couldn't go back to their bohemian roots.

At the same time, though, a carnival-like atmosphere of frivolity and fun accompanied the serious business of writing. The bohemian Village was now in full thrust. Tearooms began opening up, most of them catering to the tourists who descended upon the Village in droves. The "true" Villagers avoided most of them, with a few major exceptions, such as Romany Marie's on the corner of Thompson and Washington Square South. (It later moved to 30 West Eighth Street).

Village social life in the teens centered on tearooms, and restaurants, and cafes. "Unlike the cabarets that followed in the 1920s, the tearooms were run by Villagers who identified with the bohemian way of life and the patrons they served," writes Louis Erenberg, from the young women with their bobbed hair to the young men in their slouch hats. Writers, poets, and actors discussed politics, social trends, and the arts. Often the interiors of these tearooms were quite colorful—gaily painted in a riot of hues.

The first Village tearoom, The Mad Hatter, opened in the basement of a West Fourth Street building in 1916 with an Alice in Wonderland theme. But La Boheme, which opened in 1917, was reportedly "the first tearoom to 'affect a bohemian atmosphere,'" according to Terry Miller. By 1920, the Village contained some forty-five tearooms, most of the touristy variety. Tiny tearooms, they often were hidden away in back parlors or down dank, poorly lit basements. They sported whimsical names with a mishmash of styles, from the homey to the bizarre. Playing up the Henry Murger/Trilby connection, many had names like La Boheme, the Trilby Waffle Shop, and the Garret.

Others were known for their eccentricity, such as the Crumperie on Sheridan Square. Run by Mary Alletta Crump and her elderly mother, it attracted a largely theatrical and well-heeled clientele. The younger Crump entertained her customers on the ukulele and crooned sing-alongs in an endearingly disheveled setting full of antiques and chipped teacups.

Some became successful because of the personality of the owner. Famous for its huge portions at cheap prices, Polly's was staffed by radicals and beloved by its bohemian customers. Polly Holladay, a free spirit who originally hailed from Evanston, Illinois, opened her popular restaurant in the basement of the Liberal Club in the early teens. "The most fun-loving of the Village artists, intellectuals, and political thinkers ate at Polly's before ascending the stairs for one-act plays, poetry readings, or political and cultural arguments at the Liberal Club," notes Erenberg.

By this time, though, the Village was becoming a parody of itself. Various hucksters and entrepreneurial types offered tours of bohemian haunts and hangouts. Busloads of tourists converged on the Village to gawk at "authentic" bohemians as all-too-willing Villagers dressed up in stereotypical bohemian garb: the perfunctory

artist's smock, long skirt (for women at least), and open-toed sandals. (A similar situation would arise decades later during the Beat
era when visitors scoured Village streets in search of "beatniks"). In
1917, Sinclair Lewis, a then obscure writer, satirized Village mores
and customs with his tongue-in-cheek *Hobohemia*, which started
out in the pages of the *Saturday Evening Post* before being adapted
for the stage.

Two years later *The Greenwich Village Follies* opened at the
Greenwich Village Theatre on Sheridan Square, featuring the Village troubadour Bobby Edwards. Started by John Murray Anderson, the *Follies* was a musical revue that spoofed bohemian life,
from Freud to free love—two perennial Village favorites. It was a
huge, unqualified success and, like other successful Village productions, moved uptown to attract even greater crowds. "Like
Harlem, Greenwich Village was now seen by many as a kind of
permanent carnival, an exotic entertainment center where the ordinary rules of behavior were suspended," writes Brooks McNamara
in *Greenwich Village: Counter and Counterculture*.

During the mid-20s, young professionals and members of the
middle class began returning to the Village, driving many of the
artists out. Soon it simply became too costly for them to live there.
By the 1930s most of the major literary names had left.

And yet others came, including Tennessee Williams, who
took a course in playwriting at the New School, as well as fellow
Southerners Allen Tate and Caroline Gordon. Journalist and
novelist Josephine Herbst referred to these Southerners as
the real expatriates who "reminded you of the fluctuations of
time, and coming upon Allen Tate, suddenly, as he sat in
his apartment without seeing you arrive, you seemed to be looking at a figure, enhanced by fair skin and a noble bulging forehead, that could have belonged to an exiled dauphin of France,
dreaming of the forfeits history had demanded." James Baldwin
moved down from Harlem and worked as a waiter in a restaurant called the Calypso run by a jovial West Indian woman
on Sullivan Street. Richard Wright moved to the Village with his
family in late 1945.

Post–World War II

After World War II the Village enjoyed a literary renaissance as an influx of young writers arrived. In those days the social life centered around several bars, including the San Remo, Minetta's, the Cedar Tavern, and the White Horse Tavern. During the 1950s the White Horse Tavern in particular became the favorite watering hole of the Village literary set. It was a Sunday afternoon tradition for members of the newly-founded *Village Voice*, for example, including founders Dan Wolf, Ed Fancher, and Norman Mailer, to meet there. Others came too: Hortense Calisher, William Styron, Herman Wouk, James Jones, and Dan Wakefield.

The San Remo was an Italian restaurant at the corner of Bleecker and MacDougal streets and a rather scruffy one at that, frequented by seamen, communists, socialists, potheads, and, of course, writers, that dated back to 1925. Brawls between patrons and bartenders were frequent. Regulars included James Agee, James Baldwin, Maxwell Bodenheim, Michael Harrington, and William Styron. Jack Kerouac, William S. Burroughs, Allen Ginsberg, Gregory Corso, and other Beats were also known to quaff a few drinks there as well. Even though many of the Beats, including Ginsberg and Kerouac, lived on what would later be called the East Village, they preferred to do their drinking in the West Village.

Edward Albee continued the Village playwrighting tradition by settling in the Village in the late 1940s, spending his evenings in Village coffeehouses and bars. Albee can rightly be considered the Village heir to Eugene O'Neill. His first play, *The Zoo Story*, premiered at the Provincetown Playhouse in January 1960. A year later he moved to an apartment on West Twelfth Street where he wrote his masterpiece, *Who's Afraid of Virginia Woolf?* According to Albee, he received the inspiration for the play's cryptic title when he saw "Who's Afraid of Virginia Woolf?" scrawled in soap on a mirror in the downstairs bar of a tavern on Tenth Street between Greenwich Avenue and Waverly Place.

During the 1950s a flurry of noncommercial theatres opened in the Village. Some critics place the origins of off-Broadway to a

Greenwich Village production of Tennessee Williams' *Summer and Smoke* at the Circle in the Square. This growing predilection toward radical theater continued throughout the decade and into the 1960s with the success of several now legendary theaters, particularly Julian Beck and Judith Malina's Living Theatre and Joe Cino's Caffe Cino.

Caffe Cino was a dark, smoky coffeehouse on Cornelia Street. Considered to be the first Off-Off-Broadway theater and the city's first gay theater, it became a favorite hangout for people like Lanford Wilson, Sam Shepard, Robert Patrick, and John Guare. Terry Miller offers a vivid description in his book, *Greenwich Village and How It Got That Way*:

> *Cappuccino cost forty cents and was artfully served in shaving mugs. The artworks on the walls were changed monthly, and the occasional poetry reading served to distract patrons from noticing how uncomfortable the cramped, dimly lit tables were.*

Similarly, the Living Theatre, although perhaps not quite as outrageous as Caffe Cino, was just as adventurous. Julian Beck and his wife Judith Malina founded it. Both had performed at the Cherry Lane Theatre in the Village before starting the Living Theatre on Fourteenth Street. Avowed pacifists and anarchists, they mounted numerous controversial productions, without concern for their physical welfare or economic well-being.

Other important theater groups with ties to the Village include Joseph Chaikin's Open Theatre and Al Carmines's Judson Poets' Theatre. By the early 1970s most of the radical theater could be found outside the Village. Many in fact had moved east to the East Village, such as Ellen Stewart's La Mama or Joseph Papp's Public Theatre.

In the mid-1950s several artists and writers opened their own coffeehouses. Rienzi at 107 MacDougal Street was probably the most popular. The success of Rienzi led, in turn, to a plethora of coffeehouses, invariably frequented by youth in black turtlenecks who listened to folk music and talked about serious issues over endless cups of coffee or a game of chess. Poetry readings were held at places like the Gaslight Cafe in the basement of 116 Mac-Dougal Street. Every important Beat read here, from Ginsberg to Ferlinghetti. Le Figaro opened in the late 1950s and is still there. The granddaddy of them all, Caffe Reggio, opened in 1927.

Another favorite literary haunt was Chumley's, a former speakeasy that was opened in 1928 by a Chicago labor organizer. Among the regulars were Edna St. Vincent Millay, F. Scott Fitzgerald, Edmund Wilson, Theodore Dreiser, John Dos Passos, Ring Lardner, Willa Cather, Eugene O'Neill, Djuna Barnes, John Cheever, William S. Burroughs, Jack Kerouac, Anais Nin, James Thurber, and, most recently, Calvin Trillin. Its walls are decorated with the book jackets of mostly dead writers and former patrons.

The New York School of painters flocked to the original Cedar Tavern, on University Place off Eighth Street. They included Jackson Pollock, Willem de Kooning, Franz Kline, Mark Rothko, and Larry Rivers. It was also a favorite hangout of Beat authors Allen Ginsberg, Jack Kerouac, Gregory Corso, Ted Joans; poets Diane di Prima; Kenneth Koch; Leroi Jones, Frank O'Hara; Hubert Selby and Paul Goodman; Living Theatre founders Julian Beck and Judith Malina and composer and musician David Amram. Men often behaved badly at the Cedar. Pollock was banned for a month for allegedly kicking in the door of the men's room. Kerouac was banished altogether for urinating in public. It's uncertain whether he answered nature's call by using the services of a stand-up ashtray or a sink.

The Village experienced a decline in population during the 1940s and 1950s as residents moved north or left the city altogether for the leafy suburbs. The 1960s witnessed continued friction between various segments of the population. By this time a considerable number of gays had moved into the Village. Occasional street violence broke out, most severely during the famous riot outside the Stonewall Inn in 1969. During the early 1970s crime increased overall in the Village.

During the Vietnam War era Washington Square Park was the focal point for rallies and protest marches, as well as a popular gathering spot for musicians, hippies, druggies, and marginal characters. The folk boom was in full swing and at places such as The Bitter End on Bleecker Street and Gerde's Folk City, everyone from Phil Ochs to Bob Dylan and from Peter, Paul, and Mary to Tom Paxton performed night after night to appreciative crowds.

Living up to the Village's reputation as a bastion of outrageous behavior, the Greenwich Village Halloween Parade began as an arts project in the early 1970s. Now it is an annual event, a cheerfully hedonistic street pageant done up in the way that only the Village could do it and the closest thing to Mardi Gras north of the Mason-Dixon Line.

Everything goes in cycles, and that includes literary movements. During the 1980s and 1990s the gentrification of the Village continued its upward spiral, driving real estate prices to astronomical heights. And still another indication that things weren't quite what they used to be was the announcement that the *Village Voice*—that bastion of alternative living and thought—had been sold to an investor group, a money management firm with offices in New York and San Francisco.

If writers are no longer as prevalent in the Village as they once were and if the creative atmosphere lacks the electricity of earlier generations, if all this is true, which it probably is, what remains, what is left behind, is the essential character of the Village. For no matter who resides behind the drawn blinds and closed shutters, no matter who eats in its restaurants or drinks in its taverns and coffeehouses, it will always be the Village, forever haunted by a trail of literary ghosts. From Walt Whitman to Eugene O'Neill, from Henry James to Edith Wharton, from Djuna Barnes to Edna St. Vincent Millay, from Norman Mailer to Jack Kerouac, from Dawn Powell to Mary Cantwell, from Richard Wright to James Baldwin, from Edward Hoagland to Edmund White, the Village's literary legacy is genuine, an invaluable legacy that has been passed along through the generations.

Whether a resident or just passing through, anyone who considers themselves a writer must surely owe a huge debt to the idea of Greenwich Village. America's literary past lies here and, in some significant way, so does her future.

—JUNE SKINNER SAWYERS
Chicago, Illinois
September 2001

James D. McCabe

(1842–1883)

An early piece on Bleecker Street by a veteran journalist finds the Village on rather shaky ground, as the more respectable folk move out only to be replaced by artistic types.

"Bleecker Street" from *Lights and Shadows of New York Life: or, the Sights and Sensations of the Great City*

Perhaps very few people out of the great city know Bleecker Street at all; perhaps they have passed it a dozen times or more without noticing it, or if they have marked it at all have regarded it only as a passably good-looking street going to decay. But he who does not know Bleecker Street does not know New York. It is of all the localities of the metropolis, one of the best worth studying.

It was once the abode of wealth and fashion, as its fine old time mansions testify. Then Broadway north of it was the very centre of the aristocracy of the island, and Bond Street was a primitive Fifth Avenue. Going west from the Bowery, nearly to Sixth Avenue, you will find rows of stately mansions on either hand, which speak

James D. McCabe. "Bleecker Street" from *Lights and Shadows of New York Life: or, the Sights and Sensations of the Great City* (Philadelphia: National Publishing Co., 1872).

eloquently of greatness gone, and as eloquently of hard times present. They have a strange aspect too, and one may read their story at a glance. Twenty-five years ago they were homes of wealth and refinement. The most sumptuous hospitality was dispensed here, and the stately drawing rooms often welcomed brilliant assemblages. Now a profusion of signs announce that hospitality is to be had at a stated price, and the old mansions are put to the viler uses of third-rate boarding houses and restaurants.

In many respects Bleecker Street is more characteristic of Paris than of New York. It reminds one strongly of the Latin Quarter, and one instinctively turns to look for the *Closerie des Lilas*. It is the headquarters of Bohemianism, and Mrs. Grundy now shivers with holy horror when she thinks it was once her home. The street has not entirely lost its reputation. No one is prepared to say it is a vile neighborhood; no one would care to class it with Houston, Mercer, Greene, or Water Streets; but people shake their heads, look mysterious, and sigh ominously when you ask them about it. It is a suspicious neighborhood, to say the least, and he who frequents it must be prepared for the gossip and surmises of his friends. No one but its denizens, whose discretion can be absolutely trusted, knows anything with certainty about its doings or mode of life, but every one has his own opinions. Walk down it at almost any hour of the day or night, and you will see many things that are new to you. Strange characters meet you at every step; even the shops have a Bohemian aspect, for trade is nowhere so much the victim of chance as here. You see no breach of the public peace, no indecorous act offends you; but the people you meet have a certain air of independence, of scorn of conventionality, a certain carelessness which mark them as very different from the throng you have just left on Broadway. They puzzle you, and set you to conjecturing who they are and what they are, and you find yourself weaving a romance about nearly every man or woman you meet.

That long-haired, queerly dressed young man, with a parcel under his arm, who passed you just then, is an artist, and his home is in the attic of that tall house from which you saw him pass out.

It is a cheerless place, indeed, and hardly the home for a devotee of the Muse; but the artist is a philosopher, and he flatters himself that if the world has not given him a share of its good things, it has at least freed him from its restraints, and so long as he has the necessaries of life and a lot of jolly-good fellows to smoke and drink and chat with him in that lofty dwelling place of his, he is content to take life as he finds it.

If you look up to the second floor, you may see a pretty, but not over fresh looking young woman, gazing down into the street. She meets your glance with composure, and with an expression which is a half invitation to "come up." She is used to looking at men, and to having them look at her, and she is not averse to their admiration. Her dress is a little flashy, and the traces of rouge are rather too strong on her face, but it is not a bad face. You may see her tonight at the _____ Theatre, where she is the favorite. Not much of an actress, really, but very clever at winning over the dramatic critics of the great dailies who are but men, and not proof against feminine arts. This is her home, and an honest home, too. To be sure it would be better had she a mother or a brother, or husband—some recognized protector, who could save her from the "misfortune of living alone," but this is Bleecker Street, and she may live here according to her own fancy, "and no questions asked."

On the floor above her dwells Betty Mulligan, a pretty little butterfly well known to the lovers of the ballet as Mademoiselle Alexandrine. No one pretends to know her history. She pays her room rent, has hosts of friends, but beyond this no one knows anything. Surmises there are by the score, and people wonder how mademoiselle can live so well on her little salary; but no charges are made. People shrug their shoulders, and hint that ballet girls have resources unknown to the uninitiated. The rule here is that everyone must look after himself, and it requires such an effort to do this that there is no time left to watch a neighbor's shortcomings.

In the same house is a fine-looking woman, not young, but not old. Her "husband" has taken lodgings here for her, but he comes to see her only at intervals, and he is not counted in the landlady's

3

bill. Business keeps him away, and he comes when he can. Bleecker Street never asks madame for her marriage certificate, nor does it seek to know why her numerous friends are all gentlemen, or why they come only when the "husband" is away.

Honest, hard-working men come here with their families. Their earnings are regular, but small, and they prefer the life of this street to the misery of the tenement house. Others there are who live in the street, and occupy whole dwellings with their families, who stay here from force of habit. They are "slow" people, dull of comprehension, and to them the mysteries of their neighborhood are a sealed book. Yet all are regarded as persons whose characters are "not proven," by the dwellers outside the street.

Money is power in Bleecker Street. It will purchase anything. Much is spent by those who do not dwell here, but come here to hide their secrets. Women come here to meet other men besides their husbands, and men bring women here who are not their wives. Bleecker Street asks no questions, but it has come to suspect the men and women who are seen in it.

Indeed, so long as its tenants do not violate the written law of the land to an extent sufficient to warrant the interference of the police, they may do so as they please. Thus it has come to pass that the various personages who are a law unto themselves have gradually drifted into Bleecker Street, unless they can afford better quarters, and even then the freedom of the locality has for them a fascination hard to be resisted. No one loses caste here for any irregularity. You may dress as you please, live as you please, do as you please in all things, and no comments will be made. There is no "society" here to worry your life with its claims and laws. You are a law unto yourself. Your acts are exclusively your own business. No complaints will be made against you. You are absolutely your own master or mistress here. Life here is based on principles which differ from those which prevail in other parts of the city.

Yet, as I have said, no one dares call the street "bad." Let us say it is "irregular," "free," "above scandal," or "superior to criticism" but let us not venture to term it "bad," as its neighbors Greene and

Mercer are "bad." I cannot say it would be shocked by such a charge, for Bleecker Street is never shocked at anything. It would, no doubt, laugh in our faces, and scornfully ask for our proofs of its badness, and proofs of this sort are hard to bring to light in this thoroughfare.

—1872

Charles DeKay

(1848–1935)

In his role as art critic for the New York Times, *Charles DeKay knew firsthand of the smoky Village cafes and restaurants and the denizens of the night that frequented them. Of particular interest to him were the various artist's clubs that so epitomized the dichotomy between the artistic classes. The bohemian Expressionists, dressed in "velvet jackets, loose cravats, and slouch hats" gathered to satirize the uptown "Philistines" and make wicked fun of their crass and vulgar pursuit of bald-faced materialism.* The Bohemian, *published in 1878, is not only one of the earliest depictions of so-called bohemian life in the Village but also, according to historian Christine Stansell, the earliest American novel of bohemia. It is still an entertaining read.*

from *The Bohemian: A Tragedy of Modern Life*

I.

Dawn was breaking over the housetops on Washington Square as two young men stopped for a moment by the fountain to bid each other good-by. Both were in the frame of mind which is called happy for a long time after the real enjoyment that belongs to mild potations and unstinted argument and song is evaporated. Though neither had taken enough to intoxicate, they held each other closely

Charles DeKay. From *The Bohemian: A Tragedy of Modern Life* (New York: Charles Scribner's Sons, 1878).

embraced, keeping up a tacit effort the convivial spirit which, so far, had inspired the meetings of the Expressionists.

The shorter and broader of the two was the originator of the Expressionists, as a definite, if not chartered, corporation. That was the name of a little band composed of writing men, artists, and, as the writers and artists often called them, outsiders. It was the genius of Harpalion Bagger that had evolved from the leveling atmosphere of New York a small club, in which perfect freedom of discussion reigned at all times of the night, and on all subjects, except those in which a difference of opinion would have offended the president. Among the most enthusiastic Expressionists was reckoned the taller and younger man of the two, remarkable for his large dark eyes, curling hair, and spare wiry frame. The president was Harpalion Bagger, and he it was who did most of the speaking at this early hour in the Square.

"See, De Courcy," he said, pointing a long thick forefinger at the sky, whitening fast behind the picturesque line of house and church tops. "See! Is not the dawn like some superb, luxurious woman, leaning voluptuously, yet chastely, from amid her satin pillows, and drawing aside her silken curtains with one great dimpled arm, on which, perhaps, there is still some mark of, ah! too warm a kiss—a kiss with a sting in it!—is not the dawn like some such proudly peerless one? What a poem I could make of that! Why do I not always carry with me a tablet, like the ancient Greeks, and a stylus? Then I could jot down at any moment these precious thoughts that surge through my brain! Ah, De Courcy, you little know, fortunate fellow that you are! the misery of forgetting greater sonnets than any other living man—I say it soberly—than any other living man can write. It is agony. You are sure that the forgotten thought is a tremendous idea—you hark back—it is all gone! Your sonnet is lost!"

Harpalion cast his head upon his breast with the gesture of Edwin Booth when acting the melancholy Dane, and sighed deeply.

"But, Master," said the other, timidly, "perhaps you overrate the value of what you have forgotten."

"Overrate it!" cried Harpalion, raising his head quickly, and opening his well-fed lips in surprise; "not I. The trouble with me is, that I continually underrate myself. I have not self-assertion enough. De Courcy, in this brain there are wonderful things unfolding, unfolding. Ah, to think that I—such a genius as I am—should have to wait, cap in hand, before a mere editor of a magazine! Faugh!"

"But your book will change all that," said De Courcy. "Cheer up, old man. I will take ten copies. One shall go to a friend of mine on the Richmond press, another to a Professor in Baltimore—you shall hear from them, I promise you!"

"Do you think them sufficiently advanced to appreciate me?" said Harpalion, gloomily. "But even if they should deal fairly with me, there are so many jealous fellows on the press of New York!"

"Confound them!" said De Courcy.

"They are lying in wait to harm me! You have no idea of the ferocious malignity of literary critics—they are all disappointed writers themselves, and they love nothing better than to bury a real man of letters under the inexhaustible ordure of their mud-throwing machines. But some day I shall be even with them!"

At this heartrending outburst from Harpalion, they took leave of each other: with affection and humility on the side of De Courcy, kindness and condescension on the part of him who had been addressed as master. To De Courcy, whose full name was De Courcy Plantagenet Lee, the figure of Harpalion was glowing with all the hues of greatness with which an ardent, unsophisticated nature endows the first man who appears to it a genius. Lee was one of those rare characters in which the word chivalry still appears something more than a hollow word, convenient as a cloak to hide egotism, and often, sin. To him Harpalion was a realization of what a poet should be, full of beautiful words and images, a denouncer, in a vague way, to be sure, of the shams of the world, and a believer in a life founded upon sentiments and personal worth, not on station or wealth. De Courcy thought himself possessed of excellent birth—what Virginian does not? He knew he was very poor; but neither consideration weighed anything in his ideal. He was a cashier in a large dry-goods house on Broadway, and earned a meagre salary by close attention to work which was neither interesting to him nor recognized as particularly honorable by some people with whom he might otherwise have associated. But that only made more refreshing the occasional meetings of the Expressionists, and added a greater charm to their guiding spirit, Harpalion. For did not Harpalion often relate that he had refused the warmest invitations from haughty ladies of fashion, in order to revel in the witty literary and art talk of his fellow Bohemians? The Expressionists, to a man, claimed to be Bohemians, and were proud of the name. But when Harpalion gave vent to cynical remarks on the manners and true life of fashionable people, the Expressionists applauded; they readily pardoned the young poet for his desertion to the enemy. So great a man must see the world, must be allowed to come and go at will. There could be no doubt whatever that he was a great poet, the greatest America had yet produced. Lee was the first to make the singular discovery that his very name, Harpalion, was a predestination to lyric fame, and brought forward that idea in a sonnet as bad as the idea, addressed "To the Master." It was read with enthusiasm by the Expressionists. Their president assumed a statuesque attitude of proud humility, and, considering the circumstances, could not have been expected to reveal the fact that Harpalion was a name assumed by him at the tender age of nine years, when he first began to write odes upon his slate. He was christened Seth— Seth Bagger—after a solid Uncle Seth in Marblehead. But no one can deny that Harpalion is a much more harmonious name, especially when pronounced with a broad sound of the *a*. Moreover, it has served a good purpose in distinguishing him forever from all the other Baggers spread abroad over the face of North America.

Lee had no time that morning for a nap. After a bath and breakfast, it was necessary to leave the vulgar boardinghouse in which he dwelt, for the retail shop which employed him. He felt keenly the dull commonplace of his dwelling and the monotonous character of his business. He knew quite well that he was not in his right sphere. Nervous and impressible by nature, he was properly gloomy in his own mind at his prospects in life. Yet there was to-day a briskness in his gait and a half-formed song between his lips which did not argue a total absence of gayety. Life had dealt hard with him, but its bitterness had never yet forced the citadel of his character. His heart was still unwrung. Seated behind the gilt railing of the open-work box where his desk stood, and at work, on his accounts, in the hubbub that was beginning for the day, his thoughts wandered this way and that, now to the old days when, as a schoolboy, he poled a flatboat through the shallow reaches of the Susquehanna, then to the dear good-for-nothing father who wrote him pompous letters of advice from Virginia, next to the blood-thirsty critics who made wretched the life of Harpalion the Great, and again to the odious necessity he was under of being penned up like a wild animal all day long for the sake of a very moderate salary.

II.

A week later, on the day of the meeting of the Expressionists, De Courcy was about to run up the steps of his boardinghouse, when a tall figure arose from a sitting position and grasped his arm.

"Why! Major Lee!" cried De Courcy in a tone more astonished than gratified.

"My son, it is I," said the tall man, in the deep voice which the tragedian Forrest used in his thrilling effects. "I did declare that I never would set foot in this capital of mudsills, but—here I am!"

"Well, father, I am glad to see you looking so well," said De Courcy. "How were they all at home?"

"Ah, my son, I have never been a well man since your mother died. Things go from bad to worse. How is it with you?"

"The same old story. But it's better than nothing. Come in."

"To think," said the Major pathetically, addressing the empty street, "that a son of mine, a member of as fine a family as exists on the face of the globe, should become a counter-jumper! I am not what I once was, De Courcy. I am a poor miserable old man, or I should never allow you to work as you do. I came on to talk things over."

"I am glad you did," said the son, wondering what the trouble could be now. "Come in and take dinner with me. Afterward we will treat ourselves to the theatre, and then"—here De Courcy's tone grew proudly triumphant—"then I will take you to a meeting of the Expressionists!"

. . .

With the exception of their president, the little band of Expressionists was assembled in the back room of a well-known restaurant. The place owed its fame to its dinginess and dirt. The natural accumulations of smoke and dust, the spattering from beefsteaks broiled under the noses of the guests, and accretions of other kinds easily imagined, were increased and deepened by the presence of various incongruous articles disposed about the walls and ceilings.

From the rafters of the back room hung a pair of ancient boots, on which grew the mold of a score of years; rusty horseshoes were nailed with careful heedlessness on a projecting jamb; a curious litter of kitchen and household articles crammed the raised alcove, in which the sly-faced host was perched during the day. The tables were of the coarsest description; the crockery thick and rough; the beer was served in battered pewter mugs. Many an innocent American, yearning for a whiff of the ancient and time-honored, had deserted the clean service and good viands of other eating-houses for this frowsy den, believing in his soul that the chops tasted better and the ale "from the wood" had a flavor unknown elsewhere. Such tricks will the imagination play upon us at times and for a season.

When De Courcy entered, the young artists who entertained the deepest disrespect for Academicians, the young newspaper fellows who alluded to the proprietors of the great journals by their first names, the comic men on the funny illustrated, who came with gloomy faces to extract a little amusement out of the proceedings of the Expressionists, and were aching to have a jibe at them in print, not to forget that necessary element to fill up the chinks—the outsiders—all had their beer before them, and were talking at the top of their voices. They stopped long enough to allow De Courcy to present to the company Major James de Courcy Lee, of Lynchburg.

His father had assumed more than usual of his grand air. This was due not merely to the number of times since dinner that he had performed the sacrificial rite practiced in bar-rooms: it was also

11

meant to impress the young men—who were, if not actually mudsills themselves, then of rank mudsill stock—with an idea of the deportment belonging to a Southern gentleman of honor. Great gravity of face, severe uprightness of carriage, a labored slowness in bowing and speaking were necessary to this object. With the grace of a cavalier and the dignity of a Spaniard, Major Lee removed his broad felt hat from the gray locks that hung nearly to his shoulders, and saluted the company. His pendant mustache framed a straight mouth, whose lower lip protruded slightly above a rather long and prominent chin. His small dark eyes looked with suspicion and defiance from under thick, tufted eyebrows. He was long in the legs and very short-waisted. Major Lee had more Irish blood than Scotch, and more Scotch than English, but he shared the common prejudice of the world that worships prosperity, and preferred to consider his lineage purely English. Hardly was he seated, when a stir in the room heralded the approach of some person of note. The door was flung open, and Harpalion entered with a swift, stealthy gait, such as Dante may have used when hurried along by great thoughts. His features were wrapped in abstraction. His loose necktie was thrown this way and that in an agitated fashion, and his hair had been tumbled artistically above his forehead, which was high and broad at the top; otherwise he was scrupulously well dressed and neat. The whole assembly, with the exception of Major Lee, rose and said: "Hail, Master!"

Harpalion responded to this flattering mark of homage by an inclination of his head, and took his seat at the end of the long table in a pensive attitude of ardent agitation. He was, indeed, the great man of the club, the origin of which was due to him alone. He had long mourned the absence in New York of a Quartier Latin. The Expressionists were to form his Quartier Latin. Bohemians in New York were so few or so scattered that their existence was sometimes denied. The Expressionists were to afford the needed element. Bohemians wore velvet jackets, loose cravats, and slouch hats, sang songs in derision of staid burgesses and drank confusion to the Philistine in a smoky restaurant. All these things, or some of them, should be done by the Expressionists, even if it were hard to find in New York any one class of people more than another, upon whom the odious term *bourgeois* could fasten. On Sunday, however, a keen observer would have seen the Expressionists wending their way to church, clothed in the fashion of the day, for all the world like everybody else. This was the real reason that all, with the exception of De Courcy and a solitary artist, wore their hair very short. Long hair was almost a necessity to the complete outfit of a Bohemian. But what are you to do, if your Sunday friends are scandalized? Hair will not grow in a week. So the Expressionists conceded that much to the foolish prejudices of the Philistines.

—1878

Henry James

(1843–1916)

*Henry James was born in New York in 1843. His father was the promi-
nent theologian and philosopher; his older brother a noted philosopher.
James attended schools in New York, London, Paris, and Geneva and
studied law at Harvard. In 1865 he began to contribute reviews and short
stories to various American publications. A decade later he moved to Paris
for a short time before settling in London. James became a British citizen
in 1915. He died the following year. A prolific writer, his many works of
fiction include* The Europeans, The Portrait of a Lady, The Bostoni-
ans, The Wings of the Dove, *and* The Ambassadors. *The classic*
Washington Square *takes place in the Old New York of his boyhood (the
story was told to him by the English actress Fanny Kemble) and remains
a literary favorite. In 1997 a film adaptation starring Jennifer Jason Leigh
and Ben Chaplin was released.*

from *Washington Square*

As a child she had promised to be tall; but when she was sixteen
she ceased to grow, and her stature, like most other points in her
composition, was not unusual. She was strong, however, and
properly made, and, fortunately, her health was excellent. It had
been noted that the Doctor was a philosopher, but I would not
have answered for his philosophy if the poor girl had proved a
sickly and suffering person. Her appearance of health consti-
tuted her principal claim to beauty; and her clear, fresh complexion, in which white and red were equally distributed, was,

Henry James. From *Washington Square*. First published in 1880.

indeed, an excellent thing to see. Her eye was small and quiet, her features were rather thick, her tresses brown and smooth. A dull, plain girl she was called by rigorous critics—a quiet, lady-like girl, by those of the more imaginative sort; but by neither class was she very elaborately discussed. When it had been duly impressed upon her that she was a young lady—it was a good while before she could believe it—she suddenly developed a lively taste for dress: a lively taste is quite the expression to use. I feel as if I ought to write it very small, her judgment in this matter was by no means infallible; it was liable to confusions and embarrassments. Her great indulgence of it was really the desire of a rather inarticulate nature to manifest itself; she sought to be eloquent in her garments, and to make up for her diffidence of speech by a fine frankness of costume. But if she expressed herself in her clothes, it is certain that people were not to blame for not thinking her a witty person. It must be added that, though she had the expectation of a fortune—Doctor Sloper for a long time had been making twenty thousand dollars a year by his profession, and laying aside the half of it—the amount of money at her disposal was not greater than the allowance made to many poorer girls. In those days, in New York, there were still a few altar-fires flickering in the temple of Republican simplicity, and Doctor Sloper would have been glad to see his daughter present herself, with a classic grace, as a priestess of this mild faith. It made him fairly grimace, in private, to think that a child of his should be both ugly and overdressed. For himself, he was fond of the good things of life, and he made a considerable use of them; but he had a dread of vulgarity, and even a theory that it was increasing in the society that surrounded him. Moreover, the standard of luxury in the United States thirty years ago was carried by no means so high as at present, and Catherine's clever father took the old-fashioned view of the education of young persons. He had no particular theory on the subject; it had scarcely as yet become a necessity of self-defence to have a collection of theories. It simply appeared to him proper and reasonable that a well-bred young woman should not carry half her fortune on her back. Catherine's back was a broad one, and would have carried a good deal; but to the weight of the paternal displeasure she never ventured to expose it, and our heroine was twenty years old before she treated herself, for evening wear, to a red satin gown trimmed with gold fringe; though this was an article which, for many years, she had coveted in secret. It made her look, when she sported it, like a woman of thirty; but oddly enough, in spite of her taste for fine clothes, she had not a grain of coquetry, and her anxiety when she put them on was as to whether they, and not she, would look well. It is a point on which history has not been explicit, but the assumption is warrantable; it was in the royal raiment just mentioned that she presented herself at a little entertainment given by her aunt, Mrs Almond. The girl was at this time in her twenty-first year, and Mrs Almond's party was the beginning of something very important.

Some three or four years before this, Doctor Sloper had moved his household gods up town, as they say in New York. He had been living ever since his marriage in an edifice of red brick, with granite copings and an enormous fan-light over the door, standing in a street within five minutes' walk of the City Hall which saw its best days (from the social point of view) about 1820. After this, the tide of fashion began to set steadily northward, as, indeed, in New York, thanks to the narrow channel in which it flows, it is obliged to do, and the great hum of traffic rolled farther to the right and left of Broadway. By the time the Doctor changed his residence, the murmur of trade had become a mighty uproar, which was music in the ears of all good citizens interested in the commercial development, as they delighted to call it, of their fortunate isle. Doctor Sloper's interest in this phenomenon was only indirect—though, seeing that, as the years went on, half of his patients came to be overworked men of business, it might have been more immediate—and when most of his neighbors' dwellings (also ornamented with granite copings and large fan-lights) had been converted into offices, warehouses, and shipping agencies, and otherwise applied to the base uses of commerce, he determined to look out for a quieter home. The ideal of quiet and of genteel retirement, in 1835, was found in Washington Square, where the Doctor built himself a handsome, modern, wide-fronted house, with a big balcony before the drawing-room windows, and a flight of white marble steps ascending to a portal which was also faced with white marble. This structure, and many of its neighbors, which it exactly resembled, were supposed, forty years ago, to embody the last results of architectural science, and they remain to this day very solid and honorable dwellings. In front of them was the square, containing a considerable quantity of inexpensive vegetation, enclosed by a wooden paling, which increased its rural and accessible appearance; and round the corner was the more august precinct of the Fifth Avenue, taking its origin at this point with a spacious and confident air which already marked it for high destinies. I know not whether it is owing to the tenderness of early associations, but this portion of New York appears to many persons the most delectable. It has a kind of established repose which is not of frequent occurrence in other quarters of the long, shrill city; it has a riper, richer, more honorable look than any of the upper ramifications of the great longitudinal thoroughfare—the look of having had something of a social history. It was here, as you might have been informed on good authority, that you had come into a world which appeared to offer a variety of sources of interest; it was here that your grandmother lived, in venerable solitude, and dispensed a hospitality which commended itself alike to the infant imagination and the infant palate; it was here that you took your first walks abroad, following the nursery-maid with unequal step, and sniffing up the strange odor of the ailanthus-trees which at that time formed the principal umbrage of the Square, and diffused an aroma that you were not yet critical enough to dislike as it deserved; it was here, finally, that your first school, kept by a broad-bosomed, broad-based old lady with a ferule, who was always having tea in a blue cup, with a saucer that didn't match, enlarged the circle both of your observations and your sensations. It was here, at any rate, that my heroine spent many years of her life; which is my excuse for this topographical parenthesis.

Catherine listened for her father when he came in that evening, and she heard him go to his study. She sat quiet, though her heart was beating fast, for nearly half an hour; then she went and knocked at his door—a ceremony without which she never crossed the threshold of this apartment. On entering it now, she found him in his chair beside the fire, entertaining himself with a cigar and the evening paper.

"I have something to say to you," she began very gently; and she sat down in the first place that offered.

"I shall be very happy to hear it, my dear," said her father. He waited—waited, looking at her—while she stared, in a long silence, at the fire. He was curious and impatient, for he was sure she was going to speak of Morris Townsend; but he let her take her own time, for he was determined to be very mild.

"I am engaged to be married!" Catherine announced at last, still staring at the fire.

The Doctor was startled; the accomplished fact was more than he had expected; but he betrayed no surprise. "You do right to tell me," he simply said. "And who is the happy mortal whom you have honored with your choice?"

"Mr Morris Townsend." And as she pronounced her lover's name Catherine looked at him. What she saw was her father's still gray eye and his clear-cut, definite smile. She contemplated these objects for a moment, and then she looked back at the fire; it was much warmer.

"When was this arrangment made?" the Doctor asked.

"This afternoon—two hours ago."

"Was Mr Townsend here?"

'Yes, father; in the front-parlor." She was very glad that she was not obliged to tell him that the ceremony of their betrothal had taken place out there under the bare ailanthus-trees.

"Is it serious?" said the Doctor.

"Very serious, father."

Her father was silent a moment. "Mr Townsend ought to have told me."

"He means to tell you to-morrow."

"After I know all about it from you? He ought to have told me before. Does he think I didn't care, because I left you so much liberty?"

"Oh no," said Catherine; "he knew you would care. And we have been so much obliged to you for—for the liberty."

The Doctor gave a short laugh. "You might have made a better use of it, Catherine."

"Please don't say that, father!" the girl urged, softly, fixing her dull and gentle eyes upon him.

He puffed his cigar awhile, meditatively. "You have gone very fast," he said, at last.

'Yes," Catherine answered, simply; "I think we have."

Her father glanced at her an instant, removing his eyes from the fire. "I don't wonder Mr Townsend likes you; you are so simple and so good."

"I don't know why it is; but he *does* like me. I am sure of that."

"And are you very fond of Mr Townsend?"

"I like him very much, of course, or I shouldn't consent to marry him."

"But you have known him a very short time, my dear."

"Oh," said Catherine, with some eagerness, "it doesn't take long to like a person—when once you begin."

"You must have begun very quickly. Was it the first time you saw him—that night at your aunt's party?"

"I don't know, father," the girl answered. "I can't tell you about that."

"Of course; that's your own affair. You will have observed that I have acted on that principle. I have not interfered; I have left you your liberty; I have remembered that you are no longer a little girl—that you have arrived at years of discretion."

"I feel very old—and very wise," said Catherine, smiling faintly.

"I am afraid that before long you will feel older and wiser yet. I don't like your engagement."

"Ah!" Catherine exclaimed, softly, getting up from her chair.

"No, my dear. I am sorry to give you pain; but I don't like it. You should have consulted me before you settled it. I have been too easy with you, and I feel as if you had taken advantage of my indulgence. Most decidedly you should have spoken to me first."

Catherine hesitated a moment, and then—"It was because I was afraid you wouldn't like it," she confessed.

"Ah, there it is! You had a bad conscience."

"No, I have not had a bad conscience, father!" the girl cried out, with considerable energy. "Please don't accuse me of anything so dreadful!" These words, in fact, represented to her imagination something very terrible indeed, something base and cruel, which she associated with malefactors and prisoners. "It was because I was afraid—afraid—" she went on.

"If you were afraid, it was because you had been foolish."

"I was afraid you didn't like Mr Townsend."

"You were quite right. I don't like him."

"Dear father, you don't know him," said Catherine, in a voice so timidly argumentative that it might have touched him.

"Very true; I don't know him intimately. But I know him enough; I have my impression of him. You don't know him either."

She stood before the fire with her hands lightly clasped in front of her; and her father, leaning back in his chair and looking up at her, made this remark with a placidity that might have been irritating.

I doubt, however, whether Catherine was irritated, though she broke into a vehement protest. "I don't know him?" she cried. "Why, I know him—better than I have ever known any one!"

"You know a part of him—what he has chosen to show you. But you don't know the rest."

"The rest? What is the rest?"

"Whatever it may be, there is sure to be plenty of it."

"I know what you mean," said Catherine, remembering how Morris had forewarned her. "You mean that he is mercenary."

Her father looked up at her still, with his cold, quiet, reasonable eye. "If I meant it, my dear, I should say it! But there is an error I wish particularly to avoid—that of rendering Mr Townsend more interesting to you by saying hard things about him."

20

"I won't think them hard if they are true," said Catherine.

"If you don't, you will be a remarkably sensible young woman!"

"They will be your reasons, at any rate, and you will want me to hear your reasons."

The Doctor smiled a little. "Very true. You have a perfect right to ask for them." And he puffed his cigar a few moments. "Very well, then; without accusing Mr Townsend of being in love only with your fortune—and with the fortune that you justly expect—I will say that there is every reason to suppose that these good things have entered into his calculation more largely than a tender solicitude for your happiness strictly requires. There is, of course, nothing impossible in an intelligent young man entertaining a disinterested affection for you. You are an honest, amiable girl, and an intelligent young man might easily find it out. But the principal thing that we know about this young man—who is, indeed, very intelligent—leads us to suppose that, however much he may value your personal merits, he values your money more. The principal thing we know about him is that he has led a life of dissipation, and has spent a fortune of his own in doing so. That is enough for me, my dear. I wish you to marry a young man with other antecedents—a young man who could give positive guarantees. If Morris Townsend has spent his own fortune in amusing himself, there is every reason to believe that he would spend yours."

The Doctor delivered himself of these remarks slowly, deliberately, with occasional pauses and prolongations of accent, which made no great allowance for poor Catherine's suspense as to his conclusion. She sat down at last, with her head bent and her eyes still fixed upon him; and strangely enough—I hardly know how to tell it—even when she felt that what he said went so terribly against her, she admired his neatness and nobleness of expression. There was something hopeless and oppressive in having to argue with her father; but she too, on her side, must try to be clear. He was so quiet; he was not at all angry; and she, too, must be quiet. But her very effort to be quiet made her tremble.

"That is not the principal thing that we know about him," she said; and there was a touch of her tremor in her voice. "There are

21

other things—many other things. He has very high abilities—he wants so much to do something. He is kind, and generous, and true," said poor Catherine, who had not suspected hitherto the resources of her eloquence. "And his fortune—his fortune that he spent—was very small."

"All the more reason he shouldn't have spent it," cried the Doctor, getting up with a laugh. Then, as Catherine, who had also risen to her feet again, stood there in her rather angular earnestness, wishing so much and expressing so little, he drew her toward him and kissed her. "You won't think me cruel?" he said, holding her a moment.

This question was not reassuring; it seemed to Catherine, on the contrary, to suggest possibilities which made her feel sick. But she answered coherently enough, "No, dear father; because if you knew how I feel—and you must know, you know everything—you would be so kind, so gentle."

"Yes, I think I know how you feel," the Doctor said. "I will be very kind—be sure of that. And I will see Mr Townsend tomorrow. Meanwhile, and for the present, be so good as to mention to no one that you are engaged."

—1880

William Dean Howells

(1837–1920)

*To many literary historians the decision of William Dean Howells to re-
sign as editor of the* Atlantic Monthly *in Boston to devote himself to his
own writing in New York led to the demise of New England as literary
capital of the United States. Several of Howells' so-called New York novels were set in the Village, including* A Hazard of New Fortunes *(1890)
and* The Coast of Bohemia *(1893). In the latter, we follow the adventures of an aspiring New York art student, Charmian Maybough, and her
friends as they try their damndest to put on bohemian airs.*

from *The Coast of Bohemia*

Cornelia found herself in the last of a long line of sections or stalls
which flanked a narrow corridor dividing the girl students from
the young men, who were often indeed hardly more than boys.
There was a table stretching from this corridor to a window looking down on the roofs of some carpenter shops and stables; on the
board before her lay the elementary shape of a hand in plaster,
which she was trying to draw. At her side that odd-looking girl,
who had stared so at her on the stairs the day before, was working
at a block foot, and not getting it very well. She had in fact given it
up for the present and was watching Cornelia's work and watching her face, and talking to her.

William Dean Howells. From *The Coast of Bohemia* (New York: Harper & Brothers,
1901).

"What is your name?" she broke off to ask, in the midst of a monologue upon the social customs and characteristics of the Synthesis.

Cornelia always frowned, and drew her breath in long sibillations, when she was trying hard to get a thing right. She now turned a knotted forehead on her companion, but stopped her hissing to ask, "What?" Then she came to herself and said, "Oh! Saunders."

"I don't mean your last name," said the other, "I mean your first name."

"Cornelia," said the owner of it, as briefly as before.

"I should have thought it would have been Gladys," the other suggested.

Cornelia looked up in astonishment and some resentment. "Why in the world should my name be Gladys?" she demanded.

"I don't know," the other explained. "But the first moment I saw you in the office, I said to myself, 'Of course her name is Gladys.' Mine is Charmian."

"Is it?" said Cornelia, not so much with preoccupation, perhaps, as with indifference. She thought it rather a nice name, but she did not know what she had to do with it.

"Yes," the other said, as if she had somehow expected to be doubted. "My last name's Maybough." Cornelia kept on at her work without remark, and Miss Maybough pursued, as if it were a branch of autobiography, "I'm going to have lunch; aren't you?"

Cornelia sighed dreamily, as she drew back for an effect of her drawing, which she held up on the table before her, "Is it time?"

"Do you suppose they would be letting me talk so to you if it weren't? The monitor would have been down on me long ago."

Cornelia had noticed a girl who seemed to be in authority, and who sat where she could oversee and overhear all that went on.

"Is she one of the students?" she asked.

Miss Maybough nodded. "Elected every month. She's awful. You can't do anything with her when she's on duty, but she's a little dear when she isn't. You'll like her." Miss Maybough leaned toward her, and joined Cornelia in a study of her drawing. "How

24

splendidly you're getting it. It's very *chic*. Oh, anybody can see that *you've* got genius!"

Her admiration made no visible impression upon Cornelia, and for a moment she looked a little disappointed; then she took a basket from under the table, and drew from it a bottle of some yellowish liquid, an orange and a bit of sponge cake. "Are you going to have yours here?" she asked, as Cornelia opened a paper with the modest sandwich in it which she made at breakfast, and fetched from her boarding-house. "Oh, I'm so glad you haven't brought anything to drink with you! I felt almost sure you hadn't, and now you've got to share mine." She took a cup from her basket, and in spite of Cornelia's protest that she never drank anything but water at dinner, she poured it full of tea for her. "I'll drink out of the bottle," she said. "I like to. Some of the girls bring chocolate, but I think there's nothing like cold tea for the brain. Chocolate's so clogging; so is milk; but sometimes I bring that; it's glorious, drinking it out of the can." She tilted the bottle to her lips, and half drained it at a draught. "I always feel that I'm working with inspiration after I've had my cold tea. Of course they won't let *you* stay here long," she added.

"Why?" Cornelia fluttered back in alarm.

"When they see your work they'll see that you're fit for still-life, at least."

"Oh!" said Cornelia, vexed at having been scared for nothing. "I guess they won't be in any great hurry about it."

"How magnificent!" said Miss Maybough. "Of course, with that calm of yours, you can wait, as if you had eternity before you. Do you know that you are *terribly* calm?"

Cornelia turned and gave her a long stare. Miss Maybough broke her bit of cake in two, and offered her half, and Cornelia took it mechanically, but ate her sandwich. "*I* feel as if I had eternity *behind* me, I've been in the Preparatory so long."

On the common footing this drop to the solid ground gave, Cornelia asked her how long.

"Well, it's the beginning of my second year, now. If they don't let me go to round hands pretty soon, I shall have to see if I can't get the form by modelling. That's the best way. I suppose it's my imagination; it carries me away so, and I don't see the thing as it is before me; that's what they say. But with the clay, I'll *have* to, don't you know. Well, you know some of the French painters model their whole picture in clay and paint it, before they touch the canvas, any way. I shall try it here awhile longer, and then if I can't get to the round in any other way, I'll take to the clay. If sculpture concentrates you more, perhaps I may stick to it altogether. Art is one, anyhow, and the great thing is to *live* it. Don't you think so?"

"I don't know," said Cornelia. "I'm not certain I know what you mean."

"You will," said Miss Maybough, "after you've been here awhile, and get used to the atmosphere. I don't believe I really knew what life meant before I came to the Sythesis. When you get to realizing the standards of the Synthesis, then you begin to breathe freely for the first time. I expect to pass the rest of my days here. I shouldn't care if I stayed till I was thirty. How old are you?"

"I'm going to be twenty," said Cornelia. "Why?"

"Oh, nothing. You can't begin too young; though some people think you oughtn't to come before you're eighteen. I look upon my days before I came here as simply wasted. Don't you want to go out and sit on the stairs awhile?"

"I don't believe I do," said Cornelia, taking up her drawing again, as if she were going on with it.

"Horrors!" Miss Maybough put her hand out over the sketch. "You don't mean that you're going to carry it any farther?"

"Why, it isn't finished yet," Cornelia began.

"Of *course* it isn't, and it never ought to be! I hope you're not going to turn out a *niggler! Please* don't! I couldn't bear to have you. Nobody will respect you if you *finish.* Don't! If you won't come out with me and get a breath of fresh air, do start a new drawing! I want them to see this in the rough. It's *so* bold."

Miss Maybough had left her own drawing in the rough, but it could not be called bold; though if she had seen the block hand with a faltering eye, she seemed to have had a fearless vision of many other things, and she had covered her paper with a fantastic

26

medley of grotesque shapes, out of that imagination which she had given Cornelia to know what so fatally mischievous to her in its uninvited activities. *"Don't* look at them!" she pleaded, when Cornelia involuntarily glanced at her study. "My only hope is to hate them. I almost *pray* to be delivered from them. Let's talk of something else." She turned the sheet over. "Do you mind my having said that about your drawing?"

"No!" said Cornelia, provoked to laughter by the solemnity of the demand. "Why should I?"

"Oh, I don't know. Do you think you shall like me? I mean, do you care if I like *you*—very, *very* much?"

"I don't suppose I could stop it if I did, could I?" asked Cornelia.

The Sphinx seemed to find heart to smile. "Of course, I'm ridiculous. But I do hope we're going to be friends. Tell me about yourself. Or, have some more tea!"

After all, Ludlow decided that he would paint Charmian in her own studio, with the accessories of her peculiar pose in life about her; they were factitious, but they were genuine expressions of her character; he could not realize her so well away from there.

The first afternoon was given to trying her in this light and that, studying her from different points. She wished to stand before her easel, in her Synthesis working-dress, with her palette on her thumb, and a brush in her other hand. He said finally, "Why not?" and Cornelia made a tentative sketch of her.

At the end of the afternoon he waited while the girl was putting on her hat in Charmian's room, where she smiled into the glass at Charmian's face over her shoulder, thinking of the intense fidelity her friend had shown throughout to her promise of unconsciousness.

"Didn't I do it magnificently?" Charmian demanded. "It almost killed me; but I meant to do it if it did kill me; and now his offering to see you aboard the car shows that *he* is determined to do it, too, if it kills *him*. I call it masterly."

"Well, don't go and spoil it now," said Cornelia. "And if you're going to ask me every day how you've done"—

"Oh, I'm not! Only the first day and the last day!"

"Well!"

As Ludlow walked with Cornelia toward the point where she was to take her car down town, he began, "You see, she is *so* dramatic, that if you tried to do her in any other way—that is, simply—you would be doing her artificially. You have to take her as she is, don't you think?"

"I don't know as I think Charmian is acting all the time, if that's what you mean," said Cornelia. "Or any of the time, even."

Ludlow wished she had said she did not know that instead of as, but he reflected that ninety Americans out of a hundred, lettered or unlettered, would have said the same. "Oh, I don't at all mean that she is, intentionally. It's because it's her nature that I want to recognize it. You think it *is* her nature, don't you?" he asked deferentially.

"Oh, I suppose it is," she answered; it amused her to have him take such a serious tone about Charmian.

"I shall have to depend a great deal on your judgment in this matter," he went on. "You won't mind it, I hope?"

"Not if you won't mind it's not being worth anything."

"It will be worth everything!"

"Or if you won't care for my not giving it, sometimes."

'I don't understand."

"Well, I shouldn't want to seem to talk her over."

"Oh, no! You *don't* think I expected you to do that? It was merely the right point of view I wanted to get."

"I don't know as I object to that," said Cornelia.

The car which she wished to take came by, and he stopped it and handed her aboard. She thought he might decide to come with her, but he bowed his goodnight, and she saw him walking on down town as she passed him.

At the end of a fortnight Ludlow had failed to get his picture of Charmian; at the end of a month he began with a new pose and a fresh theory. That quality of hers which he hoped to surprise with

Cornelia's help, and which was to give verity and value to his portrait, when once he expressed it there, escaped him still.

She was capable of perfect poses, but they were mere flashes of attitude. Then the antique mystery lurking in her face went out of it, and she became *fin de siecle* and romantic, and young ladyish, and uninteresting to Ludlow.

She made tea every afternoon when they finished, and sometimes the talk they began with before they began work prolonged itself till the time for the tea had come. On the days when Mr. Plaisdell dropped in for a cup, the talk took such a range that the early dark fell before it ended, and then Cornelia had to stay for dinner and to be sent home in Mrs. Maybough's coupé.

She had never supposed there was anything like it in all the world. Money, and, in a certain measure, the things that money could buy, were imaginable in Pymantoning; but joys so fine, so simple as these, were what she could not have forecast from any ground of experience or knowledge. She tried to give her mother a notion of what they said and did; but she told her frankly she never could understand. Mrs. Saunders, in fact, could not see why it was so exciting; she read Cornelia's letters to Mrs. Burton, who said she could see, and she told Mrs. Saunders that she would like it as much as Cornelia did, if she were in her place; that she was a kind of Bohemian herself.

She tried to explain what Bohemian meant, and what Bohemia was; but this is what no one can quite do. Charmian herself, who aimed to be a perfect Bohemian, was uncertain of the ways and means of operating the Bohemian life, when she had apparently thrown off all the restrictions, for the afternoon, at least, that prevented its realization. She had a faultless setting for it. There never was a girl's studio that was more like a man's studio, an actual studio. Mr. Ludlow himself praised it; he said he felt at home in it, and he liked it because it was not carried a bit too far. Charmian's mother had left her free to do what she wished, and there was not a convention of Philistine housekeeping in the arrangement of the place. Everything was in the admired disorder of an artist's environment; but Mrs. Maybough

29

insisted upon neatness. Even here Charmian had to submit to a compromise. She might and did keep things strewn all about in her studio, but every morning the housemaid was sent in to sweep it and dust it. She was a housemaid of great intelligence, and an imperfect sense of humor, and she obeyed with unsmiling scrupulosity the instructions she had to leave everything in Miss Charmian's studio exactly as she found it, but to leave it clean. In consequence, this home of art had an effect of indescribable coldness and bareness, and there were at first some tempestuous scenes which Cornelia witnessed between Charmian and her mother, when the girl vainly protested:

"But don't you *see*, mamma, that if you have it regularly dusted, it never can have any sentiment, any atmosphere?"

"I don't see how you can call *dust* atmosphere, my dear," said her step-mother. "If I left your studio looking as you want it, and there should be a fire, what would people think?"

"Well, if there should happen to be anybody from Wilbraham, Mass.," Charmian retorted, "they might criticise, but I don't think the New York Fire Department would notice whether the place had been dusted or not. But, go on, mamma! *Some* day I shall have a studio out of the house—Cornelia and I are going to have one— and then I guess you won't have it dusted!"

"I'm sure Miss Saunders wouldn't let it get dusty," said Mrs. Maybough, and then, in self-defense, Charmian gave Cornelia the worst character for housekeeping that she could invent from her knowledge of Cornelia's room.

She begged her pardon afterwards, but she said she had to do it, and she took what comfort she could in slamming everything round, as she called it, in her studio, when she went with Cornelia to have her coffee there. The maid restored it to its conscious picturesqueness the next day.

Charmian was troubled to decide what was truly Bohemian to eat, when they became hungry over their work. She provided candy and chocolate in all their forms and phases, but all girls ate candy and chocolate, and they were so missish, and so indistinctive, and they both went so badly with tea, which she must have because of the weird effect of the spirit-lamp under the kettle, that she disused them after the first week. There remained always crackers, which went with anything, but the question was what to have with them. Their natural association with cheese was rejected because Charmian said she should be ashamed to offer Mr. Ludlow those insipid little Neufchatel things, which were made in New Jersey, anyway, and the Gruyére smelt so, and so did Camembert; and pine-apple cheese was Philistine. There was nothing for it but olives, and though olives had no savor of originality, the little crescent ones were picturesque, and if you picked them out of the bottle with the end of a brush-handle, sharpened to a point, and the other person received them with their thumb and finger, the whole act was indisputably Bohemian.

There was one day when they all got on particularly well, and Charmian boldly ordered some champagne for a burst. The man brought back Apollinaris water, and she was afraid to ask why, for fear he should say Mrs. Maybough sent it. Ludlow said he never took champagne, and was awfully glad of the Apollinaris, and so the change was a great success, for neither Charmian nor Cornelia counted, in any case; they both hated every kind of wine.

Another time, Cornelia, when she came, found Charmian lighting one of the cigars kept for show on her mantel. She laughed wildly at Cornelia's dismay, and the smoke, which had been going up her nose, went down her throat in a volume, and Cornelia had to run and catch her; she was reaching out in every direction for help.

Cornelia led her to the couch, which was still waiting its rugs to become a bed, and she lay down there, very pale and still, and was silent for a long time, till Cornelia said, "Now, if I could find a mouse somewhere to run over you," and they both burst into a shriek of laughter.

"But I'm going to *learn*," Charmian declared. "Where did that cigar go?" She sprang up to look for it, but they never could find it, and they decided it must have gone into the fire, and been burnt up; that particular cigar seemed essential to the experiment, or at least Charmian did not try another.

31

They were both very grave after Ludlow came. When he went away, he said, with an absent look at Charmian, "You have a magnificient pallor to-day, Miss Maybough, and I must compliment you on keeping much quieter than usual."

"Oh, thank you," said Charmian, gravely, and as soon as the door closed upon him she flung herself into Cornelia's arms, and they stifled their laughter in each other's necks. It seemed to them that nothing so wildly funny had ever happened before; they remained a long while quaking over the question where there was smell of smoke enough in the room to have made him suspect anything, and whether his congratulations were not ironical. Charmian said that her mistake was in not beginning with a cigarette instead of a cigar; she said she was ready to begin with a cigarette then, and she dared Cornelia to try one, too. Cornelia refused the challenge, and then she said, well, she would do it herself, some day.

There was a moment when it seemed to her that the Bohemian ideal could be realized to a wild excess in pop-corn. She bought a popper and three ears of corn, and brought them home tied up in paper, and fastened to some canvases she got for Cornelia. She insisted that it was part of the bargain that she should supply Cornelia's canvases. But the process of popping made them all very red in the face; they had to take it by turns, for she would not let Ludlow hold the popper the whole time. They had a snowy heap of corn at last, which she put on the hearth before them in the hollow of a Japanese shield, detached from a suit of armor, for that use. They sat on the hearth to eat it, and they told ghost-stories and talked of the most psychological things they could think of. In all this Charmian put Cornelia forward as much as she dared, and kept herself in a sort of impassioned abeyance. If Cornelia had been the most jealous and exacting of principals she could not have received from her second a more single and devoted allegiance. Charmian's joy in her fortunately mounted in proportion to the devotion she paid her, rather than Cornelia's gratitude for it. She did not like to talk of herself, and these séances were nothing if not strictly personal; but Charmian talked for her, and represented her in phases of interest which Cornelia repudiated with a laugh, or denied outright, without scruple, when the invention was too bold. Charmian contrived that she should acquire the greater merit, from her refusals of it, and went on to fresh self-sacrifices in her behalf.

Sometimes she started the things they talked of; not because she ever seemed to have been thinking of them, or of anything, definitely, but because she was always apparently letting her mind wander about in space, and chanced upon them there. Mostly, however, the suggestions came from Ludlow. He talked of art, its methods, its principles, its duties to the age, the people, the civilization; the large moral uses, which kindled Charmian's fancy, and made Cornelia laugh when Charmian proposed a scheme for the relief and refinement of the poor on the East Side, by frescoing the outsides of the tenement houses in Mott Street and Mulberry Bend, with subjects recalling the home life of the dwellers there: rice-fields and tea-plantations for the Chinese, and views of Etna and Vesuvius and their native shores for the Sicilians and Neapolitans, with perhaps religious histories.

Ludlow had to explain that he had not meant the employment of any such direct and obvious means, but the gradual growth of a conscience in art. Cornelia thought him vague, but it seemed clear to Charmian. She said, "Oh, yes; *that*," and she made tea, and had him set fire to some pieces of Southern lightwood on her hearth, for the sake of the murky fumes and the wreaths of dusky crimson flame, which she said it was so weird to sit by.

In all matters of artistic theory and practice she set Cornelia the example of grovelling at the master's feet, as if there could be no question of anything else; but in other things Cornelia sometimes asserted herself against this slavish submission with a kind of violence little short of impertinence. After these moral paroxysms, in which she disputed the most obviously right and reasonable things, she was always humiliated and cast down before his sincerity in trying to find meaning in her difference from him, as if he could not imagine the nervous impulse that carried her beyond the bounds of truth, and must accuse himself of error. When this happened she would not let Charmian take her to task for her behavior; she would not own that she was wrong; she put the blame on him, and found him arrogant and patronizing. She had always known he was that kind of person, and she did not mean to be treated like a child in everything, even if he was a genius.

By this time they were far away from that point in Charmian's romance where the faithful friend of the heroine remains forever constant to her vow not to speak to the heroine of the hero's passion for her, and in fact rather finds it a duty to break her vow, and enjoys being snubbed for it. As the transaction of the whole affair took place in Charmian's fancy, Cornelia had been obliged to indulge her in it, with the understanding that she should not let it interfere with their work, or try to involve her visibly or palpably in it.

With all their idling they had days when they worked intensely, and Ludlow was as severe with Cornelia's work as he was with his own. He made her rub out and paint out, and he drew ruthless modifications of her work all over it, like the cruelest of the Synthesis masters. He made her paint out every day the work of the day before, as they did in the Synthesis; though sometimes he paused over it in a sort of puzzle. Once he said, holding her sketch into the light he wanted, at the close of the afternoon, "If I didn't know you had done that to-day, I should say it was the one you had done yesterday."

Toward the end of the month he recurred to this notion again. "Suppose," he said, "we keep this, and you do another to-morrow."

The next day he said, in the same perplexity, "Well, keep this, and do another."

After a week he took all her canvases, and set them one back of another, but so that he could see each in nearly the same light. He stood looking at them silently, with the two girls behind him, one at either shoulder.

"It's as lovely as standing between two mirrors," Charmian suggested dreamily.

"Pretty much of a sameness," Cornelia remarked.

"Mm," Ludlow made in his throat. He glanced over the shoulder next her, and asked, as if Charmian were not there, "What makes you do her always alike?"

"Because she *is* always alike."

"Then I've seen her wrong," said Ludlow, and he stared at Charmian as if she were a lay-figure. She bore his scrutiny as impassively as a lay-figure could.

He turned again to Cornelia's sketches, and said gloomily, "I should like to have Wetmore see these."

"Oh!" said Cornelia.

Charmian came to life with another "Oh!" and then she demanded, "When? We must have something besides tea for Mr. Wetmore."

"I think I'll ask him to step round in the morning," said Ludlow, with authority.

Charmian said "Oh!" again, but submitted with the eagerness of a disciple; all phases of the art-life were equally precious, and even a snub from such a master must be willingly accepted.

He went away and would not have any tea; he had an air of trouble—almost of offence. "Isn't he grand, gloomy and peculiar?" Charmian said. "I wonder what's the matter?"

She turned to Ludlow's picture which he had left standing on the chair where he painted at it in disdain of an easel, and silently compared it with Cornelia's sketches. Then she looked at Cornelia and gave a dramatic start.

"What is the matter?" asked Cornelia. She came up and began to look at the pictures, too.

Charmian demanded. "Don't you see?"

"No, I don't see anything," said Cornelia, but as she looked something became apparent which she could not deny. She blushed violently and turned upon Charmian. "You ought to be ashamed," she began, and she tried to take hold of her; she did not know why.

Charmian escaped, and fled to the other end of the room with a wild laugh, and stood there. Cornelia dropped into the chair before the picture, with her head fallen on her elbow. She seemed to be laughing, too, and Charmian went on:

"What is there to be ashamed of? I think it's glorious. It's one of the most romantic things I ever heard of. He simply couldn't help it, and it proves everything I've said. Of course that was the reason

35

he couldn't see *me* all along. Why, if such a thing had happened to me, I should go round shouting it from the house-tops. I don't suppose he knew what he was doing, or else he didn't care; perfectly desperate. What *fun!*"

Cornelia kept laughing, but Charmian stopped and waited a moment and listened. "Why, Cornelia!" she said remorsefully, entreatingly, but she remained the length of the room away. Then she approached tentatively, and when Cornelia suddenly ceased to laugh she put her hand on her head, and tenderly lifted her face. It was dabbled with tears. "Cornelia!" she said again.

Cornelia sprang to her feet with a fierceness that sent her flying some yards away. "Charmian Maybough! Will you ever speak of this to any living soul?"

"No, no! Indeed I won't"—Charmian began.

"Will you ever *think* of it!"

"No"—

"Because I don't choose to have you think I am such a fool as to—to"—

"No, indeed, I don't."

"Because there isn't anything of it, and it wouldn't mean anything, if there were."

"No," said Charmian. "The only thing is to tear him out of your heart; and I will help you!" She made as if she were ready to begin then, and Cornelia broke into a genuine laugh.

"Don't be ridiculous. I guess there isn't much to tear."

"Then what are you going to do?"

"Nothing! What can I! There isn't anything to do anything about. If it's there, he knows it, and he's left if there because he didn't care what we thought. He was just trying something. He's always treated me like a perfect—child. That's all there is of it, and you know it."

"Yes," Charmian meekly assented. Then she plucked up a spirit in Cornelia's behalf. "The only thing is to keep going on the same as ever, and show him we haven't seen anything, and don't care if we have."

"No," said Cornelia sadly, "I shall not come any more. Or, if I do, it will just be to—I'm not certain yet what I shall do." She provisionally dried her eyes and repaired her looks at the little mirror which hung at one side of the mantel, and then came back to Charmian who stood looking at Cornelia's sketches, still in the order Ludlow had left them in. She stole her arm round Cornelia's waist. "Well, anyway, he can't say *you've* returned the compliment. They're perfectly magnificent, every one; and they're all *me*. Now we can *both* live for art."

—1893

O. Henry

(1862–1910)

Born William Sydney Porter in Greensboro, North Carolina, by the age of nineteen Porter would already show signs of the tuberculosis that killed his mother and thus was sent to work on a sheep and cattle ranch in Texas to breathe in the fresh air and improve his health. He then spent some ten years in Austin, where he married and worked as a bank teller, until he was finally able to purchase a newspaper, the Rolling Stone. *By this time he was also writing for the* Houston Post. *The paper failed, however, and Porter was accused of embezzling bank funds. He fled to Honduras to avoid prosecution and returned in 1897 when he found out his wife was dying. He then served three years of a five-year prison term in a Columbus, Ohio, penitentiary. It was here where he began writing under the pseudonym of O. Henry. Released from prison in 1901, he moved to the anonymity of New York. A prolific writer, he often wrote one story a week. His first book,* Cabbages and Kings, *was published in 1904. Despite his great success, Porter always considered himself a fraud. He drank heavily in later life and died, in poverty, an alcoholic at the age of forty-eight. O. Henry is the master of the ironic twist. "The Last Leaf" is a good example. Written in 1902 and set in the Village, it is the story of a young sickly woman, who, on the verge of death, is restored to health by a painter who sacrifices his life for hers.*

"The Last Leaf"

In a little district west of Washington Square the streets have run crazy and broken themselves into small strips called "places." These "places" make strange angles and curves. One street crosses

O. Henry. "The Last Leaf" (1902).

itself a time or two. An artist once discovered a valuable possibility in this street. Suppose a collector with a bill for paints, paper and canvas should, in traversing this route, suddenly meet himself coming back, without a cent having been paid on account!

So, to quaint old Greenwich Village the art people soon came prowling, hunting for north windows and eighteenth-century gables and Dutch attics and low rents. Then they imported some pewter mugs and a chafing dish or two from Sixth Avenue, and became a "colony."

At the top of a squatty, three-story brick Sue and Johnsy had their studio. "Johnsy" was familiar for Joanna. One was from Maine; the other from California. They had met at the *table d' hote* of an Eighth Street "Delmonico's," and found their tastes in art, chicory salad and bishop sleeves so congenial that the joint studio resulted.

That was in May. In November a cold, unseen stranger whom the doctors called Pneumonia, stalked about the colony touching one here and there with his icy fingers. Over on the east side this ravager strode boldly, smiting his victims by scores, but his feet trod slowly through the maze of the narrow and moss-grown "places."

Mr. Pneumonia was not what you would call a chivalric old gentleman. A mite of a little woman with blood thinned by California zephyrs was hardly fair game for the red-fisted short-breathed old duffer. But Johnsy he smote; and she lay scarcely moving, on her painted iron bedstead, looking through the small Dutch window-panes at the blank side of the new brick house.

One morning the busy doctor invited Sue into the hallway with a shaggy, gray eyebrow.

"She has one chance in—let us say, ten," he said, as he shook down the mercury in his clinical thermometer. "And that chance is for her to want to live. The way people have of lining-up on the side of the undertaker makes the entire pharmacoeia look silly. Your little lady has made up her mind that she's not going to get well. Has she anything on her mind?"

"She—she wanted to paint the Bay of Naples some day," said Sue.

"Paint?—bosh! Has she anything on her mind worth thinking about twice—a man, for instance?"

"A man?" said Sue, with a jew's-harp twang in her voice. "Is a man worth—but, no, doctor; there is nothing of the kind."

"Well, it is the weakness, then," said the doctor. "I will do all that science, so far as it may filter through my efforts, can accomplish. But whenever my patient begins to count the carriages in her funeral procession I subtract 50 percent from the curative power of medicines. If you will get her to ask one question about the new winter styles in cloak sleeves I will promise you a one-in-five chance for her, instead of one in ten."

After the doctor had gone Sue went into the workroom and cried a Japanese napkin to a pulp. Then she swaggered into Johnsy's room with her drawing board, whistling ragtime.

Johnsy lay, scarcely making a ripple under the bedclothes, with her face toward the window. Sue stopped whistling, thinking she was asleep.

She arranged her board and began a pen-and-ink drawing to illustrate a magazine story. Young artists must pave their way to Art by drawing pictures for magazine stories that young authors write to pave their way to Literature.

As Sue was sketching a pair of elegant horseshow riding trousers and a monocle on the figure of the hero, an Idaho cowboy, she heard a low sound, several times repeated. She went quickly to the bedside.

Johnsy's eyes were wide open. She was looking out the window and counting—counting backward.

"Twelve," she said, and a little later "eleven": and then "ten," and "nine"; and then "eight" and "seven," almost together.

Sue looked solicitously out of the window. What was there to count? There was only a bare, dreary yard to be seen, and the blank side of the brick house twenty feet away. An old, old ivy vine, gnarled and decayed at the roots, climbed half way up the brick wall. The cold breath of autumn had stricken its leaves from the vine until its skeleton branches clung, almost bare, to the crumbling bricks.

"What is it, dear?" asked Sue.

"Six," said Johnsy, in almost a whisper. "They're falling faster now. Three days ago there were almost a hundred. It made my head ache to count them. But now it's easy. There goes another one. There are only five left now."

"Five what, dear? Tell your Sudie."

"Leaves. On the ivy vine. When the last one falls I must go, too. I've known that for three days. Didn't the doctor tell you?"

"Oh, I never heard of such nonsense," complained Sue, with magnificent scorn. "What have old leaves to do with your getting well? And you used to love that vine, so, you naughty girl. Don't be a goosey. Why, the doctor told me this morning that your chances for getting well real soon were—let's see exactly what he said—he said the chances were ten to one! Why, that's almost as good a chance as we have in New York when we ride on the street cars or walk past a new building. Try to take some broth now, and let Sudie go back to her drawing, so she can sell the editor man with it, and buy port wine for her sick child, and pork chops for her greedy self."

"You needn't get any more wine," said Johnsy, keeping her eyes fixed out the window. "There goes another. No, I don't want any broth. That leaves just four. I want to see the last one fall before it gets dark. Then I'll go, too."

"Johnsy, dear," said Sue, bending over her, "will you promise me to keep your eyes closed, and not look out the window until I am done working? I must hand those drawings in by to-morrow. I need the light, or I would draw the shade down."

"Couldn't you draw in the other room?" asked Johnsy coldly.

"I'd rather be here by you," said Sue. "Besides, I don't want you to keep looking at those silly leaves."

"Tell me as soon as you have finished," said Johnsy, closing her eyes, and lying white and still as a fallen statue, "because I want to see the last one fall. I'm tired of waiting. I'm tired of thinking. I want to turn loose my hold on everything, and go sailing down, down, just like one of those poor, tired leaves."

"Try to sleep," said Sue. "I must call Behrman up to be my model for the old hermit miner. I'll not be gone a minute. Don't try to move 'til I come back."

Old Behrman was a painter who lived on the ground floor beneath them. He was past sixty and had a Michael Angelo's Moses beard curling down from the head of a satyr along the body of an imp. Behrman was a failure in art. Forty years he had wielded the brush without getting near enough to touch the hem of his Mistress's robe. He had been always about to paint a masterpiece, but had never yet begun it. For several years he had painted nothing except now and then a daub in the line of commerce or advertising. He earned a little by serving as a model to those young artists in the colony who could not pay the price of a professional. He drank gin to excess, and still talked of his coming masterpiece. For the rest he was a fierce little old man, who scoffed terribly at softness in any one, and who regarded himself as especial mastiff-in-waiting to protect the two young artists in the studio above.

Sue found Behrman smelling strongly of juniper berries in his dimly lighted den below. In one corner was a blank canvas on an easel that had been waiting there for twenty-five years to receive the first line of the masterpiece. She told him of Johnsy's fancy, and how she feared she would, indeed, light and fragile as a leaf herself, float away, when her slight hold upon the world grew weaker.

Old Behrman, with his red eyes plainly streaming, shouted his contempt and derision for such idiotic imaginings.

"Vass!" he cried. "Is dere people in de world mit der foolishness to die because leafs dey drop off from a confounded vine? I haf not heard of such a thing. No, I will not bose as a model for your fool hermit-dunderhead. Vy do you allow dot silly pusiness to come in der brain of her? Ach, dot poor leetle Miss Yohnsy."

"She is very ill and weak," said Sue, "and the fever has left her mind morbid and full of strange fancies. Very well, Mr. Behrman, if you do not care to pose for me, you needn't. But I think you are a horrid old—old flibbertigibbet."

"You are just like a woman!" yelled Behrman. "Who said I will not bose? Go on. I come mit you. For half an hour I haf been trying to say dot I am ready to bose. Gott! dis is not any place in which one so goot as Miss Yohnsy shall lie sick. Some day I vill baint a masterpiece, and ve shall all go away. Gott! yes."

Johnsy was asleep when they went upstairs. Sue pulled the shade down to the window-sill, and motioned Behrman into the other room. In there they peered out the window fearfully at the ivy vine. Then they looked at each other for a moment without speaking. A persistent, cold rain was falling, mingled with snow. Behrman, in his old blue shirt, took his seat as the hermit miner on an upturned kettle for a rock.

When Sue awoke from an hour's sleep the next morning she found Johnsy with dull, wide-open eyes staring at the drawn green shade.

"Put it up; I want to see," she ordered, in a whisper.

Wearily Sue obeyed.

But, lo! after the beating rain and fierce gusts of wind that had endured through the livelong night, there yet stood out against the brick wall one ivy leaf. It was the last on the vine. Still dark green near its stem, but with its serrated edges tinted with the yellow of dissolution and decay, it hung bravely from a branch some twenty feet above the ground.

"It is the last one," said Johnsy. "I thought it would surely fall during the night. I heard the wind. It will fall to-day, and I shall die at the same time."

"Dear, dear!" said Sue, leaning her worn face down to the pillow, "think of me, if you won't think of yourself. What would I do?"

But Johnsy did not answer. The lonesomest thing in all the world is a soul when it is making ready to go on its mysterious, far journey. The fancy seemed to possess her more strongly as one by one the ties that bound her to friendship and to earth were loosed.

The day wore away, and even through the twilight they could see the lone ivy leaf clinging to its stem against the wall. And then, with the coming of the night the north wind was again loosed, while the rain still beat against the windows and pattered down from the low Dutch eaves.

When it was light enough Johnsy, the merciless, commanded that the shade be raised.

The ivy leaf was still there.

Johnsy lay for a long time looking at it. And then she called to Sue, who was stirring her chicken broth over the gas stove.

"I've been a bad girl, Sudie," said Johnsy. "Something has made the last leaf stay there to show me how wicked I was. It is a sin to want to die. You may bring me a little broth now, and some milk with a little port in it, and—no; bring me a hand-mirror first, and then pack some pillows about me, and I will sit up and watch you cook."

An hour later she said:

"Sudie, some day I hope to paint the Bay of Naples."

The doctor came in the afternoon, and Sue had an excuse to go into the hallway as he left.

"Even chances," said the doctor, taking Sue's thin, shaking hand in his. "With good nursing you'll win. And now I must see another case I have downstairs. Behrman, his name is—some kind of an artist, I believe. Pneumonia, too. He is an old, weak man, and the attack is acute. There is no hope for him; but he goes to the hospital to-day to be made more comfortable."

The next day the doctor said to Sue: "She's out of danger. You've won. Nutrition and care now—that's all."

And that afternoon Sue came to the bed where Johnsy lay, contentedly knitting a very blue and very useless woolen shoulder scarf, and put one arm around her, pillows and all.

"I have something to tell you, white mouse," she said. "Mr. Behrman died of pnemonia to-day in the hospital. He was ill only two days. The janitor found him on the morning of the first day in his room downstairs helpless with pain. His shoes and clothing were wet through and icy cold. They couldn't imagine where he had been on such a dreadful night. And then they found a lantern, still lighted, and some scattered brushes, and a palette with green and yellow colors mixed on it, and—look out the window, dear, at the last ivy leaf on the wall. Didn't you wonder why it never fluttered or moved when the wind blew? Ah, darling, it's Behrman's masterpiece—he painted it there the night that the last leaf fell."

—1902

44

John Reed

(1887–1920)

Born in Portland, Oregon, in 1887, John Reed moved to the Village in 1911, straight out of Harvard. In a significant way, the Village was an extension of the camaraderie he so much enjoyed back in Cambridge. With his easy charm and boyish good looks, he soon became the Golden Boy of the Village. "Within a block of my house was all the adventure in the world; within a mile every foreign country," wrote Reed in his long comic poem, "The Day in Bohemia," a paean to life as lived in the dilapidated rooming houses of Washington Square where he and his Harvard mates had settled. The third selection honors the Village poet and fellow free spirit, Harry Kemp. Reed started a short-lived but passionate affair with literary maven Mabel Dodge before marrying Louise Bryant. Reed left the frivolous life of the Village behind when he began writing dispatches on the Mexican and Russian revolutions as a war correspondent for the New York World, *the* Masses, *and other publications. The latter revolt inspired his greatest work,* Ten Days That Shook the World. *Reed died of typhus in Moscow in 1920, where he received a hero's funeral in the Kremlin, the only American to be buried along the Kremlin Wall.*

John Reed. From *The Day in Bohemia, or Life Among the Artists* (New York: Printed for the Author, January 1913).

from *The Day in Bohemia, or Life among the Artists in Manhattan's Quartier Latin*

"The Day in Bohemia"

Muse, you have got a job before you,—
Come, buckle to it, I implore you.
I would embalm in deathless rhyme
The great souls of our little time:
Inglorious Miltons by the score,—
Mute Wagners,—Rembrandts, ten or more,—
And Rodins, one to every floor.
In short, those unknown men of genius
Who dwell in third-floor-rears gangrenous,
Reft of their rightful heritage
By a commercial, soulless age.
Unwept, I might add,—and unsung,
Insolvent, but entirely young.

Twixt Broadway and Sixth Avenue,
And West perhaps a block or two,—
From Third Street up, and Ninth Street down,
Between Fifth Avenue and the Town,—
Policeman walk as free as air,
With nothing on their minds but hair,
And life is very, very fair,
In Washington Square.

Bohemia! Where dwell the Sacred Nine,
Who landed, steerage from the White Star Line,—
(For, when the Sacred Springs dried up in Italy
They packed their duds and emigrated prettily,

46

And all the Ladies, donning virile-jeans,
Became the Editors of Magazines.)

Bohemia! There, hiding neath the Arch,
Acteon on Diana steals a march;
Glimpsing the Huntress at her weekly tub
In the round fountain near the Little Club.
(She with a watchful eye out for the cop
Who haunts the corner where the busses stop.)
Or Dionysus, prone from many drams,
Praises the vine in gulping dithyrambs;
Till some official Pentheus, billy drawn,
Fans the loud-cursing God, and bids him "On!"
While that old Maenad, with disordered hair,
Each Sabbath eve careens around the Square.
Beneath the trees, when summer-nights are hot,
Bray shawn and psaltery, if you will or not;
Out swarm light-hearted Dagos by the millions
Gay neapolitans and dark Sicilians—
Shouting and laughing, slowly they creep on
Like a drab frieze about an East Side Parthenon!

Say! unenlightened bards whom I deride,
Defend your Gramercy or Morningside,
As fitter spots for poets to reside?
Nay, you know not where Virtue doth abide!
DO GLACKENS, FRENCH, WILL IRWIN linger
    there?
Nay, they would scorn your boasted Uptown air!
Are marble bathtubs your excuse ingenious?
In God's Name, what are bathtubs to a genius!
What restaurant have you that to compare is
With the cool garden back of PAGLIERI'S?
I challenge you to tell me where you've et
Viands more rare than at the LAFAYETTE!
Have you forgot the BENEDICK,—the JUDSON,

(Purest of hostelries this side the Hudson)
The Old BREVOORT, for breakfast late on Sunday,
The CRULLERY, where poor men dine on Monday?
You don't remember THOMPSON STREET. For
    shame!
Nor WAVERLY PLACE, nor, (classic, classic name!)
MACDOUGAL ALLEY, all of stables built
Blessed home of Art and MRS. VANDERBILT.

JOHN REED

"Forty-Two
Washington Square"

In winter the water is frigid,
In summer the water is hot;
And we're forming a club for controlling the tub
For there's only one bath to the lot.
You shave in unlathering Croton,
If there's water at all, which is rare,—
But the life isn't bad for a talented lad
At Forty-Two Washington Square!

The dust it flies in at the window,
The smells they come in at the door,
Our trousers lie meek where we threw 'em last week
Bestrewing the maculate floor.
The gas isn't all that it should be,
It flickers,—and yet I declare
There's pleasure or near it for young men of spirit
At Forty-Two Washington Square!

But nobody questions your morals,
And nobody asks for the rent,—
There's no one to pry if we're tight, you and I,
Or demand how our evenings are spent.
The furniture's ancient but plenty,
The linen is spotless and fair,
O life is a joy to a broth of a boy
At Forty-Two Washington Square!

[Harry Kemp]

The unkempt Harry Kemp now thumps our door;
He who has girdled all the world and more.
Free as a bird, no trammels him can bind,
He rides a boxcar as a hawk in the wind,—
A Man, who with ideals himself begirds;
Fresh from a fiery ordeal that has paved
The Pit anew—from terrors trebly braved
He rises, burning to avenge the wrong
By flooding all the stupid earth with song.
Here's to you HARRY, in whatever spot!
True poet, whether writing it or not.

—1913

Theodore Dreiser

(1871–1945)

Novelist and journalist of the naturalist school, Dreiser was considered an American pioneer although he was also criticized by some for his pedantic and clumsy writing style. Born in Terre Haute, Indiana, Dreiser was a reporter for the Chicago Daily Globe *in 1892 and drama editor and correspondent for the* St. Louis Republic *from 1893 to 1894. In 1900 he wrote* Sister Carrie, *the story of a small town girl named Carrie Meeber who moves to Chicago and then to New York where she makes a name for herself on Broadway. The publisher withdrew the book from circulation after public outcry over the novel's portrayal of characters who go unpunished for their sins and sexual transgressions. After the publication of his second novel,* Jenny Gerhardt, *in 1911, Dreiser was able to devote himself to full-time writing. His greatest success came in 1925 with the release of* An American Tragedy. *The character of Eugene Witla in* The "Genius" *is said to be partly autobiographical as well as based on the life of Village painter Everett Shinn. Published in 1915, it was banned the following year by the Society for the Suppression of Vice.*

from *The "Genius"*

The art world of New York is peculiar. It was then and for some time after, broken up into cliques with scarcely any unity. There was a world of sculptors, for instance, in which some thirty or forty sculptors had part—but they knew each other slightly, criticized each other severely and retired for the most part into a background

Theodore Dreiser. From *The "Genius"* (New York: World Publishing Co., 1915).

of relatives and friends. There was a painting world, as distinguished from an illustrating world, in which perhaps a thousand alleged artists, perhaps more, took part. Most of these were men and women who had some ability—enough to have their pictures hung at the National Academy of Design exhibition—to sell some pictures, get some decorative work to do, paint some portraits. There were studio buildings scattered about various portions of the city; in Washington Square; in Ninth and Tenth Streets; in odd places, such as Macdougal Alley and occasional cross streets from Washington Square to Fifty-ninth Street, which were filled with painters, illustrators, sculptors and craftsmen in art generally. This painting world had more unity than the world of sculptors and, in a way, included the latter. There were several art clubs—the Salmagundi, the Kit-Kat and the Lotus—and there were a number of exhibitions, ink, water color, oil, with their reception nights where artists could meet and exchange the courtesies and friendship of their world. In addition to this there were little communal groups such as those who resided in the Tenth Street studios; the Twenty-third Street Y.M.C.A.; the Van Dyck studios, and so on. It was possible to find little crowds, now and then, that harmonized well enough for a time and to get into a group, if, to use a colloquialism, one *belonged*. If you did not, art life in New York might be a very dreary thing and one might go a long time without finding just the particular crowd with which to associate.

Beside the painting world there was the illustrating world, made up of beginners and those who had established themselves firmly in editorial favor. These were not necessarily a part of the painting or sculpture worlds and yet, in spirit, were allied to them, had their clubs also, and their studios were in the various neighborhoods where the painters and sculptors were. The only difference was that in the case of the embryo illustrators they were found living three or four in one studio, partly because of the saving expense, but also because of the love of companionship and because they could hearten and correct one another in their work. A number of such interesting groups were in existence when Eugene arrived, but of course he did not know of them.

It takes time for the beginner to get a hearing anywhere. We all have to serve an apprenticeship, whatever field we enter. Eugene had talent and determination, but no experience, no savoir faire, no circle of friends and acquaintances. The whole city was strange and cold, and if he had not immediately fallen desperately in love with it as a spectacle he would have been unconscionably lonely and unhappy. As it was the great fresh squares, such as Washington, Union and Madison; the great streets, such as Broadway, Fifth Avenue and Sixth Avenue; the great spectacles, such as the Bowery at night, the East River, the water front, the Battery, all fascinated him with an unchanging glamour.

He was hypnotized by the wonder of this thing—the beauty of it. Such seething masses of people! Such whirlpools of life! The great hotels, the opera, the theaters, the restaurants, all gripped him with a sense of beauty. These lovely women in magnificent gowns; these swarms of cabs, with golden eyes, like monstrous insects; this ebb and surge of life at morning and evening, made him forget his loneliness. He had no money to spend, no immediate hope of a successful career, he could walk these streets, look in these windows, admire these beautiful women; thrill at the daily newspaper announcements of almost hourly successes in one field or another. Here and there in the news an author had made a great success with a book; a scientist with a discovery; a philosopher with a new theory; a financier with an investment. There was news of great plays being put on; great actors and actresses coming from abroad; great successes being made by debutantes in society; great movements forwarded generally. Youth and ambition had the call—he saw that. It was only a question of time, if you had talent, when you would get your hearing. He longed ardently for his but he had no feeling that it was coming to him quickly, so he got the blues. It was a long road to travel.

One of his pet diversions these days and nights was to walk the streets in rain or fog or snow. The city appealed to him, wet or white, particularly the public squares. He saw Fifth Avenue once in a driving snowstorm and under sputtering arc lights, and he hurried to his easel next morning to see if he could not put it down in black and white. It was unsuccessful, or at least he felt so, for after an hour of trying he threw it aside in disgust. But these spectacles were drawing him. He was wanting to do them—wanting to see them shown somewhere in color. Possible success was a solace at a time when all he could pay for a meal was fifteen cents and he had no place to go and not a soul with whom to talk.

It was an interesting phase of Eugene's character that he had a passion for financial independence. He might have written home from Chicago at times when he was hard pressed; he might have borrowed some money from his father now, but preferred to earn it—to appear to be further along than he was. If anyone had asked him he would have said he was doing fine. Practically he so wrote to Angela, giving as an excuse for further delay that he wanted to wait until he had ample means. He was trying all this time to make his two hundred dollars go as far as possible and to add to it by any little commissions he could get, however small. He figured his expenses down to ten dollars a week and managed to stay within that sum.

The particular building in which he had settled was really not a studio building but an old, run-down boarding and apartment house turned partially to uses of trade. The top floor contained three fair sized rooms and two hall bedrooms, all occupied by lonely individuals plying some craft or other. Eugene's next door neighbor chanced to be a hack illustrator, who had had his training in Boston and had to set up his easel here in the hope of making a living. There were not many exchanges of courtesies between them at first, although, the door being open the second day he arrived, he saw that an artist worked there, for the easel was visible.

No models applying at first he decided to appeal to the Art Students' League. He called on the Secretary and was given the names of four, who replied to postal cards from him. One he selected, a young Swedish American girl who looked somewhat like the character in the story he had in mind. She was neat and attractive, with dark hair, a straight nose and pointed chin, and Eugene immediately conceived a liking for her. He was ashamed of his surroundings, however, and consequently diffident. This particular model was properly distant, and he finished his pictures with as much expedition and as little expense as he possibly could.

Eugene was not given to scraping odd acquaintances, though he made friends fast enough when the balance of intellect was right. In Chicago he had become friendly with several young artists as a result of working with them at the Institute, but here he knew no one, having come without introductions. He did become acquainted with his neighbor, Philip Shotmeyer. He wanted to find out about local art life from him, but Shotmeyer was not brilliant, and could not supply him with more than minor details of what Eugene desired to know. Through him he learnt a little of studio regions, art personalities; the fact that young beginners worked in groups. Shotmeyer had been in such a group the year before, though why he was alone now he did not say. He sold drawings to some of the minor magazines, better magazines than Eugene had yet had dealings with. One thing he did at once for Eugene which was very helpful: he admired his work. He saw, as had others before him, something of his peculiar distinction as an artist, attended every show and one day he gave him a suggestion which was the beginning of Eugene's successful magazine career. Eugene was working on one of his street scenes—a task which he invariably essayed when he had nothing else to do. Shotmeyer had drifted in and was following the strokes of his brush as he attempted to portray a mass of East Side working girls flooding the streets after six o'clock. There were dark walls of buildings, a flaring gas lamp or two, some yellow lighted shop windows, and many shaded, half seen faces—bare suggestions of souls and pulsing life.

"Say," said Shotmeyer at one point, "that kind o' looks like the real thing to me. I've seen a crowd like that."

"Have you?" replied Eugene.

"You ought to be able to get some magazine to use that as a frontispiece. Why don't you try *Truth* with that?"

"Truth" was a weekly which Eugene, along with many others in the West, had admired greatly because it ran a double page color insert every week and occasionally used scenes of this character. Somehow he always needed a shove of this kind to make him act when he was drifting. He put more enthusiasm into his work because of Shotmeyer's remark, and when it was done decided to carry it to the office of *Truth*. The Art Director approved it on sight, though he said nothing, but carried it in to the Editor.

"Here's a thing that I consider a find in its way."

He set it proudly upon the editorial desk.

"Say," said the Editor, laying down a manuscript, "that's the real thing, isn't it? Who did that?"

"A young fellow by the name of Witla, who has just blown in here. He looks like the real thing to me."

"Say," went on the Editor, "look at the suggestion of faces back there! What? Reminds me just a little of the masses in Dore's stuff. It's good, isn't it?"

"It's fine," echoed the Art Director. "I think he's a comer, if nothing happens to him. We ought to get a few center pages out of him."

"How much does he want for this?"

"Oh, he doesn't know. He'll take almost anything. I'll give him seventy-five dollars."

"That's all right," said the Editor as the Art Director took the drawing down. "There's something new there. You ought to hang on to him."

"I will," replied his associate. "He's young yet. He doesn't want to be encouraged too much."

He went out, pulling a solemn countenance.

"I like this fairly well," he said. "We may be able to find room for it. I'll send you a check shortly if you'll let me have your address."

Eugene gave it. His heart was beating a gay tattoo in his chest. He did not think anything of price, in fact it did not occur to him. All that was in his mind was the picture as a double page spread. So he had really sold one after all and to *Truth!* Now he could honestly say he had made some progress. Now he could write Angela and tell her. He could send her copies when it came out. He could really have something to point to after this and best of all, now he knew he could do street scenes.

He went out into the street treading not the grey stone pavement but air. He threw back his head and breathed deep. He thought of other scenes like this which he could do. His dreams were beginning to be realized—he, Eugene Witla, the painter of a double page spread in *Truth*! Already he was doing a whole series in his imagination, all he had ever dreamed of. He wanted to run and tell Shotmeyer—to buy him a good meal. He almost loved him, commonplace hack that he was—because he had suggested to him the right thing to do.

"Say, Shotmeyer," he said, sticking his head in that worthy's door, "you and I eat tonight. *Truth* took that drawing."

"Isn't that fine," said his floor-mate, without a trace of envy. "Well, I'm glad. I thought they'd like it."

Eugene could have cried. Poor Shotmeyer! He wasn't a good artist, but he had a good heart. He would never forget him.

The chief trouble with his present situation, and with the entrance of these two women into his life, and it had begun to be a serious one to him, was that he was not making money. He had been able to earn about $1200 the first year; the second he made a little over two thousand, and this third year he was possibly doing a little better. But in view of what he saw around him and what he now knew of life, it was nothing. New York presented a spectacle of material display such as he had never known existed. The carriages on Fifth Avenue, the dinners at the great hotels, the constant talk of society functions in the newspapers, made his brain dizzy. He was inclined to idle about the streets, to watch the handsomely dressed crowds, to consider the evidences of show and refinement everywhere, and he came to the conclusion that he was not living at all, but existing. And as he had dreamed of it, art had seemed not only a road to distinction but also to affluence. Now, as he studied those about him, he found that it was not so. Artists were never tremendously rich, he learned. He remembered reading in Balzac's story "Cousin Betty," of a certain artist of great distinction who had been allowed condescendingly by one of the rich families of Paris to marry a daughter, but it was considered a great come down for her.

He had hardly been able to credit the idea at the time, so exalted was his notion of the artist. But now he was beginning to see that it represented the world's treatment of artists. There were in America a few who were very popular—meretriciously so he thought in certain cases—who were said to be earning from ten to fifteen thousand a year. How high would that place them, he asked himself, in that world of real luxury which was made up of the so-called *four hundred*—the people of immense wealth and social position. He had read in the papers that it took from fifteen to twenty-five thousand dollars a year to clothe a debutante. It was nothing uncommon, he heard, for a man to spend some fifteen to twenty dollars on his dinner at the restaurant. The prices he heard that tailors demanded— that dressmakers commanded, the display of jewels and expensive garments at the opera, made the poor little income of an artist look like nothing at all. Miss Finch was constantly telling him of the show and swagger she met with in her circle of acquaintances; for her tact and adaptability had gained her the friendship of a number of society people. Miss Channing, when he came to know her better, made constant references to things she came in contact with— great singers or violinists paid $1000 a night, or the tremendous salaries commanded by the successful opera stars. He began, as he looked at his own meager little income, to feel shabby again, and run down, such as he had during those first days in Chicago. Why, art, outside the fame, was nothing. It did not make for real living. It made for a kind of mental blooming, which everybody recognized, but you could be a poor, sick, hungry, shabby genius—you actually could. Look at Verlaine, who had recently died in Paris.

A part of this feeling was due to the opening of a golden age of luxury in New York, and the effect the reiterated sight of it was having on Eugene. Huge fortunes had been amassed in the preceding fifty years and now there were thousands of residents in the great new city who were worth anything from one to fifty and in some instances a hundred million dollars. The metropolitan area, particularly Manhattan Island above Fifty-ninth Street, was growing like a weed. Great hotels were being erected in various parts of the so-called "white light" district. There was beginning, just then, the first organized attempt of capital to supply a new need—the modern sumptuous, eight, ten and twelve story apartment house, which was to house the world of newly rich middle class folk who were pouring into New York from every direction. Money was being made in the West, the South and the North, and as soon as those who were making it had sufficient to permit them to live in luxury for the rest of their days they were moving East, occupying these expensive apartments, crowding the great hotels, patronizing the sumptuous restaurants, giving the city its air of spendthrift luxury. All the things which catered to showy material living were beginning to flourish tremendously, art and curio shops, rug shops, decorative companies dealing with the old and the new in hangings, furniture, objects of art; dealers in paintings, jewelry stores, china and glassware houses—anything and everything which goes to make life comfortable and brilliant. Eugene, as he strolled about the city, saw this, felt the change, realized that the drift was toward greater population, greater luxury, greater beauty. His mind was full of the necessity of living *now*. He was young *now*; he was vigorous *now*; he was keen *now*; in a few years he might not be— seventy years was the allotted span and twenty-five of his had already gone. How would it be if he never came into this luxury, was never allowed to enter society, was never permitted to live as wealth was now living! The thought hurt him. He felt an eager desire to tear wealth and fame from the bosom of the world. Life must give him his share. If it did not he would curse it to his dying day. So he felt when he was approaching twenty-six.

The effect of Christina Channing's friendship for him was particularly to emphasize this. She was not so much older than he, was possessed of very much the same temperament, the same hopes and aspirations, and she discerned almost as clearly as he did the current of events. New York was to witness a golden age of luxury. It was already passing into it. Those who rose to distinction in any field, particularly music or the stage, were likely to share in a most notable spectacle of luxury. Christina hoped to. She was sure she would. After a few conversations with Eugene she was inclined to feel that he would. He was so brilliant, so incisive.

"You have such a way with you," she said the second time he came. "You are so commanding. You make me think you can do almost anything you want to."

"Oh, no," he deprecated. "Not as bad as that. I have just as much trouble as anyone getting what I want."

"Oh, but you will though. You have ideas."

It did not take these two long to reach an understanding. They confided to each other their individual histories, with reservations, of course, at first. Christina told him of her musical history, beginning at Hagerstown, Maryland, and he went back to his earliest days in Alexandria. They discussed the differences in parental control to which they had been subject. He learned of her father's business, which was that of oyster farming, and confessed on his part to being the son of a sewing machine agent. They talked of small town influences, early illusions, the different things they had tried to do. She had sung in the local Methodist church, had once thought she would like to be a milliner, had fallen in the hands of a teacher who tried to get her to marry him and she had been on the verge of consenting. Something happened—she went away for the summer, or something of that sort, and changed her mind.

After an evening at the theater with her, a later supper one night and a third call, to spend a quiet evening in her room, he took her by the hand. She was standing by the piano and he was looking at her cheeks, her large inquiring eyes, her smooth rounded neck and chin.

"You like me," he said suddenly a propos of nothing save the mutual attraction that was always running strong between them. Without hesitation she nodded her head, though the bright blood mounted to her neck and cheeks.

"You are so lovely to me," he went on, "that words are of no value. I can paint you. Or you can sing me what you are, but mere words won't show it. I have been in love before, but never with anyone like you."

"Are you in love?" she asked naively.

"What is this?" he asked and slipped his arms about her, drawing her close.

She turned her head away, leaving her rosy cheek near his lips. He kissed that, then her mouth and her neck. He held her chin and looked into her eyes.

"Be careful," she said, "mamma may come in."

"Hang mamma!" he laughed.

"She'll hang you if she sees you. Mamma would never suspect me of anything like this."

"That shows how little mamma knows of her Christina," he answered.

"She knows enough at that," she confessed gaily. "Oh, if we were only up in the mountains now," she added.

"What mountains," he inquired curiously.

"The Blue Ridge. We have a bungalow up at Florizel. You must come up when we go there next summer."

"Will mamma be there?" he asked.

"And papa," she laughed.

"And I suppose Cousin Annie."

"No, brother George will be."

"Nix for the bungalow," he replied, using a slang word that had become immensely popular.

"Oh, but I know all the country round there. There are some lovely walks and drives." She said this archly, naively, suggestively, her bright face lit with an intelligence that seemed perfection.

"Well—such being the case!" he smiled, "and meanwhile . . . are." She nodded her head towards an inside room where Mrs. Channing was lying down with a slight headache. "Mamma doesn't leave me very often."

Eugene did not know exactly how to take Christina. He had never encountered this attitude before. Her directness, in connection with so much talent, such real ability, rather took him by surprise. He did not expect it—did not think she would confess affection for him; did not know just what she meant by speaking the way she did of the bungalow and Florizel. He was flattered, raised in his own self-esteem. If such a beautiful, talented creature as this could confess her love for him, what a personage he must be. And she was thinking of freer conditions—just what?

61

He did not want to press the matter too closely then and she was not anxious to have him do so—she preferred to be enigmatic. But there was a light of affection and admiration in her eye which made him very proud and happy with things just as they were.

As she said, there was little chance for love-making under conditions then existing. Her mother was with her most of the time. Christina invited Eugene to come and hear her sing at the Philharmonic Concerts; so once in a great ballroom at the Waldorf-Astoria and again in the imposing auditorium of Carnegie Hall and a third time in the splendid auditorium of the Arion Society, he had the pleasure of seeing her walk briskly to the footlights, the great orchestra waiting, the audience expectant, herself arch, assured—almost defiant, he thought, and so beautiful. When the great house thundered its applause he was basking in one delicious memory of her.

"Last night she had her arms about my neck. Tonight, when I call and we are alone she will kiss me. That beautiful, distinguished creature standing there bowing and smiling loves me and no one else. If I were to ask her she would marry me—if I were in a position and had the means."

"If I were in a position—" that thought cut him, for he knew that he was not. He could not marry her. In reality she would not have him knowing how little he made—or would she? He wondered.

The studio of Messrs. Smite, MacHugh and Witla in Waverley Place was concerned the following October with a rather picturesque event. Even in the city the time when the leaves began to yellow and fall brings a sense of melancholy, augmented by those preliminaries of winter, gray, lowery days, with scraps of paper, straws, bits of wood blown about by gusty currents of air through the streets, making it almost disagreeable to be abroad. The fear of cold and storm and suffering among those who have little was already apparent. Apparent too was the air of renewed vitality common to those who have spent an idle summer and are anxious to work again. Shopping and marketing and barter and sale were at high key. The art world, the social world, the manufacturing world, the professional worlds of law, medicine, finance, literature, were bubbling with a feeling of the necessity to do and achieve. The whole city, stung by the apprehension of winter, had an atmosphere of emprise and energy.

In this atmosphere, with a fairly clear comprehension of the elements which were at work making the color of the life about him, was Eugene, digging away at the task he had set himself. Since leaving Angela he had come to the conclusion that he must complete the jointings for the exhibition which had been running in his mind during the last two years. There was no other way for him to make a notable impression—he saw that. Since he had returned he had gone through various experiences: the experience of having Angela tell him that she was sure there was something wrong with her; an impression sincere enough, but based on an excited and overwrought imagination of evil to follow, and having no foundation in fact. Eugene was as yet, despite his several experiences, not sufficiently informed in such affairs to know. His lack of courage would have delayed him from asking if he had known. In the next place, facing this crisis, he had declared that he would marry her, and because of her distressed condition he thought he might as well do it now. He had wanted time to do some of the pictures he was working on, to take in a little money for drawing, to find a suitable place to live in. He had looked at various studios in various sections of the city and had found nothing, as yet, which answered to his taste or his purse. Anything with a proper light, a bath, a suitable sleeping room, and an inconspicuous chamber which might be turned into a kitchen, was difficult to find. Prices were high, ranging from fifty to one hundred and twenty-five and one hundred and fifty a month. There were some new studios being erected for the rich loungers and idlers which commanded, so he understood, three or four thousand dollars a year. He wondered if he should ever attain to any such magnificence through his art.

Again, in taking a studio for Angela and himself there was the matter of furniture. The studio he had with Smite and MacHugh was more or less of a camp. The workroom was bare of carpets or rugs. The two folding beds and the cot which graced their individual chambers were heirlooms from ancient predecessors—substantial but shabby. Beyond various drawings, three easels, and a chest of drawers of each, there was no suitable household equipment. A woman came twice a week to clean, send out the linen, and make up the beds.

To live with Angela required, in his judgment, many and much more significant things. His idea of a studio was some such one as that now occupied by Miriam Finch or Norma Whitmore. There ought to be furniture of a period—old Flemish or Colonial, Heppelwhite or Chippendale or Sheraton, such as he saw occasionally knocking about in curio shops and secondhand stores. It could be picked up if he had time. He was satisfied that Angela knew nothing of these things. There ought to be rugs, hangings of tapestry, bits of brass, pewter, copper, old silver, if he could afford it. He had an idea of someday obtaining a figure of the Christ in brass or plaster, hung upon a rough cross of walnut or teak, which he could hang or stand in some corner as one might a shrine and place before it two great candlesticks with immense candles smoked and dripping with wax. These lighted in a dark studio, with the outlines of the Christ flickering in the shadows behind would give the desired atmosphere to his studio. Such an equipment as he dreamed of would have cost in the neighborhood of two thousand dollars.

Of course this was not to be thought of at this period. He had no more than that in ready cash. He was writing to Angela about his difficulties in finding a suitable place, when he heard of a studio in Washington Square South, which its literary possessor was going to quit for the winter. It was, so he understood, handsomely furnished, and was to be let for the rent of the studio. The owner wanted someone who would take care of it by occupying it for him until he should return the following fall. Eugene hurried round to look at it and, taken with the location, the appearance of the square from the windows, the beauty of the furnishings, felt that he would like to live here. This would be the way to introduce Angela to New York. This would be the first and proper impression to give her. Here, as in every arranged studio he had yet seen were books, pictures, bits of statuary, implements of copper and some few of silver.

There was a great fish net dyed green and spangled with small bits of mirror to look like scales which hung as a veil between the studio proper and an alcove. There was a piano done in black walnut, and odd pieces of furniture, Mission, Flemish, Venetian of the sixteenth century and English of the seventeenth, which, despite that diversity offered a unity of appearance and a harmony of usefulness. There was one bedroom, a bath, and a small partitioned section which could be used as a kitchen. With a few of his pictures judiciously substituted he could see a perfect abode here for himself and his wife. The rent was fifty dollars. He decided that he would risk it.

Having gone so far as to indicate that he would take it—he was made to feel partially resigned to marriage by the very appearance of the place—he decided that he would marry in October. Angela could come to New York or Buffalo—she had never seen Niagara Falls—and they could be married there. She had spoken recently of visiting her brother at West Point. Then they could come here and settle down. He decided that this must be so, wrote to her to that effect, and vaguely hinted to Smite and MacHugh that he might get married shortly.

This was a great blow to his partners in art, for Eugene was very popular with them. He had the habit, with those he liked, of jesting constantly. "Look at the look of noble determination on Smite's brow this morning," he would comment cheerfully on getting up; or "MacHugh, you lazy lout, crawl out and earn your living."

MacHugh's nose, eyes and ears would be comfortably buried in the folds of a blanket.

"These hack artists," Eugene would sigh disconsolately. "There's not much to be made out of them. A pile of straw and a couple of boiled potatoes a day is all they need."

"Aw, cut it out," MacHugh would grunt.

"To hell, to hell, I yell, I yell," would come from somewhere in the voice of Smite.

"If it weren't for me," Eugene would go on, "God knows what would become of this place. A lot of farmers and fishmen trying to be artists."

"And laundry wagon drivers, don't forget that," MacHugh would add, sitting up and rubbing his tousled head, for Eugene had related some of his experiences. "Don't forget the contribution made by the American Steam Laundry Company to the world of true art."

"Collars and cuffs I would have you know is artistic," Eugene at once declared with mock dignity, "whereas plows and fish is trash."

Sometimes this "kidding" would continue for a quarter of an hour at a stretch, when some one remark really brighter than any other would dissolve the whole in laughter. Work began after breakfast, to which they usually sallied forth together, and would continue unbroken save for necessary engagement or period of entertainment, lunch and so on, until five in the afternoon.

They had worked together now for a couple of years. They had, by experience, learned of each other's reliability, courtesy, kindness and liberality. Criticism was free, generous, and sincerely intended to be helpful. Pleasure trips, such as walks on grey, lowery days, or in rain or brilliant sunshine, or trips to Coney Island, Far Rockaway, the theatres, the art exhibitions, the odd and peculiar restaurants of different nationalities, were always undertaken in a spirit of joyous camaraderie. Jesting as to morality, their respective abilities, their tendencies and characteristics were all taken and given in good part. At one time it would be Joseph Smite who would come in for a united drubbing and excoriation on the part of Eugene and MacHugh. At another time Eugene or MacHugh would be the victim, the other two joining forces vigorously. Art, literature, personalities, phases of life, philosophy, were discussed by turn. As with Jerry Mathews, Eugene had learned of new things from these men—the life of fisher-folk, and the characteristics of the ocean from Joseph Smite; the nature and spirit of the great West from MacHugh. Each appeared to have an inexhaustible fund of experiences and reminiscences which refreshed and entertained the trio day by day year in and year out. They were at their best strolling through some exhibit or preliminary view of an art collection offered for sale, when all their inmost conviction of what was valuable and enduring in art would come to the surface. All three were intolerant of reputations as such, but were strong for individual merit whether it carried a great name or not. They were constantly becoming acquainted with the work of some genius little known here, and celebrating his talents, each to the others. Thus Monet, Degas, Manet, Ribera, Monticelli, by turns came up for examination and praise.

When Eugene then, toward the end of September, announced that he might be leaving them shortly, there was a united wail of opposition. Joseph Smite was working on a sea scene at the time, doing his best to get the proper color harmony between the worm-eaten deck of a Gold Coast trading ship, a half naked West Coast Negro handling a broken wheel, and a mass of blue black undulations in the distance which represented the boundless sea.

"G'wan!" said Smite, incredulously, for he assumed that Eugene was jesting. There had been a steady stream of letters issuing from somewhere in the West and delivered here week after week, as there had been for MacHugh, but this by now was a commonplace, and apparently meant nothing. "You marry? What the hell do you want to get married for? A fine specimen you will make! I'll come around and tell your wife."

"Sure," returned Eugene. "It's true, I may get married." He was amused at Smite's natural assumption that it was a jest.

"Stow that," called MacHugh, from his easel. He was working on a country corner picture, a group of farmers before a country post office. "You don't want to break up this shack, do you?" Both of these men were fond of Eugene. They found him inspiring, helpful, always intensely vigorous and apparently optimistic.

"I don't want to break up any shack. But haven't I a right to get married?"

"I vote no, by God!" said Smite emphatically. "You'll never go out of here with my consent. Peter, are we going to stand for anything like that?"

"We are not," replied MacHugh. "We'll call out the reserves if he tries any game like that on us. I'll prefer charges against him. Who's the lady, Eugene?"

"I bet I know," suggested Smite. "He's been running up to Twenty-sixth Street pretty regularly." Joseph was thinking of Miriam Finch, to whom Eugene had introduced both him and MacHugh.

"Nothing like that, surely," inquired MacHugh, looking over at Eugene to see if it possibly could be so.

"It's all true, fellers," replied Eugene, "—— as God is my judge. I'm going to leave you soon."

"You're not really talking seriously, are you, Witla?" inquired Joseph soberly.

"I am, Joe," said Eugene quietly. He was studying the perspective of his sixteenth New York view,—three engines coming abreast into a great yard of cars. The smoke, the haze, the dingy reds and blues and yellows and greens of kicked about box cars were showing with beauty—the vigor and beauty of raw reality.

"Soon?" asked MacHugh, equally quietly. He was feeling that touch of pensiveness which comes with a sense of vanishing pleasures.

"I think some time in October, very likely," replied Eugene.

"Jesus Christ, I'm sorry to hear that," put in Smite.

He laid down his brush and strolled over to the window. MacHugh, less expressive in extremes, worked on meditatively.

"When'd you reach that conclusion, Witla?" he asked after a time.

"Oh, I've been thinking it over for a long time, Peter," he returned. "I should really have married before if I could have afforded it. I know how things are here or I wouldn't have sprung this so suddenly. I'll hold up my end on the rest here until you get someone else."

"To hell with the rent," said Smite. "We don't want anyone else, do we, Peter? We didn't have anyone else before."

Smite was rubbing his square chin and contemplating his partner as if they were facing a catastrophe.

"There's no use talking about that," said Peter. "You know we don't care about the rent. Do you mind telling us who you're going to marry? Do we know her?"

"You don't," returned Eugene. "She's out in Wisconsin. It's the one who writes the letters. Angela Blue is her name."

"Well, here's to Angela Blue, by God, say I," said Smite, recovering his spirits and picking up his paintbrush from his board to hold aloft. "Here's to Mrs. Eugene Witla, and may she never reef a sail to a storm or foul an anchor, as they say up Nova Scotia way."

"Right oh," added MacHugh, catching the spirit of Smite's generous attitude. "Them's my sentiments. When d'you expect to get married really, Eugene?"

"Oh I haven't fixed the time exactly. About November first I should say. I hope you won't say anything about it though, either of you. I don't want to go through any explanations."

"We won't, but it's tough, you old walrus. Why the hell didn't you give us time to think it over? You're a fine jellyfish, you are."

He poked him reprimandingly in the ribs.

"There isn't anyone any more sorry than I am," said Eugene. "I hate to leave here, I do. But we won't lose track of each other. I'll still be around here."

"Where do you expect to live? Here in the city?" asked MacHugh, still a little gloomy.

"Sure. Right here in Washington Square. Remember that Dexter studio Weaver was telling about? The one in the third floor at sixty-one? That's it."

"You don't say!" exclaimed Smite. "You're in right. How'd you get that?"

Eugene explained.

"Well, you sure are a lucky man," observed MacHugh. "Your wife ought to like that. I suppose there'll be a cozy corner for an occasional strolling artist?"

"No farmers, no sea-faring men, no artistic hacks—nothing!" declared Eugene dramatically.

"You to Hell,' said Smite. "When Mrs. Witla sees us—"

"She'll wish she'd never come to New York," put in Eugene.

"She'll wish she'd seen us first," said MacHugh.

After the quiet of a small town, the monotony and simplicity of country life, the dreary, reiterated weariness of teaching a country school, this new world into which Angela was plunged seemed to her astonished eyes to be compounded of little save beauties, curiosities and delights. The human senses, which weary so quickly of reiterated sensory impressions, exaggerate with equal readiness the beauty and charm of the unaccustomed. If it is new, therefore it must be better than that which we have had of old. The material details with which we are able to surround ourselves seem at times to remake our point of view. If we have been poor, wealth will seem temporarily to make us happy; when we have been amid elements and personages discordant to our thoughts, to be put among harmonious conditions seems, for the time being to solve all our woes. So little do we have that interior peace which no material conditions truly affect or disturb.

When Angela awoke the next morning, this studio in which she was now to live seemed the most perfect habitation which could be devised by man. The artistry of the arrangement of the rooms, the charm of the conveniences—a bathroom with hot and cold water next to the bedroom; a kitchen with an array of necessary utensils. In the rear portion of the studio used as a dining-room a glimpse of the main studio gave her the sense of art which dealt with nature, the beauty of the human form, colors, tones—how different from teaching school. To her the difference between the long, low rambling house at Blackwood with its vine ornamental windows, its somewhat haphazard arrangement of flowers and its great lawn, and this peculiarly compact and ornate studio apartment looking out upon Washington Square, was all in favor of the latter. In Angela's judgment there was no comparison. She could not have understood if she could have seen into Eugene's mind at this time how her home town, her father's single farm, the blue waters of the little lake near her door, the shadows of the tall trees on her lawn were somehow, compounded for him not only with classic beauty itself, but with her own charm. When she was among these things she partook of their beauty and was made more beautiful thereby. She did not know how much she had lost in leaving them behind. To her all these older elements of her life were shabby and unimportant, pointless and to be neglected. This new world was in its way for her an Aladdin's cave of delight. When she looked out on the great square for the first time the next morning, seeing it bathed in sunlight, a dignified line of red brick dwellings to the north, a towering office building to the east, trucks, carts, cars and vehicles clattering over the pavement below, it all seemed gay with youth and energy.

"We'll have to dress and go out to breakfast," said Eugene. "I didn't think to lay anything in. As a matter of fact I wouldn't have known what to buy if I had wanted to. I never tried housekeeping for myself."

"Oh, that's all right," said Angela, fondling his hands, "only let's not go out to breakfast unless we have to. Let's see what's here," and she went back to the very small room devoted to cooking purposes to see what cooking utensils had been provided. She had been dreaming of housekeeping and cooking for Eugene, of petting and spoiling him, and now the opportunity had arrived. She found that Mr. Dexter, their generous lessor, had provided himself with many conveniences—breakfast and dinner sets of brown and blue porcelain, a coffee percolator, a charming dull blue teapot with cups to match, a chafing dish, a set of waffle irons, griddles, spiders, skillets, stew and roasting pans, and knives and forks of steel and silver in abundance. Obviously, he had entertained from time to time, for there were bread, cake, sugar, flour and salt boxes and a little chest containing, in small drawers, various spices.

"Oh, it will be easy to get something here," said Angela, lighting the burners of the gas to see whether it was in good working order. "We can just go out to market if you'll come and show me once and get what we want. It won't take a minute. I'll know after that." Eugene consented gladly.

She had always fancied she would be an ideal housekeeper and now that she had her Eugene she was anxious to begin. It would be such a pleasure to show him what a manager she was, how everything would go smoothly in her hands, how careful she would be of his earnings—their joint possessions.

She was sorry, now that she saw that art was no great producer of wealth, that she had no money to bring him, but she knew that Eugene in the depth of his heart thought nothing of that. He was too impractical. He was a great artist, but when it came to practical affairs she felt instinctively that she was much the wiser. She had bought so long, calculated so well for her sisters and brothers.

71

Out of her bag (for her trunks had not yet arrived) she extracted a neat house dress of pale green linen which she put on after she had done up her hair in a cozy coil, and together with Eugene for a temporary guide, they set forth to find the stores. He had told her, looking out the windows, that there were lines of Italian grocers, butchers and vegetable men in the side streets, leading south from the square, and into one of these they now ventured. The swarming, impressive life of the street almost took her breath away, it was so crowded. Potatoes, tomatoes, eggs, flour, butter, lamb chops, salt—a dozen little accessories were all purchased in small quantities, and then they eagerly returned to the studio. Angela was a little disgusted with the appearance of some of the stores, but some of them were clean enough. It seemed so strange to her to be buying in an Italian street, with Italian women and children about, their swarthy leathern faces set with bright, almost feverish eyes. Eugene in his brown corduroy suit and soft green hat, watching and commenting at her side, presented such a contrast. He was so tall, so exceptional, so laconic.

"I like them when they wear rings in their ears," he said at one time.

"Get the coal man who looks like a bandit," he observed at another.

"This old woman here might do for the witch of Endor."

Angela attended strictly to her marketing. She was gay and smiling, but practical. She was busy wondering in what quantities she should buy things, how she would keep fresh vegetables, whether the ice box was really clean; how much delicate dusting the various objects in the studio would require. The raw brick walls of the street, the dirt and slops in the gutter, the stray cats and dogs hungry and lean, the swarming stream of people, did not appeal to her as picturesque at all. Only when she heard Eugene expatiating gravely did she begin to realize that all this must have artistic significance. If Eugene said so it did. But it was a fascinating world whatever it was, and it was obvious that she was going to be very, very happy.

There was a breakfast in the studio then of hot biscuit with fresh butter, an omelet with tomatoes, potatoes stewed in cream, and coffee. After the long period of commonplace restaurant dining which Eugene had endured, this seemed ideal. To sit in your own private apartment with a charming wife opposite you ready to render you any service, and with an array of food before you which revived the finest memories in your gustatory experience, seemed perfect. Nothing could be better. He saw visions of a happy future if he could finance this sort of thing. It would require a lot of money, more than he had been making, but he thought he could make out. After breakfast Angela played on the piano, and then, Eugene wanting to work, she started housekeeping in earnest. The trunks arriving gave her the task of unpacking and with that and lunch and dinner to say nothing of love she had sufficient to do.

It was a charming existence for a little while. Eugene suggested that they should have Smite and MacHugh to dinner first of all, these being his closest friends. Angela agreed heartily for she was only too anxious to meet the people he knew. She wanted to show him she knew how to receive and entertain as well as anyone. She made great preparations for the Wednesday evening following—the night fixed for the dinner—and when it came was on the qui vive to see what his friends were like and what they would think of her.

The occasion passed off smoothly enough and was the occasion of considerable jollity. These two cheerful worthies were greatly impressed with the studio. They were quick to praise it before Angela, and to congratulate him on his good fortune in having married her. Angela, in the same dress in which she had appeared at dinner in Buffalo, was impressive. Her mass of yellow hair fascinated the gaze of both Smith and MacHugh.

"Gee, what hair!" Smite observed secretly to MacHugh when neither Angela nor Eugene were within hearing distance.

"You're right," returned MacHugh. "She's not at all bad looking, is she?"

"I should say not," returned Smite who admired Angela's simple, good-natured western manners. A little later, more subtly, they expressed their admiration of her, and she was greatly pleased.

Marietta, who had arrived late that afternoon, had not made her appearance yet. She was in the one available studio bedroom making her toilet. Angela, in spite of her fine raiment, was busy superintending the cooking, for although through the janitor she had managed to negotiate the loan of a girl to serve, she could not get anyone to cook. A soup, a fish, a chicken and a salad, were the order of procedure. Marietta finally appeared, ravishing in pink silk. Both Smite and MacHugh sat up and Marietta proceeded to bewitch them. Marietta knew no order or distinctions in men. They were all slaves to her—victims to be stuck on the spit of her beauty and broiled in their amorous uncertainties at her leisure. In after years Eugene learned to speak of Marietta's smile as "the dagger." The moment she appeared smiling he would say, "Ah, we have it out again, have we? Who gets the blade this evening? Poor victim!"

Being her brother-in-law now, he was free to slip his arm about her waist and she took this family connection as license to kiss him. There was something about Eugene which held her always. During these very first days she gratified her desire to be in his arms, but always with a sense of reserve which kept him in check. She wondered secretly how much he liked her.

Smite and MacHugh, when she appeared, both rose to do her service. MacHugh offered her his chair by the fire. Smite bestirred himself in an aimless fashion.

"I've just had such a dandy week up at West Point," began Marietta cheerfully, "dancing, seeing dress parades, walking with the soldier boys."

"I warn you two, here and now," began Eugene, who had already learned to tease Marietta, "that you're not safe. This woman is dangerous. As artists in good standing you had better look out for yourselves.

"Oh, Eugene, how you talk," laughed Marietta, her teeth showing effectively. "Mr. Smite, I leave it to you. Isn't that a mean way to introduce a sister-in-law? I'm here for just a few days too, and have so little time. I think it cruel!"

"It's a shame!" said Smite, who was plainly a willing victim. "You ought to have another kind of brother-in-law. If you had some people I know now——"

"It's an outrage," commented MacHugh. "There's one thing though. You may not require so very much time."

"Now I think that's ungallant," Marietta laughed. "I see I'm all alone here except for Mr. Smite. Never mind. You all will be sorry when I'm gone."

"I believe that, " replied MacHugh, feelingly.

Smite simply stared. He was lost in admiration of her cream and peaches complexion, her fluffy, silky brown hair, her bright blue eyes and plump rounded arms. Such radiant good nature would be heavenly to live with. He wondered what sort of a family this was that Eugene had become connected with. Angela, Marietta, a brother at West Point. They must be nice, conservative, well-to-do western people. Marietta went to help her sister, and Smite, in the absence of Eugene, said: "Say, he's in right, isn't he? She's a peach. She's got it a little on her sister."

MacHugh merely stared at the room. He was taken with the complexion and arrangement of things generally. The old furniture, the rugs, the hangings, the pictures, Eugene's borrowed maid-servant in a white apron and cap, Angela, Marietta, the bright table set with colored china and an arrangement of silver candlesticks— Eugene had certainly changed the tenure of his life radically within the last ten days. Why he was marvelously fortunate. This studio was a wonderful piece of luck. Some people—and he shook his head meditatively.

"Well," said Eugene, coming back after some final touches to his appearance, "what do you think of it, Peter?"

"You're certainly moving along, Eugene. I never expected to see it. You ought to praise God. You're plain lucky."

Eugene smiled enigmatically. He was wondering whether he was. Neither Smite nor MacHugh nor anyone could dream of the conditions under which this came about. What a sham the world was anyhow. Its surface appearances so ridiculously deceptive! If anyone had known of the apparent necessity when he first started to look for an apartment, of his own mood toward it!

Marietta came back, and Angela. The latter had taken kindly to both these men, or boys as she already considered them. Eugene had a talent for reducing everybody to "simply folks" as he called them. So these two capable and talented men were mere country boys like himself—and Angela caught his attitude.

"I'd like to have you let me make a sketch of you some day Mrs. Witla," MacHugh said to Angela when she came back to the fire. He was essaying portraiture as a sideline and he was anxious for good opportunities to practice.

Angela thrilled at the invitation, and the use of her new name, Mrs. Witla, by Eugene's old friends.

"I'd be delighted," she replied, flushing.

"My word, you look nice, Angel-Face," exclaimed Marietta catching her about the waist. "You paint her with her hair down in braids, Mr. MacHugh. She makes a stunning Gretchen."

Angela flushed anew.

"I've been reserving that for myself, Peter," said Eugene, "but you try your hand at it. I'm not much in portraiture anyhow."

Smite smiled at Marietta. He wished he could paint her, but he was poor at figure work except as incidental characters in sea scenes. He could do men better than he could women.

"If you were an old sea captain now, Miss Blue," he said to Marietta gallantly, "I could make a striking thing out of you."

"I'll try to be, if you want to paint me," she replied gaily. "I'd look fine in a big pair of boots and a raincoat, wouldn't I Eugene?"

"You certainly would, if I'm any judge," replied Smite. "Come over to the studio and I'll rig you out. I have all those things on hand."

"I will," she replied, laughing. "You just say the word."

MacHugh felt as if Smite were stealing a march on him. He wanted to be nice to Marietta, to have her take an interest in him.

"Now, looky, Joseph," he protested. "I was going to suggest making a study of Miss Blue myself."

"Well, you're too late," replied Smite. "You didn't speak quick enough."

Marietta was greatly impressed with this atmosphere in which Angela and Eugene were living. She expected to see something artistic, but nothing so nice as this particular studio. Angela explained to her that Eugene did not own it, but that made small difference in Marietta's estimate of its significance. Eugene had it. His art and social connections brought it about. They were beginning excellently well. If she could have as nice a home when she started on her married career she would be satisfied.

They sat down about the round teak table which was one of Dexter's prized possessions, and were served by Angela's borrowed maid. The conversation was light and for the most part pointless, serving only to familiarize these people with each other. Both Angela and Marietta were taken with the two artists because they felt in them a note of homely conservatism. These men spoke easily and naturally of the trials and triumphs of art life, and the difficulty of making a good living, and seemed to be at home with personages of repute in one world and another, its greatest reward.

During the dinner Smite narrated experiences in his sea-faring life, and MacHugh of his mountain camping experiences in the West. Marietta described experiences with her beaux in Wisconsin and characteristics of her yokel neighbors at Blackwood, Angela joining in. Finally MacHugh drew a pencil sketch of Marietta followed by a long train of admiring yokels, her eyes turned up in a very shy, deceptive manner.

"Now I think that's cruel," she declared, when Eugene laughed heartily. "I never look like that."

"That's just the way you look and do," he declared. "You're the broad and flowery path that leadeth to destruction."

"Never mind, Babyette," put in Angela. "I'll take your part if no one else will. You're a nice, demure, shrinking girl and you wouldn't look at anyone, would you?"

Angela got up and was holding Marietta's head mock sympathetically in her arms.

"Say, that's a dandy pet name," called Smite, moved by Marietta's beauty.

"Poor Marietta," observed Eugene. "Come over here to me and I'll sympathize with you."

"You don't take my drawing in the right spirit, Miss Blue," put in MacHugh cheerfully. "It's simply to show how popular you are."

77

Angela stood beside Eugene as her guests departed, her slender arm about his waist. Marietta was coquetting finally with MacHugh. These two friends of his, thought Eugene, had the privilege of singleness to be gay and alluring to her. With him that was over now. He could not be that way to any girl anymore. He had to behave— be calm and circumspect. It cut him, this thought. He saw at once it was not in accord with his nature. He wanted to do just as he had always done—make love to Marietta if she would let him, but he could not. He walked to the fire when the studio door was closed.

"They're such nice boys," exclaimed Marietta. "I think Mr. MacHugh is as funny as he can be. He has such droll wit."

"Smite is nice too," replied Eugene defensively.

"They're both lovely—just lovely," returned Marietta.

"I like Mr. MacHugh a little the best—he's quainter," said Angela, "but I think Mr. Smite is just as nice as he can be. He's so old fashioned. There's not anyone as nice as my Eugene, though," she said affectionately, putting her arm about him.

"Oh, dear, you two!" exclaimed Marietta. "Well, I'm going to bed."

Eugene sighed.

They had arranged a couch for her which could be put behind the silver-spangled fish net in the alcove when company was gone.

Eugene thought what a pity that already this affection of Angela's was old to him. It was not as it would be if he had taken Marietta or Christina. They went to their bedroom to retire and then he saw that all he had was passion. Must he be satisfied with that? Could he be? It started a chain of thought which, while persistently interrupted or befogged, was really never broken. Momentary sympathy, desire, admiration, might obscure it, but always fundamentally it was there. He had put his head in a noose. He had subjected himself to conditions which he did not sincerely approve of. How was he going to remedy this—or could it ever be remedied?

—1915

Harry Kemp

(1883–1960)

Called the "tramp poet," Harry Kemp lived the life of the quintessential bohemian through most of his days. He came to the Village in 1912 and soon earned a place in that vaunted neighborhood for his eccentricity and singular personality. A born entrepreneur and self-promoter, he set out on his picaresque journeys across America before Carl Sandburg, before Vachel Lindsay, and thus followed in the tradition of a Walt Whitman, a Robert Service, or a Jack London. For these reasons, this traveler on the open road of life has been referred to as the spiritual forebear of Jack Kerouac, the King of the Beats. Kemp's autobiography, Tramping on Life *(1922), has been called a minor classic of "intellectual vagabondage," to borrow a phrase from fellow bohemian Floyd Dell. Its sequel,* More Miles *(1926), didn't do quite as well but still was pure Kemp. Harry Kemp never made much money from his writings, though he did write for a surprisingly diverse number of publications, ranging from the* Smart Set *and the* Saturday Evening Post *to the* Masses *and the* Quill. *During the late teens Kemp started his own theater troupes, first at the Thimble Theater and then at Harry Kemp's Playhouse at 8 Minetta Street, prompting Village troubadour and the editor of the* Quill, *Bobby Edwards, to bill Kemp "the Shakespeare of Minetta Street." Kemp spent his last years in Provincetown, living in a tiny shack on the dunes, donning a black cape and proclaimed himself the "Poet of the Dunes."*

The first two selections are from Chanteys and Ballads: *one describes the spartan surroundings of his humble Greenwich Village dwelling, the other commemorates the street lamp lighters on Charles Street in the Village. The third poem is a parody of Whitman that originally appeared in the May 1914 issue of the* Masses.

Harry Kemp. "A Poet's Room: Greenwich Village 1912" (1912) and "Street Lamp: Greenwich" from *Chanteys and Ballads* (1912) and "Leaves of Burdock" from the *Masses* (May 1914).

"A Poet's Room
Greenwich Village 1912"

I have a table, cot and chair
And nothing more. The walls are bare
Yet I confess that in my room
Lie Syrian rugs rich from the loom,
Stand statues poised on flying toe,
Hang tapestries with folk a-flow
As the wind takes them to and fro.
And workman Fancy has inlaid
My walls with ivory and jade.

Though opening on a New York street
Full of cries and hurrying feet
My window is a faery space
That gives on each imagined place;
Old ruins lost in desert peace;
The broken fanes and shrines of Greece;
Aegean islands fringed with foam;
The everlasting tops of Rome;
Troy flowing red with skyward flame,
And every spot of hallowed fame.

Outside my window I can see
The sweet blue lake of Galilee,
And Carmel's purple-regioned height
And Sinai clothed with stars and night.

But this is told in confidence,
So not a word when you go hence,
For if my landlord once but knew
My attic fetched so large a view,
The churl would never rest content
Till he had raised the monthly rent.

—1912

"Street Lamps: Greenwich Village"

Softly they take their being, one by one,
From the lamp-lighter's hand, after the sun
Has dropped to dusk . . . like little flowers they bloom
Set in long rows amid the growing gloom. . . .

Who he who lights them is, I do not know,
Except that, every eve, with footfall slow
And regular, he passes by my room
And sets his gusty flowers of light a-bloom.

—1912

"Leaves of Burdock"

Three cheers for God and six more for Infinity. . . .
By God I shall sing the entire universe, and no
one shall stop me!
Rocks, stones, stars, wash-tubs, axe-handles, red-
wood trees, the Mississippi—everything!
Hurrah for me! Superbos, optimos, . . . I, seeing eidolons, proclaim myself, and, through
myself, all men!
By God, I say I *shall* sing!
I tell you that everything is good . . . Life, death,
burial, beer, birth, marriage, wedding certifi-
cates, polygamy, polyandry . . . and he who
denies himself is also right in his way. . . .
Who said that evil is evil? I say that evil is
good!
Ultime Thule, Ne Plus Ultra, E Pluribus Unum!
Good is both good and evil . . . evil is both evil
and good!
Everything is nothing, and nothing is everything . . .
I salute you, camarados, eleves, Americanos, Pis-
tachios, Cascaretos Mios—I salute you!
I come singing, strong, contemptuous, virile, and
having hair on my chest as abundant as a hay-
stack . . .
I, imperturbe, aplomb, sangfroid . . . Hurrah,
hurrah!

—May 1914

82

Hippolyte Havel

(1858–1950)

The resident Village anarchist, Hippolyte Havel was a ubiquitous figure on the Village streets during the nineteen teens. Allen Churchill in The Improper Bohemians *describes him as "a tiny man with spectacles, a pointed goatee, and ferocious mustaches, who possessed a notable record of incarceration for anarchist activity both in this country and abroad." Polly Holladay hired him as a cook and waiter at her famous Village eatery. Havel pulled no punches toward the customers of the restaurant, which he disdainfully dismissed as members of the dreaded capitalist class. "Bourgeois pigs!" he would snarl into their faces. To visitors, though, it was all part and parcel of the Village scene. "Greenwich Village," he once said, "is a state of mind, it has no boundaries." The Hungarian-born Havel, who was also Emma Goldman's lover, later served on the editorial board of the* Masses *and contributed articles to Goldman's* Mother Earth *and Guido Bruno's* Greenwich Village: A Fortnightly, *from which the following selection is taken.*

"The Spirit of the Village" from *Greenwich Village: A Fortnightly*

When I speak of Greenwich Village I have no geographical conception in mind. The term Greenwich Village is to me a spiritual

Hippolyte Havel. "The Spirit of the Village" in *Greenwich Village: A Fortnightly*, January 20, 1915.

zone of the mind. Is there any raison d'etre for the existence of a spiritual Greenwich Village? I believe there is. Those fellow wanderers who pawned their last coat in rue Franc Bourgeoise, who shivered in rue St. Jacques and searched for the cheapest brasserie in rue Lepic, those who crowded the Olympe in rue de la Gaiete, will understand the charm of the Village. A ramble along Charlton and Varick Streets is a reverie not to speak of the sounds of—how do Minetta Lane, Patchin Place, Sheridan Square and Gay Street strike you?

To be sure the native of the Village has no especial distinction. He is just as dull as the native of Bronx, or the native of Hoboken. The apaches of the Village are more crude than the gangs of upper Riverside. So are, in proportion, the alguecils of the Village more vicious and brutal than their confreres in other precincts. The Village has also its sneaking reformers and neighborhood centers full of apostles in male and female petticoats, good people who clean out certain parts of their territory from outcasts and drive those poor dregs of humanity into other parts of the city. The joints of the Village compare favorably with Doctor's and Barney Flynn's emporiums on the Bowery and Chatham Square.

The soothsayers of yesteryear assured us that the Village is doomed. . . . No danger so far, though the subterranean barbarians are busy in reconstructing Seventh Avenue and building a subway for the men in a hurry. True also, the "Grapevine" has disappeared and we miss the pewters of creamy ale. But take courage, ye tipplers, there are other heavenly retreats in the Village. "Grifou" is dead, but there is a new brasserie de Lilla, yea, even a cafe Grossenwahn. Josiah Flint, if he should awaken from his grave would not be lonesome in the Village.

If you lose your illusions and the devil takes hold of your soul, you leave your garret on the sacred Butte and rent a studio near Parc Monceau, you leave Soho and take your domicile in Chelsea, or you become a traitor to Greenwich Village and move into an apartment on Riverside Drive. You will smile pityingly over the folly of the poor devils who lose their lives in ugly holes on Washington Square, or find pleasure in cheap restaurants among pickpockets on Carmine Street. But some evening, after the West Indian has pushed you up to your steamheated apartment and after you have gone over your bank account, you will fall into reverie and you will sigh for the dear old haunts of the Village. Old reminiscences will float before your vision and old names will strike chords in your damned soul, and you will envy the silly chaps who remained true to the Village. Like a sneak thief you will return secretly some evening and you will look up the dear old places. But the charm will be gone. Even the Caravanserie on Thirty-first Street and the Zukunftstatt on Seventy-seventh Street will close their portals to you. Then you have lost your illusions, your enthusiasm and your idealism. Greenwich Village is a spiritual conception and shopkeepers are not interested in dreamers. The Village is the rallying point for new ideas. Its spirit reaches the heathenish belly worshippers of Harlem, even nature fakers near the Zoo in the Bronx. The Bronxite points proudly to Poe's cottage, but come to the Village, young man, caro mio, and I will point out to you "Grub Street" where another iconoclast, Thomas Paine, earned his bread and his fame in daily struggles with the economic devil.

True, there are literary and artistic coteries and cliques in the Village. Pity, envy and spiteful enmity reign in certain circles. Gossip seems supreme. Ye gods, what an avalanche of gossip! To quote that illustrious gentleman, Don Quixote of La Mancha, "there is more mischief in the Village than comes to one's ears." Also the braggart, the chevalier d'Industrie are to be found here. George Moore would have found in the Village more material and more gossip than he discovered in Paris or Dublin.

But notwithstanding all these human traits, there is a wonderful atmosphere in this part of Manhattan. In the squalid studios and garrets, ideals are forged into new forms. If your eyes are open and your heart sympathetic, you will see Francois Villon spending the borrowed dime in the "Working-girl's Home." You will note Villers de L'Isle Adam contemplating his twentieth attempt at suicide. With Peter Hille you could tramp towards Nirvana. Raskolnikoff pursues his own shadow and Bassaroff proclaims here his philosophy while Sanin celebrates his orgies.

The "Grub Street" of Greenwich Village has as many tragedies as Boul' Mich, and Soho. Chatterton and Francis Thompson are here but you must look carefully for them. Even Arctino could add here a few tricks to his Bible of criticism. Van Gogh and Gauguin are formulating their ideas. And Verlaine is to be met, if you have the divine spark in your soul. The city which hasn't a Greenwich Village is to be pitied. It has no life, no illusion, no art. Greenwich Village is a world in itself. It has its own ethics, its special morals, its distinct individuality.

We have suffered with the men and women in the attics and studios. We know them well and I am sure of their sincerity and their enthusiasm for a higher form of life. They try to forge their ideas, revolutionary ideas, mind you, into new rhythmic forms and this, to me, is the supreme effort. The knight errants of the social revolution, those fighters against capitalistic society are also to be met in Greenwich Village; they are the boon companions of the craftsmen of the chisel, the brush and the pen.

This, indeed, is a revelation. Experienced connoisseurs have told us many times that we do not need to worship at the shrines of the Old World. Here in our sordid surroundings we find the material and thought a-plenty to discover our artistic soul. If you have the artistic spark, you will find in Greenwich Village a sympathetic echo and splendid fellow workers. A Greenwich Village can be found in every part of the world; on the Seine, on the Thames, on the Yser, on the Danube, on the Tiber. Why my friend Ben Ali Yussef assures me that there is a Greenwich Village in Jerusalem!

If the Village did not exist, we would have to invent it.

—January 20, 1915

Djuna Barnes

(1892–1982)

Today she is considered one of the most important writers of the twen-
tieth century, but for most of her working life Djuna Barnes remained,
as she herself once admitted, "the most famous unknown of the cen-
tury." She was beautiful and brilliant and blessed with a corrosive wit.
Although a private woman, Barnes was a familiar figure in Greenwich
Village and well known within its literary and lesbian circles. She
worked as a journalist in New York from 1913 to 1931 on such period-
icals as the New York Morning Telegraph Sunday Magazine, *the*
New York Tribune, *the* New York American, *and the* Brooklyn
Daily Eagle. *In 1919 she joined the Provincetown Players as both an*
actress and a playwright. In the early 1930s she left New York for Paris,
where she wrote her most famous work, the darkly satirical Night-
wood. *Barnes wrote several articles on Greenwich Village in 1916:*
"The Last Petit Souper" described the numerous bohemian cafes, "Be-
coming Intimate with the Bohemians" reveled in the public's insatiable
interest in all things bohemian, and "How the Villagers Amuse Them-
selves" was a tongue-in-cheek "exposé" on so-called bohemian life. In
"Greenwich Village As It Is," Barnes describes such then Village land-
marks as the Brevoort, the Cafe Lafayette, and the Liberal Club.

"Greenwich Village As It Is"

A friend once told me of an artist who had committed suicide because his colors had begun to fade. His canvases were passing like

Djuna Barnes. "Greenwich Village As It Is," *Pearson's Magazine,* October 1916.

flowers. People looking upon them sighed softly, whispering—"This one is dying," while someone in the background added: "That one is dead." It was the unfulfilled fortune of his future. If he had been less enthusiastic, if he had studied what constitutes permanent color and what does not, he might have left some of those somber pictures that seem to grow daily more rigid and "well preserved." The earliest nudes executed with the most irreproachably permanent colors seem to be clothing themselves slowly with that most perdurable costume—the patina of time. Turner is among those who live by the death of his canvases.

And so people are standing before Greenwich Village murmuring in pitying tones: "It is not permanent, the colors will fade. It is not based on good judgment. It is not of that sturdy and healthy material form which, thank providence, we of the real Manhattan have been fashioned." There are a few who sigh: "It is beautiful in places!" while others add: "That is only an accident."

How charming an answer it was of Nature to make most of her mistakes lovely. Christianity seems to be quite a reprehensible experiment. Yet, what brings tears so quickly to the eyes as two pieces of wood shaped as a cross?

Why has Washington Square a meaning, a fragrance, so to speak, while Washington Heights has none? The square has memories of great lives and possibilities therefore; while the Heights are empty and Fifth Avenue is only a thoroughfare. Here on the North side are stately houses, inhabited by great fortunes, the Lydigs and Guinesses and all those whose names rustle like silk petticoats, and on the other side a congeries of houses and hovels passing into rabbit-warrens where Italians breed and swarm in the sun as in Naples, where vegetables and fruits are sold in the street as on the Chiaja and ice-cream is made in the bedrooms and spaghetti on the cellar floor. Here is the den where the gunmen conspired recently to shoot down the free trade butcher and here the row of houses whose inhabitants provide the Women's Night Court with half its sensations. Satin and motor cars on this side, squalor and push carts on that, it is the contrast which gives life, stimulates imagination, incites to love and hatred.

The greater past of New York is as soulless as a department store; but Greenwich Village has recollections like ears filled with muted music and hopes like sightless eyes straining to catch a glimpse of the Beatific Vision.

On the benches in the square men and women resting; limbs wide-flung, arms pendent, listless; round the fountains and on the corners children, dark-eyed Italian children shrieking now with Yankee-cockney accent, a moment later whispering to their deep-bosomed mothers in the Tuscan of Dante. Here is a bunch of Jewish girls like a nosegay, there a pair of Norwegian emigrants, strong of figure and sparing of speech; a colored girl on the sidewalk jostles a Japanese servant and wonders whether he too is colored or is he thought to be white like "dem Dagos."

On every corner you can see a new type; but strange to say no Americans are to be discovered anywhere. New York is the meeting place of the peoples, the only city where you can hardly find a typical American.

The truth has never been penned about Washington Square and Greenwich Village—names which are now synonymous. To have to tell the truth about a place immediately puts that place on its defense. Localities and atmospheres should be let alone. There are so many restaurants that have been spoiled by a line or two in a paper. We are in that same danger. What can we do? Nothing. The damage has been done, we find, and the wing of the butterfly is already crumbling into dust.

I, personally, have never seen one really good article on Washington Square. The commonest spot is not recognizable. The most daring designs in the shops have all been wrongly colored. As for the long hair of the men and the short hair of the women, that type is to be found on Broadway. Cigarette smoking goes on uptown just as much as it does here. The drinking of wine is just as public; the harmless vanities are displayed in other places quite as blatantly as they are here. The business of making love is conducted under the table beyond Fourteenth Street, but does that establish a precedent forbidding the business of holding hands above the table? Is the touch of kid more harmful than the pressure of boot leather? Of course there are pretenders, hypocrites, charlatans among us. But where are the records that state that all malefactors and hypocrites have been caught within the limits of what we call our Bohemia? And as for crime, have all its victims been found murdered in the beds of Waverley Place and Fourth Street?

Oh! Out upon it, this silly repetition about the impossible people living here. Because we let you see us in our curl papers, must you perforce return to your paternal oil stove crying that you never in your life have done your own front hair up in a bang? And must you play forever the part of the simpering Puritan who never heard of sex relations? What little story is it that is ringing in your ears, told you one night by your mother about Dad, as she sat in the evening yielding up reminiscences, which by day appear to be right or wrong, but at night are only clever little anecdotes, timid or sweet adventures of a man now too old for his youth and too wise to try to repeat those things that have made youth the world over the finest and saddest part of life? So forever we rob ourselves of ourselves. We should be born at the age of seventy and totter gracefully down into youth.

Is the beggar of Paris or of Naples any better off than the beggar of Washington Square? And is it not by our beggars that the similarity of a race as well as a group shall be known? These beggars who are the city's finger bowls, wherein the hands of greed have dipped!

What then? We have our artists, but we also have our vendors. We have our poets but we also have our undertakers. We have our idlers, but, have we not also our scrub women? We have our rich and our poor. We are wealthier by a mendicant and wiser by a poet.

In reality, Washington Square and Greenwich Village are not one. They have become one above the pavement at the height where men's heads pass; but measured out in plain city blocks the Village does not run past Sixth Avenue. It begins somewhere around Twelfth Street and commits suicide at the Battery.

There are many artists living off the Square as on it. Some shops are mentioned as these artists are mentioned, because they have caught a certain something that for want of a better word we call atmosphere!

We always speak of Daisy Thompson's shop, of the "Treasure Box," of the "Village Store" and of the "Oddity Cellar"—just as many pretty things, however, are to be seen in a small shop on Eighth Street between Fifth and Sixth Avenues. Why is it not also mentioned? Because it is in, and not of, the Village.

There is the pleasant nightlife of the Café Lafayette. The Brevoort is loved for its basement, where one can catch the lights gleaming between the shrubbery. There too is the waiter who has been serving you for ten years past. There is a certain familiarity in everything you eat. You can tell just where you are by closing your eyes. The cold cuts of the Lafayette are superior to those of the Brevoort; the New Orleans "Fizzes" are abominable at the latter and delightful at the former. There is a chance that you may meet someone you do not like and there is a probability that you will meet someone that you do. You decide beforehand what kind of a sneer you are going to throw Billy, just how coldly you are going to look past Bobbie or freeze the spinal column of Louise, who has been your next door neighbor for months.

The Cholera scare populated the place, but the atmosphere entered not much earlier than the advent of one Bobbie Edwards. In nineteen hundred and six he turned what was then the "A Club" into what later was known as the "Crazy Cat Club" or the "Concolo Gatti Matti"—at a restaurant run by Paglieri at 64 West Eleventh Street.

Edwards introduced the habit of pushing the tables back and organizing an after-dinner dance. He sent out cards of invitation to his friends, and they in their turn sent out invitations to their acquaintances. Leroy Scott, Howard Brubaker and Mary Heaton Vorse were among its earliest members. Thus came the first filterings of what was to be Bohemia.

Yet what does one know of a place if one does not know its people intimately. I know of nothing that I can offer as a substitute that will fit unless it is an anecdote—the skeleton of life.

This is the story of a dancer who came down here on a bus one day last summer, to live here. What she had done in her past we did not ask—what her eyes did not tell we knew was not worth knowing,—yet she was vastly frank. One night this girl arose from the table (it was at Polly's) to answer the phone. At her side sat a young Russian and as she went out she said to him: "Now remember, none of your dirty Slavic tricks, don't you put your fingers in my coffee while I'm gone—mind!" and someone at the other side of the table called out to the boy thus addressed: "Well, you Cossack, you, what are you going to do about that?" Instantly the dancer had run back and flinging her arms about the boy's neck, cried: "A Cossack, how glorious! I have heard of your brutalities."

And so now having eased my mind by having made at least an attempt to dispel some of the false notions, I can find heart to give this place a body.

On Macdougal Street just above the Dutch Oven is the Liberal Club. It is one more of those things that have come to us from uptown. Margaret Wilson was one of its founders, but needless to say it has changed its tone since its change of locality. Members may bring their friends if they do not bring them too often. Many people have met here, fought, loved and passed out. The candles of many intellects have been snuffed here to burn brighter for a space until they too have given place to newer candles. Here Dreiser has debated, and Bordman Robinson sketched, and Henrietta Rodman has left the sound of her sandaled feet. Harry Kemp has posed for his bust only to find on turning round that no one was doing it. Jack Reed and Horace Traubel have been seen here; Kreymborg, Ida Rohe, Max Eastman, Bob Minor and Maurice Becker—a hundred others.

Whitman dinners are held every thirty-first of May in a private room of the Brevoort. Two seasons ago the heart of the Washington Square Players began to beat here, though the theatre itself was located uptown. A little later Charles Edison, who can really afford to be known for himself, only wearing his father as a decoration—started the Thimble Theater with the great Guido Bruno for manager. If they had no successes aside from *Miss Julia*, that was of sufficient importance to have warranted the venture.

Bruno started to make a personal paper, entitled *Greenwich Village*. Allan Norton soon followed with the harmless little *Rogue*, which went out for a while but which is scheduled to return in October or November. Kreymborg put out *Others*—a magazine of verse—blank—the moods of many; a sort of plain-bread-of-poetry,—called *vers libres*; and though it was printed in the Bronx it was reeking with the atmosphere of the studios along the South side of the Square.

Clara Tice burst into print, and so did Bobbie Locher. The Baron de Meyer began to be seen above a glass of "Yvette" in the cafes, among a score of faces that may have had addresses out of the Village itself, but were Bohemians. After all, it is not where one washes one's neck that counts, but where one moistens one's throat. And still things are coming, expanding. The very air seems to be improving. There is a rumor that "King" McGrath, or otherwise Jack, backed by some society people, is going to open a tavern on Sheridan Square and Jack adds to those who will listen "*With* a license."

George Newton is also planning to erect a Toy Theatre on the same Square. Newton has started a new paper, selling at two cents. The first issue will be out in August. Ah, you see! After all you cannot put out the sun by spitting on its shadow.

And our studio buildings? Our apartment houses? The Judson on the South Side of the Square, the hotel Holly, the hotel Earle, the Washington; the promised building where now stands the Village soda fountain and Guido Bruno's garret. The Washington Mews has already been partly demolished to arise again. And of recent past history what of Louis' at Sixty Washington Square South? It is held in the memory, as only a dead woman or a past hostelry can be held; the one for its clasp on the heart, the other for its hold on the mind. Louis' had not only Louis, it also had Christine, a woman who, had she not been born in this century, would have been some great heavy goddess whose presence would have been justice without word of mouth. Louis' was closed because it was running without a license. Perhaps that was one of its charms! Drink there was not mere drink, it was wine *libre*.

And there is the Candlestick Tea Room, and there is Confarone's, and there is the Red Lamp, Mori's, Romano's, the Red Star, and Mazzini's.

And so you of the outer world be not so hard on us, and above all forbear to pity us—good people. We have all that the rest of the world has in common commodities and we have that better part: men and women with a new light flickering in their eyes, or on their foreheads the radiance of some unseen splendor.

—1916

Anna Alice Chapin

(1880–1920)

Of the many guidebooks written about the Village during the first few decades of the twentieth century, Anna Alice Chapin's was certainly one of the most detailed of portraits. She not only describes the many restaurants and tearooms that flourished in the Village during this period, she paints quick sketches of the owners and idiosyncratic patrons that frequented them. The result is an entertaining guide to Village cultural landmarks circa 1917.

"Restaurants, and the Magic Door" from *Greenwich Village*

I

What scenes in fiction cling more persistently in the memory than those that deal with the satisfying of man's appetitie? Whoever heard of a dyspeptic hero? Are not your favourites beyond the Magic Door all good trenchermen?

—ARTHUR BARTLETT MAURICE

It was O. Henry, I believe, who spoke of restaurants as "literary landmarks." They are really much more than that—they are signposts,

Anna Alice Chapin. "Restaurants, and the Magic Door" from *Greenwich Village* (New York: Dodd, Mead and Company, 1922).

psychical rather than physical, which show the trend of the times—or of the neighborhood. I suppose nothing in Greenwich Village could be more significantly illuminating than its eating places. There are, of course, many sorts. The Village is neither so unique nor so uniform as to have only one sort of popular board. But in all the typical Greenwich restaurants you will find the same elusive something, the spirit of the picturesque, the untrammeled, the quaint and charming—in short, the *different!*

The Village is not only a locality, you understand, it is a point of view. It reaches out imperiously and fastens on what it will. The Brevoort basement—after ten o'clock at night—is the Village. So is the Lafayette on occasion. During the day they are delightful French hostelries catering to all the world who like heavenly things to eat and the right atmosphere in which to eat them. But as the magic hour strikes, presto!—they suffer a sea change and become the quintessence of the Spirit of the Village!

It is 10:20 p.m. at the Brevoort in the restaurant upstairs. All the world and his wife—or his sweetheart—are fully represented. Most of the uptowners—the regulation clientele—are going away, having finished gorging themselves on delectable things; some few of them are lingering, lazily curious; a certain small number are still coming in, moved by that restless Manhattan spirit that hates to go home in the dark.

Among these is a discontented, well-dressed couple, seen half an hour before completing their dinner a block away at the Lafayette. The headwaiter at that restaurant explained to them nonchalantly, not to say casually: "It is the gentleman who married his manicurist. Regard, then—one perceives they are not happy—eh? It is understood that she beats him."

Yonder is a moving picture star, quite alone, eating a great deal, and looking blissfully content. There is a man who has won a fortune in war brides—the one at the next table did it with carpets. There is a great lady—a very great lady indeed—who, at this season, *should* be out of town.

Swiftly moving, deft-handed waiters, the faint perfume of delicate food, the sparkle of light upon rare wine, the complex murmur of a well-filled dining room. It is so far not strikingly different, in the impression it gives, from uptown restaurants.

But the hands of the clock are pointing to the half-hour after ten.

Hasten, then, to the downstairs café—the two rooms, sunk below the level of Fifth Avenue, yet cool and airy. If you hurry you will be just in time to see the Village come in. For this is their really favorite haunt—their Mecca when their pockets will stand it—the Village Restaurant de Luxe!

Upstairs are exquisite frocks and impeccable evening clothes; good jewels and, incidentally, a good many tired faces—from uptown. Down here it is different. The crowd is younger, poorer, more strikingly bizarre—immeasurably more interesting. Everyone here does something, or thinks he does—which is just as good;—or pretends to—which is next best. There are a startling number of girls. Girls in smocks of "artistic" shades—bilious yellow-green, or magenta-tending violet; girls with hair that, red, black or blonde, is usually either arranged in a wildly natural bird's-nest mass, or boldly clubbed after the fashion of Joan of Arc and Mrs. Vernon Castle; girls with tense little faces, slender arms and an astonishing capacity as to cigarettes. And men who, for the most part, are too busy with their ideals to cut their hair; men whose collars may be low and rolling, or high and bound with black silk stocks after the style of another day; men who are, variously, affectedly natural or naturally affected, but who are nearly all of them picturesque, and, in spite of their poses, quite in earnest, after their queer fashion. They are all prophets and seers down here; they wear their bizarre haircuts and unusual clothes with a certain innocently flaunting air which rather disarms you. Their poses are not merely poses; they are their almost childlike way of showing the prosaic outer world how different they are!

Here they all flock—whenever they have the price. That may be a bit beyond them sometimes, but usually there is someone in the crowd who is "flush," and that means who will pay. For the Villagers are not parsimonious; they stand in no danger of ever making themselves rich and thus acquiring place in the accursed class called the Philistines!

It is beyond question that the French have a genius for hospitality. It must be rooted in their beautiful, national tact, that gracious impulse combining chivalry to women, friendliness to men and courtesy to all which is so characteristic of "the world's sweetheart" France. I have never seen a French restaurant where the most casual visitor was not made personally and charmingly welcome, and I have never seen such typically French restaurants as the Lafayette and the Brevoort. And the Villagers feel it too. From the shabbiest socialist to the most flagrantly painted little artist's model, they drift in thankfully to that atmosphere of gaiety and sympathy and thoughtful kindliness which is, after all, just—the air of France.

Next let us take a restaurant of quite another type, not far from the Brevoort—all the Village eating places are close together—walk across the square, a block further, and you are there.

It is not many years since Bohemia ate chiefly in the side streets, at restaurants such an Enrico's, Baroni's—there are a dozen such places. They still exist, but the Village is dropping away from them. They are good and very cheap, and the tourist—that is, the uptowner—thinks he is seeing Bohemia when he eats in them, but not many of them remain at all characteristic. Bertolotti's is something of an exception. It is a restaurant of the old style, a survival of the days when all Bohemian restaurants were Italian. LaSignora says they have been there, just there on Third Street, for twenty years. If you are a newcomer you will probably eat in the upstairs room, in cool and rather remote grandeur, and the pretty daughter with the wondrous black eyes will serve you the more elaborate of the most extraordinary named dishes on the menu. But if, by long experience, you know what is pleasant and comfortable you will take a place in the basement café. At the clean, bare table, in the shadow of the big, bright, many-bottled bar, you will eat your *Risotta alla Milanese*, your *coteletti di Vitelle*, your *asparagi*—it's probably the only place in the city where they serve asparagus with grated cheese—finally your *zambaione*—a heavenly sort of hot "flip," very foamy and seductive and strongly flavored with Marsala wine.

If you stand well with the house you may have the honor to be escorted by the Signora herself—handsome, dignified, genial, with a veritable coronal of splendid grey hair—to watch the eternal bowling in the alley back of the restaurant. I have watched them fascinated for long periods and I have never learned what it is they are trying to do with those big "bowling balls." They have no ninepins, so they are not trying to make a ten-strike. Apparently, it is a game however, for now and then a shout of triumph proclaims that someone has won. He orders the drinks and they go at it again.

"But, what *is* it?" I asked the Signora.

"Eh—oh—just a *Giocho di Bocca*," she returned vaguely, "a game of bowls—how should I know?"

Beyond the bowling alley is a long, narrow yard with bushes. It would make quite a charming summer garden with little tables for after-dinner coffee. But the Signora says that the *Chiesa,* there at the back of it, objects. The *Chiesa,* I think, is the Judson Memorial Church on Washington Square. Just why they don't want the Signora to have tables in her own back yard is not clear. She, being a Latin, shrugs her shoulders and makes no comment. Standing in the darkness, there is a real freshness in the air; there is also a delicious, gurgling sound, the music of summer streams.

"How lovely!" you whisper. "What a delightful, rippling sound."

"Yet, it is the ice plant of the big hotel," says La Signora sweetly.

There is, at Bertolotti's one of the queerest little old figures in all that part of the world, the bent and aged Italian known universally as *Castagna* (Chestnuts), because of the interminable anecdotes he tells over and over again. No one knows his real name, not even the Signor or the Signora. Yet he has worked for them for years. He wants no wages—only a living and a home. In the aforementioned back yard he has built himself a little house about the size of a dog kennel. It is a real house, and like nothing so much as the historic residence of the Three Bears. It has a window, eaves, weather-strips and a clothesline, for he does his own washing. He trots off there very happily when his light work is done, and, when his door is closed, opens it for no one. That scrap of a building is *Castagna's* castle. One evening I went to call on him, but he had put out his light. In the gleam that came from the bowling alley behind me, something showed softly red and green and white against the wooden door. I put out my hand and touched that world-famous cross. It was about six inches long, and only of paper, but it was the flag of Italy, and it kept watch outside the *Casa Castagna*. I am certain that he would not sleep well without it.

Probably the most famous Bohemian restaurant in the quarter is the Black Cat. It is not really more typical than the others,— indeed it is rather less so,—but it is extremely striking, and most conspicuous. There is, in the minds of the hypercritical, the sneaking suspicion that the Black Cat is almost too good to be true; it is too obviously and theatrically lurid with the glow of Montmartre; it is Bohemianism just a shade too much conventionalized. Just the same, it is fascinating. From the moment you pass the outer, polite portals and intermediate anterooms and enter the big, smoke-filled, deafening room at the back, you are enormously interested, excellently entertained. The noise is the thing that impresses you first. In most Village resorts you find quiet the order of the day—or rather night. Even "Polly's," crowded as it is, is not noisy. In the Brevoort there is a steady, low rumble of talk, but not actual noise. At the Black Cat it is one continual and all-pervading roar—a joyous roar, too; these people are having a simply gorgeous time and don't care who knows it. It is a wonder that the high-set rafters do not fall—that the lofty, white-washed walls of brick do not tremble, and that the little black cats set in a rigid conventional design around the whole room do not come to life in horror, and fly spitting up the short stairway and out of the door!

When you go to the Black Cat you would better check what prejudices you have as to what is formal and fitting, and leave them with your coat at the entrance. Not that it is disreputable— Luigi would pale with the shock of such a thought! It is just— Bohemian! Everyone does exactly what he wishes to do. Sometimes, one person's wishes conflict with someone else's, and then there is a fight, and the police are called, and the rest of the patrons have a beautiful time watching a perfectly good and unexpected free show! As a rule, however, this determination on the part of each one to do what he wants to has no violent results. An incident will show something of the entire liberty allowed in the Black Cat.

A man came in with two girls, and, seeing a jolly stag party at another table, decided to join them. He promptly did so, with, as far as could be seen, no word of excuse to his feminine companions. In a moment two young men strolled up to their table and sat down.

"Your friend asked us to come over here and take his place," explained one nonchalantly. "You don't object, ladies?"

The girls received them amiably. Apparently no one thought of such a formality as names or introductions. The original host stayed away for the rest of the evening, but the four new acquaintances seemed to get along quite satisfactorily without him.

A young married woman from uptown came in with her husband and two other men. A good-looking lad, much flushed and a little unsteady, stopped by her chair.

"Say, k-kid," he exclaimed, with a disarming chuckle, "you're the prettiest girl here—and you come here with three p-protectors! Say, it's a shame!"

He lurched cheerfully upon his way and even the slightly conservative husband found a grudging smile wrung out of him.

There is a pianist at the Black Cat—a real pianist, not just a person who plays the piano. She is a striking figure in a quaint, tunic-like dress, greying hair and a keen face, and a personal friend of half the frequenters. She has an uncanny instinct for the psychology of the moment. She knows just when "Columbia" will be the proper thing to play, and when the crowd demands the newest ragtime. She will feel an atmospheric change as unswervingly as any barometer, and switch in a moment from "Goodbye Girls, Goodbye" to the love duet from Faust. She can play Chopin just as well as she can play Sousa, and she will tactfully strike up "It's Always Fair Weather" when she sees a crowd of young fellows sit down at a table; "There'll Be a Hot Time in the Old Town Tonight" to welcome a lad in khaki and the very latest fox trot for the party of girls and young men from uptown, who look as though they were dying to dance. She plays the "Marseillaise" for Frenchmen, and "Dixie" for visiting Southerners, and "Mississippi" for the frequenters of Manhattan vaudeville shows. And, then, at the right moment, her skilled fingers will drift suddenly into something different, some exquisite, in-spired melody—the soul-child of some high immortal—and un-der the spell the noisy crowd grows still for a moment. For even at the Black Cat they have not forgotten how to dream.

Probably the Black Cat inspired many other Village restau-rants—the Purple Pup for instance.

The Purple Pup is a queer little place. It is in a most exclusive and aristocratic part of the Square—in the basement of one of the really handsome houses, in fact. It is, so far as is visible to the naked eye, quite well conducted, yet there is something mysterious about it. Doubtless this is deliberately stage-managed and capitalized, but it is effectively done. It is an unexpected sort of place. One evening you go there and find it in full blast; the piano tinkling, many cramped couples dancing in the two tiny rooms, and every table covered with tea cups or lemonade glasses. Another night you may arrive at exactly the same time and there will be only can-dlelight and a few groups, talking in low tones.

Here, as in all parts of the Village, the man in the rolling collar, and the girl in the smock, will be markedly in evidence. Yes; they really do look like that. Lots of the girls have their hair cut short too.

And "Polly's"!

In many minds, "Polly's" and the Village mean one and the same thing. Certainly no one could intelligently write about the one without due and logical tribute to the other. Polly Holliday's restaurant (The Greenwich Village Inn is its formal name in the telephone book) is not incidental, but institutional. It is fixed, rep-resentative and sacred, like Police Headquarters, Trinity Church and the Stock Exchange. It is indispensable and independent. The Village could not get along without it, but the Village no longer talks about it nor advertises it. It is, in fact, so obviously a vital part of Greenwich that often enough a Greenwicher, asked to point out hostelries of peculiar interest, will forget to mention it.

"How about 'Polly's'?" you remind him.

"Oh—but 'Polly's'!" he protests wonderingly. "Why, it wouldn't be the Village at all without 'Polly's'. It—why, of course, I never thought anyone had to be told about 'Polly's'!"

His attitude will be as disconcerted as though you asked him whether he was in the habit of using air to breathe,—or was accustomed to going to bed to sleep.

Polly Holliday used to have her restaurant under the Liberal Club—where the Dutch Oven is now,—but now she has her own good-sized place on Fourth Street, and it remains, through fluctuations and fads, the most thoroughly and consistently popular Village eating place extant. It is, outwardly, not original nor superlatively striking in any way. It is a clean, bare place with paper napkins and such waits between courses as are unquestionably conducive to the encouragement of philosophic, idealistic, anarchistic and aesthetic debates. But the food is excellent, when you get it, and the atmosphere both friendly and—let us admit frankly—inspiring. The people are interesting; they discuss interesting things. You are comfortable, and you are exhilarated. You see, quickly enough, why the Village could not possibly get along without its inn; why "Polly's" is so essential a part of its life that half the time it overlooks it. Outsiders always know about "Polly's." But the Villager?

"'Polly's'? But *of course* 'Polly's.'"

There it is. *Of course* "Polly's." "Polly's" is Greenwich Village in little; it is, in a fashion, cosmic and symbolic.

Under the Liberal Club, where "Polly's" used to be located, the "Dutch Oven," with its capacious fireplace and wholesome meals, now holds sway. The prices are reasonable, the food substantial and the atmosphere comfortable, so it is a real haven of good cheer to improvident Villagers.

The Village Kitchen on Greenwich Avenue is another place of the same sort. And Gallup's—almost the first of these "breakfast and lunch" shops—is another. They are not unlike a Child's restaurant, but with the rarefied Village air added. You eat real food in clean surroundings, as you do in Child's, but you do it to an accompaniment that is better than music—a sort of life-song, rather stirring and quite touching in its way—the Song of the Village. How can people be both reckless and deeply earnest? But the Villagers are both.

One of the oddest sights on earth is a typical "Breakfast" at "Polly's," the "Kitchen" or the "Dutch Oven," after one of the masked balls for which the Village has recently acquired such a passion. After you have been up all night in some of these mad masquerades—of which more anon—you may not, by Village convention, go home to bed. You must go to breakfast with the rest of the Villagers. And you must be prepared to face the cold, grey dawn of "the morning after" while still in your war paint and draggled finery. It is an awful ordeal. But "it's being done in the Village"!

Quite recently a new sort of eating place has sprung up in Greenwich Village—of so original and novel a character that we must investigate it in at least a few of its manifestations. Speaking for myself, I had never believed that such places could exist within sound of the "L" and a stone's throw from drug stores and offices.

But see what you think of them.

II

"I can't believe *that!*" said Alice.

"Can't you?" the Queen said in a pitying tone. "Try again: draw a long breath and shut your eyes."

Alice laughed. "There's no use trying," she said. "One can't believe impossible things."

"I daresay you haven't had much practice," said the Queen. "When I was your age, I always did it for half-an-hour a day. Why, sometimes I've believed as many as six impossible things before breakfast."—"Through the Looking Glass."

"But it can't be this!" I said. "You've made a mistake in the number!"

"It is this," declared my guide and companion. "This is where Nanni Bailey has her tea shop."

"But this is—is—isn't anything!"

Indeed the number to which my friend pointed seemed to indicate the entrance to a sort of warehouse, if it indicated anything at all. On peering through the dim and gloomy doorway, it appeared instead to be a particularly desolate-looking cellar. There were old barrels and boxes about, an expanse of general dusty mystery and, in the dingy distance, a flight of ladder-like steps leading upwards to a faint light.

"It's one of Dicken's impossible stage sets come true!" I exclaimed. "It looks as though it might be a burglar's den or somebody's backyard, but anyway, it isn't a restaurant!"

"It is too!" came back at me triumphantly. "Look at that sign!"

By the faint rays of a street light on nearby Sixth Avenue, I saw the shabby little wooden sign, "The Samovar." This extraordinary place was a restaurant after all!

We entered warily, having a vague expectation of pickpockets or rats, and climbed that ladder—I mean staircase—to what was purely and simply a loft.

But such a loft! Such a quaint, delicious, simple, picturesque apotheosis of a loft! A loft with the rough bricks whitewashed and the heavy rafters painted red; a loft with big, plain tables and a bare floor and an only slightly partitioned-off kitchenette where the hungry could descry piles of sandwiches and many coffee cups. And there in the middle of the loft was the Samovar itself, a really splendid affair, and one actually not for decorative purposes only, but for use. I had always thought samovars were for the ornamentation either of houses or foreign-atmosphere novels. But you could use this thing. I saw people go and get glasses-full of tea out of it.

Under the smoke-dimmed lights were curious, eager, interesting faces: a pale little person with red hair I recognized instantly as an actress whom I had just seen at the Provincetown Players—a Village Theatrical Company—in a tense and terribly tragic role. Beyond her was a white-haired man with keen eyes—a distinguished writer and socialist. A shabby poet announced to the sympathetic that he had sold something after two years of work. Immediately they set about making a real fiesta of the unusual occasion. Miss Bailey, a small, round, efficient person with nice eyes and good manners, moved about among her guests, all of whom she seemed to know. The best cheese sandwiches in New York went round. A girl in a vampire costume of grey—hooded and with long

105

trailing sleeves—got up from her solitary place in the corner. She seemed to be wearing, beneath the theatrical garment, a kimono and bedroom slippers. Obviously she had simply drifted in for sandwiches before going to bed. She vanished down the ladder.

An hour later, we, too, climbed down the ladderish stairs, my companion and I, and as we came out into the fresh quiet of Fourth Street at midnight, I had a really odd sensation. I felt as though I had been reading a fascinating and unusual book, and had—suddenly closed it for the night.

This was one of the first of the real Village eating places which I ever knew. Perhaps that is why it comes first to my memory as I write. I do not know that it is more representative or more interesting than others. But it was worth going back to.

Yet, after all, it isn't the food and drink, nor yet the unusual surroundings, that bring you back to these places. It's the—well, one has to use, once in a while, the hard-worked and generally inappropriate word "atmosphere." Like "temperament" and "individuality" and the rest of the writer-folk's old reliables, "atmosphere" is too often only a makeshift, a lazy way of expressing something you won't take the trouble to define more expressively. Dick says in "The Light That Failed" that an old device for an unskillful artist is to stick a superfluous bunch of flowers somewhere in a picture where it will cover up bad drawing. I'm afraid writers are apt to use stock phrases in the same meretricious fashion.

But this is a fact just the same. Nearly all the Greenwich Village places really have atmosphere. You can be cynical about it, or frown at it, or do anything you like about it, but it's there, and it's the real thing. It's an absolute essence and ether which you feel intensely and breathe necessarily, but which no one can put quite definitely into the concrete form of words. I have heard of liquid or solidified air, but that's a scientific experiment, and who wants to try scientific experiments on the Village which we all love?

"But such an amount of play-acting and pose!" I hear someone complain, referring to the Village with contemptuous irritation. "They pretend to be seeking after truth and liberty of thought, and that sort of thing, and yet they are steeped in artificiality."

Yes, to a certain extent that is true—true of a portion of the Village, at any rate, and a certain percentage of the Villagers. But even if it is true, it is the sort of truth that needs only a bit of understanding to make us tender and tolerant instead of scornful and hard. My dear lady, you who complained of the "play-acting," and you other who, agreeing with her, see in the whimsies and pretenses in Our Village only a spectacle of cheap affectation and artifice, have you lived so long and yet do not know that the play-acting instinct is one of the most universal of all instincts—the very first developed, and the very last, I truly believe, to die in our faded bodies? From the moment when we try to play ball with sunbeams through those intermediate years wherein we imagine ourselves everything on earth that we are not, down to those last days of all, when we live, all furtive and unsuspected, a secret life of the spirit—either a life of remembrance of a life of imagination visualizing what we have wanted and have missed,—what do we do but pretend,— make believe—pose, if you will? When we are little we pretend to be knights and ladies, pirates and fairy princesses, soldiers and Red Cross nurses, and sailors and hunters and explorers. We people the window boxes with elves and pixies and the dark corners with Red Indians and bears. The commonplace world about us is not truly commonplace, since our fancy, still fresh from eternity, can transform the dusty shrubs into an enchanted forest, and an automobile into the most deliciously formidable of the Dragon Family. A bit later, our pretending is done more cautiously. We do not confess our shy flights of imagination: we take a prosaic outward pose, and try not to advertise the fact that our geese wear (to our eyes) swans' plumage, and that our individual roles are (to our own view) always those of heroes and heroines. No one of us but mentally sees himself or herself doing something which is as impracticable as cloud-riding. No one of us but dreams of the impossible and in a shamefaced, almost clandestine, fashion pictures it and lingers over it. All make-believe, you see, only we hate to admit it! The different thing about Greenwich is that there they do admit it, quite a number of them. They accept the pretending, play-acting spirit as a perfectly natural—no, as an inevitable—part of life, and, with a certain whimsical seriousness, not unlike that of real children, they provide for it. You know children can make believe, *know* that it is make believe, yet enjoy it all the more for that. So can the Villagers. Hence, places like—let us say, as an example—"The Pirate's Den."

It is a very real pirate's den, lighted only by candles. A coffin casts a shadow, and there is a regulation "Jolly Roger," a black flag ornamented with skull and crossbones. Grim? Surely, but even a healthy-minded child will play at gruesome and ghoulish games once in a while.

There is a Dead Man's Chest too—and if you open it you will find a ladder leading down into mysterious depths unknown. If you are very adventurous you will climb down and bump your head against the cellar ceiling and inspect what is going to be a subterranean grotto as soon as it can be fitted up. You climb up again and sit in the dim, smoky little room and look about you. It is the most perfect pirate's den you can imagine. On the walls hang huge casks and kegs and wine bottles in their straw covers—all the signs manual of past and future orgies. Yet the "Pirate's Den" is "dry"—straw-dry, brick-dry—as dry as the Sahara. If you want a "drink" the well-mannered "cut-throat" who serves you will give you a mighty mug of ginger ale or sarsaparilla. And if you are a real Villager and can still play at being a real pirate, you drink it without a smile, and solemnly consider it real red wine filched at the edge of the cutlass from captured merchantmen on the high seas. On the big, dark center table is carefully drawn the map of "Treasure Island."

The pirate who serves you (incidentally he writes poetry and helps to edit a magazine among other things) apologizes for the lack of a Stevensonian parrot.

"A chap we know is going to bring one back from the South Sea Islands," he declares seriously. "And we are going to teach it to say, 'Pieces of eight! Pieces of eight!'"

If, while you are at the "Pirate's Den" you care to climb a rickety, but enchanted staircase outside the old building (it's pre-Revolutionary, you know) you will come to the "Aladdin Shop"—where coffee and Oriental sweets are specialties. It is a riot of strange and beautiful color—vivid and Eastern and utterly intoxicating. A very talented and picturesque Villager has painted every inch of it himself, including the mysterious-looking Arabian gentleman in brilliantly hued wood, who sits cross-legged luring you into the little place of magic. The wrought iron brackets on the wall are patches of vivid tints; the curtains at the windows are color-dissonances, fascinating and bizarre. As usual there is candlelight. And, as usual, there is the same delicious spirit of seriously and wholeheartedly playing the game. While you are there you are in the East. If it isn't the East to you, you can go away—back to Philistia.

And speaking of candlelight. I went into the poets' favorite "Will o' the Wisp" teashop once and found the gas jet lighted! The young girl in charge jumped up, much embarrassed, and turned it out.

"I'm so sorry!" she apologized. "But I wanted to *see* just a moment, and lighted it!"

I peered at her face in the ghostly candlelight. It was entirely and unmistakably earnest. Just the same, Mrs. Browning's warning that "colors seen by candlelight do not look the same by day" is not truly applicable to these Village shrines. Even under the searching beams of a slanting, summer afternoon sun, they are adorable. Go and see if you don't believe this.

Then take the "Mad Hatter's." The entrance alone is a monument to the make-believe capabilities of the Village. Scrawled on the stone wall beside the steps that lead down to the little basement tearoom, is an inscription in chalk. It looks like anything but English. But if you held a looking glass up to it you would find that it is "Down the Rabbit Hole" written backward! Now, if you know your "Alice" as well as you should, you will recall delightedly her dash after the White Rabbit which brought her to Wonderland, and, incidentally, to the Mad Tea Party.

You go in to the little room where Villagers are drinking tea, and the proprietress approaches to take your order. She is a good-looking young woman dressed in a bizarre red and blue effect, not unlike one of the Queens, but she prefers to be known as the "Dormouse"—not, however, that she shows the slightest tendency to fall asleep.

On the wall is scribbled, "'There's plenty of room,' said Alice."

The people around you seem only pleasantly mad, not danger-ously so. There is a girl with an enchanting scrap of a monkey; there is a youth with a manuscript and a pile of cigarette butts. The great thing here once more is that they are taking their little play and their little stage with a heavenly seriousness, all of them. You expect somebody to produce a set of flamingos at any moment and start a game of croquet among the tiny tables.

Not all of the Greenwich restaurants have definite individual characters to maintain consistently. Sometimes it is just a general spirit of picturesqueness, of adventure, that they are trying to keep up. The "Mouse Trap," except for the trap hanging outside and a mouse scrawled in chalk on the wall of the entry, carries out no par-ticular suggestion either of traps or mice. But take a look at the pro-prietress (Rita they call her), with her gorgeous Titian hair and delft-blue apron; at her son Sidney, fair, limp, slim, English-voiced, with a deft way of pouring after-dinner coffee, and hair the color of corn. They are obviously play-acting and enjoying it.

Ask Rita her nationality. She will fix you with eyes utterly de-void of a twinkle and answer: "I? I am part Scotch terrier, and part Spanish mongrel, but *mostly* mermaid!"

Rita goes to the sideboard to cut someone a slice of good-looking pie. She overhears a reference to the "Candlestick," a little eating-place chiefly remarkable for its vegetables and poetesses.

"If they eat nothing but vegetables no wonder they take to po-etry," is her comment. But still she does not smile. If you giggle, as every child knows, you spoil the game. They laugh heartily enough and often enough down in the Village, but they never laugh at the Village itself,—not because they take it so reverentially, but because they know how to make believe altogether too well.

Let me whisper here that the most fascinating hour in the "Mouse Trap" is in the late afternoon, when no one is there, and the ebony handmaiden in the big back kitchen is taking the fat, delicious-smelling cakes from the oven. Drop in some afternoon and sniff the fragrance that suggests your childhood and "sponge-cake day." You will feel that it is a trap no sane mouse would ever think of leaving! On a table beside you is a slate with, obviously, the day's specials:

"Spice cakes.
Chocolate cake.
Strawberry tarts with whipped cream."

And still as you peep through the door at the back you see more and still more goodies coming hot and fresh and enticing from the oven. White cakes, golden cakes, delicately browned pies,—if you are dieting by any chance you flee temptation and leave the "Mouse Trap" behind you. It would be impossible to give even an approximately complete inventory of the representative places of the Village. I have had to content myself with some dozen or so examples,—recorded almost haphazard, for the most part, but as I believe, more or less typical, take them all in all, of the Village eating place in its varied and rather curious manifestations.

Then there is a charming shop presided over by a pretty girl with the inevitable smock and braided hair, where tea is served in order to entice you to buy carved and painted trifles.

And then there is, or was, the place kept by Polly's brother, which was heartlessly raided by the police, and much maligned, not to say libeled, by the newspapers.

And then there was and is the "Hell Hole." Its ancient distinction used to be that it was one of the first cheap Bohemian places where women could smoke, and that it was always open. When all the other resorts closed for the night you repaired to the "Hell Hole." As to the smoking, it has taken a good while for New York to allow its Bohemian women this privilege, though society leaders have enjoyed it for ages. We all know that though most fashionable hotels permitted their feminine guests to smoke, the Haymarket of dubious memory always tabooed the custom to the bitter end!

The "Hell Hole" has always stoutly approved of cigarettes, so all honor to it! And many a happy small-hours party has brought up there to top off the night in peace without having to keep an eye on the clock.

There is a little story told about one of these restaurants of which I have been writing—never mind which. A visiting Englishman on his way from his boat to his hotel dropped in at a certain place for a drink. He found the company congenial and drifted into a little game which further interested him. It was a perfectly straight game, and he was a perfectly good sport. He stayed there two weeks. No: I shall *not* state what the place was. But I think the story is true.

Personally, I don't blame the Englishman. Even shorn of the charm of a game of chance, there is many a place in Greenwich Village which might easily capture a susceptible temperament—not merely for weeks, but for years!

The last of the teashops is the "Wigwam," in which, take note, it is the Indian game that is played. Its avowed aim is "Tea and Dancing," and it is exceedingly proud of its floor. It lives in the second story of what, for over fifty years, has been the old Sheridan Square Tavern, and its proprietors are the Mosses,—poet, editor, and incidental "pirate" on one side of the house; and designer of enchanting "art clothes" on the other. Lew Kirby Parrish, no less, has made the decorations, and he told me that the walls were grey with Indian decorations, and the ceiling a "live color." I discovered that that meant a vivid, happy orange.

The spirit of the play is always kept in the Village. Let us take the opening night of the "Wigwam" as a case in point.

The Indian note is supreme. It is not only the splendid line drawings of Indian chiefs, forming the panels of the room—those mysterious and impressive shades created by the imagination of Lew Parrish—it is the general mood. Only candles are burning— big, fat candles, giving, in the aggregate, a magical radiance.

The victrola at the end of the room begins to play a curious Indian air with an uneven, fascinating, syncopated rhythm. A graceful girl in Indian dress glides in and places a single candle on the floor, squatting before it in a circle of dim, yellow light.

She lifts her dark head with its heavy band about the brows and shades her eyes with her hand. You see remote places, far, pale horizons, desert regions of sand. There are empty skies overhead, instead of the "live-color" ceiling. With an agile movement, she rises and begins to dance about the candle, and you know that to her it is a little campfire; it is that to you, too, for the moment. Something like the west wind blows her fringed dress; there is a dream as old as life in her eyes.

Faster and faster she dances about the candle, until at last she sinks beside it and with a strange sure gesture—puts it out.

Silence and the dark. The prairie fades. . . . The little dark-wood tables with their flowers and candles begin to glow again; the next musical number is a popular one step! . . .

—1917

Sinclair Lewis

(1885–1951)

Born in 1885 in Sauk Center, Minnesota, Sinclair Lewis was educated at Yale University. From 1907 to 1916 he worked as a journalist and literary editor. A naturalist, Lewis wrote several novels such as Main Street *(1920) and* Babbitt *(1922), which criticize the lack of spiritual and creative values in American middle-class life: its stifling conformity, its fear of individuality. Later novels, such as* Elmer Gantry *(1927) and* It Can't Happen Here *(1935), address the issues of religious hypocrisy and racial intolerace, respectively. In 1930 he received the Nobel Prize for literature.*

"Hobohemia" was a satirical story originally published in the Saturday Evening Post *in 1917. It was later adapted into a three-act play and produced in 1919 at the Greenwich Village Theatre on Sheridan Square. Although a critical and commercial flop, its very production indicated the level of self-absorption and self-interest in the Village. In it, Lewis poked fun at such Village obsessions as feminism, Freud, anarchism, and the bohemian life of the "artist," parodied Village eateries and tearooms, and satirized the Provincetown Players as the Hobohemian Players.*

from "Hobohemia"

Upon the eastbound train Mr. Brown sat in his compartment and wrote short stories. Whenever he found them getting interesting to himself, he decided that they probably were lowbrow, and tore them up and took a fresh start.

Sinclair Lewis. "Hobohemia," from *The Saturday Evening Post*, April 1917.

Mr. Brown had been in New York before. He knew it as two hotels, seven theaters, six cabarets, three offices, a lumberyard and a
subway. He went airily to the Grand Royal Hotel and telephoned
to Ysetta.

She did not sound particularly welcoming as she demanded:
"What are you doing here?"

"Just got in sminit. I'm here on business. May be kept in the city
for some weeks, working up some deals."

"Deals! This isn't the city of deals! It's the city of the strong red
wine of life."

"Yeh, I know, honey," he humbly agreed. "I'm going to shoot a
beaker of that myself, as soon as I get out of this hot phone booth.
But say, Bess—Ysetta—whatcha doing to-night? Can I take you out
to dinner?"

"No, not possibly to-night. But you may come up to-morrow
afternoon, and I'll give you some tea."

Did Mr. Brown spend his first evening in wandering solitary
about the streets? No, Mr. Brown did not. Mr. Brown telephoned to
the chief lumber jobber in New York, arranged for an introduction
to the managing editor of the *Morning Chronicle*, and dined cheerful at the Hotel Gorgonzola y Vino, which is so expensive that patrons try to slip by the hat-boy without claiming their coats at all.
He attended the new musical review, *Can You Beat It, Bo?* and applauded, not like a soul recently called to the finer life, but like a
buyer who had come on without The Wife.

At midnight, very pink, and cheerful and brisk, with a carna-
tion in his buttonhole and a stick swinging, all as glossy and luxurious as the orange back of a new ten-dollar bill, Mr. Brown arrived
at the office of the *Morning Chronicle*, and talked to the managing
editor for ten minutes. He wanted, he said, to hire a good press
agent, and a man who could think up plots for stories but was too
lazy to write them.

For the publicity, the editor suggested Bill Hupp, who had
been press agent for the Vampire Film Company till the recent
consolidation. As to plots, there was Oliver Jasselby, who was
always so exhausted by telling what genius his plots showed

115

that he never wrote a thing, and had to hold down a job on the *Plumbers' Gazette*.

At seven in the morning, Mr. Brown rose to lead the life literary, and get it over. He telephoned to Bill Hupp and Oliver Jasselby to come to this hotel at nine. He hustled out, and before the real-estate offices were open he had routed out the superintendents of three buildings, examined seven offices, and engaged one. He dashed by taxi to a shop on Third Avenue which rents secondhand office equipment, and hired desks, chairs, rugs and a dictation machine. He bought carbon paper, typewriter ribbons, boxes of paper.

At nine he was prancing up and down his hotel room, planning a poem.

Bill Hupp, the press agent, was announced at nine-one.

Mr. Hupp was built on the general line of a motor van. He loomed into the room, glanced at Mr. Brown, chucked his yellow chamois gloves and fur coat on the bed, cocked his long ivory cigarette holder N.W. by N., two points N., and boomed "Well, what's the sordid task? What am I to perpetrate on the public prints? Nice line about having organized a League for the Prevention of Cruelty to the Heathen, or just plain case of breaking into society?"

"Neither. I want to be a literary genius."

"My Gawd, you don't want me. I can't help you. I'm a press agent, not a bartender."

"Sure. I'm savvy. I guess the game is bunk. But I've got a girl who is artistic, and I got to follow suit, see? Me, I'm a lumber merchant. I never wrote anything in my life but ads and letters."

"Got ye. We'll put you across. I'm engaged. Salary, one hundred a week, and all we can drag down from the padded expense account. Name's Bill Hupp."

"All right. Now I want you to put me on the very latest styles in literature. I don't want to waste time on anything that isn't dead highbrow."

"Sure. Well, first, there's this *vers libre*."

"Huh?"

"Why, *vers libre*—free verse—so called because it doesn't pay. It's choppy stuff with no rimes or rhythm. Walt Whitman in kid gloves. You've seen it—this kind of poetry that you wouldn't know it was poetry if it wasn't printed that way. Then there's these one-act plays for little theaters, like the Hobohemian Players. The plays have either got to be gruesome—cheery little jamborees, like a murder in a morgue—or else highbrow kidding stuff taking off all the playwright's friends down in Greenwich Village. Third, there's Russian realistic novels. That's all."

"Fine, Bill. Here's your first week's salary. Say, can you buy me about twenty-five dollars worth of samples of all this stuff, so we can model our own lines after them?"

"Right, boss."

Oliver Jasselby did not float in till ten. Mr. Jasselby, the plot-hound, was a small little man with sandy hair and eyeglasses on a silk ribbon. He bubbled and squeaked when he talked. He agreed to deliver weekly at the office the following raw materials: One novel plot, four short-story plots, six ideas for *vers libre*, and one outline for a morbid play.

When Bill Hupp returned with a consignment of the latest novelties in high art, Mr. Brown and he planned the first publicity. Bill suggested that Mr. Brown's first name be temporarily changed from Dennis to Denis. The newspapers were to be permitted to run modest notes to the effect that Denis Brown, the distinguished California poet and dramatist, had come to New York to live. Not that Mr. Brown did come from California, but California is a good safe place for geniuses, climate, and election returns to come from.

When Bill had gone off to supervise the furnishing of their new office Mr. Brown waded into the sample literature. By twelve, he believed that he had mastered the mechanism of the three forms of art.

He saw that *vers libre* was exactly like advertising, except that usually it was not so well done. The rules were the same—short snappy stuff, breaking away from old phrases, getting a unified impression. Now Mr. Brown had written advertisements. He remembered his masterpiece: "Who is the bugaboo man who flags you every time you dream of the Little Cottage for Two? It's your local builder!! Let us bully him for you, soz you'll get what you want, old top! Buy an Inland Portable Bungalow—you can clamp your eyes on it first, and know you're getting what you wanta get—not what Mr. Local Builder thinks you think you want. Then it's ho! for the Little House o' Dreams among the trees, with You and Her sitting out on the 10 by 22 porch in the good old twilight dreamtime."

When he had completed this advertisement, two years before, Mr. Brown had been rendered violently ill by it. But it really had sold bungalows, and now he perceived that it had in it most of the essentials of these poems about colors and twilight and mist and young women.

As regards the little plays for little theaters, he decided that they were exactly like smoking-car stories, related with gestures and snickers—except, perhaps, that the smoking-car stories were more moral.

And the final gasp in recent art, the Russian realistic novels, resembled the detailed reports on lumber-tract conditions which Mr. Brown had made for lumber companies in his early days. There was the same serious attention to dull details, the same heaviness of style, and the same pessimism about the writer's salary.

Mr. Brown chortled.

"It's just as I guessed. The reason why these guys get away with literature is because no business man has taken the trouble to go in and buck them. Oh, it's a shame to take the money."

He telephoned to Bill Hupp, at the office. "Say, Bill, if you don't mind, will you start sneaking in some press stuff about a Russian realistic novelist named Zuprushin?"

"Who's he?"

"He ain't yet. But he will be."

"Then how do I get any dope about him?"

"He's planning to come over here. His novels are being translated into English. He's an immoral old hound. Primeval brute. His latest novel is a cheery thing called *Dementia*."

"I get him. But what's the idea?"

"We'll write his novels for him. Bill, you listen to me: Inside of two months we'll have every highbrow in New York talking about

Zuprushin. From what you tell me, of these foreign authors—they're too busy talking about them. They don't even buy the books. That's done by the nice little old maids that overhear the talk. So the highbrows won't dare to let on they haven't heard of any new literary joker, and once we familiarize them with Brer Zuprushin's name, they'll all talk about him."

"Yes, but say, boss—Hello! Hello! Get—off—the—wire—will yuh, operator! But say, boss, what's the use of him, and she'll know I'm the family genius."

"Gotcha."

Mr. Brown went out, humming. In four hours and a half he had made a scholarly study of all literature, created the poet-dramatist Denis Brown, and gently guided that unfortunate child of genius, Zuprushin, through his boyhood, studenthood, and the writing of his novel *Dementia*. For a person who had not been a literary gentleman till seven o'clock that morning, Mr. Brown felt that he was not doing badly, and he was whistling loudly when he arrived at Ysetta's flat for tea.

They had dined at the Cunning Rabbit Tea Shop, Mr. Brown and Ysetta, and had witnessed four one-act plays presented by the Hobohemian Players.

Everybody in New York is always delivering something from some shackles, and the Hobohemian Players are an organization for delivering the stage from the shackles of the commercialized managers, and for developig a Native American Drama. To-night the Players presented Native American Dramas translated from the Polish, the Siamese and the Esquimo, and one apologetic little curtainraiser written in the United States.

Mr. Brown didn't care much for the plays or the acting; and the audience, which kept telling itself between acts how superior it was to Broadway audiences, made him feel feeble; but aside from that, he enjoyed the show; and afterward he obediently tagged after Ysetta to meet Mrs. Saffron and her group at the Café Liberté.

Ysetta warned him:

"Now, Dennis, I want you to be careful what you say to these people—they are so clever and subtle and all—and don't get off any of the noisy jokes you used to in Northernapolis. I'm as careful as can be what I say, till I'm admitted into their inner circle, and you—"

As Ysetta expressed her timid admiration for Mrs. Saffron, her books on eugenics, and her participation in clothing strikes; for Max Pincus, the landscapist, Jandorff Fish and Gaston Rakowsky, the novelists, and Miss Abigail Manx, the anarchist queen, Mr. Brown became nervous.

With the feeling of a small boy at a new school, he followed Ysetta into the basement of the Café Liberté. It was only a fair-to-medium basement; Mr. Brown owned as good a basement himself, in the family mansion. It was painted a plain tan, and filled with chairs and tables that looked much like other chairs and tables. But the people were terrifying. When he could make out the individuals, through the confusion of talk that sounded like a phonograph factory next to a recreation park, Mr. Brown decided that Hobohemia was not going to be easy. There were large, bland, round-faced young men, with an air of inexpressible superciliousness. Two lads in evening clothes were being humble to a dismayingly pretty girl with bobbed hair, who laughed at them and made love to a stolid hulk of a man with a dark face, weedy blue-black hair, and a mustache so much like one whole live cat that it might at any moment have been expected to fly across the room and out of a window. Seven nonchalant and good-looking women were dining together, and they looked him over till he felt shredded. Behind them were babbling millions.

"Some bunch!" said Mr. Brown weekly.

"Oh, these are just imitations—society slummers, and artists that are as disgustingly respectable as though they were merchants. The real Greenwich Villagers always go in the next room."

"Well, let's stay here in the compression chamber a minute and get used to the air pressure before we try the real wild ones," he begged, but she pushed through into an inner room. Round the table in the center were a dozen people, who bawled at her:

"*Bonsoir*, Ysette. Join us!"

Mr. Brown was conscious that they were all giving him what in less spiritual surroundings might have been called "the once-over." He timorously sat down between Ysetta and a stern, smooth, tailor-made woman of thirty-five to forty. She was introduced to him as Mrs. Saffron.

Mr. Brown had expected Mrs. Saffron to be a wild-haired bouncer in a smock. He was rather uncomfortable in the presence of her mannish efficiency. A chinless red-haired young man dropped into the seat on the other side of Mrs. Saffron, and bawled at her in a raw prairie voice:

"How are you, honey? What you drinking?"

Mrs. Saffron turned her back on Mr. Brown, and he was left alone, a child in the dark. On one side of him Ysetta was talking to Max Pincus, the painter, a short, solid young man with a heavy and pasty face. Mr. Brown instantly developed a considerable degree of dislike for Mr. Pincus, who did not talk of landscapes but of Sex, with a capital S and four exclamation points after the word. In his rolling voice Mr. Pincus was assuring Ysetta that free love was the only possible life for a genius. Ysetta was attending meekly, and smiling—with the clear chestnut eyes that Mr. Brown loved—into Mr. Pincus' glistening little eyes.

On the other side Mrs. Saffron was permitting the red-haired person to make violent love to her. She chuckled at him, and yawned. "Oh, go home, you baby; you make me tired"; but she only let him hold her hand and assure her that she was the only one in the world who encouraged him to keep up his artistic photography.

Jerry McCabe, the editor of *Direct Action*, came by and bent over to whisper to Mr. Brown: "I condole with you."

"Say, McCabe, how do I get on the inside with this bunch of in-tellectual giants?"

"Make love to Mrs. Saffron. Watch Red. He does it badly and promiscuously, yet it suffices to keep him in the foreground."

Two minutes after, when Red had departed, Mr. Brown leaned confidentially toward Mrs. Saffron and crooned—just as though she were not a radical leader:

"Honey, I could slay our young friend for monopolizing you. Why do you think I came here? To see you!"

Mrs. Saffron didn't seem in the least indignant.

"Well, you do see me, don't you?" she replied affably.

Whereupon Mr. Brown forgot that he was to be modestly retiring, and with a high percentage of perjury informed Mrs. Saffron that she was fair to gaze upon and charming to talk to, that her revolutionary efforts were the one thing that inspired him in his poetry, that he wanted to buy her some more drinks and lots more cigarettes, and that he didn't care a hang who saw them holding hands under the table.

Ysetta, who had been ignoring Mr. Brown, began to notice that he seemed to be able to get along with the lofty Mrs. Saffron. Then she discovered that the whole table listened to Mr. Brown when he told about the latest Russian novelist, Zuprushin, and his novel *Dementia*. She amazedly saw that Mrs. Saffron was urgently introducing her "nice boy," Mr. Brown, to the other nice boys, Jandorff Fish and Gaston Rakowsky, who listened feverishly as Mr. Brown outlined the plot of *Dementia*, which, apparently, had recently been translated from Russian into French.

The unlettered business man demanded fiercely of the master novelist, Jandorff Fish—temporarily employed by an interior decorator:

"Why, surely you've heard of Zuprushin?"

"Certainly I have! In fact I have one of his books at home, in French, though I haven't got to it yet."

Abigail Manx, who had joined the bunch without invitation, declared:

"Of course Zuprushin is superior to any American writer, but he doesn't compare with Artzibashef, or even Andreyeff."

Max Pincus deserted Ysetta to get on the bandwagon.

"Nonsense, nonsense!" he roared. "Mr.—Your friend, Ysetta, iss right. Zuprushin is the ver' latest manifestation of the somber Russian soul!"

"I told you so," exclaimed Mr. Brown. "Look, Pincus, you've read your Zuprushin in the original, while the rest of us only know him in French. Don't you think that *Dementia* is infinitely more— oh, you know."

"Oh, yaas!"

"But *Gray*—Zuprushin's new novel, *Gray*—the one that hasn't been translated from the Russian yet—can you tell me aboout it?"

Though he was rather vague about the plot and characters of *Gray*, Mr. Max Pincus gave a discourse on its "vital motivation" which really did him credit, considering that Zuprushin was now only about twelve hours old.

When Mr. Pincus had turned again to Ysetta, and Jandorff Fish and Abigail Manx had sunk into a bitter wrangle as to the reason why there were no Zuprushins in poor sodden America, Mr. Brown went the verbal rounds of the rest of the table, and one by one he asked the yearners whether they were good little radicals and knew their Zuprushins. They did, oh, indeed they did!

Again Mr. Brown indicated to Mrs. Saffron that he was desirous of buying her a fresh box of cigarettes and a lot more drinks, that if they two could get rid of all these Little People they would stride across the mountains together, and that he cared less than ever who saw them holding hands. To which Mrs. Saffron listened with mockery and delight.

Max Pincus, fulfilling the onerous duties of genius, had to go over to another table and make love to some girls who had just come in. Ysetta was left stranded. She turned to Mr. Brown with more interest than he had seen for many months. But he paid no'attention to her. He wanted her to be just a little jealous, and—

And he was surprised to find that he was actually enjoying making love to Mrs. Saffron. Although she devoured his compliments raw he was none too sure that she was not thoroughly on, and in the game of trying to find out what she thought he was not excited by Ysetta's native tactics. When the Liberté closed for the night Mrs. Saffron was telling him the story of her life—at least one version of the story.

The Hobohemians stood unhappily on the sidewalk—exiles with no smoky place to go, though it was only one o'clock and the talk just beginning to get interesting.

"All of you come over to my place!" cried Mrs. Saffron.

"Shall I come?" Ysetta asked timidly.

"Oh, you—you most of all, funny little child from the West!" purred Mrs. Saffron.

But as she looked over Ysetta's shoulder into the eyes of Mr. Brown her expression indicated that it wasn't Ysetta she liked best of all.

Though the socks-trade strike and the Dakota mine strike had both been planned there, Mrs. Saffron's flat was not exciting, except that pillows were used in place of chairs. The talk faltered. There were only eleven people there, instead of the jolly crowd at the Liberté, and they discussed scarcely any subjects except the war, sex, Zuprushin, Mr. Max Pincus' paintings, birth control, eugenics, psycho-analysis, the Hobohemian Players, biological research, Nona Barnes' new way of dressing her hair, sex, H. G. Wells, the lowness of the popular magazines, Zuprushin, Mr. Max Pincus' poetry, and a few new aspects of sex. So the party broke up as early as two-thirty, and they all went home to get a good night's sleep for a change.

Mrs. Saffron had invited Mr. Brown to come in for tea, and bring "your nice little friend, Ysetta."

Ysetta had overheard this, and after a strained silence in the taxi on the way home, she observed:

"Dennis, do you know that you forced your attention on Mrs. Saffron to such an extent that one would almost have thought it was you that took me to the Liberté! And you promised to be so careful. What were you talking to her about anyway?"

"Oh, about Zuprushin."

"Well. . . . Well, I must read some more Zuprushin too. . . . When I get the time. . . . "

124

"Sure."

Mr. Brown grinned in the darkness. But he was in turmoil, whereof these were the component parts:

Three hours of mixed drinks and cigarette smoke.

A feeling that Ysetta would have to be thoroughly spanked.

A feeling that he ought to feel that Mrs. Saffron was a crank, but—

A feeling that he would jolly well like to know whether she really liked him or was merely having a good time with him.

—April 1917

Willa Cather

(1873–1947)

One of the country's major writers, novelist Willa Cather was born near Winchester, Virginia. At age ten she moved with her family to Red Cloud, Nebraska. After graduating from the University of Nebraska she turned to journalism. She found work as a teacher in Pittsburgh but then went to New York in 1906 to work as an editor on McClure's *Magazine. Her first book, a collection of verse entitled* April Twilights, *was published in 1903 and was followed two years later by a collection of stories,* The Troll Garden. *She did not write her first novel,* Alexander's Bridge, *until 1912. Soon thereafter she left* McClure's *to devote her energies to full-time writing. Among her best known works are* O Pioneers! *(1913),* The Song of the Lark *(1915), and* My Antonia *(1918). Many consider* Death Comes for the Archbishop *(1927), about the missionary experiences of a Roman Catholic bishop among the Native Americans of New Mexico, to be her greatest novel. Cather wrote many of her novels in her spacious Greenwich Village apartment on Bank Street, including* My Antonia. *Her long short story, "Coming, Aphrodite!," is one of the few of her works that is actually set in the Village.*

"Coming, Aphrodite!"

Don Hedger had lived for four years on the top floor of an old house on the south side of Washington Square, and nobody had ever disturbed him. He occupied one big room with no outside exposure except on the north, where he had built in a many-paned

Willa Cather. "Coming, Aphrodite!" from *Willa Cather: Stories, Poems, and Other Writings* (New York: The Library of America, 1992).

studio window that looked upon a court and upon the roofs and walls of other buildings. His room was very cheerless, since he never got a ray of direct sunlight; the south corners were always in shadow. In one of the corners was a clothes closet, built against the partition, in another a wide divan, serving as a seat by day and a bed by night. In the front corner, the one farther from the window was a sink, and a table with two gas burners where he sometimes cooked his food. There, too, in the perpetual dusk, was the dog's bed, and often a bone or two for his comfort.

The dog was a Boston bull terrier, and Hedger explained his surly disposition by the fact that he had been bred to the point where it told on his nerves. His name was Caesar III, and he had taken prizes at very exclusive dog shows. When he and his master went out to prowl about University Place or to promenade along West Street, Caesar III was invariably fresh and shining. His pink skin showed through his mottled coat, which glistened as if it had been rubbed with olive oil, and he wore a brass-studded collar, bought at the smartest saddler's. Hedger, as often as not, was hunched up in an old striped blanket coat, with a shapeless felt hat pulled over his bushy hair, wearing black shoes that had become grey, or brown ones that had become black, and he never put on gloves unless the day was biting cold.

Early in May, Hedger learned that he was to have a new neighbour in the rear apartment—two rooms, one large and one small, that faced the west. His studio was shut off from the larger of these rooms by double doors, which, though they were fairly tight, left him a good deal at the mercy of the occupant. The rooms had been leased, long before he came there, by a trained nurse who considered herself knowing in old furniture. She went to auction sales and bought up mahogany and dirty brass and stored it away here, where she meant to live when she retired from nursing. Meanwhile, she sub-let her rooms, with their precious furniture, to young people who came to New York to "write" or to "paint"— who proposed to live by the sweat of the brow rather than of the hand, and who desired artistic surroundings. When Hedger first moved in, these rooms were occupied by a young man who tried

127

to write plays,—and who kept on trying until a week ago, when the nurse had put him out for unpaid rent.

A few days after the playwright left, Hedger heard an ominous murmur of voices through the bolted double doors: the ladylike intonation of the nurse—doubtless exhibiting her treasures— and another voice, also a woman's, but very different; young, fresh, unguarded, confident. All the same, it would be very annoying to have a woman in there. The only bath-room on the floor was at the top of the stairs in the front hall, and he would always be running into her as he came and went from his bath. He would have to be more careful to see that Caesar didn't leave bones about the hall, too; and she might object when he cooked steak and onions on his gas burner.

As soon as the talking ceased and the women left, he forgot them. He was absorbed in a study of paradise fish at the Aquarium, staring out at people through the glass and green water of their tank. It was a highly gratifying idea; the incommunicability of one stratum of animal life with another,—though Hedger pretended it was only an experiment in unusual lighting. When he heard trunks knocking against the sides of the narrow hall, then he realized that she was moving in at once. Toward noon, groans and deep gasps and the creaking of ropes, made him aware that a piano was arriving. After the tramp of the movers died away down the stairs, somebody touched off a few scales and chords on the instrument, and then there was peace. Presently he heard her lock her door and go down the hall humming something; going out to lunch, probably. He stuck his brushes in a can of turpentine and put on his hat, not stopping to wash his hands. Caesar was smelling along the crack under the bolted doors; his bony tail stuck out hard as a hickory withe, and the hair was standing up about his elegant collar.

Hedger encouraged him. "Come along, Caesar. You'll soon get used to a new smell."

In the hall stood an enormous trunk, behind the ladder that led to the roof, just opposite. The dog flew at it with a growl of hurt amazement. They went down three flights of stairs and out into the brilliant May afternoon.

Behind the Square, Hedger and his dog descended into a basement oyster house where there were no tablecloths on the tables and no handles on the coffee cups, and the floor was covered with sawdust, and Caesar was always welcome,—not that he needed any such precautionary flooring. All the carpets of Persia would have been safe for him. Hedger ordered steak and onions absent-mindedly, not realizing why he had an apprehension that this dish might be less readily at hand hereafter. While he ate, Caesar sat beside his chair, gravely disturbing the sawdust with his tail.

After lunch Hedger strolled about the Square for the dog's health and watched the stages pull out;—that was almost the very last summer of the old horse stages on Fifth Avenue. The fountain had but lately begun operations for the season and was throwing up a mist of rainbow water which now and then blew south and sprayed a bunch of Italian babies that were being supported on the outer rim by older, very little older, brothers and sisters. Plump robins were hopping about the soil; the grass was newly cut and blindly green. Looking up the Avenue through the Arch, one could see the young poplars with their bright, sticky leaves, and the Brevoort glistening in its spring coat of paint, and shining horses and carriages,—occasionally an automobile, mis-shapen and sullen, like an ugly threat in a stream of things that were bright and beautiful and alive.

While Caesar and his master were standing by the fountain, a girl approached them, crossing the Square. Hedger noticed her because she wore a lavender cloth suit and carried in her arms a big bunch of fresh lilacs. He saw that she was young and handsome,—beautiful, in fact, with a splendid figure and good action. She, too, paused by the fountain and looked back through the Arch up the Avenue. She smiled rather patronizingly as she looked, and at the same time seemed delighted. Her slowly curving upper lip and half-closed eyes seemed to say: "You're gay, you're exciting, you are quite the right sort of thing; but you're none too fine for me!"

In the moment she tarried, Caesar stealthily approached her and sniffed at the hem of her lavender skirt, then, when she went south like an arrow, he ran back to his master and lifted a face full of emotion and alarm, his lower lip twitching under his sharp white teeth and his hazel eyes pointed with a very definite discovery. He stood thus, motionless, while Hedger watched the lavender girl go up the steps and through the door of the house in which he lived.

"You're right, my boy, it's she! She might be worse looking, you know."

When they mounted to the studio, the new lodger's door, at the back of the hall, was a little ajar, and Hedger caught the warm perfume of lilacs just brought in out of the sun. He was used to the musty smell of the old hall carpet. (The nurse-lessee had once knocked at his studio door and complained that Caesar must be somewhat responsible for the particular flavour of that mustiness, and Hedger had never spoken to her since.) He was used to the old smell, and he preferred it to that of the lilacs, and so did his companion, whose nose was so much more discriminating. Hedger shut his door vehemently, and fell to work.

Most young men who dwell in obscure studios in New York have had a beginning, come out of something, have somewhere a home town, a family, a paternal roof. But Don Hedger had no such background. He was a foundling, and had grown up in a school for homeless boys, where book-learning was a negligible part of the curriculum. When he was sixteen, a Catholic priest took him to Greensburg, Pennsylvania, to keep house for him. The priest did something to fill in the large gaps in the boy's education,—taught him to like "Don Quixote" and "The Golden Legend," and encouraged him to mess with paints and crayons in his room up under the slope of the mansard. When Don wanted to go to New York to study at the Art League, the priest got him a night job as packer in one of the big department stores. Since them, Hedger had taken care of himself; that was his only responsibility. He was singularly unencumbered; had no family duties, no social ties, no obligations toward any one but his landlord. Since he travelled light, he had travelled rather far. He had got over a good deal of the earth's surface, in spite of the fact that he never in his life had more than three hundred dollars ahead at any one time, and he had already outlived a succession of convictions and revelations about his art.

Though he was now but twenty-six years old, he had twice been on the verge of becoming a marketable product; once through some studies of New York streets he did for a magazine, and once through a collection of pastels he brought home from New Mexico, which Remington, then at the height of his popularity, happened to see, and generously tried to push. But on both occasions Hedger decided that this was something he didn't wish to carry further,—simply the old thing over again and got nowhere,—so he took enquiring dealers' experiments in a "later manner," that made them put him out of the shop. When he ran short of money, he could always get any amount of commercial work; he was an expert draughtsman and worked with lightning speed. The rest of his time he spent in groping his way from one kind of painting into another, or travelling about without luggage, like a tramp, and he was chiefly occupied with getting rid of ideas he had once thought very fine.

Hedger's circumstances, since he had moved to Washington Square, were affluent compared to anything he had ever known before. He was now able to pay advance rent and turn the key on his studio when he went away for four months at a stretch. It didn't occur to him to wish to be richer than this. To be sure, he did without a great many things other people think necessary, but he didn't miss them, because he had never had them. He belonged to no clubs, visited no houses, had no studio friends, and he ate his dinner alone in some decent little restaurant, even on Christmas and New Year's. For days together he talked to nobody but his dog and the janitress and the lame oysterman.

After he shut the door and settled down to his paradise fish on that first Tuesday in May, Hedger forgot all about his new neighbour. When the light failed, he took Caesar out for a walk. On the way home he did his marketing on West Houston Street, with a one-eyed Italian woman who always cheated him. After he had cooked his beans and scallopini, and drunk half a bottle of Chianti, he put his dishes in the sink and went up on the roof to smoke. He was the only person in the house who ever went to the roof, and he had a secret understanding with the janitress about it. He was to have "the privilege of the roof," as she said, if he opened the heavy trapdoor on sunny days to air out the upper hall, and was watchful to close it when rain threatened. Mrs. Foley was fat and dirty and hated to climb stairs,—besides, the roof was reached by a perpendicular iron ladder, definitely inaccessible to a woman of her bulk, and the iron door at the top of it was too heavy for any but Hedger's strong arm to lift. Hedger was not above medium height, but he practiced with weights and dumb-bells, and in the shoulders he was as strong as a gorilla.

So Hedger had the roof to himself. He and Caesar often slept up there on hot nights, rolled in blankets he had brought home from Arizona. He mounted with Caesar under his left arm. The dog had never learned to climb a perpendicular ladder, and never did he feel so much his master's greatness and his own dependence upon him, as when he crept under his arm for the perilous ascent. Up there was even gravel to scratch in, and a dog could do whatever he liked, so long as he did not bark. It was a kind of Heaven, which no one was strong enough to reach but his great, paint-smelling master.

On this blue May night there was a slender, girlish looking young moon in the west, playing with a whole company of silver stars. Now and then one of them darted away from the group and shot off into the gauzy blue with a soft little trail of light, like laughter. Hedger and his dog were delighted when a star did this. They were quite lost in watching the glittering game, when they were suddenly diverted by a sound,—not from the stars, though it was music. It was not the Prologue to Pagliacci, which rose ever and anon on hot evenings from an Italian tenement on Thompson Street, with the gasps of the corpulent baritone who got behind it; nor was it the hurdy-gurdy man, who often played at the corner in the balmy twilight. No, this was a woman's voice, singing the tempestuous, over-lapping phrases of Signor Puccini, then comparatively new in the world, but already so popular that even Hedger recognized his unmistakable gusts of breath. He looked about over the roofs; all was blue and still, with the well-built chimneys that were never used now standing up dark and mournful. He moved softly toward the yellow quadrangle where the gas from the hall shone up through the half-lifted trapdoor. Oh yes! It came up through the hole like a strong draught, a big, beautiful voice, and it sounded rather like a professional's. A piano had arrived in the morning, Hedger remembered. This might be a very great nuisance. It would be pleasant enough to listen to, if you could turn it on and off as you wished; but you couldn't. Caesar, with the gas light shining on his collar and his ugly but sensitive face, panted and looked up for information. Hedger put down a reassuring hand.

"I don't know. We can't tell yet. It may not be so bad."

He stayed on the roof until all was still below, and finally descended, with quite a new feeling about his neighbour. Her voice, like her figure, inspired respect,—if one did not choose to call it admiration. Her door was shut, the transom was dark; nothing remained of her but the obtrusive trunk, unrightfully taking up room in the narrow hall.

II

For two days Hedger didn't see her. He was painting eight hours a day just then, and only went out to hunt for food. He noticed that she practiced scales and exercises for about an hour in the morning then she locked her door, went humming down the hall, and left him in peace. He heard her getting her coffee ready at about the same time he got his. Earlier still, she passed his room on her way to her bath. In the evening she sometimes sang, but on the whole she didn't bother him. When he was working well he did not notice anything much. The morning paper lay before the door until he reached out for his milk bottle, then he kicked the sheet inside and it lay on the floor until evening. Sometimes he read it and sometimes he did not. He forgot there was anything of importance going on in the world outside of his third floor studio. Nobody had ever taught him that he ought to be interested in other people; in the Pittsburgh steel strike, in the Fresh Air Fund, in the scandal about the Babies' Hospital. A grey wolf, living in a Wyoming canyon, would hardly have been less concerned about these things than was Don Hedger.

One morning he was coming out of the bathroom at the front end of the hall, having just given Caesar his bath and rubbed him into a glow with a heavy towel. Before the door, lying in wait for him, as it were, stood a tall figure in a flowing blue silk dressing gown that fell away from her marble arms. In her hands she carried various accessories for the bath.

"I wish," she said distinctly, standing in his way, "I wish you wouldn't wash your dog in the tub. I never heard of such a thing! I've found his hair in the tub, and I've smelled a doggy smell, and now I've caught you at it. It's an outrage!"

Hedger was badly frightened. She was so tall and positive, and was fairly blazing with beauty and anger. He stood blinking, holding on to his sponge and dog-soap, feeling he ought to bow very low to her. But what he actually said was:

"Nobody has ever objected before. I always wash the tub,— and, anyhow, he's cleaner than most people."

"Cleaner than me?" her eyebrows went up, her white arms and neck and her fragrant person seemed to scream at him like a band of outraged nymphs. Something flashed through his mind about a man who was turned into a dog, or was pursued by dogs, because he unwittingly intruded upon the bath of beauty.

"No, I didn't mean that," he muttered, turning scarlet under the bluish stubble of his muscular jaws. "But I know he's cleaner than I am."

"That I don't doubt!" Her voice sounded like a soft shivering of crystal, and with a smile of pity she drew the folds of her voluminous blue robe close about her and allowed the wretched man to pass. Even Caesar was frightened, he darted like a streak down the hall, through the door and to his own bed in the corner among the bones.

Hedger stood in the doorway, listening to indignant sniffs and coughs and a great swishing of water about the sides of the tub. He had washed it; but as he had washed it with Caesar's sponge, it

134

was quite possible that a few bristles remained; the dog was shedding now. The playwright had never objected, nor had the jovial illustrator who occupied the front apartment,—but he, as he admitted, "was usually pye-eyed, when he wasn't in Buffalo." He went home to Buffalo sometimes to rest his nerves.

It had never occurred to Hedger that any one would mind using the tub after Caesar;—but then, he had never seen a beautiful girl caparisoned for the bath before. As soon as he beheld her standing there, he realized the unfitness of it. For that matter, she ought not to step into a tub that any other mortal had bathed in; the illustrator was sloppy and left cigarette ends on the moulding.

All morning as he worked he was gnawed by a spiteful desire to get back at her. It rankled that he had been so vanquished by her disdain. When he heard her locking her door to go out for lunch, he stepped quickly into the hall in his messy painting coat, and addressed her.

"I don't wish to be exigent, Miss,"—he had certain grand words that he used upon occasion—"but if this is your trunk, it's rather in the way here."

"Oh, very well!" she exclaimed carelessly, dropping her keys into her handbag. "I'll have it moved when I can get a man to do it," and she went down the hall with her free, roving stride.

Her name, Hedger discovered from her letters, which the postman left on the table in the lower hall, was Eden Bower.

III

In the closet that was built against the partition separating his room from Miss Bower's, Hedger kept all his wearing apparel, some of it on hooks and hangers, some of it on the floor. When he opened his closet door now-a-days, little dust-colored insects flew out on downy wing, and he suspected that a brood of moths were hatching in his winter overcoat. Mrs. Foley, the janitress, told him to bring down all his heavy clothes and she would give them a beating and hang them in the court. The closet was in such disorder that he shunned the encounter, but one hot afternoon he set him-self to the task. First he threw out a pile of forgotten laundry and tied it up in a sheet. The bundle stood as high as his middle when he had knotted the corners. Then he got his shoes and overshoes together. When he took his overcoat from its place against the par-tition, a long ray of yellow light shot across the dark enclosure,—a knot hole, evidently, in the high wainscoting of the west room. He had never noticed it before, and without realizing what he was do-ing, he stooped and squinted through it.

Yonder, in a pool of sunlight, stood his new neighbor, wholly unclad, doing exercises of some sort before a long gilt mirror. Hedger did not happen to think how unpardonable it was of him to watch her. Nudity was not improper to any one who had worked so much from the figure, and he continued to look, simply because he had never seen a woman's body so beautiful as this one,—positively glorious in action. As she swung her arms and changed from one pivot of motion to another, muscular energy seemed to flow through her from her toes to her fingertips. The soft flush of exercise and the gold of afternoon sun played over her flesh together, enveloped her in a luminous mist which, as she turned and twisted, made now an arm, now a shoulder, now a thigh, dissolve in pure light and instantly recover its outline with the next gesture. Hedger's fingers curved as if he were holding a crayon; mentally he was doing the whole figure in a single running line, and the charcoal seemed to explode in his hand at the point where the energy of each gesture was discharged into the whirling disc of light, from a foot or shoulder, from the up-thrust chin or the lifted breasts.

He could not have told whether he watched her for six minutes or sixteen. When her gymnastics were over, she paused to catch up a lock of hair that had come down, and examined with solicitude a little reddish mole that grew under her left armpit. Then, with her hand on her hip, she walked unconcernedly across the room and disappeared through the door into her bedchamber.

Disappeared—Don Hedger was crouching on his knees, staring at the golden shower which poured in through the west windows, at the lake of gold sleeping on the faded Turkish carpet. The spot was enchanted; a vision out of Alexandria, out of the remote pagan past, had bathed itself there in Helianthine fire.

When he crawled out of his closet, he stood blinking at the grey sheet stuffed with laundry, not knowing what had happened to him. He felt a little sick as he contemplated the bundle. Everything here was different; he hated the disorder of the place, the grey prison light, his old shoes and himself and all his slovenly habits. The black calico curtains that ran on wires over his big window were white with dust. There were three greasy frying pans in the sink, and the sink itself. . . . He felt desperate. He couldn't stand this another minute. He took up an armful of winter clothes and ran down four flights into the basement.

"Mrs. Foley," he began, "I want my room cleaned this afternoon, thoroughly cleaned. Can you get a woman for me right away?"

"Is it company you're having?" the fat, dirty janitress inquired. Mrs. Foley was the widow of a useful Tammany man, and she owned real estate in Flatbush. She was huge and soft as a feather bed. Her face and arms were permanently coated with dust, grained like wood where the sweat had trickled.

"Yes, company. That's it."

"Well, this is a queer time of the day to be asking for a cleaning woman. It's likely I can get you old Lizzie, if she's not drunk. I'll send Willy round to see."

Willy, the son of fourteen, roused from the stupor and stain of his fifth box of cigarettes by the gleam of a quarter, went out. In five minutes he returned with old Lizzie—she smelling strong of spirits and wearing several jackets which she had put on one over the other, and a number of skirts, long and short, which made her resemble an animated dish-clout. She had, of course, to borrow her equipment from Mrs. Foley, and toiled up the long flights, dragging mop and pail and broom. She told Hedger to be of good cheer, for he had got the right woman for the job, and showed him a great leather strap she wore about her wrist to prevent dislocation of tendons. She swished about the place, scattering dust and splashing soapsuds, while he watched her in nervous despair. He stood over

Lizzie and made her scour the sink, directing her roughly, then paid her and got rid of her. Shutting the door on his failure, he hurried off with his dog to lose himself among the stevedores and dock laborers on West Street.

A strange chapter began for Don Hedger. Day after day, at that hour in the afternoon, the hour before his neighbor dressed for dinner, he crouched down in his closet to watch her go through her mysterious exercises. It did not occur to him that his conduct was detestable; there was nothing shy or retreating about this unclad girl,—a bold body, studying itself quite coolly and evidently well pleased with itself, doing all this for a purpose. Hedger scarcely regarded his action as conduct at all; it was something that had happened to him. More than once he went out and tried to stay away for the whole afternoon, but at about five o'clock he was sure to find himself among his old shoes in the dark. The pull of that aperture was stronger than his will,—and he had always considered his will the strongest thing about him. When she threw herself upon the divan and lay resting, he still stared, holding his breath. His nerves were so on edge that a sudden noise made him start and brought out the sweat on his forehead. The dog would come and tug at his sleeve, knowing that something was wrong with his master. If he attempted a mournful whine, those strong hands closed about his throat.

When Hedger came slinking out of his closet, he sat down on the edge of the couch, sat for hours without moving. He was not painting at all now. This thing, whatever it was, drank him up as ideas had sometimes done, and he sank into a stupor of idleness as deep and dark as the stupor of work. He could not understand it; he was no boy, he had worked from models for years, and a woman's body was no mystery to him. Yet now he did nothing but sit and think about one. He slept very little, and with the first light of morning he awoke as completely possessed by this woman as if he had been with her all the night before. The unconscious operations of life went on in him only to perpetuate this excitement. His brain held but one image now—vibrated, burned with it. It was a heathenish feeling; without friendliness, almost without tenderness.

138

Women had come and gone in Hedger's life. Not having had a mother to begin with, his relations with them, whether amorous or friendly, had been casual. He got on well with janitresses and wash-women, with Indians and with the peasant women of foreign countries. He had friends among the silk-skirt factory girls who came to eat their lunch in Washington Square, and he sometimes took a model for a day in the country. He felt an unreasoning antipathy toward the well-dressed women he saw coming out of big shops, or driving in the Park. If, on his way to the Art Museum, he noticed a pretty girl standing on the steps of one of the houses on upper Fifth Avenue, he frowned at her and went by with his shoulders hunched up as if he were cold. He had never known such girls, or heard them talk, or seen the inside of the houses in which they lived; but he believed them all to be artificial and, in an aesthetic sense, perverted. He saw them enslaved by desire of merchandise and manufactured articles, effective only in making life complicated and insincere and in embroidering it with ugly and meaningless trivialities. They were enough, he thought, to make one almost forget woman as she existed in art, in thought, and in the universe.

He had no desire to know the woman who had, for the time at least, so broken up his life,—no curiosity about her every-day personality. He shunned any revelation of it, and he listened for Miss Bower's coming and going, not to encounter, but to avoid her. He wished that the girl who wore shirtwaists and got letters from Chicago would keep out of his way, that she did not exist. With her he had naught to make. But in a room full of sun, before an old mirror, on a little enchanted rug of sleeping colors, he had seen a woman who emerged naked through a door, and disappeared naked. He thought of that body as never having been clad, or as having worn the stuffs and dyes of all the centuries but his own. And for him she had no geographical associations; unless with Crete, or Alexandria, or Veronese's Venice. She was the immortal conception, the perennial theme.

The first break in Hedger's lethargy occurred one afternoon when two young men came to take Eden Bower out to dine. They went into the music room, laughed and talked for a few minutes, and then took her away with them. They were gone a long while, but he did not go out for food himself; he waited for them to come back. At last he heard them coming down the hall, gayer and more talkative than when they left. One of them sat down at the piano, and they all began to sing. This Hedger found absolutely unendurable. He snatched up his hat and went running down the stairs. Caesar leaped beside him, hoping that old times were coming back. They had supper in the oysterman's basement and then sat down in front of their own doorway. The moon stood full over the Square, a thing of regal glory; but Hedger did not see the moon; he was looking, murderously for men. Presently two, wearing straw hats and white trousers and carrying canes, came down the steps from his house. He rose and dogged them across the Square. They were laughing and seemed very much elated about something. As one stopped to light a cigarette, Hedger caught from the other:

"Don't you think she has a beautiful talent?"

His companion threw away his match. "She has a beautiful figure."

They both ran to catch the stage.

Hedger went back to his studio. The light was shining from her transom. For the first time he violated her privacy at night, and peered through that fatal aperture. She was sitting, fully dressed, in the window, smoking a cigarette and looking out over the housetops. He watched her until she rose, looked about her with a disdainful, crafty smile, and turned out the light.

The next morning, when Miss Bower went out, Hedger followed her. Her white skirt gleamed ahead of him as she sauntered about the Square. She sat down behind the Garibaldi statue and opened a music book she carried. She turned the leaves carelessly, and several times she glanced in his direction. He was on the point of going over to her, when she rose quickly and looked up at the sky. A flock of pigeons had risen from somewhere in the crowded Italian quarter to the south, and were wheeling rapidly up through the morning air, soaring and dropping, scattering and coming together, now grey, now white as silver, as they caught or intercepted the sunlight. She put up her hand to shade her eyes and followed them with a kind of defiant delight on her face.

Hedger came and stood beside her. ""You've surely seen them before?"

"Oh, yes," she replied, still looking up. "I see them every day from my windows. They always come home about five o'clock. Where do they live?"

"I don't know. Probably some Italian raises them for the market. They were here long before I came, and I've been here four years."

"In that same gloomy room? Why didn't you take mine when it was vacant?"

"It isn't gloomy. That's the best light for painting."

"Oh, is it? I don't know anything about painting. I'd like to see your pictures sometime. You have such a lot in there. Don't they get dusty, piled up against the wall like that?"

"Not very. I'd be glad to show them to you. Is your name really Eden Bower? I've seen your letters on the table."

"Well, it's the name I'm going to sing under. My father's name is Bowers, but my friend Mr. Jones, a Chicago newspaper man who writes about music, told me to drop the 's.' He's crazy about my voice."

Miss Bower didn't usually tell the whole story,—about anything. Her first name, when she lived in Huntington, Illinois, was Edna, but Mr. Jones had persuaded her to change it to one which he felt would be worthy of her future. She was quick to take suggestions, though she told him she "didn't see what was the matter with 'Edna.'"

She explained to Hedger that she was going to Paris to study. She was waiting in New York for Chicago friends who were to take her over, but who had been detained. "Did you study in Paris?" she asked.

"No, I've never been in Paris. But I was in the south of France all last summer, studying with C———. He's the biggest man among the moderns,—at least I think so."

Miss Bower sat down and made room for him on the bench. "Do tell me about it. I expected to be there by this time, and I can't wait to find out what it's like."

141

Hedger began to relate how he had seen some of this French-man's work in an exhibition, and deciding at once that this was the man for him, he had taken a boat for Marseilles the next week, go-ing over steerage. He proceeded at once to the little town on the coast where his painter lived, and presented himself. The man never took pupils, but because Hedger had come so far, he let him stay. Hedger lived at the master's house and every day they went out together to paint, sometimes on the blazing rocks down by the sea. They wrapped themselves in light woolen blankets and didn't feel the heat. Being there and working with C——— was being in Paradise, Hedger concluded; he learned more in three months than in all his life before.

Eden Bower laughed. "You're a funny fellow. Didn't you do anything but work? Are the women very beautiful? Did you have awfully good things to eat and drink?"

Hedger said some of the women were fine looking, especially one girl who went about selling fish and lobsters. About the food there was nothing remarkable,—except the ripe figs, he liked those. They drank sour wine, and used goat butter, which was strong and full of hair, as it was churned in a goat skin.

"But don't they have parties or banquets? Aren't there any fine hotels down there?"

"Yes, but they are all closed in summer, and the country people are poor. It's a beautiful country, though."

"How, beautiful?" she persisted.

"If you want to go in, I'll show you some sketches, and you'll see."

Miss Bower rose. "All right. I won't go to my fencing lesson this morning. Do you fence? Here comes your dog. You can't move but he's after you. He always makes a face at me when I meet him in the hall, and shows his nasty little teeth as if he wanted to bite me."

In the studio Hedger got out his sketches, but to Miss Bower, whose favorite pictures were Christ Before Pilate and a red-haired Magdalen of Henner, these landscapes were not at all beautiful, and they gave her no idea of any country whatsoever. She was careful not to commit herself, however. Her vocal teacher had already convinced her that she had a great deal to learn about many things.

"Why don't we go out to lunch somewhere?" Hedger asked, and began to dust his fingers with a handkerchief—which he got out of sight as swiftly as possible.

"All right, the Brevoort," she said carelessly. "I think that's a good place, and they have good wine. I don't care for cocktails."

Hedger felt his chin uneasily. "I'm afraid I haven't shaved this morning. If you could wait for me in the Square? It won't take me ten minutes."

Left alone, he found a clean collar and handkerchief, brushed his coat and blacked his shoes, and last of all dug up ten dollars from the bottom of an old copper kettle he had bought from Spain. His winter hat was of such a complexion that the Brevoort hall boy winked at the porter as he took it and placed it on the rack in a row of fresh straw ones.

IV

That afternoon Eden Bower was lying on the couch in her music room, her face turned to the window, watching the pigeons. Reclining thus she could see none of the neighboring roofs, only the sky itself and the birds that crossed and recrossed her field of vision, white as scraps of paper blowing in the wind. She was thinking that she was young and handsome and had had a good lunch, that a very easy-going, light-hearted city lay in the streets below her; and she was wondering why she found this queer painter chap, with his lean, bluish cheeks and heavy black eyebrows, more interesting than the smart young men she met at her teacher's studio.

Eden Bower was, at twenty, very much the same person that we all know her to be at forty, except that she knew a great deal less. But one thing she knew: that she was to be Eden Bower. She was like some one standing before a great show window full of beautiful and costly things, deciding which she will order. She understands that they will not all be delivered immediately, but one by one they will arrive at her door. She already knew some of the many things that were to happen to her; for instance, that the Chicago millionaire who was going to take her abroad with his sister as chaperone, would eventually press his claim in quite another manner. He was the most circumspect of bachelors, afraid of everything obvious, even of women who were too flagrantly handsome. He was a nervous collector of pictures and furniture, a nervous patron of music, and a nervous host; very cautious about his health, and about any course of conduct that might make him ridiculous. But she knew that he would at last throw all his precautions to the winds.

People like Eden Bower are inexplicable. Her father sold farming machinery in Huntington, Illinois, and she had grown up with no acquaintances or experiences outside of that prairie town. Yet from her earliest childhood she had not one conviction or opinion in common with the people about her,—the only people she knew. Before she was out of short dresses she had made up her mind that she was going to be an actress, that she would live far away in great cities, that she would be much admired by men and would have everything she wanted. When she was thirteen, and was already singing and reciting for church entertainments, she read in some illustrated magazine a long article about the late Czar of Russia, then just come to the throne or about to come to it. After that, lying in the hammock on the front porch on summer evenings, or sitting through a long sermon in the family pew, she amused herself by trying to make up her mind whether she would or would not be the Czar's mistress when she played in his Capital. Now Edna had met this fascinating word only in the novels of Ouida,—her hardworked little mother kept a long row of them in the upstairs storeroom, behind the linen chest. In Huntington, women who bore that relation to men were called by a very different name, and their lot was not an enviable one; of all the shabby and poor, they were the shabbiest. But then, Edna had never lived in Huntington, not even before she began to find books like "Sapho" and "Mademoiselle de Maupin," secretly sold in paper covers throughout Illinois. It was as if she had come into Huntington, into the Bowers family, on one of the trains that puffed over the marshes behind their back fence all day long, and was waiting for another train to take her out.

As she grew older and handsomer, she had many beaux, but these small-town boys didn't interest her. If a lad kissed her when he brought her home from a dance, she was indulgent and she rather liked it. But if he pressed her further, she slipped away from him, laughing. After she began to sing in Chicago, she was consistently discreet. She stayed as a guest in rich people's houses, and she knew that she was being watched like a rabbit in a laboratory. Covered up in bed, with the lights out, she thought her own thoughts, and laughed.

This summer in New York was her first taste of freedom. The Chicago capitalist, after all his arrangements were made for sailing, had been compelled to go to Mexico to look after oil interests. His sister knew an excellent singing master in New York. Why should not a discreet, well-balanced girl like Miss Bower spend the summer there, studying quietly? The capitalist suggested that his sister might enjoy a summer on Long Island; he would rent the Griffiths' place for her, with all the servants, and Eden could stay there. But his sister met this proposal with a cold stare. So it fell out, that between selfishness and greed, Eden got a summer all her own,— which really did a great deal toward making her an artist and whatever else she was afterward to become. She had time to look about, to watch without being watched; to select diamonds in one window and furs in another, to select shoulders and moustaches in the big hotels where she went to lunch. She had the easy freedom of obscurity and the consciousness of power. She enjoyed both. She was in no hurry.

While Eden Bower watched the pigeons, Don Hedger sat on the other side of the bolted doors, looking into a pool of dark turpentine, at his idle brushes, wondering why a woman could do this to him. He, too, was sure of his future and knew that he was a chosen man. He could not know, of course, that he was merely the first to fall under a fascination which was to be disastrous to a few men and pleasantly stimulating to many thousands. Each of these two young people sensed the future, but not completely. Don Hedger knew that nothing much would ever happen to him. Eden Bower understood that to her a great deal would happen. But she did not guess that her neighbor would have more tempestuous adventures sitting in his dark studio than she would find in all the capitals of Europe, or in all the latitude of conduct she was prepared to permit herself.

V

One Sunday morning Eden was crossing the Square with a spruce young man in a white flannel suit and a panama hat. They had been breakfasting at the Brevoort and he was coaxing her to let him come up to her rooms and sing for an hour.

"No, I've got to write letters. You must run along now. I see a friend of mine over there, and I want to ask him about something before I go up."

"That fellow with the dog? Where did you pick him up?" the young man glanced toward the seat under a sycamore where Hedger was reading the morning paper.

"Oh, he's an old friend from the West," said Eden easily. "I won't introduce you, because he doesn't like people. He's a recluse. Goodbye. I can't be sure about Tuesday. I'll go with you if I have time after my lesson." She nodded, left him, and went over to the seat littered with newspapers. The young man went up the Avenue without looking back.

"Well, what are you going to do today? Shampoo this animal all morning?" Eden inquired teasingly.

Hedger made room for her on the seat. "No, at twelve o'clock I'm going out to Coney Island. One of my models is going up in a balloon this afternoon. I've often promised to go and see her, and now I'm going."

Eden asked if models usually did such stunts. No, Hedger told her, but Molly Welch added to her earnings in that way. "I believe," he added, "she likes the excitement of it. She's got a

146

good deal of spirit. That's why I like to paint her. So many models have flaccid bodies."

"And she hasn't, eh? Is she the one who comes to see you? I can't help hearing her, she talks so loud."

"Yes, she has a rough voice, but she's a fine girl. I don't suppose you'd be interested in going?"

"I don't know," Eden sat tracing patterns on the asphalt with the end of her parasol. "Is it any fun? I got up feeling I'd like to do something different today. It's the first Sunday I've not had to sing in church. I had that engagement for breakfast at the Brevoort, but it wasn't very exciting. That chap can't talk about anything but himself."

Hedger warmed a little. "If you've never been to Coney Island, you ought to go. It's nice to see all the people; tailors and bartenders and prize-fighters with their best girls, and all sorts of folks taking a holiday."

Eden looked sidewise at him. So one ought to be interested in people of that kind, ought one? He was certainly a funny fellow. Yet he was never, somehow, tiresome. She had seen a great deal of him lately, but she kept wanting to know him better, to find out what made him different from men like the one she had just left— whether he really was as different as he seemed. "I'll go with you," she said at last, "if you'll leave that at home." She pointed to Caesar's flickering ears with her sunshade.

"But he's half the fun. You'd like to hear him bark at the waves when they come in."

"No, I wouldn't. He's jealous and disagreeable if he sees you talking to anyone else. Look at him now."

"Of course, if you make a face at him. He knows what that means, and he makes a worse face. He likes Molly Welch, and she'll be disappointed if I don't bring him."

Eden said decidedly that he couldn't take both of them. So at twelve o'clock when she and Hedger got on the boat at Desbrosses street, Caesar was lying on his pallet, with a bone.

Eden enjoyed the boat-ride. It was the first time she had been on the water, and she felt as if she were embarking for France. The light warm breeze and the plunge of the waves made her very wide awake, and she liked crowds of any kind. They went to the balcony of a big noisy restaurant and had a shore dinner, with tall steins of beer. Hedger had got a big advance from his advertising firm since he first lunched with Miss Bower ten days ago, and he was ready for anything.

After dinner they went to the tent behind the bathing beach, where the tops of two balloons bulged out over the canvas. A red-faced man in a linen suit stood in front of the tent, shouting in a hoarse voice and telling the people that if the crowd was good for five dollars more, a beautiful young woman would risk her life for their entertainment. Four little boys in dirty red uniforms ran about taking contributions in their pillbox hats. One of the balloons was bobbing up and down in its tether and people were shoving forward to get nearer the tent.

"Is it dangerous, as he pretends?" Eden asked.

"Molly says it's simple enough if nothing goes wrong with the balloon. Then it would be all over, I suppose."

"Wouldn't you like to go up with her?"

"I? Of course not. I'm not fond of taking foolish risks."

Eden sniffed. "I shouldn't think sensible risks would be very much fun."

Hedger did not answer, for just then everyone began to shove the other way and shout, "Look out. There she goes!" and a band of six pieces commenced playing furiously.

As the balloon rose from its tent enclosure, they saw a girl in green tights standing in the basket, holding carelessly to one of the ropes with one hand and with the other waving to the spectators. A long rope trailed behind to keep the balloon from blowing out to sea.

As it soared, the figure in green tights in the basket diminished to a mere spot, and the balloon itself, in the brilliant light, looked like a big silver-grey bat, with its wings folded. When it began to sink, the girl stepped through the hole in the basket to a trapeze that hung below, and gracefully descended through the air, holding to the rod with both hands keeping her body taut and her feet close together. The crowd, which had grown very large by this time, cheered vociferously. The men took off their hats and waved, little boys shouted, and fat old women, shining with the heat and a beer lunch, murmured admiring comments upon the balloonist's figure. "Beautiful legs, she has!"

"That's so," Hedger whispered. "Not many girls would look well in that position." Then, for some reason, he blushed a slow, dark, painful crimson.

The balloon descended slowly, a little way from the tent, and the red-faced man in the linen suit caught Molly Welch before her feet touched the ground, and pulled her to one side. The band struck up "Blue Bell" by way of welcome, and one of the sweaty pages ran forward and presented the balloonist with a large bouquet of artificial flowers. She smiled and thanked him, and ran back across the sand to the tent.

"Can't we go inside and see her?" Eden asked. "You can explain to the door man. I want to meet her." Edging forward, she herself addressed the man in the linen suit and slipped something from her purse into his hand.

They found Molly seated before a trunk that had a mirror in the lid and a "make-up" outfit spread upon the tray. She was wiping the cold cream and powder from her neck with a discarded chemise.

"Hello, Don," she said cordially. "Brought a friend?"

Eden liked her. She had an easy, friendly manner, and there was something boyish and devil-may-care about her.

"Yes, it's fun. I'm mad about it," she said in reply to Eden's questions. "I always want to let go, when I come down on the bar. You don't feel your weight at all, as you would on a stationary trapeze."

The big drum boomed outside, and the publicity man began shouting to newly arrived boatloads. Miss Welch took a last pull at her cigarette. "Now you'll have to get out, Don. I change for the next act. This time I go up in a black evening dress, and lose the skirt in the basket before I start down."

"Yes, go along," said Eden. "Wait for me outside the door. I'll stay and help her dress."

Hedger waited and waited, while women of every build bumped into him and begged his pardon, and the red pages ran about holding out their caps for coins, and the people ate and per-spired and shifted parasols against the sun. When the band began to play a two-step, all the bathers ran up out of the surf to watch the ascent. The second balloon bumped and rose, and the crowd began shouting to the girl in a black evening dress who stood lean-ing against the ropes and smiling. "It's a new girl," they called. "It ain't the Countess this time. You're a peach, girlie!"

The balloonist acknowledged these compliments, bowing and looking down over the sea of upturned faces,—but Hedger was determined she should not see him, and he darted behind the tent-fly. He was suddenly dripping with cold sweat, his mouth was full of the bitter taste of anger and his tongue felt stiff behind his teeth. Molly Welch, in a shirtwaist and a white tam-o'-shanter cap, slipped out from the tent under his arm and laughed up in his face. "She's a crazy one you brought along. She'll get what she wants!"

"Oh, I'll settle with you, all right!" Hedger brought out with difficulty.

"It's not my fault, Donnie. I couldn't do anything with her. She bought me off. What's the matter with you? Are you soft on her? She's safe enough. It's as easy as rolling off a log, if you keep cool." Molly Welch was rather excited herself, and she was chewing gum at high speed as she stood beside him, looking up at the floating sil-ver cone. "Now watch," she exclaimed suddenly. "She's coming down on the bar. I advised her to cut that out, but you see she does it first-rate. And she got rid of the skirt, too. Those black tights show off her legs very well. She keeps her feet together like I told her, and makes a good line along the back. See the light on those silver slippers—that was a good idea I had. Come along to meet her. Don't be a grouch; she's done it fine!"

Molly tweaked his elbow, and then left him standing like a stump, while she ran down the beach with the crowd.

Though Hedger was sulking, his eye could not help seeing the low blue welter of the sea, the arrested bathers, standing in the surf, their arms and legs stained red by the dropping sun, all shad-ing their eyes and gazing upward at the slowly falling silver star.

Molly Welch and the manager caught Eden under the arms and lifted her aside, a red page dashed up with a bouquet, and the band struck up "Blue Bell." Eden laughed and bowed, took Molly's arm, and ran up the sand in her black tights and silver slippers, dodging the friendly old women, and the gallant sports who wanted to offer their homage on the spot.

When she emerged from the tent, dressed in her own clothes, that part of the beach was almost deserted. She stepped to her companion's side and said carelessly: "Hadn't we better try to catch this boat? I hope you're not sore at me. Really, it was lots of fun."

Hedger looked at his watch. "Yes, we have fifteen minutes to get to the boat," he said politely.

As they walked toward the pier, one of the pages ran up panting. "Lady, you're carrying off the bouquet," he said, aggrievedly.

Eden stopped and looked at the bunch of spotty cotton roses in her hand. "Of course. I want them for a souvenir. You gave them to me yourself."

"I give 'em to you for looks, but you can't take 'em away. They belong to the show."

"Oh, you always use the same bunch?"

"Sure we do. There ain't too much money in this business."

She laughed and tossed them back to him. "Why are you angry?" she asked Hedger. "I wouldn't have done it if I'd been with some fellows, but I thought you were the sort who wouldn't mind. Molly didn't for a minute think you would."

"What possessed you to do such a fool thing?" he asked roughly.

"I don't know. When I saw her coming down, I wanted to try it. It looked exciting. Didn't I hold myself as well as she did?"

Hedger shrugged his shoulders, but in his heart he forgave her.

The return boat was not crowded, though the boats that passed them, going out, were packed to the rails. The sun was setting. Boys and girls sat on the long benches wish their arms about each other, singing. Eden felt a strong wish to propitiate her companion, to be alone with him. She had been curiously wrought up by her balloon trip, it was a lark, but not very satisfying unless one came back to something after the flight. She wanted to be admired and adored. Though Eden said nothing, and sat with her arms limp on the rail in front of her, looking languidly at the rising silhouette of the city and the bright path of the sun, Hedger felt a strange drawing near to her. If he brushed her white skirt with his knee, there was an instant communication between them, such as there had never been before. They did not talk at all, but when they went over the gangplank she took his arm and kept her shoulder close to his. He felt as if they were enveloped in a highly charged atmosphere, an invisible network of subtle, almost painful sensibility. They had somehow taken hold of each other.

An hour later, they were dining in the back garden of a little French hotel on Ninth Street, long since passed away. It was cool and leafy there, and the mosquitoes were not very numerous. A party of South Americans at another table were drinking champagne, and Eden murmured that she thought she would like some, if it were not too expensive. "Perhaps it will make me think I am in the balloon again. That was a very nice feeling. You've forgiven me, haven't you?"

Hedger gave her a quick straight look from under his black eyebrows, and something went over her that was like a chill, except that it was warm and feathery. She drank most of the wine; her companion was indifferent to it. He was talking more to her tonight than he had ever done before. She asked him about a new picture she had seen in his room; a queer thing full of stiff, supplicating female figures. "It's Indian, isn't it?"

"Yes. I call it Rain Spirits, or maybe Indian Rain. In the Southwest, where I've been a good deal, the Indian traditions make women have to do with the rain-fall. They were supposed to control it, somehow, and to be able to find springs, and make moisture come out of the earth. You see I'm trying to learn to paint what people think and feel; to get away from all that photographic stuff. When I look at you, I don't see what a camera would see, do I?"

"How can I tell?"

"Well, if I should paint you, I could make you understand what I see." For the second time that day Hedger crimsoned unexpectedly, and his eyes fell and steadily contemplated a dish of little radishes. "That particular picture I got from a story a Mexican priest told me; he said he found it in an old manuscript book in a monastery down there, written by some Spanish Missionary, who got his stories from the Aztecs. This one he called "The Forty Lovers of the Queen," and it was more or less about rain-making."

"Aren't you going to tell it to me?" Eden asked.

Hedger fumbled among the radishes. "I don't know if it's the proper kind of story to tell a girl."

She smiled; "Oh, forget about that! I've been balloon riding today. I like to hear you talk."

Her low voice was flattering. She had seemed like clay in his hands ever since they got on the boat to come home. He leaned back in his chair, forgot his food, and, looking at her intently, began to tell his story, the theme of which he somehow felt was dangerous tonight.

The tale began, he said, somewhere in Ancient Mexico, and concerned the daughter of a king. The birth of this Princess was preceded by unusual portents. Three times her mother dreamed that she was delivered of serpents, which betokened that the child she carried would have power with the rain gods. The serpent was the symbol of water. The Princess grew up dedicated to the gods, and wise men taught her the rain-making mysteries. She was with difficulty restrained from men and was guarded at all times, for it was the law of the Thunder that she be maiden until her marriage. In the years of her adolescence, rain was abundant with her people. The oldest man could not remember such fertility. When the Princess had counted eighteen summers, her father went to drive out a war party that harried his borders on the north and troubled his prosperity. The King destroyed the invaders and brought home many prisoners. Among the prisoners was a young chief, taller than any of his captors, of such strength and ferocity that the King's people came a day's journey to look at him. When the Princess beheld his great stature, and saw that his arms and breast were covered with the figures of wild animals, bitten into the skin and colored, she begged his life from her father. She desired that he should practice his art upon her, and prick upon her skin the signs of Rain and Lightning and Thunder, and stain the wounds with herb juices, as they were upon his own body. For many days, upon the roof of the King's house, the Princess submitted herself to the bone needle, and the women with her marvelled at her fortitude. But the Princess was without shame before the Captive, and it came about that he threw from him his needles and stains, and fell upon the Princess to violate her honor, and her women ran down from the roof screaming, to call the guard which stood at the gateway of the King's house, and none stayed to protect their mistress. When the guard came, the Captive was thrown into bonds, and he was gelded, and his tongue was torn out, and he was given for a slave to the Rain Princess.

The country of the Aztecs to the east was tormented by thirst, and their king, hearing much of the rain-making arts of the Princess, sent an embassy to her father, with presents and an offer of marriage. So the Princess went from her father to be the Queen of the Aztecs, and she took with her the Captive, who served her in everything with entire fidelity and slept upon a mat before her door.

The King gave his bride a fortress on the outskirts of the city, whither she retired to entreat the rain gods. This fortress was called the Queen's House, and on the night of the new moon the Queen came to it from the palace. But when the moon waxed and grew toward the round, because the god of Thunder had had his will of her, then the Queen returned to the King. Drought abated in the country and rain fell abundantly by reason of the Queen's power with the stars.

When the Queen went to her own house she took with her no servant but the Captive, and he slept outside her door and brought her food after she had fasted. The Queen had a jewel of great value, a turquoise that had fallen from the sun, and had the image of the sun upon it. And when she desired a young man whom she had seen in the army or among the slaves, she sent the Captive to him with the jewel, for a sign that he should come to her secretly at the Queen's House upon business concerning the welfare of all. And some, after she had talked with them, she sent away with rewards; and some she took into her chamber and kept them by her for one night or two. Afterward she called the Captive and bade him conduct the youth by the secret way he had come, underneath the chambers of the fortress. But for the going away of the Queen's lovers the Captive took out the bar that was beneath a stone in the floor of the passage, and put in its stead a rush-reed, and the youth stepped upon it and fell through into a cavern that was the bed of an underground river, and whatever was thrown into it was not seen again. In this service nor in any other did the Captive fail the Queen.

But when the Queen sent for the Captain of the Archers, she detained him four days in her chamber, calling often for food and wine, and was greatly content with him. On the fourth day she went to the Captive outside her door and said: "Tomorrow take this man up by the sure way, by which the King comes, and let him live."

In the Queen's door were arrows, purple and white. When she desired the King to come to her publicly, with his guard, she sent him a white arrow; but when she sent the purple, he came secretly, and covered himself with his mantle to be hidden from the stone gods at the gate. On the fifth night that the Queen was with her lover, the Captive took a purple arrow to the King, and the King came secretly and found them together. He killed the Captain with his own hand, but the Queen he brought to public trial. The Captive, when he was put to the question, told on his fingers forty men that he had let through the underground passage into the river. The Captive and the Queen were put to death by fire, both on the same day, and afterward there was scarcity of rain.

Eden Bower sat shivering a little as she listened. Hedger was not trying to please her, she thought, but to antagonize and frighten her by his brutal story. She had often told herself that his lean, big-boned lower jaw was like his bull-dog's, but tonight his face made Caesar's most savage and determined expression seem an affectation. Now she was looking at the man he really was. Nobody's eyes had ever defied her like this. They were searching her and seeing everything; all she had concealed from Livingston, and from the millionaire and his friends, and from the newspaperman. He was testing her, trying her out, and she was more ill at ease than she wished to show.

"That's quite a thrilling story," she said at last, rising and winding her scarf about her throat. "It must be getting late. Almost everyone has gone."

They walked down the Avenue like people who have quarreled, or who wish to get rid of each other. Hedger did not take her arm at the street crossings, and they did not linger in the Square. At her door he tried none of the old devices of the Livingston boys. He stood like a post, having forgotten to take off his hat, gave her a harsh, threatening glance, muttered "goodnight" and shut his own door noisily.

There was no question of sleep for Eden Bower. Her brain was working like a machine that would never stop. After she undressed, she tried to calm her nerves by smoking a cigarette, lying on the divan by the open window. But she grew wider and wider-awake, combating the challenge that had flamed all evening in Hedger's eyes. The balloon had been one kind of excitement, the wine another, but the thing that had aroused her, as a blow rouses a proud man, was the doubt, the contempt, the sneering hostility with which the painter had looked at her when he told his savage story. Crowds and balloons were all very well, she reflected, but woman's chief adventure is a man. With a mind over active and a sense of life over strong, she wanted to walk across the roofs in the starlight, to sail over the sea and face at once a world of which she had never been afraid.

Hedger must be asleep; his dog had stopped sniffing under the double doors. Eden put on her wrapper and slippers and stole softly down the hall over the old carpet; one loose board creaked just as she reached the ladder. The trapdoor was open, as always on hot nights. When she stepped out on the roof she drew a long breath and walked across it, looking up at the sky. Her foot touched something soft; she heard a low growl, and on the instant Caesar's sharp little teeth caught her ankle and waited. His breath was like steam on her leg. Nobody had ever intruded upon his roof before, and he panted for the movement or the word that would let him spring his jaw. Instead, Hedger's hand seized his throat.

"Wait a minute. I'll settle with him," he said grimly. He dragged the dog toward the manhole and disappeared. When he came back, he found Eden standing over by the dark chimney, looking away in an offended attitude.

"I caned him unmercifully," he panted. "Of course you didn't hear anything; he never whines when I beat him. He didn't nip you did he?"

"I don't know whether he broke the skin or not," she answered aggrievedly, still looking off into the west.

"If I were one of your friends in white pants, I'd strike a match to find whether you were hurt, though I know you are not, and then I'd see your ankle, wouldn't I?"

"I suppose so."

He shook his head and stood with his hands in the pockets of his old painting jacket. "I'm not up to such boy-tricks. If you want the place to yourself, I'll clear out. There are plenty of places where I can spend the night, what's left of it. But if you stay here and I stay here—" He shrugged his shoulders.

Eden did not stir, and she made no reply. Her head drooped slightly, as if she were considering. But the moment he put his arms about her they began to talk, both at once, as people do in an opera. The instant avowal brought out a flood of trivial admissions. Hedger confessed his crime, was reproached and forgiven, and now Eden knew what it was in his look that she had found so disturbing of late.

Standing against the black chimney, with the sky behind and blue shadows before, they looked like one of Hedger's own paintings of that period; two figures, one white and one dark, and nothing whatever distinguishable about them but that they were male and female. The faces were lost, the contours blurred in shadow, but the figures were a man and a woman, and that was their whole concern and their mysterious beauty,—it was the rhythm in which they moved, at last, along the roof and down into the dark hole; he first, drawing her gently after him. She came down very slowly.

157

The excitement and bravado and uncertainty of that long day and night seemed all at once to tell upon her. When his feet were on the carpet and he reached up to lift her down, she twined her arms about his neck as after a long separation, and turned her face to him, and her lips, with their perfume of youth and passion.

One Saturday afternoon Hedger was sitting in the window of Eden's music room. They had been watching the pigeons come wheeling over the roofs from their unknown feeding grounds.

"Why," said Eden suddenly, "don't we fix those big doors into your studio so they will open? Then, if I want you, I won't have to go through the hall. That illustrator is loafing about a good deal of late."

"I'll open them, if you wish. The bolt is on your side."

"Isn't there one on yours, too?"

"No. I believe a man lived there for years before I came in, and the nurse used to have these rooms herself. Naturally, the lock was on the lady's side."

Eden laughed and began to examine the bolt. "It's all stuck up with paint." Looking about, her eye lighted upon a bronze Buddha which was one of the nurse's treasures. Taking him by his head, she struck the bolt a blow with his squatting posteriors. The two doors creaked, sagged, and swung weakly inward a little way, as if they were too old for such escapades. Eden tossed the heavy idol into a stuffed chair. "That's better," she exclaimed exultantly. "So the bolts are always on the lady's side? What a lot society takes for granted!"

Hedger laughed, sprang up and caught her arms roughly. "Whoever takes you for granted—Did anybody, ever?"

"Everybody does. That's why I'm here. You are the only one who knows anything about me. Now I'll have to dress if we're going out for dinner."

He lingered, keeping his hold on her. "But I won't always be the only one, Eden Bower. I won't be the last."

"No, I suppose not," she said carelessly. "But what does that matter? You are the first."

As a long, despairing whine broke in the warm stillness, they drew apart. Caesar, lying on his bed in the dark corner, had lifted his head at this invasion of sunlight, and realized that the side of his room was broken open, and his whole world shattered by change. There stood his master and this woman, laughing at him! The woman was pulling the long black hair of this mightiest of men, who bowed his head and permitted it.

VI

In time they quarreled, of course, and about an abstraction,—as young people often do, as mature people almost never do. Eden came in late one afternoon. She had been with some of her musical friends to lunch at Burton Ives' studio, and she began telling Hedger about its splendors. He listened a moment and then threw down his brushes. "I know exactly what it's like," he said impatiently. "A very good department-store conception of a studio. It's one of the show places."

"Well, it's gorgeous, and he said I could bring you to see him. The boys tell me he's awfully kind about giving people a lift, and you might get something out of it."

Hedger started up and pushed his canvas out of the way. "What could I possibly get from Burton Ives? He's almost the worst painter in the world; the stupidest, I mean."

Eden was annoyed. Burton Ives had been very nice to her and had begged her to sit for him. "You must admit that he's a very successful one," she said coldly.

"Of course he is! Anybody can be successful who will do that sort of thing. I wouldn't paint his pictures for all the money in New York."

"Well, I saw a lot of them, and I think they are beautiful."

Hedger bowed stiffly.

"What's the use of being a great painter if nobody knows about you?" Eden went on persuasively. "Why don't you paint the kind of pictures people can understand, and then, after you're success-ful, do whatever you like?"

"As I look at it," said Hedger brusquely, "I am successful."

Eden glanced about. "Well, I don't see any evidences of it," she said biting her lip. "He has a Japanese servant and a wine cellar, and keeps a riding horse."

Hedger melted a little. "My dear, I have the most expensive luxury in the world, and I am much more extravagant than Burton Ives, for I work to please nobody but myself."

"You mean you could make money and don't? That you don't try to get a public?"

"Exactly. A public only wants what has been done over and over. I'm painting for painters,—who haven't been born."

"What would you do if I brought Mr. Ives down here to see your things?"

"Well, for God's sake, don't! Before he left I'd probably tell him what I thought of him."

Eden rose. "I give you up. You know very well there's only one kind of success that's real."

"Yes, but it's not the kind you mean. So you've been thinking me a scrub painter, who needs a helping hand from some fashion-able studio man? What the devil have you had anything to do with me for then?"

"There's no use talking to you," said Eden walking slowly to-ward the door. "I've been trying to pull wires for you all afternoon, and this is what it comes to." She had expected that the tidings of a prospective call from the great man would be received very dif-ferently, and had been thinking as she came home in the stage how, as a magic wand, she might gild Hedger's future, float him out of his dark hole on a tide of prosperity, see his name in the papers and his pictures in the windows on Fifth Avenue.

Hedger mechanically snapped the midsummer leash on Cae-sar's collar and they ran downstairs and hurried through Sulli-van Street off toward the river. He wanted to be among rough, honest people, to get down where the big drays bumped over stone paving blocks and the men wore corduroy trousers and kept their shirts open at the neck. He stopped for a drink in one of the sagging barrooms on the waterfront. He had never in his life been so deeply wounded; he did not know he could be so hurt. He had told this girl all his secrets. On the roof, in these warm, heavy summer nights, with her hands locked in his, he had been able to explain all his misty ideas about an unborn art the world was waiting for; had been able to explain them better than he had ever done to himself. And she had looked away to the chattels of this uptown studio and coveted them for him! To her he was only an unsuccessful Burton Ives.

Then why, as he had put it to her, did she take up with him? Young, beautiful, talented as she was, why had she wasted herself on a scrub? Pity? Hardly; she wasn't sentimental. There was no explaining her. But in this passion that had seemed so fearless and so fated to be, his own position now looked to him ridiculous; a poor dauber without money or fame,—it was her caprice to load him with favors. Hedger ground his teeth so loud that his dog, trotting beside him, heard him and looked up.

While they were having supper at the oysterman's, he planned his escape. Whenever he saw her again, everything he had told her, that he should never had told anyone, would come back to him; ideas he had never whispered even to the painter whom he worshipped and had gone all the way to France to see. To her they must seem his apology for not having horses and a valet, or merely the puerile boastfulness of a weak man. Yet if she slipped the bolt tonight and came through the doors and said, "Oh, weak man, I belong to you!" what could he do? That was the danger. He would catch the train out to Long Beach tonight, and tomorrow he would go on to the north end of Long Island, where an old friend of his had a summer studio among the sand dunes. He would stay until things came right in his mind. And she could find a smart painter, or take her punishment.

When he went home, Eden's room was dark; she was dining out somewhere. He threw his things into a holdall he had carried about the world with him, strapped up some colors and canvases, and ran downstairs.

VII

Five days later Hedger was a restless passenger on a dirty, crowded Sunday train, coming back to town. Of course he saw now how unreasonable he had been in expecting a Huntington girl to know anything about pictures; here was a whole continent full of people who knew nothing about pictures and he didn't hold it against them. What had such things to do with him and Eden Bower? When he lay out on the dunes, watching the moon come up out of the sea, it had seemed to him that there was no wonder in the world like the wonder of Eden Bower. He was going back to her because she was older than art, because she was the most overwhelming thing that had ever come into his life.

He had written her yesterday, begging her to be at home this evening, telling her that he was contrite, and wretched enough.

Now that he was on his way to her, his stronger feeling unaccountably changed to a mood that was playful and tender. He wanted to share everything with her, even the most trivial things. He wanted to tell her about the people on the train, coming back tired from their holiday with bunches of wilted flowers and dirty daises; to tell her that the fish-man, to whom she had often sent him for lobsters, was among the passengers, disguised in a silk shirt and a spotted tie, and how his wife looked exactly like a fish, even to her eyes, on which cataracts were forming. He could tell her, too, that he hadn't as much as unstrapped his canvases,—that ought to convince her.

In those days passengers from Long Island came into New York by ferry. Hedger had to be quick about getting his dog out of the express car in order to catch the first boat. The East River, and the bridges, and the city to the west, were burning in the conflagration of the sunset; there was that great homecoming reach of evening in the air.

The car changes from Thirty-Fourth Street were too many and too perplexing; for the first time in his life Hedger took a hansom cab for Washington Square. Caesar sat bolt upright on the worn leather cushion beside him, and they jogged off, looking down on the rest of the world.

It was twilight when they drove down lower Fifth Avenue into the Square, and through the Arch behind them were the two long rows of pale violet lights that used to bloom so beautifully against the grey stone and asphalt. Here and yonder about the Square hung globes that shed a radiance not unlike the blue mists of evening, emerging softly when daylight died, as the stars emerged in the thin blue sky. Under them the sharp shadows of the trees fell on the cracked pavement and the sleeping grass. The first stars and the first lights were growing silver against the gradual darkening, when Hedger paid his driver and went into the house,—which, thank God, was still there! On the hall table lay his letter of yesterday, unopened.

He went upstairs with every sort of fear and every sort of hope clutching at his heart; it was all as if tigers were tearing him. Why was there no gas burning in the top hall? He found matches and the gas bracket. He knocked, but got no answer; nobody was there. Before his own door were exactly five bottles of milk, standing in a row. The milk-boy had taken spiteful pleasure in thus reminding him that he forgot to stop his order.

Hedger went down to the basement; it, too, was dark. The janitress was taking her evening airing on the basement steps. She sat waving a palm-leaf fan majestically, her dirty calico dress open at the neck. She told him at once that there had been "changes." Miss Bower's room was to let again, and the piano would go tomorrow. Yes, she left yesterday, she sailed for Europe with friends from Chicago. They arrived on Friday, heralded by many telegrams. Very rich people they were said to be, though the man had refused to pay the nurse a month's rent in lieu of notice,—which would have been only right, as the young lady had agreed to take the rooms until October. Mrs. Foley had observed, too, that he didn't overpay her or Willy for their trouble, and a great deal of trouble they had been put to, certainly. Yes, the young lady was very pleasant, but the nurse said there were rings on the mahogany table where she had put tumblers and wine glasses. It was just as well she was gone. The Chicago man was uppish in his ways, but not much to look at. She supposed he had poor health, for there was nothing to him inside his clothes.

Hedger went slowly up the stairs—never had they seemed so long, or his legs so heavy. The upper floor was emptiness and silence. He unlocked his room, lit the gas, and opened the windows. When he went to put his coat in the closet, he found, hanging among his clothes, a pale, flesh-tinted dressing gown he had liked to see her wear, with a perfume—oh, a perfume that was still Eden Bower! He shut the door behind him and there, in the dark, for a moment he lost his manliness. It was when he held this garment to him that he found a letter in the pocket.

The note was written with a lead pencil, in haste: She was very sorry that he was angry, but she still didn't know just what she had done. She had thought Mr. Ives would be useful to him; she guessed he was too proud. She wanted awfully to see him again, but Fate came knocking at her door after he had left her. She believed in Fate. She would never forget him, and she knew he would become the greatest painter in the world. Now she must pack. She hoped he wouldn't mind her leaving the dressing gown; somehow, she could never wear it again.

After Hedger read this, standing under the gas, he went back into the closet and knelt down before the wall; the knot hole had been plugged up with a ball of wet paper,—the same blue note-paper on which her letter was written.

He was hard hit. Tonight he had to bear the loneliness of a whole lifetime. Knowing himself so well, he could hardly believe that such a thing had ever happened to him, that such a woman had lain happy and contented in his arms. And now it was over. He turned out the light and sat down on his painter's stool before the big window. Caesar, on the floor beside him, rested his head on his master's knee. We must leave Hedger thus, sitting in his tank with his dog, looking up at the stars.

COMING, APHRODITE! This legend, in electric lights over the Lexington Opera House, had long announced the return of Eden Bower to New York after years of spectacular success in Paris. She came at last, under the management of an American Opera Company, but bringing her own *chef d'orchestre.*

One bright December afternoon Eden Bower was going down Fifth Avenue in her car, on the way to her broker, in Williams Street. Her thoughts were entirely upon stocks,—Cerro de Pasco, and how much she should buy of it,—when suddenly she looked up and re-alized that she was skirting Washington Square. She had not seen the place since she rolled out of it in an old-fashioned four-wheeler to seek her fortune, eighteen years ago.

"*Arretez, Alphonse. Attendex moi,*" she called, and opened the door before he could reach it. The children who were streaking over the asphalt on roller skates saw a lady in a long fur coat, and short, high-heeled shoes, alight from a French car and pace slowly about the Square, holding her muff to her chin. This spot, at least, had changed very little, she reflected; the same trees, the same fountain, the white arch, and over yonder, Garibaldi, draw-ing the sword for freedom. There, just opposite her, was the old red brick house.

"Yes, that is the place," she was thinking. "I can smell the car-pets now, and the dog,—what was his name? That grubby bath-room at the end of the hall, and that dreadful Hedger—still, there was something about him, you know—" She glanced up and blinked against the sun. From somewhere in the crowded quar-ter south of the Square a flock of pigeons rose, wheeling quickly upward into the brilliant blue sky. She threw back her head, pressed her muff closer to her chin, and watched them with a smile of amazement and delight. So they still rose, out of all that dirt and noise and squalor, fleet and silvery, just as they used to rise that summer when she was twenty and went up in a balloon on Coney Island!

Alphonse opened the door and tucked her robes about her. All the way down town her mind wandered from Cerro de Pasco, and she kept smiling and looking up at the sky.

When she had finished her business with the broker, she asked him to look in the telephone book for the address of M. Gaston Jules, the picture dealer, and slipped the paper on which he wrote it into her glove. It was five o'clock when she reached the French Galleries, as they were called. On entering she gave the attendant her card, asking him to take it to M. Jules. The dealer appeared very promptly and begged her to come into his private office, where he pushed a great chair toward his desk for her and signaled his secretary to leave the room.

"How good your lighting is in here," she observed, glancing about. "I met you at Simon's studio, didn't I? Oh, no! I never forget anybody who interests me." She threw her muff on his writing table and sank into the deep chair. "I have come to you for some information that's not in my line. Do you know anything about an American painter named Hedger?"

He took the seat opposite her. "Don Hedger? But, certainly! There are some very interesting things of his in an exhibition at V——'s. If you would care to——."

She held up her hand. "No, no. I've no time to go to exhibitions. Is he a man of any importance?"

"Certainly. He is one of the first men among the moderns. That is to say, among the very moderns. He is always coming up with something different. He often exhibits in Paris, you must have seen——"

"No, I tell you I don't go to exhibitions. Has he had great success? That is what I want to know."

M. Jules pulled at his short grey moustache. "But, Madame, there are many kinds of success," he began cautiously.

Madame gave a dry laugh. "Yes, so he used to say. We once quarreled on that issue. And how would you define his particular kind?"

M. Jules grew thoughtful. "He is a great man with all the young men, and he is decidedly an influence in art. But one can't definitely place a man who is original, erratic, and who is changing all the time."

She cut him short. "Is he much talked about at home? In Paris, I mean? Thanks. That's all I want to know." She rose and began buttoning her coat. "One doesn't like to have been an utter fool, even at twenty."

"*Mais, non!*" M. Jules handed her her muff with a quick, sympathetic glance. He followed her out through the carpeted show-

166

room, now closed to the public and draped in cheesecloth, and put her into her car with words appreciative of the honor she had done him in calling.

Leaning back in the cushions, Eden Bower closed her eyes, and her face, as the street lamps flashed their ugly orange light upon it, became hard and settled, like a plaster cast; so a sail, that has been filled by a strong breeze, behaves when the wind suddenly dies. Tomorrow night the wind would blow again, and this mask would be the golden face of Aphrodite. But a "big" career takes its toll, even with the best of luck.

—1920

Randolph Bourne

(1886–1918)

Social critic and essayist Randolph Bourne was considered one of America's greatest intellectuals. He wrote frequently on education, politics, pacifism, the right to dissent, and, in particular, the cult of youth, which made him a popular figure in the Village. Hampered by severe physical deformities—he suffered a "messy" birth and then contracted spinal tuberculosis as a child—Bourne was published in the Atlantic *even before he graduated from Columbia University in 1913. The following year he joined the staff of the* New Republic. *"Bourne became a regular and welcome sight along Charles Street, his misshapen body concealed by the black cape that became his trademark," writes Terry Miller in* Greenwich Village and How It Got That Way. *Bourne left the* New Republic *prior to the outbreak of World War I because he opposed President Woodrow Wilson's neutral stance. He went on to criticize government policy in the pages of the* Seven Arts *magazine, a short-lived Village publication. After the war, he was one of the victims of the worldwide influenza epidemic that took over 600,000 lives in America alone during the winter of 1918–1919. He was only thirty-two.*

from *History of a Literary Radical*

For a man of culture, my friend Miro began his literary career in a singularly unpromising way. Potential statesmen in log cabins

Randolph Bourne. From *History of a Literary Radical and Other Essays* (1920).

might miraculously come in touch with all the great books of the world, but the days of Miro's young school life were passed in innocence of Homer or Dante or Shakespeare, or any of the other traditional mind-formers of the race. What Miro had for his nourishment, outside the Bible, which was a magical book that you must not drop on the floor, or his school-readers, which were like lightning flashes of unintelligible scenes, was the literature that his playmates lent him—exploits of British soldiers in Spain and the Crimea, the death-defying adventures of young filibusters in Cuba and Nicaragua. Miro gave them a languid perusing, and did not criticize their literary style. Huckleberry Finn and Tom Sawyer somehow eluded him until he had finished college, and no fresher tale of adventure drifted into his complacent home until the era of "Richard Carvel" and "Janice Meredith" sharpened his wits and gave him a vague feeling that there was such a thing as literary art. The classics were stiffly enshrined behind glass doors that were very hard to open—at least Hawthorne and Irving and Thackeray were there, and Tennyson's and Scott's poems—but nobody ever discussed them or looked at them. Miro's busy elders were taken up with the weekly *Outlook* and *Independent* and *Christian Work*, and felt they were doing much for Miro when they provided him and his sister with *St. Nicholas* and *The Youth's Companion*. It was only that Miro saw the black books looking at him accusingly from the case, and a rudimentary conscience, slipping easily over from Calvinism to culture, forced him solemnly to grapple with "The Scarlet Letter" or "Marmion." All he remembers is that the writers of these books he browsed among used a great many words and made a great fuss over shadowy offenses and conflicts and passions that did not even stimulate his imagination with sufficient force to cause him to ask his elders what it was all about. Certainly the filibusters were easier.

At school Miro was early impressed with the vast dignity of the literary works and names he was compelled to learn. Shakespeare and Goethe and Dante lifted their plaster heads frowningly above the teacher's, as they perched on shelves about the room. Much was said of the greatness of literature. But the art of phonetics and the complications of grammar swamped Miro's early school years. It was not until he reached the High School that literature began really to assume that sacredness which he had heretofore felt for Holy Scripture. His initiation into culture was made almost a religious mystery by the conscientious and harassed teacher. As the Deadwood Boys and Henty and David Harum slipped away from Miro's soul in the presence of Milton's "Comus" and Burke "On Conciliation," a cultural devoutness was engendered in him that never really died. At first it did not take Miro beyond the stage where your conscience is strong enough to make you uncomfortable, but not strong enough to make you do anything about it. Miro did not actually become an omnivorous reader of great books. But he was filled with a rich grief that the millions pursued cheap and vulgar fiction instead of the best that has been thought and said in the world. Miro indiscriminately bought cheap editions of the English classics and read them with a certain patient incomprehension.

As for the dead classics, they came to Miro from the hands of his teachers with a prestige even vaster than the books of his native tongue. No doubt ever entered his head that four years of Latin and three years of Greek, an hour a day, were the important preparation he needed for his future as an American citizen. No doubt ever hurt him that the world into which he would pass would be a world where, as his teacher said, Latin and Greek were a solace to the aged, a quickener of taste, a refreshment after manual labor, and a clue to the general knowledge of all human things. Miro would as soon have doubted the rising of the sun as have doubted the wisdom of these serious, puckered women who had the precious manipulation of his cultural upbringing in their charge. Miro was a bright, if a rather vague, little boy, and a fusion of brightness and docility gave him high marks in the school where we went together.

No one ever doubted that these marks expressed Miro's assimilation of the books we pored over. But he told me later that he had never really known what he was studying. Caesar, Virgil, Cicero, Xenophon, Homer, were veiled and misty experiences to him. His mind was a moving present, obliterating each day what it had read the day before, and piercing into a no more comprehended future. He could at no time have given any intelligible account of Aeneas's wanderings or what Cicero was really inveighing against. The *Iliad* was even more obscure. The only thing which impressed him deeply was an expurgated passage, which he looked up somewhere else and found to be about Mars and Venus caught in the golden bed. Caesar seemed to be at war, and Xenophon wandering somewhere in Asia Minor, with about the same lengthiness and hardship as Miro suffered in reading him. The trouble, Miro thought afterwards, was that these books were to his mind flickering lights in a vast jungle of ignorance. He does not remember marveling at the excessive dullness of the stories themselves. He plodded his faithful way, using them as his conscientious teachers did, as exercises in language. He looked on Virgil and Cicero as essentially problems in disentangling words, which had unaccountably gotten into a bizarre order, and in recognizing certain rather amusing and ingenious combinations, known as "constructions." Why these words took so irritating an order Miro never knew, but he always connected the problem with those algebraic puzzles he had elsewhere to unravel. Virgil's words were further complicated by being arranged in lines which one had to "scan." Miro was pleased with the rhythm, and there were stanzas that had a roll of their own. But the inexorable translating that had to go on tore all this fabric of poetry to pieces. His translations were impeccable, but, as he never wrote them down, he had never before his eyes the consecutive story.

Translations Miro never saw. He knew that they were implements of deadly sin that boys used to cheat with. His horror of them was such as a saint might feel towards a parody of the Bible. Just before Miro left school, his sister in a younger class began to read a prose translation of the Odyssey, and Miro remembers the scorn with which he looked down on so sneaking an entrance into the temple of light. He knew that not everyone could study Latin and Greek, and he learned to be proud of his knowledge. When at last he had passed his examination for college—his Latin composition and grammar, his syntax and his sight-reading, and his Greek composition and grammar, his Greek syntax and sight-reading, and his translation of Gallic battles and Anabatic frosts, and Dido's farewell and Cicero's objurgations—his zealous rage did not abate. He even insisted on reading the Bucolics, while he was away on his vacation, and a book or two in the *Odyssey*. His family was a little chilled by his studiousness, but he knew well that he was laying up cultural treasures in heaven, where moth and rust do not corrupt, neither do thieves break in and steal.

Arrived at college, Miro expanded his cultural interests on the approved lines. He read Horace and Plato, Lysias and Terence, impartially, with faithful conscience. Horace was the most exciting because of the parodies that were beginning to appear in the cleverer newspapers. Miro scarcely knew whether to be amused or shocked at "Odi Persicos" or "Integer Vitae" done into current slang. The professors, mild-mannered men who knew their place and kept it, never mentioned these impudent adventures, but for Miro it was the first crack in his Ptolemaic system of reverences. There came a time when his mind began to feel replete, when this heavy pushing through the opaque medium of dead language began to fatigue him. He should have been able to read fluently, but there were always turning up new styles, new constructions, to plague him. Latin became to him like a constant diet of beefsteak, and Greek like a constant diet of fine wheaten bread. They lost their taste. These witty poets and ostentatious orators—what were they all about? What was their background? Where did they fit into Miro's life? The professors knew some history, but what did that history mean? Miro found himself surfeited and dissatisfied. He began to look furtively at translations to get some better English than he was able to provide. The hair-splittings of Plato began to bore him when he saw them in crystal-clear English, and not muffled in the original Greek. His apostasy had begun.

It was not much better in his study of English literature. Miro was given a huge anthology, a sort of press-clipping bureau of *belles-lettres*, from Chaucer to Arthur Symons. Under the direction of a professor who was laying out a career for himself as poet— or "modern singer," as he expressed it—the class went briskly through the centuries sampling their genius and tasting the various literary flavors. The enterprise reminded Miro of those books of woolen samples which one looks through when one is to have a suit of clothes made. But in this case, the student did not even have the pleasure of seeing the suit of clothes. All that was expected of him, apparently, was that he should become familiar, from these microscopic pieces, with the different textures and patterns. The great writers passed before his mind like figures in a crowded street. There was no time for preferences. Indeed the professor strove diligently to give each writer his just due. How was one to appreciate the great thoughts and the great styles if one began to choose violently between them, or attempt any discrimination on grounds of their peculiar congeniality for one's own soul? Criticism had to spurn such subjectivity, scholarship could not be willful. The neatly arranged book of "readings," with its medicinal doses of inspiration, became the symbol of Miro's education.

These early years of college did not deprive Miro of his cultural loyalty, but they deadened his appetite. Although most inconceivably docile, he found himself being bored. He had come from school a serious boy, with more than a touch of priggishness in him, and a vague aspiration to be a "man of letters." He found himself becoming a collector of literary odds-and-ends. If he did not formulate this feeling clearly, he at least knew. He found that the literary life was not as interesting as he had expected. He sought no adventures. When he wrote, it was graceful lyrics or polite criticisms of William Collins or Charles Lamb. These canonized saints of culture still held the field for Miro, however. There was nothing between them and that popular literature of the day that all good men bemoaned. Classic or popular, "highbrow" or "lowbrow," this was the choice, and Miro unquestioningly took the orthodox heaven. In 1912 the most popular of Miro's English professors had never heard of Galsworthy, and another was creating a flurry of scandal in the department by recommending Chesterton to his classes. It would scarcely have been in college that Miro would have learned of an escape from the closed dichotomy of culture. Bored with the "classic," and frozen with horror at the "popular," his career as a man of culture must have come to a dragging end if he had not been suddenly liberated by a chance lecture which he happened to hear while he was at home for the holidays.

The literary radical who appeared before the Lyceum Club of Miro's village was none other than Professor William Lyon Phelps, and it is to that evening of cultural audacity Miro thinks he owes all his later emancipation. The lecturer grappled with the "modern novel," and tossed Hardy, Tolstoi, Turgenev, Meredith, even Trollope, into the minds of the charmed audience with such effect that the virgin shelves of the village library were ravished for days to come by the eager minds upon whom these great names dawned for the first time. "Jude the Obscure" and "Resurrection" were of course kept officially away from the vulgar, but Miro managed to find "Smoke" and "Virgin Soil" and "Anna Karenina" and "The Warden" and "A Pair of Blue Eyes" and "The Return of the Native." Later at college he explored the forbidden realms. It was as if some devout and restless saint had suddenly been introduced to the Apocrypha. A new world was opened to Miro that was neither "classic" nor "popular," and yet which came to one under the most unimpeachable auspices. There was, at first, it is true, an air of illicit adventure about the enterprise. The lecturer who made himself the missionary of such vigorous and piquant doctrine had the air of being a heretic, or at least a boy playing out of school. But Miro himself returned to college a cultural revolutionist. His orthodoxies crumbled. He did not try to reconcile the new with the old. He applied pick and dynamite to the whole structure of the canon. Irony, humor, tragedy, sensuality, suddenly appeared to him as literary qualities in forms that he could understand. They were like oxygen to his soul.

If these qualities were in the books he had been reading, he had never felt them. The expurgated sample-books he had studied had passed too swiftly over the Elizabethans to give him a sense of their lustiness. Miro immersed himself voluptuously in the pessimism of Hardy. He fed on the poignant torture of Tolstoi. While he was reading "Resurrection," his class in literature was making an "intensive" study of Tennyson. It was too much. Miro rose in revolt.

He forswore literary courses forever, dead rituals in which anaemic priests mumbled their trite critical commentary. Miro did not know that to naughtier critics even Mr. Phelps might eventually seem a pale and timid Gideon, himself stuck in moral sloughs. He was grateful enough for that blast of trumpets which made his own scholastic walls fall down.

The next stage in Miro's cultural life was one of frank revolt. He became as violent as a heretic as he had been docile as a believer. Modern novels merely started the rift that widened into modern ideas. The professors were of little use. Indeed, when Miro joined a group of radicals who had started a new college paper, a relentless vendetta began with the teachers. Miro and his friends threw over everything that was mere literature. Social purpose must shine from any writing that was to rouse their enthusiasm. Literature flavor was to be permissible only where it made vivid high and revolutionary thought. Tolstoi became their god, Wells their high priest. Chesterton infuriated them. They wrote violent assaults upon him which began in imitation of his cool paradoxicality and ended in incoherent ravings. There were so many enemies to their new fervor that they scarcely knew where to begin. There were not only the old tables of stone to destroy, but there were new and threatening prophets of the eternal verities who had to be exposed. The nineteenth century which they had studied must be weeded of its nauseous moralists. The instructors consulted together how they might put down the revolt, and bring these sinners back to the faith of cultural scripture.

It was of no avail. In a short time Miro had been converted from an aspiration for the career of a cultivated "man of letters" to a fiery zeal for artistic and literary propaganda in the service of radical ideas. One of the results of this conversion was the discovery that he really had no standards of critical taste. Miro had been reverential so long that he had felt no preferences. Everything that was classic had to be good to him. But now that he had thrown away the books that were stamped with the mark of the classic mint, and was dealing with the raw materials of letters, he had to become a critic and make selection. It was not enough that a book should be radical. Some of the books he read, though impeccably revolutionary as to ideas, were clearly poor as literature. His muffled taste began to assert itself. He found himself impressionable where before he had been only mildly acquisitive. The literature of revolt and free speculation fired him into a state of spiritual explosiveness. All that he read now stood out in brighter colors and in sharper outlines than before. As he reached a better balance, he began to feel the vigor of literary form, the value of sincerity and freshness of style. He began to look for them keenly in everything he read. It was long before Miro realized that enthusiasm not docility had made him critical. He became a little proud of his sensitive and discriminating reactions to the modern and the unsifted.

This pursuit had to take place without any help from the college. After Miro graduated, it is true that it became the fashion to study literature as the record of ideas and not merely as a canon of sacred books to be analyzed, commented upon, and absorbed. But no dent was made upon the system in Miro's time, and, the inventory of English criticism not going beyond Stevenson, no college course went beyond Stevenson. The Elizabethans had been exhumed and fumigated, but the most popular attention went to the gallery of Victorians, who combined moral soundness with literary beauty, and were therefore considered wholesome food for young men. The instructors all remained in the state of reverence which saw all things good that had been immemorially taught. Miro's own teacher was a fragile, earnest young man, whose robuster parents had evidently seized upon his nature as a fortunate pledge of what the family might produce in the way of an intellectual flower that should surpass in culture and gentility the ambitions of his parents. His studiousness, hopeless for his father's career as grocer, had therefore been capitalized into education.

The product now shone forth as one of the most successful and promising younger instructors in the department. He knew his subject. Card-indexes filled his room, covering in detail the works, lives, and deaths of the illustrious persons whom he expounded, as well as everything that had been said about them in the way of appreciation or interpretation. An endless number of lectures and courses could be made from this bountiful store. He never tried to write himself, but he knew all about the different kinds of writing, and when he corrected the boys' themes he knew infallibly what to tell them to avoid. Miro's vagaries scandalized his teacher all the more because during his first year in college Miro had been generally noticed as one with the proper sobriety and scholarly patience to graduate into a similar priestly calling. Miro found scant sympathy in the young man. To the latter, literary studies were a science not an art, and they were to be treated with somewhat the same cold rigor of delimitation and analysis as any other science. Miro felt his teacher's recoil at the idea that literature was significant only as the expression of personality or as interpretation of some social movement. Miro saw how uneasy he became when he was confronted with current literature. It was clear that Miro's slowly growing critical sense had not a counterpart in the scholastic mind.

When Miro and his friends abandoned literary studies, they followed after the teachers of history and philosophy, intellectual arenas of which the literary professors seemed scandalously ignorant. At this ignorance Miro boiled with contempt. Here were the profitable clues that would give meaning to dusty literary scholarship, but the scholars had not the wits to seize them. They lived along, playing what seemed to Miro a rather dreary game, when they were not gaping reverently at ideas and forms which they scarcely had the genuine personality to appreciate. Miro felt once and for all free of these mysteries and reverences. He was to know the world as it has been and as it is. He was to put literature into its proper place, making all "culture" serve its apprenticeship for him as interpretation of things larger than itself, of the course of individual lives and the great tides of society.

Miro's later cultural life is not without interest. When he had finished college and his architectural course, and was making headway in his profession, his philosophy of the intellectual life began to straighten itself out. Rapid as his surrender of orthodoxy had been, it had taken him some time to live down that early education. He found now that he would have to live down his heresies also, and get some coherent system of tastes that was his own and not the fruit of either docility or the zeal of propaganda.

177

The old battles that were still going on helped Miro to realize his modern position. It was a queer, musty quarrel, but it was enlisting minds from all classes and of all intellectual fibers. The "classics" were dying hard, as Miro recognized whenever he read, in the magazines, attacks on the "new education." He found that professors were still taken seriously who declared in passion that without the universal study of the Latin language in American schools all conceptions of taste, standards, criticism, the historic sense itself, would vanish from the earth. He found that even as late as 1917 professional men were gathering together in solemn conclave and buttressing the "value of the classics" with testimonials from "successful men" in a variety of vocations. Miro was amused at the fact that the mighty studies once pressed upon him so uncritically should now require, like the patent medicines, testimonials as to their virtue. Bank presidents, lawyers, and editors had taken the Latin language regularly for years, and had found its effects painless and invigorating. He could not escape the unconscious satire that such plump and prosperous Americans expressed when they thought it admirable to save their cherished intellectual traditions in any such fashion.

Other conservatives Miro saw to be abandoning the line of opposition to science, only to fall back on the line of a defensive against "pseudo-science," as they seemed to call whatever intellectual interests had not yet come indubitably reputable. It was a line which would hold them rather strongly for a time, Miro thought, because so many of the cultural revolutionists agreed with them in hating some of these arrogant and mechanical psychologies and sociologies that reduced life to figures or organisms. But Miro felt also how obstructive was their fight. If the "classics" had done little for him except to hold his mind in an uncomprehending prison, and fetter his spontaneous taste, they seemed to have done little more for even the thorough scholars. When professors had devoted scholarly lives to the "classics" only to exhibit in their own polemics none of the urbanity and intellectual command which were supposed by the believer somehow to rub off automatically on the faithful student, Miro had to conclude an absence of causal connection between the "classics" and the able modern mind. When, moreover, critical power or creative literary work became almost extinct among these defenders of the "old education," Miro felt sure that a revolution was needed in the materials and attitudes of "culture."

The case of the defenders was all the weaker because their enemies were not wanton infidels, ignorant of the holy places they profaned. They were rather cultural "Modernists," reforming the church from within. They had the classic background, these young vandals, but they had escaped from its flat and unoriented surface. Abreast of the newer objective, impersonal standards of thinking, they saw the weakness of these archaic minds which could only appeal to vested interests in culture and testimonials from successful men.

The older critics had long since disavowed the intention of discriminating among current writers. These men, who had to have an Academy to protect them, lumped the younger writers of verse and prose together as "anarchic" and "naturalistic," and had become, in these latter days, merely peevish and querulous, protesting in favor of standards that no longer represented our best values. Every one, in Miro's time, bemoaned the lack of critics, but the older critics seemed to have lost all sense of hospitality and to have become tired and a little spitefully disconsolate, while the newer ones were too intent on their crusades against Puritanism and philistinism to have time for a constructive pointing of the way.

Miro had a very real sense of standing at the end of an era. He and his friends had lived down both their old orthodoxies of the classics and their new orthodoxies of propaganda. Gone were the priggishness and self-consciousness, which had marked their teachers. The new culture would be more personal than the old, but it would not be held as a personal property. It would be democratic in the sense that it would represent each person's honest spontaneous taste. The old attitude was only speciously democratic. The assumption was that if you pressed your material long enough and winningly enough upon your cultivable public, they would acquire it. But the material was something handed down, not grown in the garden of their own appreciations. Under these conditions the critic and appreciator became a mere impersonal register of orthodox opinion. The cultivated person, in conforming his judgments to what was authoritatively taught him, was really a member of the herd—a cultivated herd, it is true, but still a herd. It was the mass that spoke through the critic and not his own discrimination. These authoritative judgments might, of course, have come—probably had come—to the herd through discerning critics, but in Miro's time judgment in the schools had petrified. One believed not because one felt the original discernment, but because one was impressed by the weight and reputability of opinions. At least so it seemed to Miro.

Now just as the artists had become tired of conventions and were breaking through into new and personal forms, so Miro saw the younger critics breaking through these cultural conventions. To the elders the result would seem mere anarchy. But Miro's attitude did not want to destroy; it merely wanted to rearrange the materials. He wanted no more second-hand appreciations. No one's cultural store was to include anything that one could not be enthusiastic about. One's acquaintance with the best that had been said and thought should be encouraged—in Miro's ideal school—to follow the lines of one's temperament. Miro, having thrown out the old gods, found them slowly and properly coming back to him. Some would always repel him, others he hoped to understand eventually. But if it took wisdom to write the great books, did it not also take wisdom to understand them? Even the Latin writers he hoped to recover, with the aid of translations. But why bother with Greek when you could get Euripides in the marvelous verse of Gilbert Murray? Miro was willing to believe that no education was complete without at least an inoculation of the virus of the two orthodoxies that he was transcending.

As Miro looked around the American scene, he wondered where the critics were to come from. He saw, on the one hand, Mr. Mencken and Mr. Dreiser and their friends, going heavily forth to battle with the Philistines, glorying in pachydermatous vulgarisms that hurt the polite and cultivated young men of the old school. And he saw these violent critics, in the rage against Puritanism, becoming themselves moralists, with the same bigotry and tastelessness as their enemies. No, these would never do. On the other hand, he saw Mr. Stuart P. Sherman, in his youthful if somewhat belated ardor, revolting so conscientiously against the "naturalism" and crude expression of current efforts that, in his defense of *belles-lettres*, of the fine tradition of literary art, he himself became a moralist of the intensest brand, and as critic plumped for Arnold Bennett, because that clever man had a feeling for the proprieties of human conduct. No, Mr. Sherman would do even less adequately. His fine sympathies were as much out of the current as was the specious classicism of Professor Shorey. He would have to look for the critics among the young men who had an abounding sense of life, as well as a feeling for literary form. They would be men who had not been content to live on their cultural inheritance, but had gone out into the modern world and amassed a fresh fortune of their own. They would be men who were not squeamish, who did not feel the delicate differences between "animal" and "human" conduct, who were enthusiastic about Mark Twain and Gorski as well as Romain Rolland, and at the same time were thrilled by Copeau's theater.

Where was a better program for culture, for any kind of literary art? Culture as a living effort, a driving attempt both at sincere expression and at the comprehension of sincere expression wherever it was found! Appreciation to be as far removed from the "I know what I like!" as from the textbook impeccability of taste! If each mind sought its own along these lines, would not many find themselves agreed? Miro insisted on liking Amy Lowell's attempt to outline the tendencies in American poetry in a form which made clear the struggles of contemporary men and women with the tradition and against "every affectation of the mind." He began to see in the new class-consciousness of poets the ending of that old division which "culture" made between the chosen people and the gentiles. We were not to form little pools of workers and appreciators of similar temperaments and tastes. The little magazines that were starting up became voices for these new communities of sentiment. Miro thought that perhaps at first it was right to adopt a tentative super-ciliousness towards the rest of the world, so that both Mr. Mencken with his shudders at the vulgar Demos and Mr. Sherman with his obsession with the sanely and wholesomely American might be shut out from influence. Instead of fighting the Philistine in the name of freedom, or fighting the vulgar iconoclast in the name of wholesome human notions, it might be better to write for one's own band of comprehenders, in order that one might have something genuine with which to appeal to both the mob of the "bourgeois" and the ferocious vandals who had been dividing the field among them. Far better a quarrel among these intensely self-conscious groups than the issues that had filled the *Atlantic* and the *Nation* with their dreary obsolescence. Far better for the mind that aspired towards "culture" to be told not to conform or worship, but to search out its group, its own temperamental community of senti-ment, and there deepen appreciations through sympathetic contact.

It was no longer a question of being hospitable towards the work of other countries. Miro found the whole world open to him, in these days, through the enterprise of publishers. He and his friends felt more sympathetic with certain groups in France and Russia than they did with the variegated "prominent au-thors" of their own land. Winston Churchill as a novelist came to seem more of an alien than Artzbybashev. The fact of culture be-ing international had been followed by a sense of its being. The old cultural attitude had been hospitable enough, but it had im-ported its alien culture in the form of "comparative literature." It was hospitable only in trying to mould its own taste to the or-thodox canons abroad. The older American critic was mostly in-terested in getting the proper rank and reverence for what he borrowed. The new critic will take what suits his community of sentiment. He will want to link up not with the foreign canon, but with that group which is nearest in spirit with the effort he and his friends are making. The American has to work to inter-pret and portray the life he knows. He cannot be international in the sense that anything but the life in which he is saturated, with its questions and its colors, can be the material for his art. But he can be international—and must be—in the sense that he works with a certain hopeful vision of a "young world," and with certain ideal values upon which the younger men, stained and revolted by war, in all countries are agreeing.

Miro wonders sometimes whether the direction in which he is tending will not bring him around the circle again to a new classicism. The last stage in the history of the man of culture will be that "classic" which he did not understand and which his mind spent its youth in overthrowing. But it will be a classicism far different from that which was so unintelligently handed down to him in the American world. It will be something worked out and lived into. Looking into the future he will have to do what Van Wyck Brooks calls "inventing a usable past." Finding little in the American tradition that is not tainted with sweetness and light and burdened with the terrible patronage of bourgeois society, the new classicist will yet rescue Thoreau and Whitman and Mark Twain and try to tap through them a certain eternal human tradition of abounding vitality and moral freedom, and so build out the future. If the classic means power with restraint, vitality with harmony, a fusion of intellect and feeling, and a keen sense of the artistic conscience, then the revolutionary world is coming out into the classic. When Miro sees behind the minds of the *Masses* group a desire for form and for expressive beauty, and sees the radicals following Jacques Copeau and reading Chekhov, he smiles at the thought of the American critics, young and old, who do not know yet that they are dead.

—1920

Edith Wharton

(1862–1937)

Born Edith Newbold Jones in "Old New York," Wharton grew up in Europe; Newport, Rhode Island; and New York City. Although not wealthy by New York society standards, she certainly enjoyed a comfortable and privileged upbringing. After her father's death in 1881, Wharton lived briefly in Washington Square. In 1905 she published The House of Mirth, *considered her first "New York book." Her masterpiece,* The Age of Innocence *(1920), is set in the New York of the 1870s. Like the society that is vanishing around him, its hero, Newland Archer, is a passionate man who falls victim to the conventions and restrictions of his time.* The Age of Innocence *won a Pulitzer Prize and, in 1993, was adapted into a movie starring Daniel Day-Lewis and Michelle Pfeiffer and directed by Martin Scorsese.*

from *The Age of Innocence*

Old-fashioned New York dined at seven, and the habit of after-dinner calls, though derided in Archer's set, still generally prevailed. As the young man strolled up Fifth Avenue from Waverley Place, the long thoroughfare was deserted but for a group of carriages standing before the Reggie Chiverses' (where there was a dinner for the Duke), and the occasional figure of an elderly gentleman in heavy overcoat and muffler ascending a brownstone doorstep and disappearing into a gas-lit hall. Thus, as Archer crossed Washington Square, he remarked that old Mr. du Lac was calling on his cousins the Dagonets, and turning down the corner of West Tenth Street he saw Mr. Skipworth, of his own firm, obviously bound on a visit to

Edith Wharton. From *The Age of Innocence* (1920).

184

the Miss Lannings. A little farther up Fifth Avenue, Beaufort appeared on his doorstep, darkly projected against a blaze of light, descended to his private brougham, and rolled away to a mysterious and probably unmentionable destination. It was not an Opera night, and no one was giving a party, so that Beaufort's outing was undoubtedly of a clandestine nature. Archer connected it to his mind with a little house beyond Lexington Avenue in which beribboned window curtains and flower-boxes had recently appeared, and before whose newly painted door the canary-coloured brougham of Miss Fanny Ring was frequently seen to wait.

Beyond the small and slippery pyramid which composed Mrs. Archer's world lay the almost unmapped quarter inhabited by artists, musicians and "people who wrote." These scattered fragments of humanity had never shown any desire to be amalgamated with the social structure. In spite of odd ways they were said to be, for the most part, quite respectable; but they preferred to keep to themselves. Medora Manson, in her prosperous days, had inaugurated a "literary salon"; but it had soon died out owing to the reluctance of the literary to frequent it.

Others had made the same attempt, and there was a household of Blenkers—an intense and voluble mother, and three blowsy daughters who imitated her—where one met Edwin Booth and Patti and William Winter, and the new Shakespearean actor George Rignold, and some of the magazine editors and musical and literary critics.

Mrs. Archer and her group felt a certain timidity concerning these persons. They were odd, they were uncertain, they had things one didn't know about in the background of their lives and minds. Literature and art were deeply respected in the Archer set, and Mrs. Archer was always at pains to tell her children how much more agreeable and cultivated society had been when it included such figures as Washington Irving, Fitz-Greene Halleck and the poet of "The Culprit Fay." The most celebrated authors of that generation had been "gentlemen"; perhaps the unknown persons who succeeded them had gentlemanly sentiments, but their origin, their appearance, their hair, their intimacy with the stage and the Opera, made any old New York criterion inapplicable to them.

185

"When I was a girl," Mrs. Archer used to say, "we knew everybody between the Battery and Canal Street; and only the people one knew had carriages. It was perfectly easy to place any one then; now one can't tell, and I prefer not to try."

Only old Catherine Mingott, with her absence of moral prejudices and almost *parvenu* indifference to the subtler distinctions, might have bridged the abyss; but she had never opened a book or looked at a picture, and cared for music only because it reminded her of gala nights at the *Italiens*, in the days of her triumph at the Tuileries. Possibly Beaufort, who was her match in daring, would have succeeded in bringing about a fusion; but his grand house and silk-stockinged footmen were an obstacle to informal sociability. Moreover, he was as illiterate as old Mrs. Mingott, and considered "fellows who wrote" as the mere paid purveyors of rich men's pleasures; and no one rich enough to influence his opinion had ever questioned it.

Newland Archer had been aware of these things ever since he could remember, and had accepted them as part of the structure of his universe. He knew that there were societies where painters and poets and novelists and men of science, and even great actors, were sought after as Dukes; he had often pictured to himself what it would have been to live in the intimacy of drawing-rooms dominated by the talk of Mérimée (whose "Letres a une Inconnue" was one of his inseparables), of Thackeray, Browning or William Morris. But such things were inconceivable in New York, and unsettling to think of. Archer knew most of the "fellows who wrote," the musicians and the painters: he met them at the Century, or at the little musical and theatrical clubs that were beginning to come into existence. He enjoyed them there, and was bored with them at the Blenkers', where they were mingled with fervid and dowdy women who passed them about like captured curiosities; and even after his most exciting talks with Ned Winsett he always came away with the feeling that if his world was small, so was theirs, and that the only way to enlarge either was to reach a stage of manners where they would naturally merge.

He was reminded of this by trying to picture the society in which the Countess Olenska had lived and suffered, and also—perhaps—tasted mysterious joys. He remembered with what amusement she had told him that her grandmother Mingott and the Wellands objected to her living in a "Bohemian" quarter given over to "people who wrote." It was not the peril but the poverty that her family disliked; but that shade escaped her, and she supposed they considered literature compromising.

She herself had no fears of it, and the books scattered about her drawing-room (a part of the house in which books were usually supposed to be "out of place"), though chiefly works of fiction, had whetted Archer's interest with such new names as those of Paul Bourget, Huysmans, and the Goncourt brothers. Ruminating on these things as he approached her door, he was once more conscious of the curious way in which she reversed his values, and of the need of thinking himself into conditions incredibly different from any that he knew if he were to be of use in her present difficulty.

Nastasia opened the door, smiled mysteriously. On the bench in the hall lay a sable-lined overcoat, a folded opera hat of dull silk with a gold J. B. on the lining, and a white silk muffler: there was no mistaking the fact that these costly articles were the property of Julius Beaufort.

Archer was angry: so angry that he came near scribbling a word on his card and going away; then he remembered that in writing to Madame Olenska he had been kept by excess of discretion from saying that he wished to see her privately. He had therefore no one but himself to blame if she had opened her doors to other visitors; and he entered the drawing-room with the dogged determination to make Beaufort feel himself in the way, and to outstay him.

The banker stood leaning against the mantelshelf, which was draped with an old embroidery held in place by brass candelabra containing church candles of yellowish wax. He had thrust his chest out, supporting his shoulders against the mantel and resting his weight on one large patent-leather foot. As Archer entered he was smiling and looking down on his hostess, who sat on a sofa placed at right angles to the chimney. A table banked with flowers formed a screen behind it, and against the orchids and azaleas which the young man recognised as tributes from the Beaufort hot-houses, Madame Olenska sat half-reclined, her head propped on a hand and her wide sleeve leaving the arm bare to the elbow.

It was usual for ladies who received in the evenings to wear what were called "simple dinner dresses": a close-fitting armour of whale-boned silk, slightly open in the neck, with lace ruffles filling in the crack, and tight sleeves with a flounce uncovering just enough wrist to show an Etruscan gold bracelet or a velvet band. But Madame Olenska, heedless of tradition, was attired in a long robe of red velvet bordered about the chin and down the front with glossy black fur. Archer remembered, on his last visit to Paris, seeing a portrait by the new painter, Carolus Duran, whose pictures were the sensation of the Salon, in which the lady wore one of these bold sheath-like robes with her chin nestling in fur. There was something perverse and provocative in the notion of fur worn in the evening in a heated drawing-room, and in the combination of a muffled throat and bare arms; but the effect was undeniably pleasing.

"Lord love us—three whole days at Skuytercliff!" Beaufort was saying in his loud sneering voice as Archer entered. "You'd better take all your furs, and a hot-water bottle."

"Why? Is the house so cold?" she asked, holding out her left hand to Archer in a way mysteriously suggesting that she expected him to kiss it.

"No; but the missus is," said Beaufort, nodding carelessly to the young man.

"But I thought her so kind. She came herself to invite me. Granny says I must certainly go."

"Granny would, of course. And *I* say it's a shame you're going to miss the little oyster supper I'd planned for you at Delmonico's next Sunday, with Campanini and Scalchi and a lot of jolly people."

She looked doubtfully from the banker to Archer.

"Ah—that does tempt me! Except the other evening at Mrs. Struthers's I've not met a single artist since I've been here."

"What kind of artists? I know one or two painters, very good fellows, that I could bring to see you if you'd allow me," said Archer boldly.

"Painters? Are there painters in New York?" asked Beaufort, in a tone implying that there could be none since he did not buy their pictures; and Madame Olenska said to Archer, with her grave smile: "That would be charming. But I was really thinking of dramatic artists, singers, actors, musicians. My husband's house was always full of them."

She said the words "my husband" as if no sinister associations were connected with them, and in a tone that seemed almost to sigh over the lost delights of her married life. Archer looked at her perplexedly, wondering if it were lightness or dissimulation that enabled her to touch so easily on the past at the very moment when she was risking her reputation in order to break with it.

"I do think," she went on, addressing both men, "that the *imprévu* adds to one's enjoyment. It's perhaps a mistake to see the same people every day."

"It's confoundedly dull, anyhow; New York is dying of dullness," Beaufort grumbled. "And when I try to liven it up for you, you go back on me. Come—think better of it! Sunday is your last chance, for Campanini leaves next week for Baltimore and Philadelphia; and I've a private room, and a Steinway, and they'll sing all night for me."

"How delicious! May I think it over, and write to you tomorrow morning?"

She spoke amiably, yet with the least hint of dismissal in her voice. Beaufort evidently felt it, and being unused to dismissals, stood staring at her with an obstinate line between his eyes.

"Why not now?"

"It's too serious a question to decide at this late hour."

"Do you call it late?"

She returned his glance coolly. "Yes; because I have still to talk business with Mr. Archer for a little while."

"Ah," Beaufort snapped. There was no appeal from her tone, and with a slight shrug he recovered his composure, took her hand, which he kissed with a practiced air, and calling out from the threshold: "I say, Newland, if you can persuade the Countess to stop in town of course you're included in the supper," left the room with his heavy important step.

For a moment Archer fancied that Mr. Letterblair must have told her of his coming; but the irrelevance of her next remark made him change his mind.

"You know painters, then? You live in their *milieu*?" she asked, her eyes full of interest.

"Oh, not exactly. I don't know that the arts have a *milieu* here, any of them; they're more like a very thinly settled outskirt."

"But you care for such things?"

"Immensely. When I'm in Paris or London I never miss an exhibition. I try to keep up."

She looked down at the tip of the little satin boot that peeped from her long draperies.

"I used to care immensely too: my life was full of such things. But now I want to try not to."

"You want to try not to?"

"Yes: I want to cast off all my old life, to become just like everybody else here."

Archer reddened. "You'll never be like everybody else," he said.

She raised her straight eyebrows a little. "Ah, don't say that. If you knew how I hate to be different!"

Her face had grown as sombre as a tragic mask. She leaned forward, clasping her knee in her thin hands, and looking away from him into remote dark distances.

"I want to get away from it all," she insisted.

He waited a moment and cleared his throat. "I know. Mr. Letterblair has told me."

"Ah?"

"That's the reason I've come. He asked me to—you see I'm in the firm."

She looked slightly surprised, and then her eyes brightened. "You mean you can manage it for me? I can talk to you instead of Mr. Letterblair? Oh, that will be so much easier!"

Her tone touched him, and his confidence grew with his self-satisfaction. He perceived that she had spoken of business to Beaufort simply to get rid of him; and to have routed Beaufort was something of a triumph.

"I am here to talk about it," he repeated.

She sat silent, her head still propped by the arm that rested on the back of the sofa. Her face looked pale and extinguished, as if dimmed by the rich red of her dress. She struck Archer, of a sudden, as a pathetic and even pitiful figure.

"Now we're coming to hard facts," he thought, conscious in himself of the same instinctive recoil that he had so often criticised in his mother and her contemporaries. How little practice he had had in dealing with unusual situations! Their very vocabulary was unfamiliar to him, and seemed to belong to fiction and the stage. In face of what was coming he felt awkward and embarrassed as a boy.

After a pause Madame Olenska broke out with unexpected vehemence: "I want to be free; I want to wipe out all the past."

"I understand that."

Her face warmed: "Then you'll help me?"

"First—" he hesitated—"perhaps I ought to know a little more."

She seemed surprised. "You know about my husband—my life with him?"

He made a sign of assent.

"Well—then—what more is there? In this country are such things tolerated? I'm a Protestant—our church does not forbid divorce in such cases."

"Certainly not."

They were both silent again, and Archer felt the spectre of Count Olenski's letter grimacing hideously between them. The letter filled only half a page, and was just what he had described it to be in speaking of it to Mr. Letterblair: the vague charge of an angry blackguard. But how much truth was behind it? Only Count Olenski's wife could tell.

"I've looked through the papers you gave to Mr. Letterblair," he said at length.

"Well—can there be anything more abominable?"

"No."

She changed her position slightly, screening her eyes with her lifted hand.

"Of course you know," Archer continued, "that if your husband chooses to fight the case—as he threatens to—"

"Yes—?"

"He can say things—things that might be unpl—might be disagreeable to you: say them publicly, so that they would get about, and harm you even if—"

"If—?"

"I mean: no matter how unfounded they were."

She paused for a long interval; so long that, not wishing to keep his eyes on her shaded face, he had time to imprint on his mind the exact shape of her other hand, the one on her knee, and every detail of the three rings on her fourth and fifth fingers; among which, he noticed, a wedding ring did not appear.

"What harm could such accusations, even if he made them publicly, do me here?"

It was on his lips to exclaim: "My poor child—far more harm than anywhere else!" Instead, he answered, in a voice that sounded in his ears like Mr. Letterblair's: "New York society is a very small world compared with the one you've lived in. And it's ruled, in spite of appearances, by a few people with—well, rather old-fashioned ideas."

She said nothing, and he continued: "Our ideas about marriage and divorce are particularly old-fashioned. Our legislation favours divorce—our social customs don't."

"Never?"

"Well—not if the woman, however injured, however irreproachable, has appearances in the least degree against her, has exposed herself by an unconventional action to—to offensive insinuations—"

She drooped her head a little lower, and he waited again, intensely hoping for a flash of indignation, or at least a brief cry of denial. None came.

A little travelling clock ticked purringly at her elbow, and a log broke in two and sent up a shower of sparks. The whole hushed and brooding room seemed to be waiting silently with Archer.

"Yes," she murmured at length, "that's what my family tell me."

He winced a little. "It's not unnatural—"

"*Our* family," she corrected herself; and Archer coloured. "For you'll be my cousin soon," she continued gently.

"I hope so."

"And you take their view?"

He stood up at this, wandered across the room, stared with void eyes at one of the pictures against the old red damask, and came back irresolutely to her side. How could he say: "Yes, if what your husband hints is true, or if you've no way of disproving it."

"Sincerely—" she interjected, as he was about to speak.

He looked down into the fire. "Sincerely, then—what should you gain that would compensate for the possibility—the certainty—of a lot of beastly talk?"

"But my freedom—is that nothing?"

It flashed across him at that instant that the charge in the letter was true, and that she hoped to marry the partner of her guilt. How was he to tell her that, if she really cherished such a plan, the laws of the State were inexorably opposed to it? The mere suspicion that the thought was in her mind made him feel harshly and impatiently toward her. "But aren't you as free as air as it is?" he returned. "Who can touch you? Mr. Letterblair tells me the financial question has been settled—"

"Oh, yes," she said indifferently.

"Well, then: is it worth while to risk what may be infinitely disagreeable and painful? Think of the newspapers—their vileness! It's all stupid and narrow and unjust—but one can't make over society."

"No," she acquiesced; and her tone was so faint and desolate that he felt a sudden remorse for his own hard thoughts.

"The individual, in such cases, is nearly always sacrificed to what is supposed to be the collective interest: people cling to any convention that keeps the family together—protects the children, if there are any," he rambled on, pouring out all the stock phrases that rose to his lips in his intense desire to cover over the ugly reality which her silence seemed to have laid bare. Since she would not or could not say the one word that would have cleared the air, his wish was not to let her feel that he was trying to probe into her secret. Better keep on the surface, in the prudent old New York way, than risk uncovering a wound he could not heal.

"It's my business, you know," he went on, "to help you to see these things as the people who are fondest of you see them. The Mingotts, the Wellands, the van der Luydens, all your friends and relations: if I didn't show you honestly how they judge such questions, it wouldn't be fair of me, would it?" He spoke insistently, almost pleading with her in his eagerness to cover up that yawning silence.

She said slowly, "No; it wouldn't be fair."

The fire had crumbled down to greyness, and one of the lamps made a gurgling appeal for attention. Madame Olenska rose, wound it up and returned to the fire, but without resuming her seat.

Her remaining on her feet seemed to signify that there was nothing more for either of them to say, and Archer stood up also.

"Very well; I will do what you wish," she said abruptly. The blood rushed to his forehead; and, taken aback by the suddenness of her surrender, he caught her two hands awkwardly in his.

"I—I do want to help you," he said.

"You do help me. Good night, my cousin."

He bent and laid his lips on her hands, which were cold and lifeless. She drew them away, and he turned to the door, found his coat and hat under the faint gas-light of the hall, and plunged out into the winter night bursting with the belated eloquence of the inarticulate.

—1920

Guido Bruno

(1884–1942)

Self-prompter. Charlatan. Huckster. The adjectives describing Guido Bruno have rarely been kind. Some say he was a fraud, a phony committed to squeezing every penny out of visitors eager to experience first-hand any example of "Greenwich Thrillage." A few admirers though did acknowledge his contribution to American arts and letters—he was the first to publish verses by Hart Crane, he "discovered" Djuna Barnes, and he published Alfred Kreymborg's imagist poems. Born Curt Josef Kisch in 1884 in what is now the Czech Republic, he came to America in 1907. After several years in Detroit and Chicago, he arrived in the Village in 1913, adopting the unlikely name of Guido Bruno, and in the best tradition of Henri Murger, set up headquarters in a two-story wooden shack at 58 Washington Square South over a candy and cigar store. From here, in his three-roomed "garret," he published, at various times, several publications, including Bruno's Bohemia, Bruno's Weekly, Greenwich Village, *and issued a series of chapbooks. He also sponsored art exhibits, weekly cabarets, and lectures, started the Thimble Theatre with Charles Edison, the inventor's son, and in general played the role of bohemian to the hilt. Bruno died in late 1942.*

Guido Bruno. From *Fragments from Greenwich Village* (New York: Published Privately by the Author, 1921).

from *Fragments from Greenwich Village*

"Just Time"

My garret had six windows. Through every one the sun is shining, bathing the table with my typewriter in a shower of pure golden rays. The laundry that hangs along wash lines between the houses of little Italy near by seems real white; swinging joyfully to the rhythm of a teasing wind. A few of my neighbors seem to love vivid, glaring colors. There is one red nightshirt, on which I feast my eyes every other week. Its owner must be a giant with long arms. I fancy he brought it from Naples or Sicily. The shirt will fade and go the way of all shirts and he'll buy nice flannel pajamas—all Italians wear pajamas, there are dozens of them on the lines in front of my window—and he will forget his sunny Italy, lose his sun-browned cheeks, and how long and he will be one of those thousands of pale uniformly clad New Yorkers?

Doing the same work, shoulder to shoulder with thousands of others makes people uniform. Some elevate themselves up to the standard of the average, some come down to the standard of the average. But after a while all will be equal, they will all wear the same clothes, walk in the same manner, eat the same kind of food, make the same gestures, use the same language; all for one purpose: to make their daily bread.

Over there across the backyard in front of my garret a woman leans over the washtub. She never looks up to the forget-me-not blue sky; she doesn't see the sparrows on the fence fighting for crumbs of bread. Her husband somewhere in a shop leans over his work and is angry because tiny little rays of the kind sun peep through the blinded windows fascinated by the needle in his hand and dance in jolly circles over his work. To be poor is not the tragedy that kills happiness, transforms proud and free humans into bent and worn slaves; that creates human automatons.

It is the lack of time that makes millions wretched. They cannot look up to the skies and see the passing clouds—they have no time.

They do not admire the beauty of flowers nor do they inhale their fragrance—they have no time.

They don't hear the birds singing; they don't hear the cooing of babies and the heart gladdening chattering of children—they have no time.

Time, time—just a little time to live is the real plea of the poor man.

"The Village Paper"

It was in 1913. I was broke, had come from the West where I had sold the monthly magazine that caused my ruin for the price of a ticket to New York. My search for friends had proved futile. I used to live on Washington Square and there I sat now on a bench, with $1.50 in my pocket and a large store of ideals, ambitions, energy. . . . I wanted to do something.

There is not a lovelier place in the city than Washington Square. It carries a touch of intimacy that makes dear the boudoir of our beloved one. It has the dignity of a church and the friendliness of an inn-keeper who values us as gladly-sheltered guests.

It was a wonderful evening and I took in the romance of it all. All at once it came to me! Over there the university; on the north side of the square all the aristocratic mansions; on the south side the aristocracy of mind in shabby lodging houses and studio buildings! Of course, *this* is the Quartier Latin of America. And I thought of the curious people that I knew lived in the neighborhood. How they worked: how they spent their lives in the happy solitude of creating. I made up my mind to tell the world about this strange spot in the most commercial business city on earth. I decided then and there that I would start a paper, call it *Greenwich Village*, and make it a picture of this neighorhood; quaint, most intimate, dignified, peculiar in spots, learned here and there but also with a ragged edge. I had to talk to somebody. The only shop I could see in the neighborhood was the very ice cream store which is still opposite the terminal station of the Fifth Avenue busses. I found the Rossi Brothers there very nice chaps, who seemed enthusiastic about my idea of a Greenwich Village magazine. "I am a printer," interrupted a rather rugged looking Italian who had listened to our conversation. "I have type and an old press; if the paper isn't too big in size I would like to print it."

I accompanied him to his shop, a little room two by four, everything most primitive; but I had no money and so I decided to take advantage of the offer. Next morning I went out soliciting advertisements to cover the expense of my first number. I found everybody willing to advertise in my new paper. The Episcopal-Methodist Church, a few Italian groceries, a real estate firm, a German bakery on Sixth Avenue. Those were hard days. I helped to set the type, to print the paper, and what a long weary process it was! But finally we got it out. The first number was issued in five hundred copies. I took them around to the newsdealers and left them there on consignment. I lived on the floor above the ice cream parlor; the rent then was about a tenth of what it is today. Somebody called it Bruno's Garret, and the name stuck. I rather liked the intimacy of it and printed beneath the title page of the next issue of my paper, *"Published in Bruno's Garret on Washington Square."* I never thought my paper would interest others, but the old residents of artists and writers who lived here mostly because it was cheaper than anywhere else in town. The New York *Times* commented on it in several columns of its news pages. The other dailies followed the lead. Soon I received a crop of letters from all over the United States requesting sample copies. All this was very encouraging, but did not enable me to pay my rent and pay for my food. The French pastry cook who kept a little shop on Fourth Street was my only friend. He gave me unlimited credit, and I actually lived almost two months on French pastry. It was the most dreadful period of my life. I had tea and French pastry for breakfast; tarts and napoleons, biscuits and cream rolls for lunch and for dinner. I worked from early morning till late at night, writing next week's issue from cover to cover, going about gathering advertisements and inspiration, trying to impress my advertisers with my prosperity, never asking for payment in advance, and when the money came in, I had to pay the printer (and mighty little he got) and buy paper for the next issue. About Christmas I moved to the old house on the corner of Washington Square and Thompson Street and announced that any artist who was doing serious work could hang his pictures on exhibition in my "Garret," free of charge; any poet could come any Wednesday and Saturday afternoon and read his poetry to an audience that I would get for him. This was new then in New York and artists and poets came to take advantage of my offer. In the course of two years and a half I had forty-six exhibitions by forty-six different people, and all are now well-known. Clara Tice with her little nudes attracted in my garret for the first time the attention of a public and of the Society for the Prevention of Vice. Bernhard Wall, who recently etched a portrait of President Wilson, had his humble first exhibition here. Newspapers wrote miles of funny and serious stories about Bruno's Garret. After the start of the world war English, French, German and Italian artists made their headquarters in the garret and attributed greatly to its cosmopolitan independent atmosphere. The poetry readings were a great success. I printed for the first time contributions of the since universally recognized free verse poets. Alfred Kreymborg's "Mushrooms" (as he called his unusual poetry) caused the paragraphers and calumnists everywhere to poke fun at my garret. My poetry readings became the rendezvous of the most fashionable people in New York.

And inside of nine months my correspondence was brought in big mail bags, the sight-seeing busses stopped in front of my old little frame building, which by the way, had been erected a hundred and fifty years ago by the first public grave digger of New York, Washington Square then being Potter's Field.

One day Charles Edison, who had patronized the garret frequently, unknown to me by name, asked me if the same things that I was doing for painters and writers couldn't be done for musicians. We formed a partnership, built Edison's Thimble Theatre opposite the Brevoort Hotel and issued an appeal to all musicians and composers of America. Any one could come here and play or sing to audiences which we got for them. There was no admission fee charged, and everybody remembers what a pretty and intimate show house the Thimble Theatre is. Soon I thought of utilizing the theatre for little plays. I got a small group of excellent professionals together, called them the *Bruno Players*, and we had memorable performances. This again being the first attempt of a small intimate theatre in Greenwich Village. Unmolested by the police we played Strindberg's "Countess Julie," Sada Cowen's "The State Forbids," an astonishingly free birth-control play; we had Japanese actors and a play by George Bernard Shaw. Charles Edison gave concerts on Washington Square twice a week. On two afternoons each week we gathered all the children of Greenwich Village on the Square and had dancing teachers arrange for them delightful open-air dances. *Greenwich Village* had been published fortnightly; now it became *Bruno's Weekly*. Its circulation was 32,000 a week, distributed all over the United States. This happy activity had continued for almost two years and a half. Others came down to the village, started art galleries and art shops, tea rooms, dancing halls, book shops, purely commercial places. A sort of Coney Island grew up almost over night; the quiet of the village was disturbed. The sacred peace was broken. Money changers had invaded holy ground. Slumming parties came nightly to "do the village." The police had to interfere very often with the "high life" in basements and cellars. Artists, writers, and old residents fled as fast as they could. And then we entered into the war. More serious business called us.

We had our fun and, I believe, done a good deal to foster everything new in art and literature. *Bruno's Weekly* had given ideas to editors all over the country. The art exhibitions in Bruno's Garret, which had been looked upon as freak creations of ultra-modern painters, moved up-town to respectable art galleries. The Garret had fulfilled its mission. Little theatres grew up everywhere, and so the little Thimble Theatre had fulfilled its mission. Charles Edison became manager of Thomas A. Edison, Inc., and left for good.

But the village flourishes today. Rents have gone sky-high. Greenwich Village had established its reputation, and the undesirable elements disappeared as quickly as they had come. Here it is after the war, the "gay corner" of New York.

Did you say you wished to "tour" Greenwich Village?

You must come down in the evening.

Then it is that village of which you dream, the background to so many big things, the essential in so many big lives, the one part of this city where you can forget the city and seven million co-inhabitants of yours. There is the arch with its simple architecture, the monumental gateway to the Square. Lights here and there. High up on the tower of a hotel an electric-lighted cross and still higher a few stars, and if you are lucky and the night is clear, the moon.

The square is deserted and only a few passengers, waiting for the next bus, make up the small group beneath the arc light. But the streets are peopled with men and women who stand around the Italian grocery shops and pastry bakeries; they worked all day and kept silent; now they live their own real life. There are cafes as you can see on the rivas of small Italian coast cities where you really drink coffee and eat pastry and play dominoes. Turning one of those streets and unexpectedly, like the background of a miniature playhouse, a little chapel looms up before you. The doors are open, candles before the altars are a testimony that the saints are not forgotten. Women are sitting on the stairs selling rosaries, little statues and paper flowers. Men, women and children are passing and passing out. Follow the thundering elevated and turn again to the Square. As many windows as you see lighted in these mansions of yore used now as rooming and lodging houses—so many homes do they contain.

Can you help thinking: "If I were a poet or an artist, I surely would live here and nowhere else?"

But, dear reader, because of your living here you would not be a poet or an artist.

"The Passing of Bruno's Garret"

November 8, 1916.

The old frame house on the corner of Washington Square South and of Thompson Street, which was known as Bruno's Garret, shows no more the big black signs inviting you in white letters to drop in and see an exhibition of works of some artist or other, or to stop in and listen to some poet read his own poetry.

The Garret was closed on November 1st.

I am not a friend of prospectuses and of announcements. Two years ago I conceived the idea of having a place where I could publish a magazine whose pages would be open to everybody who has something to say, whose walls would choose to bring to it; a place where poets could come and read their poetry to an audience that had strolled in accidentally as had they themselves. I did not send out prospectuses and announcements. But I opened my doors and sent out my invitations, and whoever wanted to come, came. The Garret became known, at first in New York, and later all over the United States, and it made friends in England, and Germany, in Austria and France, in Italy. The Slavic countries sent their friendly messages, and even China and Japan were represented by artists and by poets. The war brought over many refugees, artists and writers who came to Bruno's Garret before they went out to make the rounds of art galleries and magazine editors in the city.

I could fill pages with reminiscences and memories vibrating with the sentiment of obsequies. I could write a book of melancholic sadness in verse libre while leaving these rooms that have become so dear to me. I could picture to you, dear reader, in tear-wet words how badly I feel at abandoning the place where I have worked two of the best years of my life. In turn you would feel sad and you would send me a few sad thoughts of sympathy.

I love deeds and no matter if well or badly done, verily they are better than words.

And so I say, the Garret has fulfilled its mission. Here has been the debut of men and women who have made their mark in arts and letters since. The Garret has earned its place in the history of contemporary art and letters. It will live in the memory of those who used to gather there. The literature that bears its imprint is the testimony of its spirit.

Everything I undertook there was done upon its own merit. I never asked for anything without giving value for value.

I opened up the Garret and I closed it.

Per aspera ad astra.

—1921

Edna St. Vincent Millay

(1892–1950)

Born in Rockland, Maine, and educated at Vassar College, Edna St. Vincent Millay was a figure of such beauty that she remains one of the more elusive of literary figures to be associated with the Village. She arrived in 1917, the same year that her first book Renascence and Other Poems *was published. She wrote and acted in several plays for the Provincetown Players, but she is best known for her lyric poetry. Among her works are "Thistles" (1920), "Second April" (1921), and "The Ballad of the Harp Weaver" (1922), for which she won a Pulitzer Prize for poetry in 1923.* Collected Sonnets *was published in 1941,* Collected Lyrics *in 1943. Her affair with Floyd Dell was said to be the inspiration for "Weeds." Interest in Millay has never really flagged—in 2001 two biographies were published,* Savage Beauty *by Nancy Milford and* What Lips My Lips Have Kissed *by Daniel Epstein.*

"First Fig"

My candle burns at both ends;
    It will not last the night;
But ah, my foes, and oh, my friends—
    It gives a lovely light!

Edna St. Vincent Millay. "First Fig," "Macdougal Street," and "Weeds" from *A Few Figs from Thistles* (1922).

EDNA ST. VINCENT MILLAY

"Macdougal Street"

As I went walking up and down to take the evening air,
    (Sweet to meet upon the street, why must I be
        so shy?)
I saw him lay his hand upon her torn black hair;
    ("Little dirty Latin child, let the lady by!")

The women squatting on the stoops were slovenly
        and fat,
    (Lay me out in organdie, lay me out in lawn!)
And everywhere I stepped there was a baby or a cat;
    (Lord God in Heaven, will it never be dawn?)

The fruit-carts and clam-carts were ribald as a fair,
    (Pink nets and wet shells trodden under heel)
She had haggled from the fruit-man of his rotting ware;
    (I shall never get to sleep, the way I feel!)

He walked like a king through the filth and the clutter,
    (Sweet to meet upon the street, why did you glance
        me by?)
But he caught the quaint Italian quip she flung him from
        the gutter;
    (What can there be to cry about that I should lie
        and cry?)

He laid his darling hand upon her little black head,
    (I wish I were a ragged child with ear-rings in
        my ears!)
And he said she was a baggage to have said what she
        had said;
    (Truly I shall be ill unless I stop these tears!)

"Weeds"

White with daisies and red with sorrel
    And empty, empty under the sky!—
Life is a quest and love a quarrel—
    Here is a place for me to lie.

Daisies spring from damnéd seeds,
    And this red fire that here I see
Is a worthless crop of crimson weeds,
    Cursed by farmers thriftily.

But here, unhated for an hour,
    The sorrel runs in ragged flame,
The daisy stands, a bastard flower,
    Like flowers that bear an honest name.

And here a while, where no wind brings
    The baying of a pack athirst,
May sleep the sleep of blesséd things,
    The blood too bright, the brow accurst.

—1922

Alfred Kreymborg

(1883–1966)

A native New Yorker, Kreymborg was a poet, critic, and editor. He edited several Village literary magazines, including Glebe *and* Others. *The latter published the work of Wallace Stevens, Marianne Moore, and William Carlos Williams. He also edited* Broom *with Harold Loeb, the model for Robert Cohen in Ernest Hemingway's* The Sun Also Rises, *and was a playwright and producer with the Provincetown Players and The Other Players. In this selection from* Troubadour, *Kreymborg refers to himself in the third person, as Krimmie.*

"Greenwich Village" from *Troubadour: An Autobiography*

Not only had American artists begun to use villages as the subject matter of their work, but they made awkward, communal efforts toward the formation of small colonies of their own. The desire of congregating in sympathetic groups was a natural development of the craving of solitude for companionship in the wilderness. The fact that most of these colonies quickly fell into mutual admiration societies or herds of bickering porcupines did not detract from the genuineness of the original impulse. The failures simply demonstrate that the average artist is an anti-social person, and when he turns sociable it is usually at the expense of some compromise with his inner

Alfred Kreymborg. "Greenwich Village" from *Troubadour: An Autobiography* (New York: Boni and Liveright, 1925).

being. He was therefore better off in isolated places like Spoon River and Winesburg than he might be in the midst of his kin, where too much love or too much envy tended to soften or harden the integrity of his ego. Nevertheless, the poignant need of the artist in the days of darkness immediately antedating the war called for some point of contact with his fellows, in protection against the prevailing opinion held by American society that such a man was a wastrel, a pariah, a superfluous blot on an otherwise united democracy. Out of the demand for a bit of soil for the free development of the individual, colonies had grown in Carmel by the sea in California, Taos in prehistoric New Mexico, Peterboro in the hills of New Hampshire, Provincetown at the tip of Cape Cod. Krimmie had heard of these places and, on a hasty trip to Boston some years before, wandered among the beautiful remains of their forerunner in the quiet town of Concord on the Merrimac. Treading the circuitous paths of Sleepy Hollow, he lingered most of all near the smallest stone in the cemetery, a semi-circular slab marked David, leaning over the burial ground of the hermit of the Concord group, Henry David Thoreau.

The Greenwich Village Krimmie now visited was not a new confraternity. Artists had come there in the past and settled among the unostentatious relics of a primitive aristocracy. At different times, Henry James, William Dean Howells, Stephen Crane, Mark Twain, John Masefield, Theodore Dreiser and many others had lived there. It was inevitable, with the arrival of an era of a more concerted consciousness, that the village should draw a heterogeneous host of men and women from all over the country pointing their hobby-horses in the direction of Washington Square. The network of crooked streets surrounding the square was the most charming section of the city. It provided an ideal locality for artists no matter how poverty-stricken. But when the community grew more and more self-conscious, engaged in the national evils of standardized advertising and was exploited by the real estate boomers, it lapsed into a hometown, B. P. O. E. persuasion on a par with Los Angeles. Most of the artists fled elsewhere.

The first haunt Krimmie called at was the Washington Square Bookshop on MacDougal Street. The two proprietors, Albert and

Charles Boni, were mere striplings, swarthy, volatile and venturesome. He eyed the fantastic placards and posters on the walls of the shop. Who were these people, these groups—The Liberal Club, Guido Bruno and his garret, *The Masses*, *The New Republic*, The Washington Square Players, The Washington Square Gallery, Polly's Restaurant? And these men who came in the Boni boys introduced him to: Horace Traubel, who never wore a hat or an overcoat, the suave Adonis, Max Eastman, Thomas Seltzer, who turned out to be the boy's uncle, the huge, gentle, one-eyed Bill Heywood, John Reed, whom everybody adoringly called Jack? And the masculine Henrietta Rodman, the histrionic Helen Westley, the Chinese dowager, Bee Shostac, the polemical Margaret Sanger? How long had this been going on? Had his friend been right in dubbing him Rip?

The Bonis gossiped about the aims of the two new magazines, *The New Republic* and *The Masses*, and pointed out the three latest magazines from London, *The New Freewoman* (soon to be changed to the *Egoist*), *Poetry and Drama*, and *Rhythm*. He wondered whether he ought not tell the boys about *The Glebe*, but was sidetracked by an invitation to attend a general meeting of the Washington Square Players for the purpose of discussing ways and means of establishing a little theatre for the production of one-act plays. The group had put on an occasional play, usually concerning this new theme, sex, in one of the rooms of The Liberal Club, while the audience sat in the other. There was no scenery, and except for some chairs and an occasional table, props were taboo. The general meeting took place at Ida Rauh's studio, but as Krimmie had nothing immediate to contribute to the group, he drifted into the background and never attended another meeting. But he had enjoyed listening to the leaders of the venture, Edward Goodman, Sam Eliot, Jr., Philip Moeller, Lucy Huffaker, Helen Westley, Ida Rauh, and was delighted to learn that they had rented a little theatre uptown, The Bandbox, for their opening season of public productions. Patriotic villagers decried this move and maintained that The Washington Square Players should have rented and renovated one of the stables on MacDougal Street. It remained for the Provincetown Players to attempt this experiment a few years later.

Down in Polly's Restaurant, Krimmie met other pioneers of the village, and among them no man afforded more amusement than the big blond Bohemian, Guido Bruno. This eccentric finally proved the greatest menace to the village itself, and his garret on Washington Square brought down the wrath of the older settlers. It was he who started the advertising boom and enticed hopefuls and charlatans from all parts of the country by spreading lurid propaganda throughout his various sheets, *The Greenwich Village Weekly*, *The Bruno Chapbooks* and *Bruno's Weekly*. Krimmie also visited another haunt, The Washington Square Gallery, founded by the late Robert J. Coady. The pugnacious, redheaded Irishman not only had incisive ideas about modern art, but, a year or two later, founded an aggressive magazine called *The Soil*, which ran through five brilliant numbers and more or less prophesied the advent of several subsequent publications. Of all the haunts, however, Krimmie returned most frequently to The Boni Bookshop.

He now had several conferences with the Bonis with reference to *The Glebe*, as a result of which the boys agreed to finance the venture and let him edit it. He wrote a short manifesto on the aims of the venture, while the new publishers struck off placards bearing Ray's abstract design and arguing the novel benefits of one-man shows in the American magazine field. They also planned to bind a few hundred copies of each number in boards and sell them at a dollar a copy. Like Krimmie, the Bonis had some manuscripts to submit for discussion, and out of deference to them as new publishers he agreed that the honor of introducing the idea should go to a man in California who had sent in his collected poems for Albert and Charles to read. His name was George Cronyn. The second issue recalled *The American Quarterly*; it was devoted to the one-act comedy by Charles Demuth, the painter. Then followed, in some sort of monthly succession, *Des Imagistes*, Krimmie's novelette, *Erna Vitek*, the Collects of Walt Whitman's friend and conservator, Horace Traubel, and the pathetic autobiography of Wallace E. Baker, *The Diary Of A Suicide*. Young Baker, thoroughly disheartened with America, the literary game and the attendant hardships of earning his livelihood, had mailed this document to B. Russell

Herts, "that it may help, if published in part or whole, to ease the way for some who come after." Then he went down to one of the New York pleasure resorts, strode out into the sea and shot himself. The desperately courageous entries in the journal passed from Herts (no longer editor of *The Forum*) to Leonard D. Abbott, an editor of *Current Opinion*, and from Abbott to Krimmie. Baker won considerable posthumous glory for a while and then his sole literary record vanished like himself.

With the entrance of a play from the Russian, Andreyev's *Love of One's Neighbor*, translated by Thomas Seltzer, Krimmie began to lose interest in *The Glebe*. Notwithstanding his love for the expressions of modern Europe, he felt that his job as an editor, actual or potential, consisted in pursuing the ideal he had set himself from the start: the continued discovery and advancement of the unknowns on this side of the Atlantic. But the tremendous influx of translations from abroad had set in, and the Bonis, quite right from their point of view, wished to foster it in *The Glebe*. With the next two issues, translations by Sam Eliot, Jr., of plays by Frank Wedekind, *Erdgeist* and *Pandora's Box*, Krimmie resigned. Incidentally, these were the last issues of The Glebe, and the Bonis retired from the publishing field, until, a few years later, they joined a certain handsome, adventurous gentleman in the formation of the firm of Boni and Liveright.

Meanwhile, Guido Bruno had devoted three of his *Chapbooks* to Krimmie's writings: a group of slender poems called *Mushrooms*, a group still more slender, *To My Mother*, and finally the notorious *Edna*. Krimmie realized he was courting antagonism in allowing his first poems to be issued by the Bohemian sensation-monger; nor were there any financial considerations in the transaction. But they were things the new editors had rejected, and Krimmie, fairly weary of the ineffectual trips down to his mailbox, decided to give them away rather than wait forever for the recognition of editorial minds. Bruno was delighted with the poems. His florid speeches were such strange elements in Krimmie's experience, and he was so anxious to rid his desk of these things and get some perspective on them in cold type, that he resigned himself to Bruno's methods.

The sixteen mushrooms met with instantaneous disapprobation. The town guffawed over them, while columnists and their readers outvied one another in contriving grotesque parodies and vitriolic commentaries. Krimmie more or less enjoyed his sudden notoriety, though some of the attacks hurt him secretly. They ridiculed intimate confessions he had committed to paper in momentary moods of sorrow. In some curious way whose subconscious workings had developed a spirit of detachment, he was able to see his sorrows as the antics of a being somewhat foreign to himself. He expressed some of his moods in a mode of the frankest comedy, no matter how profound the suffering which had motivated the writing. He found this so-called comedy an egregiously difficult medium. It would have been easier to say outright how badly he was feeling. But this would not have taken into consideration the fact that he saw his suffering in relation to his surroundings. He recognized himself as only one of many egos struggling for room and recognition and, by a transference of the personal self to the worldly, achieved that aloofness which he felt to be the essence of the comic consciousness. He was not amazed, therefore, that people laughed at his mushrooms.

He would have liked it better had they reasoned about their laughter and analyzed the possible motives which had set him to playing with his emotions. But this would have been asking too much at once. There might come a time when readers would discover that there is nothing so tragic as comedy. Until that awareness arrived, he must be content with the impression his work had made and maintain the strictest silence no matter how tempting the provocation for saying something in his own defense. He derived considerable consolation from a laughing philosopher he happened to be reading. "We have more poets than judges and interpreters of poetry. It is easier to write than to understand." This was certainly as true of the America in which he was living as it was of the France of the era of Michel de Montaigne. He felt that he had no right to ask for more so early in a game so new to them all. . . .

—1925

Harold E. Stearns

(1891–1943)

Harold Stearns was a Harvard-educated journalist and critic who had worked on the Dial *magazine. Dissatisfied and frustrated by what he considered the slim opportunities for Americans to pursue a life in the literary arts, he assembled a group of mostly New Yorkers to offer their opinions on the topic. The result was the seminal* Civilization in the United States *(1922), which featured essays by some thirty writers including Lewis Mumford and Clarence Britten. By the time of its publication, Stearns had already left for Paris to join the contingent of Village exiles in the City of Light, a literary exodus that Malcolm Cowley called "a great migration eastward into new prairies of the mind." Stearns had lived in the Village for nearly four years, which he describes in this selection from* The Street I Know.

"When Greenwich Village Was Youth" from *The Street I Know*

Though it lasted almost four years—from just after the war started in Europe until eight months after we had entered it ourselves—my typical Bohemian existence of that time in Greenwich Village is not easy to recall either in detail or chronologically. For during all that period my nearest approach to a "regular" job was that of being a "salaried contributor" to the *New Republic*, and that

Harold Stearns. "When Greenwich Village Was Youth" from *The Street I Know* (New York: Lee Furman, Inc., 1935).

213

job, furthermore, did not materialize until after I had already been back home a couple of years. Of course, for some time before I got that particular job I had been contributing quite regularly to the magazine, and I sold an occasional article to other magazines or newspaper syndicates.

In a word, it was the characteristic pot-boiling existence of the time—except that I had few of the proper ingredients to put in the pot, even when I could find it. What I could do best was too special, perhaps too intellectual, for the kind of helter-skelter life of an occasional article here, a little piece or interview for a newspaper there, a book review somewhere else. I never could—and I didn't then—make a go of it; for I am a person, naturally, of pretty regular habits (above all, regular habits of work). If those habits are broken, or if I am not allowed to form them, I am miserable and unhappy. Yet somehow I managed to survive.

For I was still young; I was still flexible and adaptable. Occasionally I picked up the oddest kind of publicity jobs. I played poker well enough to make a profit on it with fair regularity—when there was any money in the crowd. Living was cheap, too—incredibly cheap, when compared with today's prices. There were days of hunger, it goes without saying, but there were windfalls, too. My girl—for I soon acquired one, of course—was a good fashion artist and made more than her share of what was needed to keep up the semblance of a menage, though as a matter of fact she lived out of town and "commuted," hence her contribution to the menage was more in the nature of a manager than a resident. She bought everything; she prepared some of my meals; she paid the bills and saw to it that I had new clothes when my old ones could not any longer be repaired—and all this, as if it were the most natural thing in the world. I made more than enough to cover my modest expenses, but there were occasional celebrations—at Polly's (the old one on West Fourth Street), and at the Brevoort. These celebrations my girl considered her share or, perhaps, her pleasure. I taught her French and history and English literature—so well, in fact, that later on she was able to edit trade magazines successfully and competently at really decent salaries. In fact, she can still do so today, and will almost proudly tell anybody, who might be so indiscreet as to ask her, that she was taught by me.

Many people have their own memory of Greenwich Village. Mine, at least, has the merit of being extensive. There was the old Boni bookshop on Macdougal Street, and there was the famous Liberal Club. There were the different corner saloons, especially the one at the corner of Sixth Avenue and Fourth Street (now an empty lot) where in the back room hung a photograph of a nude lady looking out through the blinds of the window of a darkened room. Eugene O'Neill and Art Young and Jack Reed (when he was in town) and Walter Franzen (whom we have lost) and Peggy Johns and Clara Tice and Thorne Smith and God knows how many of the others, some of them still living today (and some not), may even remember that picture. I hate to think of the number of drinks I have had at the table directly beneath it.

Polly's restaurant was then the real meeting-place, and some of the poker games that went on around the big table in the kitchen—after the restaurant was closed—still remain vivid in my memory. On occasion Barney Gallant [Holladay's business partner] would play, and I shall never forget how when—on a "bluff"—he was finally forced to call. "Well, what have you got?" asked Barney. "Aces," said his opponent. "How many?" demanded Barney. "One," confessed his opponent, starting to throw his hand away. Barney looked long and thoughtfully at his cards—"That wins," he said, and there was tragedy in his voice, though of course everybody else roared with delight. But it worked:—I mean, ever after that, whenever Barney *had* a good hand, nobody would believe it—and would pay high for the privilege of seeing himself beaten. Advertising pays, sometimes. "Sept" Wilson was really master of ceremonies at these poker games, and the way he would and could control the game—"Come on there, Shaky Bill," he would say, "make up your mind whether you've got a chance to fill that inside straight"—was an example of how far diplomacy could make invective agreeable.

Before I had acquired my girl, while the poker games were still going on—interspersed with contributions to the *New Repub-*

215

lic, the old *Seven Arts* magazine, reviews for the Boston *Transcript*, anything I could pick up—I lived for a time in an old rooming house on Greenwich Avenue. Walter Franzen, whom I had known in Cambridge my last year at Harvard, was a roommate of mine there for a time. Those were the days when the game room of the Lafayette was popular with everybody in the Village, as were the bar and restaurant of the Brevoort. In some respects the game room was more popular, for it was purely an after-dinner place for coffee and liqueurs and games and conversation; you could sit there and talk with the Villagers, both the successful and the indigent young hopefuls, without it costing very much. And on your way home, usually, you might "look in" at the Brevoort to see who was there also and who, by some miracle of selling a story, a picture, or an "idea," was for the moment solvent. Walter and I were often at the Lafayette together in those days.

Walter was a tall, young, handsome lad with a slight scar across his face, which, rather than detracting from his appearance, set in relief his fine, delicate features. In addition, he had one of the best minds—a gift of God, if ever there was one—I have known; it was quick, analytic, perceptive, and humorous. He had read a great deal—and in German and French as well as in English—but he always had retained consistently his own highly personal point of view. He had physical as well as intellectual courage, and he was not afraid of man or the devil, though in manner he was unassuming, almost self-deprecatory. Now as I look back on it, I do not wonder that he was so attractive to women; he combined genuine romantic qualities in a fashion to be encountered only once or twice in a lifetime.

Luckily, too, Walter was tolerant—he needed to be with me. The constant worry as to how to "get by" would be enough to make anyone jumpy and irascible, let alone one with a rather high-strung temperament, such as I was the unfortunate possessor of at that period. But Walter was merely amused when I got drunk one night, wandered out late onto Greenwich Avenue clad only in my underwear, and somehow found my way back to our room by climbing an old-fashioned fire escape. If I had missed my footing, or—what was more likely—mistaken the window and gone into the wrong room (they all looked alike), the consequences might have been quite other than comic. However, what bothered conventional people never bothered Walter—but goodbye to his friendship with you, if you lied to him, or if you made either scholarly or intellectual pretenses that you couldn't justify.

It was while living with Walter on Greenwich Avenue that I first met Charles Ashleigh—an English Jew, who, in spite of his conversational cleverness and personal charm, always gave me a slightly uneasy feeling, especially when he talked about the wrongs of the exploited laborers of the world, for Charlie's interest in "labor" was obviously debonair and unreal, as it so often is with a certain type of romanticist. (I mean, simply, real laborers have few illusions about their work; for the most part, despite it, and invariably will quit it, when they get the opportunity.) But Charles had done considerable "bumming"; he knew "the Jungles," Bill Haywood, and all the I.W.W. jargon of that period. Over and above that, he had considerable native intellectual power, and could understand—and quite frankly admire—anybody clearly and dramatically his intellectual superior, like Walter. Later on, Charlie paid dearly for his espousal of the cause of the workers, as he would put it. He was sentenced to a Federal prison along with the others in that famous and disgraceful I.W.W. case, where ten or fifteen years was considered mild punishment. But when reason came back, after the war, and all of them were pardoned, he returned to London. (Bill Haywood, you may recall, went to Russia, where he ate his heart out for a time trying to understand the whole business in a strange land among people whose language he couldn't speak and whose habits he couldn't understand.) Years later I met Charlie in Paris, over on a holiday from London, where he was editing a Communist sheet and having a good time. The memories of Leavenworth had faded; now that something much more extreme than the old I.W.W. idea was functioning in Russia and really working, Charlie was mellow and assured. We talked of "the old days" on the sidewalk café of the Dome that afternoon, but only once did we mention Walter—it was too painful for both of us that he was gone.

217

For in those early days on Greenwich Avenue Walter seemed too vital—too inevitably destined for great things instead of destined, as it turned out to be, for a mysterious death on the rocks below a cliff overlooking the sea in England. That he was adventurous and restless did not then seem at all strange to me. But if one wanted an indictment of modern education and modern civilization, I still believe that the fact that Walter Franzen was permitted to wander around New York, without finding any outlet for his great talents, would furnish a better indictment than all the Socialist orators have ever been able to draw up since before Debs. Sometimes, when discouraged at the difficulties always faced in this country by anybody trying to do honest and unbiased intellectual work, I think of Walter—and, if perhaps not all the bitterness, the discouragement goes. At least, I have been permitted to survive, though, perhaps, that is because I have not quite the same kind of courage he had. Or better luck.

Shortly after the spring had come in 1915 Walter was off again on one of his trips—this time to Canada and a lumber camp. And it was then I moved into a little room on Washington Place—the house is still there, but has been made over—only a few doors from where I was to be living later on that tragic January day when I received news of my wife's death. But I had not even met my future wife then, and the thought of marriage was far from my mind. Those were my Bohemian days—the truly Bohemian days. And even at this late date I find it impossible to look back upon them with anything like what many people might consider the proper degree of regret—I suppose they were wasted; I suppose I was "getting nowhere." But I'll be damned, if I am sorry for them. For in certain ways, due to that Bohemian experience I can never be "taken in" by conventional people in quite the same way as the average citizen, even if that involves, as Chesterton would inevitably point out, that you are often left out in the cold. Well, I have always preferred cold clearness to confused warmth—perhaps that is my one serious anti-social trait.

Before I could realize it, the summer of 1916 had swung into calendar reality—and it was then I had the strangest job of my whole career: The job of companion. Herbert Croly obtained it for me. I was to go out to Roslyn, Long Island, and more or less make myself somebody to talk to (and with) the elderly Mr. Bryce, the father of Mrs. Pinchot, now wife of the Governor of Pennsylvania. I was, of course, to live with and be one of the family—though I could come into town any time I liked. Croly advised me to go, saying that the social duties would not be onerous, which, in fact, they proved not to be. And rather to my surprise, Mr. Bryce, despite his age and obvious weakness, was intellectually quite alert—at least on certain subjects—and had a fund of reminiscences from his diplomatic career that were vastly entertaining and sometimes enlightening. At dinner, too, there were usually guests of political and social importance. Above all, it was the summer of 1916—the summer when the elder Roosevelt was denouncing Wilson as a pacifist—and with election coming on in the autumn, discussion was sometimes heated. "He kept us out of war" was a slogan that infuriated many who thought we ought to be in it, just as it pleased the fundamentally pacific American majority—indeed, as I look back on it now, I feel certain that that slogan re-elected Wilson, ironical as that may seem today. And doubly ironical, as it seemed after April, 1917, was the *then* popular song, "I Didn't Raise My Boy To Be a Soldier."

There were things I learned about the Long Island squire-archy during those summer months that I have never forgotten. One thing particularly impressed me—the democratic notion of social equality was all a sham with most of these people, especially when they didn't know it and talked loudest about their democratic sentiments. Another thing was their abysmal ignorance of American history and economic theory. Their whole life was anecdotal and really devoted to the serious task of avoiding being bored; and politics was just another form of diversion, as social service is often a form of diversion with other and less monetarily endowed people who have nothing to do with their time. A real aristocracy—I mean, a genuine one of blood—began to look terribly attractive to me after a few weeks on Long Island. Failing that, what we used to call "Bolshevism" with an accent of terror, seemed mighty good to me, too. In fact, anything looked good to me which was not like that pretentious and ignorant vulgarity, flattering itself with unctuous "liberal" sentiments. It was then that I learned to be suspicious of all people who have not at some time been hungry and cold— hungry and cold in the midst of plenty, because they *have* to be, not merely as a social service thrill-teaser.

During the summer I kept up my tutorial work with my girl—let us call her Felicia—by correspondence. I saw her, of course, whenever I came into town, but I made her do her work in French by herself and submit the results in writing regularly. She was reading, at my suggestion, Romain Rolland's "Jean Christophe" in the original, and certain chapters I made her translate, with explanatory notes as to why she chose certain English expressions and substituted one tense for another, or, sometimes, deliberately altered the tense in order to obtain an *equivalent* effect in English. My object was threefold: To introduce her to an important and interesting book, to make her familiar with narrative and descriptive French prose, and, finally, to give her some sense of the immense resources of our mother tongue. Part of her work, in addition to this, was a reading of the newspapers and preparation of summaries on topics I might choose— much as we see in *Time* these later days. Only, remember, *she* had to do it—it was not done for her. I forbade her to read the *Literary Digest* of any periodical that summed up the news, even going so far as to tell her to "lay off" the editorials in the *New Republic* (an occasional one of which I might write myself) and read only the frankly reportorial articles. Book reviews, too, were forbidden. "If you are not a perfect fool," I used to say to her, "all you want are publishers' bare announcements. You can go into any bookstore and in ten minutes tell for yourself—after all, you live in New York, where bookstores are handy."

Towards the end of that summer, Mr. Bryce had a bad heart attack—and it was obvious that what he needed was a doctor and not a companion. During my curious sojourn in the rich pastures of Roslyn I had met a Mrs. Cram—a strange, friendly, fluttery little woman of enormous goodwill, who interested herself in "causes" very much like that famous caricature depicted by Don Marquis in "The Almost Perfect State." But when I said goodwill, I meant it: She hated war and she hated exploitation of labor. There was a strike going on in the iron-ore mines on the Mesaba Range, near Duluth, Minnesota, which the I.W.W. were exploiting for their own purposes, and, if I remember correctly, Elizabeth Gurly Flynn was one of the chief "agitators." Anyway, Mrs. Cram asked me to go out and investigate for her—and if I could, write an article on the strike for the *New Republic*. As my work with Mr. Bryce was finished and nothing else engaged me beyond my occasional book reviews for that paper, I accepted and went.

That trip left three indelible impressions on my mind—first, of the unspeakable dreariness of those little industrial iron-mine towns out in the wilds of Minnesota, only a few miles from the border of Canada, where there were green woods, game, lakes, and natural loveliness; second, of Chicago itself during a record-breaking "heat wave," and third, of what sensuality might mean—from an experience in Chicago with a pretty young woman I had known only by sight before at the old Liberal Club in New York.

Even today, when I want to remind myself of what industrialism can do—I mean, of course, industrialism untempered by anything more gracious than a desire for all the profits going—I think of those ugly, dreary, desolate blights on the "open-pit" scarred earth of those iron towns near Duluth. I remember saying to myself then, "If civilization, after several centuries, has been able to bring into existence anything as ugly, hopeless, and cheap as this town, then it would have been a thousand times better had we remained in the pastoral state." I had seen ugly places in New England, like Lawrence and Lowell and Pawtucket and Brockton, but even at their worst, there was always something to redeem them—relatively speaking. But these iron towns near Duluth had nothing. The population, too, was something of a shock, for English was almost a foreign language among the people I encountered, that is to say, the strikers themselves or the workers, if you wish so to phrase it. I suppose it was something like the "Black Country" of industrial England—only I hadn't dreamed that it existed in my own country.

221

The more dramatic ironworkers' slums of industrial Pittsburgh were known to me, but at least they were alive. These towns, though they furnished the sinews of iron without which all our so called gracious living would collapse, were not dramatic and— except for this temporary strike, which was lost—were dead. I am glad I went, though. I knew for the first time what Socialist orators meant when they talked about "exploitation."

Returning through Chicago, I had a chance for my first and only interview with big, one-eyed Bill Haywood, whom—I must say—I liked enormously. I understood his power over men after five minutes' conversation, and I learned, too, as I have said elsewhere, what sabotage really meant. What I hadn't seen for myself on the iron range he told me and I knew that when I arrived back in New York I should have quite enough material for an article.

Also, I had my first experience, as I have already hinted, with real sensuality. It left an impression, a purely sensuous impression, almost as vivid as those we read about with startled shamefaced recognition in later adolescent years in the confessions of Rousseau. And here again I find our whole moralistic approach to such things not so much true or false as quite beside the point, and, when you come to analyze it, irrelevant. Morals, after all, are concerned with action in its social significance—they are not, or at least ought not to be, concerned with personal sensations that have no general implications. These are matters of psychological interest perhaps, as some people are more sensitive to music than are others. But I came back from Chicago a changed, in the deepest sense, a grown-up man. Intellectual, sensual, emotional naivete was gone forever.

The *New Republic* liked my article on the strike and the conditions in the iron mines, and featured it. Whether Mrs. Cram liked it or not I cannot say, or whether she thought she got her money's worth. Probably she did, for later on she asked me to help her to do some publicity work against war—yes, that was almost the phrase she used—at the rather indelicate period just following our own declaration, and I wrote a booklet for her on the civilian rights that soldiers still retained, despite being soldiers, in a democracy—

a booklet she had printed and distributed in draft camps, unless it was confiscated, which, had I been an officer, it certainly would have been, since it was subversive of any kind of discipline, although I seemed blissfully unaware of it just then—but that, after all, was a later period.

On my return from Chicago and the mines I took a little flat on Charles Street—not a stone's throw from the house in which I am living today. And in that house, until I again went to Chicago, this time to assume editorship of the *Dial,* I spent some of the happiest months of my life. The *New Republic* had at last put me on a regular salary, which, though small, enabled me to live modestly—together with the help of a few articles, here and there, for other magazines. Felicia took a small apartment in the same house, a floor above me, so that I had all the advantages, whatever they may be, of "living with" a girl, and at the same time of being independent and having a place of my own to which I could invite my friends occasionally for dinner. It was in that little Charles Street house that I brought up the famous cat, Mademoiselle Rabelaise, whom I had plucked out of the gutter at a tender age—an abandoned little pathetic dirty meauw. But she developed into a famous cat with a personality so strong and definite that I feel safe in saying that many people, like Alvin Johnson and Alfred Kuttner and George Soule, will remember her even to this day.

It was while living in that house that the memorable "close" election of 1916 took place—and I might as well confess that I, too, voted for Wilson. I fell for the "He kept us out of war" stuff, just as did so many others, though I had my suspicions, even at the start. The work on the *New Republic* was interesting at that time. I remember with enjoyment many of those late afternoon walks from the office on West 21st Street over to Sixth Avenue with Francis Hackett, Philip Littell, Walter Lippmann, Alvin Johnson, George Soule, Charles Merz, and the others. Littell was always good-natured, always amusing, and he was forever teasing Francis Hackett on his complete ignorance of any literature, even including his own, that is to say, Irish literature. But Francis didn't care and always came back with a good one in reply—I had the impression then that there was considerable affection between them. Walter, of course, was a little more stuffy and bowed down with the cares of the world, but even he would unbend occasionally long enough to laugh at one of Alvin Johnson's wisecracks—for Alvin had a merciless tongue, when he wanted so to use it. I think all of them looked upon me at the time as something of the "bad boy" of the office, and they refused—sometimes with a casualness that drove me to furious anger—to take any of my opinions seriously, but I think they all were fond of me rather than the reverse. I know that once Felicia and I worked for two days planning and scheming to serve a good dinner to Alvin Johnson the night he came to my little Charles Street apartment on my invitation.

No, those were happy days in Greenwich Village—perhaps the happier because we were all under the uneasy shadow of the war and vaguely felt that at any time it might reach out and draw us in, too. Walter Franzen had come back from his last adventure tour and was a frequent visitor. It was "boom" time, and even those who weren't making much money were always on the verge of doing so—and prices had not gone soaring either. Prohibition had not yet arrived to trouble anybody, though that, too, was ominous and in the wings ready to do its preposterous song and dance act. John Reed was doing some of his best reportorial work on the war; the Washington Square Players were beginning to function; Max Eastman and Art Young and the other of the *Masses* crowd were busy lambasting the life out of the war profiteers and capitalism in general—of course at a time when nobody cared. And for me, too, that period remains vivid, when otherwise it might become dim in memory, when I think of Florence Deshon, who was still alive, still so beautiful; she, too, would come to see me once in a while; Randolph Bourne was doing some of his freshest and most penetrating work; Floyd Dell was in New York, too, at work on his first novel. Who of that crowd can forget those evening meetings in Alyce Gregory's little apartment in Patchin Place?—where some of the wittiest and shrewdest conversation and comment of our day was to be heard almost any time?

Though I knew all about it, I have not mentioned the more pub-
licized and spectacular side of the Greenwich Village of those
days—the Pagan Rout balls at Webster Hall, characterized by nudity, intoxication, and the envy of rich "uptowners"; the spectacular performances of "Doris, the Dope"; the Sunday breakfast carni-
vals at the Brevoort; the hear-burnings of the young painters and
writers, many of whom have since become so famous that they actually repudiate their Bohemian days. Bobby Edwards was still
singing "Way Down South in Greenwich Village"; Thorne Smith
had not yet written a single one of his hilarious books; Jack Mac-
grath was seen by and known to everybody (what has happened to
him, too?); Clara Tice was doing her line drawings for the "flossy"
magazines and parading up the Avenue with her two famous grey-
hounds. I could go on indefinitely, but for those who remember the
old Village at all this will be enough to summon up a picture and a
recollection that they can themselves recreate. It has, to tell the
truth, struck me as curious that nobody has already done it in a
book, in spite of the fact that there have been several attempts.

I think it is because it is our lost youth, when the world was
young and amusing—that strange world before we entered the
war and became one of the great nations of the earth; the world
when "isolation" for us was a reality, at least as far as our feelings and hopes and memories could go. Sometimes I wish it
could come back.

—1935

Caroline F. Ware

(1899–1990)

In this seminal social history of Greenwich Village originally published in 1935, sociologist Caroline Ware examines the tension between the native American population and the subsequent generations that invaded the Village, from Irish and Italian immigrants and their children who swarmed the Village streets, to the "bohemians" with their disdain for traditional values and virtues.

"The Villagers"
from *Greenwich Village 1920–1930: A Comment on American Civilization in the Post-War Years*

Art and Sex as Avenues of Escape

During these years, the Village acted as a magnet which drew to it a wide variety of people with one quality in common, their repudiation of the social standards of the communities in which they had been reared. Here gathered in these years a whole range of individuals who had abandoned their home pattern in protest against its hollowness or its dominance, and had set out to make for themselves individually civilized lives according to their own conceptions. They had found the traditional Anglo-Protestant values inapplicable and the money drive offensive. In the Village, some sought to discover other positive values upon which to reconstruct a social system in America; many carried on those activities, especially artistic, which had little or no place in a civilization dominated either by the remains of the Calvinistic ethic or by the purely acquisitive impulse; an increasing proportion simply sought escape, and brought with them little negative values, throwing over more or less completely whatever smacked of 'Puritanism' or 'Babbittry'; the more serious sought some compromise which would enable them to avoid the features which they did not like, but to retain those which they consciously or unconsciously cherished.

The Village was not the only place where those who repudiated their traditions took refuge during these years. Although it was the most notorious of such places, its counterpart could be found in Chicago, San Francisco, and other large cities, and elsewhere in New York. Its notoriety did not make it unique, but only made it an advantageous point from which to observe the disintegration of old American culture in the post-War years in an acute, and, therefore, clearly visible form.

The Villager population, in 1930 and the years preceding it, included at one end of the scale those who cherished old American values, but found them so lost or submerged in the bourgeois world that they took refuge from the pressures of that world and sought the opportunity to re-create the old values in their own lives. At the other extreme were those who threw over altogether both the American and the bourgeois patterns and sought complete freedom, defiance, or escape in flight to Greenwich Village. In between these two elements was the great mass of Village residents whose repudiation of their background was only partial and who consequently presented various conflict situations where that which they had retained interfered with that which they had cast aside. The first of these groups was the one which discovered the

Village in its early, unsung days. The second gave it its reputation. The third made up by 1930 the largest element in its Villager population. Though these groups were not completely separated from each other, and lines between them were not hard and clear, they presented essentially distinct forms of adaptation and associated in groups which roughly followed these lines. All, however, shared certain basic common qualities which distinguished them both from their neighbors in that other social world and from their home communities—namely, a disregard for money values and for prestige based on either income or conspicuous expenditure, an awareness of some sort of cultural values, and tolerance of unconventional conduct even when their own habits were more constrained.

Unconventionality, especially in the matter of sex, was taken for granted, and attitudes ranged from tolerance of experimentation to approval rather than from condemnation to tolerance. The sober superintendents of 'respectable' apartment houses made no bones about enumerating 'girls and their fellers' among the occupants of their houses when trying to rent an apartment to a middle-aged lady. Villagers of conventional tastes were distinctly on the defensive in explaining to the interviewer that 'all the people in Greenwich Village aren't the kind that you expect to find. There are plenty of ordinary respectable people like us.' No one felt called upon to be on the defensive about the opposite type of conduct.

All types of Villagers were intensely individualistic in both their social relations and their point of view. Their social contacts were confined to more or less purposeful relations with those who had common interests. Independent of virtually all institutions and scorning the joining habit, taking full advantage of both the selectiveness and the anonymity which the city offered, they avoided the usual casual contacts with family, neighbors, or members of the same economic or social class and the relations growing out of institutional connections. Instead, they maintained individual ties with friends scattered all over the city. If they had professional or artistic interests, these were apt to furnish a basis for their social life. The pursuit of an avocation or common tastes in recreation brought others together.

It was not always easy or possible to make connections with those of common interests. In the early days of the Village, when numbers were few and most Villagers had common interests in art or social reform, it had been possible for newcomers to find their way, chiefly via eating-houses, into congenial company. As more people and more different types came in, newcomers could no longer count on falling in with congenial company. Yet at each stage in the Village's history some one group was identified with the locality and offered easy contacts to newcomers. In 1930, it was the pseudo-bohemians and especially the Lesbians, into whose group it was easily possible for strangers to find their way.

To trace the modification of traditional American behavior patterns during these years by means of any sort of statistical sample of Villagers would be impossible, because the essence of their effort at adjustments was its extreme individualism. Whereas among the other elements in the community it was usually possible to reconstruct the essentials of their social attitudes from a knowledge of certain parts, many of the Villagers had gone so far in their repudiation that their values followed no pattern. In the case of the young people in whom the Village abounded, moreover, there was no way of predicting their future, and their Village life was difficult to analyze without a knowledge of whether they would return to their small home communities, settle down to a bourgeois existence in the suburbs, make some successful form of city adaptation, or drift from bar to bar for the rest of their lives. As this community, like other city neighborhoods, furnished a refuge for many persons who were psychologically mal-adapted, a heavy overlay of psychological problems frequently obscured sociological implications of the position and attitudes of many Villagers.

—1935

Mabel Dodge

(1879–1962)

Born in Buffalo, Mabel Dodge arrived in New York with her estranged husband Edwin Dodge in 1912 and moved into a second-floor apartment at 23 Fifth Avenue. Den mother and muse to artists, she had already lived for several years in an Italian villa near Florence and was an old hand at the fine art of entertaining. In early 1913 she began hosting the first of her Wednesday evening gatherings. Some consider her apartment the most successful salon in American literary history. Dressed in a flowing silk gown and floppy hat, Dodge welcomed her famous guests into her large parlor. Everything was white: the ceiling, wallpaper, woodwork, porcelain chandelier, bearskin rug, and marble fireplace. Later, she moved to Taos, New Mexico, where she died in 1962.

"The Evenings"
from *Movers and Shakers: Intimate Memories*

Imagine, then, a stream of human beings passing in and out of those rooms; one stream where many currents mingled together for a little while.

Socialists, Trade-Unionists, Anarchists, Suffragists, Poets, Relations, Lawyers, Murderers, "Old Friends," Psychoanalysts, I.W.W.'s, Single Taxers, Birth Controlists, Newspapermen,

Mabel Dodge Luhan. *"The Evenings"* from *Movers and Shakers: Intimate Memories*, vol. 3 (New York: Harcourt Brace, 1933–1937).

Artists, Modern-Artists, Clubwomen, Woman's-place-is-in-the-home Women, Clergymen, and just plain men all met there and stammering in an unaccustomed freedom a kind of speech called Free, exchanged a variousness in vocabulary called, in euphemistic optimism, Opinions!

I kept meeting more and more people, because in the first place I wanted to know everybody and in the second place everybody wanted to know me. I wanted, in particular, to know the Heads of things. Heads of Movements, Heads of Newspapers, Heads of all kinds of groups of people. I became a Species of Head Hunter, in fact. It was not dogs or glass I collected now, it was people. Important People. I vaguely believed that anyone who reached eminence in the community, raised themselves above the level of others, and also individuality, difference, originality, any tendency that showed above the old tribal pattern. Each of these "leaders" brought his or her group along, for they had heard about the Evenings (by this time called a Salon) and they all wanted to come.

I had a little speech I made whenever I met a new, interesting person: "We're having an informal meeting of poets on Thursday at my house. If you or any of your friends are interested in Poetry, won't you come?" And they always did. Nearly always . . .

I sturdily maintained my attitude in letting It decide. I suppose I found this quite an easy way of solving the problem. And I would sit in the background and silently smile with a look of understanding printed on my face. I never uttered a word during my Evenings beyond the remote "How do you do?" or the low "Good-by."

I had a little formula for getting myself safely through the hours without any injury to my shy and suspicious sensibilities. As people flowed in, I stood apart, aloof and withdrawn, dressed in long, white dresses with maybe an emerald chiffon wrapped around me, and gave each one my hand—and a very small smile. It was the merest mask of cordiality—impersonal and remote. . . . "I hope you will come again if you enjoyed it."

Flushed and moist, with slightly disarrayed hair (often gray locks), with foggy spectacles ad quickened breath, those who, so they believed, said what they thought about things, wrung my unrevealing hands as they passed along. It was a wonderful new game, this Salon, and fired many people who had thought but hadn't the habit of saying what they thought, with a quite exciting sense of life.

—1933–1937

Hutchins Hapgood

(1869–1944)

Born in Chicago in 1869, Hutchins Hapgood received his bachelors degree from Harvard in 1892 and even taught at the university for a short time before realizing that the academic life was not for him. Moving to New York, he took up an offer from muckraker Lincoln Steffens to join the staff of the Commercial Advertiser, *where he wrote human interest stories and fraternized with the lower classes. Embracing the bohemian way of life, he valued good wine, the art of conversation, and sexual pleasures. He later worked for the* New York Morning Telegraph, *the* New York Evening Post, *the* New York Press, *and the* New York Globe. *Along with his wife, Neith Boyce, he wrote and acted in several plays by the Provincetown Players, including "Enemies," a portrayal of their troubled marriage. Despite his bohemian proclivities, he considered himself thoroughly Victorian, "a Victorian in the modern age."*

"The Stream of the World" from *A Victorian in the Modern World*

My old friend Hippolyte Havel, the anarchist philosopher, journalist, and bohemian whom I had met in Chicago years before when I was working with Anton Johannsen on *The Spirit of Labor*, had come to New York, and centering about his personality there

Hutchins Hapgood. "The Stream of the World" from *A Victorian in the Modern World* (New York: Harcourt, Brace, 1939).

appeared a little basement café on the west side of Washington Square. It was, I believe, the original of the later innumerable Village cafes. It was also Polly's first restaurant. But before it started I had just met Hippolyte again at a little apartment where two girls were living; one was Polly Holladay and the other was Rose Strunsky. Hippolyte and I were frequent visitors here, and I soon perceived that Polly and Hippolyte loved one another, and they started a menage together. Then came Hippolyte's idea of the little café-restaurant; his friends, among whom were Bavard Boyesen, Theodore Dreiser, and many others, patronized the place and it prospered. The little puzzled-looking gypsy from the real Bohemia of the old world, with his mass of waving black hair, was the life of the place. Polly's subsequent adventures in starting restaurants at which the faithful met, the growing crowd of Villagers, were always successful—particularly the one she had with Hippolyte in Provincetown the year the War broke out. For Greenwich Village is not so much a physical locality as a symbol of a new American Bohemia that appeared all over the country. Wherever a group of individuals—the men animated by a dislike of regular business or professional life, inclined toward the freedom of art and literature, the women of the same type, bored by some small place in the Middle West, the business office or domesticity, filled with restless ambition to lead their own lives—came together, there was the Village.

Hippolyte, although a fiery little man with a violent tongue and extremely jealous temperament, was yet honorable and responsible, when not drunk. As long as Polly had him as her right-hand man, she was at least fairly treated by her associate. But in the long list of her restaurant adventures, in which she showed great success in gathering the faithful around her, not by an means all of the men who helped her were as honorable as Hippolyte. Although they quarreled, she remained with him for some years. I remember vividly the first quarrel, when they were running the little café on the west side of Washington Square, Polly showed a vivid interest in some of the men who frequented her restaurant, and Hippolyte, although theoretically tolerant of other people's love affairs, was possessed of a surprising jealousy; so much so that he would frequently make terrible scenes in the restaurant, thus interfering with Polly's business. One night after the restaurant had closed I walked home with Polly to the little apartment where she and Hippolyte lived. On the way she bitterly complained of her lover. Her main grievance seemed to be that Hippolyte had not committed suicide. "He promised me," she said, "over and over again, but he just won't keep his word."

To show Hippolyte's great ability in promoting Bohemia let me tell of the day when he was sitting at the Brevoort with Baynard Boyesen and myself and suggested having a *Trimordeur* evening. I don't to this day know exactly what *Trimordeur* means, but Hippolyte meant by it the knights-errant of the spirit of wine and dance. He drew up a little paper, announcing a meeting of the Trimordeurs at an Italian restaurant on Mulberry Street for a certain evening. We sent postcards to many of our friends after having reserved the big room of the restaurant for our party. We had expected perhaps ten or fifteen people, but to our amazement there were at least seventy—not only those to whom we had sent cards but also their friends. There were plenty of antipasti, spaghetti, and red wine, even for the crowd, who so filled up the room that when we began dancing after dinner, we had to remove the tables and chairs. Then there was a dance, the first I ever saw, that was wholly a matter of spontaneous rhythm. The whole crowd was caught in it; it resembled the cellar-dances in the Dutch paintings of the seventeenth century, except the crowd was larger and the pattern more complex. There was no leader to give directions but, by natural right, Will Irwin among the men and Fanny Lehman, a little anarchist girl, took the lead. Fanny danced with all the fire of the coming Russian Revolution and Will Irwin was not behind in wild rhythmical abandon. I knew Irwin for many years, meeting him here and there among liberals, journalists, and especially suffragettes; but I never again got so strong an impression of his personality as when he led the dance of the Trimordeurs. At this meeting all the elements were perfect, typical of the Village that was beginning. There were writers, artists, journalists, liberals, suffragettes, feminists, some of them men and women; and there was especially another group who were merely women. And by that I don't mean any of the underworld or outcast groups, but women who belonged among the artists, the serious socially-minded, the writers; but who were themselves none of these; just women intended through their grace or imagination to be the cohesive element of human society.

There was one other meeting of the Trimordeurs, this time conducted by Theodore Dreiser. He sent out many more announcements but somehow the response wasn't nearly so great. The original Trimordeurs were there, of course, and a few others. But either the spirit had flown or Dreiser's personality, socially unimaginative, had introduced individuals who didn't combine in the movement of the whole.

—1939

Joseph Mitchell

(1908–1996)

Born in 1908 on a cotton and tobacco farm near Fairmont, North Carolina, Joseph Mitchell moved to New York in 1929 to work as a newspaperman. In 1930 he joined the Herald Tribune *and then shortly after jumped to* The World-Telegram *before bolting to* The New Yorker. *He stayed at the* New Yorker *until the early 1960s. Mitchell first wrote about Joseph Gould, the Village bohemian, in 1942 and again in 1964. Gould's life's work,* An Oral History of the World, *never truly existed. Mitchell describes Gould as "an ancient, enigmatic, spectral figure, a banished man. I never saw him without thinking of the Ancient Mariner or of the Wandering Jew or of the Flying Dutchman." Mitchell's* Up in the Old Hotel collection *consists of "McSorley's Wonderful Saloon" (1943), "Old Mr. Flood "(1948), "The Bottom of the Harbor" (1960), and "Joe Gould's Secret" (1965). Mitchell profile of Gould, "Profesor Sea Gull," originally appeared in the December 1942 issue of the* New Yorker *and made Gould an instant attraction. In 2000* Joe Gould's Secret, *a film directed and starring Stanley Tucci, based on the unusual friendship between Mitchell and Gould, was released. In 2001, Pantheon Books reissued two Mitchell collections,* My Ears Are Bent *and* McSorley's Wonderful Salon.

"Professor Sea Gull"

Joe Gould is a blithe and emaciated little man who has been a notable in the cafeterias, diners, barrooms, and dumps of Greenwich Village for a quarter of a century. He sometimes brags rather wryly that he is the last of the bohemians. "All the others fell by the wayside," he says. "Some are in the grave, some are in the loony bin, and some are in the advertising business." Gould's life is by no means carefree; he is constantly tormented by what he calls "the three H's"—homelessness, hunger, and hangovers. He sleeps on benches in subway stations, on the floor in the studios of friends, and in quarter-a-night flophouses on the Bowery. Once in a while he trudges up to Harlem and goes to one of the establishments known as "Extension Heavens" that are operated by followers of Father Divine, the Negro evangelist, and gets a night's lodging for fifteen cents. He is five feet four and he hardly ever weighs more than a hundred pounds. Not long ago he told a friend that he hadn't eaten a square meal since June, 1936, when he bummed up to Cambridge and attended a banquet during a reunion of the Harvard class of 1911, of which he is a member. "I'm the foremost authority in the United States," he says, "on the subject of doing without." He tells people that he lives on "air, self-esteem, cigarette butts, cowboy coffee, fried-egg sandwiches, and ketchup." Cowboy coffee, he says, is strong coffee drunk black without sugar. "I've long since lost my taste for good coffee," he says. "I much prefer the kind that sooner or later, if you keep on drinking it, your hands will begin to shake and the whites of your eyes will turn yellow." While having a sandwich, Gould customarily empties a bottle or two of ketchup on his plate and eats it with a spoon. The countermen in the Jefferson Diner, on Village Square, which is one of his hangouts, gather up the ketchup bottles and hide them the moment he puts his head in the door. 'I don't particularly like the confounded stuff," he says, "but I make it a practice to eat all I can get. It's the only grub I know of that's free of charge."

Gould is a Yankee. His branch of the Goulds has been in New England since 1635, and he is related to many of the other early New England families, such as the Lawrences, the Clarkes, and the Storers. "There's nothing accidental about me," he once said. "I'll tell you what it took to make me what I am today. It took old Yankee blood, an overwhelming aversion to possessions, four years of Harvard, and twenty-five years of beating the living hell out of my insides with bad hooch and bad food." He says that he is out of joint with the rest of the human race because he doesn't want to own anything. "If Mr. Chrysler tried to make me a present of the Chrysler Building," he says, "I'd damn near break my neck fleeing from him. I wouldn't own it; it'd own me. Back home in Massachusetts I'd be called an old Yankee crank. Here I'm called a bohemian. It's six of one, half a dozen of the other." Gould has a twangy voice and a Harvard accent. Bartenders and countermen in the Village refer to him as the Professor, the Sea Gull, Professor Sea Gull, the Mongoose, Professor Mongoose, or the Bellevue Boy. He dresses in the castoff clothes of his friends. His overcoat, suit, shirt, and even his shoes are all invariably a size or two too large, but he wears them with a kind of forlorn rakishness. "Just look at me," he says. "The only thing that fits is the necktie." On bitter winter days he puts a layer of newspapers between his shirt and undershirt. "I'm snobbish," he says. "I only use the *Times*." He is fond of unusual headgear—a toboggan, a beret, or a yachting cap. One summer evening he appeared at a party in a seersucker suit, a polo shirt, a scarlet cummerbund, sandals, and a yachting cap, all hand-me-downs. He uses a long black cigarette holder, and a good deal of the time he smokes butts picked up off the sidewalks.

Bohemianism has aged Gould considerably beyond his years. He has got in the habit lately of asking people he has just met to guess his age. Their guesses range between sixty-five and seventy-five; he is fifty-three. He is never hurt by this; he looks upon it as proof of his superiority. "I do more living in one year," he says, "than ordinary humans do in ten." Gould is toothless, and his lower jaw swivels from side to side when he talks. He is bald on top, but the hair at the back of his head is long and frizzly, and he has a bushy, cinnamon-colored beard. He wears a pair of spectacles that are loose and lopsided and that slip down to the end of his nose a moment after he puts them on. He doesn't always wear them on the street and without them he has the wild, unfocussed stare of an old scholar who has strained his eyes on small print. Even in the Village many people turn and look at him. He is stooped and he moves rapidly, grumbling to himself, with his head thrust forward and held to one side. Under his left arm he usually carries a bulging, greasy, brown pasteboard portfolio, and he swings his right arm aggressively. As he hurries along, he seems to be warding off an imaginary enemy. Don Freeman, the artist, a friend of his, once made a sketch of him walking. Freeman called the sketch "Joe Gould versus the Elements." Gould is as restless and footloose as an alley cat, and he takes long hikes about the city, now and then disappearing from the Village for weeks at a time and mystifying his friends; they have never been able to figure out where he goes. When he returns, always looking pleased with himself, he makes a few cryptic remarks, giggles, and then shuts up. "I went on a bird walk along the waterfront with an old countess," he said after his most recent absence. "The countess and I spent three weeks studying seagulls."

Gould is almost never seen without his portfolio. He keeps it on his lap while he eats and in flophouses he sleeps with it under his head. It usually contains a mass of manuscripts and notes and letters and clippings and copies of obscure little magazines, a bottle of ink, a dictionary, a paper bag of cigarette butts, a paper bag of bread crumbs, and a paper bag of hard, round, dime-store candy of the type called sour balls. "I fight fatigue with sour balls," he says. The crumbs are for pigeons; like many other eccentrics, Gould is a pigeon feeder. He is devoted to a flock which makes its headquarters atop and around the statue of Garibaldi in Washington Square. These pigeons know him. When he comes up and takes a seat on the plinth of the statue, they flutter down and perch on his head and shoulders, waiting for him to bring out his bag of crumbs. He has given names to some of them. "Come here, Boss Tweed," he says. "A lady in Stewart's Cafeteria didn't finish her whole-wheat toast this morning and when she went out, bingo, I snatched it off her plate especially for you. Hello, Big Bosom. Hello, Popgut. Hello, Lady Astor. Hello, St. John the Baptist. Hello, Polly Adler. Hello, Fiorello, you old goat, how're you today?"

Although Gould strives to give the impression that he is a philosophical loafer, he has done an immense amount of work during his career as a bohemian. Every day, even when he has a bad hangover or even when he is weak and listless from hunger, he spends at least a couple of hours working on a formless, rather mysterious book that he calls "An Oral History of Our Time." He began this book twenty-six years ago, and it is nowhere near finished. His preoccupation with it seems to be principally responsible for the way he lives; a steady job of any kind, he says, would interfere with his thinking. Depending on the weather, he writes in parks, in doorways, in flophouse lobbies, in cafeterias, on benches on elevated-railroad platforms, in subway trains, and in public libraries. When he is in the proper mood, he writes until he is exhausted, and he gets into this mood at peculiar times. He says that one night he sat for six or seven hours in a booth in a Third Avenue bar and grill, listening to a beery old Hungarian woman, once a madam and once a dealer in narcotics and now a soup cook in a city hospital, tell the story of her life. Three days later, around four o'clock in the morning, on a cot in the Hotel Defender, at 300 Bowery, he was awakened by the foghorns of tugs on the East River and was unable to go back to sleep because he felt that he was in the exact mood to put the old soup cook's biography in his history. He has an abnormal memory; if he is sufficiently impressed by a conversation, he can keep it in his head, even if it is lengthy and senseless, for many days, much of it word for word. He had a bad cold, but he got up, dressed under a red exit light, and, tiptoeing so as not to disturb the men sleeping on cots all around him, went downstairs to the lobby.

He wrote in the lobby from 4:15 A.M. until noon. Then he left the Defender, drank some coffee in a Bowery diner, and walked up to the Public Library. He plugged away at a table in the genealogy

241

room, which is one of his rainy-day hangouts, and which he says he prefers to the main reading room because it is gloomier, until it closed at 6 P.M. Then he moved into the main reading room and stayed there, seldom taking his eyes off his work, until the Library locked up for the night at 10 P.M. He ate a couple of egg sandwiches and a quantity of ketchup in a Times Square cafeteria. Then, not having two bits for a flophouse and being too engrossed to go to the Village and seek shelter, he hurried into the West Side subway and rode the balance of the night, scribbling ceaselessly while the train he was aboard made three round trips between the New Lots Avenue station in Brooklyn and the Van Cortlandt Park station in the Bronx, which is one of the longest runs in the subway system. He kept his portfolio on his lap and used it as a desk. He has the endurance of the possessed. Whenever he got too sleepy to concentrate, he shook his head vigorously and then brought out his bag of sour balls and popped one in his mouth. People stared at him, and once he was interrupted by a drunk who asked him what in the name of God he was writing. Gould knows how to get rid of inquisitive drunks. He pointed at his left ear and said, "What? What's that? Deaf as a post. Can't hear a word." The drunk lost all interest in him. "Day was breaking when I left the subway," Gould says. "I was coughing and sneezing, my eyes were sore, my knees were shaky, I was as hungry as a bitch wolf, and I had exactly eight cents to my name. I didn't care. My history was longer by eleven thousand brand-new words, and at that moment I bet there wasn't a chairman of the board in all New York as happy as I."

Gould is haunted by the fear that he will die before he has the first draft of the Oral History finished. It is already eleven times as long as the Bible. He estimates that the manuscript contains 9,000,000 words, all in longhand. It may well be the lengthiest unpublished work in existence. Gould does his writing in nickel composition books, the kind that children use in school, and the Oral History and the notes he has made for it fill two hundred and seventy of them, all of which are tattered and grimy and stained with coffee, grease, and beer. Using a fountain pen, he covers both sides of each page, leaving no margins anywhere, and his penmanship is poor; hundreds of thousands of words are legible only to him. He has never been able to interest a publisher in the Oral History. At one time or another he has lugged armfuls of it into fourteen publishing offices. "Half of them said it was obscene and outrageous and to get it out of there as quick as I could," he says, "and the others said they couldn't read my handwriting." Experiences of this nature do not dismay Gould; he keeps telling himself that it is posterity he is writing for, anyway. In his breast pocket, sealed in a dingy envelope, he always carries a will bequeathing two-thirds of the manuscript to the Harvard Library and the other third to the Smithsonian Institution. "A couple of generations after I'm dead and gone," he likes to say, "the Ph.D.'s will start lousing through my work. Just imagine their surprise. 'Why, I be damned,' they'll say, 'this fellow was the most brilliant historian of the century.' They'll give me my due. I don't claim that all of the Oral History is first class, but some of it will live as long as the English language." Gould used to keep his composition books scattered all over the Village, in the apartments and studios of friends. He kept them stuck away in closets and under beds and behind the books in bookcases. In the winter of 1942, after hearing that the Metropolitan Museum had moved its most precious paintings to a bombproof storage place somewhere out of town for the duration of the war, he became panicky. He went around and got all his books together and made them into a bale, he wrapped the bale in two layers of oilcloth, and then he entrusted it to a woman he knows who owns a duck-and-chicken farm near Huntington, Long Island. The farmhouse has a stone cellar.

Gould puts into the Oral History only things he has seen or heard. At least half of it is made up of conversations taken down verbatim or summarized; hence the title. "What people say is history," Gould says. "What we used to think was history—kings and queens, treaties, inventions, big battles, beheadings, Caesar, Napoleon, Pontius Pilate, Columbus, William Jennings Bryan—is only formal history and largely false. I'll put down the informal history of the shirt-sleeved multitude—what they had to say about their jobs, love affairs, vittles, sprees, scrapes, and sorrows—or I'll perish in the attempt." The Oral History is a great hodgepodge and kitchen midden of hearsay, a repository of jabber, an omnium-gatherum of bushwa, gab, palaver, hogwash, flapdoodle, and malarkey, the fruit, according to Gould's estimate, of more than twenty thousand conversations. In it are the hopelessly incoherent biographies of hundreds of bums, accounts of the wanderings of seamen encountered in South Street barrooms, grisly descriptions of hospital and clinic experiences ("Did you ever have a painful operation or disease?" is one of the first questions that Gould, fountain pen and composition book in hand, asks a person he has just met), summaries of innumerable Union Square and Columbus Circle harangues, testimonies given by converts at Salvation Army street meetings, and the addled opinions of scores of park-bench oracles and gin-mill savants. For a time Gould haunted the all-night greasy spoons in the vicinity of Bellevue Hospital, eavesdropping on tired interns, nurses, orderlies, ambulance drivers, embalming-school students, and morgue workers, and faithfully recording their talk. He scurries up and down Fifth Avenue during parades, feverishly taking notes. Gould writes with great candor, and the percentage of obscenity in the Oral History is high. He has a chapter called "Examples of the So-called Dirty Story of Our Time," to which he makes almost daily additions. In another chapter are many rhymes and observations which he found scribbled on the walls of subway washrooms. He believes that these scribblings are as truly historical as the strategy of General Robert E. Lee. Hundreds of thousands of words are devoted to the drunken behavior and the sexual adventures of various professional Greenwich Villagers in the twenties. There are hundreds of reports of ginny Village parties, including gossip about the guests and faithful reports of their arguments on such subjects as reincarnation, birth control, free love, psychoanalysis, Christian Science, Swedenborgianism, vegetarianism, alcoholism, and different political and art isms. "I have fully covered what might be termed the intellectual underworld of my time," Gould says. There are detailed descriptions of night life in scores of Villge drinking and eating places, some of which, such as the Little Quakeress, the Original Julius, the Troubadour Tavern, the Samovar, Hubert's Cafeteria, Sam Swartz's T.N.T., Eli Greifer's Last Outpost of Bohemia Tea Shoppe, do not exist any longer.

Gould is a night wanderer, and he has put down descriptions of dreadful things he has seen on dark New York streets—descriptions, for example, of the herds of big gray rats that come out in the hours before dawn in some neighborhoods of the lower East Side and Harlem and unconcernedly walk the sidewalks. "I sometimes believe that these rats are not rats at all," he says, "but the damned and aching souls of tenement landlords." A great deal of the Oral History is in diary form. Gould is afflicted with total recall, and now and then he picks out a period of time in the recent past— it might be a day, a week, or a month—and painstakingly writes down everything of any consequence that he did during this period. Sometimes he writes a chapter in which he monotonously and hideously curses some person or institution. Here and there are rambling essays on such subjects as the flophouse flea, spaghetti, the zipper as sign of the decay of civilization, false teeth, insanity, the jury system, remorse, cafeteria cooking, and the emasculating effect of the typewriter on literature. "William Shakespeare didn't sit around pecking on a dirty, damned, ninety-five-dollar doohickey," he wrote, "and Joe Gould doesn't, either."

The Oral History is almost as discursive as "Tristram Shandy." In one chapter, "The Good Men Are Dying Like Flies," Gould begins a biography of a diner proprietor and horse-race gambler named Side-Bet Benny Altschuler, who stuck a rusty icepick in his hand and died of lockjaw; and skips after a few paragraphs to a story a seaman told him about seeing a group of lepers drinking and dancing and singing on a beach in Port-of-Spain, Trinidad; and goes from that to an anecdote about a demonstration held in front of a moving-picture theatre in Boston in 1915 to protest against the showing of "The Birth of a Nation," at which he kicked a policeman; and goes from that to a description of a trip he once made through the Central Islip insane asylum, in the course of which a woman pointed at him and screamed, "There he is! Thief! Thief! There's the man that picked my geraniums and stole my mamma's mule and buggy"; and goes from that to an account an old stumble-bum gave of glimpsing and feeling the blue-black flames of hell one night while sitting in a doorway on Great Jones Street and of seeing two mermaids playing in the East River just north of Fulton Fish Market later the same night; and goes from that to an explanation made by a priest of Old St. Patrick's Cathedral, which is on Mott Street, in the city's oldest Little Italy, of why so many Italian women always wear black ("They are in perpetual mourning for our Lord"); and then returns at last to Side-Bet Benny, the lock-jawed diner proprietor.

Only a few of the hundreds of people who know Gould have read any of the Oral History, and most of them take it for granted that it is gibberish. Those who make the attempt usually bog down after a couple of chapters and give up. Gould says he can count on one hand or on one foot those who have read enough of it to be qualified to form an opinion. One is Horace Gregory, the poet and critic. "I look upon Gould as a sort of Samuel Pepys of the Bowery," Gregory says. "I once waded through twenty-odd composition books, and most of what I saw had the quality of a competent high-school theme, but some of it was written with the clear and won-derful veracity of a child, and here and there were flashes of hard-bitten Yankee wit. If someone took the trouble to go through it and separate the good from the rubbish, as editors did with Thomas Wolfe's millions of words, it might be discovered that Gould actu-ally has written a masterpiece." Another is e. e. Cummings, the poet, who is a close friend of Gould's. Cummings once wrote a poem about Gould, No. 261 in his "Collected Poems," which con-tains the following description of the history:

> . . . *a myth is as good as a smile but little joe gould's quote oral history unquote might (publishers note) be entitled a wraith's progress or mainly awash while chiefly submerged or an amoral morality sort-of-aliveing by innumerable kind-of-deaths*

Throughout the nineteen-twenties Gould haunted the office of the *Dial*, now dead, the most highbrow magazine of the time. Fi-

nally, in its April, 1929, issue, the *Dial* printed one of his shorter essays, "Civilization." In it he rambled along, jeering at the buying
and selling of stocks as "a fuddy-duddy old maid's game" and referring to skyscrapers and steamships as "bric-a-brac" and giving
his opinion that "the auto is unnecessary." "If all the perverted ingenuity which was put into making buzz-wagons had only gone
into improving the breed of horses," he wrote, "humanity would
be better off." This essay had a curious effect on American literature. A copy of the *Dial* in which it appeared turned up a few
months later in a second-hand bookstore in Fresno, California, and
was bought for a dime by William Saroyan, who then was twenty
and floundering around, desperate to become a writer. He read
Gould's essay and was deeply impressed and influenced by it. "It
freed me from bothering about form," he says. Twelve years later,
in the winter of 1941, in Don Freeman's studio on Columbus Circle, Saroyan saw some drawings Freeman had made of Gould for
Don Freeman's Newsstand, a quarterly publication of pictures of odd
New York scenes and personalities put out by the Associated
American Artists. Saroyan became excited. He told Freeman about
his indebtedness to Gould. "Who the hell is he, anyway?" Saroyan
asked. "I've been trying to find out for years. Reading those few
pages in the *Dial* was like going in the wrong direction and running into the right guy and then never seeing him again." Freeman
told him about the Oral History. Saroyan sat down and wrote a
commentary to accompany the drawings of Gould in *Newsstand*.
"To this day," he wrote, in part, "I have not read anything else by
Joe Gould. And yet to me he remains one of the few genuine and
original American writers. He was easy and uncluttered, and almost all other American writing was uneasy and cluttered. It was
not at home anywhere; it was trying too hard; it was miserable; it
was a little sickly; it was literary; and it couldn't say anything simply. All other American writing was trying to get into one form or
another, and no writer except Joe Gould seemed to have imagination enough to understand that if the worst came to the worst you
didn't need to have any form at all. You didn't need to put what
you had to say into a poem, an essay, a story, or a novel. All you

had to do was say it." Not long after this issue of *Newsstand* came out, someone stopped Gould on Eighth Street and showed him Saroyan's endorsement of his work. Gould shrugged his shoulders. He had been on a spree and had lost his false teeth, and at the moment he was uninterested in literary matters. After thinking it over, he decided to call on Saroyan and ask him for help in getting some teeth. He found out somehow that Saroyan was living at the Hampshire House, on Central Park South. The doorman there followed Gould into the lobby and asked him what he wanted. Gould told him that he had come to see William Saroyan. "Do you know Mr. Saroyan?" the doorman asked. "Why, no," Gould said, "but that's all right. He's a disciple of mine." "What do you mean, disciple?" asked the doorman. "I mean," said Gould, "that he's a literary disciple of mine. I want to ask him to buy me some teeth." "Teeth?" asked the doorman. "What do you mean, teeth?" "I mean some store teeth," Gould said. "Some false teeth." "Come this way," said the doorman, gripping Gould's arm and ushering him to the street. Later Freeman arranged a meeting, and the pair spent several evenings together in bars. "Saroyan kept saying he wanted to hear all about the Oral History," Gould says, "but I never got a chance to tell him. He did all the talking. I couldn't get a word in edgewise."

As long as he can remember, Gould has been perplexed by his own personality. There are a number of autobiographical essays in the Oral History, and he says that all of them are attempts to explain himself to himself. In one, "Why I Am Unable To Adjust Myself to Civilization, Such As It Is, or Do, Don't, Do, Don't, A Hell Of A Note," he came to the conclusion that his shyness was responsible for everything. "I am introvert and extrovert all rolled in one," he wrote, "a warring mixture of the recluse and the Sixth Avenue auctioneer. One foot says do, the other says don't. One foot says shut your mouth, the other says bellow like a bull. I am painfully shy, but try not to let people know it. They would take advantage of me." Gould keeps his shyness well hidden. It is evident only when he is cold sober. In that state he is silent, suspicious, and constrained, but a couple of beers or a single jigger of gin will untie his tongue and put a leer on his face. He is extraordinarily responsive to alcohol. "On a hot night," he says, "I can walk up and down in front of a gin mill for ten minutes, breathing real deep, and get a jag on."

Even though Gould requires only a few drinks, getting them is sometimes quite a task. Most evenings he prowls around the saloons and dives on the west side of the Village, on the lookout for curiosity-seeking tourists from whom he can cadge beers, sandwiches, and small sums of money. If he is unable to find anyone approachable in the tumultuous saloons around Sheridan Square, he goes over to Sixth Avenue and works north, hitting the Jericho Tavern, the Village Square Bar & Grill, the Belmar, Goody's, and the Rochambeau. He has a routine. He doesn't enter a place unless it is crowded. After he is in, he bustles over to the telephone booth and pretends to look up a number. While doing this, he scrutinizes the customers. If he sees a prospect, he goes over and says, "Let me introduce myself. The name is Joseph Ferdinand Gould, a graduate of Harvard, *magna cum difficultate*, class of 1911, and chairman of the board of Weal and Woe, Incorporated. In exchange for a drink, I'll recite a poem, deliver a lecture, argue a point, or take off my shoes and imitate a sea gull. I prefer gin, but beer will do." Gould is by no means a bum. He feels that the entertainment he provides is well worth whatever he is able to cadge. He doesn't fawn, and he is never grateful. If he is turned down politely, he shrugs his shoulders and leaves the place. However, if the prospect passes a remark like "Get out of here, you bum," Gould turns on him, no matter how big he is, and gives him a shrill, nasal, scurrilous tongue-lashing. He doesn't care what he says. When he loses his temper, he becomes fearless. He will drop his portfolio, put up his fists, and offer to fight men who could kill him with one halfhearted blow. If he doesn't find an audience on the trip up Sixth, he turns west on Eleventh and heads for the Village Vanguard, in a cellar on Seventh Avenue South. The Vanguard was once a sleazy rendezvous for arty people, but currently it is a thriving night club. Gould and the proprietor, a man named Max Gordon, have known each other for many years and are on fairly good terms much of the time. Gould always hits the Vanguard last. He is sure of it, and he keeps it in reserve. Since it became prosperous, the place annoys him. He goes down the stairs and says, "Hello, Max, you dirty capitalist. I want a bite to eat and a beer. If I don't get it, I'll walk right out on the dance floor and throw a fit." "Go argue with the cook," Gordon tells him. Gould goes into the kitchen, eats whatever the cook gives him, drinks a couple of beers, fills a bag with bread crumbs, and departs.

Despite his shyness, Gould has a great fondness for parties. There are many people in the Village who give big parties fairly often. Among them are a rich and idiosyncratic old doctor, a rich old spinster, a famous stage designer, a famous theatrical couple, and numbers of painters and sculptors and writers and editors and publishers. As often as not, when Gould finds out that any of these people are giving a party, he goes, and as often as not he is allowed to stay. Usually he keeps to himself for a while, uneasily smoking one cigarette after another and stiff as a board with tenseness. Sooner or later, however, impelled by a drink or two and by the desperation of the ill at ease, he begins to throw his weight around. He picks out the prettiest woman in the room, goes over, bows, and kisses her hand. He tells discreditable stories about himself. He becomes exuberant; suddenly, for no reason at all, he cackles with pleasure and jumps up and clicks his heels together. Presently he shouts, "All in favor of a one-man floor show, please say 'Aye'!" If he gets the slightest encouragement, he strips to the waist and does a hand-clapping, foot-stamping dance which he says he learned on a Chippewa reservation in North Dakota and which he calls the Joseph Ferdinand Gould Stomp. While dancing, he chants an old Salvation Army song, "There Are Flies on Me, There Are Flies on You, but There Are No Flies on Jesus." Then he imitates a sea gull. He pulls off his shoes and socks and takes awkward, headlong skips about the room, flapping his arms and letting out a piercing caw with every skip. As a child he had several pet sea gulls, and he still spends many Sundays on the end of a fishing pier at Sheepshead Bay observing gulls; he claims he has such a thorough understanding of their cawing that he can translate poetry into it.

"I have translated a number of Henry Wadsworth Longfellow's poems into sea gull," he says.

Inevitably, at every party Gould goes to, he gets up on a chair or a table and delivers some lectures. These lectures are extracts from chapters of the Oral History. They are brief, but he gives them lengthy titles, such as "Drunk as a Skunk, or How I Measured the Heads of Fifteen Hundred Indians in Zero Weather" and "The Dread Tomato Habit, or Watch Out! Down with Dr. Gallup!" He is skeptical about statistics. In the latter lecture, using statistics he claims he found in financial sections in newspapers, he proves that "the eating of tomatoes by railroad engineers was responsible for fifty-three per cent of the train wrecks in the United States during the last seven years." When Gould arrives at a party, people who have never seen him before usually take one look at him and edge away. Before the evening is over, however, a few of them almost always develop a kind of puzzled respect for him; they get him in a corner, ask him questions, and try to determine what is wrong with him. Gould enjoys this. "When you came over and kissed my hand," a young woman told him one night, "I said to myself, 'What a nice old gentleman.' A minute later I looked around and you were bouncing up and down with your shirt off, imitating a wild Indian. I was shocked. Why do you have to be such an exhibitionist?" "Madam," Gould said, "it is the duty of the bohemian to make a spectacle of himself. If my informality leads you to believe that I'm a rum-dumb, or that I belong in Bellevue, hold fast to that belief, hold fast, hold fast, and show your ignorance."

Gould is a native of Norwood, Massachusetts, a suburb of Boston. He comes from a family of physicians. His grandfather, Joseph Ferdinand Gould, for whom he was named, taught in the Harvard Medical School and had a practice in Boston. His father, Clarke Storer Gould, was a general practitioner in Norwood. He served as a captain in the Army Medical Corps and died of blood poisoning in a camp in Ohio during the First World War. The family was well-to-do until Gould was about grown, when his father invested unwisely in the stock of an Alaska land company. Gould says he went to Harvard only because it was a family custom. "I did not want to go," he wrote in one of his autobiographical essays. "It had been my plan to stay home and sit in a rocking chair on the back porch and brood." He says that he was an undistinguished student. Some of his classmates were Conrad Aiken, the poet; Howard Lindsay, the playwright and actor; Gluyas Williams, the cartoonist; and Richard F. Whitney, former president of the New York Stock Exchange. His best friends were three foreign students—a Chinese, a Siamese, and an Albanian.

Gould's mother had always taken it for granted that he would become a physician, but after getting his A.B. he told her he was through with formal education. She asked him what he intended to do. "I intend to stroll and ponder," he said. He passed most of the next three years strolling and pondering on the ranch of an uncle in Canada. In 1913, in an Albanian restaurant in Boston named the Scanderbeg, whose coffee he liked, he became acquainted with Theofan S. Noli, an archimandrite of the Albanian Orthodox Church, who interested him in Balkan politics. In February, 1914, Gould startled his family by announcing that he planned to devote the rest of his life to collecting funds to free Albania. He founded an organization in Boston called the Friends of Albanian Independence, enrolled a score or so of dues-paying members, and began telegraphing and calling on bewildered newspaper editors in Boston and New York City, trying to persuade them to print long treatises on Albanian affairs written by Noli. After about eight months of this, Gould was sitting in the Scanderbeg one night, drinking coffee and listening to a group of Albanian factory workers argue in their native tongue about Balkan politics, when he suddenly came to the conclusion that he was about to have a nervous breakdown. "I began to twitch uncontrollably and see double," he says. From that night on his interest in Albania slackened.

After another period of strolling and pondering, Gould took up eugenics. He has forgotten exactly how this came about. In any case, he spent the summer of 1915 as a student in eugenical field work at the Eugenics Record Office at Cold Spring Harbor, Long Island. This organization, endowed by the Carnegie Institution, was

engaged at that time in making studies of families of hereditary de-
fectives, paupers, and town nuisances in several highly in-bred
communities. Such people were too prosaic for Gould; he decided
to specialize in Indians. That winter he went out to North Dakota
and measured the heads of a thousand Chippewas on the Turtle
Mountain Reservation and of five hundred Mandans on the Fort
Berthold Reservation. Nowadays, when Gould is asked why he
took these measurements, he changes the subject, saying, "The
whole matter is a deep scientific secret." He was happy in North
Dakota. "It was the most rewarding period of my life," he says.
"I'm a good horseman, if I do say so myself, and I like to dance and
whoop, and the Indians seemed to enjoy having me around. I was
afraid they'd think I was batty when I asked for permission to
measure their noggins, but they didn't mind. It seemed to amuse
them. Indians are the only true aristocrats I've ever known. They
ought to run the country, and we ought to be put on the reservations." After seven months of reservation life, Gould ran out of
money. He returned to Massachusetts, and tried vainly to get funds
for another head-measuring expedition. "At this juncture in my
life," he says, "I decided to engage in literary work." He came to
New York City and got a job as assistant Police Headquarters reporter for the *Evening Mail*. One morning in the summer of 1917, after he had been a reporter for about a year, he was basking in the
sun on the back steps of Headquarters, trying to overcome a hangover, when the idea for the Oral History blossomed in his mind. He
promptly quit his job and began writing. "Since that fateful morning," he once said, in a moment of exaltation, "the Oral History has
been my rope and my scaffold, my bed and my board, my wife and
my floozy, my wound and the salt on it, my whiskey and my as-
pirin, and my rock and my salvation. It is the only thing that matters a damn to me. All else is dross."

Gould says that he rarely has more than a dollar at any one time,
and that he doesn't particularly care. "As a rule," he says, "I despise money." However, there is a widely held belief in the Village that he is rich and that he receives an income from inherited

property in New England. "Only an old millionaire could afford to go around as shabby as you," a bartender told him recently. "You're one of those fellows that die in doorways and when the cops search them their pockets are just busting with bankbooks. If you wanted to, I bet you could step over to the West Side Savings Bank right this minute and draw out twenty thousand dollars." After the death of his mother in 1939, Gould did come into some money. Close friends of his say that it was less than a thousand dollars and that he spent it in less than a month, wildly buying drinks all over the Village for people he had never seen before. "He seemed miserable with money in his pockets," Gordon, the proprietor of the Vanguard, says. "When it was all gone, it seemed to take a load off his mind." While Gould was spending his inheritance, he did one thing that satisfied him deeply. He bought a big, shiny radio and took it out on Sixth Avenue and kicked it to pieces. He has never cared for the radio. "Five minutes of the idiot's babble that comes out of those machines," he says, "would turn the stomach of a goat."

During the twenties and the early thirties Gould occasionally interrupted his work on the Oral History to pose for classes at the Art Students' League and to do book-reviewing for newspapers and magazines. He says there were periods when he lived comfortably on the money he earned this way. Burton Rascoe, literary editor of the old *Tribune*, gave him a lot of work. In an entry in "A Bookman's Daybook," which is a diary of happenings in the New York literary world in the twenties, Rascoe told of an experience with Gould. "I once gave him a small book about the American Indians to review," Rascoe wrote, "and he brought me back enough manuscript to fill three complete editions of the Sunday *Tribune*. I especially honor him because, unlike most reviewers, he has never dogged me with inquiries as to why I never run it. He had his say, which was considerable, about the book, the author, and the subject, and there for him the matter ended." Gould says that he quit book-reviewing because he felt that it was beneath his dignity to compete with machines. "The Sunday *Times* and the Sunday *Herald Tribune* have machines that review books," he says. "You put a book in one of those machines and jerk down a couple of levers and a review drops out." In recent years Gould has got along on less than five dollars in actual money a week. He has a number of friends—Malcolm Cowley, the writer and editor; Aaron Siskind, the documentary photographer; Cummings, the poet; and Gordon, the night-club proprietor, are a few—who give him small sums of money regularly. No matter what they think of the Oral History, all these people have great respect for Gould's pertinacity.

Gould has a poor opinion of most of the writers and poets and painters and sculptors in the Village, and doesn't mind saying so. Because of his outspokenness he has never been allowed to join any of the art, writing, cultural, or ism organizations. He has been trying for ten years to join the Raven Poetry Circle, which puts on the poetry exhibition in Washington Square each summer and is the most powerful organization of its kind in the Village, but he has been blackballed every time. The head of the Ravens is a retired New York Telephone Company employee named Francis Lambert McCrudden. For many years Mr. McCrudden was a collector of coins from coin telephones for the telephone company. He is a self-educated man and very idealistic. His favorite theme is the dignity of labor, and his major work is an autobiographical poem called "The Nickel Snatcher." "We let Mr. Gould attend our readings, and I wish we could let him join, but we simply can't," Mr. McCrudden once said. "He isn't serious about poetry. We serve wine at our readings, and that is the only reason he attends. He sometimes insists on reading foolish poems of his own, and it gets on your nerves. At our Religious Poetry Night he demanded permission to recite a poem he had written entitled 'My Religion.' I told him to go ahead, and this is what he recited:

> *'In winter I'm a Buddhist,*
> *And in summer I'm a nudist.'*

And at our Nature Poetry Night he begged to recite a poem of his entitled 'The Sea Gull.' I gave him permission, and he jumped out of his chair and began to wave his arms and leap about and scream, 'Scree-eek! Scree-eek! Scree-eek!' It was upsetting. We are serious poets and we don't approve of that sort of behavior." In the summer of 1942 Gould picketed the Raven exhibition, which was held on the fence of a tennis court on Washington Square South. In one hand he carried his portfolio and in the other he held a placard on which he had printed: "JOSEPH FERDINAND GOULD, HOT-SHOT POET FROM POETVILLE, A REFUGEE FROM THE RAVENS, POETS OF THE WORLD, IGNITE! YOU HAVE NOTH-ING TO LOSE BUT YOUR BRAINS!" Now and then, as he strutted back and forth, he would take a leap and then a skip and say to passers-by, "Would you like to hear what Joe Gould thinks of the world and all that's in it? Scree-eek! Scree-eek! Scree-eek!"

—1942

Floyd Dell

(1887–1969)

Born in Barry, Illinois, and raised in Quincy, Illinois, and Davenport, Iowa, Floyd Dell was the quintessential young Midwesterner who left his hometown to seek fortune and fame back East. Like many young men of his time, he chose to settle in Greenwich Village. First, though, he cut a literary swath in Chicago. As editor of the influential Friday Literary Review, *he created what many considered one of the finest literary outlets in Chicago. In the teens he moved to New York where he joined the staffs of the* Masses *and, later, the* Liberator. *A celebrated novelist, critic, editor, poet, and playwright, Dell wrote more than twenty books, several plays, and an autobiography,* Homecoming. *The epitome of the Modern Man, he was a proponent of free love and an advocate of several Greenwich Village "isms": feminism, socialism, and Freudianism.*

"Rents Were Low in Greenwich Village"

Rents were low in Greenwich Village; that was why artists and writers lived there. This was explained to me on my arrival, in 1913, by one of my Village "aunts." In Greenwich Village, as in every small community, there were "aunts" who were familiar with Village history, knew all about everyone, and, kindly but severe, were intent upon maintaining community standards. I, a favorite but wayward nephew, was called on the carpet more than

Floyd Dell. "Rents Were Low in Greenwich Village," *American Mercury*, December 1947.

once by my Village "aunts." The one I have here in mind was a leading member of the Village intelligentsia, who disapproved of the "bohemian riff-raff" which even then threatened to give that nice little community a bad name.

But first about the low rents. As New York expanded swiftly in the nineteenth century, the middle-class residents of lower Manhattan fled uptown and out of town, leaving behind them blocks of substantially built brick houses, four stories high, to be inhabited by immigrants. The immigrant flood spread northward as far as Washington Square. The houses on the north side of the Square still maintained their aristocratic dignity, but those on the south side became part of a swarming Italian district.

It was artists and writers, I was told, who halted the northward march of immigrant poverty. They leased some of the grimy old houses on Washington Square and fixed up studios and homes in them, with a kitchen and bathroom on each floor. Artists and writers are bold and fearless carpenters, plumbers and interior decorators. Italian sub-landladies also did some modernizing, but the rents remained low because there was no central heating.

There were fireplaces in those large high-ceilinged rooms; coal and wood were brought by Nick from his cellar around the corner. Italian restaurants, where food was good, cheap and plentiful, became the social centers of artists, writers, and intelligentsia. A bohemia grew up there in the eighties and nineties, long referred to as "Washington Square" though it spread northwest into Greenwich Village, a neighborhood of narrow and crooked streets that remained a secluded island between the great streams of traffic. It was the painters, with their traditional disregard of middle-class standards, who made it a bohemia, celebrated as such by Bliss Carman and Richard Hovey in *Songs from Vagabondia*.

Those authentic bohemian glories had faded out before I came there. The oldtime bohemians, it was said, had prospered, become stuffed shirts, and moved uptown. Anyway, times had changed in the Village. Its best people were now seriously interested in social reform, votes for women, the labor movement—and, of course, in art and literature, especially the kinds devoted to social progress.

I was warned not to use the term "bohemian" in Greenwich Village circles; if I did, I would be scorned and pitied, if not ostracized. So said my earnest Village "aunt." The *real* Villagers, she pointed out, paid their bills and bathed regularly. That was certainly true. And why not? Those Greenwich Villagers were schoolteachers, college professors, social workers, doctors, lawyers, engineers and other professional people. As for the artists and writers who then lived in the Village—such as John Sloan and Art Young, Mary Heaton Vorse, Inez Haynes Gillmore, Susan Glaspell, Theodore Dreiser—they already had positions of importance in the realm of art and letters. None of those Villagers were what I called poor; some of them owned houses in the country, in Westchester County, in Connecticut, New Jersey, or on the Massachusetts coast. They had most of the familiar middle-class virtues, and in addition some of their own; they were an obviously superior lot of people.

I, a newcomer believed to be a young fellow of promise, was kindly welcomed into the Village, and was soon provided with a part-time editorial job which left me considerable freedom for my own literary work. If I burned the midnight oil and kept out of the idle company of what my earnest Village "aunt" referred to as "bohemian riff-raff," I might in due time make a name for myself, assist the upward march of humanity and own a house in the country.

But already, in my first few days, I had had some glimpses of the bohemian side of life in Greenwich Village; and it had allured and charmed me. This Village bohemia was composed in part of young people, economically insecure with uncertain or unproved talents—or with perhaps no real talents, but only artistic temperaments. Who could say? They depended chiefly on hack jobs and precarious free-lancing. Their work habits were not always good, their money habits were sometimes rash and careless. These bohemian circles were adorned and fringed by very attractive young women, who no doubt should have been getting themselves married to rising young businessmen back in their home towns but were unreasonably fond of the company of artists and writers of dubious prospects.

To me this bohemia seemed a place where improbable and delightful things could happen. And so, I found, they did, for, in spite of my good standing in the more sedate circles of the Village, I found myself drawn into bohemian life. This was in part a matter of economics. My editorial earnings long remained the same, while the cost of living—it was during World War I—rose steadily. There were periods when I was out of a job and dependent on the irregular and uncertain gains of free-lancing. I barely managed to keep my head above water; I was one of the intellectual proletariat, sure enough.

However, nobody ever starved in Greenwich Village. Some Villager restaurateurs made a point of keeping their patrons fed in their periods of hard luck; and one could always get a bountiful free lunch with a five-cent glass of beer at a saloon which we called the Working Girls' Home, where once the poet John Masefield had worked between voyages.

My tastes were simple, and if there had been no girls in Greenwich Village I could have lived there almost as inexpensively as Thoreau did in his cabin on Walden Pond. That was the worst of having little money: I hadn't much to spend on girls. But when my finances were low I could always take a girl for a ride on the Staten Island ferry, from which at night the skyscrapers with their occasional lighted windows looked magically beautiful. Or I could take her for a ride on top of a Fifth Avenue bus, stopping at a little restaurant at 110th Street, where there was good coffee with real cream in it at five cents a cup. Often I was able to stand her a spaghetti dinner with red ink. Sometimes I would take her to Broad's, on Third Street, where there was sawdust on the floor and where we would have big thick juicy steaks that cost all of sixty cents apiece. Or I would appear at her place with a paper bag filled with such a delicatessen as salami, pickles, cheese and crackers, plus a bottle of milk, which is very nourishing. And, of course, when I was flush, I would take her to a bang-up dinner in the basement of the Brevoort. Food in Greenwich Village ranked high as a form of entertainment. In addition, we had conversational resources.

When my fortunes were at their worst, I was lucky enough to get an apartment in a house at 11 Christopher Street. This was not one of the fine old brick residences, but a tiny little two-story wooden house, a relic of times long past. My ground-floor apartment cost eight dollars a month; later, I moved into the larger apartment upstairs, which cost twelve dollars. There was a cold-water tap, but no bathroom and no electric light and no furnace. Years later, in the middle twenties, when I was homesick on the French Riviera, I was told by a tourist friend that my old Christopher Street house had been razed that summer; the past came back vividly to my mind, and I wrote a sentimental ballad beginning

> Is it still there, I wonder, down in Chris-
>   topher Street,
> That little rickety house of ours where
>   life was young and sweet?

When I arrived in the Village, its intelligentsia was socially dominant, social reform was its keynote, and it was expanding to take in Union Square. But the wartime years turned the Village into a melting pot in which all group boundaries were dissolved. Artists, writers, intellectuals, liberals, radicals, IWW's, bohemians, well-to-do patrons, onlookers—all were hurled into a miscellaneous social melee in which earnestness and frivolity were thoroughly intermingled. The "real" Greenwich Village of my discriminating "aunt" was swept away in the flood. I had something to do with this transformation. I helped in organizing a series of fancy-dress balls to which I gave the name "Pagan Rout," and I wrote and produced frivolous one-act plays. Fancy-dress balls and amateur theatricals are notoriously effective in provoking social disorder.

All was not beer and skittles in my own career; as literary and dramatic critic, essayist, writer of short stories, special articles, plays and poems, I burned a good deal of midnight oil, and my writings attracted the attention of a couple of publishers who wanted to know when I would have a novel ready. I was working, by fits and starts, on a novel, *Moon-Calf*, which progressed slowly. There are sometimes more important things in life than finishing a novel, especially when one is under thirty.

I might have had time to finish that novel if there had been no girls. I myself was shy and unsocial and did not care for parties and balls. But girls seemed to like to go to parties and balls; and so I took them. I found that a few drinks made me feel less shy and more sociable. A thousand or so people seem to remember me as the fellow who shinnied up a lofty iron pillar to the ceiling of Webster Hall and unscrewed a pocketful of electric light bulbs; but I think it must have been Harry Kemp. Anyway, being somewhat conspicuously on view on public occasions of a frivolous kind, I was taken by some outsiders as a "merry Villager." Heaven knows, perhaps I was. The world was plunging through the horrors of war, and I was writing light-hearted little plays about young lovers—in one of which Edna St. Vincent Millay, a young newcomer to the Village, made her debut charmingly as an actress. The future, for all of us, was uncertain; and the more darkly uncertain it became, the higher rose the tide of gaiety in Greenwich Village.

Drafted, I went to camp, cheerfully prepared to help save the world for democracy, but was sent back to stand trial, along with Jack Reed, Max Eastman and Art Young, on a charge of attempting to overthrow the government by writing an article in defense of conscientious objectors. The government wanted us sent to prison for twenty years.

Midnight of revel
And noondays of song—

that was what Greenwich Village had been like, back in the gay nineties, as described in *Songs from Vagabondia*. Something had happened to the world since then—even to bohemia. Politics had made a conquest of the ivory towers of art and literature. As for me, I belonged to the neo-Aristotelian school of aesthetics which holds that "certainly the world should be reformed: but not by novels." My novel was still unfinished. If I went to prison for twenty years, I would have lots of time to finish it; there would be no girls to distract me there. Perhaps it was just as well that I had gone a-Maying while I had the chance.

Peace came, and it was considered that the Republic might survive even with us subversive characters at large. Flowers covered the battlefield, and many May days lay ahead for living lads and lasses. But I was thirty-one, an age when one should begin to consider one's future. There was that novel of mine, waiting to be finished, and a publisher hopefully expecting it.

Yes, I thought I must sit down and finish that novel. But a girl with yellow hair came into the Village—and I felt that the novel must wait. I took the girl for a ride on the Staten Island ferry, and to a steak dinner at Broad's. She was much too lovely and companionable a girl to be allowed to marry any rising young businessman, so I talked her into marrying me. This was a rash proceeding on my part, and still more rash on hers, for my worldly prospects were dubious in the extreme. That, however, did not deter her. A courageous girl. Well, she had a good job, and perhaps felt able to afford the luxury of a bohemian husband. She proposed to support our *menage* while I finished my novel, but I made other financial arrangements, laid off from my job for three months, and rewrote and finished that long-delayed book. It sold quite a lot of copies, and we bought a house in the country. And now here we are, with two tall sons not long out of uniform. Yet it seems only yesterday that I met that girl in Greenwich Village. As I wrote in a sonnet on our silver wedding anniversary—

> The war was over—and upon the edge
> Of doom the world could lie down and
>   forget;
> The ruined rampart was a flowering hedge,
> And life was sweet the year when first
>   we met.

After the First World War, the uptowners discovered Greenwich Village. Then the United States discovered it. Greenwich Village became known throughout the world. The time had come when America had to have a bohemia of its own, and this was it. People wanted to live in bohemia, every cellar and garret in the Village was rented, and up went the rents. Sightseeing buses came to the Village. Village restaurants provided Village atmosphere for their uptown customers, with some phony Villagers on exhibit.

Dignified ex-Villagers like me deplored this crass commercialization of the Village. In a magazine article I pronounced a funeral oration over the Village. For this I was bitterly reproached by a Village friend whose real-estate business was, he thought, threatened by my sinister utterances; and I was laughed at by other Village friends, who asked: "Dost think, because thou has turned Puritan, there shall be no more cakes and ale?"

Far be it from me to say anything against cakes and ale. But what about rents? Bohemias must be based on low rents in a blighted residential area of a large city which is a cultural center; at least, the oldtime kind of bohemia was so based. There might be a bohemia of some kind in the nice new houses of a low-cost public housing project—but it would not be the same.

For one thing, in a public housing project there would be a lot of children around. Children are very nice to have around, I think; but not in a bohemia. They would interfere seriously with bohemian love affairs.

Maybe the new-fangled bohemias of our socialized future will be better than the old bourgeois private enterprise bohemias—more sanitary, more orderly, equipped with all the modern improvements. But I think of 11 Christopher Street—

> A Japanese print and a candlestick with
> candles burning bright,
> Curtain-folds of sunny gold at windows
> left and right,
> A couch with tattered tapestry, a cig-
> arette-scarred table,
> A view from either window of an alley
> and a stable—

That was nice, too, in its oldtime way. Inconvenient, to be sure: outside toilet, baths in the kitchen sink; candlelight and kerosene lamps, wood for the little fireplace brought in a sack by Nick from around the corner. Ah well, we can't have everything.

The Greenwich Village of Theodore Dreiser, Eugene O'Neill and Edna St. Vincent Millay, of John Reed and John Sloan and Art Young, of George Cram Cook and Frank Shay, has not, it seems, receded into the mists of the past. It has become a part of American cultural history, and it has a ghostly existence, I hear, as a Tradition which the Villagers of today devoutly cherish. Golly! Well, we in our day had a Tradition, too. When we stood at the bar in the Working Girls' Home, we thought of John Masefield. In Carmine Street we thought of Edgar Allan Poe. And there were other Great Old Villagers of the past—but we were too busy living our own lives to think much about the past.

As for the future of Greenwich Village, I always expected it to be rebuilt as a modern residential quarter in which people would live in complete indifference to its bohemian past. "It will not matter to them in the least," I wrote,

> if out of the dust and grime
> Impossible beauty flamed and flowered,
>   once upon a time.
> If a boy and a girl for a year and a day
>   laughed bravely at despair,
> No one will know in Christopher Street,
>   and certainly none will care.

Well, why should they care? Those lovers of today and tomorrow, bohemian or bourgeois, ought to be much too deeply occupied with their own love affairs to be thinking about some old love affair back in the preatomic past. To all such lovers, present and future, I benevolently offer the good wishes expressed in my Christopher Street ballad:

> And so may all dear lovers that are starved
>   for love's delight
> Find rest and peace, and food and fire,
>   and a kind bed at night.

And low rents—may they find those, too. But when will they? And how can American literature flourish without low rents?

Young people still go to the Village, and, it is said, find it a romantic and enchanting place. It is picturesque; even the phoniness is picturesque, to them. What is there about Greenwich Village, anyway? What has it got that the home town hasn't got?

In Greenwich Village it is all right for people to be interested in the kinds of poetry and art and music that they like, and they can say out loud what they really think, even about foreign policy. And it seems to be a place where improbable and delightful things can happen—for which I firmly decline to take the consequences. It is their Greenwich Village, not mine, and their responsibility entirely.

—December 1947

Milton Klonsky

(b. 1921–1981)

Born in 1921 in New York, Milton Klonsky attended Brooklyn College and Columbia University. He has been a formidable figure on the Village scene for many decades and is the author of William Blake: The Seer and His Visions *(1977) and* Shake the Kaleidoscope: A New Anthology of Modern Poetry *(1973). In this important piece, he reviews Village life past and present in the wake of the Great Depression and the end of World War II.*

"Greenwich Village: Decline and Fall"

> *Rabbi Joseph ben Shalom of Barcelona maintains that in every change of form, in every transformation of reality, or every time the status of a thing is altered the abyss of Nothingness is crossed. . . . Nothing can change without coming into contact with this region of pure absolute Being which the mystics call Nothing. . . . It is the abyss which becomes visible in the gaps of existence.*
>
> —Gershom Scholem

Once last summer I was crossing north on Sheridan Square, thinking of nothing; suddenly the green light turned red, and there, dodging in the middle of traffic with me, I caught sight of a man whose face was so blotched, pitted, and scabbed by disease that, modestly (having been ravished before by so many obscene stares), he cast his eyes down with the refined coquetry of a beautiful woman. Where did he come from? And what was he doing out there in the broil of midday?—this phantom escaped from the undermind! When I reached the curb, I looked for him up and down the seven streets that radiate from the hub of the Square. But he had already disappeared, leaving behind him only a euphonious after-image which, even now still burns and holds its shape. What a laugh if this image of mine were his only claim to being—yet I chose to regard him with a straight face.

Now in the rational light uptown, on 14th Street, which is cut off from the Village like the Ego from the Id, I would have seen him for what he was. "There is the world dimensional," as Hart Crane called it, "for those untwisted by the love of things irreconcilable." But downtown, everything obvious is immediately suspect: obviously, the most hidden secrets are dressed in the loudest fashion, if you know what I mean. Even the streets of Greenwich Village have so many twists, dead end gaps, trailing ends, and sudden inspirations out of blank walls that it sometimes is years of free association to find your way around.

There is no straight way. Nobody there to be tagged—you're it! Intellectuals without glasses, poets in business suits, gynanders and androgynes, the shapes and figures blur and metamorphose like the images of a dream. *Come out from behind that beard! Ovid, old Roman spy, you haven't changed, who do you think I think you are—Sigmund Freud?*

Where was I? I was standing on Sheridan Square one night waiting for the electric horse on Jack Delaney's marquee to jump over the neon stile. But just as the lights turned, I saw, out of the corner of my eye, a drunk walk on his hind legs like a dog, stagger, fall on all fours, and heave up on the street. One of the Bleecker Street Goths who hang around this neighborhood pushed him from behind with his foot so that he slumped face down in his own stew. When he tried to jack himself up on his elbows, he was shoved down again, even harder than before. Standing there, I identified myself so closely with the poor croak that it was almost as though I had been kicked, and I who was sprawled out on the street with my head in vomit. But I knew it would be dangerous to interfere, so I swallowed my disgust and walked diagonally away across the Square.

Wherever you go you run into these young toughs, the "internal proletariat" of the Village, each one of them with a little fuse of violence smoldering under his shirt. They issue every night from the ranges of ulcerous tenements along Bleecker, Christopher, Macdougal, Sullivan, etc. in order to escape from the squalor of immigrant family life in crowded cold-water flats. Since the "nice" girls of the neighborhood are called in by their parents before the long Village night is even half over, they are forced to gather on the corners by themselves in male packs. Then to see Othello walking hand in hand with Desdemona, or the lay sodalities of fairies (a caricature of themselves), makes them ache with jealousy. They even grudge the sexual freedom of the Village artists and intellectuals who, like themselves, are barred from the commercial mills uptown. But here at least the artist and the conscientious objector to American culture have some sort of status. The Goths have none. Therefore, the drunk must eat his vomit.

Sometimes I'd come across them pitching coins against the wall of the Christopher Street poolroom and then, while the next pitch was held up until I passed, they'd look me over. *Was I a Jew? How did I do? Did I show any fear? What was I doing here?* Their philosophy is as hard as the cement under their feet. Everything is a racket; the game of life is to beat the racket; and anyone who says no is a liar or a sucker. Their true heroes are the bookies, the prizefighters, and the racketeers who once rose out of their own ranks and now operate the Nite Clubs and park their Cadillacs in front of the poolroom. One question they can never figure out, and so what never fails to impress them, is this: why anyone with a chance to play for the blue chips uptown, or why any girl born with a privileged face, should choose to live in these slums? And every year they see new recruits coming down.

The Village attracts its own from every state of the mind: some for the faded romance of La Vie Boheme; some to be free of their parents; some out of acedia or wanhope; some to trade in free love; some for art's sake; some because they are zebras on the white plains; some to hide from their failure; some because they'd rather be in Paris; some to do something about it; some for a change of mind or heart—but almost all to escape from the stunning heat and light and noise of the cultural mill grinding out the mass values of a commercial civilization.

But not all who live in the Village are at home there. There are also writers, private secretaries, dancers, copy writers, actors, illustrators, and musicians on the make, who come down from the provinces to be close to the Big Time and leave as soon as they can. Graduates of the toney Eastern colleges for women such as Vassar, Bennington, Bryn Mawr, and the rest comprise one of the steadiest sources of recruits. But after a brief flurry of excitement and uplift, these also dry up fast like summer rain. And then there are the fellow-travelers of Bohemia, whose home base may be anywhere at all, but who keep up with the Village line through the auspices of friends. Not to mention an etceterogeneous muster of characters for whom any classification would be inherently contradictory.

The places where all these people live range from the plush and marble apartment hotels on the Gold Coast of lower Fifth Avenue to the cold-water tenements with communal toilets and no baths that once housed the masses of immigrant workers at the beginning of the century. Here and there a few of the old type of one-family brick houses still stand, relics of the Henry James and Lillian Russell era when Washington Square and its environs was the hub of New York society. Most of these have been split into two or three-room flats, each one inhabited by its own colony of extraordinarily sensitive roaches with long delicate, trembling wands and Hamlet-like refinements of indecision, a breed peculiar to the Village. The interiors are furnished in a style which, through the years, has become almost as standardized as Bronx Department Store Gothic or Terre Haute monde moderne: chairs and tables and couches wavering between junk and the antique like the houses themselves; framed reproductions of Rouault's "The Old King" or Picasso's "Woman in White" or that picture by Henri Rousseau of a lion in the moonlight sniffing the feet of a sleeping gypsy; floors painted red, yellow, green, brown; collapsible shelves loaded with books on psychiatry, books of modern poetry, books of prints by the Paris school, some second-hand or inherited, but most of them borrowed and never returned; and so on. With only minor changes, it is recognizable as the period style formed at the end of the First World War—the time Greenwich Village first became self-conscious—and reflects all the nostalgia for those good old days.

As seen from the foxhole perspective of the Village during the 20's, America was a No Man's Land, the haunt of the Cyclops. Only in Europe could the good life be found:

> *Là, tout n'est qu'ordre et beaute,*
> *Luxe, Calme, et Volupté.*

The boulevards of Paris were as crowded with Villagers as Washington Square in the Spring.

By the 30's, the spiritual homeland had shifted a thousand miles to the East amid the gilded domes and cupolas of the first Workers' State. (It was at this time, incidentally, that young Jewish intellectuals from the outlying boroughs of New York entered the Village as a group.) The depression fell like an incessant damp, cold and miserable and everywhere. What remained of the enthusiasm of the 20's was sublimated into political passion: Dionysius was reborn as Nicolai Lenin. And, conversely, the café and speakeasy society of those days was transformed into cafeteria society—Life Cafeteria. Stewart's, the Waldorf—where, until far in the night, the history and destiny of mankind was measured out with coffee spoons. To the Bleecker Street Klans on the other side, who sat in the steam of tobacco smoke and watched these tables seethe and boil with Marxist pronunciamentos, appeals, denunciations, charges, and countercharges, all this talk and all this fervor were just so much sucker bait.

Still, in those first years the marriage of bohemian freemasonry and the camaraderie of the WPA was almost perfect. The open collar and the grimy pants served both as well. But afterwards the foundations of this union split so wide (corresponding to the political divorce in the Workers' State itself) that, when the bastard Stalinist type appeared with his slogans, his cast-iron frame of mind, his dog faith, and his carefully cultivated mediocrity, it was a shock to recall his parentage. And the radical splinter groups that followed with the perpetual cries of "Rape!" and their tedious apocalypses—what could be expected from them?

By the end of the 30's Lenin's mummy had begun to stink.

Not the Revolution, but the Great War itself—that was the apocalypse so much dreaded and so long anticipated it was almost a relief when it came. Greeting, "Bababadalgharaghtakamminarronnkonbronntonneronnntuonnthunntroavarawnskawntoohoohoodenenthurnuk," James Joyce said. But ah, those days of innocence! O lost Arcadia! I never saw many drooping fawns and dying swans. The war put a stop to all that. And nothing could ever be the same any more.

While the war was going on, every night in the Village was Saturday night. Soldiers and sailors of all the Allied armies jammed the bars and the main streets of Greenwich Village hunting for a wild time. But then time was gone. With the moral dikes broken everywhere, and the whole country engulfed by the flood, the Village, strangely enough, was left high and dry. All the tabooed "dirty" words had been rubbed clean by everyday use. Of course there was as much freedom in the Village as before; but since this was equaled and even surpassed by Main Street, where was the defiance and the revolt against convention which, previously, had been the spur? The celebrated Village campaign for sexual independence had ended in a strange victory: free love was driving the professionals off the streets. And the baby-faced V-girls walking arm in arm with sailors down Broadway were wearing their mothers' high heels. In this situation, only the operators of the honky-tonks on Sheridan Square and in the side alleys made sure, somehow, that the sinister reputation of Greenwich Village was preserved.

The good old days when nobody had a job and nobody cared were over. Even the panhandlers who wander down to the Village from the "smoke" joints on the Bowery would touch artists and intellectuals on the street who were never good for a nickel before. And now that there was so much money around, apocryphal stories of the Depression were revived with nostalgia: how this musician had split his personality and collected four paychecks from the WPA music project as a string quartet; how someone else had lived off the Waldorf Cafeteria for a year by demanding a free cup of hot water for a second cup of tea without buying the first, and then, by pouring in enough ketchup, had brewed a thick bowl of tomato soup on his table, etc., etc. But for the majority of the Villagers, rejected by the Army on psychoneurotic grounds, the slush money to be had uptown was irresistible; and, without too much loss of face, some erstwhile bohemians were even able to join the great herd shoving at the trough. This was not altogether a betrayal of principle. It was, I think, a means for absolving the secret guild of not being in uniform. For them the despair within had at last been equaled by the hysteria without, thus providing a precarious common ground for a *modus vivendi*. But a return later on to the past life was almost impossible, as most had, in the meantime, contracted a new apartment, an analyst, a wife, or other expensive habits.

Perfect circles of friends drifted apart and disappeared like smoke rings. And one by one the old hangouts were lost. George's Bar (the ancestor of the San Remo today) was taken over completely by sailors and their quail; and even the last remaining forum of cafeteria society, the Waldorf, fell to the Bleecker Street Goths, who now had it almost completely terrorized. Boredom followed everywhere you went: boredom, barroom hysteria, confessions regretted by morning, cracked marriages, affairs over in a week, violence for reasons forgotten during the violence. . . . Then the war suddenly ended.

After the block parties and the parades under the Arch, it was wry to see the new recruits to the Village come down expecting to find the Golden Age of the 20's or the Silver Age of the 30's, but hardly prepared for this, the Age of Lead. Morale was worse than in the army. It was impossible to rent an apartment without "pull" or a great deal of cash. Through their GI loans, some managed to open new bookshops with a room in the back: and there you could see them sitting all day and part of the night surrounded by second-hand books and piles of old literary magazines—*Partisan Review, Kenyon, Sewanee, View*, etc.—chatting with friends and customers most of whom came to see rather than to buy. A dull business, once the edge had worn off.

What they had dreamed while regimented in the army was a vision of the palmy days of Paris Bohemia with a slight admixture of the American Frontier—but by now, alas! the Left Bank had been eroded by sentiment, and the frontier had contracted to the five senses of the individual. The underground names and passwords of a generation ago were already shopworn, with the new ones kept under the counter. It was also harder to break into certain Village cliques by mere brilliant talk and the flash of personality alone. Somehow the crass slogan of American business—"How much does he make?"—had been taken over by the Village: "Where does he show?"—"What has he published?"—the bark of an official dog. Artists and the poets did their "work" like everybody else.

During the war, Greenwich Village had been exposed as never before to the total glare of American mass culture, a light that had long blinded everyone with excess of light. Then, with the liberation of Paris, came the first influx in five years of the new paintings by Picasso (with their cartoon shapes) as well as work by Braque, Bonnard, and young French painters such as Dubuffet; the poetry of Eluard and the cryptograms of Queneau; and, most astonishingly, the Existentialist philosophy of Sartre and Camus, which drew heavily for its examples on the tough-guy heroes of American fiction and gangster movies. The anticipation was nothing compared to the letdown. And when European artists and writers again came to America, guided by their customary arrogance toward the natives, they were given a close look. They were like us—only smaller, fussier, dingier, and even (O Ghost of Henry James!) more innocent of the facts of life. Despite all their bitter experience, they had not yet been through the mill of a total commercial civilization—and that was the Real Distinguishing Thing. Their day and night were not ours.

Europe had already probed the nerve ends of modern art to the points of their most exquisite attenuations, from Mallarme to Proust, from Redon to Mondrian. By seeking to re-barbarize their own culture through American jazz, movies, comic strips, etc., European artists and intellectuals had in the end redirected America up its own alley. (A final irony is that, even in this, America is still following the lead of Europe.) But now there was no turning back.

In the past, these debased forms of popular culture had been something to be poked with a long stick. Now that they had acquired such foreign respectability, their very coarseness was subtly admired. O Polyhymnia, sacred slut, sing for us (if you don't mind) of the furious drives of Dick Tracy, L'il Abner, and Moon Mullins struggling in their boxed and aimless worlds; and of the shadowy Olympus of Hollywood where the old forms of Greece are overthrown by a mechanical Prometheus; and of the soap dramas on the radio where the drabness and stupidity of life is celebrated, and the movements of the bowels are announced with trumpets. . . . Maybe the old alienation of artists and intellectuals in America could be adjusted by a common bondage. Maybe this was the way out at last. But even if this were true, the sad fact remains that a way out is not necessarily a way in, nor is "culture" a revolving door.

The way of alienation is the Jew's badge of Greenwich Village, a way apart that orients itself by negation. Life here is the ghetto life, indrawn, with its own tastes and smells, rank and dark and protected as an armpit. The native loneliness of Americans is so intensified in the Village that, paradoxically, it becomes a social cement that holds it together. For what is feared even more than alienation from American life is self-alienation, the loss of identity in the melting pot reduction to the lowest common denomination of dollar and cent values. It is from this fear that Greenwich Village protects its own. Under cover of the most ideal persuasion of self-denial, there is always a private need.

The radical movement of the 30's was engaged not only with politics but with more personal considerations; political parties were places where you met and made your friends. And the same function was served by the arty societies of the 20's. But times change—now's now and then was then.

Free and easy love in the Village is a thing of the past. The night wanderer from bar to bar searching for the rare encounter finds only wanderers like himself, always on the prowl, always restless, never satisfied. The more intellectual can spend hours sitting in the gas chambers of the New School, bored to extinction, but hoping to meet a true friend in such cultured atmosphere. The fairies are the most driven, their nervous cruises down 8th Street, 4th Street, the Park, and back again are like a man pacing up and down a room. And even when all these find what they want and still want it, the gossip spreads so fast, the Who's Had Who in the Village is faithfully compiled—although nobody cared enough to snoop before—that a lasting relationship is rare.

If the most common single event in this erotic life of Man during the past century has been the gradual disappearance of animals from the cities and farms, then the next—although probably there is no connection—has been the emergence of Woman in the rank of full and equal partner. Women in the Village are often as aggressive as the men, who are inclined to be somewhat backward as a result. The illusion of emancipation, however, satisfies most. On the corner of Greenwich and 6th Avenue stands the House of Detention, or jug, for women which hides its grim interiors behind the façade of an apartment house—even numbered, 10 Greenwich Avenue: a demure symbol and monument of the suffrage movement. Like the men of Greenwich Village, women here suffer from the fact that love is not an immolation of the self, but the proof of it: *Copulo ergo sum*. And those phrases and movements which once supplied additional proof are no longer viable.

Without any unifying political or artistic center, the Village has fragmented into small groups who go to the same parties, hold the same views, and know each other too well. The Society of Neurotics undergoing Psychoanalysis is the only one present with something of the old catholicity, yet with this important difference: it is a secret society, and the membership is hidden even from those who belong. Still, there is a connection. And it takes only a minute of those who are, or who have been, or will be analyzed to smell one another out. First, a shy query: Have you been analyzed? Then: How many years? And next: Who is he? How much does he charge? And then: What party?—Freudian, Reichian, Horneyan, Jungian? This last question is charged, and the wrong answer can explode any further conversation.

For when the political cliques of the 30's lost their passion and died, they never really died but rose to the bosom of the Father and were strangely transmogrified. Psychoanalysis is the new look, *Sartor Resartus*, wrote the body underneath is the same.

A competent analyst can read their minds from a book by Freud, which is what some of them become after two or three years on the couch. The desperation, however, is real. Looking into themselves, they've seen the Gorgon. It does no good to pat its ugly snout, or to feed it lump sugar. The monster hides deep inside covered by the muck of the undermind and with its eyes always open. In order to charm it to sleep, or to pierce its heart by a sharper insight, they lie on the psychoanalytic couch in a dark room with Perseus on his rocker behind them, his pen in hand, taking notes. *O why was I born with a different face? Why can't I find a lover? or a job? or a friend? Why don't people admire me? Why do I hate the sound of clocks? Why can't I dream? Why can't I get up in the morning? Why do I bite my toenails? Why don't you ever say anything? O tell me it's true and it's not true! Show me the open way! Make me feel that everything will be all right.* So it goes on. Job, covered with boils and sitting on a stone in the field, asked the same questions.

There is a circle apart, however, even from the Village which is itself apart, where all the answers kiss the questions and all those who are afflicted with wanhope or acedia can make peace with themselves. I mean the jazz-narcotics coteries, the "hipsters," so-called. These are drawn from the spiritually dispossessed who form the underground of Village life. Since they are unalterably against The Law, they have their own rites and passwords and worship their own forbidden God—The One Who Puts Out The Light. The Hipster societies—if they are such, since nobody in them thinks they belong—may be considered the draft-dodgers of commercial civilization, just as Villagers, in general, are the loyal opposition or "conscientious objectors." They take no stand, for any stand wold have to be inside the group and therefore against themselves, against their negative principle. The mood which infects them all is, perhaps, a tender American version of that underground nihilism which erupted in the forms of Dada and fascism in Europe—anti-art and anti-morality. What they believe in is Benzedrine, "tea," and jazz.

Jazz and "tea" (marijuana) form a bridge to Harlem, the other ghetto uptown, and many on both sides use it to cross over. The midpoint is 52nd Street where all the cats, black and white, can get together in the cellar clubs to dig the latest jive and to hear Dizzie or the Bird or the Hawk blow their valves. Black jazz is the only art whose moods and ecstasies reflect their own, whose pace is equal to the terrible inner speed of the drug. When marijuana loses its drive there are some who learn how to saddle and ride the "horse" of heroin. But once on that nightmare, as everybody knows, there is no dismounting until the other side of the Bar has been crossed. For such release, life itself is a handicap.

Around the track of all these gyres and circles in Greenwich Village, no matter where we start from we arrive at the same place in the end—beside the point. Without a common focus, images are fractured on everybody's point of view; and meanings shift without pivotal reference. The boundary between inner and outer reality is blurred. What is real or good or beautiful is a matter of taste. Since for our time, and in the Village especially, truth itself has become a sentiment, the search for an Absolute is maudlin. All the beards of authority have been cut off, and anything goes: Ovid is Freud is Karl Marx is Joe Gould is I AM. Which brings us by a commodius vicus of recirculation back to Sheridan Square and environs, like a barber's pole forever disappearing into itself.

I cut diagonally across the Square, leaving the drunk on the sidewalk, and headed for the cover of darkness in the movies. The theater was packed, people were standing five deep behind ropes, yet, somehow, probably because I was alone, the usher signaled for me to follow as soon as I arrived. While we were walking down the aisle, a sudden blow of laughter from the audience struck me so hard that, even without knowing why, I laughed along with the rest.

My seat was in the middle row, the best in the house, and, what was even more uncanny, two others right next to it were vacant! I smelled them, I looked under them, I felt them—nothing was wrong. But why wasn't anyone coming down the aisle? There was another blow of laughter, and then another even harder, the effect augmented by itself. I looked up at the screen. *A man was being hit over the head by a lead pipe.* Although he seemed in agony, every time he screwed his eyes and made mouths the laughter from the audience became louder. A woman was whispering behind my back! I turned around, but quickly she looked the other way. ME? Now the whole house was screaming. *A blindfolded man was about to walk into an open sewer.* I shut my eyes, but his after-image remained. The beam of the inner eye cast his figure onto my mind with as much power as the projector upon the movie screen. As I wavered, the women in gray and black came down the aisle. There was no other way out. I ran onto the stage, and, while my shadow wavered on the screen for a moment as though undecided whether to follow, plunged into an abyss of nothing. The man tore the bandage from his eyes and clutched at me and passed. But the film of reality which separated us was as wide as the abyss itself.

Down Fifth Avenue and under the Arch I ran to the cement circle in Washington Square. It was a bitter night without stars or a moon and the park was deserted. Then from nowhere someone called "Klonsky"—my name. I saw him then as he came walking towards me, his face so flat and black I could hardly separate the features. "Give me some skin, man," he said, "I want you to dig some of this new charge."

Ah well, ah well, it was my friend, Sam, an old viper out of Harlem, always free, always high, the kind of tea-pusher who would pull a hype on his own mother if he knew who she was. Under his sleeve his wrist was pocked with a thousand bites of the needle. He took out a long white fuse of tea from his pocket and bit open one end. Then he lit up with a deep sigh of smoke and the image of the burning match reflared in his eyes, I saw in that sudden flash of sight that they were pitch-black! they had no whites!—like the sooty fireplace with no orange flame burning inside it before which I am writing.

—November 1948

Malcolm Cowley

(1896–1989)

A native of Pittsburgh, Malcolm Cowley moved to New York in 1919 following a stint as an ambulance driver during World War I. From 1929 to 1944 he worked as an editor of the New Republic. *A prolific writer of literary criticism, essays, and poetry, Cowley edited many collections and anthologies. Today he is remembered by many as the man who edited Jack Kerouac's* On the Road. Exile's Return *is Cowley's classic work on "The Lost Generation." In this selection he writes about coming to the Village, "to the crooked streets south of Fourteenth Street . . . because living was cheap. . . because it seemed that New York was the only city where a young writer could be published."*

"The Greenwich Village Idea" from *Exile's Return: A Literary Odyssey of the 1920s*

In those days when division after division was landing in Hoboken and marching up Fifth Avenue in full battle equipment, when Americans were fighting the Bolshies in Siberia and guarding the Rhine—in those still belligerent days that followed the Armistice there was a private war between Greenwich Village and the *Saturday Evening Post*.

Other magazines fought in the same cause, but the *Post* was persistent and powerful enough to be regarded as chief of the aggressor nations. It published stories about the Villagers, editorials and articles against them, grave or flippant serials dealing with their customs in a mood of disparagement or alarm, humorous pieces done to order by its staff writers, cartoons in which the Villagers were depicted as long-haired men and short-haired women with ridiculous bone-rimmed spectacles—in all, a long campaign of invective beginning before the steel strike or the Palmer Raids and continuing through the jazz era, the boom and the depression. The burden of it was always the same: that the Village was the haunt of affectation; that it was inhabited by fools and fakers; that the fakers hid Moscow heresies under the disguise of cubism and free verse; that the fools would eventually be cured of their folly: they would forget this funny business about art and return to domesticity in South Bend, Indiana, and sell motorcars, and in the evenings sit with slippered feet while their children romped about them in paper caps made from the advertising pages of the *Saturday Evening Post*. The Village was dying, had died already, smelled to high heaven and Philadelphia. . . .

The Villagers did not answer this attack directly: Instead they carried on a campaign of their own against the culture of which the *Post* seemed to be the final expression. They performed autopsies, they wrote obituaries of civilization in the United States, they shook the standardized dust of the country from their feet. Here, apparently, was a symbolic struggle: on the one side, the great megaphone of middle-class America; on the other, the American disciples of art and artistic living. Here, in its latest incarnation, was the eternal warfare of bohemian against bourgeois, poet against propriety—Villon and the Bishop of Orleans, Keats and the quarterly reviewers, Rodolphe, Mimi and the landlord. But perhaps, if we review the history of the struggle, we shall find that the issue was other than it seemed, and the enmity less ancient.

Alexander Pope, two centuries before, had taken the side of property and propriety in a similar campaign against the slums of art. When writing *The Duncaid* and the *Epistle to Dr. Arbuthnot*, he lumped together all his enemies—stingy patrons, homosexual peers, hair-splitting pedants; but he reserved his best-considered insults for the garrett dwellers of Grub Street, the dramatists whose lives were spent dodging the bailiff, the epic poets "lulled by a zephyr through the broken pane." These he accused of slander, dullness, theft, bootlicking, ingratitude, every outrage to man and the Muses; almost the only charge he did not press home against them was that of affectation. They were not play-acting their poverty. The threadbare Miltons of his day were rarely the children of prosperous parents; they could not go home to Nottingham or Bristol and earn a comfortable living by selling hackney coaches; if they "turned a Persian tale for half a crown," it was usually because they had no other means of earning half a crown and so keeping themselves out of debtors' prison. And the substance of Pope's attack against them is simply that they were poor, that they belonged to a class beneath his own, without inherited wealth, that they did not keep a gentleman's establishment, or possess a gentleman's easy manners, or the magnanimity of a gentleman sure of tomorrow's dinner:

> Yet then did Gildon draw his venal quill;
> I wish'd the man a dinner, and sate still.
> Yet then did Dennis rave in furious fret;
> I never answer'd, I was not in debt.

Pope was a far wittier poet than any of his adversaries, but the forces he brought against them were not those of wit or poetry alone: behind him, massed in reserve, was all the prejudice of eighteenth-century gentlefolk against intruders into the polite world of letters. He was fighting a literary class war, and one that left deep wounds. To many a poor scribbler it meant the difference between starvation and the roast of mutton he lovingly appraised in a bake-shop window and promised himself to devour if his patron sent him a guinea: after *The Duncaid*, patrons closed their purses. Pope had inflicted a defeat on Grub Street but—the distinction is important—he had left bohemia untouched, for the simple reason that Queen Anne's and King George's London had no bohemia to defeat.

Grub Street is as old as the trade of letters—in Alexandria, in Rome, it was already a crowded quarter; bohemia is younger than the Romantic movement. Grub Street develops in the metropolis of any country or culture as soon as men are able to earn a precarious living with pen or pencil; bohemia is a revolt against certain features of industrial capitalism and can exist only in a capitalist society. Grub Street is a way of life unwillingly followed by the intellectual proletariat; bohemia attracts its citizens from all economic classes: there are not a few bohemian millionaires, but they are expected to imitate the customs of penniless artists. Bohemia is Grub Street romanticized, doctrinalized and rendered self-conscious; it is Grub Street on parade.

It originated in France, not England and the approximate date of its birth was 1830: thus, it followed the rise of French industry after the Napoleonic Wars. The French Romantic poets complained of feeling oppressed—perhaps it was, as Musset believed, the fault of that great Emperor whose shadow fell across their childhood; perhaps it was Science, or the Industrial Revolution, or merely the money-grubbing, the stuffy morals and stupid politics of the people about them; in any case they had to escape from middle-class society. Some of them became revolutionists; others took refuge in pure art; but most of them demanded a real world of present satisfactions, in which they could cherish aristocratic ideals while living among carpenters and grisettes. The first bohemians, the first inhabitants of that world, were the friends of Theophile Gautier and Gerald de Nerval, young men of good family, bucks and dandies with money enough to indulge their moods; but the legend of it was spread abroad, some twenty years later, by a poor hack named Henry Murger, the son of a German immigrant to Paris.

Having abandoned all hopes of a formal education when he left primary school, and feeling no desire to follow his father's trade of tailor, Murger began to write mediocre verse and paint incredible pictures, meanwhile supporting himself by his wits. Soon he joined a group that called itself the Water Drinkers because it could rarely afford another beverage. A dozen young men with little talent and extravagant ambitions, they lived in hovels or in lofts over a cow stable, worked under the lash of hunger, and wasted their few francs in modest debauchery. One winter they had a stove for the first time: it was a hole cut in the floor, through which the animal heat of the stable rose into their chamber. They suffered from the occupational diseases of poor artists—consumption, syphilis, pneumonia—all of them aggravated by undernourishment. Joseph Desbrosses died in the winter of 1844; he was an able sculptor, possibly the one genius of the group. His funeral was the third in six weeks among the Water Drinkers, and they emptied their pockets to buy a wooden cross for the grave. When the last sod clumped down, the gravediggers stood waiting for their tip. There was not a soul in the party.

"That's all right," said the gravediggers generously, recognizing the mourners. "It will be for the next time."

Spring came and their feelings rose with the mercury. One evening when his friends were making war maps in water color, Murger began unexpectedly to tell them stories. They listened, chuckled and roared for two good hours, till somebody advised him, seriously between gales of laughter, to abandon poetry for fiction. A little later he followed this advice, writing about the life of his friends, the only life he knew. Personally he hated this existence on the cold fringes of starvation and planned to escape from it as soon as he could, but for the public he tried to render it attractive.

In *Scenes de la Vie de Boheme*, he succeeded beyond his ambition. He succeeded not only in writing a popular book, one that was translated into twenty languages, successfully dramatized, candied into an opera, one that enabled its author to live in bourgeois comfort, but also in changing an image in the public mind. Grub Street, where dinnerless Gildon drew his venal quill, contemptible Grub Street, the haunt of apprentices and failures and Henry Murger, was transformed into glamorous bohemia. The unwilling expedient became a permanent way of life, became a cult with rituals and costumes, a doctrine adhered to not only by artists, young and old, rich and poor, but also in later years by designers, stylists, trade-paper sub-editors, interior decorators, wolves, fairies, millionaire patrons of art, sadists, nymphomaniacs, bridge sharks, anarchists, women living on alimony, tired reformers, educational cranks, economists, hopheads, dipsomaniac playwrights, nudists, restaurant keepers, stockbrokers and dentists craving self-expression.

Even during Murger's lifetime, the bohemian cult was spreading from France into other European countries. Having occupied a whole section of Paris—three sections, in fact, for it moved from the Boul' Mich' to Montmartre and thence to Montparnasse—it founded new colonies in Munich, Berlin, London, St. Petersburg. In the late 1850s it reached New York, where it established headquarters in Charlie Pfaff's lager-beer saloon under the sidewalk of lower Broadway. Again in 1894 the "Trilby" craze spawned forth dozens of bohemian groups and magazines; in New York a writer explained that the true bohemian may exist at millionaire's tables; in Philadelphia young married couples south of Market Street would encourage their guests: "Don't stand on ceremony; you know we are thorough bohemians." All over the Western world, bohemia was carrying on a long warfare with conventional society, but year by year it was making more converts from the ranks of the enemy.

When the American magazines launched their counteroffensive, in 1919, a curious phenomenon was to be observed. The New York bohemians, the Greenwich Villagers, came from exactly the same social class as the readers of the *Saturday Evening Post*. Their political opinions were vague and by no means dangerous to Ford Motors or General Electric: the war had destroyed their belief in political action. They were trying to get ahead, and the proletariat be damned. Their economic standards were those of the small American businessman.

The art-shop era was just beginning. Having fled from Dubuque and Denver to escape the stultifying effects of a civilization ruled by business, many of the Villagers had already entered business for themselves, and many more were about to enter it.

They would open tea shops, antique shops, bookshops, yes, and bridge parlors, dance halls, nightclubs and real estate offices. By hiring shop assistants, they would become the exploiters of labor. If successful, they tried to expand their one restaurant into a chain of restaurants, all with a delightfully free and intimate atmosphere, but run on the best principles of business accounting. Some of them leased houses, remodeled them into studio apartments, and raised the rents three or four hundred percent to their new tenants. Others clung faithfully to their profession of painting or writing, rose in it slowly, and at last had their stories or illustrations accepted by *Collier's* or the *Saturday Evening Post*. There were occasions, I believe, when Greenwich Village writers were editorially encouraged to write stories making fun of the Village, and some of them were glad to follow the suggestion. Of course they complained, when slightly tipsy, that they were killing themselves—but how else could they maintain their standard of living? What they meant was that they could not live like *Vanity Fair* readers without writing for the *Saturday Evening Post*.

And so it was that many of them lived during the prosperous decade that followed. If the book succeeded or if they got a fat advertising contract, they bought houses in Connecticut, preferably not too far from the Sound. They hired butlers; they sent their children to St. Somebody's; they collected highboys, lowboys, tester beds; they joined the local Hunt and rode in red coats across New England stone fences and through wine-red sumacs in pursuit of a bag of imported aniseed. In the midst of these new pleasures they continued to bewail the standardization of American life, while the magazines continued their polemic against Greenwich Village. You came to suspect that some of the Villagers themselves, even those who remained below Fourteenth Street, were not indignant at a publicity that brought tourists to the Pirates' Den and customers to Ye Olde Curiowe Shoppe and increased the value of the land in which a few of them had begun to speculate. The whole thing seemed like a sham battle. Yet beneath it was a real conflict of ideas and one that would soon be mirrored in the customs of a whole country.

Greenwich Village was not only a place, a mood, a way of life: like all bohemias, it was also a doctrine. Since the days of Gautier and Murger, this doctrine had remained the same in spirit, but it had changed in several details. By 1920, it had become a system of ideas that could roughly be summarized as follows:

1. The idea of salvation by the child.—Each of us at birth has special potentialities which are slowly crushed and destroyed by a standardized society and mechanical methods of teaching. If a new educational system can be introduced, one by which children are encouraged to develop their own personalities, to blossom freely like flowers, then the world will be saved by this new, free generation.
2. The idea of self-expression.—Each man's, each woman's, purpose in life is to express himself, to realize his full individuality through creative work and beautiful living in beautiful surroundings.
3. The idea of paganism.—The body is a temple in which there is nothing unclean, a shrine to be adorned for the ritual of love.
4. The idea of living for the moment.—It is stupid to pile up treasures that we can enjoy only in old age, when we have lost the capacity for enjoyment. Better to seize the moment as it comes, to dwell in it intensely, even at the cost of future suffering. Better to live extravagantly, gather June rosebuds, "burn my candle at both ends. . . . It gives a lovely light."
5. The idea of liberty.—Every law, convention or rule of art that prevents self-expression or the full enjoyment of the moment should be shattered and abolished. Puritanism is the great enemy. The crusade against puritanism is the only crusade with which free individuals are justified in allying themselves.
6. The idea of female equality.—Women should be the economic and moral equals of men. They should have the same pay, the same working conditions, the same opportunity for drinking, smoking, taking or dismissing lovers.

7. The idea of psychological adjustment.—We are unhappy because we are maladjusted, and maladjusted because we are repressed. If our individual repressions can be removed—by confessing them to a Freudian psychologist—then we can adjust ourselves to any situation, and be happy in it. (But Freudianism is only one method of adjustment. What is wrong with us may be our glands, and by a slight operation, or merely by taking a daily dose of thyroid, we may alter our whole personalities. Again, we may adjust ourselves by some such psycho-physical discipline as was taught by Gurdjieff. The implication of all these methods is the same—that the environment itself need not be altered. That explains why most radicals who became converted to psychoanalysis or glands or Gurdjieff gradually abandoned their political radicalism.)

8. The idea of changing place.—"They do things better in Europe." England and Germany have the wisdom of old cultures; the Latin peoples have admirably preserved their pagan heritage. By expatriating himself, by living in Paris, Capri or the South of France, the artist can break the puritan shackles, drink, live freely and be wholly creative.

All these from the standpoint of the business-Christian ethic then represented by the *Saturday Evening Post*, were corrupt ideas. This older ethic is familiar to most people, but one feature of it has not been sufficiently emphasized. Substantially, it was a *production* ethic. The great virtues it taught were industry, foresight, thrift and personal initiative. The workman should be industrious in order to produce more for his employer; he should look ahead to the future; he should save money in order to become a capitalist himself; then he should exercise personal initiative and found new factories where other workmen would toil industriously, and save, and become capitalists in their turn.

During the process many people would suffer privations: most workers would live meagerly and wrack their bodies with labor; even the employers would deny themselves luxuries that they could easily purchase, choosing instead to put back the money into their business; but after all, our bodies were not to be pampered; they were temporary dwelling places, and we should be rewarded in Heaven for our self-denial. On earth, our duty was to accumulate more wealth and produce more goods, the ultimate use of which was no subject for worry. They would somehow be absorbed, by new markets opened in the West, or overseas in new countries, or by the increased purchasing power of workmen who had saved and bettered their position.

That was the ethic of a young capitalism, and it worked admirably, so long as the territory and population of the country were expanding faster than its industrial plant. But after the war the situation changed. Our industries had grown enormously to satisfy a demand that suddenly ceased. To keep the factory wheels turning, a new domestic market had to be created. Industry and thrift were no longer adequate. There must be a new ethic that encouraged people to buy, a *consumption* ethic.

It happened that many of the Greenwich Village ideas proved useful in the altered situation. Thus, *self-expression* and *paganism* encouraged a demand for all sorts of products—modern furniture, beach pajamas, cosmetics, colored bathrooms with toilet paper to match. *Living for the moment* meant buying an automobile, radio or house, using it now and paying for it tomorrow. *Female equality* was capable of doubling the consumption of products—cigarettes, for example—that had formerly been used by men alone. Even *changing place* would help to stimulate business in the country from which the artist was being expatriated. The exiles of art were also trade missionaries: involuntarily they increased the foreign demand for fountain pens, silk stockings, grapefruit and portable typewriters. They drew after them an invading army of tourists, thus swelling the profits of steamship lines and travel agencies. Everything fitted into the business picture.

I don't mean to say that Greenwich Village was the source of the revolution in morals that affected all our lives in the decade after the war, and neither do I mean that big business deliberately plotted to render the nation extravagant, pleasure worshipping and reckless of tomorrow.

The new moral standards arose from conditions that had nothing to do with the Village. They were, as a matter of fact, not really new. Always, even in the great age of the Puritans, there had been currents of licentiousness that were favored by the immoderate American climate and held in check only by hellfire preaching and the hardships of settling a new country. Old Boston, Providence, rural Connecticut, all had their underworlds. The reason puritanism became so strong in America was perhaps that it had to be strong in order to checkmate its enemies. But it was already weakening as the country grew richer in the twenty years before the war; and the war itself was the puritan crisis and defeat.

All standards were relaxed in the stormy-sultry wartime atmosphere. It wasn't only the boys of my age, those serving in the army, who were transformed by events: their sisters and younger brothers were affected in a different fashion. With their fathers away, perhaps, and their mothers making bandages or tea-dancing with lonely officers, it was possible for boys and girls to do what they pleased. For the first time they could go to dances unchaperoned, drive the family car and park it by the roadside while they made love, and come home after midnight, a little tipsy, with nobody to reproach them in the hallway. They took advantage of these stolen liberties—indeed, one might say that the revolution in morals began as a middle-class children's revolt.

But everything conspired to further it. Prohibition came and surrounded the new customs with illicit glamour; prosperity made it possible to practice them; Freudian psychology provided a philosophical justification and made it unfashionable to be repressed; still later the sex magazines and the movies, even the pulpit, would advertise a revolution that had taken place silently and triumphed without a struggle. In all this Greenwich Village had no part. The revolution would have occurred if the Village had never existed, but—the point is important—it would not have followed the same course. The Village, older in revolt, gave form to the movement, created its fashions, and supplied the writers and illustrators who would render them popular. As for American business, though it laid no plots in advance, it was quick enough to use the situation, to exploit the new markets for cigarettes and cosmetics, and to realize that, in advertising pages and movie palaces, sex appeal was now the surest appeal.

The Greenwich Village standards, with the help of business, had spread through the country. Young women east and west had bobbed their hair, let it grow and bobbed it again; they had passed through the period when corsets were checked in the cloakroom at dances and the period when corsets were not worn. They were not very self-conscious when they talked about taking a lover; and the conversations ran from mother fixations to birth control while they smoked cigarettes between the courses of luncheons eaten in black-and-orange tea shops just like those in the Village. People of forty had been affected by the younger generation: they spent too much money, drank too much gin, made love to one another's wives and talked about their neuroses. Houses were furnished to look like studios. Stenographers went on parties, following the example of the boss and his girl friend and her husband. The "party," conceived as a gathering together of men and women to drink gin cocktails, flirt, dance to the phonograph or radio and gossip about their absent friends, had in fact become one of the most popular American institutions; nobody stopped to think how short its history had been in this country. It developed out of the "orgies" celebrated by the French 1830 Romantics, but it was introduced into this country by Greenwich Villagers—before being adopted by salesmen from Kokomo and the younger country-club set in Kansas City.

Wherever one turned the Greenwich Village ideas were making their way: even the *Saturday Evening Post* was feeling their influence. Long before Repeal, it began to wobble on Prohibition. It allowed drinking, petting and unfaithfulness to be mentioned in the stories it published; its illustrations showed women smoking. Its advertising columns admitted one after another of the strictly pagan products—cosmetics, toilet tissues, cigarettes—yet still it continued to thunder against Greenwich Village and bohemian immorality. It even nourished the illusion that its long campaign had been successful. On more than one occasion it announced that the Village was dead and buried: "The sad truth is," it said in the autumn of 1931, "that the Village was a flop." Perhaps it was true that the Village was moribund—of that we can't be sure, for creeds and ways of life among artists are hard to kill. If, however, the Village was really dying, it was dying of success. It was dying because it became so popular that too many people insisted on living there. It was dying because women smoked cigarettes on the streets of the Bronx, drank gin cocktails in Omaha and had perfectly swell parties in Seattle and Middletown—in other words, because American business and the whole of middle-class America had been going Greenwich Village.

—1951

Jo Davidson

(1883–1952)

Like a number of Villagers of his day, sculptor Jo Davidson had spent some time in Paris, and having achieved an element of success in his overseas adventures, returned home to the Village with renewed vigor and determination. Establishing himself in a studio at 23 MacDougal Alley, Davidson secured commission after commission. A large, robust man with a full beard, Davidson was a popular figure on the Village streets.

"Washington Square in 1911" from *Between Sittings: An Informal Autobiography of Jo Davidson*

We arrived in New York in early February of 1911. This time I thought we had come home to stay. After visiting with my family we looked around for a place to live, and naturally gravitated to Washington Square. Yvonne had lived for a time in West Eighth Street and many of my friends resided in that neighborhood. Besides, Washington Square had a feel of Paris, and the Square itself was a suitable place to air the baby.

I found an apartment in 40 Washington Square South, the top floor of the three-story building. It had a spacious L-shaped living room, with a big fireplace, which gave it a very friendly feeling. Yvonne's ingenuity had free play—she could do so much with so little—and in a few weeks' time, she made it look as if we had always lived there and intended to live there forever.

I had brought over some paintings of Jerry Blum's at his request and I hung several of them on the walls of our apartment. I wrote him that everybody admired them and that I thought I had a purchaser for one of them. I did not hear from him. Instead, he suddenly arrived in New York. "Well, what's doing?," he said.

The dining room was furnished with a long wooden table and benches. There was always room for an extra person and our friends soon discovered that Nounou was a wonderful cook. Nounou's cuisine was so popular that we found ourselves giving many dinner parties. Our friends formed the habit of dropping in for a drink in the afternoon. In fact, whenever a light was seen on the top floor of 40 Washington Square, people did not hesitate to come up. My exhibition at the New York Cooperative Society the year before had made me new friends—the addition of a wife heightened their interest and we were greeted with open arms.

Emily Grigsby brought Doris Keene, who was then playing in "The Affairs of Anatole," and Doris Keene brought Ned Sheldon, who was at work on "Romance," which he was writing for her. Among the steadies were Hutchins Hapgood, Frederick James Gregg, Ernest Lawson, George Luks and John Gregory, whose charm and wit were always an asset.

Nounou was never alone in the kitchen. Her cheery disposition attracted everyone. One of our guests, Bill MacColl, attempted to embrace Nounou while she was preparing an omelette. The omelette left the frying pan and landed on Bill's cheek—there was no trifling with Nounou.

When my sculpture arrived from Paris I had the smaller bronzes delivered to the apartment and went in search of a gallery which would give me an exhibition.

George Hellman, who had arranged my exhibition the year before, introduced me to Mr. Eugene Glaenzer. Mr. Glaenzer was the old type of cultivated Frenchman. His gallery, once the old

Harriman stables, located on Fifty-fifth Street and Fifth Avenue, was very luxurious, with tapestries, pictures and rare pieces of furniture. The main room had a glass roof, a perfect light for sculpture. Mr. Glaenzer came to Washington Square, saw my work and agreed to give me an exhibition.

The exhibition at the New York Cooperative Society had been a little affair. This was my first big exhibition, showing bronzes, terra-cottas, and a room full of drawings. The big figure, "La Terre," which had been exhibited in Paris at the Autumn Salon, was one of the main attractions. The opening of the show promised well. The press and critics discussed it seriously, and James Gibbons Huneker wrote in the *Sun*, April 13, 1911:

"This young man, who has studied in Paris, one is tempted to say, at the feet of Rodin, is a sculptor born, one who has not allowed his enormous facility to decline into dilettante methods. His touch is personal, crisply nervous, virile and not too impressionistic; the feeling for line, for structural foundation, never deserts him. That slight perpetual novelty which should season any art production, is seldom absent. There is an imaginative element, too, in his slightest effort. A torso for him is a cosmos, and he shows several that are as beautiful in their way as the Greek; indeed, when they are most beautiful they are Greek. Only this to assure you that Mr. Davidson does not manufacture those writhing, spasmodic dolls which are the fashion of the hour in Paris; nor does he waste his gifts on huge monsters, whose limbs are as bladders full of lard. He models with the plastic, not the literary idea before him; he is more rhythmic than static; yet he can achieve the effect of rigid ponderousness. His figures are evocations of poetic moods translated into legitimate sculptural terms. . . .

"His imposing exhibition definitely ranges Jo Davidson as a strongly individual artist in the field of contemporary sculpture."

—1951

Chandler Brossard

(1922–1993)

Chandler Brossard was born in Idaho Falls, Idaho, but grew up in Wash-ington, D.C. During the 1940s he worked for a number of newspapers and magazines, including the Washington Post, Time, *and* American Mer-cury. *His novel* Who Walk in Darkness *has been called the first beat novel (although others, such as John Clellon Holmes'* Go *and George Mandel's* Flee the Angry Strangers, *also lay claim). Regardless,* Dark-ness *is still considered an underground classic. Its language is spare and uncluttered, its characters moving trancelike within their own self-created existential maze. The hero of the novel is a laidback young fellow named Blake Williams, while other characters are said to resemble real-life figures (a charge resolutely denied by Brossard): Henry Porter is reportedly mod-eled after writer Anatole Broyard, Max Glazer after Milton Klonksy, and Harry Lees after William Gaddis. Brossard never quite repeated the suc-cess of* Darkness. *He died in 1993. The following selection is taken from the original unexpurgated version reissued in 2000 by Herodias.*

from *Who Walk in Darkness*

People said Henry Porter was a "passed" Negro. But nobody knew for sure. I think the rumor was started by someone who had grown up with Porter in San Francisco. He did not look part Negro to me. Latin, yes. Anyway, the rumor followed him around. I sus-pect it was supposed to explain the difference between the way he behaved and the way the rest of us behaved. Porter did not show that he knew people were talking about him this way. I must give him credit for maintaining a front of indifference that was really remarkable.

Someone both Porter and I knew quite well once told me the next time he saw Porter he was going to ask him if he did or did not have Negro blood. He said it was the only way to clear the air. Maybe so. But I said I would not think of doing it. I have always been quite willing to let people keep their secrets to themselves. I have never had the desire to uncover them. I felt that if Porter was part Negro and ever wanted that publicly settled, he would one day do so. I was willing to wait.

The story went that his father had been a seaman turned jack-of-all-trades and his mother a hostess in a restaurant. They lived together for a few weeks and then one day the old man just pulled out. Porter was given to some of his mother's relatives to raise and she went back to what she had been doing before this interruption.

Porter had been living downtown, in New York City, in the section of the Sporting Club Bar for about three years when I knew him. He had come there right from San Francisco. Until he became literary minded, Porter liked living in San Francisco. He was rather popular at school, he was a tennis champion, he was an accomplished dancer, and because he was good looking—a tall, well-built blonde—and bold he had early successes with women. He had his first affair when he was sixteen. The woman was a professional singer, a Mexican. She had two abortions before they finally broke up. She paid for the abortions herself. They cost a hundred dollars each at that time.

Porter went to college—Berkeley—for three years, quit, and was drafted into the army. When he was mustered out he returned to San Francisco and married a neighborhood girl. Her father paid for a lively neighborhood type wedding and many of her relatives gave them small presents of money.

Porter's best man was a boyhood friend, a Spanish boy. Five years later when this best man was in a hospital bleeding to death of knife wounds received in a street fight, Porter could not find the time to visit him.

The Porters had a child, a boy, but something was wrong with it and it died at three months. Porter and his wife went to the movies quite often and she spent a good deal of time in her kitchen preparing fine meals for him. He had a job in a publicity office. Soon after his child died Porter became very literary minded. He decided that his wife was a burden to him and that the life he was leading in California was nowhere. So he left. He left his job and his wife and came to New York to begin his literary career.

I was told that his wife forgave him for leaving her. She knew that he was really very fond of her but that he was ashamed of her origin and thought she would interfere with his new career. I understand they wrote friendly letters to each other until the day she remarried.

It was odd, but Porter was occasionally quite talkative about his wife. Mostly he bitched her, but not vehemently. He laughed about her fondness for housekeeping, her ignorance of cultural matters, her confusion at the contradictory feelings he had about marriage. You would think that he would have kept all this to himself too, because of the questions it might raise. But there you are.

Downtown Porter lived for a while on veterans' unemployment checks. He read a great deal and looked in nearly every bookshop he passed and he met as many people as he could. He worked hard to get rid of his Western accent. He did this by trying to "model" his accent. But the Western part was not so easily cut off, and the result of his labor on his speech was that it sounded slightly odd. Also, Porter began to dress like a Harvard man.

With what he had left of his share of his and his wife's savings, Porter bought a couple of Brooks Brothers suits. These suits are the Harvard man's identification. Henry Porter wanted to be taken for a Harvard type. This was one of the contradictions in his character. Porter hated Harvard men. Whenever he got the chance he put them down. He always said they were exotic and over-mannered and inclined to be faggy. He always secretly envied and publicly put down Harry Lees.

Unfortunately, he did not have the style for dressing this way. You have to have a certain style to go with Brooks clothes, and

Porter did not have it, that was all. And despite his hard under-studying Porter missed a point here and there. He got the wrong kind of ties. His ties were nice-looking but they were the wrong kind. And he tied the knots too big. His shirts were never exactly right either. So nobody took him for a Harvard man. He was look-ing hard for a style.

Along with the Brooks suits, Porter began to go after the kind of girls Harvard men usually go after.

One night at a big party Porter had got himself invited to [sic] he met a Bennington girl who was distantly related to Harry Lees. She was with a date and other men were following her around, but Porter, slightly tight, made use of his boldness and his expert danc-ing, and took her away from all of them. Later he took her home. He stayed with her for three months in her apartment. She was tired of over-mannered Harvard types and Porter seemed to be what she was looking for. She went for him in a big way. She wanted to marry him. But first she thought he could use a little psychoanalysis. She had four or five thousand dollars in the bank that she said she did not need and she told him he should use it for an analysis.

After some persuasion Porter finally went to an analyst, for five weeks, for kicks. He stopped going and at the same time left this girl. She never knew why. She was quite a nice girl. Being with her had convinced Porter that he could make the grade with her type. It gave him confidence to know this. It made him feel he was be-ginning to acquire style.

When his money ran out Porter got a job writing promotion copy for a publishing company. On the side he pursued his literary career by writing fiction and book reviews. His fiction was not bad. It did not knock me out, but it was not bad. Three or four of his stories were accepted by small literary magazines. This gave him some literary status. His reputation with women gave him more status though. I had to hand it to him. He could pick up almost any woman he saw.

Almost all of the people we knew well went to the Sporting Club Bar. We went there nearly every night. There were other bars around like it, but we did not go to them. I do not know why we all selected the Sporting Club instead of another place, but we did.

None of the other bars felt the same to us afterward. We did not like the people who went to them. We did not think they were very hip.

I was not working at that time. I had recently been fired from a job because I had not been able to hide my feelings that the place was no good. I should have been smarter about it, I guess, but I was not interested in being smart that way.

It was early summer. I had finished working at home and decided to go to the Sporting Club to see who was around. It was about six o'clock. I left my third-floor apartment on Dover Street and went outside. Standing on the sidewalk in front of my building were several Italians. They belonged to the Sorrento Social Club downstairs next door. They shot pool there and played cards and made bets on the horses and watched the television screen. Some of them wore large-brimmed hats with the brim turned up all around. This made them look tough and like underworld characters. They wore splashy ties. They were arguing about the Dodgers.

I walked by them. They looked at me as they always did and I looked back. We did not speak although I had seen them every day for several months. I walked on up the street to the corner of Spring Street. It was warm out. Across the street in the candy store the juke box was playing loud. The owner was standing outside the store watching the street. You could hear the juke box all the way down the block. On the corner of Spring Street in front of the bar were the three bookies and their friends. They were in front of the bar all day long taking bets. One of them was holding a baby and talking to a woman with a baby carriage. They were all Italians.

I crossed Spring Street and walked to Prince. I passed the kids playing stoop ball against the side of a red brick warehouse and ducked when one kid threw the ball to home plate as I was passing through them.

Women were leaning out of the tenement buildings and talking from building to building. I walked by the vegetable push-carts parked in the gutter facing the sidewalk, smelling the fresh, clean, fragrant smell of the fruit and the freshly watered lettuce and radishes and spring onions and dandelion greens in big boxes. Then by the fish market downstairs with the black-shelled mussels clinging in bunches and the spiraled scungili shells in bushel baskets and the big basin inside the window full of the small black live eels wriggling through the clear running water. The fish smell was strong and sharp.

I stopped to look downstairs into the store at all the different kinds of fish piled neatly in layers on the slanted shelves with chopping ice thrown over them. The store was crowded with fat women talking loud in Italian and broken English.

I crossed Prince and walked up Sullivan Street past the Jesuit school playground, past the Mills Hotel with the drunks leaning unsteadily, beaten-faced, against the walls, and the smell of piss and cheap wine hanging in the air, and on to the park.

The park was leafy green and full of children playing and their mothers sitting on the benches watching them and talking among themselves in groups. Walking by the benches I looked at all the young mothers. They were pretty and lightly dressed and looked cool and happy and desirable and I liked them very much. I wished I knew a couple of young mothers. I looked toward the big circle in the middle of the park. There had been a large fountain in the circle at one time but its flowing had been cut off and the circle was used now for sitting in. I did not see anyone I wanted to visit. A few easy-sitting hipsters and their girls were sitting on the periphery of the dry circle. I had seen them around but I did not really know them. One of them saw me and jerked his head back in a motion of hello. I did the same thing, and went on walking. Then I saw Cap Fields. He was sitting with a girl. I thought of going to sit with them, but then decided not to.

I walked south through the park, looking at the people on the benches and enjoying it every time I passed one of the young models who were always walking in the park in their absolutely stylized way, walking haughtily but obviously liking very much being looked at. I came to the south side of the park. I crossed Elkin Street and walked up the block, turned the corner, and went into the Sporting Club Bar.

No one I knew was standing at the bar. I looked around the booths. Max Glazer and Henry Porter were sitting in a booth in the corner. They were with a girl I had never seen before.

"Hey, Blake!" Porter shouted seeing me. "Come on over, old sport."

The girl looked at me, and away. I walked to the booth and sat down next to Glazer. Neither he nor I spoke to each other immediately. He always waited before greeting anybody he knew.

"What's new, man?" Porter asked me.

"Nothing," I said. The girl was quite nice-looking. Her hair was cut short like a boy's. She faced away.

"Everything is pretty dragged right now," Porter said.

"Hello there, Blake," Max said, playing with his beer glass.

"Hello, Max."

I motioned with my head to one of the two waiters standing around. He came to the booth and I ordered a glass of beer. He did not say anything. I liked him less than any waiter I had ever seen. He looked deadpan at us, and went to the bar for my beer. The Italians who worked in the restaurants down there disliked all non-Italians. Some of them disguised it better than others.

Porter and Glazer kept looking around the place. A few more people had come in now. "This is Betty Graham, Blake," Porter said suddenly. "This is Blake Williams."

We said hello. She was slightly tight-faced but rather nice-looking. Max winked at her without smiling and sipped his beer and went on glancing around. The waiter brought my beer. I took a long drink of it. It stung my nose. The waiter stood there at the booth waiting to be paid for the beer. I gave him a dime and he left. I wondered who the girl was with, Porter or Glazer.

"What are you going to do for a vacation, Blake?" Porter asked me.

"I'm not sure. Maybe I'll go to Harry Lee's father's place up on the Cape. Maybe we could all of us go there. He has a whole beach house to himself."

"That so?"

"Yes. His old man went to Europe and left him the house for a couple of months."

"He'll miss his old man," said Porter.

'You're too hard on the guy," I said. "Why don't you lay off him?"

"I don't mean anything."

"I'll ask him what the chances are of our going up there."

"Sounds great. Work on it, man."

Just then Cap Fields came in. Max watched him with sudden interest. Cap nodded to us and took a chair from a near-by table and sat down with us.

"Did you get it?" Max asked him.

Cap nodded his head. "Listen, man," he said. "This is really great charge. The best. I know. But it will cost you."

"How much?" Max asked.

"An ace for two sticks."

Cap talked thick and strange. He was really high. He moved his head in a jerky way when he was lit up and talking.

"That's steep, man," Max said. "Are you getting anything out of this?"

"No, man. Not a thing. There's nothing in this for me. You can buy it or not. I'm doing you a favor. But you should really dig this charge. It's the best."

Max looked across the booth at Porter, squinting. I used to think this was an affectation, an irritating one to most people, until I found out that he was nearsighted. He looked at Porter for a couple of seconds before speaking.

"Can you lend me some gold?" he asked Porter.

"I'm low. How much do you need?"

"Can you lend me an ace?"

Porter took the money from his watch pocket. "I want this back," he said.

"You'll get it. You'll get it."

The girl watched Porter give the money to Max. Max now looked around the place. Cap did too. Then Cap took a pack of Luckies from his shirt pocket. He offered the pack to Max. Max took the two thin sticks of marijuana from the Luckies and put them in his pocket. He slipped the dollar to Cap.

"You won't regret it," Cap said, his voice thick and funny-sounding. "It's the best in the city. You won't need more than half a stick each. I know. I've been on it for three days."

He laughed.

"You really like it, huh?" Max said, turning his head to look around the place again.

"That's what I've been saying," Cap said. He laughed again. He was really on.

Max sipped his beer, finishing it. "Want to blow this place now?" he said to the girl.

"I'm ready," she said, tight-faced.

"That was a fine pun, man," Cap said, laughing. "Want to blow this place."

I stood up so that Max could get out of the booth. The girl got up quickly. She was about nineteen.

"We'll see you around," Max said to Porter.

"O.K. Call me. Take it slow."

He looked at me, smiling slightly. "So long, Blake."

"So long."

"Thanks," he said to Cap. "I'll remember this."

"Do that," Cap said.

Max and the girl left, the girl not saying good-by to any of us. The surly waiter came up to the booth. "You want anything more?" he asked, picking up the glasses.

"I want another beer," I said. "What about you?" I said to Porter.

"None for me. I don't like the stuff."

"Cap?"

"Sure. I'll drink anything. Beer. Wine. Whisky. I love it all, Jack." He smiled and jerked his head around. "I feel so good," he said, and laughed.

Porter smiled and shook his head. The waiter left.

"Who was the chick?" Cap asked Porter.

"A girl I used to know."

"Now Glazer knows her?"

"Yes. I got her for him."

"That's very lovely, man. You really look out for your buddies. Wish somebody would look out for me." He laughed. The waiter brought our beers. I paid him and gave him a tip. He picked up the money and left.

"He's cute," said Cap. "Don't you love these surly wops? You know something? I saw this guy beat up a man one night who had only one arm. And the man was drunk too. What do you think of that?"

"They are the worst," I said.

"They're so far underground they don't need eyes any more," Porter said.

Porter waved at someone in another booth. I looked up to see who it was. It was the editor of a literary magazine Porter had done some reviewing for. I did not know him well enough to wave at him. At least that is the way I felt about it. Porter left us and went over to his booth to talk to him. Slapping the editor on the back and talking loud and laughing. Promoting something. A drunk radio writer sat down in the next booth with a girl. He began talking loud about his I.Q.

Porter came back and I asked him if he wanted to eat dinner. I was getting hungry.

"Sure. Anytime you say, sport."

"You don't want to eat here, do you?"

"No."

"Suppose we leave then. What about Enrico's?"

"Not that dump. It depresses me. Too many cornballs go there. Besides, the floor is always so dirty."

"Where do you want to go then?" I did not want to argue about a place to eat.

"What about the Eagle?"

"All right. Let's go there." I looked at Cap. "What about you, Cap? Are you hungry?"

"I'm always hungry," he said. "But I think I will stick around here for a while. Maybe something beautiful will happen to me if I stick around long enough." He laughed. He was certainly on. He probably could not even see the ground, he was so high.

Porter and I started out. Porter told Cap Fields to take it slow. I motioned so long to him with my hand. Halfway down the block we ran into Grace. She was walking toward the Sporting Club.

"Hello, Slim," Porter said, grabbing her around the waist. "Where are you headed?"

"Looking for you," Grace said. "As if you didn't know."

She was smartly dressed. She was the best-looking Italian girl I had ever seen. She did not look Italian. She had more of a Jewish beauty. Most people at first thought she was Jewish.

"See, you found me," Porter said, laughing. It was a dry ha-ha laugh. "Want to eat with us?"

"What do you think?"

"Come on then."

We walked on. I could smell Grace's perfume. She had good taste in perfume and clothes. I liked her. I felt sorry for her that she had ever connected with Porter. There were lots of people she could have gone with. You could tell in a minute that she was in some way in love with him. I was sorry for her.

"I thought you were going to call me," she said to Porter.

"I got involved," he said.

"Involved. You're really an involved person, aren't you?"

"O.K. O.K. I'm sorry."

"All right. But I expected you to call me."

She linked her arm with mine as we walked. "Let's ignore this involved person, Blake," she said "Tell me what you have been doing with yourself. Have you involved a job yet?"

"Not yet."

"Do you think he is crazy?" said Porter.

"Listen, involved. We're ignoring you. Are you worried about a job, Blake?"

"No. I don't need one for a little while yet."

"It's horrible to be worried about a job," she said.

We passed the caffe espresso place with the iron wrestlers in the window, and by the Coco Bar which the uptown tourists always crowded, and waited on the corner before crossing as a low red foreign car drove by us. Porter watched the car drive by. Grace held both our arms now.

"You're the Italian expert, Blake," he said. "Wasn't that a wop car?"

"Yes. It was a Lancia."

"They are sharp-looking but they probably don't last long."

"Are you the Italian expert?" Grace asked me. "I thought he was us."

"He says I am."

"I decided it was time somebody else was the Italian expert," Porter said. "I'll rest on my laurels."

Grace looked at him, and at me, and made a mock puzzled expression and then shrugged.

"Let's go dancing tonight," she said. "You're still the dancing expert aren't you."

"I am," said Porter. "The only one around."

"Want to go along, Blake?" she asked me.

"Fine. I'll get Joan."

Now we walked along the south side of the park. It would soon be dark. It was still warm out. Several New York University students came by. We walked through their struggling crowd and turned the corner and went south toward Sixth Avenue and the Eagle. I was trying to remember Joan's telephone number. It had slipped my mind.

Grace looked up at the sky. It was clouding up.

"I hope it doesn't rain tonight," she said.

"So do I," I said.

Porter looked up at the clouds too but he did not say anything.

—1952

John Clellon Holmes

(1926–1988)

John Clellon Holmes was born in 1926 in Holyoke, Massachusetts. Literary lore has it that, during a conversation in 1948, Jack Kerouac turned to Holmes and said, referring to the members of his generation that came of age after World War II, "So I guess you might say we're a beat generation." Four years later, in an article that ran in the New York Times Magazine, *the word entered the national bloodstream when Holmes himself used the term.* Go, *considered one of the early beat novels, was published in 1952. The characters are modeled on the lives of Kerouac (Gene Pasternak), Allen Ginsberg (David Stofsky), Neal Cassady (Hart Kennedy), and Holmes himself (Paul Hobbes). Holmes died in 1988 in Old Saybrook, Connecticut.*

from *Go*

"There hasn't been a party for three weeks, so *we* have to give one, eh?" Kathryn said with mock horror as they walked down Sixth Avenue toward West Third Street. "A lot of people staggering around breaking glasses and cluttering up my floors! And besides, Mr. Ketcham, what guarantee do we have that you'll be there?"

"But of course I'll be there. What do you mean?"

As always when Kathryn joshed him for his unreliability, Ketcham laughed with easy surprise, and replied innocently or in kind without offending her, she who was quickly offended.

Hobbes had always felt that Kathryn got along better with Arthur Ketcham than he, but he was also grateful for the fact.

"I always come when contracted. How about Friday night? Is that all right? I'll help you make out the guest list."

"Will it be that kind of party? It sounds hideous, but all right, Friday night."

Hobbes was pleased by her willingness, and credited it to the large, tasty meal they had just finished at the Normandy, a cheap French restaurant on Ninth Avenue. Then also, she had been feeling better lately. He had slept through the persistent jiggling of the phone when Stofsky called late the night before, but Kathryn, whom it had awakened, had not moved and had finally outlasted it obstinately. When she told Hobbes about it the next morning, he was surprised that she had not awakened him to share her anger.

They were on their way to meet Pasternak, who had called Hobbes during the afternoon to say that he was supposed to meet Christine in Washington Square at three o'clock, but wouldn't be able to make it. Would Hobbes, if she phoned, tell her that he was sorry and would get in touch with her? They had arranged to meet at nine that evening at Freeman's, which was a Village bar. Though Hobbes had seen Pasternak once since the night at Mannon's, the latter had tactfully made no mention of Mexico, probably concluding that "the trouble" had been worked out.

Just as Ketcham arrived at the apartment that afternoon, Christine called, and she sounded aggressive, although she made no reference to the Mexico incident either.

"That guy never turned up, Paul! He left me standing there like a goddamn fool for two hours!"

And then after Hobbes had explained: "Well, he could have reached me somehow. That makes a third time!" There was a pause and a catch in her voice. "Do you think he's getting tired of me or something? Tell me right out, won't you? I never been with a person like him before, and after I've thrown myself at his head and all. . . ! Has he got another woman?"

Hobbes tried to placate her, but he was not good at subterfuge for other people.

"Well, my God, I'm risking my baby's future for him. Doesn't he care that Max's getting worse and worse all the time? I think he even suspects. What can I do, Paul? I'm in love with that gorgon-head, that's all . . . But I didn't think he'd treat me like this . . . Then I suppose I deserve it for what I've done with him!"

But now, walking down Sixth Avenue, Ketcham was concerned about something.

"Does Gene feel I'm critical of him, I wonder? I haven't seen him for over two weeks. You see, I told him he should cut his book a little before he gave it to MacMurry's, and you know how irate he can get, in a kind of way. But I was wondering, has he been avoiding me?"

Hobbes enjoyed his desire to explain why Pasternak hadn't been around, even though he did not know the actual reason. He liked it because it placed him in a mediatory position with Ketcham, whom he envied slightly because of his orderly bachelor life, and the impeccable taste which was as evident in his conduct in relationships as it was in the books, records, and the decor of his apartment in the West Eighties, which Hobbes liked to think of as "The Firebird Suite."

There was but one flaw in the order of his life, and though everyone knew of it, and sometimes Ketcham himself would make reference to it, it was never discussed, because like all people who are reticent about themselves, he gave other people a feeling of un-easiness that only extreme delicacy on their parts could annul.

This flaw was Bianca. It was well known that they had been engaged just before she met Agatson. With Agatson, that engagement and Bianca's feeling for him had gone out of his life. He had no other women, still visited her regularly once a week, and, though he was an intellectual, modern young man, allowed himself the old fashioned virtue of being true to her despite everything, uttering no reproaches, and even endeavoring to get along with Agatson, whom she continued to adore even after he had thrown her out.

But now Hobbes set Ketcham's mind at rest in a light, bantering tone: "You know how Gene is. He gets all involved in these things and they have to run their course. Christine will probably come to the party and you can meet her then."

"I don't think she should come," Kathryn said. "She wouldn't like it at all. She's not used to the kind of people who will be there. Look at the way she was at Stofsky's party!"

"What do you mean?" Ketcham asked suavely. "She can't be more attractive than you." His charm was natural, and he was always thoughtful and attentive with women.

They met Pasternak in Freeman's and he was standing alone at the bar among the throngs of Lesbians that habituated the place. They ordered beer, and the thick, tense atmosphere was so contagious that they stood watching everything, unable to concentrate on each other.

The Lesbians were in couples, the "men," brutal, comradely, coarse; wearing badly cut business suits and loud ties. The "girls" were carbon copies, except for long hair and dresses. The bar was filled with raucous jokes, back slapping and the suck of cigarettes. A few graceful, shoulder swinging homosexuals glided in from the street, mincing, chirruping and trying to rub up against everyone.

"Christ, let's get out of here!" Ketcham exclaimed with unusual heat. "It's horrible!"

They went and the trance passed from them, and Pasternak started talking excitedly.

"Say, you know, I found Winnie this afternoon. That's why I couldn't make it in to Christine's. She's holed up in a pad out in Astoria throwing her morphine habit; just like Verger said. He gave me her address . . . It's out in a huge, stinking tenement section, and there was this Tristano record going the whole time I was there. She *lives* to bop!"

"It sounds horrible," Kathryn interjected.

"No, she was lying on the bed when I came in. She'd had ropes on herself last week. Imagine that, she'd tied herself down! And we talked and then her boy came in. This simpering little guy, some petty thief or someone, who brings her milk and a Danish every day. His name's Rocco Harmonia, or something like that; but they call him 'Little Rock' Harmony! What do you think of that? And he said to me the first thing: 'You know, man, Win's just about got the Chinaman off her back!' "

"What does that mean?" Ketcham inquired, fascinated by all of it as long as it did not come too close.

"Coming off junk! Isn't that mad? She was throwing the Chinaman off her back!"

He was still talking when they wandered into the Santa Maria, an old Italian bar that was now the hangout for crackpot painters, writers and a few miserable existentialists. The flat lighting gave everything an underdeveloped look. The place was filled with nasty arguments. Bitter, cracked voices were raised on all sides. Lonely, soft chinned young men stood around in couples, watching everyone else, and a girl at the bar was berating two boys for what she called "the lust for absolutes." There was contempt in her voice, the same scathing contempt that rolled back and forth across the room. The boys, ill dressed bohemians who wanted to talk about art, had been involved in the subject of "absolutes" against their will and sat sullenly, only half-listening. Everyone seemed to be watching everyone else.

Fortunately, Pasternak was oblivious to all this.

". . . And I got this big letter from Hart too. You remember I told you about Hart Kennedy! Well, he's driving east with a buddy of his and should be here next week."

Kennedy was a wild young man Pasternak had met on one of his previous trips to California. He had regaled Hobbes with fabulous stories of marijuana parties and crazy driving in the mountains around Denver where Kennedy was originally from. Hobbes thought of him as a sort of half-intellectual juvenile delinquent, but had never been able to get a straight impression from either Stofsky or Pasternak.

"He might be here in time for the party because he drives like a madman—absolutely the greatest driver in the world!—and he says he's got a new Cadillac. He wrote me all about this tremendous orgy he was at with a lot of Negro bop men and hipsters—"

Ketcham, though amused and interested, wanted to move on again, because the Village always irritated him. They strolled through the streets, just as a fine, sifting rain began. The bars were overflowing, music struggled with laughter. Angry people were trying to pick fights or get drunk. Young oily toughs were standing around in leering packs, watching the girls go by and hooting obscenely. Everyone traveled ceaselessly from street to street, dive to dive.

Washington Square, the trees already laden with rain, the arch hazed by a thin mist, was deserted but for a few couples sitting on the benches under umbrellas, thrusting with one another. Lonely, stoical old men, their worn corduroys soaked, crouched under the trees with sorrowful, lined faces.

They walked on and on, stopping here and there for beer, doing what they used to call, in the old days, "the grand tour of the Village"—now somehow unpleasant. Only Pasternak's enthusiasm carried them:

"And I'll get Verger to bring some weed to your party. He's gotten an oz. from a passer up on One Hundred and Twenty-fifth Street."

"Good," Kathryn said with exaggerated approval that caused the others some surprise. "I'm sick of drinking anyway. Do you think you can really get it?"

"Verger'll bring it along if you call him up."

"You do that, Paul. I've always wanted to smoke some, haven't you, Arthur?"

"Maybe it's the new taste sensation we've been looking for . . ."

They went to another place, a basement room with candles and war trophies, which was fashionable with an uptown crowd, and was not filled with motionless women in cool frocks and their inattentive companions. It was very much like a sad and unsuccessful cocktail party that had given up and moved to a working-class bar in the hope of inspiration.

"Why did you stand up Christine, Gene?" Kathryn asked brusquely. "She was phoning about it earlier."

Pasternak bunched his eyebrows, disliking the turn. "I told you, I was out seeing Winnie. I couldn't get in in time. But listen, you get Verger and his tea, and I'll see if I can round up Stofsky somewhere

. . . I don't know where the hell he's gone this time! . . . But we'll have this mad, vast party on Friday, eh? The greatest party! . . . You coming, Art?"

"Certainly, but you're not going to bring this Winnie are you?"

"No, she'll still be on the bed. Besides, she's laying low these days. This character she's with, this Little Rock, he's got her itchy about things. But I'll bring Christine, how about that?" He looked from Kathryn to Hobbes.

"Sure, Gene."

"I don't think it's a good idea at all, if there's going to be tea! I'm afraid she's going to get herself in trouble with that husband anyway, the way she's going."

Pasternak sulked. "Christ, she's okay. Why do you always dream up these things?"

They let it drop and stood having beers silently. Pasternak's joy at having found Winnie and hearing from Hart Kennedy, who was a very important friend to him, would not be dampened, and when they broke up for the evening on Eighth Street, heading for different subways, he said:

"You remember, Paul, you said you thought a new season was about to break? I guess you were right!" And he ran off through the puddles.

"Now, Arthur," Kathryn said firmly. "You be at our place at nine, or don't you come at all! I don't want you coming in dead drunk!"

Ketcham replied evenly: "What do you mean? I never get drunk," which was not true, but this was a standard game they played. "Besides, I want to see *you* get drunk. You're always saying you're going to, but then you go home!"

Kathryn was decidedly affirmative.

"I'm going to get stinking drunk and let the party take care of itself!"

"That's the only way," Ketcham laughed, although he was always worried for days before he gave one. "Just let yourself go."

—1952

315

Maxwell Bodenheim

(1893–1954)

Maxwell Bodenheim contributed greatly to the modernist movement. He is best remembered though as being one of the many Village characters. Born in Mississippi, Bodenheim (real name: Bodenheimer), moved to Chicago in 1913 during the Chicago Literary Renaissance, where he wrote plays with Ben Hecht and, along with Hecht, edited the short-lived Chicago Literary Times. *He moved to the Village in the late 1920s. A heavy drinker, his dissolute lifestyle eventually left him bereft and without funds, reduced to peddling poems for food and a few coins in Greenwich Village bars. He met a tragic end. He and his third wife were murdered by a mentally disturbed drifter whom they had befriended. His works of poetry include* Minna and Myself *(1918) and* Selected Poems, 1914–44 *(1946). His novels include* Blackguard *(1923),* Crazy Man *(1924),* Georgie May *(1928),* Sixty Seconds *(1929), and* Naked on Roller Skates *(1931). The following selections are taken from his autobiography,* My Life and Loves in Greenwich Village *(1954). In the first piece we meet Gertrude Stein, Alice B. Toklas, and an eccentric Village landlord by the name of Albert Strunsky. Born in Russia, the cantankerous Strunsky allowed impoverished artists to live rent free if he liked them. In the second, Bodenheim comments on an old Village landmark, the exceedingly ordinary Waldorf Cafeteria, a favorite hangout for everyone from Jackson Pollack to Joyce Johnson.*

Maxwell Bodenheim. "Gertrude Stein in Macdougal Alley" and "The Waldorf: A Cafeteria à la Einstein" from *My Life and Loves in Greenwich Village* (New York: Bridgehead Books, 1954).

from *My Life and Loves in Greenwich Village*

"Gertrude Stein in Macdougal Alley"

There were two great cultural forces in the thirties which collided with each other and sought to occupy the intellectual vacuum which is charitably called the bohemian mind. They were Gertrude Stein, who ruled the Village by remote control from Paris, and Albert Strunsky, the Village landlord, whose benevolent despotism extended beyond the frontiers of Sheridan Square.

When Strunsky knocked at your door on a cold, wintry morning, it was like a knock on the door of Macbeth, fraught with supernatural doom, evil-laden and irresistible because it was the echo of Heaven's judgment itself.

Strunsky was the pre-Marxist tutor of the impecunious Villagers, who taught them to place the gold of the marketplace before the gold of poetry, to put money before the Muses. At the same time Strunsky did more than any man in America, perhaps, to make the Village the cultural capital of the country.

This was the paradox of Strunsky: the sworn enemy of the arts who did more for its advancement than a flock of learned societies hoary with age and prestige. The true Villagers were "bums" to him, but whenever I have met any of these successful "bums" in California, New Mexico, Maine or Illinois, the first person they mentioned in their conversation was Albert Strunsky.

Strunsky, like Gertrude Stein, had seen the pathetic bird in the grass and cried out, "Alas! Alas!" From his bench in Washington Square park he had eyed the bleeding pigeon of the soul rise to new life on the wings of art, and the "bums" became prophets of the spirit to him, evangels of the creative future.

Strunsky, like a good father, punished with one hand and healed with the other. He was capable of ripping the hinges off

317

your door in the dead of winter, forcing you to move out with your goods and chattels, including your mistress, and then, driven to desperation by your girl's calculated weeping, he would slip you a ten-dollar bill "for breakfast" and assail you as a fool for having taken him seriously.

"The damned mortgages are bothering me," he would apologize, his rotund, apoplectic face redder than ever. "How do you expect me to hold on to my property if you bums don't pay your rent?" (He died penniless, a victim of his pity and the "bums" he secretly envied.)

While he continued to rave on, vowing vengeance on all Villagers and threatening a forced exodus from the hundreds of rooms and studios in the Village Square area, you boldly moved back your belongings—including your girl friend—to your room, while he looked on with impotent rage, yelling about his high blood pressure, and his blood-thirsty, dastardly, intractable, cannibalistic, insolent tenants.

You knew that Strunsky had seen the bleeding pigeon in the grass and that the yoke of pity had descended upon his neck, forcing him to tread forever in the path of Abel, his brother's keeper.

There were times when Strunsky's god of real estate impelled him to break with the Muses altogether and choke the angel of mercy within him. I remember one bleak dawn in November when the streets around Washington Square looked like a scene staged by an earthquake, with the help of a hurricane blowing from the Gulf of Mexico. Odd pieces of furniture, valises, trunks, pianos, bedding, caged parrots and songbirds, dogs, cats, pet monkeys, praying Buddhas, hat-boxes, canvases, statues, typewriters, models and manuscripts were piled high on the sidewalks, while the owners milled about in a state of confusion.

While the true Villagers were making the rounds of the bars, tea-rooms and cafeterias, Strunsky had hired a crew of huskies who had done a thorough job of dumping their belongings into the street. They had ambled bleary-eyed and pixillated to their homes in the Washington Square area, expecting to get a little "shut-eye" in their not-so-comfortable beds. Far from getting any sleep they found themselves a part of a living, surrealistic landscape that would have rivaled the grotesque imagination of Dali himself.

The homeless and woebegone held an emergency meeting on the Macdougal Street sidewalk and it was decided to send a delegation to Strunsky, pleading for grace and pardon. As at the convention of mice, the vital question arose, Who is going to bell the cat? The feline Strunsky was driven out of bed by the riotous clamor in his dispossessed kingdom, and he finally was persuaded to let the Village move back into its cramped rooms and studios.

The bleeding pigeon in the grass had dropped a trickle of blood on Strunsky's conscience, forcing him into the sacred precincts of pity, where humanity and the humanities hold sway over the human heart. Perhaps Gertrude Stein's bird had nothing to do with the humane emotions out of which the classical arts spring, and perhaps Miss Stein was the hard-boiled, granite-like woman she appeared to be in person, but Mr. Strunsky exhumed a deep philosophy out of her bird-in-the-glass exclamation.

Mr. Strunsky first came across Gertrude Stein by receiving a review copy of one of her books, *The Autobiography of Alice B. Toklas*, which was actually the personal memoirs of Miss Stein herself. Strunsky was not a literary reviewer, although his illiteracy led cynics like H. L. Mencken to believe that he actually wrote many book criticisms under assumed names.

It so happened that many aspiring authors in the Village, turned critics, would often pay their rent with discarded review books instead of greenbacks. Strunsky's basement apartment was cluttered with review copies of the latest books which he vowed he never read, but he often dipped into this "trash" surreptitiously, for he had a secret thirst for the very culture which he identified with spiritual and mental pauperism and degeneracy.

I had often discussed the significance of Gertrude Stein with Mr. Strunsky who was fascinated and amused by her echolalia or word-repetitions. He thought her language imitated the babble of children in Washington Square park, or the alcoholic blather of Village poets who assaulted him with demands for better living quarters when they failed to pay for their old ones. Whenever he felt a spark of meaning in the slag of her disjointed and circuitous sentences, his face lit up with a triumphant smile, as if he had entered into the great mystery of Art itself.

I thought that Miss Stein catered to the artist's need for revolt at a time when the political, economic and moral solutions to the problem of a decadent and collapsing culture were alien to him. "The eunuchs of the arts," to use a phrase of Thomas Wolfe, who had once been Strunsky's tenant, sought to overcome their impotent lust for life by alcoholic, sexual and aesthetic stimulants, brawling, squalling and falling under tables to register their protest against a business society that had not room for artists who deviated from its norm of profit hoarding.

Greenwich Villagers who rebelled against language with Miss Stein were aesthetic revolutionaries who, like the logical positivists today, imagined that the world crisis was a problem of semantics, and that if the right four-letter words were used there would be a closer harmony and understanding between nations and peoples.

Of course Miss Stein was responsible for the Hemingway school of writing in America with its elaborate, complicated efforts to achieve simplicity in literary expression, but simple words embodying the stupidities of modern fiction did not in any way retard the decay of our Puritan culture fashioned by Emerson, Melville, Hawthorne and Poe.

Strunsky would listen to my exposition of Gertrude Stein and then he would rattle off a page of Steinian prose, repeating the Hebrew word "*Messhugeh*" (crazy) till he fell into a Steinian mood and broke up his already broken English into a jumble of words and phrases that signaled his initiation into the Steinian universe where nonsense achieved the gravity of classical sense.

When Miss Stein visited America after an absence of many years (this was in '33) she was greeted like a conquering hero, for the American intelligentsia was still under the delusion that our literature could be saved by a revolution in style, even though its body had been drained of its intellectual and moral contents, deprived of its guts, and filled with the embalming fluids of Freudian pathology, like a corpse barbered, waxed and dressed for the inspection of relatives.

Miss Stein was staying at the Algonquin, the Mecca for visiting celebrities, accompanied, as usual, by her secretary and *alter ego*, Alice Toklas. A literary tea and book action was arranged by some friends with Gertrude Stein as guest of honor. Strunsky was my private guest, and when Miss Stein appeared and sat down in granite silence after a flurry of applause, she reminded me of Hawthorne's "Great Stone Face," grim, masculine and forbidding. Her grey-white hair cut to a mannish bob looked like a Colonial wig, and her dull, nondescript sweater added to her masculine appearance.

Strunsky nudged me and whispered, "She looks like George Washington at Gettysboig," meaning Valley Forge, perhaps. I myself was thinking of the Lincoln Memorial in Potomac Park. When she rose and spoke the effect was tremendous, as if a statue had come to life. The chairman was so unnerved that he introduced the celebrated Miss Stein as "Albert Einstein." Immediately, of course, he gabbled an improvised cover-up for his blunder: "—er-ah—Miss Stein had caused a revolution as great as Einstein's revolution in physics." There was not the mirth you might have expected, at the slip of the tongue. I daresay the identification with some heroic or revered image was fairly general and too impressive for laughter.

Miss Stein, not at all surprisingly to me, spoke like any other sane person, in simple English that bore not a trace nor a hint of the pathological. Max Eastman, in his essay "The Cult of Unintelligibility," tried to prove that Miss Stein's style originated in a madhouse, and that in her heroic effort to achieve simplicity of speech and purity of emotion she was doing her bit to plunge the English language into the snake-pit of insanity. At the tea party, however, Miss Stein was as logical and coherent as, at least, Hemingway, expressing that perfect absence of idea marking the aesthete who has nothing to say and says it very lucidly.

However she gave us one Steinian repetition that was all to the good. She said that the artist should be helped to tide over the depression, and she had done all she could in Paris to keep the wolf from the artists' door. She said it some dozen times and sat down to thunderous and rapturous applause. I certainly did not disagree with her, but could not help thinking of the general seriousness which greeted Coolidge's statement to the effect that the depression was due to the fact that millions were unemployed and that prosperity would return when there was more cash in the pay envelope.

The book auction was a lively affair, though a prim spinster, bidding for an "autographed copy" of Miss Stein's *Three Lives* got what proved to be a copy of *Fanny Hill*, wrapped in the jacket of the Stein opus. Strunsky had contributed many of the books to the auction, and I suspect that the embarrassing mistake was caused by his peculiar sense of humor. The edition was a particularly flagrant one with the juicy drawings by the Village's Madonna-eyed female illustrator. It was like the pornographic statue in Chekhov's story, that everybody chuckled at, then passed on to somebody else as quickly as possible, by whatever ruse was necessary. One couldn't have that thing around, even in Greenwich Village.

A few days later Alice Toklas and Gertrude Stein drove down to the Village to observe the operation of the denizens. Trying to entertain them, I suggested that we go to the Village Magistrate Court, then held in the historic and picturesque architectural oddity, called variously a monstrosity and a masterpiece, at Tenth Street and Sixth Avenue. Strunsky had been hauled before the judge for "insulting" one of his female tenants. When we arrived, Strunsky was "telling it to the judge."

"It's an outrage, your honor," he expostulated. "I didn't lay a finger on the girl."

"The charge is not assault but defamation," the magistrate explained.

"Defamation?" Strunsky queried. "Why I only called the bum a two-bit whore."

"Mr. Strunsky," said the magistrate sternly. "The complaining witness maintains that she is a respectable model."

"Your honor," said Strunsky. "Posing for artists is no fun. It's hard work. And that kind is not what you call bums—and worse in Times Square. But this kind, they call themselves models—in the Village we call them *horizontalists*: they make their living laying down."

"Now, Mr. Strunsky," the magistrate remonstrated, "I must remind you that you were at fault, legally, accepting a woman whose profession you thought to be what you have specified, as a tenant."

"Tenant?" said the fabulous landlord. "Oh, that's only in a technical sense."

"How can that be?"

"Well, according to the dictionary a tenant is 'a person who pays rent for the use of a building or an apartment.' I always read that to the bums, but they won't even believe Webster. They figure that a tenant is a person who sticks a landlord as a sucker, then goes around as a bum pretending to be an artist or a model. A real Strunsky tenant is anybody trying to get a studio rent-free."

There has been much hilarity in the courtroom, properly rebuked by the magistrate. Miss Toklas had smiled continuously, had giggled, but Miss Stein had sat looking like one of the stone lions in front of the Public Library. At this point she whispered to Miss Toklas: "It's right out of *Three Saints in Four Acts*."

"Mr. Strunsky," the judge inquired, "why do you let these 'bums' as you call them—more or less appropriately—occupy your premises rent-free, sometimes for long periods, as I know?"

"Genius is not like measles," Strunsky explained. "It doesn't break out all of a sudden. It must be nursed and taken care of like a tender plant. Sometimes I guess right and the plant grows into a beautiful bush with blossoms. But usually the plant is just a stinkweed and I get disgusted. When I'm disgusted I say things that I don't mean."

"I see," said the judge, with a look of genuine benevolence. "Is that why you moved the complaining witness back into her room after you got an order of the court to dispossess her?"

"Of course," the landlord agreed. "When I called her a two-bit whore I meant it as a compliment. At least she had the common sense to charge something for laying. Most of her Village friends go to bed with a man if he offers them a cheese sandwich. Or they'll go to bed with anybody for nothing, just because they're bored. They are tired, pathetic doves. *'A bird in the grass; alas, alas!'"*

Miss Stein's face suddenly glowed with human warmth, and she exploded with hearty laughter.

When the case was dismissed, Miss Stein, Miss Toklas, Strunsky and I made a personally conducted tour of his domain, inspecting the celebrated "Gonorrhea Mansions." Miss Stein was fascinated by the famous "duplex" studios. Strunsky explained that he had added the balconies and wooden ladders to the tiny rooms in order to accommodate an extra bed, so that a boy and girl could pool their finances and pay Strunsky a couple of dollars now and then without having to share the same studio couch.

Strunsky told Miss Stein that a young man or woman who broke the taboo and climbed the ladder to the roommate's bed would be dealt with summarily by true Villagers. There was a young woman, for instance, who posed as a lesbian, but often climbed the ladder into a strange man's bed. Usually she got away with it, the flesh being weak, but once when she scaled the ladder, she found some unknown girl had been ahead of her. The jealous girl pushed her over the balcony, and she sustained serious injuries.

Miss Toklas climbed the ladder, with a sense of curiosity and adventurous excitement. She got considerably more than she was bargaining for. When she reached the last rung and peered between the wooden stakes of the balcony she screamed bloody murder and hurried down.

"There's a tiger up there!"

In the hallway, when she had more or less composed herself, she asked, "What's the meaning of this, Mr. Strunsky?"

"Oh, one of my tenants."

"I thought you said the room was unoccupied."

"I meant there wasn't a man on the balcony. And there shouldn't have been a tiger. It's only a cub, anyway. There's a young lady who makes a living buying animals for zoos, and when she comes to New York from the jungles she always stays in one of my palatial Washington Square studios. I ordered her to get rid of the cub, and she must have hidden it up there till she could find a home—or parking space—for it."

We went to the Jumble Shop, where Miss Stein and Mr. Strunsky engaged in an argument about the nature of art. Mr. Strunsky rather hogged the floor, after a couple of cocktails. He had no use for ivory tower art, he thought that the homosexuals who painted or wrote in the Village symbolized the sterility of art divorced from life; he advocated the artifical impregnation of lesbians—that would restore them to true feminine creativity: "Make them have babies."

After a good deal of this, Miss Stein and Miss Toklas excused themselves.

Strunsky was an Old Testament character, every bit a patriarch, imbued thoroughly with the Scriptural idea that generation was in obedience to the highest law and the respective organs should be devoted to that, not to degenerate and obscene abomination. Besides, lesbians were rather more inclined than other amorous couples to burn cigarette holes in mattresses! (I do not see that, but he was in a position to know.)

Yes, Strunsky, the Greenwich Village landlord, who was pauperized by his pity, was the true artist, working with the shreds and patches of blasted lives in an effort to weave a human pattern of being that would somehow be a copy of Man made in God's image.

It is to be hoped we shall some day rediscover his prototype and then there will be many Strunskys who have made art a rhythm of thought and action rather than a framed canvas to be exhibited for sale to tourists idly staring at the Washington Square Open Air Art Show.

"The Waldorf: A Cafeteria à la Einstein"

The true Villagers who stand on their heads are like the denizens of Mars who would feel alien and uprooted if they landed in

Manhattan with the help of the spaceships provided by the exuberant authors of science fiction. They must have a familiar meeting place, a microcosm that shall reflect their world-picture of things with macrocosmic overtones. *The heart is a lonely hunter*, as a fine young woman novelist, Carson McCullers, has told us; it forever seeks other hearts, trapped in isolation, unable to join in the wild chorus of being.

Villagers for the past thirty years (as long as we can remember) have always pooled their loneliness in a centrally located cafeteria somewhere between Sheridan Square and Washington Square. Back in the middle twenties, when I upset the critics by comparing the moon to "a spilling glass of gin" and somebody else said it was a gong tolling the doom of civilization, the nerve center of the neurotic Village was Hubert's Cafeteria in Sheridan Square. It was torn down in the thirties to make room for a bank building—a prophetic reminder that the Village was fated to go bourgeois and bow to the god of Real Estate. But in the late twenties Bobby Edwards, the Village minstrel, was strumming away at his cigar box ukulele:

> In Hubert's Cafeteria
> The girls all suffer from sex-hysteria.
> They drink a glass of gin or wine
> And make a dash for Bodenheim.

When Hubert's Cafeteria gave way to the bankers' world of dollars and cents, Village group life moved across the street where the Life Cafeteria beckoned the lonely, the insulted and the damned.

The class war between the true Villagers and the owners of the Village eating-place was waged with sound and fury at Life Cafeteria. Unfortunately the owners of the huge self-service restaurant and the true Villagers differed materially on the meaning of the word "cafeteria." It is a problem in semantics which the Village has not solved even today.

According to the proprietors of "Life" the cafeteria was a business venture and not a philanthropic experiment. They had established a restaurant, not a public meeting place for true Villagers to weave endless carpets of conversation, embroidered with strange decisions for living taken from Sappho, Buddha, Plato, Oscar Wilde, T. S. Eliot, Tolstoy, the Marquis de Sade and Spengler. (Villagers discovered Marx in the thirties during the great Depression.)

They were serving not manna from heaven, but food that must be paid for with cash. The restrooms were built for certain biological functions, and not for romantic assignations between members of the third or intermediate sex.

The true Villagers argued that the owners of "Life" had made a grievous semantic mistake. A cafeteria, in the esoteric language of the Village, was primarily a refuge for talkers, not eaters, and if the talk ended on an erotic note, the restrooms were the proper places to celebrate the rites of Venus or Priapus. If a true Villager could not pay the sum punched on his meal check, he had the right to wait an hour or twenty-four hours until he was "bailed out" by a compassionate "Elk" whose heart was as open as his purse to the call of hunger. Finally, a true Villager had the divine right to filch a meal-check from an adjoining table, order up a dollar's worth of food on it and then present his own blank check to the cashier, while the "Elk" searched high and low for his missing pasteboard. Self-preservation, argued the true Villager, is the first law of nature.

The owners of "Life" insisted on their semantic definition of "cafeteria" and called in the police to back them up. But a cafeteria with a policeman at every table is not exactly a pleasant place to dine in (we might hazard a terrible pun and call it an "Arrestaurant") and Life Cafeteria was emptied of all its customers—paying and non-paying. It was forced to shut down and was broken into many store units that sell everything from bologna to books.

We do not know who persuaded the owners of the Waldorf chain of cafeterias to open one of their low-price eating places on Sixth Avenue near Eighth Street. No doubt he was fired after the tragic event, for he caused the Waldorf owners to inherit a headache bequeathed by the proprietors of Hubert's, "Life," Stewart's and other restaurant men who discovered that a Village cafeteria was not an eating place but a meeting place where people chewed the rag, roasted the latest poet or painter and made love *sub rosa* in the restrooms.

The Waldorf people sought heroically to save their lavishly appointed restaurant which the true Villagers looked upon as a cosmic cafeteria where spoons were used to point a moral and saucers flew in the direction of a philosopher to indicate a rejection of his private universe. The first innovation was to introduce a pay-as-you eat system so that no true Villager could manipulate meal-checks or occupy a seat for hours until he was "bailed out" by an accommodating "Elk."

The restrooms were nailed up, striking a blow at true Villagers with certain physiological or amatory propensities. The cash register was placed on the counter as warning to the true Villagers that they had entered a cash-register universe where the countermen rang up dimes and quarters instead of rhymes and quirks of the creative imagination. "No smoking" signs were tacked to the walls in an effort to discourage talkers who brought their sandwiches and cigarettes from their studios and managed to bum a dime for coffee.

Many true Villagers cannot talk or reminisce without blowing circles of smoke towards the ceiling, and this prohibition against smoking was challenged as a breach of a natural right—but the ban against cigarettes was strictly enforced.

Then a short-story writer who had once practiced law insisted on breaking the ban against smoking, and the manager called in one of New York's finest to have the culprit ejected. As the cop stood open-mouthed in amazement, the ex-lawyer quoted from the code dealing with the duties of restaurant owners, and the bluecoat had to admit that a diner had the legal right to put a Camel or a Chesterfield between his lips during or after meals. The Waldorf management was forced to remove the "no smoking" signs, and the semantic battle between the true Villagers and the Waldorf was switched from the tobacco to the erotic front.

An artist's model who owned a frayed mink coat—a family heirloom—was commandeered by some Villagers who had heard of the famous Venus-in-furs, with a view to bringing a blush to the managerial cheek. When she removed the coat she had on nothing but her bare skin and a pair of green pumps. The management, however, did not blush but called the police instead. The girl was carted off to Bellevue and there we hope that the staff of learned psychiatrists was able to teach her how to distinguish between the bedroom and the market place; that each locale has its own decorum and special proprieties not the least of which is the choice of suitable raiment.

Before we leave Life Cafeteria and its hoary chronicle let us give to it one more nostalgic *huzzah!* And hail to the Waldorf which whatever its original intention to establish an eatery of elegance has nobly acquiesced to bohemia.

—1954

Dawn Powell

(1897–1965)

Literary titans Edmund Wilson and Gore Vidal did us all a favor by rescuing Dawn Powell from certain oblivion. It's a shame though that this wickedly funny writer did not live long enough to experience firsthand her much-deserved renaissance. Powell was born in Mt. Gilead, Ohio. After graduating from college in the Midwest, Powell moved to New York, where she lived in the Village, at various locations, for the rest of her life. The "wicked pavilion" of the title refers to the Café Julien, which is modeled after Powell's favorite hangout, the elegant and long-defunct Cafe Lafayette, where writers, artists, and assorted hangers-on cavort until the wee hours of the morning. Herbert Muschamp in the New York Times *described her work as offering "the most luminous portrayal of life downtown in the era between Edna St. Vincent Millay and the Stonewall uprising." The Vermont-based Steerforth Press has reissued Powell's work, long out of print. Powell, like other women of her generation who had gravitated toward New York, epitomized a certain type of urban female writer: wickedly funny, bitterly sarcastic, unmercifully biting and yet leavened with a touch of human kindness.*

" . . . the farewell banquet . . . "
from *The Wicked Pavilion*

By eight o'clock it began to be apparent to even the dullest tourist that this was no ordinary night at the Café Julien. Guests who had dropped in for a single apéritif, en route to an inexpensive dinner at San Remo or Grand Ticino's in the Italian quarter, stayed on through curiosity drinking up their dinner money very slowly, ordering a new round just as importunate newcomers were about to snatch their table from under them. They could see important-looking elderly gentlemen in dinner clothes peep in the café door, then proceed onward into the private dining room at the rear. It must be the Silurian annual banquet, someone hinted, the Silurians being newspapermen who had been in the trade twenty-five years.

"How could anybody afford to dine here if he's been in newspaper work that long?" argued others. It was a dinner honoring Romany Marie, or Barney Gallant, or survivors of the Lafayette Escadrille, others said, recalling similar occasions in the past. It was a banquet of real estate men commemorating their grief in selling the Julien to a mysterious concern rumored to be about to change it into apartments. This last theory was gaining credence when the unfamiliar sight of Monsieur Julien himself gave old-timers the clue to what was going on. Yes, it was a dinner of the Friends of Julien, an association of gourmets of great distinction, and what was more sensational was the whisper that this was their farewell dinner. Photographers from newspapers and magazines were setting up impressive-looking apparatus in every corner and mousy little people who inhabited the cheap little rooms upstairs and were never seen in the glamorous café suddenly showed their frightened little faces at the door. Hoff Bemans, leading his guest panelists into the café for a rewarding drink at anybody else's expense, spotted Dalzell Sloane and beckoned his men to crowd around the table, so that when Biggs returned from the men's room he could scarcely squeeze in.

"By George, I've done it again!" Hoff exclaimed proudly. "I didn't even know the Café was going to go out of business and here I stumbled right into the big night. So that's the old master, Julien himself!"

Monsieur Julien was a gay bachelor of sixty who made enough from the café bearing his name to live and usually dine at the Plaza. He was the last of a formidable dynasty of French chefs, inheriting the great reputation without the faintest culinary interest. But after a youthful struggle against the public insistence that all Juliens must be cooks he had surrendered. Cooking contests, cook books, food columns, canned dainties, all must have his name as sponsor. Wherever he went he was questioned about this dish or that sauce. At first he had sighed candidly, "I assure you if I had a pair of eggs and a greased griddle on the stove I would still starve to death." Later on in his career he answered more archly, "Ah, if I were to tell you how I make that dish then you would be Julien and what would I be?"

His grandfather had been proprietor of the famous Julien's in Paris and had founded the New York branch early in the century. Even those who had never tasted *escargots Julien* quickly realized that they must pretend they knew, and would sniff the air and paw the ground like truffle hounds, sighing, "Ah, Julien's!" Having put by a nice fortune paying French salaries and charging American prices the old gentleman was finally done in by the shrewdness of his equally thrifty employees who sold furniture and dishes under his very nose and found many convenient ways of rewarding themselves. The Paris place vanished in World War One and the New York café had been about to give up in 1929 when a group of wealthy gentlemen from all over the eastern seaboard (and one very proud member from Seattle) decreed that the name of Julien must not perish. All those who had swooned over a Julien lobster bisque or cassoulet of duck Julien-Marie (or said they had) vowed with their hands on their checkbooks that Julien's must go on. The finest lawyers, bankers, jurists, all manner of men of affairs co-operated to insure future security. Monsieur Julien was put on salary and to keep the venture from smacking of Depression opportunism the group called itself simply the Friends of Julien, standing by the thin of the thirties to reap profits in the forties. Self-made men, lacking in clubs and college backgrounds, listed membership in the Friends of Julien beside their names in *Who's Who* for it hinted of world travel and financial standing.

Most of the Friends were by no means habitués but appeared only at the annual dinner where they toasted bygone days, the chef, the wine steward, the bartender, and above all the great Julien. Julien, who appeared in the kitchen only for photographers, always wept over these unearned tributes to his magic touch with a field salad and permitted himself to quote elegies to his skill from old rivals—Moneta, the Ambassador's Sabatini, Henry Charpentier; and he summoned sentimental memories of days when the incomparable Escoffier of London's Carlton called personally on Papa Julien to pay his respects to the only man in the world he deigned to call "Maître," or so Julien *fils* declared. The anecdotes grew more impressive each year and convinced by his own publicity Julien made himself instead of his forebears the hero.

This evening's banquet had finally gotten under way in the private room but the café guests continued to dawdle, sending emissaries back to spy on the feast and report back who was there and what was being said. The waiters' unusual speed in presenting checks as a method of clearing the café only made the guests more obstinately determined to stay on enjoying the splendid affair by proxy. Caught in the spirit of the occasion Hoff Bemans was ordering round after round of highballs, figuring that he might stick Dalzell Sloane with the check by carefully timing his own departure or if Sloane got away first there was a very young first novelist along who had been on his panel and would be too shy to protest. On the program that evening Hoff had made insulting and derogatory remarks concerning the young man's work and youthful pomposity but he vaguely felt letting him buy the drinks would atone for this. For that matter no reason why old Sloane shouldn't have it since he would be getting into Cynthia Earle's pocket any minute.

"Thought your *City Life* piece on Marius didn't quite come off," Hoff said genially to Briggs. "Some good things in it but as a whole it just didn't come off."

"Thanks," Briggs said absently. He was staring at the young novelist wondering what it felt like to have your name on a fat book, and have people talking about it as if it meant something. The novel had worried him because the author's method wasn't like his own at all. Instead of building his characters on a sensible economic structure this fellow built them on what they had to eat and drink from the breast right through Schrafft's and the Grand Central Oyster Bar; whatever they elected to eat was evidently supposed to mean something about their hidden natures. Even their retching was recorded and it didn't indicate they had had a bad oyster but meant they were having an emotional *crise*. When they weren't eating, this author's characters were all put through boarding schools and colleges, all Ivy League, no matter how poor they talked, and Briggs, having worked his way through a minor university, was irritated at having to work his way again through these fictional characters' education. What did people like about that kind of book? Maybe it was the deep sex meaning the fellow gave to those menus, for the hero was always drawing some high-bosomed girl into his arms between courses, the hot oatmeal pounding through his veins.

"I read your book," Briggs roused himself to tell the young man.

"Thanks," said the author gratefully. Briggs noted that whatever fine liquors his characters enjoyed their creator was limiting himself to simple beer, though this economy might later be regretted when he found he had to pay for his comrades' expensive tastes.

Hoff was continuing the discussion on Marius' show, pointing out errors in the critics' reviews due perhaps to their not having consulted Mr. Bemans' recent book on the subject. The *Times* critic, for example, persisted in linking Marius' work with that of Forrester and Sloane which was utterly idiotic because neither Ben nor Dalzell could paint the simplest apple to resemble Marius' touch. Hoff wished Dalzell to tell Cynthia Earle, moreover, that he felt very hurt that his contribution to the Marius Long Playing Record had been cut out and he considered that was probably the real reason the project had been such a flop. Without his key words the thing hadn't jelled, had not, as he liked to put it, "quite come off."

The café had never been noisier or more crowded. Everyone was shouting to be heard and from the private dining room there were periodic roars of applause. As the banquet progressed curious changes were taking place all over the restaurant. Certain of the banqueters were slipping out to the café between their gourmet

dishes to freshen up their palates with quick shots of rye or invigorating martinis and later on grew sociable enough to draw up
chairs and make acquaintance with the café customers. Some of
these truants urged their new friends to return to the banquet with
them, gave them their own places and went back to the café for
more informal fun. Before the dinner was even half over the personnel of the Friends' table had changed in such a surprising fashion that there was a lively sprinkling of sports jackets and dark
shirts and these strangers were being served roast duckling with
the finest of Chambertin while out in the café their legitimate highballs and rubbery canapés were being finished by distinguished
drunken Friends. It was in this interchange that Hastings Hardy
wound up at Dalzell's table while Briggs, done out of his rightful
place, found himself in the private dining room drinking toasts to
personalities he'd never heard of. He had arrived at the moment
when Monsieur Julien was making the great salad with his own
hands—that is to say he took into his own sacred hands various ingredients deftly offered by assistants and poured them personally
into the bowl. In the solemn hush induced by this traditional rite
cooks' caps could be seen bobbing around corners as they strained
to see; other diners bent their heads reverently, and down in the
lower kitchen the seafood chef was sustaining himself with mighty
swigs of Martel in his pride that Monsieur Julien had thought his
sole good enough to claim as his own handiwork.

Toasts had been made to famous dishes, countries, high-
living monarchs and again and again to Monsieur Julien until the
master was shaken to tears, and many others were moved to
blow their noses heartily. To restore calm the oldest living member rose to propose a health, he said, to that great chef, Henri
Charpentier, inventor of the *Crepe Suzette* which had brought
happiness to so many thousands. The applause inspired Monsieur Julien to interpolate that Charpentier, excellent genius
though he was, had been surpassed by Sabatini, king of them all,
next of course to Escoffier.

"'Born with the gift of laughter and a sense that the world is
mad,'" shouted one of the café intruders joyously, but a neighbor

335

yanked him down by his brown-checked coattail hissing, "You ass, not THAT Sabatini."

"Five generations of kings Sabatini served," Monsieur Julien went on unperturbed, his black eyes flashing proudly under the table, "including Umberto and the Czar of all the Russians. As for Charpentier's *Crepe Suzette,* can it really compare in delicacy and sheer originality with the *Coeur Flottant* Sabatini created especially for that queen among women, Mary Garden?"

A Friend who had spent the last three courses in the café returned in time to catch the last words and squeezing into the group snatched up Briggs's glass and shouted a ringing toast to Mary Garden, King Umberto and the Czar himself, then sat down on the nonexistent chair dragging napery, silver, dishes and six kinds of greens to the floor with him. It was too bad that the photographer chanced to get a fine shot of this disorderly scene for it spoiled the nostalgic sentimental tone of the accompanying article on "Farewell to the Café Julien" and made many ministers give thanks that this palace of sin was finally to be routed by clean-minded citizens.

It was this picture, showing Briggs wiping salad off the fallen comrade with Monsieur Julien handing him a napkin with Gallic courtesy, that turned out to be lucky for Briggs. The very day the picture appeared he was offered the job of restaurant reporter on a tabloid. It meant postponing his literary career which grieved him but was a great relief to Janie, who loved him devotedly and without illusions.

—1954

Lionel Trilling

(1905–1975)

An American educator and literary critic, Lionel Trilling spent most of his career teaching at Columbia University. A longtime contributor to the Partisan Review, *his major works include* The Liberal Imagination *(1950),* Freud and the Crisis of Our Culture *(1955),* The Opposing Self *(1955),* Beyond Culture *(1965), and* The Mind in the Modern World *(1972). He published one novel,* The Middle of the Journey *(1947), about the intellectual milieu of the 1930s and 1940s. This piece about another famous literary critic, Edmund Wilson, appeared in his autobiography,* A Gathering of Fugitives.

"Edmund Wilson: A Backward Glance" from *A Gathering of Fugitives*

In 1929 I signalized my solidarity with the intellectual life by taking an apartment in Greenwich Village. I was under no illusion that the Village was any longer in its great days—I knew that in the matter of residential preference I was a mere epigone. So much so, indeed, that my apartment was not in a brownstone house or in a more-or-less reconditioned tenement, but in a brand-new, yellow brick, jerry-built, six-story apartment building, exactly like the apartment buildings that were going up all over the Bronx and

Brooklyn. Still, the Village was the Village, there seemed no other place in New York where a right-thinking person might live, and many of my friends held the same opinion and were settled nearby. What is more, my address was Bank Street, which, of all the famous streets in the Village, seemed to me at the time to have had the most distinguished literary past, although I cannot now remember my reasons for thinking so. And to validate its present dignity, to suggest that what the Village stood for in American life was not wholly a matter of history, Edmund Wilson lived just across the way. Someone had pointed out his apartment to me and I used to take note of his evening hours at his desk.

I did not meet Wilson until later in the year, when I called on him at the offices of *The New Republic* to solicit work as a reviewer. He was at that time a rather slender young man, giving no hint of the engaging appearance of a British ship captain closely related to Henry James which he was to have a few years later. It was scarcely a meeting at all, for my admiration, and envy, of Wilson made me shy, and Wilson himself seemed shy: there were just enough years between us to make it possible that he felt the special uneasiness, which I then could not imagine, of the established senior toward the aspiring junior. He politely showed me over the rows and piles of books—those melancholy rows and piles of books in the office of the literary editor, passively waiting to be noticed—and we made no connection whatever. Nor, indeed, did we ever become at all well acquainted after other meetings during the years, but I speak of Wilson in a personal way because he had so personal an effect upon me. He seemed in his own person, and young as he was, to propose and to realize the idea of the literary life.

We are all a little sour on the idea of the literary life these days. The image of the institutionalized intellectual activity of the intellectual capital, of the man of letters in a community of his compeers, no longer pleases and commands us. And very likely there is some good reason for this feeling. But the literary life, apart from the fact that it may have its good pleasures and true rewards, is quite indispensable to civilization, and it isn't a propitious sign that we have become disenchanted with it. In

America it has always been very difficult to believe that this life really exists at all or that it is worth living. But for me, and for a good many of my friends, Wilson made it a reality and a very attractive one. He was, of course, not the only good writer of the time, but he seemed to represent the life of letters in an especially cogent way, by reason of the orderliness of his mind and the bold lucidity and simplicity of his prose—lucidity and simplicity of style seemed bold to me even then—and because of the catholicity of his interests and the naturalness with which he dealt with the past as well a with the present. One got from him a whiff of Lessing at Hamburg, of Sainte-Beuve in Paris.

I remember with great distinctness and particular gratitude a specific incident of the personal effect of Wilson's intellectual quality and position. It took place at what I think was our second meeting, which occurred in a men's room of the New School for Social Research during an intermission at some political affair of the Thirties. At that time "everybody" was involved in radical politics in one degree or another, and Wilson himself was a controversial figure because of his famous statement, made in his essay of 1932, "A Plea to Progressives," that we—that is, the progressives or liberals—should take Communism away from the Communists. I was trying to write a book about Matthew Arnold and having a bitter time of it because it seemed to me that I was working in a lost world, that nobody wanted, or could possibly want, a book about Matthew Arnold. Nor was I being what in those days would have been called "subjective"—no one did want the book. They wanted it even the less because it was to be a doctoral dissertation: there was at that time a great deal of surveillance of the dwelling places of the mind, and ivory towers were very easily inputted; the university, it is true, was just then beginning to figure in people's minds more than ever before in America, but it did not enjoy the prestige, though ambiguous, which it now has, and I was much ashamed of what I had undertaken. But Wilson asked me how my book was getting on, and not merely out of politeness but, as was clear, because he actually thought that a book on Matthew Arnold might be interesting and useful. He wanted to read it. It is impossible to overestimate the liberating effect which this had upon me, the sudden sense that I no longer had to suppose that I was doing a shameful academic drudgery, that I was not required to work with the crippling belief that I was "turning away" from the actual and miserable present to the unreal and comfortable past. The kindest and most intelligent of professors could not possibly have done this for me—it needed Wilson with his involvement in the life of the present which was so clearly not at odds with his natural and highly developed feeling for scholarship.

My first sense of Wilson has remained with me over the intervening years, in which, as is natural, I have found myself sometimes at odds with him. Any reader's relation to a critic is, and ought to be, an uneasy one, and if the reader is himself given to the practice of criticism, he is especially likely to turn a questioning mind on other critics, for he defines himself by the questions he asks and the disagreements he institutes. But in the back-and-forth of critical dialectic it has never occurred to me to alter my first estimate of Wilson's special intellectual quality or my judgment of the peculiar importance of his early work. And the rightness of that judgment is confirmed by *The Shores of Light*, the volume in which Wilson collects his essays and reviews of the Twenties and Thirties. There are things in it which seem to me quite mistaken, as when, to exemplify what he calls the "stuffed-shirt side of Wordsworth," Wilson cites "The Leech-Gatherer," which is surely one of the finest of Wordsworth's poems; or when he speaks of Samuel Butler's "queer intellectual position in attacking Darwin"—there is nothing at all queer about it. But the mistakes do not matter very much— they really never do matter much in a good critic; they may even be an element of his virtue. And Wilson's critical virtue of the Twenties and Thirties is really as large as we remember it to be. The essays and reviews, read thirty or twenty years later, are as serious, as workmanlike, as interesting, as they ever seemed. This is indeed a considerable achievement, for it is the unhappy characteristic of much work of the same period that it now seems faint and dim, unformed and tiresome.

The Shores of Light bears the subtitle "A Literary Chronicle of the Twenties and Thirties" and in the historiography of the period in which it was written and to which it refers it is a document of first importance. The period is now far enough in the past to justify its being made an object of academic study, and the notions which are held of it by students and by young teachers are often enough of a kind to make one despair of the whole possibility of literary history. Possibly Wilson's collection will do something to correct the gross misapprehensions that prevail. It constitutes the best account of the culture of the period that I know, and what it lacks in system and completeness, it more than compensates for by its intimate and accurate understanding of literary events. No academic history is likely to improve on the simplicity and directness of the understanding which Wilson gives us of such matters as the Humanist controversy, the attitude to the popular arts, the early doctrinaire nationalism of Van Wyck Brooks, the ideas about the relation of literature and politics which flourished after 1929.

Of the ninety pieces which comprise *The Shores of Light*, seventy-three first appeared in *The New Republic*, of which Wilson was for some years the literary editor. We have nothing in our intellectual life today like *The New Republic* of that time, no periodical, generally accepted by the intellectual class, serving both politics and literature on the assumption that politics and literature naturally live in a lively interconnection. After Wilson left the magazine, that assumption began to lose its vitality. It was an idea entirely beyond the comprehension of Bruce Bliven, under whose editorship it quite died. But it was taken for granted in Wilson's day, and the social, political concern of the magazine, however, we want to estimate its value in itself, made the perfect context for his literary criticism. The belief in a national moral destiny, which marked liberal social and political opinion after the first war, complemented and gave weight to the sense of a developing American culture.

This social and political context for his criticism was not the only advantage that Wilson derived from his editorial post on *The New Republic*. The authority with which he could speak by right of function as well as by right of talent; the frequency with which, as a matter of duty, his work appeared; the continuity of his writing over a considerable time—these circumstances were of great benefit to him. He was not in the situation of the merely occasional reviewer or essayist, who, if he has anything to say, is likely to say too much and to say it too hard in order to establish his identity and his authority, and this editorial situation of Wilson's had, I think, a decisive effect on his style. In the preface to *The Shores of Light*, Wilson apologizes for his frequent use of the first person singular, which, he says, was a prevailing habit of the time even among young and unknown men; but the apology is needless, and the case and number of the pronoun are exactly appropriate to his situation. "I" has its own modesty, and a more impersonal form would not have been suitable to a writer addressing himself regularly to the relatively small and essentially homogeneous group of people who read *The New Republic*. The tone of the pieces of *Classics and Commercials*, most of which appeared in *The New Yorker*, is not so felicitous, chiefly because of Wilson's natural response to the size of the audience and its heterogeneity.

One of the things that must strike the reader of *The Shores of Light* is Wilson's love of books in and for themselves. This has not changed with the years, and it is what made so many of the younger critics, when *Classics and Commercials* appeared two years ago, pass over the critical judgments they disagreed with to speak of their pleasure and relief at Wilson's passion for literature. Of this Wilson himself is aware, and about it he is militant. In 1938 he wrote one of his most amusing parodies, "The Pleasures of Literature," in which he assumed the character of Christopher Morley, a browser among dusty shelves, a devourer of delicious half-forgotten tomes, a reader under hedgerows of delightful, ever-to-be-cherished volumes; in which guise and by which device he made a plea for books in themselves, for *belles lettres* (the very name has become a sneer). In 1938 it was political seriousness and orthodoxy which stood in the way of love of books, but since that time other seriousnesses and orthodoxies have come to intervene, most especially our seriousness and orthodoxy about literature itself—in the degree that we have come to take literature with an unprecedented, a religious, seriousness, we seem to have lost our pleasure in reading. More and more young people undertake the professional study of literature; fewer and fewer like to read. It is my impression that the act of reading, which used to be an appetite and a passion, is now thought to be rather *infra dig* in people of intelligence; students make it a habit to settle on a very few authors, or, if possible, on one author, whom they undertake to comprehend entirely and to make their own; or to wait until they can conceive a "problem" suitable to their talents before they read at all.

There is indeed something very appealing in Wilson's old-fashioned, undoctrinaire voracity for print. For him a book is a book, the life blood of a spirit which may not be particularly precious but which is likely to be interesting if only for its badness. If one imputes a fault, it is that, while so many spirits are interesting to Wilson, there seem to be not quite enough that are precious. He is certainly far from being without enthusiasm or respect. He has a peculiar gentleness toward writers who are modest or minor. Where his personal feeling toward a writer is involved by reason of friendship, he has a very generous loyalty, as in the memoirs of Christian Gauss and Edna St. Vincent Millay, the two recent essays which form respectively the prologue and epilogue of *The Shores of Light*. But the fullness of his literary feeling is directed toward, as it were, the general enterprise of literature. Toward the individual writer he maintains the attitude of *nil admirare*—by which we are not to understand that he does not admire individual writers, but that he is never astonished by them, or led to surrender himself to them. I speak of this as a fault, yet it is a virtue too, of an astringent kind, at a time when all too often we are inclined to deal with literature as a spiritual revelation, less as writing than as Scripture.

It is Wilson's love of literature in general and his enormous appetite for it in all its forms that must account for his warm sympathy with Saintsbury, a critic in whom I find it hard to discover merit. The two men are of course in many respects at opposite poles from each other. For example, Wilson truly says of Saintsbury that "he had no interest in ideas," and certainly an interest in ideas, although with the years it has become rather less explicit in his work, is of the very essence of Wilson's criticism. Yet we can say of Saintsbury's response to literature that, almost by its very lack of ideas and of interest in ideas, by the very in-discriminateness of its voracity, it expresses an emotion that might seem to pass for an idea—for it affirms the swarming, multitudinous democracy of letters, and testifies to the rightness of loving civilization and culture in and for themselves and of taking pleasure in human communication almost for its own sake and of the order and peace in which men may listen to each other and have time and generosity enough to listen even to those who do not succeed in saying the absolutely best things.

And this idea, if we may call it that, is what chiefly animates the work of Edmund Wilson. It is given explicit expression in an essay which was written as long ago as 1927, "A Preface to Persius." But so early as in that quite moving essay Wilson adds to this "conservative" and "aristocratic" conception of literature an element which was beyond Saintsbury's grasp, the awareness that what constitutes the matter of literature is the discordant and destructive reality that threatens the peace which makes literature possible.

—1956

Caroline Bird

In this famous piece that originally ran in Harper's Bazaar *in February 1957, Caroline Bird examines the generation born after The Lost Generation—the so-called Silent Generation. Unlike their more bohemian forebears, Bird finds this new generation a largely humorless bunch, who take both life and themselves very seriously and where security takes precedence over self-expression. She cites several types: the Corporate Man, the Intellectual, and the Hipster.*

"Born 1930: The Unlost Generation"

The perennial cold war between middle age and the young idea has, in recent years, taken a distinctly piquant turn. In the 1920's, the young adults of the Lost Generation found their parents stuffy and distressingly inhibited. Now that these firebrands are parents themselves, they are making the same complaint about their grownup sons and daughters. They call them "The Silent Generation," "The Uncommitted Generation," "The Generation of Conformity." Edward Steichen, the great photographer, observed not long ago that the United States is suffering from a "shortage of the youngness of youth."

The young born circa 1930, like the Victorians born circa 1830, look back to the ripsnorting antics of the generation born before them and are not amused. The young writer, who, twenty-five

Caroline Bird. "Born 1930: The Unlost Generation," *Harper's Bazaar*, February 1957.

years ago, flaunted his freedom in the cafes of the Left Bank, is today apt to settle for a teaching job at a small college with facilities for his children. Youthful baseball players are staying with the team in order to be eligible at fifty for $100 a week under the new television-financed pension plan. The fifty-year olds, in fact, are being deprived of one of the headiest compensations of middle age—the pleasure of telling the young to be sensible and practical. No doubt an element of pique colors the complaints of Lost Generation veterans that their children have sold their souls for a mess of "adjustment" pottage. But this much is certain: among the 1930 generation, the quest for security takes precedence over ambition and self-expression.

What can we say factually about this group now in its midtwenties?

First of all, its members are visibly and statistically healthier, taller, heavier and handsomer than any previous generation. Numerically, they are a relatively rare species. Born during the depression trough in the birth rate, the young men now enjoy a scarcity value for the armed forces, industry and the professions, and also in relation to the larger crop of girls born just after them. The young women can take their pick of jobs, and of the older, more numerous men born during the boom years who marry them. Materially and romantically, no generation of young adults ever had it so good. One might expect them to take advantage of their favored-fewness by developing a choosy independence. In fact, they are doing nothing of the sort. They are settling down to jobs sooner, marrying earlier—and having more babies—than their parents did.

Why do these favored young seem so unambitious, so over-adjusted and apathetic? One reason is that they are on the receiving end of new techniques for the mass handling of people. They were among the first public school pupils taught to "adjust to the group" as well as to develop their minds and memories. Later, in the postwar army, they were the first soldiers trained to "voluntary cooperation" rather than directed to "Take a brace, mister." Finally, when they applied for their first jobs, they quickly discovered that the interviewer was more concerned with their ability to work with others than to do the work.

The industry which welcomed them was in the throes of a breathless discovery. "The biggest problem in industry," President John L. McCaffrey of International Harvester solemnly warns young executives, "is that it is full of human beings . . . with the same general problems of preventive maintenance, premature obsolescence, or complete operational failure that you have in machines." Industry and even the professions are applying themselves energetically to this new problem. To insure against human lapse, even such stubbornly one-mind jobs as scientific research, magazine writing, the diagnosis of human illness and the persuasion of customers are organized into team projects. To grease the relations between larger and larger aggregations of human beings, industry has invented a whole new category of jobholders: coordinators, liaison men, staff advisors, expediters. Formal courses teach bosses how to boss and beginners how to develop working personalities which will be useful to the corporation. There is plenty of time for these finishing school touches because mechanization leaves less unspecialized work for the beginner to do. For the first few years at least, he is really being paid to adjust to the corporate way of life.

Even a man's wife comes in for a kind of processing. Progressive employers size her up to see whether she is likely to be a natural ally for the corporation. Business is following the diplomatic service and the armed forces in converting the ladies' auxiliary into a serious school for wives. The high-level Hot Springs conference for managers sponsored by George Fry, management consultant, schedules "Mr. and Mrs. Executive" sessions at which wives are encouraged to discuss their role in the corporation as well as to join their husbands at panels on the art of management.

The unintended result of this so-called humanization of business is a system in which advancement depends on catching elusive clues rather than on demonstrating achievement. It was easy to see who held the power in the disciplined schoolroom, the old-style Army, the owner-operated business. In contrast, the progressive classroom, the new army, and the professionally managed corporation turn on invisible springs: no one can be quite sure who does what. There is a feeling in these institutions that one's fate is determined by faceless men, impersonally in spite of all efforts at "personalization," inscrutably in spite of house organs and handouts. To live in a Pentagon or a big corporation, one must walk on eggs— and that is something new in America.

Nevertheless, the generation born 1930 is managing it, by and large without a murmur and frequently with a smile. Why have they submitted so tamely to this loss of individuality and independence? Why don't they raise their voices against the excessive claims of a mass society as their parents once did? The answer is that it has not seemed unnatural to them that their lives should be so regulated. From nursery school to executive training squad to housing project, they have been trained to conformity, and family life—that bulwark against the claims of mass society—has not been able to halt the process. Rapid moves from house to house during the war years, and the wholesale divorces that punctuated the war's end, all made it only too natural to let one's existence be gradually reoriented toward the institution.

Americans expect the young to overthrow—in the name of progress—at least part of the values of their parents. But those born 1930 have found their parents largely without oppressive values. How are you going to rebel against a generation which made a cult of rebellion; which, in the confession of its spokesman Malcolm Cowley, felt that "our lives were directed by Puritan standards that were not our own, that society in general was terribly secure, unexciting, middle-class." The articulate members of the Lost Generation yearned for personal achievement in the arts as ardently as the country-club contingent yearned for personal success in business. Most of them wanted to throw away their parents' precepts about art and society, and they proposed to explore sex as if it were an uncharted continent. Men of the Word, defining the hero as iconoclast, led the revolution, and their idea of Utopia was a place where everyone could do as he pleased. There was only one way to revolt against so sweeping and so noisy a rebellion, and that, of course, was to repudiate the notion of rebellion itself. If their parents had called themselves lost, the young had to find a way to be unlost—which is harder. But this is exactly what the young adults are doing. They are revolting against the cult of personal experience, against sexual experiment, against infatuation with talk, against skepticism.

The Revolt Against Success

It has long been fashionable for Americans to proclaim that the price of success is too high. But until recently, there has been a strong element of hypocrisy—rather like the pity bestowed on the poor little rich girl—in this depreciation of what was, in fact, a first principle of American life. Today, however, many young adults really are rejecting the all-out struggle for success. Of half-a-dozen young men of twenty-five, pictured by *Fortune* in a story on the businessmen of tomorrow, all but one—a Negro college graduate—expected to remain employees, and not one hoped to become president of the company. Business analysts say that opportunities for setting up independent businesses are going begging because young men would rather be employed by a company that will take the responsibility.

Recent polls show that while young people have the traditional admiration for the doctor and the scientist, they don't aspire to become either: the road looks too lonely and too tough. In spite of the unprecedented prestige and rewards available to prospective scientists and engineers—at least one manufacturer is offering a bonus of $1,000 to anyone on his staff who succeeds in recruiting a scientist—the 1930 generation is critically short on these skills, a dangerous deficiency in view of Russia's growing strength. In 1955, whereas Soviet advanced technical schools turned out 80,000 graduates, the corresponding number in the United States was 37,000. Nor does this situation look like being remedied in the future. The young parents of high I.Q. children, by hesitating to let them skip grades or to send them to special schools, are encouraging yet another generation to grow up apathetic toward specialized effort. In the 1920's, educators tried to enrich the curriculum for the benefit of the gifted child, and there still are educators who hold to this line—but they are voices in the wilderness. Most bright children must learn to slow their pace to that of their duller age-mates.

The fear is that the exceptional child will become an "odd-ball" and the moral seems to be that it is dangerous to shine, dangerous to stick your neck out. By doing so, you may, as capitalist theory maintains, benefit society as a whole. But people won't like you for it, and among the 1930 generation the fear of not being liked has reached obsessive proportions.

It would not be altogether facetious to say that the old urge to keep up with the Joneses has been replaced by the need to keep *down* with the Joneses. Veblen's theory of conspicuous consumption has, among the young, been knocked into a cocked hat. They no longer dress to kill, nor are their clothes designed to fix social status. It is hard to tell which of the young women wearing blue jeans at the supermarket lives in a development and which in the more expensive reaches of exurbia. The few custom tailors left in New York say that more and more men are buying ready-made suits. That onetime mark of rank, the male hat, is fast losing its prestige: there are few men under thirty who feel socially lost without a headpiece. A growing number of the vanguard is even ashamed to flaunt that classic American advertisement of status, the flashily large and expensive car.

Money, in a capitalistic ethic, must have intrinsic glamour, or it cannot spur effort as it is supposed to do. But to the young it seems to have no symbolic value whatever. It has become merely a bookkeeping device. Time purchases are becoming a respectable convenience even among those with capital to pay cash. The people principally responsible for our twenty-nine billion-dollar installment debt on consumer goods are married couples under thirty: two-thirds of these young families are in debt. Interest rates are so high that there is often more money to be made in financing merchandise than in retailing it, yet credit men say many young marrieds don't even bother to ask what interest they are paying.

In the young menage it is usually the wife who handles the money: a recent bank survey, for example, discloses that more young wives than husbands sign the rent check. Now, according to the anthropologist, Margaret Mead, those activities in human society which are allocated to women are invariably held in lower esteem than those which are the province of the men. It would seem significant of the new attitude to money that the once-sacred male prerogative of managing it has now fallen almost exclusively into female hands.

The Revolt Against Sexual Experiment

"I'm sick of hearing about my father's generation as the lost generation," the heroine of William Styron's *Lie Down in Darkness* says of her philandering father. "They weren't lost. They were losing us." To the generation born 1930 sexual laxity no longer seems smart. Too many of today's young people have felt its results. They have rediscovered—and for the children of divorce, the hard way—that sex has social as well as individual consequences. They are less interested in experiment than in building lasting marriages, and they fervently believe that the proper end of love is a child. Their actions speak louder than their words. More young women are marrying: in 1920 almost half the girls aged 20 to 24 were single, while in 1953 the figure was down to 21 percent. Both men and women are marrying earlier: between 1930 and 1955, the median age of marriage dropped a year and a half to 22.7 for men and a little over a year, to 20.2 for women. They are also having babies sooner: 56 percent of women 21 to 25 are mothers, compared with 42 percent in 1920.

Husbands as well as wives are flocking to courses in parenthood and devouring the "how to stay married" articles that have replaced the "how to get a man" theme of slick fiction. The problem now is not how to get a mate, but what to do with a mate after you've got one. The advice doesn't shrink at physiological detail. Neither is it pornographic. If its monitory tone makes love and

351

marriage sound rather a chore, at least it has displaced the tutelage of the sentimental love story and the gutter.

The men of the Lost Generation liberated women by encouraging them to experiment sexually. The men in their twenties today are taking another tack. They are learning to *like* women, and the new sexual friendliness has loosened the hold of traditional sex roles. Thus men are not ashamed to diaper a baby or take a hand in the kitchen. Women can bring home a sizable portion of the bacon without apology. Those who worry that men are getting to be too like women and women too like men are usually Lost Generation critics concerned about maintaining the celebrated difference between the sexes. But the generation born 1930 is unworried. This is their way to stability in marriage, and by and large it is working.

The Revolt Against Criticism

The generation born 1930 grew up awash in words, victims of a generation hell-bent on explaining itself—in books, on canvas and in endlessly speculative palaver. In contrast, today's young adults are certainly not afflicted by the urge to communicate. Conversationally, they believe in playing it safe. When they consult a psychiatrist, they don't tell their friends the fascinating details. Criticism of politics and mores does not intoxicate them as it did their parents, and they are leery of verbal wit. In fact, barbed repartee—or expressive language which sharply reveals the speaker's character—is apt to strike them as in bad taste and even dangerous (i.e., not conducive to popularity). American speech is even fuzzing up its adjectives. Previous generations thought up juicy and specific cuss words for their many targets. This generation coins vague, all-purpose words of approval: adjusted, well-liked, with it, the most.

The young people seem silent because they do not protest, as vociferously as their elders did, against big business, the government, the church, or the Puritan respectability which is our American heritage. They appear uncritical because they want so very much to believe—although in just what they are not very sure. For want of an articulate faith, they seem to be making friends with the existing authorities. Some of the most popular postwar fiction urges reconciliation with the powers that be. Wouk has become the biggest selling postwar novelist as a preacher of conformity. *The Caine Mutiny* suggested the moral that it's better to obey the brass, right or wrong; *Marjorie Morningstar* preached conventional respectability to adventurous young girls. *The Man in the Gray Flannel Suit* found happiness only when he withdrew from the struggle to affirm his individuality in business and became a good Joe around the house and the office.

An elaborate opinion study made by the University of Michigan's Institute for Social Research discloses that those most favorable to big business are young people who can't remember the depression. It would seem that many young Americans—perhaps even a majority—agree with Charles Wilson that "what's good for General Motors is good for America."

More young people than ever before have been exposed to the influence of foreign travel, but they do not go abroad as rebels protesting the crudity of America. On the contrary, they are going to spread the American way as employees of oil companies, airlines, construction firms or government agencies; as servicemen or exchange students or grantees from foundations fostering international understanding.

Freud is no longer regarded as a liberator from Puritan repression, but strictly as a healer. While more young adults than ever before are seeking psychoanalytical treatment, they are looking for help in adjusting to work and authority rather than for an excuse to flout them. Group therapy is currently popular not only because it is cheaper, but because it provides practice in adjustment. The new patients don't demand spiritual rebirth. They aren't proud of their symptoms. They just want to get rid of them.

It is a moot point whether there is actually a religious revival among the young. But it is certain that more of them go to church, and nearly all young parents are, even if rather tepidly, in favor of sending the children to Sunday school. Religion, like politics and big business, is no longer a subject for heated and impassioned controversy. Rather, it is treated with a sort of vague respect, and an admiration which crystallizes, among the better read, around such figures as Albert Schweitzer and Reinhold Niebuhr, and at another level, around such "healer" types as Norman Vincent Peale. It seems likely that the generation born 1930 tends to view church-going, like psychiatry, as a means to general "adjustment" rather than as a spiritual end. Professional advisers in the "how to stay married" articles regularly recommend it as a way to "togetherness," but the emphasis is quite as much on the social activities of the church (i.e. a way of getting along in the community) as on faith itself. Religion, in short, now provides still another pattern for conformity. Whether it does more than that remains to be seen.

Corporate Man

Corporate man is easy to find. We found him through the personnel director of a multi-million dollar corporation. As an executive trainee, twenty-eight years old, he was used to being probed, polled, and tested, and he answered our inquiries with a poise beyond his years.

He took his present job, he volunteered, because the company had a reputation for treating everybody fairly and taking a real interest in you. He's happy in personnel work because he likes people. His wife likes them too—they have lots of friends in the new suburban development where they live. Her photograph comes easily out of his wallet and shows a pleasantly pretty, somewhat earnest girl in babushka and slacks, holding a baby. He talks easily, too, of their life together. He has no objections to the standardization of his home. The builders did a fair job, and he has built in his own touches of individuality—an outdoor barbecue that is different in design from his neighbor's, a storage wall that neatly includes the TV set. He speaks of the friendliness of development living, of block parties, shared responsibility for baby-sitting and car pools. He makes it clear that his is no life of quiet desperation. Its similarity to that of his neighbors doesn't depress him. In fact, he finds it reassuring: neither he nor his wife believe in being "cliquey."

Religion? They go to the Presbyterian Church because they like the minister and the Sunday school is the most popular, even though he himself was born a Unitarian. Politics? He guesses both parties are pretty much alike, but he voted Republican because he liked Ike and he's never forgotten that Ike ended the Korean War. It was the only war he was ever in, and it was enough. Reading? He wishes he had more time for it, though he subscribes to a weekly news magazine and the *Reader's Digest*. His wife manages to read most of the best-selling novels, but he prefers nonfiction. He read *Love Or Perish*, and thought there was a lot of truth in it, but in general he likes books that give you information.

The interviewer can't help feeling he's really much nicer than Babbitt—more sensitive, less ambitious, more genuine. He is a good listener, attentive to nuances of personality. Personality, in fact, is one of his words. He speaks of it as if it were a commodity, something that can be manufactured and sold. It's what he likes in entertainment figures. It's what helps you to get along (he never says "get ahead"). His own personality seems so smooth that, for all his ingenuous frankness, the interviewer has a hard time getting a purchase on him. If he had gone to Princeton, he would have been known approvingly as "tweed"—the Ivy League slang for "regular guy" which describes him in terms of his uniform and leaves one wondering whether there is an unknown and possibly quite different man inside the clothing.

The Intellectual

While today's young intellectuals would, for the most part, repudiate the notion of conformity, they are certainly less in conflict with the conventional ethos of their time—less adventurous and less embattled—than the intellectuals of the 1920's and '30's: the maverick and the Bohemian are becoming increasingly rare species among the young.

Like his contemporary in the business world, the young intellectual prefers the security of working for a large institution to the hazards and high hopes of independence, and his sights are firmly set on the universities and the foundations. As a writer, he is more apt to devote his energies to scholarship and criticism, which will further his professional status than to fiction and poetry. As a social animal, his style of dress and living, while informal, is more likely to be conventional than not. As a voter, he was probably for [Adlai] Stevenson but by and large he is leery of political involvement. For one thing, the "loyalty" inquiries of recent years—though he had strong feelings about the issues at stake—impressed upon him the danger of going out on a political limb. In the second place, the whole climate of the age is not one in which causes are flourishing.

The reading tastes of young intellectuals today are far harder to chart than they would have been three or two decades ago. The generations which were young adults in the 1920's and '30's had their well-recognized spokesmen among the novelists and their favorite prophets among the social thinkers and philosophers. The intellectuals born in 1930, broadly speaking, do not have heroes among the novelists close to them in age. Norman Mailer, Truman Capote, William Styron, perhaps half-a-dozen others approaching or just past thirty—have numerous admirers, but it is clear that the impact on young intellectuals has not been remotely comparable to that made on a previous generation by Fitzgerald, Hemingway, and Dos Passos when they were young. Authors most highly regarded as intellectuals in their mid-twenties are by and large the same as those in vogue among their elders—for instance, Henry James and Melville; Faulkner; or George Orwell, who has been so incisive a critic of philosophies of power.

Perhaps the most striking characteristic of the young intellectuals—an unusual one for this tribe—is their modesty. They are distinctly less dogmatic, assertive, exhibitionistic than their counterparts in previous eras. They are interested in their inner life, but they do not expect to interest everyone else in it.

The Hipster

Our search for the rebels of this generation led us to the hipster. The hipster is an *enfant terrible* turned inside out. In character with his time, he is trying to get back at the conformists by lying low. If it were not for the intellectuals who have discovered him, he might have succeeded in remaining invisible.

You can't interview a hipster because his main goal is to keep out of society which, he thinks, is trying to make everyone over in its own image. He takes marijuana because it supplies him with experience that can't be shared with "squares." He may affect a broad-brimmed hat or a zoot suit, but usually he prefers to skulk unmarked. The hipster may be a jazz musician; he is rarely an artist, almost never a writer. He may earn his living as a petty criminal, a hobo, a carnival roustabout or a freelance moving man in Greenwich Village, but some hipsters have found a safe refuge in the upper income brackets as television comics or movie actors. (The late James Dean, for one, was a hipster hero.)

Unlike historic rebels against society, the hipster has little use for language—he likes to communicate by gesture. He brushes his palm or points with hands at sides in greetings, moves slowly as if to signal his contempt for action. He reads little and that painstakingly, searching for the non-verbal truth behind the lines; and his taste runs to works of diffuse mysticism—Ouspensky, for instance. In company with other hipsters he sits motionlessly, absorbing the "real" interaction of the group. An example of his rare exchanges:

"Why were you putting me down?"

"Man, I wasn't putting you down."

"You weren't?" (incredulously)

Long pause.

"Then which way was it?"

It is obvious that this is a secret language, akin to the codes of school boys. "Putting down" means getting the better of, and it is always construed abstractly. The vocabulary is limited, imprecise, and loaded: "cool," "gone," "with it," "there," "crazy," are terms of approval; "beat," "drag," "nowhere," "sad," "square" are terms of disapproval. It is tempting to describe the hipster in psychiatric terms as infantile, but the style of his infantilism is a sign of the times. He does not try to enforce his will on others, Napoleon-fashion, but contents himself with a magical omnipotence never disproved because never tested. If corporate man's magic is ready-to-wear for all occasions, the hipster's must be custom-built to meet the changing threat of the moment. As the only extreme nonconformist of his generation, he exercises a powerful if underground appeal for conformists, through newspaper accounts of his delinquencies, his structureless jazz, and his emotive grunt words.

The Future

Where are these silent, smooth young people going? To their elders, they seem to be building a somewhat savorless society, lacking in individual idiosyncrasy, intellectual vitality, or even political responsibility. Certainly, they raise troubling questions for the sociologist. How, he asks, can our capitalist economy sustain its dynamism if so few are willing to take risks? What will happen to our culture if there is a continued decline in the American tradition of protest?

There is a chance that while the young seem tame, uncommitted, they may be invisibly moving in a direction so radical that we cannot as yet conceive of it. For, as the phenomenon of the United States moved Alexis de Tocqueville to say so long ago:

"Time, events, or the unaided individual action of the mind will sometimes undermine or destroy an opinion, without any outward sign of the change. As its enemies remain mute or only interchange their thoughts by stealth, they are themselves unaware for a long period that a great revolution has actually been effected; and in this state of uncertainty they take no steps; they observe one another and are silent."

—February 1957

Norman Podhoretz

(b. 1930)

Former editor in chief of Commentary *magazine, Norman Podhoretz has written more than a half a dozen books on diverse topics from an analysis of American foreign policy to his ongoing love affair with America. During the 1950s and 1960s, he belonged to a small circle of New York intellectuals, among them Allen Ginsberg, Lionel and Diana Trilling, Lillian Hellman, Hannah Arendt, and Norman Mailer, who, in his book* Ex-Friends *(1999), he considers estranged former colleagues. In this famous essay, "The Know-Nothing Bohemians," he lashes ferociously at what he considers the vacant culture and anti-intellectualism that spawned the Beats and the entire bohemian lifestyle often associated with Greenwich Village. The darling of the neoconservative set, Podhoretz is a prolific memoirist, from his famous* Making It *(1967) to* My Love Affair with America *(2000). He remains a singular voice on the contemporary literary scene.*

"The Know-Nothing Bohemians"

Allen Ginsberg's little volume of poems, *Howl*, which got the San Francisco renaissance off to a screaming start, was dedicated to Jack Kerouac ("new Buddha of American prose, who spit forth intelligence into eleven books written in half the number of years. . . . Creating a spontaneous bop prosody and original classic literature"),

Norman Podhoretz. "The Know-Nothing Bohemians," from *Doings and Undoings: The Fifties and After in American Writing* (New York: Farrar, Straus & Co., 1964).

William Seward Burroughs ("author of *Naked Lunch*, an endless novel which will drive everybody mad"), and Neal Cassady ("author of *The First Third*, an autobiography . . . which enlightened Buddha"). So far, everybody's sanity has been spared by the inability of *Naked Lunch* to find a publisher,* and we may never get the chance to discover what Buddha learned from Neal Cassady's autobiography, but thanks to the Viking and Grove Presses, two of Kerouac's original classics, *On the Road* and *The Subterraneans*, have now been revealed to the world. When *On the Road* appeared last year, Gilbert Millstein commemorated the event in the New York *Times* by declaring it to be "a historic occasion" comparable to the publication of *The Sun Also Rises* in the 1920's. But even before the novel was actually published, the word got around that Kerouac was the spokesman of a new group of rebels and Bohemians who called themselves the Beat Generation, and soon his photogenic countenance (unshaven, of course, and topped by an unruly crop of rich black hair falling over his forehead) was showing up in various mass-circulation magazines, he was being interviewed earnestly on television, and he was being featured in a Greenwich Village nightclub where, in San Francisco fashion, he read specimens of his spontaneous bop prosody against a background of jazz music.

Though the nightclub act reportedly flopped, *On the Road* sold well enough to hit the best-seller lists for several weeks, and it isn't hard to understand why. Americans love nothing so much as representative documents, and what could be more interesting in this Age of Sociology than a novel that speaks for the "young generation"? (The fact that Kerouac is thirty-five or thereabouts, was generously not held against him.) Beyond that, however, I think that the unveiling of the Beat Generation was greeted with a certain relief by many people who had been disturbed by the notorious respectability and "maturity" of post-war writing. This was more like it—restless, rebellious, confused youth living it up, instead of thin, balding, button-down instructors of English composing ironic verses with one hand while changing the baby's diapers with the

*It did, of course, find one a few years after this piece was written.

other. Bohemianism is not particularly fashionable nowadays, but the image of Bohemia still exerts a powerful fascination—nowhere more so than in the suburbs, which are filled to overflowing with men and women who uneasily think of themselves as conformists and of Bohemianism as the heroic road. The whole point of *Marjorie Morningstar* was to assure the young marrieds of Manaroneck that they were better off than the apparently glamorous *luftmenschen* of Greenwich Village, and the fact that Wouk had to work so hard at making this idea seem convincing is a good indication of the strength of prevailing doubt on the matter.

On the surface, at least, the Bohemianism of *On the Road* is very attractive. Here is a group of high-spirited young men running back and forth across the country (mostly hitchhiking, sometimes in their own second-hand cars), going to "wild" parties in New York and Denver and San Francisco, living on a shoe-string (GI educational benefits, an occasional fifty bucks from a kindly aunt, an odd job as a typist, a fruit-picker, a parking lot attendant), talking intensely about love and God and salvation, getting high on marijuana (but never heroin or cocaine), listening feverishly to jazz in crowded little joints, and sleeping freely with beautiful girls. Now and again there is a reference to gloom and melancholy, but the characteristic note struck by Kerouac is exuberance:

> We stopped along the road for a bite to eat. The cowboy went off to have a spare tire patched, and Eddie and I sat down in a kind of homemade diner. I heard a great laugh, the greatest laugh in the world, and here came this rawhide oldtimes Nebraska farmer with a bunch of other boys into the diner; you could hear his raspy cries clear across the plains, across the whole gray world of them that day. Everybody else laughed with him. He didn't have a care in the world and had the hugest regard for everybody. I said to myself, Wham, listen to that man laugh. That's the West, here I am in the West. He came booming into the diner, calling Maw's name, and she made the sweetest cherry pie in Nebraska, and I had some with a mountainous scoop of ice cream on top. "Maw, rustle me up some grub afore I have to start eatin myself or some damn silly idee like that." And he threw himself on a stool and

went hyaw hyaw hyaw hyaw. "And throw some beans on it." It was the spirit of the West sitting right next to me. I wished I knew his whole raw life and what the hell he'd been doing all these years besides laughing and yelling like that. Whooee, I told my soul, and the cowboy came back and off we went to Grand Island.

Kerouac's enthusiasm for the Nebraska farmer is part of his general readiness to find the source of all vitality and virtue in simple rural types and in the dispossessed urban groups (Negroes, bums, whores). His idea of life in New York is "millions and millions hustling forever for a buck among themselves . . . grabbing, taking, giving, sighing, dying, just so they could be buried in those awful cemetery cities beyond Long Island City," whereas the rest of America is populated almost exclusively by the true of heart. There are intimations here of a kind of know-nothing populist sentiment, but in other ways this attitude resembles Nelson Algren's belief that bums and whores and junkies are more interesting than white-collar workers or civil servants. The difference is that Algren hates middle-class respectability for moral and political reasons—the middle class exploits and persecutes—while Kerouac, who is thoroughly unpolitical, seems to feel that respectability is a sign not of moral corruption but of spiritual death. "The only people for me," says Sal Paradise, the narrator of On the Road, "are the mad ones, the ones who are mad to live, mad to talk, mad to be saved, desirous of everything at the same time, the ones who never yawn or say a commonplace thing, but burn, burn, burn like fabulous yellow roman candles exploding like spiders across the stars. . . ." This tremendous emphasis on emotional intensity, this notion that to be hopped-up is the most desirable of all human conditions, lies at the heart of the Beat Generation ethos and distinguishes it radically from the Bohemianism of the past.

The Bohemianism of the 1920's represented a repudiation of the provinciality, philistinism, and moral hypocrisy of American life— a life, incidentally, which was still essentially small-town and rural in tone. Bohemia, in other words, was a movement created in the name of civilization: its ideals were intelligence, cultivation, spiritual refinement. The typical literary figure of the 1920's was a mid-westerner (Hemingway, Fitzgerald, Sinclair Lewis, Eliot, Pound) who had fled from his home town to New York or Paris in search of a freer, more expansive, more enlightened way of life than was possible in Ohio or Minnesota or Michigan. The political radicalism that supplied the characteristic coloring of Bohemianism of the 1930's did nothing to alter the urban, cosmopolitan bias of the 1920's. At its best, the radicalism of the 1930's was marked by deep intellectual seriousness and aimed at a state of society in which the fruits of civilization would be more widely available—and ultimately available to all.

The Bohemianism of the 1950's is another kettle of fish altogether. It is hostile to civilization; it worships primitivism, instinct, energy, "blood." To the extent that it has intellectual interests at all, they run to mystical doctrines, irrationalist philosophies, and left-wing Reichianism. The only art the new Bohemians have any use for is jazz, mainly of the cool variety. Their predilection for bop language is a way of demonstrating solidarity with the primitive vitality and spontaneity they find in jazz and of expressing contempt for coherent, rational discourse which, being a product of the mind, is in their view a form of death. To be articulate is to admit that you have no feelings (for how can real feelings be expressed in syntactical language?), that you can't respond to anything (Kerouac responds to everything by saying "Wow!"), and that you are probably impotent.

At the end of the spectrum, this ethos shades off into violence and criminality, mainline drug addiction and madness. Allen Ginsberg's poetry, with its lurid apocalyptic celebration of "angel-headed hipsters," speaks for the darker side of the new Bohemianism, Kerouac is milder. He shows little taste for violence and the criminality he admires is the harmless kind. The hero of *On the Road*, Dean Moriarty, has a record: "From the age of eleven to seventeen he was usually in reform school. His specialty was stealing cars, gunning for girls coming out of high school in the afternoon, driving them out to the mountains, making them, and coming back to sleep in any available hotel bathtub in town." But

Dean's criminality, we are told, "was not something that sulked and sneered; it was a wild yea-saying overburst of American joy; it was Western, the west wind, an ode from the Plains, something new, long prophesied, long a-coming (he only stole cars for joy rides)." And, in fact, the species of Bohemian that Kerouac writes about is on the whole rather law-abiding. In *The Subterraneans*, a bunch of drunken boys steal a pushcart in the middle of the night, and when they leave it in front of a friend's apartment building, he denounces them angrily for "screwing up the security of my pad." When Sal Paradise (in *On the Road*) steals some groceries from the canteen of an itinerant workers' camp in which he has taken a temporary job as a barracks guard, he comments, "I suddenly began to realize that everybody in America is a natural-born thief"—which, of course, is a way of turning his own stealing into a bit of boyish prankishness. Nevertheless, Kerouac is attracted to criminality, and that in itself is more significant than the fact that he personally feels constrained to put the brakes on his own destructive impulses.

Sex has always played a very important role in Bohemianism: sleeping around was the Bohemian's most dramatic demonstration of his freedom from conventional moral standards, and a defiant denial of the idea that sex was permissible only in marriage and then only for the sake of a family. At the same time, to be "promiscuous" was to assert the validity of sexual experience in and for itself. The "meaning" of Bohemian sex, then, was at once social and personal, a crucial element in the Bohemian's ideal of civilization. Here again the contrast with Beat Generation Bohemianism is sharp. On the one hand, there is a fair amount of sexual activity in *On the Road* and *The Subterraneans*. Dean Moriarty is a "new kind of American saint" at least partly because of his amazing sexual powers: he can keep three women satisfied simultaneously and he can make love any time, anywhere (once he mounts a girl in the back seat of a car while poor Sal Paradise is trying to sleep in front). Sal, too, is always on the make, and though he isn't as successful as the great Dean, he does pretty well: offhand I can remember a girl in Denver, one on a bus, and another in New York, but a little research

would certainly unearth a few more. The heroine of *The Subterraneans*, a Negro girl named Mardou Fox, seems to have switched
from one to another member of the same gang and back again
("This has been an incestuous group in its time"), and we are given
to understand that there is nothing unusual about such an
arrangement. But the point of all this hustle and bustle is not freedom from ordinary social restrictions or defiance of convention
(except in relation to homosexuality, which is Ginsberg's preserve:
among "the best minds" of Ginsberg's generation who were destroyed by America are those "who let themselves be _____
in the _____ by saintly motorcyclists, and screamed with
joy, / who blew and were blown by those human seraphim, the
sailors, caresses of Atlantic and Caribbean love"). The sex in Kerouac's books goes hand in hand with a great deal of talk about
forming permanent relationships ("although I have a hot feeling
sexually and all that for her," says the poet Adam Moorad in *The
Subterraneans*, "I really don't want to get any further into her not
only for these reasons but finally, the big one, if I'm going to get involved with a girl now I want to be permanent like permanent and
serious and long termed and I can't do that with her"), and a habit
of getting married and then duly divorced and re-married when
another girl comes along. In fact, there are as many marriages and
divorces in *On the Road* as in the Hollywood movie colony (must be
that California climate): "All those years I was looking for the
woman I wanted to marry," Sal Paradise tells us. "I couldn't meet
a girl without saying to myself, What kind of wife would she
make?" Even more revealing is Kerouac's refusal to admit that any
of his characters ever makes love wantonly or lecherously—no
matter how casual the encounter it must always entail sweet feelings toward the girl. Sal, for example, is fixed up with Rita Betten-
court in Denver, whom he has never met before. "I got her in my
bedroom after a long talk in the dark of the front room. She was a
nice little girl, simple and true (naturally), and tremendously
frightened of sex. I told her it was beautiful. I wanted to prove this
to her. She let me prove it, but I was too impatient and proved
nothing. She sighed in the dark. 'What do you want out of life?'

I asked, and I used to ask that all the time of girls." This is rather touching, but only because the narrator is really just as frightened of sex as that nice little girl was. He is frightened of failure and he worries about his performance. For *performance* is the point— performance and "good orgasms," which are the first duty of man and the only duty of woman. What seems to be involved here, in short, is sexual anxiety of enormous proportions—an anxiety that comes out very clearly in *The Subterraneans*, which is about a love affair between the young writer, Leo Percepied, and the Negro girl, Mardou Fox. Despite its protestations, the book is one long agony of fear and trembling over sex:

> I spend long nights and many hours making her, finally I have her, I pray for it to come, I can hear her breathing harder, I hope against hope it's time, a noise in the hall (or whoop of drunkards next door) takes her mind off and she can't make it and laughs— but when she does make it I hear her crying, whimpering, the shuddering electrical female orgasm makes her sound like a little girl crying, moaning in the night, it lasts a good twenty seconds and when it's over she moans, "O why can't it last longer," and "O when will I when you do?"—"Soon now I bet," I say, "you're getting closer and closer"—

Very primitive, very spontaneous, very elemental, very beat.

For the new Bohemians interracial friendships and love affairs apparently play the same role of social defiance that sex used to play in older Bohemian circles. Negroes and whites associate freely on a basis of complete equality and without a trace of racial hostility. But putting it that way understates the case, for not only is there no racial hostility, there is positive adulation for the "happy, true-hearted, ecstatic Negroes of America."

> At lilac evening I walked with every muscle aching among the lights of 27th and Welton in the Denver colored section, wishing I were a Negro, feeling that the best the white world had offered was not enough ecstasy for me, not enough life, joy, kicks, darkness, music, not enough night . . . I wished I was a Denver Mexican, or even a poor overworked Jap, anything but what I was so

drearily, a "white man" disillusioned. All my life I'd had white ambitions. . . . I passed the dark porches of Mexican and Negro homes; soft voices were there, occasionally the dusky knee of some mysterious sensuous gal; and dark faces of the men behind rose arbors. Little children sat like sages in ancient rocking chairs.

It will be news to the Negroes to learn that they are so happy and ecstatic; I doubt if a more idyllic picture of Negro life has been painted since certain Southern ideologues tried to convince the world that things were just as fine as fine could be for the slaves on the old plantation. Be that as it may, Kerouac's love for Negroes and other dark-skinned groups is tied up with his worship of primitivism, not with any radical social attitudes. Ironically enough, in fact, to see the Negro as more elemental than the white man, as Ned Polsky has acutely remarked, is "an inverted form of keeping the nigger in his place." But even if it were true that American Negroes, by virtue of their position in our culture, have been able to retain a degree of primitive spontaneity, the last place you would expect to find evidence of this is among Bohemian Negroes. Bohemianism, after all, is for the Negro a means of entry into the world of the whites, and no Negro Bohemian is going to cooperate in the attempt to identify him with Harlem or Dixieland. The only major Negro character in either of Kerouac's two novels is Mardou Fox, and she is about as primitive as Wilhelm Reich himself.

The plain truth is that the primitivism of the Beat Generation serves first of all as a cover for an anti-intellectualism so bitter that it makes the ordinary American's hatred of eggheads seem positively benign. Kerouac and his friends like to think of themselves as intellectuals ("they are intellectual as hell and know all about Pound without being pretentious or talking too much about it"), but this is only a form of newspeak. Here is an example of what Kerouac considers intelligent discourse—"formal and shining and complete, without the tedious intellectualness":

We passed a little kid who was throwing stones at the cars in the road. "Think of it," said Dean, "One day he'll put a stone through a man's windshield and the man will crash and die—all on account of that little kid. You see what I mean? God exists without qualms. As we roll along this way I am positive beyond doubt that everything will be taken care of for us—that even you, as you drive, fearful of the wheel . . . the thing will go along of itself and you won't go off the road and I can sleep. Furthermore we know America, we're at home; I can go anywhere in America and get what I want because it's the same in every corner, I know the people, I know what they do. We give and take and go in the incredibly complicated sweetness zigzagging every side."

You see what I mean? Formal and shining and complete. No tedious intellectualness. Completely unpretentious. "There was nothing clear about the things he said but what he meant to say was somehow made pure and clear." *Somehow*. Of course. If what he wanted to say had been carefully thought out and precisely articulated, that would have been tedious and pretentious and, no doubt, *somehow* unclear and clearly impure. But so long as he utters these banalities with his tonguetied and with no comprehension of their meaning, so long as he makes noises that come out of his soul (since they couldn't possibly have come out of his mind), he passes the test of true intellectuality.

Which brings us to Kerouac's spontaneous bop prosody. This "prosody" is not be confused with bop language itself, which has such a limited vocabulary (Basic English is a verbal treasure-house by comparison) that you couldn't write a note to the milkman in it, much less a novel. Kerouac, however, manages to remain true to the spirit of hipster slang while making forays into enemy territory (i.e. the English language) by his simple inability to express anything in words. The only method he has of describing an object is to summon up the same half dozen adjectives over and over again: "greatest, "tremendous," "crazy," "mad," "wild," and perhaps one or two others. When it's more than just mad or crazy or wild, it becomes "really mad" or "really crazy" or "really wild." (All quantities in excess of three, incidentally, are subsumed under the rubric "innumerable," a word used innumerable times in *On the Road* but not so innumerably in *The Subterraneans*.). The same poverty of resources is apparent in those passages where Kerouac tries to handle a situation involving even slightly complicated feelings. His usual tactic is to run for cover behind cliché and vague signals to the reader. For instance: "I looked at him; my eyes were watering with embarrassment and tears. Still he stared at me. Now his eyes were blank and looking through me. . . . Something clicked in both of us. In me it was suddenly concern for a man who was years younger than I, five years, and whose fate was wound with mine across the passage of recent years; in him it was a matter that I can ascertain only from what he did afterward." If you can ascertain what this is all about, either beforehand, during, or afterward, you are surely no square.

In keeping with its populistic bias, the style of *On the Road* is folksy and lyrical. The prose of *The Subterraneans*, on the other hand, sounds like an inept parody of Faulkner at his worst, the main difference being that Faulkner usually produces bad writing out of an impulse to inflate the commonplace while Kerouac gets into trouble by pursuing "spontaneity." Strictly speaking, spontaneity is a quality of feeling, not of writing: when we call a piece of writing spontaneous, we are registering our impression that the author hit upon the right words without sweating, that no "art" and no calculation entered into the picture, that his feelings seem to have spoken themselves, seem to have sprouted a tongue at the moment of composition. Kerouac apparently thinks that spontaneity is a matter of saying whatever comes into your head, in any order you happen to feel like saying it. It isn't the *right* words he wants (even if he knows what they might be), but the first words, or at any rate the words that most obviously announce themselves as deriving from emotion rather than celebration, as coming from "life" rather than "literature," from the guts rather than the brain. (The brain, remember, is the angel of death.) But writing that springs easily and "spontaneously" out of strong feelings is *never* vague; it always has a quality of sharpness and precision because it is in the nature of strong feelings to be aroused by specific objects. The notion that a diffuse, generalized, and unrelenting enthusiasm is the mark of great sensitivity and responsiveness is utterly fantastic, an idea that comes from taking drunkenness or drug-addiction as the state of perfect emotional vigor. The effect of such enthusiasm is actually to wipe out the world altogether, for if a filling station will serve as well as the Rocky Mountains to arouse a sense of awe and wonder, then both the filling station and the mountains are robbed of their reality. Kerouac's conception of feeling is one that only a solipsist could believe in—and a solipsist, be it noted, is a man who does not relate easily to anything outside himself.

Solipsism is precisely what characterizes Kerouac's fiction. *On The Road* and *The Subterraneans* are so patently autobiographical in content that they become almost impossible to discuss as novels; if spontaneity were indeed a matter of destroying the distinction between life and literature, these books would unquestionably be It. "As we were going out to the car Babe slipped and fell flat on her face. Poor girl was overwrought. Her brother Tim and I helped her up. We got in the car; Major and Betty joined us. The sad ride back to Denver began." Babe is a girl who is mentioned a few times in the course of *On the Road*; we don't know why she is overwrought on this occasion, and even if we did it wouldn't matter, since there is no reason for her presence in the book at all. But Kerouac tells us that she fell flat on her face while walking toward a car. It is impossible to believe that Kerouac made this detail up, that his imagination was creating a world real enough to include wholly gratuitous elements; if that were the case, Babe would have come alive as a human being. But she is only a name; Kerouac never even describes her. She is in the book because the sister of one of Kerouac's friends was there when he took a trip to Central City, Colorado, and she slips in *On the Road* because she slipped that day on the way to the car. What is true of Babe who fell flat on her face is true of virtually every incident in *On the Road* and *The Subterraneans*. Nothing that happens has any dramatic reason for happening. Sal Paradise meets such-and-such people on the road whom he likes or (rarely) dislikes; they exchange a few words, they have a few beers together, they part. It is all very unremarkable and commonplace, but for Kerouac it is always the greatest, the wildest, the most. What you get in these two books is a man proclaiming that he is *alive* and offering every trivial experience he has ever had in evidence. Once I did this, once I did that (he is saying) and by God, it *meant* something! Because I *responded*! But if it meant something, and you responded so powerfully, why can't you explain what it meant, and why do you have to insist to?

I think it is legitimate to say, then, that the Beat Generation's worship of primitivism and spontaneity is more than a cover for hostility to intelligence; it arises from a pathetic poverty of feeling as well. The hipsters and hipster-lovers of the Beat Generation are rebels, all right, but not against anything so sociological and historical as the middle class or capitalism or even respectability. This is the revolt of the spiritually underprivileged and the crippled of soul—young men who can't think straight and so hate anyone who can; young men who can't get outside the morass of self and so construct definitions of feeling that exclude all human beings who manage to live, even miserably, in a world of objects; young men who are burdened unto death with the specially poignant sexual anxiety that America—in its eternal promise of erotic glory and its spiteful withholding of actual erotic possibility—seems bent on breeding, and who therefore dream of the unattainable perfect orgasm, which excuses all sexual failures in the real world. Not long ago, Norman Mailer suggested that the rise of the hipster may represent "the first wind of a second revolution in this century, moving not forward toward action and more rational equitable distribution, but backward toward being and the secrets of human energy." To tell the truth, whenever I hear anyone talking about instinct and being the secrets of human energy, I get nervous; next thing you know he'll be saying that violence is just fine, and then I begin wondering whether he really thinks that kicking someone in the teeth or sticking a knife between his ribs are deeds to be admired. History, after all—and especially the history of modern times—teaches that there is a close connection between ideologies of primitivistic vitalism and a willingness to look upon cruelty and blood-letting with complacency, if not downright enthusiasm. The reason I bring this up is that the spirit of hipsterism and the Beat Generation strikes me as the same spirit which animates the young savages in leather jackets who have been running amok in the last few years with their switchblades and

371

zip guns. What does Mailer think of those wretched kids, I wonder? What does he think of the gang that stoned a nine-year old boy to death in Central Park in broad daylight a few months ago, or the one that set fire to an old man drowsing on a bench near the Brooklyn waterfront one summer's day, or the one that pounced on a crippled child and orgiastically stabbed him over and over and over again even after he was good and dead? Is that what he means by the liberation of instinct and the mysteries of being? Maybe so. At least he says somewhere in his article that two eighteen-year-old hoodlums who bash in the brains of a candy-store keeper are murdering an institution, committing an act that "violates private property"—which is one of the most morally gruesome ideas I have ever come across, and which indicates where the ideology of hipsterism can lead. I happen to believe that there is a direct connection between the flabbiness of American middle-class life and the spread of juvenile crime in the 1950's, but I also believe that juvenile crime can be explained partly in terms of the same resentment against normal feeling and the attempt to cope with the world through intelligence that lies behind Kerouac and Ginsberg. Even the relatively mild ethos of Kerouac's books can spill over easily into brutality, for there is a suppressed cry in those books: Kill the intellectuals who can talk coherently, kill the people who can sit still for five minutes at a time, kill those incomprehensible characters who are capable of getting seriously involved with a woman, a job, a cause. How can anyone in his right mind pretend that this has anything to do with private property or the middle class? No. Being against what the Beat Generation stands for has to do with denying that incoherence is superior to precision; that ignorance is superior to knowledge; that the exercise of mind and discrimination is a form of death. It has to do with fighting the notion that sordid acts of violence are justifiable so long as they are committed in the name of "instinct." It even has to do with fighting the poisonous glorification of the adolescent in American popular culture. It has to do, in other words, with one's attitude toward intelligence itself.

—Spring 1958

John Updike

(b. 1932)

Born in Shillington, Pennsylvania, John Updike was educated at Harvard University and the Ruskin School of Drawing and Fine Art at Oxford. A staff writer for the New Yorker *from 1955 to 1957, he is best known for his exploration of suburbia and the upper middle class, particularly in the Rabbit series:* Rabbit, Run *(1960),* Rabbit Redux *(1971),* Rabbit Is Rich *(1981), for which he won the Pulitzer Prize, and* Rabbit at Rest *(1990), another Pulitzer winner. The often troubled relationships between the sexes is a favorite theme. Other titles include* The Centaur *(1963);* Of the Farm *(1965);* Couples *(1968);* The Witches of Eastwick *(1984), which was made into a film in 1987 starring Jack Nicholson, Michelle Pfeiffer, Cher, and Susan Sarandon;* In the Beauty of the Lilies *(1996); and* Gertrude and Claudis *(2000).* Hugging the Shore *(1983) is a collection of literary essays while* Bech: A Book *(1970) is a collection of interrelated essays about a writer and was followed by* Bech Is Back *(1982) and* Bech at Bay *(1998). "Snowing in Greenwich Village" explores a side of the Village not often seen in fiction since the days of Henry James and Edith Wharton: of genteel inhabitants obsessed about keeping up appearances.*

373

"Snowing in Greenwich Village" from *The Same Door and Other Stories*

The Maples had moved just the day before to West Thirteenth Street, and that evening they had Rebecca Cune over, because now they were so close. A tall, always slightly smiling girl with an absent manner, she allowed Richard Maple to slip off her coat and scarf even as she stood gently greeting Joan. Richard, moving with an extra precision and grace because of the smoothness with which the business had been managed—though he and Joan had been married nearly two years, he was still so young-looking that people did not instinctively lay upon him hostly duties; their reluctance worked in him a corresponding hesitancy, so that often it was his wife who poured the drinks, while he sprawled on the sofa in the attitude of a favored and wholly delightful guest—entered the dark bedroom, entrusted the bed with Rebecca's clothes, and returned to the living room. Her coat had seemed weightless.

Rebecca, seated beneath the lamp, on the floor, one leg tucked under her, one arm up on the Hide-a-Bed that the previous tenants had not as yet removed, was saying, "I had known her, you know, just for the day she taught me the job, but I said okay. I was living in an awful place called a hotel for ladies. In the halls they had typewriters you put a quarter in."

Joan, straightbacked on a Hitchcock chair from her parents' home in Vermont, a damp handkerchief balled in her hand, turned to Richard and explained, "Before her apartment now, Becky lived with this girl and her boyfriend."

"Yes, his name was Jacques," Rebecca said.

Richard asked, "You lived with them?" The arch composure of his tone was left over from the mood aroused in him by his successful and, in the dim bedroom, somewhat poignant—as if he were with great tact delivering a disappointing message—disposal of their guest's coat.

"Yes, and he insisted on having his name on the mailbox. He was terribly afraid of missing a letter. When my brother was in the Navy and came to see me and saw on the mailbox"—with three parallel movements of her fingers she set the names beneath one another—

"Georgene Clyde,
Rebecca Cune,
Jacques Zimmerman,

he told me I had always been such a nice girl. Jacques wouldn't even move out so my brother would have a place to sleep. He had to sleep on the floor." She lowered her lids and looked in her purse for a cigarette.

"Isn't that wonderful?" Joan said, her smile broadening help-lessly as she realized what an inane thing it had been to say. Her cold worried Richard. It had lasted seven days without improving. Her face was pale, mottled pink and yellow; this accentuated the Modiglaniesque quality established by her long neck and oval blue eyes and her habit of sitting to her full height, her head quizzically tilted and her hands palm downward in her lap.

Rebecca, too, was pale, but in the consistent way of a drawing, perhaps—the weight of her lids and a certain virtuosity about the mouth suggested it—by da Vinci.

"Who would like some sherry?" Richard asked in a deep voice, from a standing position.

"We have some hard stuff if you'd rather," Joan said to Rebecca; from Richard's viewpoint the remark, like those advertisements which from varying angles read differently, contained the quite legible declaration that this time *he* would have to mix the Old Fashioneds.

"The sherry sounds fine," Rebecca said. She enunciated her words distinctly, but in a faint, thin voice that disclaimed for them any consequence.

"I think, too," Joan said.

"Good." Richard took from the mantel the eight-dollar bottle of Tio Pepe that the second man on the Spanish sherry account had stolen for him. So all could share in the drama of it, he uncorked the bottle in the living room. He posingly poured out three glasses, half-full, passed them around, and leaned against the mantel (the Maples had never had a mantel before), swirling the liquid, as the agency's wine expert had told him to do, thus liberating the esters and ethers, until his wife said, as she always did, it being the standard toast in her parents' home, "Cheers, dears!"

Rebecca continued the story of her first apartment. Jacques had never worked. Georgene never held a job more than three weeks. The three of them contributed to a kitty, to which all enjoyed equal access. Rebecca had a separate bedroom. Jacques and Georgene sometimes worked on television scripts; they pinned the bulk of their hopes onto a serial titled *The IBI*—"I" for Intergalactic, or Interplanetary, or something—*in Space and Time*. One of their friends was a young Communist who never washed and always had money because his father owned half of the West Side. During the day, when the two young girls were off working, Jacques flirted with a young Swede upstairs who kept dropping her mop onto the tiny balcony outside their window. "A real bombardier," Rebecca said. When Rebecca moved into a single apartment for herself and was all settled and happy, Georgene and Jacques offered to bring a mattress and sleep on her floor. Rebecca felt that the time had come for her to put her foot down. She said no. Later, Jacques married a girl other than Georgene.

"Cashews, anybody?" Richard said. He had bought a can at the corner delicatessen, expressly for this visit, though if Rebecca had not been coming, he would have bought something else there on some other excuse, just for the pleasure of buying his first thing at the store where in the coming years he would purchase so much and become so well known.

"No thank you," Rebecca said. Richard was so far from expecting refusal that out of momentum he pressed them on her again exclaiming, "Please! They're so good for you." She took two and bit one in half.

He offered the dish, a silver porringer given to the Maples as a wedding present and which they had never before had the space to unpack, to his wife, who took a greedy handful and looked so pale that he asked, "How do you feel?" not so much forgetting the presence of their guest as parading his concern, quite genuine at that, before her.

"Fine," Joan said edgily, and perhaps she did.

Though the Maples told some stories—how they had lived in a log cabin in a Y.M.C.A. camp for the first three months of their married life, how Bitsy Flaner, a mutual friend, was the only girl enrolled in Bentham Divinity School, how Richard's advertising work brought him into contact with Yogi Berra—they did not regard themselves (that is, each other) as raconteurs, and Rebecca's slight voice dominated the talk. She had a gift for odd things.

Her rich uncle lived in a metal house furnished with auditorium chairs. He was terribly afraid of fire. Right before the depression he had built an enormous boat to take himself and some friends to Polynesia. All his friends lost their money in the crash. He did not. He made money. He made money out of everything. But he couldn't go on the trip alone, so the boat was still waiting in Oyster Bay, a huge thing, rising thirty feet out of the water. The uncle was a vegetarian. Rebecca had not eaten turkey for Thanksgiving until she was thirteen years old because it was the family custom to go to the uncle's house on that holiday. The custom was dropped during the war, when the children's synthetic heels made black marks all over his asbestos floor. Rebecca's family had not spoken to the uncle since. "Yes, what got me," Rebecca said, "was the way each new wave of vegetables would come in as if it were a different course."

Richard poured the sherry around again and, because this made him the center of attention anyway, said, "Don't some vegetarians have turkeys molded out of crushed nuts for Thanksgiving?"

After a stretch of silence, Joan said, "I don't know." Her voice, unused for ten minutes, cracked on the last syllable. She cleared her throat, scraping Richard's heart.

"What would they stuff them with?" Rebecca asked, dropping an ash into the saucer beside her.

Beyond and beneath the window there arose a clatter. Joan reached the windows first, Richard next, and lastly Rebecca, standing on tiptoe, elongating her neck. Six mounted police, standing in their stirrups, were galloping two abreast down Thirteenth Street. When the Maples' exclamations had subsided, Rebecca remarked, "They do it every night at this time. They seem awfully jolly, for policemen."

"Oh, and it's snowing!" Joan cried. She was pathetic about snow; she loved it so much, and in these last years had seen so little. "On our first night here! Our first *real* night." Forgetting herself, she put her arms around Richard, and Rebecca, where another guest might have turned away, or smiled too broadly, too encouragingly, retained without modification her sweet, absent look and studied, through the embracing couple, the scene outdoors. The snow was not taking on the wet street; only the hoods and tops of parked automobiles showed an accumulation.

"I think I'd best go," Rebecca said.

"Please don't," Joan said with an urgency Richard had not expected; clearly she was very tired. Probably the new home, the change in the weather, the good sherry, the currents of affection between herself and her husband that her sudden hug had renewed, and Rebecca's presence had become in her mind the inextricable elements of one enchanting moment.

"Yes, I think I'll go because you're so snuffly and peaked."

"Can't you just stay for one more cigarette? Dick, pass the sherry around."

"A teeny bit," Rebecca said, holding out her glass. "I guess I told you, Joan, about the boy I went out with who pretended to be a headwaiter."

Joan giggled expectantly. "No, honestly, you never did." She hooked her arm over the back of the chair and wound her hand through the slats, like a child assuring herself that her bedtime has been postponed. "What did he do? He imitated headwaiters?"

"Yes, he was the kind of guy who, when we get out of a taxi and there's a grate giving out steam, crouches down"—Rebecca lowered her head and lifted her arms—"and pretends he's the Devil."

The Maples laughed, less at the words themselves than at the way Rebecca had evoked the situation by conveying, in her understated imitation, both her escort's flamboyant attitude and her own undemonstrative nature. They could see her standing by the taxi door, gazing with no expression as her escort bent lower and lower, seized by his own joke, his fingers writhing demonically as he felt horns sprout through his scalp, flames lick his ankles, and his feet shrivel into hoofs. Rebecca's gift, Richard realized, was not that of having odd things happen to her but that of representing, through the implicit contrast with her own sane calm, all things touching her as odd. This evening too might appear grotesque in her retelling "Six policemen on horses galloped by and she cried, 'It's snowing!' and hugged him. He kept telling her how sick she was and filling us full of sherry."

"What else did he do?" Joan asked.

"At the first place we went to—it was a big night club on the roof of somewhere—on the way out he sat down and played the piano until a woman at a harp asked him to stop."

Richard asked, "Was the woman *playing* the harp?"

"Yes, she was strumming away." Rebecca made circular motions with her hands.

"Well, did he play the tune she was playing? Did he *accompany* her?" Petulance, Richard realized without understanding why, had entered his tone.

"No, he just sat down and played something else. I couldn't tell what it was."

"Is this *really* true?" Joan asked, egging her on.

"And then at the next place we went to, we had to wait at the bar for a table and I looked around and he was walking among the tables asking people if everything was all right."

"Wasn't it *awful*?" said Joan.

"Yes. Later he played the piano there, too. We were sort of the main attraction. Around midnight he thought we ought to go out to Brooklyn to his sister's house. I was exhausted. We got off the subway two stops too early, under the Manhattan Bridge. It was deserted, with nothing going by except black limousines. Miles above our head"—she stared up, as though at a cloud, or the sun— "was the Manhattan Bridge and he kept saying it was the el. We finally found some steps and two policemen who told us to go back to the subway."

"What does this amazing man do for a living?" Richard asked.

"He teaches school. He's quite bright." She stood up, extending in stretch a long, silvery white arm. Richard got her coat and said he'd walk her home.

"It's only three-quarters of a block," Rebecca protested in a voice free of any insistent inflection.

"You must walk her home, Dick," Joan said. "Pick up a pack of cigarettes." The idea of his walking in the snow seemed to please her, as if she were anticipating how he would bring back with him, in the snow on his shoulders and the coldness of his face, all the sensations of the walk she was not well enough to risk.

"You should stop smoking for a day or two," he told her.

Joan waved them goodbye from the head of the stairs.

The snow, invisible except around street lights, exerted a fluttering romantic pressure on their faces.

"Coming down hard now," he said.

"Yes."

At the corner, where the snow gave the green light a watery blueness, her hesitancy in following him as he turned to walk with the light across Thirteenth Street led him to ask, "It is this side of the street you live on, isn't it?"

"Yes."

"I thought I remembered from the time we drove you down from Boston." The Maples had been living in the West Eighties then. "I remember I had an impression of big buildings."

"The church and the butcher's school," Rebecca said. "Every day about ten when I'm going to work the boys learning to be butchers come out for an intermission all bloody and laughing."

Richard looked up at the church; the steeple was fragmentarily silhouetted against the scattered lit windows of a tall improvement on Seventh Avenue. "Poor church," he said. "It's hard in this city for a steeple to be the tallest thing."

Rebecca said nothing, not even her habitual "Yes." He felt rebuked for being preachy. In his embarrassment he directed her attention to the first next thing he saw, a poorly lettered sign above a great door. "Food Trades Vocational High School," he read aloud.

"The people upstairs told us that the man before the man before *us* in our apartment was a wholesale meat salesman who called himself a Purveyor of Elegant Foods. He kept a woman in the apartment."

"Those big windows up there,' Rebecca said, pointing up at the third story of a brownstone, "face mine across the street. I can look in and feel we are neighbors. Someone's always there; I don't know what they do for a living."

After a few more steps they halted, and Rebecca, in a voice that Richard imagined to be slightly louder than her ordinary one, said, "Do you want to come up and see where I live?"

"Sure." It seemed implausible to refuse.

They descended four concrete steps, opened a shabby orange door, entered an overheated half-basement lobby, and began to climb four flights of wooden stairs. Richard's suspicion on the street that he was trespassing beyond the public gardens of courtesy turned to genuine guilt. Few experiences so savor of the illicit as mounting stairs behind a woman's fanny. Three years ago, Joan had lived in a fourth-floor walkup, in Cambridge. Richard never took her home, even when the whole business down to the last intimacy, had become formula, without the fear that the landlord, justifiably curious, would leap from his door and devour him as they passed.

Opening her door, Rebecca said, "It's hot as hell in here," swearing for the first time in his hearing. She turned on a weak light. The room was small; slanting planes, the underside of the building's roof, intersecting the ceiling and walls, cut large prismatic volumes from Rebecca's living space. As he moved further forward, toward Rebecca, who had not yet removed her coat, Richard perceived, on his right, an unexpected area created where the steeply slanting roof extended itself to the floor. Here a double bed was placed. Tightly bounded on three sides, the bed had the appearance not so

381

much of a piece of furniture as of a permanently installed, blanketed platform. He quickly took his eyes from it and, unable to face Rebecca at once, stared at two kitchen chairs, a metal bridge lamp around the rim of whose shade plump fish and helm wheels alternated, and a four-shelf bookcase—all of which, being slender and proximate to a tilting wall, had an air of threatened verticality.

"Yes, here's the stove on top of the refrigerator I told you about," Rebecca said. "Or did I?"

The top unit overhung the lower by several inches on all sides. He touched his fingers to the stove's white side. "This room is quite sort of nice," he said.

"Here's the view," she said. He moved to stand beside her at the windows, lifting aside the curtains and peering through tiny flawed panes into the apartment across the street.

"That guy *does* have a huge window," Richard said. She made a brief agreeing noise of n's.

Though all the lamps were on, the apartment across the street was empty. "Looks like a furniture store," he said. Rebecca had still not taken off her coat. "The snow's keeping up."

"Yes. It is."

"Well"—this word was too loud; he finished the sentence too softly—"thanks for letting me see it. I—have you read this?" He had noticed a copy of *Auntie Mame* lying on a hassock.

"I haven't had the time," she said.

"I haven't read it either. Just reviews. That's all I ever read."

This got him to the door. There, ridiculously, he turned. It was only at the door, he decided in retrospect, that her conduct was quite inexcusable: not only did she stand unnecessarily close, but, by shifting the weight of her body to one leg and leaning her head sidewise, she lowered her height several inches, placing him in a dominating position exactly fitted to the broad, passive shadows she must have known were on her face.

"Well—" he said.

"Well." Her echo was immediate and possibly meaningless.

"Don't, don't let the b-butchers get you." The stammer of course ruined the joke, and her laugh, which had begun as soon as she had seen by his face that he would attempt something funny, was completed ahead of his utterance.

As he went down the stairs she rested both hands on the banister and looked down toward the next landing.

"Good night," she said.

"Night." He looked up; she had gone into her room. Oh but they were close.

—1959

Jane Jacobs

(b. 1916)

Born in 1916 in Scranton, Pennsylvania, Jane Jacobs moved to New York during the height of the Depression. She held various jobs, but also experienced various periods of unemployment before finding work in journalism, writing for the New York Herald Tribune *and* Vogue. *During World War II she worked for the Office of War Information and later joined the staff of* Architectural Forum. *After more than thirty years in New York, Jacobs moved to Toronto in 1968, to escape the Vietnam War.* The Death and Life of Great American Cities *is both her first book and her best known and most respected work. Although she has no professional training in urban planning, she was never afraid to express her opinion, and is credited with launching the concept of New Urbanism. A forceful advocate of creating and sustaining livable cities, Jacobs condemned the work and principles of such earlier urban planners as Sir Patrick Geddes, Lewis Mumford, and others like them, who she felt were largely responsible for turning people away from city life. Her other books include* The Nature of Economies *(2000),* Cities and the Wealth of Nations *and* Systems of Survival: A Dialogue on the Moral Foundations of Commerce and Politics *(1992), and* The Question of Separatism *(1980).*

from *The Death and Life of Great American Cities*

Under the seeming disorder of the old city, wherever the old city is working successfully, is a marvelous order for maintaining the safety of the streets and the freedom of the city. It is a complex order. Its essence is intricacy of sidewalk use, bringing with it a constant succession of eyes. This order is all composed of movement and change, and although it is life, not art, we may fancifully call it the art form of the city and liken it to the dance—not to a simple-minded precision dance with everyone kicking up at the same time, twirling in unison and bowing off en masse, but to an intricate ballet in which the individual dancers and ensembles all have distinctive parts which miraculously reinforce each other and compose an orderly whole. The ballet of the good city sidewalk never repeats itself from place to place, and in any one place is always replete with new improvisations.

The stretch of Hudson Street where I live is each day the scene of an intricate sidewalk ballet. I make my own first entrance into it a little after eight when I put out the garbage can, surely a prosaic occupation, but I enjoy my part, my little clang, as the droves of junior high school students walk by the center of the stage dropping candy wrappers. (How do they eat so much candy so early in the morning?)

While I sweep up the wrappers I watch the other rituals of morning: Mr. Halpert unlocking the laundry's handcart from its mooring to a cellar door, Joe Cornacchia's son-in-law stacking out the empty crates from the delicatessen, the barber bringing out his sidewalk folding chair, Mr. Goldstein arranging the coils of wire which proclaim the hardware store is open, the wife of the tenement's superintendent depositing her chunky three-year-old with a toy mandolin on the stoop, the vantage point from which he is learning the English his mother cannot speak. Now the primary children, heading for St. Veronica's Cross, heading to the west, and the children for P.S. 41, heading toward the east. Two new entrances are being made from the wings: well-dressed and even elegant women and men with brief cases emerge from doorways and side streets. Most of these are heading for the bus and subways, but some hover on the curbs, stopping taxis which have miraculously appeared at the right moment, for the taxis are part of a wider morning ritual: having dropped passengers from midtown in the downtown financial district, they are now bringing downtowners up to midtown. Simultaneously, numbers of women in house-dresses have emerged and as they crisscross with one another they pause for quick conversations that sound with either laughter or joint indignation, never, it seems, anything between. It is time for me to hurry to work too, and I exchange my ritual farewell with Mr. Lofaro, the short, thick-bodied, white-aproned fruit man who stands outside his doorway a little up the street, his arms folded, his feet planted, looking solid as earth itself. We nod; we each glance quickly up and down the street, then look back to each other and smile. We have done this many a morning for more than ten years, and we both know what it means: All is well.

The heart-of-the-day ballet I seldom see, because part of the nature of it is that working people who live there, like me, are mostly gone, filling the roles of strangers on other sidewalks. But from days off, I know enough of it to know that it becomes more and more intricate. Longshoremen who are not working that day gather at the White Horse or the Ideal or the International for beer and conversation. The executives and business lunchers from the industries just to the west throng the Dorgene restaurant and the Lion's Head coffee house; meat-market workers and communications scientists fill the bakery lunchroom. Character dancers come on, a strange old man with strings of old shoes over his shoulders, motor-scooter riders with big beards and girl friends who bounce on the back of the scooters and wear their hair long in front of their faces as well as behind, drunks who follow the advice of the Hat Council and are always turned out in hats, but not hats the Council would approve. Mr. Lacey, the locksmith, shuts up his shop for a while and goes to exchange the time of day with Mr. Slube at the cigar store. Mr. Koochagian, the tailor, waters the luxuriant jungle of plants in his window, gives them a critical look from the outside, accepts a compliment on them from two passers-by, fingers the leaves on the plane tree in front of our house with a thoughtful gardener's appraisal, and crosses the street for a bite at the Ideal where he can keep an eye on customers and wigwag across the message that he is coming. The baby carriages come out, and clusters of everyone from toddlers with dolls to teen-agers with homework gather at the stoops.

When I get home after work, the ballet is reaching its crescendo. This is the time of roller skates and stilts and tricycles, and games in the lee of the stoop with bottletops and plastic cowboys; this is the time of bundles and packages, zigzagging from the drug store to the fruit stand and back over to the butcher's; this is the time when teen-agers, all dressed up, are pausing to ask if their slips show or their collars look right; this is the time when beautiful girls get out of MG's; this is the time when the fire engines go through; this is the time when anybody you know around Hudson Street will go by.

As darkness thickens and Mr. Halpert moors the laundry cart to the cellar door again, the ballet goes on under lights, eddying back and forth but intensifying at the bright spotlight pools of Joe's side-walk pizza dispensary, the bars, the delicatessen, the restaurant and the drug store. The night workers stop now at the delicatessen, to pick up salami and a container of milk. Things have settled down for the evening but the street and its ballet have not come to a stop.

I know the deep night ballet and its seasons best from walking long after midnight to tend a baby and, sitting in the dark, seeing the shadows and hearing the sounds of the sidewalk. Mostly it is a sound like infinitely pattering snatches of party conversation and, about three in the morning, singing, very good singing. Sometimes there is sharpness and anger or sad, sad weeping, or a flurry of search for a string of beads broken. One night a young man came roaring along, bellowing terrible language at two girls whom he had apparently picked up and who were disappointing him. Doors opened, a wary semicircle formed around him, not too close, until the police came. Out came the heads, too, along Hudson Street, of-fering opinion, "Drunk . . . Crazy . . . A wild kid from the suburbs."*

Deep in the night, I am almost unaware how many people are on the street unless something calls them together, like the bagpipe. Who the piper was and why he favored our street I have no idea.

---

* He turned out to be a wild kid from the suburbs. Sometimes, on Hudson Street, we are tempted to believe the suburbs must be a difficult place to bring up children.

The bagpipe just skirled out in the February night, and as if it were a signal the random, dwindled movements of the sidewalk took on direction. Swiftly, quietly, almost magically a little crowd was there, a crowd that evolved into a circle with a Highland fling inside it. The crowd could be seen on the shadowy sidewalk, the dancers could be seen, but the bagpiper himself was almost invisible because his bravura was all in his music. He was a very little man in a plain brown overcoat. When he finished and vanished, the dancers and watchers applauded, and applause came from the galleries too, half a dozen of the hundred windows on Hudson Street. Then the windows closed, and the little crowd dissolved into the random movements of the night street.

The strangers on Hudson Street, the allies whose eyes help us natives keep the peace of the street, are so many that they always seem to be different people from one day to the next. That does not matter. Whether they are so many always-different people as they seem to be, I do not know. Likely they are. When Jimmy Rogan fell through a plate-glass window (he was separating some scuffling friends) and almost lost his arm, a stranger in an old T shirt emerged from the Ideal bar, swiftly applied an expert tourniquet and, according to the hospital's emergency staff, saved Jimmy's life. Nobody remembered seeing the man before and no one has seen him since. The hospital was called in this way: a woman sitting on the steps next to the accident ran over to the bus stop, wordlessly snatched the dime from the hand of a stranger who was waiting with his fifteen-cent fare ready, and raced into the Ideal's phone booth. The stranger raced after her to offer the nickel too. Nobody remembered seeing him before, and no one has seen him since. When you see the same stranger three or four times on Hudson Street, you begin to nod. This is almost getting to be an acquaintance, a public acquaintance, of course.

I have made the daily ballet of Hudson Street sound more frenetic than it is, because writing it telescopes it. In real life, it is not that way. In real life, to be sure, something is always going on, the ballet is never at a halt, but the general effect is peaceful and the general tenor even leisurely. People who know well such animated city streets will know how it is. I am afraid people who do not will always have it a little wrong in their heads—like the old prints of rhinoceroses made from travelers' descriptions of rhinoceroses.

On Hudson Street, the same as in the North End of Boston or in any other animated neighborhoods of great cities, we are not innately more competent at keeping the sidewalks safe than are the people who try to live off the hostile truce of Turf in a blind-eyed city. We are the lucky possessors of a city order that makes it relatively simple to keep the peace because there are plenty of eyes on the street. But there is nothing simple about that order itself, or the bewildering number of components that go into it. Most of those components are specialized in one way or another. They unite in their joint effect upon the sidewalk, which is not specialized in the least. That is its strength.

—1961

Dan Balaban

The Village Voice was born on October 26, 1955, in Greenwich Village, the offspring of Edwin Fancher and Daniel Wolf. Fancher and novelist Norman Mailer provided the funding for the paper (Mailer withdrew in 1956 after penning a serious of incendiary essays). Almost from the start the Voice, which prided itself on attracting journalists who didn't quite fit in anywhere else, was a national publication. Over the years it has published some of the finest and quirkiest writers in America, including e. e. cummings, Ezra Pound, and Katherine Anne Porter. Cartoonist Jules Feiffer was a regular contributor. Bill Manville, John Wilcock, Seymour Krim, Allen Churchill, Howard Smith, Jack Newfield, Nat Hentoff, and, more recently, Ann Powers have also lent their singular voices to the literary brew. In this piece, Voice regular Dan Balaban looks at one of the Village's many characters, "Romany Marie" (real name: Marie Marchand). A native of Moldavia, she opened a number of exotic tearooms in the Village in 1912, offering a cozy and intimate atmosphere (including tea-leaf readings and palmistry). "Romany Marie" was a favorite haunt of Village regulars.

"The 'Gypsy' Lady Who Fed Bohemia"

Some people bow three times toward Mecca. Romany Marie's friends greet her with: "Ah, Marie, Marie, Marie." It is a triple-tongued orison to nostalgia, to the time the Village was what it has been trying to live up to ever since.

Dan Balaban. "The 'Gypsy' Lady Who Fed Bohemia," from *The Village Voice Reader: A Mixed Bag from the Greenwich Village Newspaper* (New York: Grove Press, 1962).

Romany Marie was the gold band in which the gems shone. For three decades—the 20's, the 30's, and the 40's—she ran a coffee house-restaurant type of place where the great and the brilliant and the people who clustered about them used to gather.

Technically she had seven "Romany Marie's" during her career: on Sheridan Square, on Christopher Street, 8th Street, Washington Square, Minetta Lane, Waverly Place, and Grove Street. But as she remembers them, "All the seven places were one place. . . . When I moved there would be a sign saying 'My caravan has gone to . . .' And they would follow."

It is more than seven years since Romany Marie sold her last place and retired from active business. But she dresses still as she always did—like a gypsy. Ankle-length, aqua-blue dress, cerise shawl, dangling earrings and jangling bracelets. Her face is warm and vivid; her voice is deeper than most men's.

How she came by Romany Marie—her real name is Marie Marchand—her gypsy style, and even her career as a restaurateur is explained by her early history. She was born 73 years ago in Roumania, "in the primitive part near a forest where the gypsies lived. My mother had an inn for gypsies and that's why I had a place for artists. They go hand in hand. When I was three years old I used to dance in my mother's place. I loved my mother so much I found myself imitating her in many ways. Bohemia means 'land of gypsies,' and when I found myself in New York I thought what better thing than to do like my mother did."

Romany Marie has managed to preserve her Roumanian accent through the 55 years she has been in America. "I spoke seven languages when I came here, and lost them all trying to learn English.

"My husband," she continued, "spoke 300 dialects and languages, and gave me an inferiority complex. A natural philologist, he even made up languages. He was an interpreter on Ellis Island for 16 years. But he was many other things. I was 45 years with him, and every day a romance. I'm a quarter of myself since he's gone." Dr. Marchand died about four years ago. It was to take care of him during his last illness that Romany Marie left the restaurant business. His photograph hangs on the wall above her easy chair—an independent-looking man with strong, heavy moustaches.

She and her husband first moved to the Village in 1914. "I recognized that was the place for me and I didn't leave it since." She enrolled in an art class and her home became open house for her fellow students. When Ellis Island became an internment camp during the First World War and her husband lost his job as interpreter, her artist friends urged her to open a place they could patronize instead of exploiting her home. "My husband was against it, but I did it anyway."

The first Romany Marie's started as a little coffee shop serving sandwiches and five or six kinds of coffee. But the warm "gypsy" proprietor with her interest in creative people, the easy unhurried atmosphere, attracted more and more people—from the Village, from the city, from all over. "I discovered there was a hunger for the kind of place I had." She expanded her menu, adding broilings ("many customers liked to turn their own steaks"), special European dishes—"with distinctive herbs and flavors and sauces"—and her *piéce de résistance*, Ciorba, a thick Roumanian vegetable soup made with leeks and fresh dill.

"The whole world came to me. They made appointments in Paris to meet at my place. A lot of people I meet, we fall on each other's necks. But I don't know their names. There were so many of them. People used to say to me: 'Why don't you have two places, so we'll have another place to go to?'"

She tells a story about a banker who used to frequent Romany Marie's. He had a very beautiful wife who one day went to France, fell in love with Paris, and decided to live there. She wouldn't come home. The banker's work kept him in New York, so he couldn't join her. He begged her to come back, but she refused. Things went from bad to worse until finally there was nothing to do but divorce. However, the banker was very much in love with his wife, and became more and more depressed. Finally he said: "Marie, I am going to take my roadster and go to the Sahara desert and I shall not return until I have driven this woman from my mind."

Months later a letter came which read: "Marie, Marie, Marie. To have known your place once is never to be lonely again, even in the Sahara desert. I was motoring along in the desert when I met a girl riding the other way on a bicycle. We looked at each other and she said: 'Romany Marie's! I don't know who you are, but I've seen you at Romany Marie's.' We smoked a cigarette and I was no longer alone."

"Things were different then," says Marie, reflecting. "There was more spacing, not so much building." There were also places with strange, vanished names: The Pirate's Den, Aladdin's Lamp, The Three Thieves, Will o' the Wisp.

Her first place near 1 Sheridan Square—"on the third floor, up a winding staircase"—was right in the middle of the teeming tourist track. "Greenwich Village was like Coney Island then. I had artists, and they drew sightseers. It was such a mix-up. The sightseers would crowd into my place.

"All my places had an inner circle," she explained. "A special corner with a fireplace where all the creative people sat. They weren't permitted to buy anything. People would ask: "How do I qualify to get in there?' I would say: 'Be creative!' Two kinds of people came to my place, those who were creative and those who could pay for their food." Romany Marie used to have a $200 circulating fund—"never more"—which was always being emptied or replenished according to the changing fortunes of creativity.

With a wonderful infectious smile she says: "People used to walk and look into the windows and say: 'When I *know* something, then I'll go there.' Some would come in and say: 'This isn't the place for me.' They would eliminate themselves."

A night at Romany Marie's: You enter a crowded restaurant, well-lit by overhead light and little lanterns placed throughout the dining room. There are wooden tables and benches for 60 patrons; 200 will have come and gone before the evening is over. The walls are decorated with paintings by artists who eat there, with hanging Roumanian rugs and beautiful plates and earthenware from many countries.

In the kitchen of the dining room, Romany Marie, in gay gypsy clothes, will be before the stove watching the broiling steaks. Her husband might be nearby making sandwiches, which he was fond of doing, or checking the larder to see what was needed. Standing by Romany Marie, "Varese would be telling me about his music, an artist would be talking about a painting. Bodenheim—how many times I threw him out—he used to read his poetry to me all night."

If it were in the early days, Eugene O'Neill would be at one table. "He used to come in right from the beginning." He would have come over from the Hell Hole, a saloon on 4th Street, bringing with him a crowd of young people, "who used to look up to him like God. He made notes on his sea plays in my place."

Quite possibly Alfred Kreymborg and his crowd would be there, eating, talking, and carving their names in the table top.

Or it might be one of the nights for their periodic banquets. They would hold their sessions at either the Waldorf or Romany Marie's. "The old fossils used to say: 'What is this? Greenwich Village?' Vilhjalmur Stefansson would be among them. "He met his wife in my place." So would Peter Freuchen and Philip Plant—"He had his wedding dinner there."

Marie would in time leave the cooking to an employee—"No matter who cooked, I would always taste the food"—and go into the dining room to do the hostessing she loved. She might sit with Fannie Hurst and read her fortune in Turkish coffee grounds—"Tea leaves is a New England invention"—or she might sit and chat with Ruth St. Denis, Segovia, Enesco. She would avoid the tall, very handsome, blue-eyed fellow. That would be Hunt Diedrich, the wealthy sculptor who during the Nazi era "used to complain that Jews were sitting on his property and he couldn't get them off."

A short, sturdy, cheerful-looking fellow with a round beard and lively eyes might hail her flamboyantly with: "oh, mother of the arts in America!" This was Brancusi—"He never came to New York without seeing me." Or she might point out a very tall, beautifully built, Indian-faced fellow working absorbedly over some diagrams. That was Howard Scott, one of the founders of Technocracy. "He made his first charts at my place. They call me the mother of Technocracy. They call me the mother of everything," she recalls happily.

Or you might see William Saroyan there during the years he was writing *The Beautiful People* and *The Daring Young Man on the Flying Trapeze*. "He was very enthusiastic and, I would say, satiric." It might have been the night Dr. Marchand read Saroyan's palm and told him: "You're a piece of cheese," and Saroyan answered: "I never heard such a truth about myself."

If Eddie Albert were there, he would be easy to single out. "He was an Ohio farm boy with a play under his arm. I used to give him hot milk and toast because he needed nourishment." She sent Albert to George Abbott—"I was very good at spotting people who ought to meet." In her way Romany Marie was also the mother of "Room Service" and "Brother Rat."

You might ask her who that tall thin fellow with the moustache was, but she couldn't have told you. "I used to see Sherwood Anderson often, but I didn't know who he was." She finally met him at a party and told him this, and still treasures his answer: "I'm so happy to meet someone who doesn't know me and notices me."

But she could have pointed out to you Ernest Hemingway, Elliot Paul, William Rose and Stephen Vincent Benét, Burl Ives— "He was very poor then"—Gjon Mili, famous *Life* photographer, Leonard D. Abbot, editor of the *Literary Digest*, Theodore Dreiser, Witter Bynner, Walter Duranty, Leger, Stuart Davis, Marsden Hartley, E. E. Cummings, Isadora Duncan, Charles Demuth, Niles Spencer, Joseph Stella.

You might have noticed a young man sitting on the stairs as you left. "Clifford Odets used to wait for Harry Kemp on my doorstep. Kemp"—leader of Bohemia in the 20's and author of *Tramping on Life* and *More Miles*—"was his early influence."

Although she loved her clientele and was very proud of them, she still retains her own independent critical opinion. Edna Millay, for example, she thought beautiful, with her red hair and blue eyes. "I couldn't stop looking at her. She was delightful. She was nicer than her work."

Of Thomas E. Dewey she says: "Dewey used to come to my place before he was married with his girl. He didn't know whether to become a singer or a politician. He would have made a fine opera singer."

Romany Marie now lives on West 18th Street, just outside her beloved Village. She feels very much at home. There are many reminders of the golden years. Her walls are covered with paintings by old friends: Stuart Davis, Mark Tobey, Preston Dickinson, De Hirsch Margulies, Aronzo Gasparo.

The house in which she lives had been occupied by Oona O'Neill, no stranger to Romany Marie, up to the time she married another of Marie's famous clients, Charlie Chaplin.

She lives with Edith Corwin, who off and on for over 10 years had been a waitress at Romany Marie's. Downstairs, Miss Corwin, a painter and former dancer, and her artist husband, Jake Taggart, run a crafts workshop called A Place to Know. Miss Corwin is devoted to Romany Marie and often entertains visitors with her, seated on the arm of Marie's easy chair, patting her hand with daughter-like affection. Romany Marie is still among her "creative people."

When Lee De Forest, the inventor and a former patron of hers, visited New York from California after a 25-year absence, he asked his secretary to arrange a dinner for himself and friends at Romany Marie's. He had not known that she was retired. When Romany Marie heard about it, she arranged the dinner. At El Charro's.

After her husband died, Romany Marie used to spend her evenings at El Charro. Dressed in her gypsy raiment, she used to receive her visitors there. She is very fond of Maria and Garcia, the proprietors of El Charro. "They are peasants from Asturias, Spain, where the nicest gypsies come from. Of all the people I knew, they had the deepest understanding of me. Maria used to bring me hot soup when I was ill."

Her illness was a heart attack she suffered a year ago and which has somewhat restricted her activities. "The great doctor told me I have a weak heart. I contradicted him. I don't have a weak heart, I have a tired heart. So I'm going to give it a rest and then I'll be back."

Romany Marie was an integral part of the glory that was Greenwich Village. But this fact does not wed her to the past. There is no mourning for the good old days.

"There weren't then so many cultural places—off-Broadway theatre and art galleries," she recalls. "I think the Village is culturally better now."

The Village she sees as having developed from the time "it was misunderstood as a phony Latin Quarter with cafes and all, like Montmartre. But it has become more like Montparnasse, where worthwhile artists come to live."

Her explanation for this reveals a thoughtful perspective on her life experience. "The feeling used to be more that people wanted release from sordidness. The release was not to creativity, but to superficial gaiety. Now they've tasted war, and the release is deeper, more cultural. The needs of people are deeper now because they are preparing for a new world."

—1962

Howard Smith

Howard Smith was a veteran Village Voice *staffer. In this piece, he describes Jack Kerouac's famous stint at that Village standby, the Village Vanguard, during the height of his literary fame.*

"Jack Kerouac: Off the Road, Into the Vanguard, and Out" from the *Village Voice*

Out front the J. J. Johnson Quartet heats up the buzzing, jammed-in, packed house to a supercharged, pregnant pitch. In a back alcove, near the men's room, sits Jack Kerouac, who has come off his road into the spotlight of the literary world and his sometime home, Greenwich Village, for a stay at the Village Vanguard that was supposed to be indefinite—and was. It lasted seven nights.

His receding hair touseled, sweating enough to fill a wine cask, Kerouac looks like a member in good standing of the generation he called "beat." Anxious drags on cigarette after cigarette, walking around in tight little circles, fast quick talk to anyone nearby, swigs from an always handy drink, gulps of an always handy coffee, tighten Paisley tie, loosen tie, tighten tie.

Howard Smith. "Jack Kerouac: Off the Road, Into the Vanguard, and Out" from *The Village Voice Reader: A Mixed Bag from the Greenwich Village Newspaper* (New York: Grove Press, 1962).

"What am I going to read?" . . . and he leafs through a suit-caseful and suddenly realizes no one remembered to bring a copy of his own *On the Road*. His combination manager-literary agent talks slowly and carefully in the assuring way they get paid to talk in, but the girl jazz singer is lilting a flip version of "Look to the Rainbow," and Jack knows he's on next.

He leafs through lots of little pads filled with the tiniest hand-lettered notes. "When I write I print everything in pencil. My fa-ther was a printer. He lost his shop on the horses. If he didn't, I'd be a printer today. I'd probably be publishing the fresh, young poets. . . ."

He's getting more nervous, but his speech comes easy in an-swer to certain questions."You don't know what a square is? Well, old Rexroth says I'm a square. If he means because I was born a French Canadian Catholic . . . sometimes devout . . . then I guess that makes me a square. But a square is someone who ain't hip. Hipness? Him" (pointing to me) "and I, we're hip."

Trying to keep up with the questions, he goes on at an even faster rate. "I was sitting with Steve Allen out front for a while; he said he wished he had his old 'Tonight' show, so he could put me on. I told him he should wire Jack Paar. . . . Jazzmen and poets are both like babies. . . . No, I decided not to read to music because I feel they don't mix. . . . Well, maybe Allen will sit in on the piano for a while, though. . . . Yair, whatever I write about is all true. . . . I think Emily Dickinson is better than Whitman, as a wordman, that is."

The drink, the sweat, the smoke, the nerves are taking effect. It's time for him to go on. He grabs some of those pads and begins making his way through the maze of tiny night-club tables. They all came to see him, and a few tieless buddies from the old days, a little proud and a little jealous, the fourth estate, the agents, the handshakers, the Steve Allens, the Madison Avenue bunch trying to keep ultra-current; all treating him like a Carmine DeSapio or Floyd Patterson.

He's shorter than they expected, this writer who has been likened to Sandburg but looks like a frightened MC on his first job.

They applaud wildly for this 35-year-old who was drunk for the first three weeks that his book made the bestseller list, and now stands before them wearing an outfit of fair middle-class taste, but with a thick, hand-tooled, large-buckled leather belt.

"I'm going to read like I read to my friends." A too-easy murmur of laughter, the crowd is with him. He reads fast, with his eyes untheatrically glued to the little pad, rapidly, on and on as if he wants to get it over with. "I'll read a junky poem." He slurs over the beautiful passages as if not expecting the crowd to dig them, even if he went slower. "It's like kissing my kitten's belly. . . ." He begins to loosen up and ad lib, and the audience is with him. A fast 15 minutes and he's done.

The applause is like a thunderstorm on a hot July night. He smiles and goes to sit among the wheels and the agents, and pulls a relaxed drag on his cigarette.

He is prince of the hips, being accepted in the court of the rich kings who, six months ago, would have nudged him closer to the bar, if he wandered in to watch the show. He must have hated himself in the morning—not for the drinks he had, but because he ate it all up the way he really never wanted to.

As I was leaving I heard some guy in an old Army shirt, standing close to the bar, remark: "Well, Kerouac came off the road in high gear . . . I hope he has a good set of snow tires."

—1962

Max Eastman

(1883–1969)

For a short period of time, from 1911 to 1917, the Masses *was the most famous, most read radical magazine in America. Edited by Max Eastman, it featured the work of John Sloan, John Reed, Sherwood Anderson, and many others. The* Liberator *succeeded the* Masses, *but it did not quite match its predecessor, lacking both its fire and its sense of innocence. Its purpose was, according to frequent contributor John Reed, "to attack old systems, old morals, old prejudices . . . and to set up new ones in their place." The* Masses *started in Greenwich Village in 1911 and ended its short reign when the post office effectively shut it down in 1917 for its opposition to America's entry into World War I. Brought to trial twice, both instances resulted in hung juries.*

Eastman was educated at Williams College, in Williamstown, Massachusetts, and taught logic and philosophy at Columbia University for four years. After the demise of the the Masses, *he edited and published the* Liberator. *He also wrote several books on the Soviet Union and translated Leon Trotsky's* History of the Russian Revolution. *The following selection from his autobiography,* Love and Revolution, *recalls a time when the Village was not yet quite "the Village" of legend but rather a charming and intimate neighborhood of "low houses, transformed bakeries and livery stables, and streets that meandered around until they ran at times almost into themselves."*

Max Eastman. "An Achievement of Love" from *Love and Revolution: My Journey through an Epoch* (New York: Random House, 1964).

"An Achievement of Love" from *Love and Revolution: My Journey through an Epoch*

I was happy as only the immortals are supposed to be in the years approaching our entrance into the First World War. So happy that I found solemnly written in a notebook of those days: "My life began in January 1917."

In order to make this understandable, I must give some little account of my early inhibitions. Although lucky in home and circumstances, I was a neurotic child. I was a prey to sleepwalking dreams and midnight fears, and was abnormally timid. My nightmares, frequently repeated, were visions of some undefined awfulness groping towards me, descending upon me, threatening to envelop me; in later years this awfulness assumed the form of a woman, still too undelineated to be called a hag, but dreadful in a softly implacable way. After these nightmares I would be found roaming the house, fast asleep with my eyes open. Even in the daytime I was morbidly—I would almost say, pathologically—shy. I suppose my grown-up boldness of opinion might be roughly described as an overcorrection of this clutching demon of self-consciousness that would jell my limbs and make me speechless in social situations. Combined with a rabidly puritanical upbringing, it so inhibited me in my physical relations with girls that I was deprived, in its proper season, of the joys of adolescence.

My marriage set me free belatedly in this respect, but it did not make me happy in spirit. The girl I married, Ida Rauh, was gifted and graceful, thoughtfully witty, ambitious of freedom, which a moderate income enabled her to enjoy, and very good to look at. But something in me having irresistible power rejected my commitment to her as soon as it became overt. That happens often, I tried to think, and told myself that a fruitful everyday companionship would hush it down or silence it. But our companionship was not fruitful. Through some accident of her temperament or mine, Ida damped in me the creative verve and zest for being by which I live. I delighted in her witty and intellectual charms, her rare dramatic and artistic talents. I enjoyed and admired her, but I was not enhanced by her love—not lifted up to myself and set forward on what I might become.

We were married in 1911, and in the spring and summer of 1916, while still living with her and our three-year old son in a Greenwich Village apartment, I was seeking a feeling of my independent self in solitude. I had rented a separate room which I called my study, and was spending most of my energetic hours away from home.

Greenwich Village, I pause to say, was a visibly distinct region then, a region of low houses, transformed bakeries and livery stables, and streets that meandered around until they ran at times almost into themselves. It contained alleys; it contained nooks and crannies. Studios sat in back and you had to go through a tunnel under the street front to reach them. We were living in one of these in-back studios on Thirteenth Street just west of Seventh Avenue when my son Daniel was born. The diminutive red brick house in front was occupied by two charming and sophisticated old maids, Helen Marot, Ida's best friend, and Caroline Pratt, who founded the City and Country School. The cement-lined tunnel under their house was not wide enough to extend your elbow in, but there was room in the back yard for a game of catch, had there been anybody to play catch with.

My memory goes back to the time when people first began to talk of "the Village" and call themselves "Villagers." I never used the term, and I disliked it. I disliked group-consciousness of any kind. I disliked belonging. I still wanted to live as an individual and nowhere but in the universe. Moreover when I became a socialist, a fighter, supposedly, with the working class for a universal "Big Change," I was on principle opposed to the anarchist flavor in the cult of Bohemianism. I was conscious of this—rather priggishly conscious of it, I fear, for after all I *was* a Villager, I did live in the Village. I enjoyed its free and easy mode of life. It was, in fact, the mode of life that I hoped, when we got rid of classes and class rule, would become universal.

At the time I was writing of, when I was drifting from matrimony into what I called solitude, we have moved. Ida and I and the baby and the baby's nurse, into a third floor at 118 Waverly Place, just west of Washington Square. My "separate" study was a small partitioned-off piece of a dusty attic on West Tenth Street. To reach it, I had to walk along the stately north side of the Square, around Mrs. Philip Lydig's handsome red brick mansion on the corner of Fifth Avenue—where, by the way, in a memorable moment I exchanged a few words with Sarah Bernhardt and looked into her tragically beautiful eyes—then three blocks along the tranquil south end of Fifth Avenue, with Mark Twain's house and the old black-brick Brevoort Hotel opposite.

Besides renting that separate nook on Tenth Street, I had in the same year, 1916, bought with my own money—and my father's—a tiny house and barn at the crest of Mount Airy Road in Croton-on-the-Hudson. The house had four small rooms, one of which I turned into a bathroom, and it had an uncovered porch from which you could look down through forest trees to the river. Beside the porch, and overarching it almost like a roof, was an Osage orange tree some twenty feet high, the only one I ever saw in our part of the world. I got Philip Schnell, Croton's good-natured carpenter, whose benignly keen smile was as satisfying as the work he did, to make me a long oak dining table, heavy enough to live the year round outdoors on that roofless porch. When weather permitted, the porch was the dining room, and the catbirds would come and eat butter out of the dish in front of us. Philip told me my house was the second oldest in Croton, and showed me how strangely it was built, with yellow clapboards outside and papered walls inside, but between them a concealed solid wall of brick. For further isolation, I had him fix me up a little study in the barn. And below the Osage orange tree I carved out from my rough acre of sloping land an excellent tennis court—a little short for professionals, but with plenty of room for a hot game by first-class amateurs.

Ida would come up to Croton sometimes with the baby, and even helped me to plant things in the run-down flowerbeds, but she knew in her heart how deeply the whole thing was mine. My zeal for the tennis court told her that, for she had no interest whatever in play. In October of 1916 I was saying to my typewriter:

The flowers we planted in the tender spring,
And through the summer watched their blossoming,
Died with our love in autumn's thoughtful weather,
Died and dropped downward altogether.

I was spending more and more of my time there alone with that typewriter—and with a few neighbors (for Mount Airy Road was already assuming the traits of a rural Greenwich Village). My house had once been a cider mill and it backed up for the convenience of the apples straight into the road up the hill. "He was a friend to man, and he lived in a little house by the side of the road," I used to say, conceiving myself to be something very different from what I am. It was a romantic conception borrowed from a classic source; and that at least was characteristic. For I tend to elude the distinction between classic and romantic. To myself, at least, I seem to contain them both in a state of warring equilibrium.

During that year, I was very much overplaying the romantic. I was dwelling in dreams of young love as steadily as I had during my junior year in college. I was undergoing a second adolescence. I remember passing one day on Thirty-fourth Street a dark-eyed girl of the Leonardo type walking rapidly eastward, carrying over her head a gaily-painted Japanese parasol. I was coming down Madison Avenue as she approached, and I stopped still because the unconventionality of the act pleased me, and because she was so beautiful. She was by far the most beautiful being I had ever seen—so I sincerely thought. And I turned mechanically as she passed and walked beside her, believing she must look up and give me a chance, or a genuine impulse, to say something. But she quickened her pace and kept her eyes down, and I dropped back. All that evening I was tormented with sadness because I had lost in a vast city the most beautiful girl I would ever have the luck to see.

In the same shy, baffled, boyish way I yearned over the beautiful girls I saw on the stage. For weeks I was in love with three, at least, of Isadora Duncan's pupils, but especially with Lisa, whose lithe golden beauty in motion was as perfect an embodiment of music in its lightly melodious forms as Isadora was of all music. Isadora and her five pupils dancing to a great orchestra combined art with nature, restraint with abandon, in the very proportions that bring me the feeling of perfection. But I cannot pretend that my emotion about the half-naked bodies of those girls, so simple in their little Green tunics, so dedicated to nature that their hair hung free, their feet were bare, and their armpits unshaven, was what is called purely aesthetic. I was passionately desirous of them. I was sure, moreover, that with the opportunity to choose, I could find a true-live friend in one of them. Irma, Anna, Lisa—it would be one of those three, and probably Lisa.

But when I went one day to their studio and actually met them, I could not think of a thing to say. They spoke English imperfectly then, and Ida was there, and Mabel Dodge, who always embarrassed me, and a crowd of radicals—the antiwar party. I only murmured a word of congratulation to Lisa and passed on to the high priestess, toward which my adoration was indeed purely aesthetic. That evening I was sad again with a sense of frustration. If I could only meet a girl like Lisa alone by accident, everything, I was sure, would turn out well. But I did not possess even in this second and adult adolescence the audacity to scheme up such an accident, still less to go to the girl, propelled frankly by the principle of causation, and ask if we might have a cup of tea together, or even perhaps a drink.

So I would drop back from these obsessing dreams to the home life with Ida, and to my now surprisingly comfortable affection for our baby, as one returns to sobriety after a debauch. With a great muster of resolution, I would be "realistic"—until some new vision of nubile beauty would tempt and torment me back into the mood of romance.

The most startling of these visions appeared, without forewarning, at the *Masses* ball, which was held in Tammany Hall, of all places, on December 15, 1916. Fate, in preparing its path, made firm in Ida's heart a whimsical decision not to go. Those balls were gay and tumultuous affairs put on for money-raising purposes by our business manager. They were a reflection, within the frame of American morals, of the "Quat's Arts" balls in Paris. All bars against "Greenwich Villageism" were let down and many curious visitors came from uptown to see them. Among the curious on this occasion was the popular novelist, John Fox, Jr., author of a wildly best seller, *The Trail of the Lonesome Pine*. He brought with him to the ball a young actress named Florence Deshon who had just won acclaim in the movies—playing the lead in a film version of *Jaffery*, a popular novel by William J. Locke. Here once again—and this time it was not just a romantic notion of mine but a general opinion—was as beautiful a girl as I would ever have the luck to see. Her hair and eyes were dark brown, her features keenly chiseled, her coloring rich yet delicate, and she wore the ghost of a pout. There was the merest suggestion of something wantonly sulky in her beauty.

We danced together while John Fox sat at a table sipping highballs and looking on in what I chose to regard as a fatherly manner. We talked fervently as we danced, and our minds flowed together like two streams from the same source rejoining. She was twenty-one, and was in exactly that state of obstreperous revolt against artificial limitations, which I had expressed, in my junior and senior essays at college. Even in my wish to transcend patriotism she outran me in our conversation, describing with happy laughter how she had almost caused a riot in a theater by refusing to stand up when they played "The Star-Spangled Banner."

"What do I care about a flat? I'm living in the world, not a country!" she exclaimed. And there was no zealotry in the exclamation, just a joyous overflowing of bounds.

I walked rather dizzily home in the dawn from that *Masses* ball. I went to sleep believing that I had miraculously found what all young men forever vainly dream of, the girl who is at once ravishingly beautiful and admirable to what lies deepest in their minds and spirits. At noon, when I awoke in my home, I realized that this could hardly be true. To prove it was not true, I remembered a certain unmanageable excess and impetuosity in her judgments which troubled what is classic in my nature. No one person could really fulfill the ideals of another. Besides, she was John Fox's girl, and here was I, the husband of a faithful wife, father and dutiful teller of bunny-rabbit stories to a three-year old baby. I kept the telephone number she gave me and the address—111 East Thirty-fourth Street—where she lived with her mother. I kept them very carefully, but I lacked the force of character to use them. Shyness, the dread of disillusionment, the inhibiting weight of Ida's emotions, my sense of guilt—I could not make a habit of drifting away and them coming back to her—these things all held me in a tight circle which I called "reality." There was no place in it, obviously, for pure romance.

Nevertheless, it so happened that during that same month, for reasons unconnected with romance either in dream or reality, my home life became so filled with anger that on the day after Christmas I summoned the courage to walk out—just walk down the stairs and abandon married life, as I thought, forever. I gave up my study and moved with a small bundle of clothing into a room offered to me by my close friend, Eugene Boissevain, a vacant room in his apartment at 12 East Eighth Street. There I came down with a fever, a mixture of influenza with homesickness, which made my bare lonely room look for a time like the end of the world. But my convalescence was rapid, and I was soon brave enough to go up to Croton to my little house by the side of the road, and enter with classic reality into that lonely life as a friend-to-man which had been my romantic dream. I considered myself set free from love and dedicated to a hermit's life—with occasional interludes—for many years to come. I would marry my art, my science, my evangel of liberty. That would be enough.

Just out of fidelity, however, to an underlying dogma that life must be adventurously lived, I did, in a mood of Calvinistic self-discipline, push myself into a telephone booth and ring the number that Florence Deshon had given me a month before at the *Masses* ball. By that act, my dedication was disrupted, my romantic dream of a classic life exploded, the whole temper and tenor of my living changed.

Florence had, besides that mixture of the sculpturesque and wayward which made her beauty so startling, a richly melodious voice. Her laughter was a riotous tumble of jewelly tone qualities poured out like colors in a kaleidoscope. I don't know what she said, or I, but she filled the whole telephone booth, and filled me, with mirthful excitement. We agreed to meet for dinner the next day and I came from the telephone in a state of credulous wonder. Could it be true then, after all, my midnight dream of finding a girl utterly beautiful, and yet possessing the qualities of mind and feeling I adore? Could the whole dance-elated invention have been true! Of that large proposition I was convinced by the tones of her voice in the telephone and her few words deftly and joyously spoken.

For journeys to Croton, I had bought a disintegrating Model T Ford car in which I could, with a noise like Gettysburg and a similar recklessness of human life, go forty miles an hour—almost as fast as a railroad train! It was not the vehicle in which John Fox would have called for a movie star, and I was arrogantly aware of that as I drove over to 111 East Thirty-fourth Street—past the corner where I had been turned around and pulled mutely along like an iron filing by the girl with the Japanese parasol. That girl had been a wish; this one was a reality, and I was on the way in my actual self to see her. Perhaps only those tormented as I am by an irrepressible romanticism combined with an obdurate allegiance to fact will understand what was happening to me. I was *believing* that reality might conceivably live up to a dream. I was facing it out with the Ascending Moon. I was giving nature a chance to be divine.

I pushed the bell believing, but when the buzzer gave a loud roar, my belief faltered and I went up the two tight little flights of stairs with businesslike steps. Florence herself opened the door. She had on a slim dress of heavy black silk that clung softly to the body. She wore no jewelry. Her incomparable colors and precisely carved features, and the lustrous dark waves natural to her hair, were beyond adorning. I drew a breath that I think was almost a gasp when I saw her, she was so startling in her beauty, and so simple.

She introduced me to a bright-eyed Hungarian mother, whom she called Caroline and treated more like a child than a mother. I made aimless conversation with Caroline, while Florence put on a hat and coat in an adjoining room. Then we went down the two flights of stairs together and climbed into my old Ford car, admiring its good points with a little laughter and wondering with a like mixture of whim and honest perplexity where it was going to take us.

There is no reason why I should recite these simple details of our coming together, except that their simplicity was a fact of importance to my emotions. Once again, and even more explicit than at the *Masses* ball, we seemed to have poured from a common source. We seemed to be, underneath the thrill of our strangeness, surprisingly alike. She was not, at least, rich or poor, humbled by her social position or proud of it and neither was I.

The old Ford took us across town to Mouquin's famous restaurant that stood opposite a dance hall called the Haymarket on Sixth Avenue at Twenty-ninth Street. The Haymarket was the sole place in New York where one could, without fear of police interference, make a date with a prostitute. This mysteriously unique fact made that street corner a little like Montmartre in Paris, and Mouquin's restaurant, although perfectly respectable, partook of the French atmosphere. It occupied an old-fashioned wooden clapboard house, dull yellow and rambling as no house in New York rambles any longer. You climbed the porch stairs to get in, and dined in any one of three or four once stately living rooms. It wasn't very expensive either—not too expensive for me to entertain Florence with a "Jack Rose" cocktail, a four-course French dinner, a bottle of wine, and enough brandy to keep us talking about ourselves, and finding out with continuing astonishment how much akin we were, for three or four hours. As though this miracle of impetuous communion, adjoined to her unutterable beauty, were not enough to unsettle all the points of my compass, luck had to add to it one last touch of divinely contrived romance.

She had been expressing petulantly, almost in the language of my college essay, "O Mores!" her scorn of men's slavery to custom, and to illustrate their sheeplike conformity, she said: "You can't do any little thing to please your own taste in this town without starting a riot. I once got a present of a little Japanese silk parasol. It was becoming to me, and I thought it would be fun to carry it. Do you know I never got farther than Fifth Avenue—I had to turn back home, it caused such a commotion!".

We could not part when the restaurant closed. I had told her about the house in Croton. It was waiting. And the car was waiting to take us there. We slept side-by-side in the corner bed by the big moonlit window, a very tranquil tenderness filling our hearts. Florence was extremely chaste and reticent in her instincts, and I was still diffident and inexpert in the art of unfamiliar love. But in this relation, too, which seemed to me the farthest that magic could reach; we were mysteriously not unfamiliar. The night gave to our bodily union the same instinctive simplicity, that quality of the destined, the awaited, which had marked the flowing together of our minds. The sense of having come from the same source, of finding ourselves in each other, the flame of "very ownness" burning in both our hearts dissolved all the little problems of reticence and self-consciousness. In each of us, for the first time, the ideal rapture and the physical achievement of love were so blended as to be indistinguishable.

—1964

Jack Kerouac

(1922–1969)

Born of French-Canadian parents in the Massachusetts mill town of Lowell, Jack Kerouac attended Columbia University on an athletic scholarship before dropping out to pursue the life of a writer. While at Columbia he met Lucien Carr, Allen Ginsberg, and William S. Burroughs, and, later, Neal Cassady and Herbert Huncke—all important members of what would be called the Beat Generation. Whether in New York or traveling back and forth across the country, he transformed his bohemian adventures into fiction. His first novel—and the most conventional—the Thomas Wolfe–inspired The Town and the City *was published in 1950. He wrote his most famous novel,* On the Road, *in about three weeks, which turned him almost overnight into the first Beat celebrity, a position that made him feel uncomfortable. Kerouac's distinctive prose style was profoundly influenced by modern jazz, its staccato rhythms and jarring juxtapositions that left the reader with a slightly unsettled feeling. His other works include* The Subterraneans *(1958),* Dharma Bums *(1958),* Doctor Sax *(1959),* Mexico City Blues, *and* Visions of Cody *(1972). This selection is from* Desolation Angels, *one of his most autobiographical novels, which he completed in 1964; it was published the following year. Irwin Garden is based on Ginsberg, Bull Hubbard on Burroughs, Julien on Carr, Cody Pomeray on Cassady, Raphael Urso on Gregory Corso, Ruth Heaper on Helen Weaver, and Alyce Newman on Joyce Johnson. Johnson describes her first real-life encounter with Kerouac as thus: "I walked into the Howard Johnson's on Eighth Street in Greenwich Village and there at the counter was Jack Kerouac in a red-and-black checked lumberjack shirt. Though his eyes were a startling light blue, he too seemed all red and black, with his ruddy, sunburned complexion and his gleaming dark hair."*

from *Desolation Angels*

I was about to come across a belly of wheat myself which would make me forget about death for a few months—her name was Ruth Heaper.

It happened like this; we arrived in Manhattan on a freezing November morning, Norman said goodbye and there we were on the sidewalk, the four of us, coughing like tuberculars from lack of sleep and too much resultant concomitative smoking. In fact I was sure I had T.B. And I was thinner than ever in my life, about 155 pounds (to my present 195), with hollowed cheeks and really sunken eyes in a cavernous eye bone. And it was *cold* in New York. It suddenly occurred to me we were all probably going to die, no money, coughing, on the sidewalk with bags, looking in all four directions of regular old sour Manhattan hurrying to work for pizza night comforts.

"Old Manhattoes"—"bound round by flashing tides"—the deep VEEP or VEEM of freighter stack whistles in the channel or at the dock. Hollow eyed coughing janitors in candy stores remembering the greater glory . . . somewhere . . . Anyway: "Irwin, what the hell are we gonna do now?"

"Dont worry, we'll ring Phillip Vaughan's doorbell just two blocks away on Fourteenth"—Phillip Vaughan aint in—"We could have camped on his wall-to-wall French translation rug till we found rooms. Let's try two girls I know down here."

That sounds good but I expect to see a couple of suspicious sandy uninterested Dikes with sand for us in their hearts—But when we stand there and yell up at cute Chelsea District Dickensian windows (our mouths blowing fog in the icy sun) they stick their two pretty brunette heads out and see the four bums below surrounded by the havoc of their inescapable sweatsmelling baggage.

"Who is that?"

"Irwin Garden!"

"Hello Irwin!"

"We just got back from Mexico where women are serenaded just like this from the street."

"Well sing a song, just dont stand there coughing."

"We'd like to come up and make a few phonecalls and rest a minute."

"Okay."

Minute indeed . . .

We puffed up four flights and came into the apartment which had a wooden creaky floor and a fireplace. The first girl, Ruth Erickson, stood greeting us, I suddenly remembered her:—Julien's old girlfriend before he got married, the one he said had Missouri River mud running through her hair, meaning he loved her hair and loved Missouri (his home state) and loved brunettes. She had black eyes, white skin, black black hair and big breasts: what a doll! I think she'd grown taller since the night I got drunk with her and Julien and her roommate. But out of the other bedroom steps Ruth Heaper in her pajamas yet, brown sleek hair, black eyes, little pout and who are you and what for? And built. Or as Edgar Cayce says, builded.

But that's all right but when she throws herself in a chair in such a way I see her pajama bottom I go mad. There's also something about her face I never saw before:—a strange boyish mischievous or spoiled pucky face but with rosy woman lips and soft cheek of fairest apparel of morning.

"Ruth Heaper?" I say when introduced. "Ruth who heaped the heap of corn?"

"The same," she says (or I guess she said, I dont remember). And meanwhile Erickson has gone downstairs to fetch the Sunday papers and Irwin is washing in the bathroom, so we all read the paper but I cant keep my thoughts off the sweet thighs of Heaper in those pajamas right there in front of me.

Erickson is actually a girl of tremendous consequence in our Manhattan now who heaps lots of influence with phonecalls and dreams and plots over beers to cupid up people, and makes men guilty. Because (making men guilty) she is an irreproachaby sensitive open lady tho I suspect her of evil motives right off. But as for Heaper, she has wicked eyes too, but that's only because she's been spoiled by her self made grandfather, who sends her like Television sets for Christmas for her apartment and she's not impressed at all—Only later I learned she also walked around Greenwich Village with boots on, carrying a whip. But I cant see that the reason is congenital.

All four of us are trying to make her, the four coughing ugly bums of their doorstep, but I can see I got the upper hand just by staring into her eyes with my hungry want-you campy "sexy" look which nevertheless is as genuine as my pants or yours, man or woman—I *want* her—I'm out of my mind with weariness & goop— Erickson brings me a darling beer—I'm going to make love to Heaper or die—She knows it—She however starts singing all the tunes from *My Fair Lady* perfectly, imitating Julie Andrews perfectly, the Cockney accent and all—I realize now this little Cockney was a boy in my previous lifetime as a Boy Pimp and Thief in London—She's come back to me.

Gradually, like always the case, the four of us boys get to use the bathroom and shower and clean up suitably somewhat, even shaves—We're all going to have a gay night now to find some old friend of Simon's in the Village, with the happy Ruths, walk around in cold lovely New York winds in love—Oh boy.

What a way to end that horrible trip up.

And where's my "peace"? Ah, there it is in that belly of pajama wheat. That naughty kid with shiny black eyes who knows I love her. We all go out to the Village streets, bang on windows, find "Henry," walk around Washington Square Park and at one point I demonstrate my best ballet leap to my Ruth who loves it—We go arm in arm behind the gang—I think Simon is a little disappointed she hasnt chosen him—For God's sake Simon give me *something*— Suddenly Ruth says just the two of us oughta go up and hear the whole album of *My Fair Lady* again, meet the others later—Walking arm in arm I point to upstairs windows of my delirious Manhattan and say: "I wanna write about everything that happens behind every one of those windows"

"Great!"

415

On the floor of her bedroom as she starts the record player I just kiss her, down to the floor, like a foe—she responds foe-like by saying that if she's gonna make love it aint gonna be on the floor. And now, for the sake of a 100% literature, I'll describe our loving.

It's like a big surrealistic drawing by Picasso with this and that reaching for this and that—even Picasso doesnt want to be too accurate. It's the Garden of Eden and anything goes. I cant think of anything more beautiful in my life (& aesthetic) than to hold a naked girl in my arms, sideways on a bed, in the first preliminary kiss. The velvet back. The hair, in which Obis, Parañas & Euphrates run. The nape of the neck the original person now turned into a serpentine Eve by the Fall of the Garden where you feel the actual animal soul personal muscles and there's no sex—but O the rest so soft and unlikely—If men were as soft I'd love them as so— To think that a soft woman desires a hard hairy man! The thought of it amazes me: where's the beauty? But Ruth explains to me (as I asked, for kicks) that because of her excessive softness and bellies of wheat she grew sick and tired of all that, and desired roughness—in which she saw beauty by contrast—and so like Picasso again, and like in a Jan Müller Garden, we mortified Mars with our exchanges of hard & soft—With a few extra tricks, politely in Vienna—that led to a breathless timeless night of sheerly lovely delight, ending with sleep.

We ate each other and plowed each other hungrily.

The next day she told Erickson it was the first *extase* of her career and when Erickson told me that over coffee I was pleased but really didnt believe it. I went down to 14th Street and bought me a red zipper sweat jacket and that night Irwin and I and the kids had to go look for rooms. At one point I almost bought a double room in the Y.M.C.A. for me and Laz but I thought better of it realizing he'd be a weight on my few remaining dollars. We finally found a Puerto Rican roominghouse room, cold and dismal, for Laz, and left him there dismally. Irwin and Simon went to live with rich scholar Phillip Vaughan. That night Ruth Heaper said I could sleep with her, live with her, sleep with her in bedroom every night, type all morning while she went to work in an agency and talk to Ruth Erickson all afternoon over coffee and beer, till she got back home at night, when I'd rub her new skin rash with unguents in the bathroom.

With only ten dollars left I go down to the corner drugstore on 5th Avenue to buy a pack of butts, figuring I can buy a roast chicken that night and eat it over my typewriter (borrowed from Ruth Heaper). But in the drugstore the character says "How are things in Glacamora? You living around the corner or in Indiana? You know what the old bastard said when he kicked the bucket . . ." But later when I get back to my room I find he's only given me change for a five. He has pulled the shortchange hype on me. I go back to the store but he's off duty, gone, and the management is suspicious of me. "You've got a shortchange artist working in your store—I dont wanta put the finger on anybody but I want my money back—I'm *hungry*!" But I never got the money back and I shoulda stuck the finger up my ass. I went on typing on just coffee. Later I called Irwin and he told me to call Raphael's uptown girl because maybe I could live with her as she was already sick of Raphael.

"Why's she sick of Raphael?"

"Because he keeps laying around on the couch saying 'Feed Raphael'! *Really!* I think she'd like you. Just be cool nice Jack and call her." I called her, Alyce Newman by name, and told her I was starving and would she meet me in Howard Johnson's on 6th Avenue and buy me two frankfurters? She told me okay, she was a short blonde in a red coat. At 8 P.M. I saw her walk in.

She bought me the hotdogs and I gobbled them up. I'd already looked at her and said "Why dont you let me stay at your apartment, I've got a lot of typing to do and they cheated me out of my money in a drugstore today."

"If you wish."

But it was the beginning of perhaps the best love affair I ever had because Alyce was an interesting young person, a Jewess, el-

417

egant middleclass sad and looking for something—She looked Polish as hell, with the peasant's legs, the bare low bottom, the *torque* of hair (blond) and the sad understanding eyes. In fact she sorta fell in love with me. But that was only because I really didnt impose on her. When I asked her for bacon and eggs and applesauce at two in the morning she did it gladly, because I asked it sincerely. Sincerely? What's insincere about "Feed Raphael"? Old Alyce (22) however said:

"I s'pose you're going to be a big literary god and everybody's going to eat you up, so you should let me protect you."

"How do they go about eating lit'ry gods?"

"By bothering them. They gnaw and gnaw till there's nothing left of you."

"How do you know about all this?"

"I've read books—I've met authors—I'm writing a novel my-self—I think I'll call it *Fly Now, Pay Later* but the publishers think they'd get trouble from the airlines."

"Call it *Pay Me The Penny After*."

"That's nice—Shall I read you a chapter?" All of a sudden I was in a quiet home by lamplight with a quiet girl who would turn out to be passionate in bed, but my God—*I dont like blondes.*

"I dont like blondes," I said.

"Maybe you'll like me. Would you like me to dye my hair?"

"Blondes have soft personalities—I've got whole future life-times left to deal with that softness—"

"Now you want hardness? Ruth Heaper actually isnt so great as you think, she's only after all a big awkward girl who doesnt know what to do."

I had me a companion there, and more so I saw it the night I got drunk in the White Horse (Norman Mailer sitting in the back talk-ing anarchy with a beer mug in his hand, my God will they give us beer in the Revolution? or Gall?)—Drunk, and in walks Ruth Heaper walking Erickson's dog and starts to talk to me persuading me to go home with her for the night.

"But I'm living with Alyce now—"

"But dont you still love me?"

"You said your doctor said—"

"Come on!" But Alyce somehow arrives at the White Horse and drags me forcibly as if by the hair, to a cab to her home, from which I learn: Alyce Newman is not going to let anybody steal her man from her, no matter who he will be. And I was proud. I sang Sinatra's "I'm a Fool" all the way home in the cab. The cab flashed by oceangoing vessels docked at the North River piers.

—1965

Maeve Brennan

(1917–1993)

A native of Ireland, Maeve Brennan settled in New York in 1949, where she joined the staff of the New Yorker. *She contributed book reviews, essays, and short stories. Between 1954 and 1981 she contributed to the popular "The Talk of the Town" column, a series of sketches about daily life in Manhattan, primarily the area around Times Square and Greenwich Village.* The Long-Winded Lady *features most of those pieces. In addition, she published two collections of short fiction,* In and Out of Never-Never Land *(1969) and* Christmas Eve *(1974), and, in 1997,* The Springs of Affection: Stories of Dublin. *Maeve Brennan died in 1993, at the age of seventy-six. She is most remembered for her uncanny ability to transform the ordinary events of daily life into something quite extraordinary.* The Long-Winded Lady *is full of these moments of recognition, literary snapshots of New York street life.*

"The Farmhouse That Moved Downtown" from *The Long-Winded Lady:* Notes from the *New Yorker*

Tonight, Sunday, March 6, I heard on the radio that a two-hundred-year-old wooden farmhouse was moved this morning from Seventy-first Street and York Avenue all the way down to Charles Street, in the Village—a five-mile journey. The move was a rescue. The farmhouse was about to be demolished, because it was in the way of a new building plan. I am staying in the Village, and I thought I'd walk over and see the house—see how it was standing up to its first night away from its birth site. Charles Street is a nice street, a good place for a house to move to. When I left my apartment, it was raining; it has been raining all day today—a long, dim, passive Sunday, with daylight ebbing from minute to minute, blurring the edges of the roofs and making the long distances of the avenues mysterious. Last night, it snowed a little, and tonight it is very dark out. I live on a small street off Washington Square Park, a street where there are always people walking, because it connects the park with Sixth Avenue, but tonight, when I walked out of my house, at a minute or so after ten o'clock, the street was deserted, wet, and lonely, and so was the park, when I glanced over there before turning toward Sixth Avenue, but the tall neon sign over Marta's Restaurant glowed cheerfully, its red color made foggy and yet intensified by the rain. Important people built these houses for their families years ago, but they have been apartments for a long time now, and Marta's is one of the old Village places that started out as speakeasies. I walked along Sixth Avenue to Greenwich Avenue, where the big open fruit-and-vegetable market is, and although it is Sunday, the market was busy, as it always is, full of color and of big, good-natured men in aprons weighing and counting and sorting oranges and apples and nuts and green peas and all the other things—pomegranates and avocados and melons, all the delicious food they have heaped up there. I stayed on Greenwich Avenue until I got to Charles Street, and when I turned into Charles I immediately began looking for the farmhouse. I couldn't imagine where they had put it. Charles is a narrow old street that starts at Greenwich Avenue and would run into the Hudson River except that the West Side Highways stop it. Along Charles, for the most part, are old houses now containing apartments, and an occasional heavy-looking big apartment building. It is an attractive street, except that, like all small New York streets, it takes on a dead, menacing air at night, because of the lines and lines of cars that are parked along its sidewalks—cars jammed together, bumper to bumper, stealing all the life and space out of the place. Even so, it is pleasant to walk there. Some of the residents hadn't drawn their curtains, so I had glimpses of comfortable, peaceful interiors: corners of rooms, parts of armchairs, nice ceilings, mantelpieces, shelves of books, paintings, people moving about—New Yorkers at home. But I saw no sign of the farmhouse. No sign of it between Greenwich Avenue and Seventh, or between Seventh and West Fourth, or between West Fourth and beautiful, bountiful Bleecker Street. After I crossed Bleecker, Charles Street seemed darker and more deserted. I was walking toward Hudson Street and the warehouse district—the West Village, which is gradually becoming the best part of the Village to live in as people slowly move away from the deteriorating part that was once the heart of the Village. Hudson Street is an awful street to cross, wide and grim and desolate, like an exaggeration of a big-city highway in a gangster movie. But when I stepped up on the sidewalk on the northwest corner of Hudson and Charles Street I saw the house. It was up in the air, a ghost shape, at the end of the block, on the northeast corner of Charles Street and Greenwich Street. The eastern wall of the farmhouse is painted a dark color, but the front wall, facing Charles Street, is white, and as I approached it I got a sidewise glimmer of it that defined the whole tiny structure. It was a *very* tiny house—much smaller than I had expected. That must have been a very small farmer who built it. It was sitting up high on a sturdy cage, or raft, of heavy wooden beams, on a wedge-shaped, weedy lot, with the old brick warehouses towering over it like burly nursemaids. It was a crooked little house—askew on its perch but crooked anyway—and it looked as plain and as insubstantial as a child's chalk drawing, but it was a real house, with a chimney sticking out of it. They hadn't nailed its western wall back on—it leaned, waiting, against the nearest warehouse—but they had covered the west end of the house with a big sheet of plastic, which flapped and glistened in the rain tonight. Across Greenwich Street, the big arched windows over the loading platforms of Tower's Warehouses, Inc., stared solemnly back with a darker and more solid shine. The house was protected by a high fence of metal net, going all the way around the corner, and outside the fence, all the way around, there were yellow wooden barricades with POLICE LINE DO NOT CROSS lettered on them. The farmhouse met Importance when it arrived down here. The lot it stands on is in an angle formed by the massive side wall of an enormous Greenwich Street warehouse and the narrower side wall of an old Charles Street apartment house. Both of these sheltering walls are blank, with no windows (no eyes to watch, no sneaks to throw garbage into the lot at night), and it is as though the old farmhouse had found itself in one corner of a gigantic brick-walled garden. It is a very private place, with those big walls to the north and east, and with warehouses across both streets, Charles and Greenwich, but I saw domestic lights in the tall windows of the house diagonally across from the farmhouse, on Greenwich Street, and there are people living in the houses going back toward Hudson Street, so it is not deserted there at night or during the weekends. The house could hardly have found a better place to settle in.

It was raining very hard by this time, and as I walked away, a police car came along, driving slowly west, and the two policemen inside peered out at the farmhouse—to see if it was still there, I suppose. I walked back the way I'd come and stopped at the newsstand at the corner of Eighth Street and Sixth Avenue to buy the *News* and the *Times*. When I reached home, I read the news stories about the house, and looked at a picture showing it in its old place at Seventy-first and York, where it was surrounded by towering walls filled with apartment windows. It's much better off down here with the warehouses, and with the river so close. I read my horoscope in the *News*, and I read the gossip columns, and then I read this story:

12 STARVING CATS
SPARE PIGEON PAL

BUDAPEST, March 5 (AP)—Friendship proved stronger than hunger for the 13 pets of an elderly Hungarian woman. Sealed for eight days in a Budapest apartment after their owner died, the pets were rescued when neighbors broke in. The neighbors found the woman's 12 cats lying around a room, weak with hunger. The 13th pet, a pigeon, was unharmed, although it lay defenseless in a low chair.

Except in our minds, there is no connection between the little American farmhouse and the Hungarian cats and the Hungarian pigeon, but in our minds these stories remind us that we are always waiting, and remind us of what we are waiting for—a respite, a touch of grace, something simple that starts us wondering. I am reminded of Oliver Goldsmith, who said, two hundred years ago, "Innocently to amuse the imagination in this dream of life is wisdom."

—March 18, 1967

Seymour Krim

(1922–1989)

Born in New York in 1922 and orphaned at the age of ten, Seymour Krim spent a short time at the University of North Carolina before returning to his hometown to pursue a career as an editor and writer. He contributed to the New Yorker *and was a consulting editor to the* Evergreen Review. *He edited* Manhattan: Stories of a Great City *(1954) and* The Beats *(1960).* Views of a Nearsighted Cannoneer, *which consists of essays, some short fiction, and critical reviews, was originally published in 1961 and is now recognized as a landmark in American avant-garde writing. In the foreword to the 1961 edition Norman Mailer calls Krim "the child of our time, he is New York in the middle of the 20th Century, a city man, his prose as brilliant upon occasion as the electronic beauty of our lights, his shifts and shatterings of mood as searching and true as the grinding of wheels in a subway train."*

"Two Teachers—Nuts, Two Human Beings!" from *Views of a Nearsighted Cannoneer*

I first met Milton Klonsky in probably the early spring of 1945. I had inherited a (to me) charming small apartment at 224 Sullivan Street from a girl I had been dating who suddenly winked at

Seymour Krim. "Two Teachers—Nuts, Two Human Beings!" from *Views of a Nearsighted Cannoneer* (New York: E. P. Dutton & Co., 1968).

me in bed one morning and said with a smile that she was getting married. She had realistically been cheating on my remarkable self-conceit that I was irresistible and had nabbed herself, while I was absorbed in making love to me, a guy much more of this world and less mirror-riveted than yours truly. So she moved out in a bridal rush and I moved into this clean swinging little hideaway with a feeling of delight (once I told my bruised ego it had no case). What the hell, women were replaceable but groovy apartments were something else!

I didn't know then as they say in the old stories that my 2 to 3 years at 224 Sullivan were going to radically change my formless young life, but they did. I was wide-open for it though. Full of bounce, full of fanatical seriousness about writing and ready and willing for every mother-loving experience—"black, white, a zebra or anything new they can invent!" as a laughing call-girl once nailed it to the door—I was able to overcome my native shyness and red-hot anxieties and blossom to the point where my clean little pad became a nest for Vassar-Bryn Mawr chicks to make fairly happy weekends for me. I got mostly literary types when secretly I thirsted for expensive, well-stacked, fine-assed royalty, but I had no kicks coming since I knew how half-man I was in the deep dark cellar of psychic me. Not that I was queer, baby, but that I often felt as unreal as Kafka and neurotic as Proust and shaky as a leaf in the privacy of my own head. I take little pride in spelling it out but I was bugged, fearful, "sensitive as a baby's ass" (as Klonsky once described me with that fearlessness of intellect that could allow you to take a personal insult and not flip because you saw the truth-clicking mind behind the words) and at the mercy of a fireworks-livid imagination; but the big thing was that I was a kid, 23, and in spite of everything the world and Eternity were just ripe dandelions waiting for me to pluck. Everything lay before me, I felt (what 23-year-old globe-eater hasn't?) and now that I was out of the rooming-houses and chance 3-week flops in friends' apartments and the whole general weirdness of living that made the war years over here a night-and-day rollercoaster I was feeling feisty and ready to ride herd on everything that plagued me. Man, the world was going to part and bow low for me! Neuroses look out, cause Krim's gonna boot you puny little assassinators right out of his life! I had never really had my own adult-decent place before and I took tremendous pride in keeping it shining and kept clapping myself on the forehead, in effect, and saying over and over to myself, "You don't believe it but it's yours, yours!"

Billie Holiday blew her blues from my new record player (I took over my ex-girlfriend's first-rate modern furniture and equipment, too, when I moved in and still owe her $48 on the deal although I haven't seen her in 15 years), Miro prints danced on the wall, a lovely pungent undefinable furniture-and-straw-rug odor smelled through the place, and the optimistic merriment of having this nice new apartment really picked me up high. I had made the Village scene 2 years before, but in a much more squalid depressing way. I had lived with the first important girl in my life, Connie S_____ (now just out of a Midwestern brainlockup, as I served my time in a Manhattan one, having gone back out of awful need to a convent-girl brand of Roman Catholicism and following priestly bluntness after being one of the Village's most wide-open soul-sisters) in a lousy one-room bohemian fantasy on Cornelia Street. I had felt excited about it all when we took the place because Jim Agee had lived on Cornelia when I first visited him while in high school (he was now down on King Street) and I was a book-hugging literary romantic who got high inside identifying with my crushes, but Connie's and my little stint on Cornelia was a savage bust. Nothing worked for us. I was scared of the Italian street-threat that used to psychically de-ball all us violin-souled Jewish boys who had fled downtown, I was wildly insecure and neurotic as was Connie, and together we managed to stagger through an unreal man-wife for about a year before it became a comic tearful enraged nightmare and she pulled out (for she had personal integrity, God bless her).

But here I was now in my new Village cozy-pad on the second floor of F Building overlooking the clean-swept courtyard—there were and are 5 small buildings built around a courtyard sporting a concrete goldfish tureen in the center and the whole scheme is

427

protected in a Shangrila kind of way by a big gate which locks out the Sullivan Street strong-arm locals —and it was a pleasure to get up in the morning these days, leg-tangled or alone. I was pulling down nearly $85 per week at the OWI writing war news, going dutifully to an analyst with the usual boyscout dreams of solving all my "problems" (the echo of Klonsky's chanting quotation of Blake's "O why was I born with a different face? Why was I not born like the rest of my race?" coming back to me as I write this, for he had a profound sense of tragedy and wasn't snowed by pleasant theories of mortal amelioration) and I was full of the immense future-kissing conviction of glory that your average U.S. writing nut of 23 usually glows with.

Going in and out of this lovely courtyard I used to see with increasing regularity—since I had my eyes peeled for it by now, especially when I was wearing my glasses (for I used to wear them and not wear them in the usual nearsighted hang-up that is almost a universal small symbol of uncertainty and shame among the boys and girls of my generation)—a strange shortish lithe dark-looking cat who would brush by me at the entrance with brusqueness and what seemed like hostility, but also looking me over in a grudging way. There was an under-the-rock air of furtiveness, reptilianism, about the guy; his eyes would never meet mine, never signal hello, but out of their squinting holes they'd flick off my buttons so to speak in one razor-swipe and then stare stonily beyond. Frankly I'd feel like melting sheet every time I ran into this dark trigger-man and it jarred me—ME, brilliant, handsome, proud, a Beethovian earth-shaker missing heartbeats because some dark snot didn't know who I was and stared through me! I resented this creep and steeled myself when I had to walk past the inhuman guns of his eyes, but even then— in spite of myself and my pride—I thought they were great eyes, green-grey, catlike, opaque, the possessors of some secret knowledge of mystery which later reminded me almost exactly of the hypnotizing eyes we see in photographs of Rimbaud.

This was Milt Klonsky, although I didn't know his name at the time. I also didn't know that part of the deadly looks he'd shoot me there in the courtyard-entrance was due to his own my-opia and the accompanying bitching pressure of having to squint and almost bore holes in the air in order to see clearly—or else be forced to wear the anti-heroic, anti-moviestar, ANTI-CHIC glass over his unusual eyes. (He was and is less nearsighted than my-self and has never fully resolved the problem downward as I have had to do because I was fingered by that dear old maniac, Mother Nature, as Dr. Chandler Brossard once dubbed her.) I knew nothing about Klonsky except that I was scared of him, aware of him, the cat was creepy—where did he get off acting so stony, rude, the hard-guy? I was mattressed sweet right then in my own terrifically self-important world—new pad, fears held at bay, fawncy-voiced eastern college pusserino tumbling (some), me not getting killed in the war and also living out an old news-paperman-dream via my OWI trick, some prose steaming in the Remington Portable at home and great-writer fantasies gassing me even as I shaved in my new hospital-slick john— and I didn't want some alley-hustler off the streets, some foreign-looking Mafia slitter, threatening my ego this way godamnit!

There was no doubt after a couple of weeks of these minor eye-crises at the doorway to 224 that the two of us had sniffed each other out, the way hipsters or Beards or Negro chicks who refuse to get their hair conked will get animal-feelers toward a member of the same club walking down the block. We knew, baby! I don't re-member exactly how it happened, whether it was a muttered de-fensive word (both of us shy) exchanged near the mailbox of a mu-tual friend like the now-gone Isaac Rosenfeld who placed a hand on both our shoulders and drew us together (although I doubt it), but soon, unexpectedly, easily, we were speaking and digging each other. Even though he was only about a half year older than my-self, Klonsky immediately (the classic take-over guy) buttoned up the role of older brother and with good reason: he was wiser in the ways of the world—although a consummate practical fuckup like myself—wiser about women (he was then in the process of teeter-ing on the brink with Rhoda Jaffe Klonsky, his first wife who has long since split with him and remarried), wiser, in fact, period.

429

Once I was able to penetrate the hard shell he grew for the world and swing with him I confirmed that there was nothing a hair's-width false in this wisdom except for the occasional high paraboles of thought, as in all under-30 visionaries, not backed up by enough experience to give them the body needed to support such rarity. Other than that the man was a masked literary marvel. He had matured much earlier than myself, especially in the minds he had trained with—difficult English poets like Donne, Marvell, Christopher Smart, his much-quoted Blake; the French symbolists, Rimbaud, Baudelaire, Valery, Laforgue, all the way up to Michaux; plus the most formidable of the contemporary headache-makers like Kafka, Eliot, Pound, Auden, Joyce, Yeats, Stevens and critics like Coleridge, Blackmur, Tate, I. A. Richards (with a Trilling read for mere entertainment like a mystery). Klonsky's mind seemed to contain the ENTIRE hip literary-intellectual university and closely grasped with an IQ that could stutter your butter too. When we got more relaxed and informal with each other after the initial feeling-out sparring—"Whodya like in prose right now? Chicks: Bennington or spade? Dig a tenor or a trumpet? You a Giant fan? What about Matisse?"—I got the downhome gooseflesh warning that I was on the way in for the most significant human and intellectual experience of my life up to then.

I wasn't wrong. Klonsky's personality was a subtle, forceful and later I was to recognize deeply profound one and it entered my being—tore through it actually—like a torpedo into the unguarded gut of a battle-innocent smug cruiser. I had never met anyone even remotely like him nor could I have conceived him in my imagination. Instead of being direct (my holy-grail kick at that time, encouraged by the prose of Hemingway, Eliot, Pound, which made a glistening literary virtue of straightforwardness and which I translated into an ethical ideal—even then trying to convert beauty into life-action!) he was indirect, elusive, paradoxical, frowning, iceberg-cheerless often. And yet one always had the impression, felt the impression I should really say, of a fine and deep mind that was fixed like a rule beyond every flare of mood, behind his furrowed swarthy face (now Roman-looking, now Jewish, now Spanish) and

430

in back of those special catlike eyes. The guy's strangeness, unique-
ness, was heaped further on my barometric apparatus by his style:
although quotations from Blake or Hart Crane or Wordsworth—in
fact most of the whole noble repertoire of English-speaking verse—
sprang to his dark purplish cracked lips at appropriate moments,
he electrically bit out the language of the ballpark and streets too.
The combination was fascinating to me, jazzing my ear and mind
with such new contrasts and perspectives on reality that I felt my
simple-minded conceits blushing out of embarrassment. When I
later found out that Klonsky was a hard-driving stud also, a refined digger of modern painting, a rigorous ace at mathematics
and logical thinking (I know this sounds too good to be true but it
was greased perfection), I willingly doffed my inner fedora all the
way. I had never met anyone my own age before Milt who I didn't
think I could top as a writer and ultimately as a man—a psychotic
piece of egomania (shared by you too, my self-worshipping pals!)
to set down yet true; but with Klonsky I had more than met my
match and although I felt that hard lump of frustration at his being
better and righter about so many things, something I was to feel at
different times angrily or casually over the next 15 years, I was able
to leash in my envy at his more perfect image and become a happy
sidekick and admirer.

—1968

Diane di Prima

(b. 1934)

Diane di Prima is a terrific writer who has become one of the most cele-brated of contemporary poets and writers. Born in New York in 1934, di Prima, the granddaughter of Italian immigrants, dropped out of Swarth-more College to become a writer. Hettie and Leroi Jones published her first collection of poetry, This Kind of Bird Flies Backward, *in 1958. She was associated with The Living Theatre and also helped found the New York Poet's Theatre, which produced one-act plays by poets with sets de-signed by the likes of Alex Katz and Larry Rivers. In 1964 she founded Poets Press, publishing the early work of Herbert Huncke, among others. Among her poetry collections is* Dinners and Nightmares *(1961). In 1993 she received an Award for Lifetime Achievement in Poetry from the National Poetry Association and, in 1999, an honorary doctorate from St. Lawrence University. To some, di Prima's* Memoirs of a Beatnik, *a bru-tally frank underground classic, smacks of pornography; to others it is simply the unconventional story of a young woman coming of age in the New York of the 1950s in a time and place dominated by men. In 2001, di Prima published another memoir of her New York years,* Recollections of My Life as a Woman.

from *Memoirs of a Beatnik*

You never do get to go back to anything, but it really takes a long time to learn that . . .

When I stepped off the bus at 40th Street and Eighth Avenue, it was like arriving at a foreign port. The city, steaming and tropical, resounded with music: guitars, harmonicas, an occasional horn, radios blaring, children playing in the dark, women talking together on the sidewalks or stoops, or calling to each other from the windows. The night was pregnant with lust and violence, and the small, dark men stalked softly. It was a universe away from the world of home-fries and roadwork that I had left only an hour and a half earlier, and yet it was the same, exactly the same—crowded together and seen in the dark.

Downtown the streets were filled with youngsters who had made their way to the Village over the summer months. You could hear the drumming blocks from Washington Square, and when you stepped into the crowd around the fountain, you saw the young men barefoot and naked to the waist, and the young women, their skirts held high, stomping and dancing together in the heavy night.

I had no luggage and I had no pad. The apartment had been lost for non-payment of rent while I was away, and O'Reilley had moved my "stuff"—mostly books—to a West Tenth Street apartment where a little street-hustler-ballet-dancer named René Strauss lived. I joined the kids at the fountain, chanting and clapping, greeting friends and acquaintances, hearing the news. Finally, the crowd thinned, the musicians all went home, and I wandered over to René's and fell out.

I spent the next few days casing the scene. The city was really crowded; there were, simply, no pads to be had, and rather than hassle I took to sleeping in the park.

At that time no laws had been passed limiting a citizen's right of access to the public parks, no curfews were in effect. By two o'clock in the morning Washington Square was usually clear of its usual crowd: folksingers, faggots, and little girls from New Jersey on the make, and I would stretch out on the steps by the fountain and sleep peacefully until just after dawn, when a Park Department man with a big broom would come by and wake me. He swept my bed and went away again, and I and the half-dozen other people, all complete strangers, who shared these quarters, would exchange dazed greetings and go back to sleep till ten or so, when people started to arrive.

There was a regular crew of about eight of us who slept there, four to six of the eight being there on any given night, and we all got to know each other pretty well, as far as moods and habits and aura went, but we never spoke. Something about the intimacy of our shared space and the code of coolness in effect at that time would have made it unseemly for us to know each other by name, or have anything more to say to each other than the minimum morning greeting. It would have been intrusion, filling each other's turf and head with rattling chatter and conversation, and the inevitable unfolding of our emotional lives would have destroyed the space that the indifference of the city gave each and every one as her most precious gift.

At ten I would get up, stretch, look around me, and read for an hour or so till I was thoroughly awake. Then, stuffing all my accoutrements into the attaché case that served as my portable home and contained a raincoat, a toothbrush, notebooks, pens, and a change of underwear, I would pick it up and set off for the Chinese laundry on Waverly Place. I kept all my clothes there on separate tickets: one pair of slacks and one shirt on each ticket. I would take out a ticket's worth, and, carrying now attaché case and laundry package, I'd amble to Rienzi's, which opened at eleven, and order a breakfast, usually some kind of sweet and espresso coffee, though occasionally I'd splurge and treat myself to eggs and English muffins, or even some sausages or bacon. While the order was making, I'd find my way to the bathroom which was hidden away downstairs; down a rank, damp staircase with oozing walls, and along a corridor straight out of the *Count of Monte Cristo* to a tiny, cramped room, fortunately vaguely cleaned, where I would wash my face and feet and hands, brush my teeth, and change clothes, stuffing the dirty ones into a paper bag I carried in the attaché case for that purpose. Would then pull a brush through my hair and tie it up, and, feeling vaguely human, would grope my way up the stairs and to my breakfast.

Great pleasure it is to sit in an unhurried, uncrowded shop, drinking good, strong coffee and reading while your friends come in and out and the morning draws to a close and you write stray words in a notebook. I would linger as long as I could, usually a couple of hours, leaving finally to go to my afternoon's "work." The man to whom Duncan Sinclair had been selling his pictures, a real porn tycoon named Nelson Swan, had been busted, and that market was dead for the moment, but I had found it simpler and pleasanter, though much less lucrative, to work for some of the older painters on the scene—painters who were one or two generations older than the abstract expressionists, and still used models.

They were gentle, friendly folk who had come of age during the depression and were given to painting what in the thirties had been known as "Social Realism"—people with a sad, haunting sense that the world had changed since their "day," and a persistent kindly determination to discover of what the change consisted. Most of them were within walking distance of Washington Square, and I would walk up to the studio where I was expected, stopping along the way to drop off the bag with my yesterday's clothes at the Chinese laundry. I would perch on a high stool, or recline on a couch, in Moses Soyer's studio, while his wife rattled in and out chattering and Moses told me the gossip about his other models: who was going to have a baby, who was leaving for San Francisco, and almost one could believe oneself in that haunting and haunted world of nineteenth-century Paris, would catch the bold and flashy faces from *La Boheme* out of the corners of one's eyes. The money I got for two hours modeling was enough to buy me dinner and next morning's breakfast and to take another outfit out of the laundry, and, as I had no other needs, I thought myself quite rich.

After a while a certain number of luxuries attached themselves to this routine: I met Victor Romero, a young photographer with a job and an apartment, and he gave me a key to his place, which had a shower; and occasionally I would work two jobs in one day and take René or O'Reilley out to dinner; and I got a card at the New York Public Library, which varied my reading considerably.

Then one day I wandered into the Quixote Bookstore on MacDougal Street and Norman Verne, the proprietor, offered me a job: he and his wife Gypsy wanted to go canoeing on the Canadian lakes for a month, and would I like to manage the store? The store came with a kitchen in the back, complete with stove and refrigerator, and there was an army cot to set up in the middle of the back room, where one could sleep in comparative luxury. The rains and thunderstorms of late August had begun, and the park was neither as pleasant nor as convenient as it had been, so I accepted, gave a few days' notice to all my painters, and moved in, attaché case and all, and Norm and Gypsy took off.

After they were gone, I discovered that the store also came with its own built-in junkie: a very beautiful, ghost-like blonde boy named Luke Taylor, who played a very heavy shade blues guitar and shot a lot of heroin—"horse" as we called it then. I had seen Luke around the scene for some time—he used to frequent the Saturday night "rent parties" that were held in a loft around Twentieth Street and Seventh Avenue—and I had eyes for him from the first time I heard him sing. Something about the supercool, wasted look: the flattened, broken nose, the drooping green eyes, thin pinched junkie face with its drawn mouth—the mixture of hunger and bitter—cut right through me, and left me wanting to touch, to fondle, to somehow warm that chilly flesh. I was in love with Luke then, and for some time to come.

On the first night that I was taking care of the store—it opened around four in the afternoon and stayed open till midnight in order to cover the tourist trade—I was standing in the doorway, looking out at the scene on MacDougal Street. The Village had gotten tougher as the summer had worn on. It was one of those years in the middle of the nineteen-fifties when the Italians who lived below Bleecker Street, getting more and more uptight behind the huge influx of "new Bohemians" (the word "beatnik" had not yet been coined) were beginning to retaliate with raids and forays into what we had traditionally considered our territory: the streets north of Bleecker. On their side, it must be admitted that we were invading, moving into their turf *en masse*. Many new apartments on Sullivan Street, Thompson Street, etc., had been opened up to us by real estate moguls. They were cheap, convenient to the Village scene, and in the heart of the Italian neighborhood. Into them flocked unheeding the boys and girls of the new Village: men who wore sandals, or went barefoot, and sometimes wore jewelry, girls who favored heavy eye makeup and lived with a variety of men, outright faggots, and—worst crime of all to the Italian slum mind—racially mixed couples.

The police were run by Tammany Hall, and Tammany was itself the heart of the Italian Village, and so they tended to ignore the escapades of the Italian youth. Only two days before, I had stood in Washington Square and watched a police car cruise slowly up the block and away, while about twenty young men pursued Francois, a quiet, pale-skinned mulatto boy from the Bahamas, into a building then under construction. The twenty hoodlums milled about in the empty lot next door, shouting obscenities and afraid to enter the building, till someone started, and they all took up, the chant "Get a pipe! Get a pipe!" The police car pulled smoothly away to the tune of this bloodthirsty chant, with never a backward glance. Francois, whom I knew slightly, had been making it with Linda, a pretty white chick of about sixteen, since he hit the Village at the beginning of the summer.

On this particular evening, I stood on the steps of my new store and watched three young faggots get beaten up by their dago brothers. A not unusual evening's entertainment. A cool breeze was coming up and many people were out enjoying the soft summer air. Scuffling and screams. The police pulled up. They bravely entered the building, arrested the three gay men and drove away. About three minutes later, the young gangsters emerged from the building and continued their stroll up the block.

Somebody came into the shop and asked for *Vestal Lady on Brattle*, Gregory Corso's first book, which had just been printed in Cambridge. There was no "beat poetry" as yet, it was just another poetry book. After the customer left, I settled down on the stoop to read a copy. I was deep into Gregory's peculiarly beautiful head when Luke appeared, guitar in hand.

"Where's Norm?" he asked hoarsely. His voice was always hoarse, was hardly more than a whisper, with that peculiar junk roughness.

"He's gone," I said, "for four weeks. Gone camping with Gypsy in Canada."

Luke muttered some obscenity, started to take off, then came back and sat down beside me on the metal steps.

"You watching the store?" he asked.

I nodded.

"You gonna be sleeping here?" he persisted, edging toward the thing that was on his mind.

I nodded again. Supercool, me too.

"Oh," he said. He was silent for a few minutes, and we both watched the street.

Then he said, "I was living in back here. Didn't Norm tell you?"

Now, Norm had told me nothing—whether because he wanted to cool the scene with Luke and was hoping I would get rid of him, or for whatever reasons of his own, I didn't know.

"No," I said. I was quite surprised. One of the things I had really been looking forward to was having that combination kitchen-bedroom all to myself, and cooking little things, and puttering, and playing the hi-fi: playing house, for all the world as if it were mine, and mine alone. After you've been on the streets for a while, living alone becomes the ultimate luxury.

I was quiet, but Luke, I was sure, could hear me thinking, with that telepathy people develop when they are continually at the mercy of others. I glanced sidelong at him and my heart went out to him. I wanted to touch those long, skinny, dirty fingers—beautifully articulate hands with the mercifully bitten nails. A pang of desire shot like lightning through my groin.

"No, I didn't know you were staying here," I said softly, "but if you want to, I guess you still can. I mean—we can figure something out so we both fit." I didn't look at him. "Why don't you go on back and stash your guitar?"

"Yeah," he said, and I met his eyes, and he flashed a smile. "Yeah, thanks. All I want to do right now is fall out."

I went back with him, and helped him set up the cot, and he flung himself across it, declining blankets and food, and in a moment was deeply asleep.

The street got dark, a few people came and bought books. I read the rest of *Vestal Lady on Brattle*, but all the while my head was in the back room with Luke, anticipating the night. I felt as if someone had laid a rare gift in my hands.

At last it was midnight and I locked the front door and turned out the lights in the front of the store. I poked my head in back and Luke was still sound asleep, so I decided to go out for a while and ramble. The street was extraordinarily quiet and, after checking out the scene at Rienzi's and the Limelight, I realized that I hadn't eaten supper and was very hungry, and that Luke would probably be hungry too when he woke up. There was a deli on Seventh Avenue that was open all night, and there I bought frozen potato pancakes and jars of apple sauce and cokes for a late meal.

When I got back to the store on MacDougal Street it was about three in the morning. I let myself in and groped my way to the narrow back room without turning any lights on. I found the refrigerator and stuck the bag of groceries in without unpacking it. The light from inside fell across Luke's face, and he stirred and half-opened his eyes. He had been up for a while, I figured, because the amplifier of the hi-fi set was glowing orange in the dark. I switched it off, and slipped out of my clothes, terribly aware of Luke, awake and silent in the dark.

—1969

Anais Nin

(1903–1977)

A writer and diarist, Anais Nin was born in Paris of a Catalan father and a Danish mother. She lived in New York as a teenager but spent the twenties and thirties in Paris, where she met the American novelist Henry Miller, who became her lover and friend. She returned to New York in the early 1940s and moved to a studio in the Village at 145 MacDougal Street and started a small printing press. The author of avant garde novels in the French surrealistic style, she is best known for her diaries, The Diary of Anais Nin, Vols. 1–7 *and* The Early Dairies of Anais Nin: Vols. 1–4.

from *The Diary of Anais Nin, Volume Three, 1939–1944*

[September, 1940]

After much searching I found an apartment I could afford. Sixty dollars a month, a skylight studio, on the top floor of 215 West Thirteenth Street. Five flights up. A very large, high-ceilinged room, half of the ceiling an inclined skylight, the whole length of it, twelve windows in all. A small kitchen, with barely enough room for stove and icebox. A small bathroom. A door opening on a terrace about nine by twelve feet, overlooking back yards and the back of a factory, but one can smell the Hudson when there is a breeze.

Anais Nin. From *The Diary of Anais Nin, Volume Three, 1939–1944* (New York: Harcourt Brace Jovanich, Inc. 1969).

I bought simple unpainted furniture, beds, large worktables. The previous tenants left a brown wall-to-wall carpet. I covered this with American Indian serapes.

Beautiful autumn days. I love the Village. I love the Italian shops selling homemade spaghetti and fresh cheese, the vegetable carts which sell small fruit, small vegetables, not the tasteless giant ones. Macdougal Street is colorful. The Mews, and Macdougal Alley, with beautiful small houses of another era, cobblestone streets and old street lamps. On Macdougal Street there are night clubs where they play a subtle, low-keyed jazz which occasionally explodes.

I sat on a bench in Washington Square and wrote the story of Artaud, a composite of real fragments from the diary and imaginary conversations.

The studio is A-shaped, and flooded with light. Next to my bed, I have a bookcase filled with books on one side, and on the other a table I bought in an antique shop. It is painted with scenes from Spanish history, and the top of it is like a tray with handles of wrought iron. Two lanterns are stuck at each end. Gonzalo tells me it is a feast table. On feast days it was carried to the entrances of churches and set up to sell refreshments. Candles were lighted inside the small lanterns.

It stands in the ascetic studio like a magical jewel in the plainest setting.

The first night I moved in there was a storm. A violent thunderstorm. I felt it was a bad omen. Is the war coming here, too? What is happening in the world is monstrous. Just as people are learning the use of gas masks, I feel I have to wear a mask of oxygen-giving dreams and work to keep alive the cells of creation as a defense against devastation. I do not want to become hard and callous as other people are doing around me. They shrug their shoulders and don another layer of indifference.

Henry [Miller] is preparing to leave for his tour of America. People have not responded to his marvelous book on Greece [*The Colossus of Maroussi*].

Sometimes I think of Paris not as a city but as a home. Enclosed, curtained, sheltered, intimate. The sound of rain outside the window, the spirit and the body turned towards intimacy, to friendships and loves. One more enclosed and intimate day of friendship and love, an alcove. Paris intimate like a room. Everything designed for intimacy. Five to seven was the magic hour of the lovers' rendezvous. Here it is the cocktail hour.

New York is the very opposite of Paris. People's last concern is with intimacy. No attention is given to friendship and its development. Nothing is done to soften the harshness of life itself. There is much talk about the "world," about millions, groups, but no warmth between human beings. They persecute subjectivity, which is a sense of inner life; an individual's concern with growth and self-development is frowned upon.

Subjectivity seems to be in itself a defect. No praise or compliments are given, because praise is politeness and all politeness is hypocrisy. Americans are proud of telling you only the bad. The "never-talk-about-yourself" taboo is linked with the most candid, unabashed self-seeking, and selfishness.

If people knew more about psychology they would have recognized in Hitler a psychotic killer. Nations are neurotic, and leaders can be psychotic.

The ivory tower of the artist may be the only stronghold left for human values, cultural treasures, man's cult of beauty.

[December, 1941]

Gonzalo and I searched for a job he could do and like. It was a dismal search, and Gonzalo grew more and more despairing. The only work he responded to was printing, because he had been associated with that on his brother's newspaper in Lima. He loved first editions, fine printing, and everything connected with it. But he could not get a job because he had no experience.

As we talked, I began to think again it might be good to have our own press. He could do my books or whatever else he wanted to do for his political beliefs, his Latin poet friends.

We saw secondhand presses for seventy-five and one hundred dollars. One of them operated like an old-fashioned sewing machine, by a foot pedal. The inking had to be done by hand. The man said we could turn out Christmas cards on it, but not fine books. Gonzalo was sure it would work. We would have to find one hundred dollars for type and trays.

I talked it over with Frances Steloff [founder of the legendary Gotham Book Mart]. She would lend me seventy-five if I could find the rest of the money.

Thurema Sokol lent me a hundred dollars.

I spent days looking for a loft. At the end of one afternoon of hunting, I tried a real estate agent on Washington Square. He took me to Macdougal Street, across the way from the Provincetown Theater. It was an old house. We climbed the front stairs, then three flights to the top floor. As soon as he opened the door I knew it was the right place. It was a skylight studio, ideal for the work. An attic, with a ceiling slanting down to the windows on Macdougal Street. It was old, uneven, with a rough wood floor, painted black, walls painted yellow. There was a very small kitchenette. It was all a little askew, it had character, like the houseboat. It had a fireplace. Past tenants had left a big desk and a couch. Thirty-five dollars a month. I took it immediately. Gonzalo was ecstatic. It looks like the houseboat! We had seen so many places which we hated, dusty, plain, faceless, shabby, like prisons, with narrow windows, cold, damp.

The doors were uneven. The house was so old it had settled. The windows on the street opened outward, like French casement windows. The houses across the way were also small and intimate, a little like Montmartre. Everywhere there was a casual, artist life. One could see windows open on paintings, on pottery, on looms.

Gonzalo hung some of his own drawings on the walls.

—1969

John Gruen

(b. 1926)

In the early 1960s, John Gruen was a music and art critic for the New
York Herald Tribune, *a position that he held until the paper's demise in
1969. He was also a senior editor at* Dance Magazine *and has served as
contributing editor to* ARTNews Magazine. *He is the author of several
books, including* People Who Dance, The Private World of Leonard
Bernstein, *and* The New Bohemia. *As far as he and his wife were concerned, the only place to live was in the Village. In the following selection
of his memoirs, he discusses those early days in the Village, when everything seemed exciting and hopeful. He closes with the story about a very
drunk Dylan Thomas, who had just embarked on a literary tour of the
United States.*

from *The Party's Over Now:*
Reminiscences of the Fifties—
New York's Artists, Writers,
Musicians, and Their Friends

The year is 1949, one year after my marriage to Jane Wilson. I have
just received a master's degree in art history. My thesis was entitled, "Peter Paul Rubens: Collector and Antiquarian," a subject of
limited relevance to my own or anybody else's life, but unusual

enough to have won me a scholarship for Ph.D. study at New York University's Institute of Fine Arts.

The kind of life Jane and I were planning to lead could not be lived in any other section of New York except Greenwich Village. It was the legendary place for star-bound people such as ourselves. We began looking around for an inexpensive brownstone apartment, and found one located at 319 West Twelfth Street, near Hudson Street. It was a parlor floor, and we were attracted by the red-brick building, the two long inviting French windows facing the street, and by the small park in nearby Abingdon Square. The rent was twelve dollars a week, and the entire apartment consisted of one single furnished room. It measured approximately twelve by fifteen feet, and its only bow to elegance was a wood-burning fireplace. Its furnishings suggested a motley crew of previous tenants: two sagging couches of indeterminate color and age, three wooden chairs, a square, peeling table, and a folding screen that had seen cleaner and better days. When our landlord showed us the place, we stood somewhat less than dazzled in our new home. I remember Jane tentatively looking around for the kitchen. The smiling landlord informed us that there wasn't any kitchen, but that the rent included cooking privileges.

"And is there a bathroom?" Jane inquired. "Certainly," said the landlord. "It's just down the hall, and only the tenants living on this floor are allowed to use it."

But at twenty-one a parlor floor in Greenwich Village without a kitchen or private bath is decidedly not the end of the world. So we bought a solitary hot plate, upon which we dreamed of cooking fabulous meals for the legion of accomplished and celebrated friends we would shortly acquire.

We did, of course, wonder what had happened to the rest of the parlor floor, and soon discovered, through noises emanating from behind our parlor's wall, that it was occupied by an Italian couple. They turned out to be the best neighbors two newly married people could have. As it turned out, the husband worked as a delivery man for the Duvernoy Bakery Company, which supplied bread, rolls, cakes, etc., to restaurants around town.

Our Italian friends proved the sanest people in 319 West Twelfth Street. The rest of the tenants could easily be considered slightly mad. On the three floors above us, there lived, for one, a short, heavily rouged actress attending drama classes at the Stella Adler School of Acting, who supported herself as a hostess at the Five Oaks Restaurant in the Village. There was an outrageously handsome dancer, studying with Martha Graham; there was a fashion model from California who was deep in Reichian analysis and could be found in her orgone box at all hours of the day and night; and a male couple, whose sexual penchant was of the noisily sadomasochistic variety.

Two weeks passed, during which Jane, in her impulsive way, made life bearable in our apartment by painting the walls white, rearranging the "décor," buying bunches of flowers, and beginning to paint a few pictures, which I insisted we hang on our bare walls. The big problem, of course, was money. We were practically penniless, and it was at this moment that we began to depend on the kindness of strangers. Our splendid Italian neighbors, hearing our stomachs growl through the thin walls between us, would invite us in for spaghetti dinners. The kindly truck-driver would leave bags of fresh rolls, danishes, bread, and cake in front of our door, before leaving for his rounds. Finally, Jane wrote to her father asking him for some tiding-over money, which, mercifully, arrived within a few days. We could go on living for several more weeks.

Looming ahead of us were our separate careers. I would now have to make my first appearance at the Institute of Fine Arts. Jane had already written several letters to private New York schools and colleges regarding a teaching post in art history. There had been few replies—and the pay offered was so meager that she held on, deciding to wait it out until something more substantial came her way.

In the meantime, I started going to classes. The first of these was conducted by a professor whose German accent was so impenetrable that I could barely make out a word he was saying. The subject at hand, on that first meeting, was the study of cathedral ground plans. Sitting in the darkened hall, with slide after slide passing be-

447

fore my eyes, and incomprehensible verbiage floating past my ears, I knew in my heart of hearts that my student days were over. I was, after all, living in New York City. I had heard about new artistic movements rising to the fore—movements created by living painters and sculptors working in studios only a few blocks from us, and I could not reconcile myself to being in an ambiance of dead art, no matter how lofty or noble, while New York was already in the grips of abstract expressionism.

On that first day at the institute—the moment my first class was over—I marched into the dean's office, thanked him profusely for my scholarship, and announced that due to unforeseen circumstances I could no longer take advantage of it. My reasons were extremely vague, and the man no doubt considered my motives highly suspect. Somehow I could not bring myself to tell him that two or three more years of art history would result in one student's intellectual and emotional strangulation. I realized, of course, that I would cease receiving the small stipend attached to the scholarship, but I figured that poverty would be mine with or without it. So I brazenly walked away from the opportunity that might have resulted in the world's calling me Dr. Gruen.

Jane and I celebrated my willful loss of a doctorate by throwing our first New York party. The guests were the tenants of 319 West Twelfth Street. Our actress-friend announced she would be delighted to do a scene from Oscar Wilde's *Salome*—a scene she had only that afternoon rehearsed in Stella Adler's class. We were thrilled, and proceeded to arrange our room in a manner suggesting an Art Nouveau set. We lit dozens of candles and draped our screen with a wild assortment of thrift-shop throws. We burned incense, and as the event was about to begin, bade everyone sit quietly around the room. The actress announced she would do Salome's last love-crazed scene. She went behind our screen, then emerged wearing tons of black lace, her hair combed out wildly. She entered carrying a large round tray upon which the imaginary head of Saint John the Baptist was supposedly resting. She slunk into the center of the room, placed the tray on the floor, and began crouching over it like a tigress in heat. Finally, she began to speak her lines.

The room was tense with expectation. The candles flickered ominously in the darkness. The actress was, indeed, speaking her lines, but not a single person in the room could hear what she was saying. The girl had elected to do the entire scene in one prolonged whisper. The fact that her head was practically buried in the tray before her made audibility even more impossible. The more impassioned her sinuous movements on the floor, the less she could be heard. This would all have been simply amusing, had the soliloquy not taken nearly an hour. At last it was over, and we regaled her with endless compliments. She agreed that it was one of the best performances of the scene she had ever given. After a while, we clustered in groups, drank, smoked, and listened to the latest Frank Sinatra records.

Much later, when Jane and I were in bed, panic struck us. It hit both of us that in the morning I would have to go out and seriously start looking for a job. Our meager amount of money was definitely running out.

I had always thought that Brentano's bookstore on Fifth Avenue was the most elegant bookstore in New York. The fact that it had a branch in Paris added to its glamour. I had also heard rumors that stars of stage and screen came into Brentano's for their cultural needs, and that Garbo often paid the shop a visit. Next morning, then, I walked into Brentano's, made a beeline for the art books department, and announced that I could speak French, Italian, and German fluently, and wanted a job as book salesman. To my astonishment, I was hired on the spot. Thus began four years of living with books—first as an art book salesman, and later as an assistant to the book buyer. I started at thirty-six dollars a week, and considered myself in the mainstream of the art world.

Endless hours of pacing and dusting—the lot of the book salesman—did not nourish my spirit or my intellect. Who could read *one* book amidst so many of them? Besides, reading on duty was strictly *verboten*. So I occupied my time by getting acquainted with my fellow salesmen, wandering around from department to department, and keeping a sharp lookout for Greta Garbo and other luminaries. Then it happened. Garbo *did* walk in. Spotting her at once, I dashed to her side and said hoarsely, "May I help you?" Her reply was simple and to the point: "No." Deeply disappointed, I retreated a few paces but kept my adoring eyes glued upon her fabled face. Sensing my silent adulation, Garbo promptly walked out of the store.

My second encounter with the stars was Salvador Dali, who proved a thrilling contrast to the reticent Miss Garbo. He walked up to me and asked if I had a copy of his *Secret Life of Salvador Dali*. I quickly fetched the book and said, "Here you are, Mr. Dali." He asked whether I had read it, and I had to admit that I hadn't. He then said that he would take the book, and would I gift-wrap it. I did so with alacrity, and handed him the package. He now handed the book back to me saying, "Take it. It is my gift to you. Would you like me to autograph it for you?" I tore open the gift wrapping, found him a pen, and, in the largest possible letters, he scrawled his name—and mine—upon the frontispiece. Mr. Dali omitted one vital step in the transaction. He walked out of the shop without paying for the book. Needless to say, the book still rests upon my bookshelf—Brentano's gift to me.

My next encounter was with a very short, owl-faced gentleman whom I had observed in the store on several previous occasions. He was constantly browsing in the poetry department, fingering all the volumes, but especially the series of short, fat poetry books entitled *Oscar Williams' Little Treasuries of Poetry*. These volumes were extremely familiar to me since we had been obliged to use them as texts in English lit courses. This, then, was Oscar Williams himself, greedily checking the stock of his *Little Treasuries*. I had recognized his face from the small oval photographs of the poets which were included in each collection. Being unable to resist a "name," no matter how dimly brushed by stardust, I walked up to him and announced that I had been conversant with his *Little Treasuries* for years.

450

This was all Williams needed to hear to become my nearest and dearest friend. He was full of questions about my life, said we must meet socially, and was, in short, prepared to take me under his wing. When I told him I was married and living in Greenwich Village, he offered to pay us a visit the very next evening. I rushed to the phone and called Jane, telling her that on the next evening we would be entertaining our first honest-to-goodness celebrity.

True to his word, Oscar Williams arrived at our door, laden with two shopping bags, one containing two dozen hard-boiled eggs, the other filled with red and green plums. A man of intelligence and a certain pixy wit, Williams also had some of the less endearing qualities of a nosy spinster. There was something rather monkeyish about him, with his long arms, short body, wide cheekbones, pointed chin, and deep-set eyes framed by cold steel-rimmed glasses. He seemed not so much to walk as to scurry; not so much to talk as to squeak. He had a way of insinuating himself into other people's lives that could be trying and tiresome. This quality was particularly apparent when, some years later, he became the jealous amanuensis of the poet Dylan Thomas, who, on his first visit to New York, found Williams his overprotective guide to New York's intelligentsia.

But Oscar Williams had much kindness in him, and he found genuine pleasure in introducing Jane and me to the literary figures of the fifties—writers, poets, publishers, editors, mainly affiliated with the so-called "little magazines" of the period—publications like *Partisan Review, Hudson Review, Poetry*, et al.

Oscar Williams and his wife, the poet Gene Derwood, lived in a penthouse on Water Street in Lower Manhattan. This was actually an enormous office building which at night assumed a bizarre and frightening dimension. There were seedy bars all around, and dozens of woebegone drunks reeled in and out of them, or walked in a daze down Water Street. Visiting the Williamses was something of a trauma, particularly since we had to wait for several very long minutes before Gene Derwood made her way down in the manually operated elevator to unlock the front doors of the building. Miss Derwood was given to wearing long capes and big berets, no matter where she appeared, and she was thus attired the first night we met her. Under her beret, we could see that her hair was a frizzy gray. Her voice was raspy and rather sinister-sounding. From the first, we found her witch-like. Whenever she spoke, there seemed to be some foreboding message behind even her pleasanter words. She seemed to harbor some strange, secret knowledge which, were it probed, might produce some catastrophic augury. We recall her leading us into the cavernous depths of the building's elevator that first night. Once inside, she sat, silent and regal, on the elevator's small stool, clutching the operator's lever that levitated us up to her penthouse floor.

She ushered us into her living room, around which sat some of the literati of the period. They seemed a most sophisticated bunch, into which two awed upstarts moved with a certain phony ease. The talk centered around sensitive literary matters—style, poetic innuendoes, psychoanalysis, alcoholism—all this, as liquor flowed and words and ideas became more and more confusing and elliptical. Oscar Williams talked very little, but was the agile dispenser of drinks and food. Gene Derwood sat erect, occasionally adding some portentous and cryptic statement, the response to which was a charged collective silence. Jane and I decided we had been accepted into this esoteric milieu by virtue of our decorative appearance, and because we ventured no opinions whatever.

But the Williams/Derwood menage gave us entry into a literary world which in retrospect was as formidable as it was stifling. To be in the presence of names that one had encountered in print during college years meant being in the presence of people who had, in effect, "arrived." Yet the seriousness and humorlessness of these "names" confounded us. For myself, I wanted desperately to know about their daily lives and passions, and was more curious about their feelings than about their intellects. I voiced none of these questions, afraid of making a fool of myself.

For a period that spanned nearly two years, Jane and I sat and listened to what we assumed were profundities but were actually the ponderous, self-deluding musings of craftsmen without souls. There was a leaden, inbred, self-congratulatory, and oppressive quality to their discussions. In phrases of convoluted impenetrability, these "younger writers" of the fifties would dissect matters of style and give heavy vent to opinions that seemed eons removed from what I considered the essentials of inspired literature. This was a finicky group, bent on magnifying the minutiae of great literary minds. And when they wrote about these masters they did so under the abstruse cover of the current critical language.

Indeed, the critical essays found in the "little magazines" of the fifties, with their voluminous footnotes and annotations, seemed consistently to stand in the way of the subject at hand. Because they were basically writing for each other, and even prided themselves on being out of the mainstream of public acceptance, these writers' work—their criticism, essays, and poetry—seemed like wastelands of picayune words and arid ideas. Not that it wasn't impressive. I would read these pieces with what amounted to religious zeal. Where did they find all these words? How did they know how to fuse one complex thought to another? At the time, I was totally incapable of saying what I was beginning to feel about these writers—that they were excruciatingly dull, filled with pedantic and archaic references, delighting in obscure literary allusions, and in general giving the words "dryness" and "emotional poverty" whole new meanings.

This grim literary world was thrillingly shattered when Dylan Thomas entered the scene around 1950. The tubby, curly-headed, pink-cheeked Welsh poet was making his first visit to America, and, as I said, Oscar Williams was his shadow. At one point, you could not have access to Dylan Thomas without first being in contact with Oscar Williams. I think Thomas tolerated all this out of sheer helplessness. And Williams was helpful in introducing Thomas to a great many people who were eager to meet the famous poet.

Naturally, it was at the Water Street penthouse of the Williamses that we met Dylan Thomas. A large party had been arranged and Jane and I were among the first to be invited. It was an established fact that Thomas drank. It was an affliction that would ultimately kill him. But Thomas sober and reading his poetry was an unforgettable experience. The poetry itself was like a gust of fresh wind, compared to the dusty, contrived, and pretentious verse that we had been listening to and reading prior to Thomas's arrival in New York. Here were words touched with life. They rang true, and were filled with feeling and with singular grace. The waterbirds and herons of Thomas's poems really took wing. One could hear the whoosh of their flight as they hovered over landscapes and shorelines that shimmered through summer trees and autumn winds. Always, the poetry contained an openness and a directness, a clarity and a music, which were literally breathtaking. To hear Thomas read from his work was to be engulfed in these exhilarating climates. His voice had a ring to it, and an inflection that gave the words a full-bodied melodic timbre, far removed from the somnambulistic intonings of most of the other poets we knew.

On the evening of the party for Thomas, the Williamses asked us to come early so that we might be able to talk with him before the other guests arrived. Jane and I came at approximately 6 p.m., and when Gene Derwood opened the door she started shooshing us profusely, pointing to a prone Dylan Thomas, snoring, and, as she put it, "resting." We tiptoed into the living room, and sat in total silence for about fifteen minutes, beholding him in his red wooly shirt. Finally, Thomas stirred, rubbed eyes, and sat up. We were introduced and for the next two hours engaged in conversation. On the floor, at Thomas's feet, stood four quarts of beer.

If Thomas was suffering from a hangover, he did not show it. His conversation was as clear and as lucid as his poetry. I asked him to describe the Welsh town in which he lived, and the house that he shared with his wife Caitlin and his two small children. With precisely the same cadences that marked his poetry, Thomas went into these descriptions. Every tree, every flower, every bird assumed a life of its own. The images were so clear, so crisp, and so magical as to make the room we were sitting in appear gray and ghostly.

This was no poetic rhapsodizing from the lips of a "poet," but the simple and accurate remembrance of a place he obviously missed terribly. For nearly two hours, Dylan Thomas spoke about his birthplace. The words were simple, but the sentiments complex, made so by the quality and intensity of his recollections. As he progressed into his stories, he progressed further into the beer at his feet. At the end of the two hours, his speech became slurred and finally incomprehensible.

It was now 8 p.m. and new guests were arriving—the usual entourage of poets, critics, editors, painters, and their wives. Gene Derwood had set up a small portable easel in the center of the living room. (She had, for years, been painting small portraits of her friends—an adjunct to her life as a poet.) Miss Derwood now placed a small blank canvas board on her easel, and began busily arranging her oils and brushes. Her plan was to capture the living Dylan Thomas in a portrait that she had been planning for weeks. This seemed hardly the occasion to embark on such a project, but we could tell by her darting, flashing eyes that she was inspired— and determined. So concentrated was her activity at the easel that she paid not the slightest attention to her guests (by now some two dozen). Oscar took care of the amenities and the drinks. Dylan Thomas was practically invisible in one corner of the room, hidden by a crowd of admirers.

People were sitting on the floor, paired on single chairs, on couches, on small side tables, crouching in every available spot. We kept wondering how Gene Derwood was going to manage her masterpiece. She had just turned off every light save a small lamp covered by a red silk shade on a low coffee table near her easel. It was the only source of light for her or anybody else. Suddenly we noticed that she had sat down on a very low rocking chair, far below eye level of her easel, and was peering through the maze of people, trying desperately to catch a glimpse of her subject. Her head bobbed in every direction, and finally she began applying brushstrokes with mad urgency.

We saw one guest, the beautiful Helen Coggeshall, imploring Thomas to read some of his poems. She had in fact brought along his collected poems and had preselected several poems which she wanted him to deliver aloud. Never unmindful of a beautiful woman, Thomas listened to her beseechings and seemed ready to comply. As Mrs. Coggeshall handed him the volume, he fell to his knees, lifted her tunic, and plunged his head beneath it. Stunned, the elegant, well-bred Mrs. Coggeshall allowed the poet to nestle only momentarily. Then she gently pushed him away, pressed the open volume of poetry into his hands, and commanded, "Please, Mr. Thomas, *do* read!"

Thomas lurched to a standing position, tore the book from her, ostentatiously turned it upside down, and proceeded to give a mock reading consisting solely of loud mooselike bellows and nonsense syllables, a ten-minute blast of cacophonous sounds without, of course, any relation to the work clenched in his hand. All the while he was gesturing madly, like a Roman emperor in the throes of an epileptic seizure. It was during this oration that Gene Derwood reached the peak of her inspiration, feverishly applying stroke after stroke upon the minuscule canvas. It was also during this reading that Oscar Williams elected to serve dinner, which consisted of mashed potatoes—period. He wove zanily in and out, balancing paper plates, some of which came close to falling upon the heads of the guests.

Thomas had now finished his "reading" and collapsed into a mumbling heap onto an empty chair. Polite conversation ensued, but the atmosphere became oppressive and uncomfortable. The mashed potatoes were being consumed in a desultory manner and it became apparent that the party was over. The only person totally unperturbed by the proceedings was Gene Derwood at her easel, and we saw that she had indeed done a portrait of Dylan Thomas—a portrait of a red-haired man in a red shirt in a red light. Amazingly enough, she had caught much of the frenzy exhibited by Thomas during his performance.

Glancing over at Thomas, we now saw an unreachable, exhausted man on the brink of another long alcoholic sleep. The evening with Dylan Thomas had come to an end.

—1972

Michael Harrington

(1928–1989)

American political activist, writer, and educator, Michael Harrington was born in St. Louis and educated at Holy Cross College and the University of Chicago before moving to New York. He had both the mind of a poet and the consciousness of a social activist. In the 1950s he joined the Catholic Worker Movement, a radical organization fused with Christianity that advocated pacifism. A conscientious objector during the Korean War, Harrington became actively involved in the civil rights Vietnam War protest movements during the 1960s. In 1973 he established the Democratic Socialist Organizing Committee, which eventually merged with the new American Movement, at one time the largest socialist organization in the United States. Their goal was to work within the Democratic Party to achieve economic reforms. Harrington wrote several books, including the 1960s classic, The Other America: Poverty in the United States *(1962) and* Toward a Democratic Left: A Radical Program for a New Majority *(1968). A professor of political science at Queens College, City University of New York, Michael Harrington died in 1989. In* Fragments of the Century, *he writes of the bohemian days in the Village during the 1950s, when it was large enough to foster a sense of community yet small enough to maintain individuality.*

Michael Harrington. "The Death of Bohemia" from *Fragments of the Century: A Social Autobiography* (New York: Saturday Review Press/E. P. Dutton & Co., 1973).

"The Death of Bohemia"
from *Fragments of the Century:*
A Social Autobiography

In a frenzy of youthful discovery, I found the seacoast of Bohemia on the banks of the Mississippi River in the late 1940's, when I was a Jesuit-educated son of the Irish middle class. The port of entry was a bar called, obviously enough, Little Bohemia, on a side street just above the levee in St. Louis. I had already learned enough modernist lessons that, to the horror of sober burghers, I used to push Alexander Calder's mobile at the Art Museum to set it dancing. So it was an epiphany to join the painters and the other regulars in the back of the room at Little Bohemia where they talked about art and psychoanalysis and the motherland of Greenwich Village. There was a business and warehouse district outside and, of a summer's evening, the streets seen through the door were always lonely and deserted, perfect décor for beer and romanticism and the lyric violin passage from Falla's *El Amor Brujo* on the jukebox. Sometimes there was a party later on in an apartment painted black, with mattresses instead of furniture, and no doors, not even on the bathroom.

I had encountered Bohemia in about the one hundred and twentieth year of its existence and on the eve of its death. Bohemia could not survive the passing of its polar opposite and precondition, middle-class morality. Free love and all-night drinking and art for art's sake were consequences of a single stern imperative: thou shalt not be bourgeois. But once the bourgeoisie itself became decadent—once businessman started hanging objective art in the boardroom—Bohemia was deprived of the stifling atmosphere without which it could not breathe.

The point is not simply that executives have co-opted modernist painting (particularly when they saw a chance to make a capital gain on the art market). That was only one symptom of a much more profound sea change. All of the middle-class verities—that God is in his heaven, Adam Smith's invisible hand kindly guides the market and the nuclear family is the one true way to love, to cite but a few—are either in doubt or in shambles. An entire culture is now more lost than the Lost Generation ever was.

That is why the counterculture freaks falling off the margin of society have such a difficult task. They have no Babbitt to tell them who they are not; they lack that solemn sense of anti-values which was at the center of Bohemian irreverence. For Bohemia, even as it dressed with "aggressive political untidiness" (the phrase is Isherwood's), was always a conservative place. It appeared in France in the 1830's during the middle-class monarchy of Louis-Philippe when bankers ruled for the first time in their own name. Baudelaire wrote of those years that, as riches came to appear as the final goal of the individual, beauty and charity disappeared and debauchery was the only decent alternative. So the original Bohemians—the French thought that all gypsies came from Bohemia and that artists were becoming gypsylike—protested outlandishly in the name of artistic tradition against a boorish ruling class. That is why Baudelaire, as he smoked hashish, thought of himself as an aristocrat, a dandy in an age of upstarts. Never has immorality been so moralistic.

From Baudelaire's time until a few years ago there were all kinds of Bohemia: of aristocrats, workers, American Negroes, frauds, geniuses, dilettantes on swinging tours of poverty, and many more. Bohemia was generally left-wing in France and sometimes right-wing in Germany; it was a bitter necessity for the outcast artists in late-nineteenth-century Paris and a lark for Mabel Dodge as she featured Wobblies like Big Bill Haywood and anarchists like Emma Goldman in her Lower Fifth Avenue salon before World War I. At the University of Chicago in 1948 there was even a graduate-student Bohemia, spread out through a decaying interracial neighborhood with appropriately seedy rooms for rent (it has since been urban-renewed into academic gentility). There were bookstores, like the Red Door, which sold the littlest of little magazines, and campus organizations would raise funds by showing obscure classics of the surrealist films or documentaries on the Bolshevik Revolution. There were, of course, bars, those perpetual town meetings of any Bohemia, where blacks and whites drank together a generation ahead of the fashion and sang about the Spanish Civil War rather than of happy college days. One couple I knew kept the complete works of Trollope in the bathroom for browsing and the husband regularly broke into stream-of-consciousness monologues about the intimate details of his marriage while his wife listened serenely.

Everyone I knew at Chicago had a poem or a play or a novel in process and one history student was carefully and falsely documenting his life so that, if he ever became famous, he would drive his biographers mad. Lindy, the first girl whom I dated there, was sufficiently typical of the place. She lived with relatives and, after listening to romantic music—Sibelius' *Swan of Tuonela* was a favorite—typed her novels in the bathroom in the middle of the night. Her books were primarily about people at the university, dealt candidly with their sex lives, and sometimes used real names, a fact which enlivened meetings of the Creative Writing Club where manuscripts were read. It also brought a letter from a New York editor who rejected her novel but invited her to dinner. When we agreed, with some unpleasantness, to stop seeing one another, she threatened to write a novel about me.

Several years later I learned that Lindy had killed herself. But at the time that dark denouement and the ambiguities which were to afflict the rest of us were not yet apparent. We practiced the established rites of nonconformity of the academic underground found in places like Antioch, Sarah Lawrence, Bard, Black Mountain, Reed and Bennington. The night most of the Master's candidates in English literature stood on mailboxes along Fifty-fifth could thus be explained as a not particularly imaginative exercise in collegiate Dada. But what made Chicago unique was that all this was done under the patronage of Aristotle and Aquinas.

Robert Hutchins, the guiding genius of the university, abolished intercollegiate football in the Thirties and, with one stroke, appealed to that tiny minority who saw college, not as a four-year beer bust of middle-class trade school, but as a Left Bank of the mind where ideas, like the poems and paintings of Bohemia, were their own excuse for being. Hutchinson then added insult to injury by sponsoring an Aristotelian-Thomist revival in the middle of a Depression when most fashionable thinkers were turning toward superficial Marxism. There were, to be sure, some people at Chicago who were studying law and even business administration. And by an incredible irony the Manhattan Project conducted the first controlled nuclear fission in the history of mankind at Stagg Field. The end of intercollegiate football had facilitated the creation of the atom bomb. Yet the dominant mood of the university was Aristotelian-Thomist Bohemian and there were fierce and beery discussions of whether Eliot's *Murder in the Cathedral* was really a play according to the criteria of *The Poetics*. As long as there was an iconoclastic regard for standards and a contempt for middle-class utilitarianism, Bohemia could assimilate any content, the revolutionary as well as the conservative, the romantic and the realist, and, at Chicago in the late 1940's, even the Graeco-Medievalist.

One December evening in 1949, I was walking home to cram for a crucial exam the next day and bought a copy of Joseph Conrad's *Victory* on the way, a book which had nothing to do with the test or any other course of mine. When I got to my room, I decided to read a few pages of the novel before I got down to the serious business of studying. At four in the morning I finished Conrad's poignant account of how a man cannot hide himself from life and love. That was the spirit of Chicago in those days: there were even some students who waited for months to go to the Registrar's to find out their grades on the grounds that a professor's opinion of their work was an irrelevance. And there was a rage to talk, to discuss, to articulate, that surged through bars and drugstores and love affairs.

Our Aristotelian-Thomist Bohemia was not, however, a bizarre Shangri-la in the Midwest. It was also a part of a major cultural movement in the America of the Thirties and Forties.

There was no basis for a right-wing Bohemia in this country because there was no feudal past with which the opponents of middle-class morality could identify. Instead there was the spiritual domination of white, small-town, Protestant America, the rule, not of a bourgeoisie which was bad enough, but, in Mencken's word, of a booboisie, which was worse. So in the years before World War I the political and cultural revolutionaries were comrades. In Greenwich Village there was a promiscuous confraternity of dissidence: of free love and free verse, socialism and anarchism, John Reed's radical journalism and Eugene O'Neill's realistic theatre, of painters from the Ashcan School and muckrakers, of Max Eastman's *Masses* with its anti-capitalist cartoons and Margaret Anderson's *Little Review* with its imagist poems and Ezra Pound's latest European discovery.

But by the Thirties all that had changed. The Stalinization of communism had poisoned the political as well as the literary left. Indeed, it turned out that Babbitt and Stalin had quite similar views on the arts: they wanted symphonies that could be whistled and paintings that told stories with morals. They only differed as to what non-artistic values art should serve, the one favoring Midwestern boosterism, the other Russian totalitarianism. It was a group of intellectuals around *Partisan Review* who, in keeping with Bohemian tradition, rose up against the new Philistines of the left in the name of high standards. They simultaneously defended Marxism in politics and nonrepresentationalism in the arts; they admired T. S. Eliot, the self-proclaimed classicist, royalist and Anglo-Catholic, and Leon Trotsky, the organizer of the October Revolution.

Some years later, in 1952, I got a glimpse of the twilight of that *Partisan Review* world. There was a party at Dwight Macdonald's apartment in an old brownstone on the eastern fringe of the Village. There was intense literary-political talk, but the feature of the evening was a tiny opera company under the direction of Noah Greenberg—once the leader of a Trotskyist fraction in the seaman's union, later the founder of the Pro Musica, a group which specialized in Renaissance music—which performed Purcell's *Dido and Aeneas* in the living room. This synthesis, in which the lions and lambs of Marxism and high culture lay down together, was breaking up even as I observed it at that party. For instance, Macdonald, who had edited the anarcho-pacifist magazine, *Politics*, was now writing for *The New Yorker*. But it had dominated the best of American intellectual life in the Thirties and Forties and it was one reason why the Bohemian style and Aristotelian-Thomist content at Chicago were not so contradictory after all.

I was not looking for historical trends on the evening in 1949 when I first arrived from Chicago—then, as always, the second city—put down my bags, and went out to find Greenwich Village. I wandered in and out of a few bars around Sheridan Square and drifted into a place called Café Bohemia on Barrow Street. It was in a lesbian phase (the police and organized crime, which jointly supervised such things in the Village, rarely allowed a homosexual haunt to run for more than a few years) and, like all straight young men from the Middle West, I found that fascinating. I got into conversation with an attractive young woman, but then her girlfriend appeared, angry with my heterosexual poaching. "You don't belong here, buddy," she said. "You're a San Remo type." The next night I went to the Remo and found out that she was right.

The San Remo was an Italian restaurant at the uneasy intersection of Greenwich Village and Little Italy, with bad, yellowed paintings over the bar and the Entr'Acte from Wolf-Ferrari's *Jewels of the Madonna* on the jukebox. In 1949, it was the united front of the Village. There were a few old Bohemians, like Maxwell Bodenheim, the poet and novelist who dated back to the pre-World War I ferment in Chicago and was not a shouting, mumbling, drunken, hollow-eyed memory of himself. (Bodenheim and his last wife, Ruth, were to be murdered by a psychotic a few years later.) There were seamen on the beach, the most important single contingent from working-class Bohemia. Some of them had fought in Spain; one had been a leading Communist in the National Maritime Union, but he broke from the Party and was later expelled from the union. They all combined two seemingly antagonistic life-styles: the militant and the vagabond. At that time, most of the radical seamen were being driven out of their jobs by the loyalty program and had plenty of time to drink and reminisce about Spain in the Remo.

Among the other regulars there were heterosexuals on the make; homosexuals who preferred erotic integration to the exclusively gay bars then on Eighth Street; Communists, Socialists and Trotskyists; potheads; writers of the older generation, like James Agee, and innovators of the future like Allen Ginsberg, and Julian Beck and Judith Malina, who were to found the Living Theatre. There was only one really important element from the Village missing: the painters, like de Kooning, Klein and Pollack, who at that moment were taking over the artistic leadership of the world from Paris, drank at the Cedar over on University Place, along with some of the Black Mountain poets.

The Remo was, of course, interracial, as far as that was possible in the late Forties. One night after I had been in residence for about a year I brought the fiancee of a friend of mine in St. Louis to see the "real" Village in the San Remo. As we walked into the bar I could feel her stiffen. It was not because there were obvious homosexuals, both male and female, or because some of the girls were barefoot or there was a hum of four-letter words. "Are those two white girls over there," she asked with some agitation, and oblivious of the exotic flora and fauna around her, "on a date with those Negroes they're sitting with?"

There were only a few remittance men among us, so the strategies for survival varied: over the years I worked doing articles for *The Columbia Encyclopedia*, as a writer trainee for *Life*, as a soda jerk hiring out by the day, as a machine operator in a shop owned by socialist friends where the bosses and the workers discussed the Russian Revolution at lunch break, as a functionary in a civil-liberties organization, and as a free-lance writer-researcher for a foundation. When one was forced into the workday world there was always the anticipation of the joys of socialized Bohemianism to come: unemployment insurance. I called my twenty-six weeks on the dole my Thomas E. Dewey Fellowship in honor of the Governor and spent it studying the Italian Renaissance. Later on one friend made some money on the side by appearing on the quiz show, *The $64,000 Question*, and proved something about middle-class morality by being the only participant to quit when he found

464

out that it was rigged. And there were crews of Village jocks, alcoholics and repatriated expatriates who provided the most raffish moving van service in the world.

The object was to avoid the routine of nine-to-five, to find a space in which to think, to write, perhaps to dribble away a life. In the afternoons the sweet smell of pot perfumed the balcony air of the Loew's Sheridan, perhaps the only commercial movie house in New York where a passing reference to Leon Trotsky could provoke a small ovation. Sometimes the conversations literally lasted until dawn. Every night at the Remo, Tony, who ran the tiny after-hours joint in the rear of a luncheonette around the corner, came in for his ice and we sometimes followed him back at four in the morning. On Third Street there was another speak-easy, a marvelous demimonde of mobsters, call girls and transvestites. They charged $1.25 for a beer, the standard extortion in the Mafia bars of the period, so we used to sneak in a last bottle from the Remo under our coats and drink it while watching the customers, the best floorshow in the Village.

I remember one party with over a hundred people in a huge loft, all naked. The party was in honor of Winny, a striking black woman who, legend had it, had once indulged her penchant for public disrobing by boarding a Sixth Avenue bus in the nude. She had, of course, stripped to receive birthday greetings and it seemed to her guests that it was the gentlemanly and ladylike thing to follow her example. So it was that they found a milling mass of drinking, chatting, naked people. In one of the most extreme demonstrations of official aplomb I have ever witnessed they did not once refer to that extraordinary fact. But as they left one officer winked.

At Winny's party one could meet a good portion of the Bohemian cadre in New York. For the Village—and I stress now one of the crucial differences between Bohemia and the counterculture of the Sixties and Seventies—was small, organized on a human scale. Take a not untypical chain of circumstances. Through friends at the Remo (whom I still see from time to time, more than twenty years later) I met a young woman, Barbara Bank. She invited me to a party at Norman Mailer's huge loft over on

First Avenue where, only two years out of St. Louis and goggle-eyed I talked with writers and painters and gallery owners and even saw Marlon Brando. Mailer—and I mean no harm to his image as an enfant terrible—is one of the nicest men I have ever known, with a marvelous memory for names of young nobodys from St. Louis. In the world which he dominated I became friends with Dan Wolf and Ed Fancher, who were to found *The Village Voice*; met Susan Sontag, who was teaching philosophy then, and the playwright, Maria Irene Fornes and the poet, Denise Levertov; and glimpsed visiting celebrities, like Alberto Moravia and William Styron, across the room at crowded parties.

We were a handful of voluntary exiles from a middle-class which itself was still fairly small. But then in the Sixties three major trends intersected: the post-World War II baby boom began to come of age; there was a relative affluence which gave the new armies of the young more economic independence than any generation in human history: and there was the near collapse of almost every institution of social control, including the church, the family and, for a significant number, the discipline of the labor market, where it was no longer true that he who does not work shall not eat. As a result, the freaks of the Sixties and Seventies came in hordes and rebelled in confusion against liberal permissiveness. The clothes, the hostility to middle-class values, were very much like those of Bohemia. But they were a mass movement on an uncharted social frontier; we, who preceded them by only ten or twenty years, had been a self-appointed saving remnant within the citadel of traditional banality.

So Christopher Jencks was wrong when he wrote, "Instead of one Greenwich Village in New York, populated by a handful of rebels from traditional homes, America developed scores of campus Villages populated by young people whose values were shaped by the ideals espoused by their liberal parents." That is to miss one of the most crucial and Hegelian of truths about contemporary culture: that increases in quantity eventually become a change in quality, that a Bohemia that enrolls a good portion of a generation is no longer a Bohemia.

My point, for reasons utterly beyond my control, is elitist. It could not, alas, have been otherwise. When the great majority of people were kept in the cultural darkness and the rulers were taste-less makers of money, the enclaves of art had to be the refuge of an outcast minority of aesthetic aristocrats even when some of them were starving. One of the virtues of that cruel necessity was that the Bohemian scale was intimate. To recognize, and even celebrate, that fact is not to apologize for the outrageous maldistribution of economic, and therefore spiritual, resources which gave rise to it. A love of Renaissance painting and sculpture hardly makes one an accomplice of the Borgias.

So it was good that, on a warm Sunday afternoon in the early Fifties when the folk singers were performing over by the fountain, I would know half of the people in Washington Square Park on sight. (In 1961 we even took on the police in the "Folk Song Riots" to defend their right to sing.) The Village was large enough to have a sense of community, of society, and small enough for everyone to remain an individual. It is something else again—and not Bo-hemia—when hundreds of thousands of young people gather at a Woodstock Festival to listen to highly paid super-stars in commer-cialized and collectivized rites of liberation. That does not mean that I want to go back to the old injustices where the many were hungry and the happy few could be sensitive. I fought for the so-cial programs which freed those young people to go to Woodstock and do not think the laws we won went halfway far enough. But that does not change the fact that, in preparing the way for some-thing utterly unprecedented, a mass counterculture, they de-stroyed the possibility of Bohemia.

Do I romanticize that sheltered little nonconformist world of my youth? Here is William Gaddis' bitter description of the San Remo in *The Recognitions*: "And by now they were at the door of the Viareggio [the Remo's pen name in the novel], a small Italian bar of nepotistic honesty before it was discovered by the exotics. Neighborhood folk still came, in vanquished numbers and mostly in the afternoon, before the two small dining rooms and the bar were taken over by the educated classes, an ill-dressed, underfed, overdrunken group of squatters with minds so highly developed that they were excused from good manners, tastes so refined in one direction that they were excused from having none in any other, emotions so cultivated that the only aberration was normality, all afloat here on sodden pools of depravity calculated only to manifest the pricelessness of what they were throwing away, the three sexes in two colors, a group of people all mentally and physically the wrong size."

Mary McCarthy was not quite so unflattering. She toured the Village for the New York *Post* in the Winter of 1950 and found the Remo to be an American Café de Flore. (The Flore was the café in Saint-Germain-des-Pres where Sartre and de Beauvoir held existentialist court right after World War II.) But still she did not find much substance in the Village, but only a place "where young people throng for a few years before settling down to 'real life,' where taxis full of tourists pursue the pleasure-principle outside of ordinary time, as on a steamer, where bands of teenage nihilists, outside of everything, from nowhere, rove the streets like a potential mob, and where certain disabled veterans of life, art, and politics exercise mutual charity and philosophize all night long, as though already translated into the next world."

Gaddis and McCarthy were partly right and utterly wrong, having failed to understand one of the most crucial single truths about Bohemia. There were certainly "overdrunken squatters" around the Village then even if the "sodden pools of depravity" are a bit melodramatic. And there were "disabled veterans of life, art, and politics." But those things are obvious and inevitable. In Bohemia throughout its history the poseurs, the failures and the frauds have always overwhelmingly outnumbered the serious artists. Theophile Gautier, that quintessential literary man of the age of Baudelaire, had identified one of the Remo types almost a century before Gaddis and McCarthy noticed him: "In admiring beauty, he forgot to express it, and whatever he felt deeply, he believed that he had given form."

Indeed it is a cruel truth of the history of all art and literature that most would-be poets, writers and painters fail. The genuine man or woman of real talent is rare, the born genius rarer still. For every book that survives the merciless judgment of time, there are nine hundred and ninety-nine rotting unread in libraries and nine thousand and ninety-nine which were never written in the first place. It is thus an insight of no particular value to say that most of the conversations at the Remo were, at best, cultured superficialities and usually not even that good. It could not have been otherwise.

And yet—and here again the contrast with the counterculture is marked—our phoniness had had standards. We postured about the first-rate, about Proust and Joyce and Kafka, the later Beethoven quartets and Balanchine choreography, Marx and Lenin. So there was always the possibility that the sophisticated inanities could become serious and substantial, that one would hear or say a truth or even be incited to create. The proof is in the production. Over the years the people I knew in the Village worked to considerable effect. I think, for example, of the writers and performers I knew when I went to the White Horse, the Remo's successor, every night for more than ten years.

At first glance the saga of the Horse in those days confirms the worst fears of Gaddis and McCarthy. It was a party that lasted longer than a decade. In the early Fifties it was the haunt of Irish longshoremen, Catholic liberals and radicals, socialists and Communists. Norman Mailer used to hold Sunday afternoons there for a varied assortment of writers like Vance Bourjaily, Calder Willingham and William Styron. A little later on Dylan Thomas began telling audiences that he drank there and every English major in the Northeast corridor began to make a pilgrimage to the White Horse. Still later on it became a rollicking hangout for folk singers.

It was a party in the sense that on any given night, or week, or month, you knew you would see the same people. In the middle of that public bar, even when it was jammed on a post-Dylan Thomas weekend, there was an invisible space which the regulars inhabited like a London club. Pretty girls could enter it rather easily, men much less so, and the faces changed slowly. We had our tabs, our phone messages, even our mail, and 1961 was not that different from 1951. So the White Horse fulfilled a classic Bohemian function; it was, to borrow from a German writer, "a kind of organization of disorganization."

The women were sexually liberated in the Twenties' and Thirties' sense of the word: they recognized their own erotic needs and slept with men whom they loved, or just liked. If a couple left the Horse together at closing time it was taken as probable that they would share a bed; if they drank together two nights in a row they achieved the social status of—to use the period's favorite cliché—a relationship. In the early Fifties you would sometimes meet a Wilhelm Reichian in search of the ultimate orgasm—though it often seemed to me that the Reichian girls were trying to shout down their own tightness and timidity with incantations to the uncontrollable rhythms of life. But for all the casual intimacy of those days the scene was not depraved or sluttish and it actually produced a fair number of marriages. Now, of course, our daring experimentation is the sexual orthodoxy of college students.

For some that ten-year party was a moral disaster, an amusing waste of life. (Our own legend had it, with some truth I suspect, that one group moved from their table in the front room of the Horse to the South of France without interrupting their conversation and musical beds.) For others it was, just as Mary McCarthy said, an episode, a prelude to entering the world of "real life." For instance I used to drink in the White Horse with Bernard Cornfeld, then a socialist, later the ill-fated financial genius of Investors Overseas Services. But there was also a significant number for whom the Horse was a place to relax after serious work. I think of just a few of them, some regulars, some occasionals, all part of the scene: there were writers like Mailer, James Baldwin, Dan Wakefield and Richard Farina; musicians and performers like The Clancy Brothers and Tommy Makem, Bob Dylan, Carolyn Hester, David Amram; poets like Joel Oppenheimer and Delmore Schwartz.

I know my own case best, I was in the Horse during more than ten years every night I was in New York. As the people of Konigsberg were said to set their clocks by Immanuel Kant's walks, you would see me, punctually dissolute, appear on weeknights at midnight and on weekends at one o'clock. At two in the morning you could usually observe me engaged in an intense conversation of no great importance and at a distance I must have seemed one of Gaddis' squatters. But if I slept until eleven or noon every day, I worked for twelve hours after I got up, reading, writing or doing socialist organizing. The late night was a gregarious, potentially erotic release from a disciplined existence. The world of nine-to-five was a routine; of twelve-to-twelve, a choice.

There were obviously a good number of people in the Village following the same kind of internal schedule on the inside of a seemingly discombobulated life. In addition to the portion I've already mentioned there were Dan Wolf and Ed Fancher who created a new style of journalism at *The Village Voice*; Jose Quintero, Ellen Stewart and Ted Mann, who were part of the Off-Broadway theatre renaissance; and the painters one would see around the Cedar— Pollack, de Kooning, Klein, Rivers—who helped make New York the art center of the world.

And there was Dylan Thomas. The White Horse was his home away from home when he was in New York and, from the point of view of the regulars, the fame he brought to it was calamitous with crowds. Old Ernie, the owner, even stopped giving out the chess sets. Anyone with a vision of the poet divinely drunk upon the midnight might ponder Thomas' final evenings at the Horse. He was a slobbering, incomprehensible man slumped over the table and surrounded by a retinue of sycophants and young girls who wanted to go to bed with immortality. ("These little maggots," he had written in a denunciation of his own Bohemianism in 1934, "are my companions for most of the time.") That last night at the Horse he was half carried out and taken to the Chelsea Hotel where he began to die the death he had been so long preparing for himself. Old Ernie took up a collection for Thomas' widow and one longshoreman gave and another didn't. "Who's that for?" said the one who didn't. "Oh," his friend answered, "some drunk who used to hang around here just died."

But the non-Bohemian world was not always as indifferent, or even tolerant, as those longshoremen. Malcolm Cowley was right in the Thirties to notice that the traditional American mores were being subverted and to argue that the destruction of middle-class morality would mark the end of Bohemia. He was, however, a generation premature. In the late Forties and Fifties the basic institution of American righteousness—belief in God, family and the holy destiny of the nation—were still intact. Old Ernie asked me one night if we couldn't sing more of the radical songs in German and French rather than English so the other patrons couldn't understand the words. It was less amusing on another night when a group of us sat singing labor songs in a working-class bar around the corner from the Horse. Eventually management phoned the police to protect our exit from a back door. We had persuaded the trade-union regulars there, not of our solidarity with them, but that we were Communists.

And on a number of occasions during the Joe McCarthy years Irish working-class kids from the neighborhood made fist-swinging, chair-throwing raids on the Horse. They used to scream that we were Commies and faggots, the latter epithet expressing their fury that we were always in the company of good-looking and liberated women while they drank in the patriotic virility of all-male groups. Jimmy Baldwin suffered most from the hostility. One night Baldwin, Dick Bagley, the cameraman who made *On the Bowery* and a regular at the White Horse, and two girls were drinking at the Paddock, a bar up the street [For another account of this incident, see the Dan Wakefield selection]. Some of the working-class patrons were furious to see a black man sitting next to a white woman and they jumped Baldwin and Bagley.

Some years later, in Paris in the Winter of 1963, Baldwin and some friends and I were talking of the black movement in the States and he went back in horrified reminiscence to that night in the Paddock. He remembered how, as a man tried to kick him in the genitals, he tried to squeeze himself into a ball in the dirt under the bar. It was, he said, a terrible confirmation of his knowledge that he would never be safe in white America, that someone was always lying in wait. [In his novel, *Another Country*, which is partially set in the Village, Baldwin's protagonist, the African-American jazz

472

musician Rufus Scott, sarcastically dismisses the Village as "the place of liberation."] In Jane Jacobs' account of the neighborhood in *The Death and Life of Great American Cities*—she lived a few doors down from the Horse—all these tensions are omitted and the street life of the place is praised for making it safe. She apparently did not realize that the friendly tavern across from her, The Ideal, was nicknamed The Ordeal by the White Horse regulars who used to go there when Ernie closed early. It was the scene of tense confrontations between Bohemia and square America.

But then, somewhere around the early Sixties, America lost that faith in its own philistine righteousness and Bohemia began to die. One of the beginnings of that end, I now realize, was the night a young gawky kid named Bob Dylan showed up at the Horse in a floppy hat.

Robert Shelton, a regular and then the folk-music critic of the *New York Times*, had been among the very first to recognize Dylan's talent. Once, quite late after the Horse closed, we all went over to McGowan's on Greenwich Avenue and, at Shelton's urging, Dylan gave an impromptu concert. I heard the future and I didn't like it. Dylan's singing had a diffidence, a studied artlessness, which was, I suspect, one of the reasons for his impact upon his generation. But it was lost on me, at least at first. (Later, standing before the State House in Montgomery on the last day of Martin Luther King Jr.'s Selma March and listening to *Blowin' in the Wind* speak for that vast multitude, I learned with a shiver to appreciate his genius.)

Indeed, Dylan's singing was like the speechmaking in Students for a Democratic Society in the early years. At the time I privately called it the stutter style. It assumed that any show of logic or rhetorical skill was prima facie proof of hypocrisy and dishonesty, the mark of the manipulator. The sincere man was therefore supposed to be confused and half articulate and anguished in his self-revelation. By that standard the fact that Dylan did not have a good voice in any conventional sense of the word was one of the highest recommendations of his singing.

To be sure, Dylan, particularly in the first period of his fame, looked back to Woody Guthrie and the tradition of the political vagabond. That impulse was very much alive in the Village when he arrived. I remember one Sunday afternoon in 1961 over at Sheridan Square when Guthrie's friends and admirers—Freddy Hellerman and Lee Hays from The Weavers, Oscar Brand, Will Geer and Logan English and many others—gathered around him. He sat, slumped and emaciated and dying, while they sang him a farewell in the words of his own songs. Dylan had, of course, absorbed that Guthrie spirit and it infused his early work and even his lifestyle. But even then his calculated indifference was a portent of the Sixties rather than an echo of Guthrie's passionate Thirties. It was no accident that so many of his contemporaries mistook him for a major poet. Modernism, which had always had its links with Bohemia, was proud of the demands it made upon its tiny public. Now, however, popular songs were to be regarded as high poetry, much as ecstasy was thought to be all rolled up in a pill or a joint.

Perhaps Allen Ginsberg was even more symptomatic of that change than Dylan. He had been around the Remo when I arrived in 1949, but I did not meet him until 1964 when he and Peter Orlovsky and another friend came to our apartment to see my wife, who was then on the staff of the *Voice*. They had just been picketing in the snow in front of the Women's House of Detention as part of their campaign to legalize marijuana. I was working on a book review of a study of cannabis and, after having hung his socks on the radiator to dry, Ginsberg sat there and cited court decisions, official inquiries and academic analyses with the authority of a scholar and the enthusiasm of a militant.

For Ginsberg has deep roots in American tradition. He traces himself back, of course, to Walt Whitman and he has obvious affinities with the Bohemia of personal exploration typified by Henry Miller. But his penchant for organization and detail—he functioned as sort of an international address book and courier for the Beat Generation—was part of his radical political background. So in one respect Ginsberg is a literary-political rebel on the model of the pre-World War I Villager, an innovator in art, social attitudes and lifestyle. The young who turned him into a guru tended to ignore his traditionalism and critical standards. They imitated only the flamboyant and mad poet chanting mantras or casually incanting a description of homosexual orgasm before a large crowd.

This one-sided reading of Ginsberg was part of a new sensibility that Irving Howe has brilliantly defined: "It is impatient with literary structures of complexity and coherence, only yesterday the catchwords of our criticism. It wants instead works of literature— though literature may be the wrong word—that will be as absolute as the sun, as unarguable as orgasm, and as delicious as a lollipop."

Without getting too McLuhanesque about the point, I wonder if the mass counterculture may not be a reflection of the very hyped and videotaped world it professes to despise. As early as 1960, Ned Polsky, the sociologist of deviance, discovered that the Beats around the Village had a quality that set them off from all previous generations of Bohemia: they did not read. More recently, Theodore Roszak, the theorist of the counterculture, has rejected all of the mainstream assumptions of the West since the scientific revolution of the seventeenth century. Roszak's emphasis is upon personal experience, mysticism, drugs. The intricacies of literature and symbolism have as little a place in that universe as they do in the instantaneous world of the media.

As Don McNeill, the brilliant participant-observer of the counterculture who died tragically at twenty-three, wrote of the East Village: "The transient rut is not a creative way. It is a fertilizing, procreative experience for a few. It is an interim for a few. For more, it is a long road down, laced with drugs, especially amphetamine. Many dig the descent; oblivion can be seductive. There is a fascination in being strung out for days on amphetamine, a fascination in Rolling Stones echoes, a fascination in the communal chaos of the Lower East Side, as far removed from Westchester as is India. If you wade in too deep, you may learn that the East Side undertow is no myth."

Bohemia died in that undertow. Walking around the East Village in the Summer of 1966 was like attending a huge Halloween party. The streets were alive with frontiersmen and guerrillas and painters from the 1830's. There were bearded homosexuals aggressively holding hands, girls with long straight hair walking barefoot on filthy sidewalks to prove their organic oneness with nature, and teenagers panhandling or sitting and staring blankly, strung out on drugs. Gangs of Puerto Ricans and blacks sometimes clashed with the flower children and the brutal law of the drug pushers was already in evidence. The aging Russians and Ukrainians whose lives once centered upon Tompkins Square Park were bewildered by all these comings and goings and terrified by the "love" the young offered them (it was, to paraphrase a remark of Paul Goodman's, love spoken through clenched teeth and the flowers they sometimes pressed upon the startled old people there might as well have been bricks.)

Now all that is gone. Within five years the myth died because it never had very deep roots. There are fewer runaways and no one in that East Side jungle with its ubiquitous junkie rip-offs believes in love anymore. Roszak had talked of the proclamation of "a new heaven and a new earth," but Woodstock turned into Altamont in a matter of months and the community was witness not to love but to a murder.

In 1970 my wife and I were on our way to *The Village Voice* Christmas party. Once those annual get-togethers were held in Ed Fancher's railroad flat on Christopher Street and had been the celebration of a family. But now the *Voice* had become a successful national institution. Its friends and employees needed the vast space of Howard Moody's Judson Memorial Church for their revels. As our cab crossed Bleecker Street toward Washington Square we passed the corner where the Remo had stood. It had become a Howard Johnson's.

—1973

Edmund Wilson

(1895–1972)

Regarded as one of the premier literary critics of the twentieth century, Edmund Wilson wrote in many genres—novels, short stories, drama, verse, biography, and history. More than anything, though, he was a social and literary critic. Born in Red Bank, New Jersey, he was educated at Princeton University and later became an editor with Vanity Fair *and the* New Republic *and a book reviewer for* The New Yorker. *He married Mary McCarthy in the late thirties. His first major work,* Axel's Castle *(1931), examines the work of T. S. Eliot, James Joyce, and others. His other works include* The American Jitters: A Year of the Slump *(1932) and the novel* I Thought of Daisy *(1929).* Memoirs of Hecate County *(1946), a collection of short stories, was banned for being obscene. His notebooks on the literary life that he knew so well were published posthumously as* The Twenties *(1975),* The Thirties *(1980),* The Forties *(1983),* The Fifties *(1986), and* The Sixties *(1993). An incorrigible namedropper, they are entertaining vignettes—miniature portraits—of a time and place long since vanished.*

from *The Twenties*
From Notebooks and
Diaries of the Period

Eugene O'Neill was still married to and living with his second wife, Agnes—to whom he referred to as Aggie. I saw quite a lot of

Edmund Wilson. From *The Twenties: From Notebooks and Diaries of the Period* (1975). Excerpts from "Return to New York" copyright © 1975 by Elena Wilson. Reprinted by permission of Farrar, Straus, and Giroux, LLC.

Agnes O'Neill because she was a friend of Mary Blair's. Her father was English, a painter, and she was an English type, sensible, practical, rather lacking in elegance but likeable and with qualities that commanded respect. She had also some literary ability and wrote a book about her marriage. O'Neill, on the other hand, in spite of an appealing boyish charm, was difficult to make contact with. I was grateful to him for persuading the Provincetown Players to produce my first play, *The Crime in the Whistler Room*, but I found conversation with him impossible. He was then completely on the wagon, and you were cautioned not to offer him anything to drink. But I got so bored with his non-responsive silence that one night, having dinner with him in a Greenwich Village restaurant, I decided to prime him with some wine, which with no hesitation he accepted. For this I paid a heavy price. We talked about Greek tragedy, and I told him that in *Oedipus at Colonus* the crimes of Oedipus seemed to have been expiated when he was somehow miraculously removed by a supernatural agency. O'Neill said that he continued to believe this: Sophocles would have had too much respect for human beings. O'Neill had a peculiar point of view on the homosexual activities of the sailors he had known on shipboard. He thought that in degrading themselves by submitting to the demands of other sailors, they were always trying to atone for some wrong which was on their conscience. He was amusing about the old female performers—Trixie Friganza and others like her—whom he had known in his early days. One of them had sat at his bedside and told him that if she hadn't been faithful to his brother, she would have come right into bed with him. Another had been warned by her friends that she would have to be very careful with the family of the groom of a pal who was having a proper wedding party at the Bellevue Stratford in Philadelphia. The friend restrained herself till the very last moment when the bride and groom were driving away in a taxi. She had collected several towels from the bathroom of the hotel and she threw them in at the window, with "I guess you'll need these."

After dinner, we went on to my apartment at 3 Washington Square North, and, once started talking, it seemed O'Neill would never stop. What was striking was that he quite lost connection with anything that was said by me or Mary. He did not answer questions or seem to recognize that we were there at all. He disregarded all our hints. We got up and crossed the room; we made remarks which with anyone else would have brought the session to a close. But his talk was an unbroken monologue. And he drank up everything we had in the house: when a bottle was set before him, he simply poured out drinks for himself, not suggesting that we might care for any. If we said we ought to go to bed, he paid no attention to this. He told us at length about a rich man who lived near him in Connecticut. He had some tragic theory about him: he was frustrated, his conscience bothered him. O'Neill, there now being nothing more to drink, did not leave until four in the morning.

Just beyond Red Bank, in late May [1927] when I slept past my station on the train—out the window the bright signs, red roofs, white walls, green foliage.

In the first week of early June in New York, I was walking among those old-fashioned crisscrossed streets—Barrow, Grove, etc.—I could smell the faintly saline, the mildly rank smell of the river, as if it had invaded the streets of the lower butt of the island, now that the people had left for the summer—for Woodstock, for Provincetown—I was looking for Fitzy (Eleanor Fitzgerald) [the manager of the Provincetown Players] on Barrow Street, but, in an unfamiliar deserted square, ran into Harold McGee, who sent me to Grove—he knew the way, I did not. —That *cavernous old house*, where Fitzy, Stark Young, Dorothea Nolan and Djuna Barnes once all lived at the same time—with its wastes and stretches of linoleum, its steep staircases and rambling halls, its balustrades, its broken skeleton hatrack in a marble-framed niche, its high square-topped radiators, its enormous vestibule doors, its mysterious inside windows covered over with cloths from within, the desolation of its corridors, the interminable and exhausting climbs of stairs, the yellow plaster and yellow woodwork, the smell of bathrooms, the sound of dripping bathtubs and defective toilets. Fitzy started trying to make the Provincetown Players go, to get it started by July 1 for next year, raise money, pay bills (she had got so she could tell the bill collectors when they came to her own apartment—because they came early in the morning and knocked with the knock of a stranger)—she was so tired—her little place in the country.

—1975

Max Gordon

(19?–1989)

Max Gordon founded the Village Vanguard in 1934. Initially the enter-tainment revolved around the poetry of such quintessential Villagers as Joe Gould, Maxwell Bodenheim, and Harry Kemp. Gordon then turned to folk music with the likes of Leadbelly, Burl Ives, and the Weavers. Later came Peter, Paul, and Mary, the Kingston Trio, and Woody Guthrie. Stand-up comics, such as Woody Allen and Lenny Bruce, were also represented. But it was jazz that put it on the map: Miles Davis, John Coltrane, Art Tatum, Dinah Washington, Charlie Parker, Thelonious Monk, Art Blakey, Dizzy Gillespie, Dexter Gordon, and Sonny Rollins all played at the Vanguard. Although he died in May 1989, Max Gordon's legacy lives on. After his death, the Village Vanguard continued under the direction of his widow, Lorraine Gordon. This selection describes his early days in the Village.

"You Don't Need Any Money" from *Live at the Village Vanguard*

Running a joint is tough, but my years in the Village before I opened one were tougher. I was living in a six-dollar-a-week room with a toilet in the hall, in the Strunsky block on West Third Street. Strunsky (I can still hear his asthmatic breathing as he climbed the stairs collecting rent) was a legendary Village landlord, the owner of a block of tenements bordered by Washington Square South and Sullivan, MacDougal, and West Third Streeets. He was the kind of

Max Gordon. "You Don't Need Any Money" from *Live at the Village Vanguard* (New York: St. Martin's Press, 1980). Reprinted by permission of Lorraine Gordon.

481

landlord you could owe a week's rent to, two weeks, even a month's. A generation of Villagers owe their survival during the Depression to Strunsky.

I hung a suit on one of the wire hangers left over by the last tenant, put my secondhand typewriter on the floor, looked around and saw it was OK for sleeping. I didn't want to spend any more time in this room than I had to.

Stewart's Cafeteria on Sheridan Square was the reigning cafeteria of the day in the Village. You could always find somebody there who'd talk to you. So I slept all day and hung out at Stewart's all night.

Now that I was in the Village, what the hell was I gonna do with myself? I had to eat, pay the rent, and the few bucks in my pocket were fast running out. I'd have to do something, find something, some job at night preferably so that I could have my days to myself to look around, flex my ego, see what might turn up. It shouldn't be a job that'd tie me down, but a stopgap job until something right came along, though what that right job might be I had no idea.

My first job was in a loft on lower Fifth Avenue, a mail-order house where I was assigned the task of reading copy on sales letters before they were "personalized" by an automatic typewriting process. I worked from six p.m. to two a.m. and hated every minute of it. At two a.m. I'd walk down to Stewart's Cafeteria and hang out till daylight.

I did this for a year. One night I decided I'd had it. So the next night I went to Grand Central, spent four days and four nights on a train, and landed home in Portland, Oregon. My father spoke to me without acrimony, and my mother cooked and baked to mark my homecoming. But I felt the cold draft of their worry and disapproval. Six months later I was back in the Village at a table in Stewart's Cafeteria.

I found a job in a one-man advertising establishment, helping the boss put together a catalogue for an electrical fixture firm on West Fourteenth Street. My job was to write brief, succinct descriptions of electrical gadgets. I was fired. Next, I walked off the street in answer to a sign in the window of a delicatessen in the fur district: Wanted, Counterman. I lasted ten minutes. I couldn't hold two cups in my left hand while working the coffee urn with my right. I could fill only one cup of coffee at a time, which wasn't enough for a busy delicatessen. I was no counterman.

Months passed when I didn't look for a job. I didn't want a job; I could get by without a job.

If you were broke, the best place I knew of to be broke in was Greenwich Village. You could always bum a cigarette, a cup of coffee, even a bed for the night.

A Villager in one of his more candid moments once told me: "I walk in to Stewart's Cafeteria, grab a check, pick up a tray, walk over to the steam table, and I order the roast beef medium-rare with two vegetables. The counterman punches my check. I carry my tray over to a table, and I sit down. When I'm through eating, I sit, and I wait. I'm in no hurry. Some days I got to sit there longer than I like. It's a good thing Stewart's is open all night. It never fails but somebody I know will drop in, somebody who's got sixty cents, and bail me out."

When things got real tough, I'd assume the old routine, scanning the want ad columns of the morning papers: the *Times*, the *World*, the *Herald-Tribune*, for likely jobs. One day I spotted this ad:

Writer wanted for small magazine catering to Madison Ave. and the financial community. No experience necessary.

It sounded like the kind of job I was looking for. I got the job. It paid no salary. I worked on a commission basis.

I'd arrive about ten a.m. in the editorial room on Beekman Street. There was a staff of five, sometimes six; the number and composition changed daily. The boss editor, a tall, lean man, his face hooded in a green eyeshade, was already there. He had searched the business and financial pages of the morning papers and was ready for us with small items, mostly personal, of what had happened overnight in the business and advertising community: A vice-president moved up to be president of a corporation;

a fat account landed by an advertising agency; a creative lady executive now bossing men who once bossed her; an old product
repackaged; a forward-looking operation involved in the takeover
of another company; men assigned to foreign parts—all these items
were ready for editorial treatment by the staff.

My job was to write a three-hundred-word congratulatory article, a puff, hailing the event that had overtaken the gentleman or
lady I'd never heard of until that very morning.

Salesmen manning telephones in the next room lost no time in
calling up the subject of the article brought in by "our investigative
reporters" to read it for omissions and corrections. Said article was
scheduled for next week's issue of the magazine, *The Commercial
Reporter*. Would they care to have copies of the article reserved for
them, their family, their friends? A hundred reprints, five hundred
reprints, a thousand reprints? Cost: thirty-five cents a reprint.
C.O.D. A messenger would deliver them pronto.

You'd be surprised how many fell for the pitch. I got twenty-
five percent of the take. I worked there six months and never saw
a published copy of *The Commercial Reporter*.

One night I met a girl named Ann at Stewart's Cafeteria. The
next night I went down to Paul's Rendezvous on Wooster Street
where she, dressed in pink pajamas, worked as a waitress for tips.
Ann was a nice, blond, sassy girl with high cheekbones and a ready
laugh. This was my first visit to Paul's.

I had never, in fact, been to a nightclub before. There weren't
any in Portland that I knew of. During my undergraduate years at
Reed, bolder students met in a clandestine apartment to drink the
local gin. I remember the awful taste of that gin. I remember a girl
holding her nose to swallow the stuff, get it down without spilling
or heaving it. That was about the extent of my nightlife experience
before I came to the Village.

Ann greeted me like an old friend, took me over to a booth
where she was sitting with some friends or customers, I couldn't
tell which, and introduced me. It was first-name Greenwich Village society, and I felt at home. She sat down next to me. When-

ever her duties as a waitress called her, she got up, then came back and took her seat.

"This used to be a real Village joint when I first came to work here," she said. "But Paul's let the Bronx and Brooklyn move in and spoil the joint. He doesn't know it, but I'm quitting the first chance I get."

Here I was thinking how great Paul's was, and Ann was telling how awful it had become.

"That's John Rose Gildea, the poet," Ann whispered. It was the first time I'd ever seen a live poet. I knew of people who wrote poetry. We had them in Portland. But this was the first time I ever saw a poet who not only was a poet but looked like a poet—large head, long hair, eager eyes, shirt open at the throat. At the moment, John was pouring himself a drink of what looked like gin.

After that, I'd go to Paul's every night and hang around till closing time, four a.m., to walk Ann home. We'd walk down West Fourth Street to Hubert's Cafeteria, an all-night Village hangout where Ann knew everybody. I'd carry a couple of cups of coffee from the counter to a table, and we'd sit down.

"I shouldn't put my foot into this joint," Ann said to me one night. "Old man Hubert is a fink: Poor Joe Gould poured himself a bowlful of ketchup and mustard, so what does old man Hubert do? He has all the mustard and ketchup bottles removed from the tables. I really should boycott this joint."

"Who's Joe Gould?" I asked her.

"He's the poet who likes mustard and ketchup," Ann laughed. "I never see him at Paul's anymore. Paul won't let him in."

Ann had come to the Village from a farm in Wisconsin, with a stopover in Chicago, about two years before. She was a sturdy, self-confident girl. When she got here, she met a musician from Iowa who was studying classical piano and driving a cab at night. She moved in with him. Some months later, when she discovered that he had taken up with a man, she moved out. She wouldn't have moved out if it'd been another woman. She could cope with another woman, but a man was different.

So Ann moved into a furnished room that fronted on Washington Square, the more expensive side of the Strunsky block. Old man Strunsky let her have it because he knew her tips at Paul's could carry the fifteen-dollar weekly rental those rooms demanded.

When I had the money, I'd buy a bottle of home brew from a super on the block and carry it upright in a paper bag to Ann's room, careful not to disturb the yeast sediment at the bottom of the bottle.

Ann's room was always crowded with friends, neighbors, weekenders from Yale. I couldn't tell whether she'd never been to bed at all or was just getting up.

On her night off from Paul's, Ann and I'd make the rounds of the other Village joints: Romany Marie's, the Gypsy Tavern, the Black Cat. Ann hated all of them. Romany Marie was a snob; the two sisters in peasant costumes who ran the Gypsy Tavern were phony; the Black Cat was dark and full of menace. Then there was the Alimony Jail on West Fourth Street. Its high-backed booths were designed for necking and fornication. "Why don't they go home if that's what they want?" said Ann. The Fifth Circle on Varick Street was a laugh. The ex-rabbi who ran it featured seminars on sex, with questions from the floor: Should a woman propose marriage to a man? "Juvenile stuff," said Ann. "The last straw is what's become of Stewart's Cafeteria. They hired a bouncer, a goon with muscles to patrol the place. There isn't a decent place left in the Village," was her verdict.

"I'm quitting Paul's," Ann announced one day. "Because what do you think happened last night? Graham Norwell, a hell of an artist, came to the door 'bout two a.m., and Paul wouldn't let him in. True, Norwell was drunk and in his bare feet. He must've lost his shoes somewhere along the way. Well, Paul wouldn't let him in. Norwell painted Paul's murals four years ago for three bottles of gin. Paul doesn't remember that. He was glad to let him in then, when he needed him.

"The trouble with Paul is," Ann went on, "he's making too damn much money. He turned his joint over to a fast, hard-drinking crowd of uptown tourists who've got plenty of money to spend. So he doesn't have room for Villagers without money anymore—the same Villagers who made him, when he was getting started five years ago. That's Paul for you. I'm splitting. I won't work for a guy like that," said Ann with finality.

"Why don't we—you and me—open a straight-ahead place in the Village? " said Ann. She was impulsive like that. "A real Village place! A no bullshit kind of place! I know everybody—all the poets: Max Bodenheim, John Gildea, Joe Gould, Eli Siegel, Bob Clairmont. They'd follow me wherever I go. It'd be terrific!"

"What do we use for money?" I asked her.

"You don't need any money to open a place in the Village," she said. "My friend Al, who likes the Bohemian atmosphere and lends money on the side—fifty bucks for sixty in return—he'll let us have a hundred. Al would like to have a stake in a Village rendezvous where he can meet girls. I know Al."

"What the hell do I know about running a Village place?"

"I'll run it. I'll show you the ropes."

I thought about it. I thought about it so hard that we opened the Village Fair on Sullivan Street in 1932. I didn't have any money except for the hundred I borrowed from Al. I didn't know what I was doing. But at first it didn't seem to matter.

I had dreamt of the kind of place I'd like to open in the Village: a quiet, gentle place, the kind of place where Sam Johnson hung out in eighteenth century London. You dropped in, met your friends, heard the news of the day, read the daily papers provided by the house. When it got crowded at night, as I hoped it would, and the conversation soared and bristled with wit and good feeling, perhaps a resident poet would rise and declaim some verses he had composed for the entertainment and edification of the guests. That's the kind of place the Village Fair was going to be.

A week after it opened, Ann disappeared and left me holding the bag. I heard from her two years later. She was living in Miami with a textbook salesman.

In those days Prohibition was rife in the land. Customers brought their own bottles. The Village Fair served tea, coffee, sandwiches, and setups. Before I knew it, without anything I did or planned, the place assumed a dimension that took my breath away.

Assorted weekend Villagers and out-of-towners discovered the Fair. They walked in with bottles of brown paper bags, ordered glasses and a bowl of ice, stared at the poets, at the "freaks," and at one another, and proceeded to get drunk, all for seventy-five cents minimum charge per person. It was cheap, handy, and the customers liked the "Bohemian atmosphere." It was no place for Dr. Johnson anymore.

During Prohibition, if you stepped out on the town for a night's entertainment, you carried a bottle with you. If you happened to forget it, or if your bottle ran dry at midnight, and you found yourself in some joint in the Village, where would you go to get another bottle?

There was always a guy in a doorway hanging outside Village joints who could get you one. You stepped outside, made the deal, went back inside, sat down and waited. Your waitress would tell you when your bottle had arrived. So you stepped outside again, passed the money to the messenger, picked up your bottle in a brown paper bag, and joined your party inside. The legal niceties were thus observed. The sale was made outside the premises and the joint was in the clear.

One night a guy in shirtsleeves who turned out to be a cop arrested me for selling him a bottle of gin. I didn't sell him a bottle of gin. I didn't have the muscle or know-how to sell booze in Prohibition New York. But this cop, acting in the line of duty, instead of going outside to complete the deal, pushed his money (larded with a massive tip) at the waitress and asked her would she please step to the door and bring him his bottle, like a good girl. That did it. The money was passed on the premises. Once an arrest was made, a cop in uniform was installed on the premises to see that the crime that hadn't happened wouldn't happen again. That's how it was done in those days. That finished the Village Fair.

Three months later when my case came up, I won a dismissal but it was too late to save the Fair.

All was not over though because now I was in demand. I was a man with a following in the nightclub business, so Frankie Starch offered me a partnership in his West Third Street speakeasy that was ailing and empty. No cash investment. "Just come in and bring that crowd from the Village Fair with you." I could draw forty a week as a partner. Frankie had status in the neighborhood as the cousin of Tony Bender, the boss of Greenwich Village.

I didn't know what I was getting into. When I discovered Frankie kept a baseball bat in the back of the bar, I thought I'd better split, even though I had his place crowded inside of a week. After two months I proposed that he keep it all himself. He didn't like it, but I made it stick.

So I was back where I started from, broke and unemployed, hanging out in Sheridan Square cafeterias, wondering when and if I'd ever get back into action again.

Without Harry the plumber I don't believe I ever would have.

—1980

Joyce Johnson

(b. 1935)

Joyce Johnson may be best known as the girlfriend of Jack Kerouac during the heyday of the Beat Generation, but she wrote her first novel, Come and Join the Dance *(1962), a full year before she even met Kerouac. While working as an editor at Farrar, Straus, and Cudahy, the Dial Press, William Morrow, and other houses, she continued to write, penning the novels* Bad Connections *in 1978 and* In the Night Cafe *in 1989, the latter about a tortured painter who lives in the Village and hangs out at the Cedar Tavern. Johnson has also been a contributing editor at* Vanity Fair *and her work has appeared in the* New Yorker, Harper's, *and* Cosmopolitan. *The aptly-named* Minor Characters *describes, luminously and with great compassion, that brief moment "of hope and energy and the feeling that anything was possible . . . that four people sitting around a table could change the world." It is a marvelous piece of writing that captures a particular place and time.*

from *Minor Characters: A Young Woman's Coming of Age in the Beat Generation*

Just when I was so eager to abandon New York, it seemed to turn before my eyes into a kind of Paris. The new cultural wave that had crested in San Francisco was rolling full force into Manhattan,

Joyce Johnson. From *Minor Characters* (1983) by Joyce Johnson. Reprinted by permission of Penguin, a division of Penguin Putnam Inc.

bringing with it all kinds of newcomers—poets, painters, photographers, jazz musicians, dancers—genuine artists and hordes of would-be's, some submerging almost instantly, others quickly bobbing to the surface and remaining visible. Young and broke, they converged upon the easternmost edges of the Village, peeling off into the nondescript district of warehouses and factory lofts, and Fourth Avenue with its used bookstores, and the broken-wine-bottle streets of the Bowery. An area with an industrial rawness about it, proletarian, unpretty—quite illegal to live in, but landlords were prepared to look the other way. An outlaw zone that silently absorbed people who'd sneak their incriminating domestic garbage out in the dead of night or hide a bed behind a rack of paintings, always listening for the knock of the housing inspector.

An older group of painters had survived here since the late 1940s. In lofts deserted by the garment industry, where sewing-machine needles could still be found in the crevices of floorboards, they'd dispensed with the confinements of the easel. Possessing space if little else, they'd tacked their canvases across larger and larger stretches of crumbling plaster, or nailed them to the floor. They threw away palettes and used the metal tops of discarded kitchen tables. Paint would rain down on the sized white surfaces—house paint, if there was no money or oils—colors running in rivulets, merging, splashing, coagulating richly in glistening thickness, bearing witness to the gesture of the painter's arm in a split second of time, like the record of a mad, solitary dance. Or like music, some said, like bop, like a riff by Charlie Parker, incorrigible junky and genius, annihilated by excess in 1955, posthumous hero of the coming moment. Or like Jack's "spontaneous prose," another dance in the flow of time. For the final issue of *Black Mountain Review*, he'd jotted down his own manifesto, which many of the New York painters soon would read: "Time being of the essence in the purity of speech, sketching language is undisturbed flow from the mind of personal secret idea-words *blowing* (as per jazz musician) on subject of image."

Substitute *painting, color, stroke,* and it was close in spirit to the way the painters defined themselves in their heated discussion at

491

"The Club," a loft on Eighth Street where they met regularly, or over beers at the Cedar Bar, continuing on into dawn over coffee at Riker's. Blearily they'd stagger back to their studios, switching on the light to stare at the new canvas up on the wall, matching it to the words still spinning in the brain, feeling exhausted or depressed or dangerously exalted—with the rent due, after all, and not enough money for the tube of cadmium red, and no gallery another goddamn year.

But Jackson Pollock had broken the ice, they said, broken it for all of them, and then died—in classic American style—in his Oldsmobile, in his new affluence and fame that seemed to mean so little to him by the time he got it that he veered off the road into a tree by the side of Montauk Highway on his way to a party with his teen-age mistress and her girlfriend. Suicide by alcohol, this accident they all still talked about obsessively even a year later. Endless Jackson stories they told, and they journeyed out to Amagansett to the grave marked by a granite boulder that had been outside Pollock's house, with his signature on it in bronze as if he'd signed his death—the name of the artist at the very end completing the painting.

Legend adheres to artists whose deaths seem the corollaries of their works. There's a perversely compelling satisfaction for the public in such perfect correspondences—like the satisfaction the artist feels upon completing an image. It was fitting that Jackson Pollock, whose paintings were explosions of furious vitality, dizzying webs of paint squeezed raw from the tube, who ground cigarette butts into his canvases with seeming brutal disrespect for the refinements of Art, would smash through a windshield at eighty miles an hour. Thirteen years later, Kerouac's quiet death in St. Petersburg would be viewed as improper, slightly embarrassing—at best, supremely ironic. Better to have died like Pollock or James Dean, or like Neal Cassady had—of exposure on the railroad tracks.

Artists are nourished by each other more than by fame or by the public, I've always thought. To give one's work to the world is an experience of peculiar emptiness. The work goes away from the artist into a void, like a message stuck into a bottle and flung into the sea. Criticism is crushing and humiliating. Pollock was hailed as a genius by the time he died, but could he have forgotten the widely repeated witticism that his paintings could have been done by a chimpanzee? As for praise, somehow it falls short, empty superlatives. The true artist knows the pitfalls of vanity. Dangerous to let go of one's anxiety. But did you *understand*? must always be the question. To like and admire is not enough: did you *understand*? And will you understand the next thing I do—the wet canvas in my studio, the page I left in my typewriter? Unreasonably, the artist would like to know this, too. Praise has to do with the past, the finished thing; the unfinished is the artist's preoccupation.

Follow roughly outlines in outfanning movement over subject, as river rock, so mindflow over jewel-center need (run your mind over it, once) arriving at pivot, where what was dim formed "beginning" becomes sharp-necessitating "ending" and language shortens in race to wire of time-race of work, following law of Deep Form, to conclusion, last words, last trickle—Night is The End.
—Jack Kerouac

It's with a fire that the summer of 1957 comes in, in my memory, a giant conflagration on Eighth Street and Broadway. I remember the night sky filling with smoke and flame and the fire engines clamoring, and that it was a Friday and, being at loose ends, I'd stayed downtown after work. Wanamaker's Department Store was burning—the massive old landmark that had stood for so long like a boundary wall between the Village and the East Side. That Friday night it burned to the ground. The famous clock I'd walked under in January on my way to meet Jack melted like one of Salvador Dali's watches.

What a strange night it was. The summer restlessness, the mobs watching the fire, the smell of ashes everywhere. On East Tenth Street a half-dozen galleries were opening that night for the first time, according to fliers pasted up around the Village. Owned and run by artists, they seemed to have come into being all at once in deserted storefronts. Gradually, the shabby block between Fourth

493

Avenue and the Bowery had become a little country of painters. Franz Kline and Willem de Kooning, men whose names had just become familiar to me, lived on that street, as did many of the totally unknown artists whose works I was about to see in the small new galleries. For me Tenth Street had the charm of foreign territory—to enter it that fiery night was like finding Washington Square all over again.

Under the strange dusky orange glare, as passing sirens wailed, groups of people moved from storefront to storefront, talking intensely, laughing, congratulating each other, gulping wine from paper cups, calling out to friends: "Have you seen the stuff at the March yet?" . . . "Hey, I'll meet you at the Camino!" . . . "Is Franz here? Anyone seen Franz?" To get into a gallery you'd first stand back from the narrow doorway to let a rush of others out, and, once inside, you'd be drawn into a slow circular progression from painting to painting and have to look at everything for at least a few moments, whether you liked what you saw or not. That seemed the unspoken rule—everyone's work must be given attention.

I didn't really know what to make of the paintings. What was I supposed to see? Where were the images? My college teachers had taught me always to look for images; but I found very few as recognizable as those in even the most difficult Picassos at the Museum of Modern Art. There was just all this paint. Sometimes you had the impression of tremendous energy or an emotion you couldn't quite put into words; sometimes nothing came to you from the canvas at all. Was this how you decided which ones were good or bad?

But goodness and badness didn't even seem important that night. It was the *occasion* that was important. What I'd wandered into wasn't the beginning of something, but the coming into light of what had been stirring for years among all these artists who'd been known only to each other.

Major or minor, they all seemed possessed by the same impulse —to break out into forms that were unrestricted and new.

—1983

Madison Smartt Bell

(b. 1957)

Born and raised in Tennessee, Bell has lived in New York, London, and, most recently, Baltimore. A graduate of Princeton University, he has taught creative writing programs in various places, including the Iowa Writers' Workshop and Johns Hopkins University writing seminars. Among his many novels are Waiting for the End of the World *(1985),* Straight Cut *(1986),* The Year of Silence *(1987),* Doctor Sleep *(1991),* Save Me, Joe Louis *(1993), and* Soldier's Joy *(1989). He has also published two collections of short stories,* Zero db *(1987) and* Barking Man *(1990). His best-known novel,* All Soul's Rising, *was nominated for a National Book Award. This selection from* The Washington Square Ensemble *takes place in the famous park of the same name. But rather than the genteel park of old, it has been transformed into a seedy, rundown corner of New York, teeming with life, including Johnny B. Goode, the charismatic leader of a small-time heroin-pushing operation.*

"Johnny B." from *The Washington Square Ensemble*

And I feel like a completely new man as I step into the northwest corner of Washington Square, ready to seek the day's fortune among the flora and fauna surrounding me, the fauna most especially. The horizon of possible futures expands all around me, and I pause in the pincers of this circular array of concrete benches, in the dense shade of tall overarching trees. It is cool and dusky and damp under these trees, in the grasp of the benches, and the air is impacted with chlorophyll. This is a genteel end of the park, on the benches I see only two old men in their loose cardigans, looking down at the liver spots on the backs of their hands, and three old ladies in tired Sunday best, talking together in vanishing voices, and one polite and listless poodle dog. They look like they're dying by inches, all five of them, but they're causing no one any inconvenience about it, least of all me.

So I don't look at them. Framed in an arch of the trees and out in the open sunlight there's a kid juggling some multicolored ninepins—three, now four, and now five, throwing them absurdly high but keeping them quite nicely under control. Outsized and garish under the sun, the ninepins loop end over end in the air, returning surely to the hands of the juggler, who never even looks at them. For that is the secret of juggling, not to think where the thrown object was or will be, but only to know where it is, a knowing that doesn't even know it knows. It's a secret which fascinates me, as you may well imagine, and I stand stock-still, spying on the trance of the juggler until something breaks it and the ninepins bounce and scatter over the lawn with the juggler scrambling after them, a magician no longer but only a redheaded freckled college kid, running and frightening pigeons.

Now I rotate my head around like an owl, but there is still no action on any of the benches, only the old people still sitting there lifeless as waxworks. Now a fat black fly comes droning into the park, bloated and sluggish from a visit to the Haagen-Dazs stand up on Eighth Street, and as he makes his first pass along the benches, the old man holding the ivory-handled cane raises one eyelash, then becomes even stiller than before. The fly loops a turn and comes back again, teasing the hair of one weary old lady, piquing the dog for a second or less, and settling finally and foolishly on the mottled knuckles that hold the white cane.

Whop—dead fly. The old man blinks, smiles to himself, and scrapes with a long brown fingernail at a spot of dirt and blood on the back of his hand. And that is the only thing that is likely to happen around here for the next hour or so, so I am going to snap out of my daze and go down into the park to find whatever is awaiting me there on this particular day.

So I go along down the diagonal path, and the trees get thinner and the shade fades out behind me. No more senior citizens on the benches along the way, but a different clientele, mixed up some but mostly black guys in sneakers and sweats, maybe basketball players from the courts on Sixth Avenue, come over for a breather and a couple of joints. And then there're the radios, big box radios, thundering at me from either side.

I walk through the noise, half-catching a couple of lyrics, and fade into the usual scrimmage at the end of the path and the edge of the trees, crossing toward the open center of the park, free ground. There's four or five guys drifting around the border, and a couple of them seem to be new enough to the area that they're trying to catch my eye.

". . . smoke, smoke, joints and bags . . ."

". . . smoke, my man, you never too old for Gold, just got to be bold . . ."

I keep walking and the two freelancers warp away around the edges of my very useful dark glasses. Eye contact is where it all begins for these guys, then they're in your pocket and smoking your cigarettes and giving you all kinds of good advice and ripping you off just as fast as they can. So you don't want to look at them, but then it's nice to know more or less where they are. Not that I care too much, they're all a bunch of lightweights and most of what they deal is garbage. They don't interest me, except that it's nice to have them around to create confusion so the cops can't find the right people when they come visiting. And then they're also a useful pool for recruiting purposes, which it now occurs to me is something I'd better start thinking about, and soon. I'm going to have to get at least one other man, and a good man too, not another Carlo. Yusuf and Santa are great as far as they go, but I really can't stretch them all over this territory. I need someone reliable, and unfortunately I don't know of anyone like that.

I come up to the edge of the fountain, turn around, and sit on the rim to watch the action. Two girls come down the diagonal, walking with difficulty because they're each twined around a boy friend. Both pairs get the runaround from the hawkers and shrug it right off, passing them by. They go, and now an old black guy I seem to see around a lot calls two freelancers over to this bench. It's the same two that tried it on me, and when the old cat says whatever he says to them, they both turn and look my way and nod their heads like puppets. He's warning them off of me, the old guy, telling them not to waste their breath. I can't quite put a name on this old guy, though I've seen him around quite a bit, and he's easy to spot by the light patches in his beard. He's operating something though, that's easy to see, and maybe those guys aren't exactly freelancers after all. It gives me a cold spot in the small of my back to have the finger laid on me like that, even though I know I'm as clean as a newborn infant, cleaner in fact. With the time I put in down here I can't avoid a little recognition, but it doesn't suit my modest and retiring disposition at all, and I especially don't enjoy being pointed out to newcomers and people passing through. Who is this guy, anyway? I could have Yusuf say something to him, but what can you do, you can't stop word-of-mouth. And I'm covered for that, I'm clean, so forget it.

The old man finishes his rap and the two kids catch themselves looking at me and stop. That's very subtle, children. I watch the old man, nodding and mumbling on his bench, and I decide that here's someone that knows what's what. And maybe he's the man to take on, but no, it's too complicated, and he's probably happier with his own show, the loose joints and that. Better I should find somebody new and working alone, but I can't think of anyone that would do, not offhand. I have to admit it, Holy Mother is going to be hard to replace, hard if not impossible. Holy Mother, Aniello, where is he now, I wonder, in the meat wagon, or already in the morgue? But I can't let my mind go wandering off in these perverse directions, because I have to get on with the day.

The day, and so far everything is as usual. This side of the fountain everything is very pluralistic, it's open territory. The long sweep of benches is full of people, all kinds of people, you can take your pick, artists and intellectuals up from downtown, teenage runaways, semiamateur musicians, lunatics, Frisbee throwers, apostles of strange beliefs, anything you want, and all melting together in the hot midday sun, a bit like human peanut brittle. Here's the balloon man, and there's the hot-dog man and also the knish man, and in and out through the crowds go a couple of amateurs with tin buckets full of cold beer, only slightly illegal, ladies and gentleman. I stand here with my back to the falling water, picking over the crowd from behind my dark glasses and looking for anything or anyone that might give me some cause for unease, but I don't see it, nothing at all to worry about at the minute. It's now twenty to one by my watch, twenty minutes to clocking-in time, and all systems are go, assuming my staff turns up when it should. I've got the car stashed a few blocks off the park, and so far I don't see anything here that shouldn't be, though I haven't yet covered all of the ground.

I walk around the other side of the fountain and spot Alex the fuzzbox guitar player sitting off in the shade, not building any audience as yet, just jerking around with a few of his friends, the volume turned down low. But here's hoping Alex will do his whole number a bit later in the day to pull in the tourists and stimulate commerce. Right now the arch spot is taken by the Trinidadian steel drummer, rolling his sticks with a great sound of bells. He's not bad, this guy, but he's not drawing anybody, I'm afraid he'll go home hungry tonight. And now I see Charlie the Joker coming down Fifth, spiffed out in red pants and a white fishnet shirt, and flanked by two bodyguards about twice his size. He's a very small guy with a very big mouth, and I'm always glad to see him around. Not only because his routine is quite funny, but also because he brings his own crowd down from the Upper West Side, all guys with money they're ready to spend. Charlie's just here to secure his spot, his show won't kick off till the late afternoon, but it will pull in the people when it does.

Hey, it's all right, it's okay, I'm going to make some money today. A yellow butterfly materializes in front of my nose and I follow him into the east end of the park, losing him finally among the trees and the stained tattered grass. It's quiet over here and not much going on. Here's a pale reedy girl sitting cross-legged, playing the flute in the general direction of the boy with a backpack who's reading Camus. Over there on a bench there's another old lady, tapping a black orthopedic shoe. A mongrel dog comes along and propositions her and she gives him a taste of the old steel toe, so he runs on ahead to check out a wino stroked out on the next bench down the line next to two black guys in knit caps, passing a joint. I follow the dog as he keeps going, now scaring an overweight pigeon into flight, now homing in on a loaf of wheat bread and a bottle of carrot juice, which sit in a circle of gray-haired hippies. So the dog blunders in and makes friends and gets some organic peanut butter for his trouble, as aging hippies believe in niceness to dogs. And there's nothing else going down in the east end, so I swing back and climb the steps to the platform patio on the south side.

I hear a buzz of wheels over brick, and a sweaty girl skater whips by my left shoulder, missing me by a hair, and when she comes out in front where I can see her she makes a snap turn and glides backward, momentum unbroken, along the curve of the street-side benches and trees. And now she pulls another two-footed turn and careens backward straight toward the small fountain there in the center, and I think she's going to break her neck for sure, but now I see she planned it. She swoops down into the basin and catches herself on the fountain's top pipe, bent over backward like a ballerina with water pouring all over her face and her red one-piece suit. A very classy way to cool off, I would say, and I am even tempted to start applauding or something like that, but then I feel eyeballs drilling into my back.

I hold still and listen, but all I can hear is a squirrel climbing around in the trees behind me, the same trees that screen this patio from the rest of the park, so that no one will see what is about to happen, if anything is. I turn around, there's four of them, Latins over from Alphabet Town, and I don't know them, but I think I know what their problem is. Their attention is bound on me by a line of need and urgency substantial enough to pull their heads after me in unison when I start moving off to the left, enough to pull them out to the edge of the bench they're sitting on. Junkies all four, and not in good shape, I'll bet they've been sitting there waiting all day. Junkies have extra senses all their own, and either that or the word-of-mouth has told them who I am and what I've got. A minute more with my back to them and they would have jumped me. Another minute and they might yet. I pull off my sunglasses and give back the stare.

It's a long strained moment, while I try to communicate by mental telepathy—patience, my friends, you'll get yours when the time comes. Meanwhile don't do anything you might regret later, and whatever you do, don't kill the goose that lays the golden eggs. Now the one nearest to me relaxes, sits back on his bench, sags until the back of his head catches on the top rail. One by one the others lean back also. It's over. They don't look at me. They look up into the trees over their heads. That's right, my children, never be hasty. First thing you learn is that you've always got to wait.

I walk down the steps on the other side, putting my glasses back on as I go, and move back toward the center of the park. I've got no symptoms of nervousness other than a couple of ligaments twitching at the backs of my knees, but I don't like little encounters like that, not at all. We're getting a lower class of customers these days, sent to us by, of all people, the cops, who in their wisdom decided to make a big push and shut down all the shooting parlors in Alphabet Town, which had the happy effect of putting all the action back into the street. It's wonderful how the cops work it out. So now we've got guys coming over to the Square who would happily cut your throat for your watch, and although I don't mind getting whatever money they may happen to have, I really don't think it's worth the bother of having them around. Maybe there's some kind of pressure play we could pull to send them all somewhere else for a while, I should talk to Holy Mother and see what we can come up with.

But there I go again, it's funny how my mind keeps running in these habitual channels, no matter what I try to do about it. I walk up to the edge of the fountain and look down into the water, not really seeing it. Repeat until learned—there is no Holy Mother, there is no Aniello Di Angelo, not anymore. I see my own face reflected from the dark water, tight-lipped and drawn and shielded behind the sunglasses. Where is he now? . . . *in the morgue, the coroner's assistant dialing the phone, holding the address book open with a scrupulously clean thumb, the receiver clamped between his shoulder and jaw, dialing for the next of kin. Next of kin, I'm sorry, I have some bad news for you, hello* . . . but enough of this. Let the thought be as dead as the man. I raise my head and look at the top of the fountain and think only of how many times I will breathe in and out before all other thoughts purl out of my mind and drown in the muttering water.

Now I snap back into the soothing singularity of my present moment, and now, void of memory, I begin constructing the world all over again and naming it to myself: this flowing substance in front of me is water, and this hard substance containing it is concrete, and the pavement I'm standing on is also concrete, and it is my feet that I'm using when I now turn around. I see the old black guy that pointed me out to the young ones, still lounging in his bench. I think I'll call him Lemon Peel, for the lemon-yellow stains in his beard around his mouth. I will, and when I've called him that enough times to enough people that will be his name, because that is the way the world works, and what you call a thing is what it is. I call this a good summer day, with plenty of sun and green grass and idling people who have certain needs that I can satisfy and others that I can't. A good day to do some good business and lay hands on some incorruptible money, and I am socking away all my spare change into AT&T stock and the money market for a nice blend of high gain and security, and probably by the time I turn forty I will be able to buy a condo in Florida and start boring myself to death in a big way. Maybe I'll do that and maybe I won't, but either way I have no problems or worries, not now, not today. I take a step forward, walk down the diagonal to the southwest corner and the chess tables.

This time the hawkers don't give me a tumble. I walk by them and Lemon Peel without getting so much as a glance. Two college kids in long cardboard streamers are chasing each other all over the playground to my left, commandos of the insane, yelling orders at each other through six-foot cardboard tubes. This place is getting really crazy, sometimes I wonder if I'm seeing what I'm seeing. But down in the chessboard circle everything is very normal. At this time of day it's so sedate that it's barely even worth checking out, but we always have to stick to the drill. So I look all around and it's the usual crowd: Chinese whiz kids from Taiwan, and computer programmers with inch-thick glasses, and random aging gents ruined by chess more surely than by liquor or women, the usual run of chess nuts, in a word.

I'm about to turn around and go back when I feel eyeballs on me again, and why should that happen down here? I turn around and scan a row, the same one where Porco was sitting last night, so maybe it is only an afterimage of Porco come back to bother me some more, not satisfied after last night and this morning. The hell he's raised with his talking rock, I'm really beginning to think I should have had him taken out. But now I spot the two guys that just don't look quite right, and looking them over for why, I see that the reason is their coats. Both of them have on thick polyester suit jackets, on a day like this when I am sweating all over my light summer shirt. I watch them at an angle, hiding behind my glasses, and as the near one reaches out to move a piece I see the fabric stretch tight over a lump in the armpit, probably not a goiter, probably a gun. Cops. These guys are absolutely cops, and about as inconspicuous as a pair of orangutans at the Metropolitan Opera. I even recognize their faces, but not quite. I've never been personally acquainted with these particular cops I don't think, though of course we may have mutual friends. Anyway, it's no use to stand here and stare at them, so I head back into the center of the park.

My little heart is going pit-a-pat and no mistake, even though I'm telling myself in all reason they're probably not after anybody here. Oh no, I'm sure they just came down here to play a little chess, with their nice plaid coats and their guns on. However, probably whoever they're after isn't me, and anyway I'm clean, so the best thing to do is wait and see if anything develops. I get back to center and drop onto a bench across the path from my man Lemon Peel, and I pat my forehead down with my handkerchief, because my sweat is beginning to chill.

And now right behind me comes one of my cops, and he gives me a half-look in passing and checks it, walking on by. I follow him from the corner of my hooded eye, watch him stop at the Sabrett wagon and talk to the vendor, then check me out to see if I've moved.

The hell with it all, my day is shot, completely and totally out the window. I start smoking a Kool for consolation, but the wind carries the spark all down one side, hotboxing it so bad I have to throw it away. Nothing, but nothing, goes right anymore. My cop lingers by the hot-dog stand for five minutes or so, marking time and still watching me. Finally he gets a box lid full of hot dogs and soda and goes away to report to his friend, leaving me sitting here chewing my lip.

My cop fades out among the chess tables and I get up and wander around the fountain, trailing my fingers along the raised rim. Two white kids arrive on the wall opposite me and plop down under a miserable stunted tree, catching my attention with the two huge Panasonic radios they're carrying, both tuned to PLJ. Blocky couple of kids they are, and don't look like they're from town. Bet you a nickel they're fagbashers in from Jersey City, sitting there with matching mean looks on their faces, waiting for dark. Not that I care, bet you a dime I'm not working this park again for a couple of days, maybe even a couple of weeks. I don't like it, but I know how to follow directions when they're written all over the wall, and when the rest of my people show up I'm just going to tell them they're all getting a vacation. Another vacation, on top of the first one Porco let us in for when he bugged out on me back in June, and both in summer prime time. This is going to get into my end of the profits, not to mention the aggravation.

The aggravation and the worry. I turn back toward the south side, but I can't see my cops at this distance. I just don't see what they're after me for, when I've been an exemplary citizen for the last ten years or so, as far as anyone knows any different, not unless somebody tipped me in. I'll have to look into that, and the first thing to do is send Holy Mother down there to see if he can make them—ah, no, not this again. I push back out of the memory through my trusted five senses, concentrating on two skaters on the volleyball court, half dancing together, half ignoring each other, and notice PLJ is playing the Pretenders . . . *while somewhere the coroner's assistant has connected his call: "Hello, sorry, I have some bad news for you"—the thumb pinning down the address book like a speciman on corkboard, and the coroner has completed the pointless autopsy, pointless because the cause of death is obvious from a cursory glance at the remains, but now he can write on a yellow form that the ratio of opiates to blood in the body of the deceased was found to be this over that* . . . and how tiresome it is that I can't shake this morbid chain of thought.

New distractions. In between me and the skaters there're some Rastas grouping up, six or eight of them, not quite enough for a good soccer game, though enough to make even Yusuf Ali think twice if anything were to occur. They're making Rastas pretty big these days. They circle together and chillum, spliff between little and ring finger, mouth over thumb. This way you get a nice air mix and can hold the smoke down longer and if you are lucky have a vision of Jah. And Jah lives, and two o'clock we play soccah, mon. I get a whiff of what they're smoking, brought to my nostrils on this cool little breeze, and it smells good and rich, like cedar. I almost wonder where they're getting it from, but then I really am not interested, the turnover you need to make money off that is much too big and too dangerous.

The paired Panasonics sound good to me, putting out a nice solid bass line, still the Pretenders. The Rastas split up and start toeing a soccer ball, and look, here comes Eva the Swede, up La Guardia Place past the Loeb Center, taking the curb neatly on her skates, and she's in the park a good three hours earlier than usual. Maybe she had a bad night herself. But she looks fresh as an ice-cream cone, and wearing blue satin, which becomes her greatly. Nice idea, Eva, and swish, she goes by, right under my nose. Sometimes I think I must be invisible, but then I suppose that I'm trying to be. Eva is communicating in body language to one of the Rastas, while the Pretenders play on. Eva pirouettes and Chrissie Hynde sings and I am drawn into this twirl—she's got my attention.

Nice spin, Eva, but I'll take Chrissie Hynde if I can get her, her voice has that fine edge of desperation which is so attractive, and her little leatherboy backup band is not at all bad. And cute too, I've seen her picture in the window down at J&R. I wonder what she takes. Eva, skating backward, raises her arms and gives her shiniest smile to a long bony Zulu with a wide-brimmed hat and a feather. Anybody but Eva would know with her back turned that this guy is nothing but trouble, and low-grade trouble at that. It depresses me to watch her dig her own grave. Time to take a walk and think about something else for a while.

So I move off down toward the south end again, shaking out my legs, which have stiffened from standing in one place for too long. Down on the corner of Fourth and MacDougal I spot that blond girl singer that's starting to come around on weekends, dancing behind her black guitar and singing so strong and proud I can hear her from where I'm standing, over the crowded noise and the passing cars. She won't be playing the parks long with the voice she's got, and writes her own stuff too, they tell me. For some reason it lightens my heart to see her down there, and I'm about to go down and throw her a bill, but then I remember my cops, and I don't want to give them another free look. Let them come up here if they want to see what I'm doing.

I stop in my tracks, feeling more than a little piqued and annoyed, because I haven't lived this long to get into a state where I can't walk across the park without having to stop for second, third, and fourth thoughts. I didn't live this long for that, no . . . *while somewhere the coroner slides the corpse into a long numbered drawer, a tag tied to its toe for double security, and the coroner's assistant returns the address book to the manila envelope with the other personal effects and waits for a claimant to arrive* . . . and the feeling now sweeping over me is not irritation this time, but panic. I'm in a box but good this time, all my efforts at keeping the horizons empty and open wasted. I'm caught in a corner between all these unlikely circumstances on the one hand and the conspiracy my treacherous mind has mounted against me on the other. I look at my watch and it's one already, my staff should appear at any moment, though I won't take an attitude if they're a little late, last night was so tough on all concerned. But I want to get out of here as soon as may be, turn over the car to Yusuf, I suppose he's the best I've got left for that job, and blow out of here before something snaps permanently. I've got to get off by myself somewhere and not think about anything for a while, because I'm so shaky right now I might do something really ridiculous, like take a shot of my own dope. And maybe a little vacation won't be so bad after all, the way things seem to be going.

I'm back at the fountain again and none of my people have come along yet, but I'm cooling out anyway, at least enough to go back to admiring the scenery. Those two Panasonics are still beating it out, and I roll around on my toes in time to it, one more device to stop myself from thinking. I see Eva has shaken the guy with the feather, and now she's holding conversation with some of the Rastas. She says something I don't catch, twirls away on the toes of her skates, wrists crossed over her head, then rolls back into the group. And what's this? One of our Rastas is hitting Eva a good solid clout across the side of her pale face, a backfist without too much weight behind it, so it's easy to see that my man has finesse when it comes to beating up women. Good woman no show armpits to other man, that would seem to be the message. Eva, sitting down on her blue satin behind with her legs stretched out before her like a child of ten, doesn't seem to get it. What could she have done to offend this gorilla with the foot-long dreadlocks, who's walking toward her now? Probably she doesn't even remember his name.

Eva has a bad-looking bruise on her left cheek, red with blue filling into it, and with her fair skin it could be a month before she can take her face out in public again, and summer will be over. And Eva is also in a bad situation at this very moment. If she was only on her feet she could be skating away at ninety miles an hour, but unfortunately she's not on her feet. Now this is Washington Square, not Union Square where you can take two

hours and torture somebody to death. Here you've got ten minutes at the outside to waste someone, then comes the man. However, time flies when you're getting badly hurt.

I'm thinking all of these thoughts on the wing, because it seems
that my legs have just walked out from under my brain. Am I dancing? No. I am walking toward this big Rasta in a businesslike way,
and with my mouth I am shouting, *"Hey, whaddaya think you're doing?"* Just exactly like a Boy Scout. My man is simply attired, wearing only Adidas, gym shorts, and muscles. He's staring at me in
sheer amazement, because nobody gets into other people's problems down here. Then he appears to wake up, and I get the backfist square in the middle of my chest, which is more or less what I
deserve for behaving like a freaking fool, and it's such a good solid
backfist that it's flipping me head over heels.

Now I land on the pavement and start rolling across my shoulder blades, tucking in my arms and legs and head so as not to get
them all broken, and while rolling out I'm making this little list on
my little mental scratch pad:

1. I still hear the Pretenders. "Mystery Achievement" now.
   What a lot of one group on one station.
2. Yusuf Ali is not here right at this moment.
3. Neither is anybody else I know and love.
4. Even if they were all here I couldn't ask them to bail me out
   of this one. Because I have to follow my own rules or life will
   become meaningless, and it's perfectly clear that I got into
   this entirely through my own stupid fault. I got myself into
   it and I will just have to get myself out.
5. In order to do this I will have to resort to the secret weapon
   I reserve for real emergencies. Not the tear-gas pen, which
   would be of very little use against six or eight people on a
   breezy day like this. Secret weapon number two.

I come out of my roll with my thoughts all in order and squat on
the balls of my feet. I've managed to put about eight feet between
me and the first Rasta, and he's only about eight feet tall. And he's

in no hurry to cover the distance. A good sport, he doesn't kick another player when he's down, or more likely he's just overconfident. Whichever it is, he'll regret it for the rest of his life, or about forty seconds, if I have my way. Now I am reaching into the loose top of my not-so-fashionable left Dingo boot and taking hold of the thing I keep there for times of real trouble. A gift from the Orient, useful for shelling rice, as well as other things. I stand up and send it lashing behind my neck and under both my arms and through my groin once for show, all too quickly for these hashheads to really see. Then I drop into a shallow crouch and hold the thing extended in front of me for them to look at for one second, holding it lightly by my fingertips like a flute.

It's not much of a thing to look at really, just two tapered sticks joined by a little piece of chain.

But check it out, my friends, I'm ready.

Ras Tafari.

—1983

Allen Ginsberg

(1926–1997)

Born in Newark, New Jersey, in 1926, Allen Ginsberg was the son of a poet and high school teacher. His mother was also a Communist and suffered a nervous breakdown during the Great Depression. Ginsberg wrote about his mother's life and death in "Kaddish," along with the controversial "Howl," one of his most anthologized poems. He attended Columbia University, where he was editor of the college's humor magazine. It was while enrolled at Columbia that he met Jack Kerouac, William S. Burroughs, Herbert Huncke, and other members of what was to be labeled the Beat Generation. In 1954 he moved to San Francisco. During the early 1960s he turned toward Buddhism and became a indefatigable promoter of the faith. In later years he was a professor of English at Brooklyn College, City University of New York. Although Ginsberg lived for many years in a Lower East Side tenement, he visited the Village often. The Minetta Tavern, described here, was one of his favorite Village haunts.

"The Old Village Before I Die"

Entering Minetta's soft yellow chroms, to the acrid bathroom
22 years ago a gold kid wrote "humankindness" contrasting
"humankind-ness" on enamel urinal where Crane's match
      skated—
Christmas subway, lesbian slacks, friend bit someone's earlobe off
tore gold ring from queer ear, weeping, vomited—
My first drunk nite flashed here, Joe Gould's beard gray
("a professional bore" said Bill cruelly—but as I was less than
      twenty,
New scene raged eternal—caricatures of ancient comedians
framed over checkertabled booths, first love struck my heart
      heavy
prophecy of THIS MOMENT I looked in the urinal mirror
      returning decades
late same heavy honey in heart—bearded hairy bald with age
soft music Smoke gets in your eyes Michele Show Me the Way to
      Go to
    Jail
from stereophonic jukebox that once echoed You Always Hurt
      The One
    You Love as dear Jack
did know under portraits of Al Smith, Jimmy Walker, Jimmy
      Durante, Billy
    Rose.

—1984

511

Judith Malina

(b. 1926)

Along with her husband Julian Beck (1925–1985), Judith Malina founded The Living Theatre in 1947, a theatrical repertory company that specialized in experimental drama and produced little known and avant-garde plays by Gertrude Stein, Luigi Pirandello, Alfred Jarry, T. S. Eliot, Jean Cocteau, August Strindberg, Bertolt Brecht, and William Carlos Williams. Avowed pacifists and anarchists, Malina and Beck produced Kenneth H. Brown's The Brig *in 1963, which criticized the armed forces. The Internal Revenue soon thereafter began hounding them for back taxes. They were tried and convicted of tax law violation and jailed briefly. In 1988 Malina married Hanon Reznikov. Together they run the latest reincarnation of The Living Theatre. These selections from Malina's diaries capture the uncertainty and impatience of the young Malina, as she ventures forward in her bold theatrical experiment. Village life comes vividly to life in these pages, from brief visits to e. e. cummings to the death of Maxwell Bodenheim.*

from *The Diaries of Judith Malina 1947–1957*

November 1, 1947

Yesterday we visited E. E. Cummings in his little house in Patchin Place. Normal trepidations at meeting the great poet who has influenced Julian so much. Rain. We entered like two dripping cats.

Judith Malina. From *The Diaries of Judith Malina, 1947–1957* (New York: Grove Press, 1984).

A tall woman opened the door and immediately dispatched Julian to the corner bakery "to get the cake for Mrs. Cummings" and disappeared into the kitchen leaving me alone in a room that was informal, almost unkempt, with figurative paintings on the walls, an ebony elephant. . . .

Cummings came in wearing work clothes and talking the way his poems read—lively, exaggerated, concise. He had a repertory of stories and comments on every subject.

Upon Julian's return we had Dubonnet and cake. We talked about language and the misuse and disrepute into which adjectives like "lovely" had fallen, about tall buildings and about the dead art of burlesque. We talked about the strangely reactionary tendency in modern poetry. He said he had heard T. S. Eliot say, at a lecture at the 92nd Street Y, that it was all right to read Milton again.

"But of course," said Cummings, "we had never stopped reading Milton."

We talked about *HIM*. And about the Living Theatre. Cummings seemed pleased with our ideas, though I thought we talked far too little about our work plans.

He gave us permission to go ahead with *HIM*.

The talk was two hours old when suddenly Cummings leapt to his feet, shook our hands, and said: "It is time for the poet to go to work."

Julian is troubled by his abrupt departure. I thought it fitting.

A few days ago Julian and I visited Paul and Sally Goodman. Paul sees swiftly through everything; he is as honest as hay. I expected a whitewashed orderly life from the author of *Communitas*. But his home is an easy, carefree setting for their baby to grow in.

He talks philosophically, deeply, wisely. He says he will be a sponsor of the Living Theatre.

We showed him Cocteau's letter about the translation of *Les Chevaliers de la Table Ronde*. He says it's his favorite Cocteau play, that he admires Cocteau even as much as I do, and will make the translation for us.

March 1, 1949

Here am I and what am I? I wait. There is nothing to do but to wait and to wait is to make time the tyrant. Time cancels everything.

These are the years that matter. This is my young life and how do I pass it, my young life, my only youth? With waiting.

Dr. Jacoby says that I rebel. I do. My rebellion is all that I have. I rebel against my impotence, against time. Must I grow old to achieve anything?

Time is occupied.

I go to the theater: Wagner's *Siegfried, Tristan and Isolde, Madwoman of Chaillot* by Giraudoux.

Sense of losing ground. I am so heavy with the pregnancy.

Julian's patient nature. And now at last, Julian's love.

January 29, 1950

A cocktail party for Anais Nin at Lawrence Maxwell's. Very crowded, hot room.

Kreymborg talks endlessly about himself. Paul Goodman is talking about the Living Theatre and Kreymborg.

There's a new magazine, *Flair*, that features a badly written article describing the "New Bohemia." It seems decadent to be part of it. Yet these are our people and I don't see any escape: This is the world we must work within. The peak we seek to scale is no higher than a thimble. Oh, vanity of vanities!

Save me from the clever conversationalist. Save me from the chic. Save me from the despair of caring so terribly.

April 17, 1950

A film called, *The Man on the Eiffel Tower*.

The City of Paris. Homesickness for a place yet unvisited. Who has not carried a little map of Paris in a notebook, reciting, and even memorizing the names of the boulevards? Unvisited, she is the phantom of unimaginable and illimitable pleasures.

November 23, 1950

When I feel that I can do all that I want to do, I become elated and industrious. Then, in my ardor, I work faster and faster until the ardor exhausts itself in nervous energy. I've just experienced such an elation, but the cycle hasn't run its course. Now I grip my pen so hard that my fingers ache and can't write quickly enough. My anxiety mounts. Impatience takes over. I'll scream. Then I don't.

Instead of turning away from the theater, I have to approach it in a different way, a way frowned on by theater people, but the only way possible for me.

I've forgotten that I'm an artist. I've forgotten that I am a woman.

Daily on my rounds I become a "character ingenue" and I'm ashamed.

April 26, 1951

Billy Budd is a morality play: Melville's story of the sea, war, the ship as small world within the world, the captain as God.

I leave the theater in that tearless state on the threshold of tears.

Dicken asks why I can't read *Moby Dick*. Is it because I have a deep cruelty in me, or that I fear cruelty too deeply that I am unable to bear it witness?

Julian and I go down to the Village. I need the buzz of populated places, that other kind of loneliness.

We go to the San Remo Cafe which I've heard so much about but where I've never been. It's a good bar, gay and intellectual, rather close to my notion of a Paris café.

Here we listen to Chester Kallman talk about *The Rake's Progress* and Stravinsky. He is highly opinionated about opera. By four in the morning, the sadness, along with all other feeling, has left me.

A Thursday: Peter Farb, Helen, Dicken, Joe and Marilyn Turner, and Jackson Mac Low. Jackson, the unhappy anarchist whose good will is trodden bare by his cynicism, stays late and we talk of the world.

May 18, 1952

I put a photograph of Modigliani on my dressing room wall because he has a beautiful face. No. Because his face shows his suffering. The sorrowful life of the bars and the unfulfilled art.

Do we idolize its victims and priests? Do we not idolize Maxwell Bodenheim although we are sometimes loath to talk to him and always ashamed of our condescension to him? the bartenders at the Remo have put a photograph of him over the bar.

What we admire is Bodenheim's refusal to resist. We fight all the time, resisting temptation. We admire those who don't. Even if it's suicidal.

Money harries us. Threatening creditors arrive with their own sad stories of deprivation. We quest even for food (a borrowed meal and peanut butter sandwiches).

A check bouncing at the San Remo upsets us. If we lost our credit at the Remo, wht would become of us?

Last week at the group session I raved.

June 25, 1952

After midnight, after rehearsals, to the San Remo. In spite of the ruthless violence of the current juke box favorites, one can sit still there.

With Weegee, the photographer of the Naked City, I go to his shabby, one-room home behind the Tombs and then to eat at Thau's. Joined by Norman and Nina and Julian, we prowl the dawn streets, and visit the catacombs below MacDougal Street and the Minetta Spring captured in the art nouveau fountain of a fashionable Washington Square hotel.

Last night in the Remo with John Cage and Lou Harrison. Lou, looking splendid in a white suit and a small Edwardian beard, boasts of his exploits like a child recounting his defiances.

Seven of the cast have left us. The recasting is arduous and boring.

And this is my good season.

"Why, this is hell nor am I out of it." The red glass bowls in the Remo's windows are little Cleopatra coals to comb through my hair.

Would we remember Faustus if he had heeded the good angel?

July 13, 1952

They sleep, the bohemians. Here in the tech room, Julian. In the dressing rooms, Frances and Bruce, and on the floor, Bill Kehoe. In the hallway on prop tables, Eric Weinberger and Bill Mullahly. In the lobby, Nina on the floor.

One night at the Remo Eric and Bill asked me if they could "flop" at the theater. They have been here ever since and they work hard. Eric, an exemplary person, is going to replace Larry Elfenbein in *Ubu*. He is admired by all. Bill Mullahly is stage manager.

Julian has gone overboard in his admiration for the haphazard way of life. He goes shoeless, which is all right, and dirty, which is not. He thinks he looks relaxed, but he looks a mess. I'm not troubled because it cannot last (this pose not being natural). Meanwhile, it's uncomfortable.

But the spirit—and that's the important part—the spirit is what matters. The work is done with communal enjoyment.

Still the communication is too superficial. Something more. Something more.

December 8, 1952

Am I not addicted to the San Remo? To a mere atmosphere? I fight it, try to stay away, to taper off, to break away cold turkey. I fail.

And are the passions that make us sick no more or less than addictions to the desired one?

There's nothing to which one can't be addicted.

February 10, 1954

The hideous death of Bodenheim blankets the Village in a funereal spirit. Who dares confess to the wrenching excitement of seeing a companion's mauled corpse on the front page of every newspaper, and all of us knowing that the worst has again triumphed?

Max and Ruth both murdered by a boy to whom they offered a bed. The ranks of the dead poets swell.

Even self-contempt when fierce enough is magnificent. The virtue of the extreme is its extremity. Nature loves extremes as much as she loathes a vacuum.

So it was for his very last birthday that Art stole the pumpkin pie from the Waldorf Cafeteria counter. . . .

—1984

Ronald Sukenick

(b. 1932)

After receiving his Ph.D. from Brandeis, Ronald Sukenick turned his back on academia in favor of pursuing the bohemian life in the Village and the Lower East Side. Later he ran the Coordinating Council of Literary Magazines and founded the American Book Review. *In this frank and robust memoir of life in the underground, we meet such familiar figures as Jack Kerouac, Allen Ginsberg, Lawrence Ferlinghetti, Andy Warhol, Norman Mailer, James Agee, Miles Davis, and Sam Shepard at such places as Stanley's Tavern, Max's Kansas City, and, in this selection, the infamous San Remo.*

"The Remo" from *Down and In: Life in the Underground*

I'm sitting in a cavernous cabaret off Bleecker Street near Washington Square called the Open Door, talking to a junkie musician named Tony Frusella who's playing here tonight. For a while now in the early fifties the Open Door is the center of the Village scene and the music scene. It books the hippest groups, and jazzmen come down to jam after they finish their gigs on Fifty-second Street. Tony plays a big mellow trumpet and he's good, though some people say he sounds too much like Miles Davis.

Ronald Sukenick. "The Remo" from *Down and In: Life in the Underground* (New York: Beech Tree Books/William Morrow, 1987). Reprinted by permission of the author.

"When I got out of the army," Tony says, "I got this hot-shit gig with Charlie Barnet. It was a big band and I was in the trumpet section. But like it was bull shit because all you'd do was get up and blow the same notes with a bunch of other guys. It was just like the army. And besides, it's like too piercing. So one day we're playing and Barnet points at us to get up and blow our notes and I don't get up. He points to me again and I refuse to blow. Everybody else in the line is blowing, see, and like I'm just sitting there. Then he starts making fun of me right on stage. Like he's got a real attitude on him. I just sit it out. Finally he fires me in front of the whole audience. Never do what they tell you just because everybody else does it."

"Shmucks," I murmur.

Who are the shmucks here? Tony? He's the hero. Charlie Barnet? No, he's the heavy. The shmucks are the guys who get up when told and play their notes together. To understand what follows, you need to know what a shmuck is. It's not just a jerk or a wimp, it has to do with a particular time and place. A shmuck is somebody with a certain way of thinking, a combination of caution, conformity, and mercenary values. An idolator of Things, a consumer at the feet of the Golden Calf. If you're Jewish like me and from Brooklyn, "shmuck" is a word without which you could not have made it across the bridge from Flatbush to a dubious salvation in the underground of Greenwich Village. "Shmuck." Or some equivalent. If you don't have a word for it in teen-age James Dean America, then you're lost. At the end of *Huckleberry Finn*, Huck forgoes the confines of the settled town to "light out for the Territory" and freedom. Huck Finns are still lighting out for the Territory. Even though there is not Territory anymore. The underground is the Territory and they keep lighting out from Fargo and L.A. and St. Louis and Brooklyn. Why?

We're all less individual than individualism permits us to imagine. The tension Twain sees in America between stability and freedom is not something peculiar to an individual or an era, but still conditions the moment. At the rough parts of the road the culture offers only a limited number of detours, of possible options. To anyone. In this respect we're interchangeable with anyone else in our generation. You can serve as that anyone as well as I, and what we have in common may be the most crucial part of our stories. Certainly it is of mine. The rest is incidental.

Any moderately well informed kid around 1950 knew about the going romance of Bohemia, with its peculiar mix of both pleasure and salvation so attractive for kids in pre-sixties puritan America, where sex was a commodity you traded for marriage. We knew about mythic figures. We knew about the artist's life, Toulouse-Lautrec's legendary penis, Pollock's fabled drunks, van Gogh's mythic ear. *La vie de bohéme.* They say that Dylan Thomas had a sweet tooth for chocolate and that when he was especially drunk he would sometimes shit in bed, usually sombody else's, so you couldn't tell whether he was wallowing in shit or chocolate or both. On the other hand Robert Creeley tells a story about waking up on the edge of the Pacific after a night of partying, Jack Kerouac looking into his face asking, "Are you pure?" Even thirty years later, if you are anything like me, you will still be moved by Gregory Corso's faith in the tradition when he tells you, "If you believe you're a poet, then you're saved."

It's 1948 and Henry Wallace is running for president on a third-party ticket. All over the United States idealistic liberals are getting behind Wallace and pushing hard. Every bright kid in Midwood High School in the middle of middle-class Brooklyn is campaigning his ass off for Henry Wallace. Henry Wallace wants peace, Henry Wallace wants social progress, Henry Wallace is against Red-baiting, Henry Wallace is a liberal's dream. *Village Voice* libertarian columnist Nat Hentoff, at fifteen heavily influenced by Arthur Koestler's anti-Stalinist *Darkness at Noon*, says, "I was very unpopular on my block in Boston when I refused to support Henry Wallace, and I gave as my reason that the Commies were running his campaign." Wallace is the guilty conscience of the well-to-do liberal establishment turning on itself, although you shouldn't put down guilty conscience. It's better than no conscience.

But if, like me, you don't feel part of that establishment or, like Hentoff, you don't like Stalinism, you don't have that kind of bad conscience. You don't like Red-baiting any more than the liberals but you also don't like pious Communist-front youthniks. Worst of all, you don't like folk-singing, or folk dancing for that matter, with its heavy ideological freight. You never dreamed you saw Joe Hill last night and the hora seems less out of step with your reality because you're Jewish. But my bit, like Hentoff's, is not especially political. For one thing, the alternative to righteous liberals at the time consists largely of reactionary fanatics, capitalist dupes, and cynically manipulative politicians, which makes Wallace boosters appetizing by comparison.

In 1948 I've just joined the middle class, or I'm trying to, having moved three blocks from the Gravesend Avenue neighborhood of the impoverished Malamud Delicatessen under the El, which was the original for the deli in Bernard's *The Assistant*, to the affluent Midwood High district at Ocean Parkway. I always seem to assume the position of an outsider looking in, even when looking in at outsiders. But the radicals are also affluent here, so who are the outsiders? One problem is that, being anti-Wallace, I'm considered deficient in social conscience concerning those less fortunate than ourselves. Besides, the ambiance of Gravesend Avenue has given me a permanent distaste for the middle-class Jewish facility for bad conscience later so well represented by the movies of Woody Allen, who attended—what else?—Midwood High School.

Down at the Gravesend of things you don't have the luxury of either no-risk liberal idealism or Jewish guilt, you have enough to contend with surviving as a Christ-killer among the local Christians. But the future firemen, postmen, mechanics, cops, and crooks of Gravesend Avenue are my pals, even if they are subject to irrational racist behavior that, however, I know cannot be put down as endemic stupidity. Stupidity is their refuge, their protection from the unreachable middle-class world beyond Gravesend, and they take me into it. If they refer to my Yiddish grandmother as a kike, they also call Blacks niggers, Hispanics spics, Irish micks, and Italians wops, even though a lot of them are Italians themselves and occasionally get sore about "wop." One time I start talking about wops in front of an older Italian kid and he grabs me by the collar and warns me, "Never call a guinea a wop."

What is the attraction of the underground for kids? Why won't Huck stay home? Midwood kids apparently thought that getting straight A's and going to Harvard Med School was all there is in life. Unreal. These were the days when any self-respecting college had strict Jewish quotas. What were they going to do with five hundred Jewish kids a year with 99.8 averages from Midwood High School alone? The resulting crazed rat race was what passed for reality at Midwood. For me, coming from Gravesend Avenue, the effect of this mad struggle was astonishment. First of all it was clear that even playing along with a system like that was participating in a racist insult in which the price of success was self-contempt—try to be better because you're actually worse—and there we are back to the joke of guilt and inferiority enacted by Woody Allen. Very funny, Woody.

My sense of unreality is verified by the great socialized-medicine debate. I already have a reputation for stupidity, the stupidity I've learned from Gravesend. Stupidity is a form of resistance, and provokes not only contempt but hostility. The irate response to me is always, "What, *you* got a hundred on your geometry regents?" "*You* won a scholarship?" But with the socialized-medicine debate I know I have it made, because I'm at least on the smart, liberal, righteous side of things. I'm emphatically in favor of socialized medicine in a big, formal high-school forum. I'm in for a shock, because when the day of the debate comes around it turns out that all those future doctors and lawyers think socialized medicine is the worst thing that could happen to a bunch of upwardly mobile dermatologists, gastroenterologists, and malpractice experts. You'd think I'd got up there and told them—ultimate insult—that they were "bujwah." Of course I will come to detect the inevitability of neoconservatism here when, decades later, these people are forced to confront their real interests, but at the time I stagger off the stage in confusion after a barrage of sarcastic and contemptuous questions, thinking, *Shmucks.*

"Shmuck" was a code word for a condition whose alternative in Flatbush was vague. But in Greenwich Village at the time there was a strong sense of alternative identity. In the underground of Greenwich Village you not only knew who They were, you also knew who We were. America was one thing and Greenwich Village another. Village people might go Uptown but it was a kind of slumming in reverse. Yoram Kaniuk, an Israeli who had already fought for Jerusalem in the War of Independence, found the promised land again in a way as a painter in underground New York of the fifties and its center, the San Remo bar. The plunge into the underground, with all its implications of the infernal, is nevertheless an attempt to resurrect the mythic Holy City within the profane polis. It involves a notion of the good life beyond "mercenary" concerns. The spiritual geography of the underground describes a promised land of freedom, illuminations, and excitement beyond the provincial ego, the constrictions of social class and ethnic heritage, beyond the conventional altogether. A new Athens, a new Jerusalem—and let's not forget Sodom either.

"Out of the bar were pouring interesting people, the night making a great impression on me," writes Jack Kerouac of his version of the San Remo in *The Subterraneans*—a book supposedly about San Francisco but actually about the Village with names changed, according to Allen Ginsberg—and here you can see not only Kerouac's romantic attraction to subterranean life, but also the kernel of his run-on, innovative, improvisational style incubated in that jazz-influenced underground scene, in his riff on the coinage or typo "birl"—"some kind of Truman-Capote-haired dark Marlon Brando with a beautiful thin birl or girl in boy slacks with stars in her eyes . . . and with them a guy with another beautiful doll, the guy's name Rob and he's some kind of adventurous Israeli soldier with a British accent whom I suppose you might find in some Riviera bar at 5 A.M. drinking everything in sight alphabetically with a bunch of interesting crazy international-set friends on a spree."

Kaniuk, graying, decades later a eminent Israeli writer, will reminisce to me in a café in Tel Aviv almost with a sense of wonder about his Village days. When, back then, he goes to a posh Uptown party for Tennessee Williams with painter Gandy Brodie it's in the spirit of an expedition among the Philistines. Brodie spots Ginger Rogers and tells her, "This guy here is Russian, and he saw you when he was in the underground, and he admired you, and he was in the KGB, and his great dream was to once be like Fred Astaire and dance with you."

"So she got all excited. And I start speaking to her in bad English, not that my English was so good but I made it worse, and I said, 'Me dreaming about you. Underground. You. Fred Astaire."

"And it was a strange thing, she looked glittery, beautiful, and when we danced together I saw that all her age was in her neck, you could see the wrinkles of her age, and she was trying to patch herself up. And I played it all the way."

Kaniuk isn't buying into Uptown, he's putting it on.

Around the time of the socialized-medicine fiasco, selling out became the hot topic among those of us in Midwood who weren't shmucks, what was selling out and what wasn't, who was selling out and who wasn't. Selling out applied to those who assumed the moral superiority of leftish views while maintaining shmuck-materialist values about money, success, and sexuality. It never occurred to any of us that shmuck materialism and dialectical materialism had any relation. The dialectical lefties were stuffy, but the shmucks were not even "subtle." We thought of ourselves as in the spirit of the true left, unaware that we might be something else, something for which there was perhaps no political category, or at least not yet. Not till the sixties, if then. So selling out came to mean not only working for advertising companies and corporations, but almost any of the normal shmuck-materialist ambitions when pursued by leftish classmates. Selling out, finally, meant becoming a doctor or a lawyer, because such choices denied the promise of a more "valid" kind of life beyond the middle class from which we all came. For some, selling out was simply the synonym for making it—at anything. *Who are the shmucks here?* "Tradition has been broken, yet there is no new standard to affirm," observes writer-intellectual Paul Goodman of "the young." We were growing up absurd, though we didn't know it till Goodman's book of that title articulated our mystique in 1960. The lack of a myth appropriate for us begat a sour negativity.

But the mystique of the Village seemed near irresistible: Money isn't important. Sex is. The value of art is taken for granted.

"I came to the Village because sex was very uptight in the fifties," says Howard Smith, longtime author of the "Scenes" column for *The Village Voice*. As such, he was the man from whom a few decades of undergrounders and would-be undergrounders picked up their cue about what was considered in—and especially, sexy and in. Smith with his rumpled five-o'clock-shadow look, has even these days a certain puppyish quality that conflicts with his pitch for raunch. "I wanted to fuck. I wanted women who would talk to me. I wanted women who didn't wear padded, wired bras with a slip over it and a sweater. I knew I was going to do something in the area of the arts with my life but I had no idea what. I came for sex. In the Village some girls didn't even wear bras. At all. God, to me that would be like seeing five fashion models walk by nude right now, that's how far out that was. At Pandora's Box, I used to go to that coffee shop all the time and this waitress would lean over and say, 'Anything else I can get you?' and she wore a low-cut peasant blouse and no bra and I would almost fall out of my chair."

"Suddenly, I *was* free, I felt," writes poet-playwright Amiri Baraka—then known as LeRoi Jones—of the first impact of the Village on him. "I could do anything I could conceive of. . . . The idea that the Village was where Art was being created, where there was a high level of intellectual seriousness, was what I thought. And the strange dress and mores that I perceived . . . I thought part of the equipment necessary to have such heavy things go on. . . . So that I did think that coffeehouse after coffeehouse and the other establishments down around West 4th and MacDougal, Bleecker or 8th Street, were filled with World Class intellectuals."

MacDougal Street in Greenwich Village was not so different in 1948 from what it would be if you fast-forwarded all the way to 1984. In thirty-six years Minetta's would still be there, and the Kettle of Fish too, if soon to close. Minetta's was where you were when you weren't in the San Remo, the bar down the block at the corner of Bleecker Street. The Rienzi, an early hip non-Italian espresso place, started by five or six artists of various kinds, would not be there, though the Figaro would, rebuilt in the same place. But way back in 1948, if you wanted a hip cup of coffee, you went to the Waldorf Cafeteria—thirty-six years after a bank—on Sixth Avenue off Eighth Street, where the artists went to snack and talk, since the Rienzi and the Figaro were not yet built. The Kettle was the bar you went to if you wanted a somewhat rougher scene, which you didn't. You wanted the Remo because the Remo was the place, in 1984 a Chinese restaurant, in 1948 the mecca for refugees from places like Midwood. You were headed for the Remo, where you'd try to look old enough to be in an actual Village-Bohemian-literary-artistic-underground-mafiaso-pinko-revolutionary-subversive-intellectual-existentialist-anti-bourgeois café. Real life at last.

I edge into the Remo, which luckily is crowded so I don't look conspicuous. I'm looking for my sister Gloria, a regular, who has left Yale Art School to become a belle of Bleecker Street. It's the kind of bar that in the 1970's ambience of accelerated nostalgia might be considered "campy," but now in 1948 it's just an aging New York bar with old wood, white-and-black-tiled floors, a pressed-tin ceiling, wooden booths, and a busy backroom restaurant. I find Gloria, wearing jeans, in the proletarian-looking crowd at the bar in the front room. She waves me toward a booth and joins me in a minute carrying a martini. Gloria, an occasional waitress and model, is maybe the first girl to scandalize the gray-flannel generation by wearing what, at the time, are still called dungarees. Jeans in 1948 are considered shocking on men, much less women. Not that I'm much aware of it then, but in retrospect it would be clear that men find Gloria's voluptuousness and curly hair insanely attractive.

"Have an espresso, they serve the strongest espresso this side of Sicily," she urges, thereby neatly avoiding the legal-drinking-age problem. She keeps waving to friends as she talks.

"It was really like the home away from home for thousands of people," she'll explain years later. "Everybody was living in cold-water flats or tiny little apartments so everybody used to gather there. Nobody spent time at home, I mean the Remo was really like the living room hearth, kind of, except there was like also a lot of heavy drinking going on. The martini scene."

"Not beer?"

"Beer was for the weekend crowd. For the hardcore drinkers a martini was the most alcohol you could get for the least amount of money. Cause everybody was always broke."

A tough Italian guy comes by and Gloria asks him to send the waiter over. "He's one of the bartenders," Gloria says. "A real ass pincher." A lot of the guys in the Remo, it seems, are "semi-Mafia-connected," what poet—then painter—Ted Joan's friends refer to as "the Minor Mafia."

The Village was much more a village in 1948 than in the sixties, when it would get to be a tourist mecca and Bleecker Street on weekends would resemble Coney Island. In 1948 it was all Italian with some underground people attracted by the Bohemian tradition, cheap rents, and its insulation from the middle-class world of Uptown, which began at Fourteenth Street with a few Village beachheads further north like the Chelsea Hotel on West Twenty-third where Dylan Thomas died. And the Italians were very insular. Tribal. Hoods loafing around storefront social clubs directing dead deadly looks at Bohemian interlopers, especially if they seemed to be gay or, in their view, worse, were like Ted Joans, Black. Pre-civil rights America. Years later Gregory Corso would remind Allen Ginsberg about an incident involving LeRoi Jones/Baraka. "Remember how we went to read in Washington, D.C.? He crawled underneath the backseat. I never saw a man in my life do that, and I said, 'Hey, LeRoi, what're you doing there?'

"He says, 'Don't you understand, I'm in Washington, D.C. I'm in a place where they don't like Blacks.'

"I said, 'What, the capital of the United States?' So he woke me up to the ball game on that. Right. This class guy."

"He wouldn't get out of the car to go into a drive-in," says Ginsberg. "And he was right at the time, I didn't realize."

"Me neither. I figure, all right, I'm Italian but at least I'm white so they can't fuck with me too much."

Thirty years later in Boulder, Colorado, I encounter a courtly Baraka, with frosting hair and beard but still formidable gull-wing eyebrows and the projection of a raging mental intensity, and I try to put together this anecdote and his history of quick-change ethnopolitical ferocity—I remember Ted Joans telling me that being friends with LeRoi is like riding the back of a shark. The two takes merge into a new image of the man.

"For a while I lived on Thompson Street," says poet Tuli Kupferberg, leading member of the dirty-talking, rabble-rousing music group the Fugs, his almost pedantic intonations belied by a mad clown face, scraggly beard, glittery eye. "That was called the South Village, less desirable and infinitely more dangerous. Racially mixed couples, if they wandered in there by mistake, they were taking their lives in their hands. I finally decided to get out when I came home very late at night and there were two people in front of the bar, badly dressed, one was on the ground, the other one was kicking him in the head. So I decided this was not a nice kind of neighborhood."

"I motioned with my head to one of the two waiters standing around," writes Chandler Brossard of his version of the Remo in his 1952 novel, *Who Walk in Darkness*. "He came to the booth and I ordered a glass of beer. He did not say anything. I liked him less than any waiter I had ever seen. He looked deadpan at us, and went to the bar for my beer. The Italians who worked in the restaurants down there disliked all non-Italians. Some of them disguised it better than others."

The Italian hoods in the Village represent a leitmotif of fear for the classless subterraneans in Brossard's book, alienated as they are from both the Downtown proletariat and the Uptown bourgeoisie. This accurately reproduces the feel of the streets at the time, and in retrospect I see it corresponds to the situation of the cultural underground in the forties and fifties, with its hostility toward the middle class and its ideological divorce from the working class in consequence of the failed socialist movements of the thirties. It was a situation that vitiated the politics of the older Bohemia and largely depoliticized the new underground until the social protest movements of ten years later, in which the always-political Living Theater took the vanguard. A de-emphasis of politics and, especially, ideology marked the transition from Bohemians to "subterraneans" who, it might be said, initially moved further underground. But for a kid like me, this enclave of hold-outs had the power of myth and the sanction of tragic genius—Poe, Rimbaud, van Gogh. If you had to choose between worldly success and tragic genius, and this scene implied that you did, you would gladly have chosen the latter.

Joe Santini, owner of the Remo, would "stand at the bar and watch all the funnies come in," says Gregory Corso, implying a contained antagonism toward the underground types in the interests of business. Corso should know. He's a native, born across the street from the Remo at 190 Bleecker, did time in an orphanage, already in jail at twelve and in Dannemora at seventeen. Corso as a member of the underground does not have the same problems with the working class as do some still measuring things by middle-class values. Anatole Broyard sees the scene, in his 1950 article "Village Café," as a sardonically romanticized Inferno whose bizarre inhabitants are paralyzed as if in the circle of ice by their own hang-ups, compared to which the bartenders seem normal. But Corso felt right at home. "One bartender, Nick Colossi, became a National League umpire. And he, whenever there was a fight in the bar, would get a baseball bat, dig it? And beat up on the fuckers. Because, you see, people from all over the city would go to that bar."

"All the bartenders were pretty tough?"

"They were Italians, Italians are like that. And I guess they had to be at that time with so many people coming in. You know why people go to bars. Either they got a problem, either they get drunk and act dumb, or they go there to pick somebody up. So these guys, especially if they're Italian—like yegods."

It's true there was a certain hostility in the air, not only in the Village but in the whole forty-eight states. It was the beginning of the cold war. Waves of superpatriotism were emanating from Washington. Pinkos and faggots were in trouble in the provinces.

The first list of subversive organizations was just out of the attorney general's office, quickly becoming a job test for members of listed groups. And from another point of view, the left, still going to demonstrations in jackets and ties, seemed hopelessly Victorian and out of touch.

"Early in the fifties I became associated with an anarchist group called Resistance," says Tuli Kupferberg. "They were still living in the Spanish Civil War. All the foreign anarchist groups, the Italians, the Jews, and the Spaniards, were much stronger than the American group. It had a lot of people who went into the War Resisters League, Ralph DiGia, Dave McReynolds, Paul Goodman, Judith Malina, and Julian Beck. But we just felt we were holding on. The Europeans were still living in Europe. I remember one guy got up once and he said—he'd fought in the Civil War—'My friends, there is only one saying. *Machine guns! Machine guns!*'"

A lot of the veterans of the old left were hanging around the Village bars, blacklisted and unable to find jobs, unemployable merchant seamen, men with memories of the Spanish Civil War. "It was really a bummer," says Gloria, "because never having had any particular personal life because they were always going to sea, they were now stuck in New York and they had no personal life, so it made for a particularly chaotic kind of scene." Writers and actors who could no longer get work drifted down to the Village. Zero Mostel took up painting.

The tone of the bars was strictly macho. Broyard writes admiringly about a bartender who "can break your nose over the bar." Judith Malina of the Living Theater records in her *Diaries* a fight involving the manager of the Remo, the owner's stepson. "Johnny Santini's face grew more and more brutal with satisfaction as he struck again and again his already unconscious opponent, crumbled on the tiles, inert. Johnny kept striking till they pulled him away." Gays were out, though Corso insists that "Thursday night is faggot night" at the Remo and Broyard says some gay activity was tolerated and that the tension with which it proceeded, "so much deeper and more equivocal than at the regular markets, is like a delicious knotting in the bowels."

531

Some people dig the edge of violence that shows in these precincts those years. You experience a knotting of the bowels, delicious or not, walking past the hoods at 121 Prince Street, where Broyard lives in a cold-water flat across the hall from Gloria, as does Carl Solomon, to whom Allen Ginsberg's *Howl* is dedicated. The building has a quirky population of Bohemians, one of whom "threw his bed out the window and painted his apartment black to end his marriage," according to Beat historian John Tytell. One of the subterraneans in Brossard's book is nearly beaten to death by hoods at the end, and Ginsberg will try to recollect close to four decades later where it was—in Minetta Lane, outside the Remo, at the West End Bar near Columbia?—that Kerouac was beat up.

"Kerouac did get beaten up at the San Remo, didn't he?" asks Ginsberg.

"No," says Gregory. Corso describes himself these days as simian, but his face has fleshed and softened in mid-age so that if you put a babushka on him he'd look more like a sly old lady. "That mother-fucking, what's that place called, across the street?"

"The Kettle of Fish," I say.

"The Kettle of Fish," Corso affirms.

"That was a rougher place anyway," I say.

"Yeah," says Corso. "I knew the guy that did it, and you know what happened? See, Jack when he spoke was like me. Open. First thought, best thought. Okay. We were walking on the street, this guy suddenly grabs Kerouac. Kerouac was much stronger than him, but he wouldn't touch him. So the guy grabs him, and I saw the worst thing in my life. He's bouncing Kerouac's head on the ground, like this"—Corso jumps up and starts acting out the scene—"and I suddenly realized. And I screamed, *'Sto-o-op!'* and he keeps on doing it, and I grabbed this motherfucker back. *Uuuh!* And he looks at me like a drunk man, and walked away. It was the scariest thing I ever saw."

"Just completely spontaneous for no reason?" I ask.

"Yeah. It was fast. All I could do was scream, 'Stop!'"

"What was the reason the guy grabbed Kerouac?" asks Ginsberg. "Because Jack, like me, we speak the unspeakable. And we feel free. We're Americans, why not? We're not insulting the guy. No, but that day his head was being bounced on the ground, I saw a smile on his face. And I knew that man never hurt anybody in his life. Monsieur Kerouac. I love him, I love him very much."

In another light, at the Cedar Tavern, painter Franz Kline, repeatedly provoked, blows his stack at his good friend Jackson Pollock and starts punching him hard in the gut. Pollock, the biggest and toughest of all the painters on the scene, does nothing but double over in pain, laugh happily, and, according to the account by writer Fielding Dawson, whisper to Kline, "Not so hard."

Despite all the aggression floating around in the warm gas of tobacco and beer filling the San Remo, there was also a certain careless freedom in the atmosphere. Carlos Castaneda would preach to a later generation of youth about the existence of alternate realities. In the fifties there was only one, challenged occasionally by, say, an old book that escaped current categories, like *Leaves of Grass* or *Tristram Shandy*, or a way of moving and talking, such as James Dean's, or the tone of a bar like the Remo. What a relief for teenage rebels fleeing across the bridges and tunnels from the rat race for success that made Sammy run from World War II and the Bomb and the Holocaust through the fifties, so frightened, his hysteria fed by McCarthyism, that he didn't stop till he got to the sixties. Reality was middle class. If you stumbled in the race and fell out, you faced the frightening prospect not so much of starvation or even of "failure," as simply of nothing. The "working class" had not been real since the decline of the working-class movements in the late thirties, the "masses" were being absorbed in the mass market. "Negroes" certainly were not real—they weren't even visible. The upper class was a myth presumably neutralized by FDR along with the monopolies, monopoly having been reduced to the status of a game. Doctors, lawyers, and especially businessmen were real, maybe even, at the limit, professors. Politicians and celebrities had a tantalizing metareality. Beyond that, you ceased to exist.

What's fascinating to me about the Remo is that the habitues are doing nothing, they're wasting time. "Hovering halfway between the pleasure principle and the death instinct"—a phrase

Broyard means as a putdown—they are at least in contact with the pleasure principle and the death instinct, something that middle-class existence at the time does not dare permit. America, innocent victim of Russian aggression, persecuted by the Rosenbergs and Alger Hiss, and sneaky subversives who hide behind the Fifth Amendment, is itself too aggressive to allow the dream, the reverie, the passive attention required to recognize its deepest impulses. The smile on the faces of Kerouac, of Pollock, as they are beaten is a smile of perverse beatitude, emblem of breakthrough to the primal pleasure of giving in, giving up, of failure, loss, defeat, the other side of the fifties drive for success.

In the underground you learn to violate the taboos that support middle-class reality. You learn not only to waste yourself, you learn to waste time, disrupting the countdown toward death implicit in the chronology of production, with the timelessness of pleasure. You have to know how to hang out. Some people have a talent for it, others learn. It requires a certain amount of stupidity, which, for those brought up to pursue middle-class ambitions, is often hard to muster. For many people, and especially those like intellectuals whose goals are internalized, hanging around doing nothing can be a trial of patience. Drinking helps, so do drugs, but at its most refined hanging out is a form of meditation. You let your mouth gape, you stare dully into space and let your mind go blank. It's not easy, but it's worth the effort. Sitting in the bars and espresso places, browsing bocce courts, the 8th Street Bookshop, Fred Leighton's Mexican boutique, Fred Braun's sandal store, or the off-beat jewelry store run by Sam Kramer with the earring in one ear on Eighth, the various pottery shops and importers of cheap exotica—hanging out in such places digging the merchandise and members of the opposite sex becomes an end in itself.

But the hanging-out place par excellence is, I quickly discover, Washington Square. Maybe its relaxed, dead-end ambience has to do with its position as cul-de-sac at the bottom of Fifth Avenue, or with the fact that it served as a pauper's graveyard around the beginning of the nineteenth century. You can almost always find anyone you want to see there if you hang out long enough. Meanwhile you can enjoy sitting on a bench watching the mix of bohoes and middle-class ladies, Italian hoods, hip sex mothers playing with their babies and hip dogs, knowing adolescent boys and newly nubile sexpots from Little Red School House down the block or private schools Uptown, preening Blacks cocksure and superior from their place in the Bohemian pecking order, intellectuals in proletarian clothing, young folk singers gazing into infinity as they let their fingers trip across their guitar strings, emaciated Bowery types, NYU college kids, and a miscellany of loafers sitting around the circular fountain in the center with a certain casual inner-than-thou look.

This was the crowd on a sunny weekday afternoon. Starting with the sixties, the Square increasingly became a place where small-time drug dealers would congregate, but those were already the days when the Hippies were lounging on the lawns, with rarely a blue uniform in view. In the old days you got tickets for sitting on the grass. Howard Smith remembers "getting tickets for my kids being nude on the grass when they were crawling, they didn't even walk yet, and the cops gave them tickets for indecent exposure."

At this time the Square is run for the gentry coming down through the Arch from Fifth Avenue and the hoods coming up from the Village past the fenced playground where NYU's Loeb Student Center will later stand. Neither group wants drugs, noise, vagrants, musicians, queers, hoboes, bohoes, or Negroes. Decadent loafers. Hanging out. Wasting time. Corrupting morals. But this is just what they start to get, plus attendant tourists in large crowds on weekends, despite the cops. In fact, the real enforcers are the Italian hoods. Anything they don't like they beat up. If it doesn't vacate the premises fast. Two swarthy types approach a wispy-looking youth who is neither with a girl nor looking like he wants one, which can mean only one thing to them.

"Hello, Mary," says the hood on the right.

"Waiting for your boyfriend?" says the hood on the left.

"Ain't he pretty?" says the hood on the right.

"*Mah-rone!*" says the hood on the left, shaking his wrist.

At this point the wispy youth remembers an urgent errand and leaves.

My first take on the underground is that it's a class of outsiders experimenting with an idea of the good life beyond stable middle-class constraints. Since I believe that to be my inclination, I'm willing to give subterraneans the benefit of every doubt. Those rebels inclined to waste their lives and get on with it, to embrace failure at the start and opt for excitement over security, are then confronted with the promised land of previously repressed impulses, a risky new underground landscape to explore consisting of everything deemed unreal by the dominant culture, which amounts to almost everything. The risk is becoming a victim, a risk that is totally taboo since the Holocaust. But those who go all the way in defeat and become victims are, like Dylan Thomas, at least victims of themselves, achieving sometimes an inverted saintliness symptomatic of the culture—the last is first and the best is worst. This underground saintliness of the beaten is a phenomenon that has been noticed by many, among them Norman Mailer and Broyard, negatively, as well as by Malamud, and above all by the Beats. As in the perverse purity of Maxwell Bodenheim, for example.

Bodenheim drifts into the Remo, poet and novelist, relic of an older Village Bohemia that thrived between Wars I and II. Gloria points him out, bummy looking, a local fixture, selling his old books. Bodenheim becomes for me, even in his seedy decline, a symbol of the dark glamour of the underground. "How dumb I was at that time," says Ted Joans, an avid collector. "Bodenheim would wander around with maybe five or six copies, hardcover copies, of his book *Naked on Roller Skates*. 'Give me thirty-five cents, son, I'll sign it, thirty-five cents.' Isn't that something, you can't even buy a copy for three hundred and fifty dollars in cash. And I, like a dummy—and I had the money—didn't buy it. Cause I looked at it wrong."

Judith Malina—who told me only half joking in Paris that the ground-breaking Living Theater, so influential in the sixties, was born in the Remo—writes in her *Diaries* in 1952 of "Bodenheim's queer remembrance of poems past, and his terrible face. There was a mocking item about him in *Time* magazine, a story of his arrest some nights ago for sleeping in the subway. With it was a picture of him much as he looks now, though sober. He passed it around and confided to me that he will sue for libel. A recent benefit for him given by some Villagers put him in possession of some money, so he bought me beer, and gin for himself, and became quickly incomprehensible."

Flash forward: We're sitting in Allen Ginsberg's slum apartment on East Twelfth Street near Avenue A, his neighborhood since the fifties, Peter Orlovsky just in from Boulder and Gregory Corso from Paris, talking about Bodenheim. "Gregory's still sleeping on my floor," says Ginsberg, thinking back thirty years. Allen now at sixty, with *terribilita*-lined Moby Dick brow in contrast with a sensual fish mouth, which possibly provokes Corso's characterization of him as guppy, has a face slightly skewed by Bell's palsy from right eye droop to mouth twist above his beard, as if distorted by a perceptive Impressionist painter to capture the interaction of poet-crazy and rabbinic moralist.

"Before us was the Bohemians," says Corso, in many ways Bodenheim's successor. "Now you know what the Bohemians did. Mr. Bodenheim would go around and sell a redundancy of a poem for fifty cents to buy a drink. He didn't join Ben Hecht or any of those assholes to whatyacall go to Hollywood and play the game," says Corso.

"No, you know why?"

"Why?" asks Corso.

"He was drinking and he took a pee in the National Academy of Arts and Letters meeting, and they kicked him out of the National Academy. My father told me because my father and mother were there. He pissed on the floor of the National Academy. Just like you," says Ginsberg laughing.

"Fuck them, man," says Corso.

"And so they drummed him out. We nominated a whole bunch of people and you know what happened? We nominated Robert Duncan, Robert Creeley, Gary Snyder, and Kenneth Koch and maybe somebody else, I forget. Not one of them made it, instead Russell Baker, E. L. Doctorow, William Gaddis—all right—Donald Justice, Charles Rosen, Paul Theroux, Lewis Thomas. Isn't that incredible?"

"I'm just happy Koch didn't make it," says Corso. "I'm happy he didn't make it because he wanted to make it. I'm happy the motherfucker didn't make it. I'm happy about Koch. I'm not a bad man, y'know, an evil man and all that shit, but I always thought he was a little ambitious. If you believe you're a poet, you don't fuck about anything, you got it made."

"Do you think that kind of ambition is always bad?" I ask.

"I think so, because you gotta know who y'are. If you believe you're a poet, then you're saved."

In a diary entry on art in relation to suffering and hedonism, Judith Malina writes, "Do we idolize its victims and priests? Do we not idolize Maxwell Bodenheim although we are sometimes loath to talk to him and always ashamed of our condescension to him? The bartenders of the Remo have put a photograph of him over the bar.

"What we admire is Bodenheim's refusal to resist," continues Malina. "We fight all the time, resisting temptation. We admire those who don't even if it's suicidal."

In the Remo, Bodenheim is this very minute reciting one of his poems over at the bar, which he does for drinks, when he's abruptly interrupted by the cry of a seagull piercing the bar noise.

Joe Gould, Harvard 1911, small, bald, toothless, gray-bearded, frail, is standing in the middle of the room, strung over his shoulders his cardboard sandwich sign that advertises poems for sale from his "Oral History of the World," carrying a huge bundle of papers, presumably the "History" itself. Gould puts down his papers and starts flapping his arms while making sea gull noises—he can imitate sea gulls. He stops when someone buys him a beer. He stops to drink the beer. Gould says he understands the language of sea gulls and claims to have translated Longfellow into Sea Gull. For this talent he has earned the name Dr. Sea Gull.

"Gould had something called 'The Oral History of the World,'" says social historian of the hip Seymour Krim, whose writings were instrumental in demystifying the old Bohemian mystique that Gould represents. "He took down what people said, it was very interesting, uncommon speech, and he was supposed to have had thousands of pages, I think selectively but I don't know what his criteria were. He used to carry around these tattered red folders."

Actually, years later, Izzy Young, impresario of the influential Folklore Center, found Gould's handwritten notebooks. "And you know what," says Howard Smith. "They stink. You know the theory was he listened to everybody's conversation, especially at Minetta's. There was also a great portrait of him in the Kettle of Fish, a kind of caricature. Izzy found tons of notebooks. This is what they said: 'Overheard woman in next booth ordering shrimp marinara. Her boyfriend said, "Want another cigarette?" She said, "No." People in booth in front of me ordered another bottle of wine. Can't make out what they're talking about.' Izzy said you had to read about six notebooks till maybe there'd be one line anyone would have been interested in. He was obviously over the hill into heavy alcoholism by then, or older age or whatever, and these notebooks were a great myth created by the guy who wrote them up in *The New Yorker*." Though as John Tytell says, Gould's method could be considered "the original tape recorder," incorporating an important principle employed later by people like Kerouac and John Cage: "No discrimination, which is a Beat as well as a Buddhist tenet, but hard to realize because of academic conditioning."

As a neophyte, I watch Gould and Bodenheim with utter fascination. After a while, I also become familiar with the strange figure of Moondog in medieval-looking leather, blanket, and Viking horns, usually stationed in the middle of the sidewalk on Broadway or Sixth Avenue, selling sheet music. Moondog, crackpot composer and inventor of bizarre instruments such as the "oo" and the "trimbas," like the clownish Puerto Rican street poet Jorge Brandon, whom I later encounter with his talking coconut in the East Village, turns out to be a fairly interesting artist, or so say those who attend his occasional rooftop concerts. Philip Glass once let Moondog live at his place when he had nowhere to go. It's not the oddball quality of these figures that attracts me, but rather the way they throw themselves on the mercy of others, their willed destruction of pride, self-respect, and even ego itself. If you are seeking distinctions from the aggressive egoism of the fifties success cult, Gould and Boden-heim are especially instructive examples.

Both Bodenheim and Gould "were clowns in a certain way," says Krim. "I mean bitter clowns, to make a dollar."

Maybe court jester would be a more appropriate category, one that Ginsberg and Corso in their poet-crazy mode have found effective, but if Gould and Bodenheim are clowns, they are so in a lineage of underground clowns descending from Dostoyevsky's *Notes from Underground*. Decades later, talking to Ginsberg, I'll suddenly realize how important Dostoyevsky is to the Beats in their formative years, and to the underground mystique. Dos-toyevsky's original subterranean, spiteful and belligerent, is also an exhibitionist who knows how to keep you amused. You tolerate his hostility while being entertained by the spectacle of his self-humiliation. The bitter clown of *Notes* pays for his contempt with total lack of respect for himself.

I would come to understand that the flagrant self-destructiveness of the underground of Bleecker Street is an expression of its total contempt for the cautious pragmatism of the middle class. Dos-toyevsky's antihero reserves for us the right to destroy ourselves in spite of all rational arguments. His psychological self-dissection may make *Notes*, after *Tristram Shandy*, one of the first self-conscious works, as defined in Postmodern fiction to denote consiousness by the narrative voice of itself. In *Notes* the insistent nonconsciousness of the normal bourgeois world would make any kind of instrospection, or even self-awareness, seem self-conscious if not downright sick. In fact "sick" was used as a strategy by the rebellious "black humor" comedians of the fifties, like Lenny Bruce and Mort Sahl—not to mention cartoonist Jules Feiffer and his "Sick, sick, sick"—who in turn influenced a number of novelists in a modest attempt to break away from established styles. Self-awareness is against the interests of a dominant class that wants to maintain power without thinking too much about motives or consequences.

However, at the end of the forties we began to see the intellec-tual chic of Auden's "age of anxiety." It attempted to domesticate the underground mystique with the housebroken fifties version of "alienation." Alienation dignified the situation of underground man with the idea that the anguish of a heroic disaffection with the culture was necessary to produce the awareness that would ultimately validate the culture. It was a doctrine that led you to reject the mainstream only in expectation of eventually being redeemed by it as a hero.

So it would become hip to be self-consciously neurotic in the fifties in opposition to the healthy, normal louts in the gray flannel suits. The fifties was the age of breakdowns. The insanity bit had a heroic hue. There were times when you felt like an outsider by the mere fact of not being in psychoanalysis. That I avoided the shrink was not because of any virtue of my own, but rather because of not having enough money. Whatever its therapeutic benefits, psychoanalysis kept you on the straight and narrow of social conformity just so you could earn enough bread to pay for it. But in the sixties even madness would get to be transvalued by R. D. Laing via Freud heretic Wilhelm Reich, by redefining madness as a form of sanity.

Reich's orgone psychology, which insists on the integrity of the human organism no matter how maladjusted to society, was throughout the fifties influential on a long list of creative people interested in resisting that society, from Bellow to Mailer to Kerouac to performance artists and dancers like Carolee Schneemann and Ann Halprin. William Burroughs, who is dubious about Reich's therapy, defends his orgonomic cancer research quite vigorously. "The function of the orgone box, as I see it, is to raise the electrical tension at the surface of the cell and that's exactly what it seems to do. You get a tingling sensation in the surface of the skin, and I think that would be definitely anticancerous. The discovery of the electrical cell theory of cancer has been enunciated by others with no acknowledgements to Reich, although it's his discovery."

Most Reichians place credence in both the healing power of the orgone box and the effectiveness of the therapy. There was a time in the Village when practically every hip apartment or loft you walked into had a restored brick fireplace and an orgone box or "accumulator," as they're called, a metal-lined wooden closet you sit in to charge up on healing orgone energy, the basic energy of the universe. But hardcore subterraneans will never, like R. D. Laing, rationalize madness as an impulse toward a higher form of normality. Gould and Bodenheim had to know that self-destruction is self-destruction, desirable only because the burn-out it leads to is preceded by incandescence.

This attitude is sardonically illustrated by a story repeated in one of Bill Manville's "Saloon Society" columns, which appeared in the early *Village Voice*. "Say, you know that hotel I'm cooling it in? The rat manager comes in this morning, he says to me: 'Sam, that blonde on the second floor, they found her this morning. She must have been on something powerful, she was dead. She was all blue from the junk, all shriveled up.' Man, you know what I said to him? I said: 'Oh, lead me to that connection!' Imagine, Bill, how strong that junk must have been. Imagine, not *only* to die—*but to turn BLUE and to die!*"

Though I don't realize it at the time, Reich's theories are appealing to me during the McCarthy era because they provide a rationale for underground values in the absence of radical politics, and encourage the Bohemian yen for Dionysian freedom. As a recent article in *Partisan Review* puts it, "Sex, for Reich, *was* politics, and the contentious language of his manifestoes . . . made his system [sound like] a regrouping for a war of liberation against the residual Puritanism and production-oriented austerities of American life." Unsparing in its critique of the authoritarianism of revolutionary society as well as the constraints of capitalism, Reich's attack on sexual repression finally links for me the apparently opposed oppressions of dialectical materialism and shmuck materialism, between which it formerly seemed necessary to make a choice. Though the middle class, de-energized by its self-imposed suppression of biological instinct, is not really free, revolution is not necessarily liberation. Despite McCarthyism, it's possible to fight the system without being a Marxist. As a friend says, "Now you can be a rebel, if not without a cause, then without a Cause." From then on for me, and I think many others, sex becomes a weapon and dissipation a form of dissent, instead of merely a way of having fun in defiance of the work ethic. I know a guy who convinces himself that seduction is a duty, though one he manages to enjoy, neatly combining the righteousness of the work ethic with the pleasure-prone underground mystique.

In the underground, hostility toward middle-class values tends to be ambivalent. In the Village bars, this envious hostility toward the middle class—even the cultivated middle class—could be seen any weekend in its attitude toward the Uptown tourists willing to buy drinks to watch the clowns perform. People remember, for example, Terry Southern coming Downtown with a bankroll, looking. And eventually finding "the funny man," as Corso calls him, Mason Hofenberg, co-author with Southern of *Candy*. In Brossard's novel an ad-agency account exec named Russell Goodwin turns up in the bar. He lives Uptown and has a charge account at Abercrombie and Fitch. He reads *The New Yorker* regularly and thinks it's "really terrific." He listens to WQXR, the classical music station, goes to the Museum of Modern Art, and prefers French films to American movies.

"'Don't *bring us down*,'" one of the underground regulars says.

"'Oh, I get it,' Goodwin said. 'I get that one. It's a jive expression. Right?'

"'You're in,' Porter said.

"'He's a very solid citizen,' Harry said. 'He makes four hundred a week.'"

Behind the self-righteousness of the subterraneans is an assumption of superior virtue, even of a certain purity. In fact, at this time in the early fifties, I am credulous enough to credit a kind of grungy purity to the Village scene in its deliberate isolation from the world of Uptown. Before Mary McCarthy's article about the Remo in the *New York Post*, which simultaneously popularizes it and puts it down—a strategy also dear to *Time-Life*, which used it on Jackson Pollock to ridicule and vulgarize him at the same time—Broyard says the bar "hadn't even an obscene scrawl in the men's toilet." It's the tourists who come to check it out who "decorated it with the images of their disappointment." There is a kind of communality down here after all, the good side of tribalism. You don't foul your own nest, you take care of your own shit. Ginsberg has the impression that the neighborhood was familial toward Corso as a native son, but even the tough bartenders at the Remo extend credit to regulars, and the bar-toughs are tender toward exotic characters like Bodenheim after they've been around long enough.

A hood comes over to sit in our booth a while talking to Gloria. This guy is a real gorilla. He communicates in gutturals and grunts, punctuated with jabs and animated gestures. After he leaves, Gloria says he's more or less a hitter for the Mafia and she didn't understand a word either. She just keeps smiling and nodding. She says he speaks a language known to only a few intimates who live on his block in Little Italy. Later, after this guy learns to talk by associating with the subterraneans, he gives up hittering and becomes a rather well known actor.

"Let's make it over to Minetta's," says Gloria. "Maybe we can eat something if Manny's there." The MacDougal Street regulars are on a shuttle between the Remo and Minetta's a block away, seeing who's where when, and what parties are happening later in the evening.

"Why do we eat only if Manny's there?" I ask out on the street.

"He lets us charge food."

Minetta's has the same kind of clientele as the Remo, sawdust on the floor, the walls covered with caricatures, many done by Franz Kline. Joe Gould is usually stationed at the door. Manny is there. He looks a lot like a grasshopper. We order eggplant Parmesan and slather it with lots of grated cheese to make a whole meal out of it. Costs around seventy-five cents and we don't leave a tip. "Every now and then somebody comes into some money, then we tip him. He's nice."

We check out the Remo again. Gloria points out jazzman Miles David nodding in a corner. The going drugs are pot and heroin. Gloria says hello to a woman who comes on as if Black. "Junkie to the musicians," says Gloria. "Supplies a lot of people with junk. And bisexual," which is not too unusual at that point because it's a very macho scene going on down there. "But she's the only one who holds her own with everybody." Judith Malina of the Remo crowd says that Paul Goodman, her guru and analyst, and whose plays she is directing, is "of the opinion a woman couldn't be an artist." Malina also has to struggle with the problem that he wants all her boyfriends. Stanley Gould of the junk-blue eyes is around as he always is, making drug deals. "'Listen, man, this is really great charge,'" says Cap Fields quaintly in Brossard's book. "'The best.'

"'How much?'

"'An ace for two sticks.'" Cap himself is already high on the weed, talking "thick and strange" as he sits down in the bar.

In her article, which I will remember because it gets a lot of attention in the Village, Mary McCarthy puts down the Remo because, she says, its habitues Do Nothing. McCarthy's generation of Bohemians, the political intellectuals around *Partisan Review*—which in any case is Upper Bohemia—is tuned in, she says, to "the battle of ideas and standards." The "ideas and standards" her group is involved with, however, are those of Modernism, which American art is about to leave on the beach. One of the tragedies of American culture is that the political intellectuals usually haven't a clue about what cutting-edge contemporaries in the arts are up to, and care less it fits into their doctrines. In his well-known study of the avant-garde, Renato Poggioli asserts that the political intelligentsia typically focuses on subject matter rather than aesthetic considerations. In painting, this period is an exception. Clement Greensberg and Harold Rosenberg, polemicists of Abstract Expressionism, demonstrate the power, for better and for worse, that intellectuals can generate when they make contact with formal developments in the arts.

The San Remo underground, succeeding the older Bohemians, besides being a new generation, which is always difficult for the preceding wave to make out, just may have been too low for a high intellopol like McCarthy to see clearly. If she could she might have spotted, for example, Paul Goodman in the Remo, musicians John Cage, George Kleinsinger, and Miles Davis, dancer Merce Cunningham, artists William Steig and Jackson Pollock, Julian Beck and Judith Malina of the Living Theater, social activist Dorothy

Day, and writers as diverse as James Agee, Brossard, Broyard, Ginsberg, Corso, Kerouac, and many others who, it might be argued, were doing something, even if it was something Miss McCarthy wasn't aware of.

It helps me to make sense of my experience with Bohemians, and it may help you with yours, to understand that when you talk about the difference between Upper and Lower Bohemia you're talking mostly about life style. Upper Bohemians happen to have radical, or at least heterodox, ideas, but they live middle class. Or even upper middle class. Or even rich. The distinction between Upper and Lower Bohemia should not be confused with the distinction between the hardcore and softcore underground. The latter is well described in Malcolm Cowley's 1934 book about the Bohemia of the 1920's, *Exile's Return.* "'They' [the hard core] had been rebels: they wanted to change the world, be leaders in the fight for justice and art, help to create a society in which individuals could express themselves. 'We' [the soft core] were convinced at the time that society could never be changed by an effort of the will. . . . But it was fun all the same. . . . We lived in top floor tenements along the Sixth Avenue Elevated because we couldn't afford to live elsewhere. Either we thought of our real home as existing in the insubstantial world of art, or else we were simply young men on the make, the humble citizens not of Bohemia but of Grub Street."

I have often been puzzled, along with many others, by the spectacle of a former subterranean known for an unconventional or even radical way of life suddenly turning up in an ad agency, say, coming on straighter than straight. Bohemia, Upper or Lower, is for softcore subterraneans only a matter of life style. They are along for the ride. When it's no fun, or a better ride is available, having no necessary stake in the underground or anything but career, they melt into the middle-class mainstream. "We took our little portion of the easy money that seemed to be everywhere," writes Cowley, "and we thereby engaged or committed ourselves without meaning to do so. We became part of the system we were trying to evade, and it defeated us from within. . . . We laughed too much, sang too much . . . and after a few years we were, in Zelda Fitzgerald's phrase, 'lost and driven now like the rest.'" Never confuse a life style with a commitment, son, or you'll end up committed to nothing but your stock portfolio. For example, Abbie Hoffman tells me that Jerry Rubin, notorious for his switch from Yippie to Yuppie and who himself seems lost and driven now like the rest, "used to always talk about his career—this is good for his career, this is bad for his career."

"Even in the old days?" I ask.

"Yeah, he used the word 'career.' And I always used to go"— Hoffman assumes a helplessly astonished expression—"'Career?!'"

Cowley himself, after zigging to support the Moscow trials and turning away from the avant-garde to endorse a Party-line cultural nationalism in the mid-thirties, zagged to recuperate the reputation of America's greatest "experimental" writer. Faulkner, in the forties, then sold Kerouac to the publishing industry in the fifties, but only after *On the Road* had been subjected to a certain amount of censorship in the name of revision. Ginsberg says the revisions were negligible, though others disagree, but he adds that Kerouac wrote *Dharma Bums* in response to Cowley's request for something the public could understand more easily.

However, Kerouac ambiguously craved the public acclaim that Cowley made possible and that helped to destroy him. He once said that fame was "like old newspapers blowing down Bleecker Street." But in a 1957 article in *The Village Voice*, Howard Smith observes Kerouac after reading from his work at the Village Vanguard: "The applause is like a thunderstorm on a July night. He smiles and goes to sit among the wheels and the agents . . . He is prince of the hips, being accepted in the court of the rich kings . . . He must have hated himself in the morning—not for the drinks he had, but because he ate it all up the way he really never wanted to." Many subterraneans want to violate the taboos of the middle class, while simultaneously needing its indulgence, as if you could bite the hand of oppression and then expect it to feed you. With those contradictory needs, success may be as unsatisfying as failure. But there are subterraneans who see the underground as providing a permanent moral perspective on the dominant culture, as well as subterraneans who are ambivalent, or even what you might call honestly opportunistic.

Cowley's career is exemplary. Cowlies are indispensable to the underground. When Ginsberg berated Cowley for not publishing *On the Road*, Cowley reminded him he was the only editor around at least trying to do so. It is the Cowlies who always sooner or later discover the commercial value of the underground and figure out how to vend it to the middle class, either diluted by time, or in denatured imitations, or filtered through a de facto censorship. So Cowley is able to rediscover Faulkner for us, whose greatest work was done twenty years earlier, and manages to "discover" Kerouac, if in a revised version. So the underground becomes "offbeat," weird but fun, or rather, weird and fun. "There must be a new ethic that encouraged people to buy, a *consumption* ethic . . . Many of the Greenwich Village ideas proved useful in the altered situation," says Cowley of the Bohemian rebellion of the twenties in a passage that previews the commercialization of the sixties "counterculture." "Thus, *self-expression* and *paganism* encouraged a demand for all sorts of products."

It's not for me, voyeur of bars, vagabond of coffeehouses, itinerant outsider, to put down the Cowlies. When your orientation is looking in, you have to accept that your position will be outside. But when you do want in, these middlemen to the middle class are among the few connections available. And why shouldn't you want in? There's a difference between selling and selling out. So what if Cowlies are sometimes only joyriders— at least they know joy when they see it. In fact, that will be part of the appeal of subterranean life in the sixties—we're having more fun than you. Why shouldn't everybody have the chance of buying into a good thing once it's discovered? But something new will soon start happening to this familiar American dynamic of cultural opportunism. To an unprecedented degree it will become the artists themselves, in a strategy that can be traced back to the French Surrealists, who sell themselves to the middle class. Norman Mailer's *Advertisements for Myself* is an obvious case in point. And when you start selling yourself, you may stop selling your art and wind up selling your life style.

On any night in the Remo you might hear about a certain ongoing party over in Sheridan Square in the West Village. There's a kind of open-house potluck dinner in progress there, supervised by this huge Black guy, an unemployed merchant-seaman Spanish Civil War vet who watches over a gigantic communal pot of something that's been on the stove continuously for weeks. Anybody who's hungry dips in; anyone with food to contribute adds it and stirs, fish, a piece of chicken, a can of baked beans, as long as it's edible. There's also one gigantic ashtray to emphasize the collective tone, from each according to his ability, etc. The Iron Curtain has closed, Tail Gunner Joe McCarthy is gearing up, and a lot of these old lefties can't get any work other than driving cabs, moving furniture, occasional carpentry.

"This isn't the time to sell out and take a steady job anyway," says a guy in a black turtleneck, munching something nameless he's fished out of the pot. "This is the time to wait and organize while the inherent contrafuckingdictions of the system start to tear it apart." He's got me trapped in a corner. People in this kind of scene like to give me advice, maybe because I'm a kid. "You got to use your head"—he taps his and gets a surprising castanet sound. "Like I used mine in the Lincoln Brigade. That's a steel plate, kid. You think things are bad but the worse they are the closer we get to the revolution. Bad is good, kid. Use your head."

I don't say anything. What can you say to a guy like that? Stay away from magnets. These guys, stuck in a stagnant ideology, are programmed for wipeout. In a few years the big Black will be living in a rathole apartment next door to a crazed alcoholic pal on the Lower East Side where they will break down the wall between the two apartments in a drunken fit and end up with a duplex rathole. "They were like so crazy," says Gloria, "the two of them. The roommate would come around to my loft pounding on my door, screaming in the street. You know, the kind of drunk where you roar and you scream and you pick up

rocks, I mean it was crazy. And I never saw him in any other condition. Ever. He was like a killer type, it was horrible."

Soon, for me, the party melts into pleasant confusion, through
which I stray dazed by beer, cheap wine, and generally overloaded
circuits. At some point I notice a blond girl sitting, knees crossed,
on a couch across the room. I say "girl" though she must be at least
five years older than me and way ahead. She's wearing her blond
hair short and straight and is the first woman I've seen dressing in
what I later come to think of as existentialist style—black stockings,
black sweater, pallid makeup. Marilyn Duport, whom I will come
to know on and off through the years of her short life, is starlet-
pretty and Bohemian-sexy, and one of the nicest people I'll meet in
the underground scene. Poised, if not a little detached, as if skating
maybe on thin ice, on this occasion she looks like she could have
walked out of Saint-Germain-des-Pres.

In fact, a lot of American painters used to drink their *demis* in
exile at the Select and the Coupole through the fifties, Sam Francis
and Ed Clarke among them, and some Black writers, including
Richard Wright used to hang out in a café near the Luxembourg
Gardens called the Tournon. There was a kind of easygoing traffic
between Montparnasse and the Village.

I see that Marilyn is rolling a cigarette and I will later remember thinking, *Shit, that must be a reefer.* The existential pallor tends
to make girls look blank-faced, as if, I always think, they're in
shock. But when Marilyn looks up and notices me staring, her face
breaks into this warm, wide smile, so I go over and get my first
taste of marijuana. Marilyn assumes an easy camaraderie with me,
despite my age, in the spirit of the giant cooking pot on the stove.
It's us against the world of gray flannel and attaché cases, I feel, the
crumbling solidarity of the underground against the triumphant
middle class, the doomed fellowship of resistance, the poverty and
isolation of losers. The romance of it, the bitter pathos of it. In fact,
no more than fifteen years later, after the last of the several acid-in-
duced institutionalizations, Marilyn would be out of friends,
money, and places to live. One vagrant night she asked an acquaintance in Brooklyn if she could crash in her apartment. When

she was turned down Marilyn walked up to the roof and jumped. You would have to realize then that the inverse of her openness and generosity was an underlying acceptance of a darker fate, and that her archetype was Marilyn Monroe, the tragic mess of de Kooning's *Marilyn* implied under the glossy image of Warhol's.

When the only energetic collective effort around is the united front of shmuck materialism, it's easy to see that Tony Frusella is right not to stand up and blow for Charlie Barnet. It's easy to see, coming from Midwood, where everything is overstuffed—the furniture, the people, the heads of the high school kids trying to make it into Columbia, Harvard, Yale—that Bohemian self-denial is virtuous. It's easy to see, coming from the conspicuous consumption of the middle class, why romantic poverty should be worn like a badge. It's easy, too easy, to see, in face of the concerted success drive of Luce's American Century, how a career of solitary self-destruction could be a heroic course. To discover these truths in a going scene, with its own sense of prestige and its own kind of tradition, is an irresistible revelation. So what if Seymour Krim starts his underground career by sweeping out a book store, when the book store is owned by Joe Klinger, who had published one of the classic literary magazines, *Pagany*, and supposedly discovered doomed, self-victimizing, visionary *poete maudit* Hart Crane? You do not question too much the bitterness of veterans of Bohemia, like the one-eyed Klinger, while fighting off the wide-eyed optimism of post-V Day booster America. You expect to be bitter, you prefer it.

Years later, over lunch in a small café in Paris, Ted Joans and I get to talking about the habit of tough independence, the adversary stance, retained by the Abstract Expressionists even after their sudden success in the early fifties.

"That strikes me as the last generation of painters that had been really completely separated from the establishment."

"That's right, that's it," says Joans.

In fact, Abstract Expressionist Adolph Gottlieb has said that "during the forties, some artists were painting with a sense of absolute despair. . . . Things were going so badly . . . I felt free to do whatever I wanted, no matter how absurd it might seem; what was there to lose?"

"Like with the writers hitting a brick wall in the fifties," I say to Joans. "You know in 1957 when *On the Road* came out, Kerouac had already written most of his novels and none of them had been published, except his first one in 1950, which wasn't real Kerouac. There was hardly any chance to become establishment."

"All of them were like that then," says Joans, almost as if he's acting everything out with his loose body and mobile face creating in the process a persona with the name of Ted Joans, to whom he often refers in third person. "See, Pollock remained a Bohemian, too, true maverick, even with money. It bothered him that he became a celebrity. In 1951, two weeks in New York, I walked into the San Remo, which is right on the corner of Bleecker, so if you came out one door you could go out the other right onto MacDougal, so I was doing one of those things instead of just going around the corner and I saw him and I said, 'Excuse me, are you . . .?' And he said, 'Yeah, yeah, I'm Jackson Pollock. Who are you?' You know, like that. Sort of like a surly John Wayne." Joans goes into a sort of shit-kicking cowboy act. Ted's a great mimic, so that for example when he does his hilarious imitation of Gregory Corso, it's so precise that I sometimes think I'm actually looking at Corso despite the difference in complexion. Now he slips into a version of himself as naive young painter.

"'Oh, oh, my name is Ted Joans, I, I just graduated from Indiana University, I studied painting there, and this is my first time in New York and I'm going to Europe.'

"'What are you going to Europe for?'

"'Well, I'm going to advance my painting.'

"'I thought you graduated.'

"'Yeah, I . . .'

"'Well, what in shit you going to Europe for? Unless you want to learn to paint the hair in somebody's nose or asshole. What's happening is happening right here. What's happening is happening right here in this goddamn United States, especially in this city. What are you drinking?'

"'Well, I don't know, I'll have the same,' I said, which was a mistake because he was slowly drinking little glasses of gin, and then washing them down slowly with beer, let me tell you."

"Looks like all those guys were doing their best to drink one another to death. How'd you know who he was?"

"From *Life* magazine! But see, he didn't want that kind of celebrity. Those guys, see, like de Kooning still refuses it."

"That's interesting, because now, at least, everybody wants to be a celebrity."

"Well, they had that tough American maverick thing, like cowboy stars. Once you become a star like that, it's like in the Wild West, somebody's gonna come up and try to outdraw you."

"Or outpaint you."

Around the Village, after the myth of collectivism had shattered and the cult of heroic individualism had grown, of necessity, out of the social rejection of the great Black jazzmen, the isolation of the early Abstract Expressionists, and a disillusion with grand social movements, I sometimes thought of the big pot. In an ambiance so fragmented that the so-called Abstract Expressionists vehemently rejected any common label and people had a hard time agreeing on common interests, much less the common good, the Spanish Civil War vet's big, communal pot seemed a lot more appetizing than it once had.

—1987

Edmund White

(b. 1940)

Edmund White was born in January 1940 in Cincinnati. His parents divorced when he was seven and he was raised in the Chicago area by his mother. He attended school at the prestigious Cranbrook Academy and studied at the University of Michigan before eventually moving to New York. At various times he worked for the Saturday Review *and* Horizon. *A prolific writer who is comfortable in many genres, he has written numerous novels, including* Forgetting Elena *(1972),* Nocturnes for the King of Naples *(1978), and* A Boy's Own Story *(1982). He is the author of several nonfiction titles, including* States of Desire: Travels in Gay America *and the coauthor of* The Joy of Gay Sex: An Intimate Guide for Gay Men to the Pleasures of a Gay Life. *More recently, he has written a biography of Jean Genet. White lived in Paris from 1983 to 1990. During that time many of his closest friends died of AIDS; White himself is HIV-positive. The selection from* The Beautiful Room Is Empty *culminates in the Stonewall riots of 1969 when a routine police raid of the Stonewall Inn on Sheridan Square on the night of June 28 turned into a full-scale riot. "Seeing their friends being dragged kicking and screaming into paddy wagons, the crowd in the street reacted, hurling epithets, then loose coins, then beer bottles and garbage cans," writes Village historian Terry Miller. White remains one of the finest stylists writing today, a brave and provocative voice in the literary wilderness. His most recent books are* The Flaneur: A Stroll Through the Paradoxes of Paris *and a biography of Marcel Proust for Viking's Penguin Lives series.*

Edmund White. From *The Beautiful Room Is Empty* (New York: Alfred A. Knopf, 1988).

from *The Beautiful Room Is Empty*

Sean didn't want to be gay, and waking up beside me was too much evidence for him that he was becoming homosexual. I suggested that we start therapy together and go straight together—slowly, I hoped. Through Ava I found a psychotherapist named Dale who specialized in a treatment based on the idea that everyone at all times was playing a game.

Sean and I were placed in separate groups in which all the other members were heterosexual. A group met once a week with Dale in her office, and one other evening without her in the apartment of a member. Unhappy marriages, celibacy, impotence, adultery, alcoholism, divorce, career frustration, the coldness of men and the hysteria of women, bankruptcy, friendships riddled by spite and envy—we watched the painful surfacing of all these problems. Like a team of midwives, we encouraged the birth of each memory.

What came harder was the shrink's theory that we must re-create among ourselves the hostilities that had divided but perpetuated our families. Listening to each other's stories was no problem; that called on the familiar American skills of shocking confession and compassionate audition. But it was trickier to point a finger at a fellow member, a housewife from Scarsdale, and shout, "You're trying to guilt-trip us by playing Poor Me."

We usually sought the origins of our pain in the unresolved conflicts of childhood. Those of us who had bad memories had to keep rereading the same old tea leaves. I was let off lightly. Since I was a homosexual, everyone knew what caused my disease (absent father and overprotective mother), so no one poked about for further explanations.

My only enemy was Simon, a recent Russian immigrant in his sixties. He'd entered therapy to convince his wife that he was making an effort to curb his rages, but he still beat her regularly. He'd even knocked out a tooth. As a Russian, Simon wasn't used to the American way of coddling people. He hated our welfare system, detested out-of-work blacks and thought they should all be sent back to Africa. He thought sexual perversion should be punished by castration or lobotomy, but he was convinced by the other group members that I was making an honest effort to go straight. In his mind the cure was simple. I should go out with girls, buy them candy, strike them, no doubt, finally marry them. Whenever I started spinning my analytic gossamer, he'd say, "But wot about de goils? I wanna hear about de goils."

I embraced Dale's system with passion and rigor. I thought about the games people play not only during sessions but also at work. In my own modest way, I even set up shop as a therapist for a few of my fellow employees. We were all so idle—and so frustrated from the company's duplication (or negation) of our efforts—that we had the time and spleen conducive to auto-analysis.

In therapy I became so expert in spotting covert games that Dale herself would sometimes ask me for my opinion. Once in a great while someone would notice that I had said nothing about myself for ages, but I was too valuable an ally to alienate. In my mind I was earning chips I'd be able to cash in one wonderful day when I would need everyone's attention and sympathy.

One night over supper with Maria I yawned and said, "Of course Maeve was just playing Yes, But."

"What do you mean?" Maria asked.

"That's one of the games people play," and I went on to explain it with majestic confidence.

Maria put her knife and fork down and grew silent. Without raising her eyes she said, "When I met you, you had one of the sharpest, most open, most skeptical minds I'd ever encountered. Now you've become the dullest sort of bigot. You see absolutely every last thing through those ridiculous therapeutic glasses. You're as smug as a Catholic convert or an American Marxist without enjoying the intellectual range and depth of either system."

"Why do you find my therapy so threatening, Maria?" I asked, already trying to label the game she was playing.

"You're my best friend, Dumpling, but I don't think I can continue this friendship if you don't change. I can't bear to see the wreck you've made of your mind. It's all because you can't accept being gay, which isn't such a big deal. You're still white, a man, handsome, charming, from a well-to-do family, intelligent—everything's been handed to you, but you—"

Keep collecting injustices, I thought, naming one of the games members sometimes played.

Maria's case interested me. I noticed how she was slowly giving up her pro-Russian stand in favor of feminism. Women's rights. I asked her what earthly rights women lacked. They could already vote, divorce, work. Maria became so angry with me that she had to swallow an extra high-blood-pressure pill. Her voice shaking, she told me how women earned half of what men made for the same work but how they were usually refused the better jobs. "The woman problem is a poverty problem," she said. "You joke around about whether to say *Miss* or *Ms.*, but the real issue is poverty. Most of the poor families in America are headed by single women, usually black."

We ordered brandies. She said, "Do you remember how we used to smile at Buddy and Betts, those two old dykes at Solitaire? We used to think it was so amusing the way Betts played the *malade imaginaire*. I just got a letter from the colony director telling me that Bett's malady was hunger. The poor old things didn't have any money, and Buddy got too old to be the sheriff. They never did have much money. Then Buddy started drinking. Last winter they both froze to death." Maria's eyes filled with tears. "Those lovable old eccentrics were starving. The real woman question is poverty."

When I'd first met Maria, she'd held in contempt everything she was—middle-class, American, artistic—in favor of a remote ideal, a Soviet Union we knew next to nothing about except that it stood for principles we considered progressive: respect for labor, division of wealth, equal opportunity for women, atheism, science. In recent years, however, we'd read more and more accounts about Russia that had disillusioned and finally appalled us.

Simultaneously, Maria had become aware that women were oppressed in every country regardless of national policies or economics. She became angry with me when I suggested that her own lesbianism made her especially sensitive to women's indignities. "Why do you have to search for a personal reason for political convictions that can be established through rational arguments? It's so demeaning."

Maria's feminism may have been objective, as she insisted, but nevertheless it provided subjective benefits to her. Because she was now defending what she was, a woman, her politics elicited pride not guilt, affirmation not chagrin. She began to paint again. Art was no longer a badge of privilege, but a quiet, deft way of making things, as one might make a new window box. She painted, listening to *Der Rosenkavalier*, as she had that first day I'd ever seen her, so many years ago, waltzing around her studio at the Eton art academy, her eyes closed.

By chance I knew a young woman who was in Sean's group. I badgered her to break the rule of secrecy and tell me what he was saying about me. She and I were seated in a cozy, dirty booth in a coffee shop on upper Broadway.

"But he's really sick," she said. "He paces up and down and talks about feeling flames along his arms—'bizarre somatic delusions' is what Dale calls them. He tries so hard to detect a heterosexual urge in himself he even pretends he's getting excited over Dale, who could be his mother and has ankles thicker than his waist."

"I know it's going to hurt," I said, "but what does he say about me?"

"He's never even mentioned you." She was polite enough to add, rather feebly, "That's the sickest thing of all."

Under pressure from the group to date girls, Sean told me the sexual part of our relationship was over. He looked so pitiful, so *flayed*, that I didn't object. I thought that a real person in my position would have said, "Fuck you. So long," and walked out for good. But I felt sorry for Sean. The report of his behavior in group made me fear he was far more disturbed than I'd imagined.

I also felt sorry for myself. I had stopped my compulsive toilet cruising since I'd met Sean. His sexual acceptance of me, paradoxically, had given me the courage to seduce other young men and take them home. In our mythology, a proper trick was more respectable than a tearoom quickie. A trick committed enough of his time to you to come home with you, mount your stairs, mount you, expose all his body, not just his penis, share a cigarette, and go through the usually empty but respectful ceremony of exchanging phone numbers.

If Sean left me, I'd be consigned back to the toilets, to my grubby, sleepwalking, streetwalking life. Since he'd been the first break in my bad luck, I assumed he'd be the last.

When we were together, I thought of nothing but strategy. I refused to give Sean reassurances, hoping he'd come back to me pleading for them.

But what I hadn't taken into account was how small a part I played in Sean's life. If he thought of me at all, he must have seen me as a nice guy though sometimes a pain in the ass, always coming on. But he was contemplating the flames dancing on his flesh, flashing on his money worries and school, brooding about going straight. He grew thinner and thinner, and Dale had to feed him with a spoon during their sessions, which had become daily, or he wouldn't eat at all.

Then she put him in St. Vincent's, in the psycho ward. He ran up and down the halls, knocking down nurses and patients, and had to be heavily medicated and put into restraints. He cried when he wasn't sleeping. Dale turned his case over to a doctor on the ward, who promptly went on vacation.

Lou, an old hand at being in bughouses, visited Sean with me. "Listen, Sean, you've got to talk to anyone and everyone around the clock," he said. "Start your own group therapy in the TV room. Psychoanalyze your roommate. Talk the psych-grad student's ear off. That's the only way to get well and get out. There's a bed shortage and it's costing the city money; they don't want you in here a second longer than necessary. There's no conspiracy."

"Is that right?" Sean asked tonelessly, his lips cracked from the dehydrating sedatives.

I cried in group, but Simon froze my tears by asking, "What about de goils?"

Eventually Sean, bloated from suffering and pills and completely silent, was shipped home to his parents in the Midwest.

I wondered how much I'd been responsible for his breakdown. The worst thing had been my inability to remember that he was weak. For an instant I would grasp he was fragile, but a second later I'd resent his intransigence, his casting me back out into the darkness.

I missed Sean so much I started to fester with it. I'd lie in bed and cry *it* and turn in *it* until I'd soiled myself with *it*. Everything, feebly, spoke *it*, even the neighbor's laundry palpitating shadows on my blinds. "Woke up this morning, blues around the bed. Sat down to eat, blues in my bread," said the song, and I sang it. I'd played a game, pretending to fall in love, but now the game had tricked me; I was caught.

I started hyperventilating, although it felt as though I was getting too little air, not too much. Pins and needles started in my hands and feet and spread upward. If the numbness reached my heart, I thought, I would die. I carried a brown paper bag and breathed into it on the subway as a way of cutting down on the amount of oxygen. My hands would jerk and fly around all on their own, and if I was in public I'd cover by pretending to pat my hair.

When the weather became warm, I lay on a towel in the park in hopes of getting a tan. I basted myself in suffering. If Sean had stopped loving me, I was unlovable. My memory would wander back to his apartment, to the blue gas jets by which he'd showered, to the salad we'd eaten out of a saucepan, to our mortally young faces in the candlelit mirror—but then I'd slap myself awake as you must treat someone who's swallowed too many sedatives.

In the park on my towel I searched for something to like. If I could find one thing in the whole world to like, I could start again. I saw a cop on a horse riding toward me and I thought, looking up at his centaur, admiring the shiny flanks and gleaming leather boots, hearing now the creak of the tack, here's something beautiful, something I can like. The cop rode up, looked down and said, "Get your shirt on, this isn't a beach. You're breaking the law."

Sean wrote me twice. Flat notes, and each sentence I saw as a safe compromise between several dangerous ways of saying things. The joke was that the great love of my life was a man who knew nothing about me and next to nothing about himself.

Suffering does make us more sensitive until it crushes us completely. I started to write about Sean, and the writing, like a searchlight sweeping wildly, almost caught my fugitive feelings. A close call, but another failure, for I was so afraid of being sentimental or self-indulgent, of not distancing myself through the appropriate irony and understatement and objectivity, that I wrote about myself in the third person. I invented a stand-in for myself but with ten points less intelligence. Yet how could I like myself or ask the reader to take seriously a love between two men? A plea for tolerance was the best I might have come up with, but I was too proud to plead for anything.

On early summer nights in the city I drifted down Christopher Street to a new dance place, the Stonewall, which had the hottest jukebox. The clientele was a bit tacky, all those black and brown boys and drags who'd attracted me at Riis Park, but they were the best dancers, the sharpest dressers, the most generous lovers. Many of my old friends didn't interest me much because they wouldn't let me talk about Sean anymore. Only Maria and Lou indulged me.

For me, the Stonewall was a place where I could watch people in the inner, darker room, sit along the wall and feel at once alone and comforted. I liked to watch a giant black man who'd twirl and slice the air dangerously with his outflung arms and pointed toes, a flailing death machine of a ballerina. I was so glad I'd bothered to acquire a nice body, since it gave me something to offer every night to a different man—the graying high-school principal, the Puerto Rican hairburner, the death machine. I went to bed with anyone who wanted me.

One night I talked with a woman who explained to me she'd had her sex changed. "My husband doesn't even suspect I was once a guy. We live in a huge housing development. We even have our own shopping center, can you believe. One day at the mall I saw another post-op also passing. She's never told her old man either. Anyway, we're best girlfriends, we watch the soaps together. But sometimes I get lonely for gay guys. You gay guys know how to have fun."

A man I'd met at a bar invited me to the house he'd rented in Cherry Grove on Fire Island. The house had a name, "The Wicked Witch's Ding-Dong," and the instant we arrived my host put on a silk caftan and mixed cocktails in the blender out of créme de menthe and milk. He made a cognac icebox pie with a graham cracker crust and started his famous key lime chicken basted in rum, but then he began to drink those cocktails with the neighbors, Bill and "Dot." We all sat on the small front porch, while the others evaluated each passing number. "She buys her polka-dot schmattes at F.A.O. Schwarz." "That one told me she's got an inner beauty, but she could die with the secret." "Here's Edwina—she lost her husband to that slut over on Tuns," naming a boardwalk in the next community, the far classier Pines, where most of the renters were still heterosexuals.

On and on they went, dishing every passerby. My host, drunk and belligerent by now, told me that the usual thing was for a guest to bring a quart of J&B scotch for the weekend. Shamefaced, I scuttled down to the liquor store and rushed back the requisite tribute.

The burned chicken was served at midnight, but we were all too smashed to do anything except toy with the cinders. We went dancing at the disco, where by local law every group of men had to include at least one woman. At last I escaped to the Meat Rack, that stretch of scrub pines and sassafras bushes that lay between the ocean and the bay.

I was so sad about losing Sean that I felt my life was over. In the mirror, we'd looked into our reflections as though we were contemplating an allegory whose symbolism had been lost but that was still replete with meaning, a serenade on the grass that may

562

speak of sacred and profane love or of the Platonic love of wisdom or of Meleager's love of Atalanta—but love in any case, some strong form of love.

In the dunes I felt sacralized. If as a child I'd known my whole long life was going to be so painful, I'd never have consented to go on leading it. At each step I had looked forward to more freedom. Paul had told me someday that I'd have too much freedom, and he was right. At least, I had too much free time. I had wanted to have fun with other gay men and to make my own money. Now I'd done that and I'd made my body beautiful, or so people told me; but I loved Sean and he wasn't even part of my life anymore. My suffering had humbled me, and his had extracted something vital out of me. I worked out every evening at the gym, wishing I could start a conversation with another man, but I lacked the confidence or necessary hope. I snatched up every issue of the *Post*, which was running a series on love, on how to give it and receive it, and I read every word.

Sean seemed like a sickness I'd contracted, a sickness such as malaria that you never get over and that gives you a spell of chills during the least expected moments. Because I had always doubted the authenticity of my feelings, I was shocked at the virulence of my love. Now I could only wander around the world, charismatic with suffering, handing myself over to whoever would have me, just as a Buddhist monk must eat whatever is placed in his begging bowl, even if it is meat, even poisoned meat (the very dish that had killed the Buddha). In the pines under the moon, listening to the surf—which was invisible, since it was on the other side of the dunes, crashing slowly and voluminously—I felt the shock of each wave in the ground under my moccasins and moved, a mendicant, eating whatever was given me. I ate all the men and didn't mind or even really notice. I cried while I sucked one cock because it was bent to one side, just as Sean's had been.

I came back to the city and my sad serenity vanished. At night, I'd be about to drift off to sleep when I'd sit straight up, gasping for air. The magazine I worked for published an editorial on homosexuality for no particular reason. It denounced the "chic new trend toward treating homosexuality as though it were a *different* way rather than a *lesser* way." The essay deplored homosexuals' "glibly self-justifying references to the ancients." It actually said, "We must blush for fifth-century Athens." In conclusion, the essay read: "Let's face the sour music: homosexuality is not a sophisticated or naughty aberration but a pathetic malady. We must make certain that in this era of drugs, free sex, and sloppy liberal rhetoric the Homintern, that conspiracy of bitter inverts who already have a stranglehold over the theater, fashion, and fiction, does not pervert the lives of decent people by glamorizing vice, neutering the female body, and making the fine old art of being a mature man or woman look dull—or as *they* would say, campy."

When I cried in group therapy about Sean, about the helplessness I felt now, Simon said, "I wanna hear about de goils."

A rage I couldn't control boiled up inside me. The other men in the group had to pull me off Simon. I knocked his chair over and was sitting on him, choking him with both hands and shouting, over and over, "Don't you *ever*, don't you *ever*—" but I didn't know how to finish the sentence.

I'd always regarded my sister as the norm. She had managed to marry, have children, settle in the suburbs and lead a respectable life. I saw her only occasionally when I was home for the holidays, and then she'd shyly press her three children forward. One Christmas Eve she and I stayed awake all night trying to sort out the parts of a tricycle to be assembled according to instructions written in English by a Japanese. I never talked to her about my real feelings or my real life, but I assumed I knew everything about hers.

Then she announced that she wanted to visit me in New York. She'd be coming without her husband but with the neighbor lady, Peg. Since by now I was making a decent living, I bought a new sofa bed for them.

My sister was in love with Peg. Awkward, bespectacled, ashamed, my sister gazed at the handsome Peg with adoration and recounted to me by the hour the sad saga of Peg's life (brutal parents, elderly husband, delinquent children, unfulfilled artistic ambitions). It was obvious to me that Peg didn't love my sister but enjoyed all the attention, something her husband wasn't providing.

The two women never stopped drinking. First thing in the morning they'd stir up a batch of bloody marys, declaring that they were on vacation and determined to whoop it up. I discovered that my sister no longer thought I was a weirdo but someone who'd had the courage to lead a free life. She seemed strangely gratified that I found Peg beautiful—my sister apparently was as obsessed with physical beauty as I. I think she also was hoping that somehow, mysteriously, things would work out between Peg and her in my presence.

I was shocked. I called Maria and said, "I had closed the books on my sister. She was the mother of three and the PTA member. Do you think she's really a lesbian? Or is she just copying me?"

Maria laughed. "Didn't you tell me she was always getting crushes on other girls? She never dated men and she married the first guy who asked her."

My sister and Maria spent a long boozy evening in New York together after Peg flew home early. "Your sister is a riot," Maria responded. "She is so extraordinarily frank—frank to the point of shocking even jaded old me. But she has no sense whatsoever of her rights as a woman. She's terribly confused. She says the worst things about herself, thinking she's being honest. She hates her husband, she never stops drinking and she's absolutely desperate about Peg, but funny at the same time. It sounds like the suburbs are a lesbian hotbed. Tomorrow night we're going to a dyke bar; your sister has already bought boots and trousers."

Another night my sister made me accompany her to a black-and-tan lesbian dance place where a lesbian band was playing. There we were, me in a coat and tie, she in her suburban pleated gray skirt and shoulder-strap bag (we'd been to the theater), trying to get past the bouncer, although we looked like a provincial husband and wife who'd strayed to the wrong door. "But we're gay!" we kept protesting, laughing. "We look square but we're a hundred percent gay." Then I added, "This is my sister and she's trying to come out and she's afraid to come in here alone." That did the trick.

I'd never felt so close to my sister before. I was no longer the younger brother but the older mentor, despite my misgivings. We sat in a corner, studied the dancers, and, hypnotized, watched a standing woman comb her seated girlfriend's hair with an Afro pick, slowly, hair by hair. The face was as rigid as a Benin bronze and the hair was caught in a lavender and gold crosslight. I asked my sister how she could give up the security of marriage.

"There's nothing secure about suffering," she said. "Dick is frustrated and wounded. He wants to have sex all the time; I never knew people could be so horny, and I can't bear for him to touch me. I sit near the window for hours hoping to catch a glimpse of Peg. I invent excuses for going over there. I'm sort of the ringleader for the whole neighborhood, all the women admire me; but I create activities just to involve Peg and have another excuse for being with her. The kids—I love the kids, but they make me nervous, and I suppose I sometimes snap at them because I think that without them I could leave Dick."

I feared my sister would suffer for years to come. Although her coming out meant that I'd lost my sole hostage to normality, at the same time her homosexuality exonerated me. There was something—genetic or psychological—in our family that had made us both gay. I asked her if she'd told our father. I wanted her to share my culpability in his eyes. But she wept and pleaded with me not to give her away. I understood that just as I was married to our mother, she was married to our father.

Maria would stop off in Chicago now to see my mother and sister on her way home to Iowa. When I was growing up, my mother had had a horror of evenings out with the girls and had frequently said, with a smile, "I like *men*." But now, without ever renouncing that theoretical preference, she grew closer and closer to Maria. And my sister, bewildered by the tough lesbian world she saw at the bars (she and Maria went back to the Volley Ball in Chicago), found in Maria someone she could emulate.

I did not travel.

I didn't experience the melancholy of tramp steamers or of mornings waking up cold in tents.

I stayed on in New York.

I went out a lot and I had new adventures, but I never forgot Sean. At last he wrote me that he'd found a lumberjack for a lover and they'd opened a dude ranch in Arizona. He said I'd been "too gay" for him. I lived too much in the "ghetto." But I hadn't caused his breakdown. His suffering had been due to money pressures, intellectual self-doubt, and the "usual" coming-out anxieties. What he liked about his lumberjack, he said, was that no one would ever guess he was gay, not in a million years.

A million years passed.

Lou called me one day. "Wanna turn a trick? I've got a double for us. Two johns from Akron in a midtown hotel room."

He gave me the address and I joined him.

Lou had been sober for the last few months. Ava had left him, not because of the boys, but because of the drugs and booze. He'd passed out in the corridor of his building. Neighbors (he didn't know which) had dragged him into his apartment and left an Alcoholics Anonymous leaflet on his chest. He joined that day. His sponsor in A.A., an eighty-year-old crime novelist, told him that she thought shrinks were for shit. She said it was obvious to her that despite whatever psychological problems might have triggered his drinking (such as growing up in a totally alcoholic family), the disease was now self-perpetuating and created the problems it pretended to solve. When Lou told her that he was afraid sobriety would make him a square, she suggested he add a new vice to his life, one irrelevant to drink, but totally unacceptable.

Lou had turned to prostitution. Although he was now earning over a hundred thousand dollars a year in advertising and was in his late thirties, he could still look like a dumb teenage drifter. After a full day of pitching a campaign, he'd change into a T-shirt and jeans right out of the dryer and a corny cowboy hat of the sort never seen west of Jersey. Then he'd stand, skinny and forlorn on Third Avenue and Fifty-First, and be picked up by married men in cars.

I met him at the hotel just off Times Square. Our customers were already drunk and playing a tape of Beethoven's Fifth they'd doctored with trippy insertions of Joni Mitchell's talkative ballads. Lou and I knew who Joni Mitchell was, but we pretended we'd never heard of Beethoven. Our clients winked at each other over our heads.

I had to put on a leather harness, stick a swan feather up my john's ass, and call him "Pretty Peacock" as he strutted proudly about, cocking his head from side to side like a bird while wanking off in an all-too-human way. Fifty bucks for me and seventy for Lou who, after all, had organized the party.

Afterward Lou and I drifted down toward the Village. We didn't despise our johns. In fact, I was flattered that I'd been able to sell it at my advanced age (I was twenty-nine). I felt for now at last as though I were one of those tough guys I'd admired at Riis Park and here at the Stonewall.

The night was hot. We gay guys had taken over all of Christopher Street; even the shops were gay. Although the bars were owned by the Mafia, we somehow thought of them as ours. Just as this street, this one street in a city of ten thousand streets, felt like ours.

Of course, stories of police violence still circulated.

In the Stonewall the dance floor had been taken over by Latins. I had a friend, Hector Ramirez, a kindergarten teacher who, because he lived with his parents in the Bronx, borrowed my apartment every afternoon after school to rehearse new dance steps with another Latin twenty-two-year-old, similarly mustached and dressed in carefully ironed beige cotton shirts over guinea T-shirts and highwaisted pleated pants held up by a thin black crocodile belt. They were here tonight, twirling out of a tight clench, hips on small pistons, faces illegibly cool. Another friend, the death machine, came up to me and rested his size-twelve black hands on my shoulders and stared into my eyes with a mad gleam: ". . . is dead."

"Who?" I shouted over the music.

"Judy. Judy Garland."

Then the music went off, and the bar was full of cops, the bright lights came on, and were all ordered out onto the street, everyone except the police working there. I suppose the police expected us to run away into the night, as we'd always done before, but we stood across the street on the sidewalk of the small triangular park. Inside the metal palisades rose the dignified, smaller-than-lifesize statue of the Civil War officer General Sheridan.

Our group drew a still larger crowd. The cops hustled half of the bartenders into a squad car and drove off, leaving several policemen behind, barricaded inside the Stonewall with the remaining staff. Everyone booed the cops, just as though they were committing a shameful act. We kept exchanging peripheral glances, excited and afraid. I had an urge to be responsible and disperse the crowd peacefully, send everyone home. After all, what were we protesting? Our right to our "pathetic malady"?

But in spite of myself a wild exhilaration swept over me, the gleeful counterpart to the rage that had made me choke Simon. Lou was already helping several black men pull up a parking meter. They twisted it until the metal pipe snapped. By accident, the dial cracked open and dimes scattered over the pavement. Everyone laughed and swooped down to snatch up the largesse; the piñata had been struck open at this growing party. Two white, middle-class men in Lacoste shirts came up to me shaking their heads in disapproval. "This could set our cause back for decades," one of them said. "I'm not against demonstrations, but peaceful ones by responsible people in coats and ties, not these trashy violent drag queens."

I nodded in sober, sorrowing agreement. But a moment later I pushed closer to see what Lou was doing. Someone beside me called out, "Gay is good," in imitation of the new slogan, "Black is beautiful," and we all laughed and pressed closer toward the door. The traffic on Christopher Street had come to a standstill.

Lou, a black grease mark on his T-shirt, was standing beside me, holding my hand, chanting, "Gay is good." We were all chanting it, knowing how ridiculous we were being in this parody of a real demonstration but feeling giddily confident anyway. Now someone said, "We're the Pink Panthers," and that made us laugh again. Then I caught myself foolishly imagining that gays might someday constitute a community rather than a diagnosis.

"This could be the first funny revolution," Lou said. "Aren't these guys great, Bunny? Lily Law should never have messed with us on the day *Judy* died. Look, they've turned the parking meter into a battering ram."

The double wooden doors to the Stonewall cracked open. I could hear the cops inside shouting over their walkie-talkies. One of them stepped out with a raised hand to calm the crowd, but everyone booed him and started shoving and he retreated back into Fort Disco.

The city trash cans were overflowing with paper cups, greasy napkins, discarded newspapers. A new group of gays rushed up, emptied a can into the splintered-open doorway, doused it with lighter fluid, and lit it. A cloud of black smoke billowed up. "They've gone too far," I said.

A black maria came around the corner of Seventh Avenue and up Christopher the wrong way. The cops cleared the sidewalk, formed a cordon, and rushed the remaining bartenders into the van past the smoldering garbage, but the crowd booed even louder. Once the van had driven off, the cops pushed us slowly back from the bar entrance.

Down the street, some of our men turned over a parked Volkswagen. The cops rushed down to it while behind them another car was overturned. Its windows shattered and fell out. Now everyone was singing the civil rights song, "We Shall Overcome."

The riot squad was called in. It marched like a Roman army behind shields down Christopher from the women's prison, which was loud with catcalls and the clatter of metal drinking cups against steel bars. The squad, clubs flying, drove the gay men down Christopher, but everyone doubled back through Gay Street and emerged behind the squad in a chorus line, dancing the can-can. "Yoo-hoo, yoo-hoo," they called.

Lou and I stayed out all night, whooping like kids, huddling in groups to plan tomorrow's strategy, heckling the army of cops who were closing off all of Sheridan Square as a riot zone and refusing to let cars or pedestrians pass through it.

I stayed over at Lou's. We hugged each other in bed like brothers, but we were too excited to sleep. We rushed down to buy the morning papers to see how the Stonewall Uprising had been described. "It's really our Bastille Day," Lou said. But we couldn't find a single mention in the press of the turning point in our lives.

—1988

Harold Norse

(b. 1916)

*Born in New York, Norse received his B.A. from Brooklyn College in
1938 and his M.A. from New York University in 1951. William Carlos
Williams called him the best poet of his generation. Among his works
include* Hotel Nirvana: Selected Poems *(1974), for which he was
nominated for a National Book Award. During the early 1960s Norse
lived in the infamous "Beat Hotel" in Paris, with William S. Burroughs, Allen Ginsberg, and Gregory Corso. There he wrote the experimental novel of the same name. Among his poetry collections are*
The Undersea Mountain, Karma Circuit, Selected Poems: Penguin Modern Poets 13, *and* Hotel Nirvana, *and* Love Poems.
Memoirs of a Bastard Angel *(1989) discusses his friendships with
W. H. Auden, Christopher Isherwood, e. e. cummings, Ned Rorem,
John Cage, Tennessee Williams, William Carlos Williams, and Dylan
Thomas, among many others. The first selection describes Norse's first
encounter with James Baldwin, who would become a close friend; the
second recalls the prophetic meeting with a virginal Allen Ginsberg
on the New York subway. In the prologue to the book he describes
Greenwich Village in the 1940s and 1950s as "loosely radical, nonconformist, and art oriented, . . . an oasis of liberation to which, from all
over America, young men and women flocked to express their socially
unacceptable life-styles."*

Harold Norse. "Greenwich Village" and "Allen Ginsberg" from *Memoirs of a Bastard Angel* (New York: William Morrow and Co., 1989).

"Greenwich Village"

from *Memoirs of a Bastard Angel*

One day a friend called Johnny Talayco brought me to a slum of decaying tenements on the Lower East Side, on First Avenue and Eleventh Street. Through a rusted iron gate we entered a courtyard of wash-laden clotheslines and reeking, overflowing garbage cans; it was known as Paradise Alley. In a cold-water flat with a grimy skylight lived a young man called Harry Herschkowitz. Scotch-taped on the walls were original watercolors by Henry Miller and pages of the outline for Harry's novel, *Alfred's Younger Brother*. Tall, emaciated, with a heroic, handsome head of curly brown hair, Harry was the stereotypic bohemian. He was the protégé of Henry Miller, had traveled many times around the globe as a merchant marine, and had endless, fascinating tales to unfold about the Persian Gulf and the Shatt al-Arab. With a single published story in *Circle* magazine, called "The Bulbul Birds" (Miller, Anais Nin, and Lawrence Durrell had also appeared in the first issue), Harry had gained legendary status. Three poems of mine had also appeared and caught the eye of Miller and Nin.

Harry had published the first issue of a magazine called *Death*. Hearing that he needed a poetry editor, I volunteered, and having admired my poems in *Circle*, he said, "You're on." All he knew about poetry, he said, he had learned in bed from women poets. "I introduced Miller to Lepska, my old lady, and they got married, which relieved us both, ha ha. I can't be tied to one woman. I want to fuck them all."

Miller and Harry flaunted their machismo, their lack of formal education, their domination of women, whom they treated with arrogant contempt. Harry repeated Henry's remark: "If you can't fuck it, eat it. If you can't eat it, piss on it." Sensitive guys. Though

I'd had few sexual relations with the opposite sex (mostly prosti-tutes), I would soon have an affair with a woman.

I never had a chance to exercise my editorial skill—*Death* died with its first issue, although *Life* almost revived it with an article; Harry's face also appeared on the cover of *Newsweek*: as spokesman for a strike of the Maritime workers. He had a natural gift for pub-licity. A decade later *Death* became reincarnated in Allen Ginsberg's *Howl*—"who ate fire in paint hotels or drank turpentine in Paradise Alley, death"—surely a reference to the magazine, although the footnote in Ginsberg's *Collected Poems* (Harper & Row, 1984) men-tions only "PARADISE ALLEY: A slum courtyard N.Y. Lower East Side, site of Kerouac's *Subterraneans*, 1958." It would come as a sur-prise if Kerouac had *not* beeen drawn by the magnetic madness of Harry, for we all drank at the San Remo, where Kerouac and I traded drunken insults and perhaps they traded women. Harry was a Jewish Neal Cassidy [sic], also born and reared in Denver. The works of Dostoevski, Miller, Nin, Michael Fraenkel, and Niet-zche (from whom Fraenkel had derived many ideas) cluttered the orange crates that served as bookshelves. But Harry had set too high a goal. Overwhelmed by too many concepts, he talked much and wrote little.

We'd meet around the fountain in Washington Square, where he knew everybody. One day he introduced me to a slender young man with a small boy in tow. "This is Bob De Niro, a talented painter," said Harry, "and his son Bobby." The boy, around four or so, jumped in and out of the watery basin making a mess. An Irish-Italian, Bob was separated from his wife, Virginia Admiral, also a painter. Broke like the rest of us, how he managed to bring up the boy I don't know. He was dreamy and bland. The other day I saw a full-page 1947 photo in *Vanity Fair* of Bob and Bobby in his lap seething with cherubic energy, just as I remember them, Bob with his wavy blond hair, handsome, languid, and wistful. The cover story, of course, was on the young De Niro, a famous film star.

Another painter I met at the fountain through Harry I had read about in Miller's monograph *The Amazing and Invariable Beauford*

Delaney. Short, stocky, bald, a middle-aged black man with the face of a shaman and air of being in touch with unconscious forces, Beauford stared as if I were a talisman or painting, never removing his large sad eyes from mine, making slow, elaborate gestures as he spoke, showing his palms as if smoothing a canvas. Beauford, said Harry, was wise and kind. Years later, after many attempts, he finally succeeded in committing suicide in Paris.

Then, one long winter night in January 1943, which began at the San Remo and ended near dawn in Bickford's Cafeteria on Fourteenth Street, I met someone who would become a very special friend. As we left the cafeteria in the fog and bitter cold, a small black youth loped swiftly toward us through the mist, a woolen navy watch cap pulled down around his ears, his wild eyes bugging out alarmingly, giving him the crazed look of a junkie about to kill for a fix. Wearing only a torn blue sweater over a thin shirt, he was shivering. He looked as if he'd gladly cut our throats for a quarter. To my surprise Harry greeted him warmly.

"Jimmy! How the hell are ya? I thought you were a mugger!"

"I was worried myself," said Jimmy with a radiant smile. "Two white men skulking in the mist in the early hours can only mean trouble for a defenseless black boy." We laughed.

"Jimmy, I want you to meet a friend of mine, a poet," said Harry. "Jimmy Baldwin meet Harold Norse."

We smiled and nodded, stamped out feet, blew into our frozen hands, and rubbed them together. "Have you been published?" Jimmy asked with interest. I had—in *Poetry, Accent,* and *Circle.* He was impressed. In those days it was hard to break into print.

"You look very young," he said archly, "no more than twenty."

"Twenty-six," I said.

He stared in fascination. "You look absurdly young," he repeated wistfully. He was nineteen. With his half-starved, gaunt face he looked much older—in the misty light of the cafeteria window his brown parchment skin reflected a silvery glow like an ancient African mask. It was impossible to imagine that in ten years this starved, threadbare black ragamuffin would become a major

575

spokesman for the civil rights movement and that his fiery essays and novels would help change the world.

Deciding on more hot coffee, we returned to the deserted cafeteria, where we talked and smoked till dawn. Jimmy had a concise, accurate way of putting things, with a rapid delivery and no trace of a southern accent. His mind was nimble, he spoke with conviction and made his points. One thing I clearly recall: Jimmy said that he felt estranged from Harlem, with its poverty and limitations and, except in the Village, felt alien in the white world. In either case he was in a ghetto, outside the mainstream, he said, an oddity in Harlem, which he had left two years earlier. Small and slight, he sounded like an educated white man and was regarded with suspicion and hostility in Harlem. "Hey, nigger! Ya wanna be white? Black ain't good enough for you? You must be crazy, boy!" Except for bohemians and radical intellectuals, with whom he lived and slept, he was discriminated against by both races. "Ya gotta disarm the enemy," Harry said. "They call you nigger, become 'the crazy nigger of Harlem.' Deal with them on *your* terms, not theirs, or you'll despise yourself. Let go like Miller, Artaud. Don't be trapped by their idea of you!"

Harry's solution held little appeal for Jimmy. He was too realistic to adopt the bizarre behavior that was common both in the Village and in Harlem, the flight into a fantasy world. He made a few conciliatory responses like "uh huh," and "perhaps," but his brows remained furrowed with concern. His protruding eyes glittered, darting from mine to Harry's. He looked to me rather than to Harry for support. I felt that I understood his predicament better, could empathize more. As the night wore on we knew that we had something in common that Harry couldn't share. When he said, "All right, Jimmy, so you're poor, black, and queer, but that's what will make you strong." Jimmy and I exchanged a look of understanding. Being queer was even worse than being black, Jewish, or poverty-stricken. Among bottom dogs gays were the bottom.

Jimmy and I saw a great deal of each other, managing to cadge drinks at the San Remo, Minetta's, and MacDougal's Tavern. The latter, a basement dive in MacDougall Alley, was a dark seedy gay bar run by Italians. A couple of doors south was a lesbian bar where drunken sailors tried to pick up women and got beat up by tough bull dykes. The sailors never understood why. A few doors north, Jimmy waited on tables for tips in a tiny restaurant called the Calypso, serving spicy, mouth-watering West Indian food. Connie Williams, the owner, was a hefty, chuckling Jamaican black woman whose motherliness and sweetness gave warmth to our lives, as did her food. Like so many others, mostly whites, she took Jimmy under her wing and fed him, clucking and chuckling like a mother hen. In the red-bulbed dim cellar the tables were always full.

One night Jimmy introduced me to a boy called Russell Edson whose father, Gus, drew the syndicated cartoon strip "The Gumps," which I had followed in childhood. Russell was only sixteen and, as I recall, had long hair, unheard of in those days. He was extremely bright and precocious and went on to become a master of the prose poem, achieving fame in a genre he made entirely his own. Whenever Jimmy, Russell, and I arrived Connie would call out in her ringing contralto, "Here comes de Gumps." Then, even if only Jimmy and I arrived, she'd call it out anyway, followed by a rippling cascade of laughter.

Another friend of Jimmy's was Mason Hoffenberg, a cantankerous youth who drank too much and had a sharp tongue that kept you laughing—if it wasn't directed at you. Like most of us, Mason was well read but indulged in the Village pastime of putting down writers with a contempt that couldn't mask ill-concealed envy. His blue eyes danced with malicious humor. Small, with a ruddy face that revealed bad temper, Mason, although not exactly ugly, was simply unbeauteous. His nasal, unpleasant whine grated on the nerves, and his merciless wit drew blood. Years later in Paris, where he had lived since 1948 with a French wife, he still greeted me with derogatory remarks. "Everybody I know has been mentioned in *Time* magazine at least once," he snarled in an encounter on the Boulevard Saint Germain. "I'll bet even *you* have been written up." I hadn't been and he was then known as the coauthor, with Terry Southern, of the bestselling novel *Candy*. Until he died he remained an old hand at making success sound like a social disease. Once, in a violent argument with Jimmy, who had just received a Saxton Fellowship to complete his first novel, Mason belittled the event and Jimmy shouted furiously, "I haven't seen *you* break into print yet!"

Even in the Village Jimmy was by no means immune to racist attacks. [See the Michael Harrington and Dan Wakefield selections for two accounts of another racially-charged attack on Baldwin.] One night, an hour or so before he waited on tables at Connie's (meals didn't begin till about 9:00 P.M.), we went to MacDougal's as usual and ordered two beers. The thickset barman stared at Jimmy a trifle sheepishly. "I can't serve you, Jimmy," he said. We thought we hadn't heard him correctly. "Two beers, Tony," Jimmy repeated. Pushing a beer toward me Tony shook his head. His face was set. "I don't understand, Tony. What have I done?" Tony ignored him. "I asked what I've done, Tony." Jimmy started to shout. "Don't make no trouble or I'll have to throw you out," growled Tony. "Come on, Jimmy," I urged. "Let's go!" But Jimmy was out of control. Fearing for his safety I seized him with both arms and pulled him kicking and screaming out the door.

"Allen Ginsberg"

In my tiny room on Horatio Street I froze in winter. In the wee hours when the streets were deserted I'd go on sorties to gather orange crates for firewood around the corner at the slaughterhouse. Old bums wrapped in newspapers slept on concrete platforms that by day held bloody beef carcasses.The gloomy racks stank like a stockyard and the meathooks glinted menacingly in the moonlight. When it snowed the bums were covered like sacks of garbage with the cold white stuff.

In my unheated two-by-four on Horatio Street I was visited by Tennessee Williams, James Baldwin, and Allen Ginsberg. Far from being monstrously famous, they were all obscure, gay, unsure of themselves. In that arctic winter of late 1944, one night I was riding the IRT subway to the hole in the wall I called home, drunk and dispirited. I can't remember where I'd been, some dull party or other in Brooklyn, where I hadn't succeeded in dragooning into service a bedmate for the night. There was nobody else in the car and I was lonely, dreaming of love and sex, which I needed every moment and had to forage for, like firewood, to keep warm. The yellow lights glowed eerily, the empty car rattled and roared—an empty train speeding to an empty room, to empty nights and meaningless days. It was a time of total war, total hate.

With a feeling of desolation stifling me, I fought back my despair. A charter member of the "Beat Generation," which would be named some ten years later, I didn't feel like a generation. I felt like a scared drunken kid in a terrifying world of murderers.

A tall skinny youth wearing a red bandana around his neck entered and took a seat directly opposite. He carried a book from which he kept reading aloud; occasionally he'd shoot a glance in my direction, not really seeing me. Always curious about people carrying books, I wanted to see the title—was it a piece of crap or the real thing? In my romantic way I hoped to meet an undiscovered genius, some teenage Rimbaud who would become my lover. Meanwhile the youth across the aisle began babbling louder, his head lolling around, glazed eyes rolling wildly behind horn-rimmed specs. But the clatter and roar of the train drowned out the words. He had thick black hair, sensual Jewish features, smooth olive skin, and a slender body—definitely attractive, I decided, at least on a cold night at three in the morning. At station stops, when the roar of the train died down, I could make out what he was reciting. It was in French. "Rimbaud!" I said at a stop. "'The Drunken Boat'!"

"You're a poet!" said Allen Ginsberg with open-mouthed astonishment. Here was the genius, though neither of us could swear to it then. I always thought there was something prophetic about the meeting. For instance, he might have sat at a far corner of the car and it wouldn't have happened. I was the first writer he had met. ("I met Kerouac about a week after I met him," Allen told me in San Francisco in 1974. "I met Burroughs ten days later.")

A virgin of eighteen and a student at Columbia, studying poetry with Mark Van Doren, Allen had nervously come to the Village to pick up a boy for the first time in his life and ended up with me. I was twenty-eight. We both wanted the same thing—a teen-aged "angel-headed hipster." I had found mine (though not a hipster) six years earlier, but [W. H.] Auden had taken him from me. It only happens once. I would never again find quite the same thing, and I'd never again be that young.

For Allen, as for us all, the Village was an oasis in the puritan desert, a watering place for the soul. The Village offered free-wheeling sex. The closet cases of America were drawn to the bars and hangouts of Bohemia, longing to fulfill their secret desires and sneak anonymously back to conventional niches. Ginsberg was no exception. The scared willowy boy came to my room and sat primly and self-consciously, and somewhat stiffly, beside me on my single cot, anxiously showing me his rhymed four-line poems, seeking my praise and approval. His quatrains, however, were in my opinion ordinary. Ironically, in view of what he would become—this was eleven years before *Howl* was written—I found his efforts too tame, too feeble, too conventional. Both in his personality and his poems he was too restrained.

Obsessed with Hart Crane's visionary homosexual mysticism and Dylan Thomas's inebriate incantatory style, I spoke of them and of Whitman, the obsessions of my youth, as masters of the spontaneous, intuitive flow of language. As we huddled together I held forth about Dionysian breath, as evidenced in "Song of Myself" and *The Bridge*, by two great "fairies" who wrote the two greatest long poems ever written by Americans. *The Waste Land* (we didn't know that Eliot wrote it for a drowned young Frenchman he was in love with) was no model for succeeding generations—like Pound's *Cantos*, it was too hermetic. It may be hard to imagine now, but during World War II almost nobody read Pound except to attack him. While Hitler was devastating Europe it was impossible to read without bias a rabid Fascist who made violent anti-Semitic harangues from Mussolini's short-wave Radio Rome. Pound praised the dictators and slandered American writers and politicians as "yids" and "kikes" or in the pay of Jews. Tennessee referred to him as "the unspeakable Mr. Pound," which summed it up.

Perhaps I influenced Allen a little that morning and perhaps I didn't. I showed him my poem "Key West" in *Poetry*, which was greeted by some critics as a neoromantic breakthrough in a concrete wall of academic dullness. Apocalyptic poetry, however, enjoyed no vogue in America. Anything British was highly regarded by the establishment, as Oscar Williams's *Little Treasuries* proved, but with the sole exception of Dylan Thomas and the surrealist David Gascoyne, the other so-called Apocalyptics produced no stylistic departures to speak of.

Allen listened, agreed, said little. Around 7:00 A.M., when I began hinting that he could stay over if he wished, he glanced at the hard narrow cot, which could comfortably accommodate two if one slept on top of the other, and with a look of alarm jumped to his feet. "I've got to get back to New Jersey," he said quickly. "I'm leaving tomorrow for Murmansk!" We both held union cards from the Maritime Commission. So Allen, who had arrived a virgin, departed a virgin. If I had resembled Peter Orlovsky, this memoir would have been longer.

That little room was a turning point in my life. There I would soon take a wrong turn that I've regretted ever since.

—1989

Herbert Huncke

(1915–1996)

Although born in Greenfield, Massachusetts, Huncke grew up in Chicago, where he trafficked in petty crime and even served as a runner for Al Capone's people. A drifter and drug addict, he sometimes made ends meet by reverting to prostitution. In 1939 he moved to New York. Five years later, he met William S. Burroughs. Burroughs reportedly modeled the character of Herman in Junkie *after Huncke while Jack Kerouac reportedly based his character Elmo Hassel in* On the Road *on Huncke. Indeed, Huncke is said to have introduced Kerouac to the term "beat." Huncke spent his last years at the infamous Chelsea Hotel in New York. He died on August 8, 1996. A collection of his writings,* The Herbert Huncke Reader, *was published in 1997. The following brief selection describes an encounter among Huncke, Kerouac, and Burroughs in Washington Square Park.*

from *Guilty of Everything: The Autobiography of Herbert Huncke*

The first time I met Kerouac was on a day not long after I had first met Bill. I was hanging out in Washington Square Park when Bill and Jack walked by. Bill introduced me, and then told me he'd picked up something in the way of a narcotic and asked me if I

Herbert Huncke. From *Guilty of Everything: The Autobiography of Herbert Huncke* (New York: Paragon House, 1990).

knew anything about it. I can't recall what the drug was but I had not heard of it. I didn't think it was something I wanted to fool with, simply because I did not know what it was.

I remember thinking Jack was green, but he was taking everything in and making little comments to Bill—mostly about the scene in general. His eyes were flashing around. Kerouac was a typical clean-cut American type. He looked to me like the Arrow-collar man. They always had these clean-cut young progressive American businessmen in their ads with their hair cut neatly and a twinkle in the eye. That was Jack.

Bill invited us up to his room over on Waverly where we decided this drug was something that should be shot intramuscularly. We did shoot it that way, and nothing happened. Bill tried to talk Kerouac into shooting up, but Jack said no, he would pass on it, though he was obviously curious about it. At that time Jack would smoke a little pot, but he was leery of the needle.

We went back outside and then we split up. They wanted to go and get coffee but I had a habit and I knew I was wasting time with them because I'd already been sounded down for money. Neither had any bread on them so I went on about my business alone.

It was through Burroughs, also, that I met Ginsberg—a man who's had a very big influence on my life. Allen, not quite twenty years old, wasn't sure what he was to become. From a practical standpoint he had decided that it would be best to become a history teacher, since he was specializing in history at Columbia. Meanwhile, he was attending a poetry course under Lionel Trilling.

At the time, too, I met Allen's brother, who was studying law and is now a lawyer. It surprised me to meet this rather conservative young man who was Allen's brother. He certainly didn't fit into the picture that Allen had surrounded himself with then. His interests were far more flamboyant. He had naturally sought out the oustanding people at Columbia at that particular time. Most of them were literary, or interested in psychiatry or journalism or things of this sort.

Ginsberg was going through a stage where he didn't know whether he was heterosexual, homosexual, autoerotic, or what. In fact, I was going through many changes myself about my homosexuality. I didn't know whether I was purely homosexual, or bisexual. I have had relationships with both men and women my entire life.

—1990

Hettie Jones

(b. 1934)

Born into a Jewish middle-class family in Queens, Hettie Cohen moved to Greenwich Village in the 1950s, where she become part of a larger community of fellow artists: painters, poets, and jazz musicians. It was in the Village where she met and married the African-American poet LeRoi Jones (who would later change his name to Amiri Baraka). Together they published a small literary magazine called Yugen, *which was made possible by the income she brought in from her position as manager of the* Partisan Review. *They also joined forces with Eli Wilentz of the Eighth Street Book Shop to publish books under the Totem Books imprint. Like many women artists of her day, she was usually relegated to the background. "In every interview with Roi or review of his work I was mentioned," she writes in* How I Became Hettie Jones. *"Sometimes I got a dependent clause: 'Jones, who is married to a white woman.' Or my name: his white wife, the former Hettie Cohen.'" Maintaining individual identity, never mind artistic identity, was always a challenge in such an atmosphere.*

from
How I Became Hettie Jones

The Mills Hotel, on Bleecker Street at Thompson, was a dank, cavernous, derelict's roost and occasional home to desperate artists. On the Thompson Street side it had a narrow café, which opened for a time as a coffeehouse called Jazz on the Wagon. Although the music was only occasional, and the place was funky and hastily

Hettie Jones. From *How I Became Hettie Jones* (New York: E. P. Dutton, 1990).

constructed of plywood and the floor slanted, a small but provocative literary group sometimes gathered at the squeezed-up, wobbly tables. They even had a name—the "Beats"—ambiguous enough to include anyone.

Jack Kerouac had thought up "the Beat Generation," in conversation with another writer, John Clellon Holmes, who later explained *beat* as "pushed up against the wall of oneself." At the readings at the Wagon—and the Gaslight, Limelight, Figaro and other Village cafés—not all the poetry beat the agony. Roi and I were almost too sane in a group where shrink-time seemed mandatory. To be beat you needed a B-movie graininess, a saintly disaffection, a wild head of hair and a beard like the poet Tuli Kupferberg, or a look of provocative angst like Jack Micheline. Ted Joans was another beat picture, a black man always dressed in black, from a black beret on down. The women, like me, had all found Goldin Dance Supply on Eighth Street, where dirt-defying, indestructible tights could be bought—made only for dancers then and only in black—which freed you from fragile nylon stockings and the cold, unreliable, metal clips of a garter belt. The Beats *looked* okay to me, and I applauded their efforts, successful or not, to burst wide open—like the abstract expressionist painters had—the image of what could be (rightly) said.

Public readings were a new, qualitatively different route for writers. Few were in print and performance counted—how you sound, as Roi said. Besides Kerouac, the other beat hero-poet was Allen Ginsberg, whose *Howl and Other Poems*—published in San Francisco, in the fall of 1956, by Lawrence Ferlinghetti's City Lights Bookshop—had been seized by Customs and the police and tried for obscenity. (It won.) Roi got Allen's address in Paris and wrote him, on toilet paper, asking if he was "for real." Allen was pleased and responded. Roi was asked to read his own work. Soon we'd met the poets Gregory Corso, Diane Di Prima, and then Frank O'Hara, who was also a curator and took us to the Cedar Tavern to meet the Tenth Street painters—Larry Rivers and Alfred Leslie are the first of those I remember but soon I recognized more than a few and picked them out of the crowd at the

Five Spot, where they also were regulars. At the Cedar we met many of the artists who'd studied and lived at Black Mountain College, the legendary home of avant-garde education, which had just closed. The days went by in a streak of events and performances. John Coltrane succeeded Monk as a main attraction. Atlantic Records advertised "the label in tune with the Beat Generation." In England a current play was described as a "soap opera of the Beat Generation, British version." One dark, jammed night at Jazz on the Wagon Roi and I were introduced to the suddenly famous Kerouac himself, a medium-sized, rather shy man. Critics had called him "a voice," but he seemed bewildered by the ardent young crowd for whom he'd spoken.

That fall, after the Russians sent up *Sputnik*, the world's first spacecraft, the suffix "nik" was added to beat, putting us square in the enemy camp. There was some humor—Ted Joans and photographer Fred McDarrah rented themselves to parties as "genuine beatniks," dressed appropriately and carrying a set of bongos, an instant symbol for Negro culture. Although like hipsters the Beats appreciated jazz, they weren't content to leave it where it had always been left—in its "place." Jack Kerouac's "spontaneous bop prosody," for instance, was an attempt to sophisticate the English language rhythmically, to make it *work*, like music. Like the writing of Martin Williams and Nat Hentoff, this did prefigure a different approach to black culture, and got on some literary nerves:

"Oh, man! man! man!" moaned Dean [in *On the Road*]. ". . . here we are at last going east together . . . Sal, think of it, we'll dig Denver together and see what everybody's doing although that matters little to us, the point being that we know what IT is and we know TIME and we know that everything is really FINE . . . Listen! Listen! . . . He was poking me furiously in the ribs to understand. I tried my wildest best. Bing, bang, it was all Yes! Yes! Yes! . . ."

It was only a ten-minute walk from the *Partisan* office to the Village hubbub. I brought what I'd learned, and judged Roi front line. Not just for love: I'd read enough to see that his voice was unique. He didn't use a lot of words, but then again he didn't have to. Sometimes, like Miles Davis says about notes, you just have to play the pretty ones. Roi wrote what he knew, from a fresh point of view. Onstage he was clear, musical, tough. He delivered.

He was also looking around for another job while finishing up at the *Changer*. Usually I met him there after work. One evening when I arrived he was on the phone. While he listened he kept gesturing at me and slapping his forehead. Then he said, "Yes, I'm well aware that he's a Negro, but he's been a fine employee. He hasn't stolen anything, if that's what you mean."

I gaped at him.

"We'd be glad to vouch," he said pleasantly, but with an expression that was new to me. His jaw muscles jumped, repeatedly and noticeably, as if he were gnashing his teeth while the rest of his face remained calm. It was a look I would come to know.

And this was the story: a record collector he'd seen about a job had just called the *Changer* to ask for a recommendation. Dick wasn't in. Thinking to get himself hired, Roi had pretended to be someone else.

Of course we laughed. But it brought home how suspect he was, simply being his competent self. Like, though so *unlike*, most of our new friends. Yet often what he said about them applied to him most: "The freaks are fascinating," wrote one critic, "although they are hardly part of our lives."

My own life still worried me a little. Beside my desk at *Partisan* I kept a big green metal waste can, where most of my lunchtime attempts to write got filed. I was too ashamed to show them. I didn't like my tone of voice, the twist of my tongue. At the open readings, where anyone could stand up, I remained in the cheering audience. Roi was so much better; everyone else was so much better. Only one poem I wrote then survives, a sort-of-but-not-too haiku.

Nevertheless I didn't feel down for the count. All the Beats found it funny that I worked for the *Partisan* titans. Sometimes I hired Diane Di Prima, who had become a friend, to stuff envelopes and keep me company. I was able to bring Roi books and magazines. And at *Partisan* I could already see a stir of reaction, a gearing-up of the generations. William [William Phillips, one of the *Partisan Reviews* founding editors] was considering poems by Allen Ginsberg and Gregory Corso. I felt happy to have landed— by remarkable, marvelous chance—in the middle.

But it was slick little Roi himself who made me feel most needed and wanted and appreciated, and it didn't seem (though this would change) that he loved me any less for my silence. But I did begin learning how to cook. My first pot of brown rice was inedible—a gummy off-tan mush. The two of us, hungry, stood peering into the pot in the little corner air-shaft kitchen on Morton Street. "What'd you do?" he said. "I don't know," I said. Still I felt nothing but hope in the future.

—1990

Dan Wakefield

(b. 1932)

Dan Wakefield is the author of many books, including the best-selling nov-els Going All the Way *and* Starting Over *and several nonfiction works with spiritual themes,* Returning: A Spiritual Journey *and* Creating from the Spirit. New York in the 1950s *tells the story of a young Mid-western boy in New York City at a time when the Village offered a thriv-ing cultural scene. Like the bohemian Village of pre–World War I, partic-ular topics were hot, from free love and cool jazz to radical politics and psychoanalysis. A documentary film based on the book was released in early 2001. In this selection he describes one of his favorite Village haunts, the White Horse Tavern, and its cast of regulars, including Michael Har-rington, Seymour Krim, Norman Mailer, and James Baldwin.*

"Home to the Village" from *New York in the Fifties*

> *"The birds did warble from every tree*
> *The song they sang was old Ireland free"*

It was in the back room of the White Horse Tavern on Hudson Street that I learned and sang songs of Irish rebellion as if they were the anthems of my own and my friends' personal struggles. In a way they were, for I'd never been to Ireland and knew next to noth-ing of its history or politics except that it seemed to be in a continuous state of rebellion against oppression, and my friends and I identified with the Irish as underdogs battling the mighty British Empire. We regulars in the back room thought of ourselves as underdogs and rebels in Eisenhower's America, and so we lustily joined in the songs, sometimes led by the Clancy Brothers (they were real Irishmen and understood the whole thing), who made the White Horse their headquarters.

The Horse was like a social club or informal fraternity, and veterans took pride in telling something of the history of the place to novices. On one of my first visits a habitue volunteering as host showed me the table where Dylan Thomas, one of the legendary patrons, had his last drink (the shot that killed him?). My host then pointed out the window to St. Vincent's Hospital, up the street, and explained with hushed reverence that there the great Welsh poet was taken to die at age thirty-nine. The proximity of the tavern to the hospital seemed a real convenience, giving assurance to a newcomer that if he, too, were to drink himself to oblivion at one of these historic tables, an emergency room was not far away.

I was twenty-three at the time, and the whole thing seemed not only tragic but glamorous and wise, for life after forty sounded so far off as to seem superfluous, and most great poets died young anyway, didn't they? Whenever I could, I tried to get a seat at Dylan Thomas's "last table" and told the story to impress people new to the place, especially girls. Sometimes I took a date there and then back to my apartment to play her my Caedmon record of Thomas reciting his passionate poetry. As seductive as any record of Sinatra singing "In the Wee Small Hours" or even the sexy June Christy throatily crooning "Something Cool" was the poet himself telling us not to go gentle into that good night.

I always wondered how Thomas had discovered the White Horse in the first place, which before he came was mainly known as a longshoremen's hangout and had no literary aura at all. An old-time Village friend told me the novelist David Markson, who wrote *Springer's Progress*, *The Ballad of Dingus Magee*, and *Wittgenstein's Mistress*, was the one who first brought the Welshman to the bar on Hudson Street, but Markson says it was the other way around—it was Thomas who took *him* to the White Horse.

"I was a graduate student at Columbia when Dylan Thomas gave a reading there in 1952," Markson remembers. "I went backstage because I wanted to see a real writer, up close and in the flesh. I don't know where I got the chutzpah, but I asked him if he wanted to have some drinks with a couple of would-be writers at the West End bar. He said he had to go to a party first, given by the critic William York Tyndall, who taught at Columbia, but he said, 'If you wait, I'll be out of there soon.' We didn't think he'd really come to drink with us, but he did.

"The next time I saw him I was supposed to meet him at a bar next door to the Chelsea Hotel, where he was staying, and he said, 'Let's go down to the White Horse.' I went there a number of times with him, and people would be sitting around staring at him—and then at me, wondering who the hell I was because I was with Dylan. People would be eight deep at the bar, all because Dylan Thomas was there."

John Malcolm Brinnin, the poet and teacher who escorted Thomas on his American reading tour and wrote about it in *Dylan Thomas in America*, says it was really the Scottish poet Ruthven Todd who introduced Thomas to the White Horse. Brinnin explains that "the British who came to New York liked the White Horse because it reminded them of a pub. Before Todd took Dylan to the Horse, I'd been trying to keep him in check, take him to places like the Blarney Stone, which wasn't all that interesting, didn't have a lot of people for him to talk to, but when he got to the White Horse it was all over."

Thomas's patronage of the White Horse is immortalized now on the bar's menu, which boasts, "Over 100 years old, the White Horse Tavern found favor as the favorite watering hole of Welsh poet Dylan Thomas. (In fact, his final collapse came a few staggering steps from the front door). The White Horse remains a fascinating collection of history, color, charm, and character . . ." There's a plaque on the wall now indicating the table where the poet had his last drink, but in the old days it was one of an insider's privileges to *know*, and reveal the sacred spot to newcomers.

The literary fame of the bar was enhanced soon after Thomas started drinking there, when one of the young novelists to emerge after World War II, Vance Bourjaily (*The End of My Life* was an influential novel of the period), organized a regular Sunday afternoon gathering of writers at the White Horse. One of them was Norman Mailer.

"The group didn't have a name," Mailer recalls, "but on any given Sunday we got together—probably twenty times or more. There was Vance, and me, Calder Willingham, John Aldridge, John Clellon Holmes, even Herman Wouk came a few times—he was the most successful author we knew. The only woman who was part of the group was Rosalind Drexler. She was a lady wrestler as well as a writer, and we were agog with the idea we had a woman wrestler in our group. It was like she was a creature from a carnival—we were scared stiff, knowing that if she wanted to she could throw any one of us across the room. She was bright, and she realized we'd come to gawk. In this quiet voice she told us we really didn't care about her writing, and she wasn't going to come anymore. The group finally petered out, I think because there were no themes, no literary discussion, no ongoing arguments. Vance was disappointed—he had more of the collegial spirit than I did."

The White Horse wasn't the only popular bar in the Village, of course. In those days people made the rounds, going to several bars for an evening's entertainment, but it seemed the Horse was on the route of everyone I knew, and usually served as the final stop, the high point of the evening.

Art d'Lugoff, who started the Village Gate nightclub, says, "I used to make the rounds of the bars—Julius's for those fat hamburgers on toast, then the San Remo, the Kettle of Fish, and the White Horse. Booze was a social thing. The bar scene wasn't just to get drunk. It was like the public square in a town or a sidewalk café in Paris—comradely meeting and talking."

The *Village Voice* columnist and reporter Mary Nichols also made the rounds. "When I still lived in East Harlem with the Swarthmore graduates in the el cheapo apartment, before I worked for the *Voice*, I took the El to the Village every night and went to the

San Remo, where my friends hung out. We had a regular route, from the Remo to Minetta's to Louis' and then the White Horse.

David Amram, the musician who managed to cross comfortably between the worlds of writing and painting, frequented the Cedar Tavern. "I met de Kooning, Rivers, Kline, and Alfred Leslie there. The White Horse was all Dylan Thomas fans and people who liked writing. Also, I met the Clancy Brothers there and began playing Irish music, backing them up.

Ed Fancher, the cofounder and original publisher of the *Village Voice*, says, "There was a smaller bohemian world in the fifties—the writers were at the White Horse or the Remo, the artists were at the Cedar. There's nothing comparable today."

Most often when I went to the White Horse I was waved to a table by Mike Harrington, the author and activist who served as the informal host of an ongoing seminar on culture and politics, dispensing information and opinion interspersed with great anecdotes about left-wing labor leaders and colorful factional fights of political splinter groups that I could never keep straight, with exotic designations like Schactmanites, Sweezyites, Browederites, Musteites, and Cochranites, not to speak of Trotskyites, Socialist-Laborites, and "Yipsuls" (of the YPSL, or Young People's Socialist League).

The added charm and fascination of hearing all this radical political exotica from Mike Harrington was that in looks, voice, and manner he could have passed for an older version of Huck Finn, or even Jack Armstrong, the All-American Boy. This was the era in which McCarthyism had brought about the fear that anything left of the mainstream of politics or ideology was—that ugly word—un-American. But here was Mike, a lanky, straightforward guy with freckles, a boyish grin, and broomstraw hair, speaking in a strong Missouri twang, continuing in a time of conformity the great American tradition of questioning the status quo, caring about the underdog, challenging the powers that be. Had it not been for Mike's taking over the nearly moribund Socialist youth factions, forming the Young Socialist League in 1954 and leading with dignity and intelligence the Socialist movement in America until his death in 1989, it is hard to imagine that tradition surviving the fifties.

Mike lived and worked for a while at the Catholic Worker hospitality house, and the young idealists and intellectuals who were drawn to the place joined Mike's table at the Horse after the Friday night sessions on Chrystie Street. When he became the head of the YSL, the people who heard him speak and lead those meetings also followed him to the Horse.

One night Mike was engaged in a lively colloquy with a Yale professor named Robert Bone, who wrote for *Dissent* and shunned the Whiffenpoofs for the Clancy Brothers at the White Horse whenever he could escape New Haven. He and Mike were discussing the arcane factions of the Spanish civil war—as popular a topic here as the Irish rebellion—when they noticed that two young women none of us knew had appeared at the big table and seemed obviously in the dark.

It was not all that common for girls to show up at the Horse unless they were part of a group like the Catholic Workers or the YSL and knew the regulars, or were brought here on a date by a man; these young women were by themselves and new on the scene. Mike graciously asked what they did, and they said they were telephone operators. There was an uneasy silence as everyone tried to figure out how they happened to wander into this bar, and how we could make them feel at home, since attractive girls showing up in the back room was a happy and welcome event. What could they be told that would make them feel part of a discussion on the intricacies of the Spanish civil war? It was painfully clear the subject was about as familiar to them as nuclear physics.

Bob Bone suddenly brightened and broke the awkward silence: "Telephone operators! Why, telephone operators played a key role in the fighting in Barcelona during the Spanish civil war. Franco's troops were trying to cut off all communications, but the workers at the Barcelona telephone exchange kept the lines open in spite of being under attack." The men smiled with relief and approval, and the girls perked up, honored by this revelation of the noble behavior of their Catalonian sisters. Pints of arf 'n' arf were ordered for them, and soon the table broke into some song of Irish rebellion, which cut the tension altogether and allowed everyone to relax.

595

(In the back room, after many pints of ale, the Irish rebellion and the Spanish civil war seemed to blend together in one grand battle of noble underdogs against tyrant oppressors, waged from the dawn of history, and any rousing song of freedom stood just as well for the brave lads of Spain and Ireland, either one—or for any of us who had left home to come to the Village).

I was asked to write book reviews for *Commonweal*, the liberal Catholic magazine, when I drank with its editors in the back room of the Horse, where they sat at a table with Harrington or at one of their own, in a kind of continuous editorial meeting. I never knew exactly where the office of *Commonweal* was—somewhere downtown, I thought—but I considered the White Horse its true headquarters. It was there I met the editors Jim, Finn, John Cogley, Wilfred "Bill" Sheed, and a friendly man described by the *Village Voice* writer Seymour Krim as "a tolerant and sympathetic book editor named Bill Clancy."

I could echo Krim's experience with Clancy, who, Krim said, "sensed I was not a native or orthodox critic but nevertheless brought out of me some of the best I could do because he had a taste for fullness of expression rather than the narrower, stricter conception of criticism then at its height." Krim felt that as a Jew, "even writing for a Roman Catholic magazine like *Commonweal* I literally had much more freedom of expression than in *Commentary*. . . . I took the life out of a young American-Jewish writer to do a piece for them."

As an unaffiliated WASP, I myself enjoyed a sense of freedom when I later began writing for both the Catholic and the Jewish magazines. The publication I would have felt stifled writing for in those days was the *Indianapolis Star*!

I'd been following the jazzy, electric prose of Seymour Krim in the *Voice*; he used his personal experience as material—often like raw wounds—to comment on the literature, culture, and politics of the time. Krim was an unsung father of what was later called the New Journalism, and his pieces from the fifties were collected at the end of the decade in *Views of a Nearsighted Cannoneer*, which had a real influence on other writers. He always worked out on the frontier of trends and lingo; he coined the term "radical chic" before Tom Wolfe made it famous, and his essay "Making It" preceded Podhoretz's book of that title. Krim's souped-up style was similar to Norman Mailer's nonfiction riffs, which were also appearing in the *Voice* in those days. In a foreword to *Cannoneer* Mailer wrote: "Krim in his odd honest garish sober grim surface is a child of our time. I think sometimes, as a matter of style, he is *the* child of our time, he is New York in the middle of the 20th century, a city man, his prose as brilliant upon occasion as the electronic beauty of our lights, his shifts and shatterings of mood as searching and true as the grinding wheels in a subway train. He has the guts of New York, old Krim."

I met Seymour Krim at the White Horse, in the most embarrassing "literary encounter" of my life, one that almost turned into a brawl. Surprisingly, for a bar of steadily drinking patrons, continually engaged in passionate discussions, there weren't many bad scenes, and only a few times I know of when fights were even threatened.

Murray Kempton had quoted something from Dostoevsky in his column in the *Post* that day, and I was holding forth on how great it was. Just as I was reaching a crescendo of praise, I heard a high, squeaky female voice screech from a few tables away: "I just can't *stand* Murray Kempton!"

When I heard the slur, a kind of calm, trancelike state came over me. I got up from my chair, took my nearly full pint, walked with deliberate steps to the table where the woman sat with several other people, raised my glass above her, and poured the contents over her head. As she screamed, I calmly walked back to my own table and took up the conversation as if nothing had happened. In my trance, I did not expect any further response. I somehow thought I had simply taken the only appropriate action called for under the circumstances.

I was surprised when two pairs of hands yanked me roughly from my seat. Two men who'd been sitting with the screecher had come to defend her honor. We started shouting at each other: "Why you goddam—who the hell do you think you are!" Then one of the men, a tall, intellectual-looking guy wearing horn-rims, grabbed me by the collar and said, "I know who you are, Wakefield. I've seen you around. I never thought you'd—" Now I grabbed his collar and demanded, "Who the hell are you?" When he told me he was Seymour Krim, I said, "No kidding? I read your stuff in the *Voice*," and he said, "Yeah? I read your stuff in *The Nation*." We were still gripping each other by the collar and snarling through our teeth. "Great piece you did on Bellevue," I said, and he said, "I dug the one you did on Kerouac," but everyone was watching and we couldn't release ourselves from our roles as ferocious antagonists. We both admitted later how relieved we were when a big waiter came over and broke us apart, which allowed us to sit down without losing face.

Krim became a friend in the Village whose work I read and enjoyed discussing over beers at the Horse, and over veal scallopini at John's, a marvelous restaurant he introduced me to on East 10th Street. It was handy to Krim's dinky, book-erupting studio apartment on the same street where, to the everlasting amusement of his friends, he once entertained Paul Newman and Joanne Woodward by turning a couple of garbage cans upside down for them to sit on—the only seats in the place.

What Mailer described as Krim's "odd honest garish sober grim surface" was created in part by those thick black-rimmed glasses beneath a head of matted-down wavy black hair. He always seemed to be wearing the same black corduroy sport jacket with a thin tie, as if he were a hip diplomat of the literary fringe come to negotiate his ideas with you. Behind that formal surface was a healthy sense of humor that broke out in his prose as well as his conversation, in quirky, jazzy phrasings like the description of his friend Milton Klonsky, a legendary Village poet-genius of the forties, who Krim claimed had "an IQ that would stutter your butter."

I felt a bond with Krim because we had both known the urge and passion to write early on. He started publishing in high school—DeWitt Clinton in the Bronx—where he wrote for the school magazine, *The Magpie*, and coedited a more avant-garde mimeographed sheet called *expression* ("Man, were we swingingly lowercase back in 1939," he later said). We also shared a devotion to the Village, where Krim, a decade older than I, had moved in 1943 at age twenty-one, thrilled to find a "one-room bohemian fantasy on Cornelia Street." One of his literary heroes, James Agee, had lived on that street, and Krim as a high school student made a pilgrimage there to meet and interview him.

In an odd and unexpected way, Krim's love of the Village and his feeling for it as home saved him from a downward personal spiral that started in the summer of 1955, when he experienced what we called then a "crack-up" or "nervous breakdown." He describes in his unforgettable essay "The Insanity Bit" how he was handcuffed and taken to Belluvue, and sent from there to "a private laughing academy in Westchester," where he was given insulin shock treatments. A few months after his release he confessed to a psychologist a suicide attempt he'd planned but didn't carry out, and was dispatched "this time to another hedge-trimmed bin in Long Island," where "electric shock clubbed my good brain into needless unconsciousness" (as it did to some of the great Negro jazz musicians of the time, damaging or altogether destroying their ability, as in the case of Bud Powell).

When, after the battering of electric shock, the house psychiatrists battered at Krim's belief in his own powers of reason, intelligence, and talent—one of them wanted him to, Krim wrote, "accept my former life, which had produced some good work, as a lie to myself"—and tried to get him to "equate sanity with the current cliches of adjustment," he was almost, for the second time, "humbled, ashamed, willing to stand up before the class and repeat the middle-class credo of limited expressiveness." He might have been incarcerated for many more years, or come out so robbed of his beliefs that he wouldn't have written again, but the road to his recovery of confidence came when one of the house psychiatrists finally went too far. The shrink described Greenwich Village as a "psychotic community."

They might pin some label of nuttiness on *him*, but not the Village! When he heard that, he "saw with sudden clarity that *insanity* and *psychosis* can no longer be respected as meaningful definitions—but are used by limited individuals in positions of social power to describe ways of behaving and thinking that are alien, threatening, and *obscure* to them."

After that Krim wasn't taking any more. He argued for his "basic right to the insecurity of freedom," and with the help of a friend who "did the dirty fighting," got his release from the sanatorium. A year later he brought a woman psychiatrist friend to the San Remo, one of his favorite Village bars, and she told him with a straight face that it reminded her of "the admissions ward at Bellevue," where she had been an intern.

Krim felt the "incommunicable helplessness" of the gap between her and a well-known poet whom he'd had a drink with two weeks before at the Remo: "The poet was at home, or at least the heat was off there; while the psychiatrist felt alien and had made a contemptuous psycho-sociological generalization." Yet both the poet and the psychiatrist were "intelligent and honest human beings, each of whom contributed to my life."

To the benefit of all concerned—especially the fans of his work and the many writers, like myself, whom Krim gave so much help as a friend, editor, and reviewer—he remained at the Remo, the White Horse, and other such havens of the Village, never again to return to Belluvue.

> *"The birds did warble from every tree*
> *The song they sang was old Ireland free"*

If at Chumley's nostalgia-filled bar you saw book jackets and photographs of authors from the twenties, at the White Horse you saw in the flesh the writers of books you had read just a week or a year before. One night, through the haze of smoke in the back room, I recognized the face of an author I'd recently seen on a book, not on the back but filling the whole front cover.

What had struck me when I first saw the photo were the eyes. They were large and looked very wise, older than the face in which they were set. There was a sadness about them, but more than that, a power and strength that survived whatever blows—physical or psychic—had caused the deep shadows around them, giving them the bruised look of a fighter who'd been punched. It might, in fact, have been the face of a fighter, a young black man with a thin mustache who had boxed his way out of the ghetto. He had actually done just that, but with words rather than fists. I knew the name that was set in yellow letters across the top of the black-crowned head in the photograph: James Baldwin. His face stared up at me from the book of essays, *Notes of a Native Son*, on a rack of new paperbacks at the bookstore in Sheridan Square in 1958.

I picked up the book, flipped through the Autobiographical Notes at the beginning, and was as quickly transfixed by the writing as I had been by the eyes on the cover. The words, like the eyes, burned with a special intensity. Though I didn't spend money lightly on books, or on anything else in those days, and this was one of those large, expensive paperbacks priced at $1.25, I bought it and rushed back to my apartment to read it, alive with that heightened excitement of having discovered something so powerful I sensed it could change my own thinking and writing, my very life.

The direct simplicity of the prose, the radiant clarity of it, delivered a message I adopted as a creed. The final sentence of that blazing introduction was not about race relations or what was then called the Negro Question. It seemed to be about how I, as a young journalist aspiring to write novels, might try to conduct myself as a human being in a murderous and corrupting world: "I want to be an honest man and a good writer."

There was the author at the next table.

He was older than the face in the picture. The rather scraggly mustache was gone, and he looked more mature and self-assured. He was thirty-three at the time, and I was twenty-five, a gap that made him seem like a wise elder. His big, staring eyes were like a trademark, an appropriate symbol for the way his unrelenting gaze as a writer penetrated the walls and disguises of a whole social structure. The eyes seemed almost to protrude from his face in a look of unsparing inquiry. (Later, I was shocked to learn that as a child Baldwin had been told he was ugly, and believed it; I thought he was beautiful.) When he turned those eyes

601

on me, I felt that he could see through me, into my mind, read my thoughts, and that I would never be able to avoid or even shade the truth in his presence.

One of the regulars introduced me. Jimmy, he was called, which surprised me. The diminutive didn't seem to suit his natural dignity, the way he held himself so straight, alert, giving his rather small frame a sense of the greater stature he had as a writer and as a man. There was an authority about him, not aggressiveness or pomposity but the earned authority of the Whitman line he quoted as the epigraph of *Giovanni's Room*: "I was the man, I suffered, I was there." You felt that authority in his prose, in the sureness of it, and in his own speech, so that his use of slang or idiom, which would have sounded pretentious or cute from anyone else, seemed right coming from Baldwin. He was the only man I've ever known who could call me "baby" without making me wince.

At the time I met him I was writing *Island in the City*. Baldwin had read some of my pieces in *The Nation* about the emerging civil rights struggle in the South, and he expressed an appreciative interest in my Spanish Harlem book, rather than the condescension or challenge that a black writer born in Harlem might well have presented to a white outsider presuming to report on that scene. He treated me not as an interloper but as a like-minded colleague, a fellow writer. In the same spirit, he also invited me to come by his apartment in the Village and have a drink some afternoon.

Baldwin lived on Horatio Street, in a high-ceilinged studio that was clean and sparsely furnished—all I remember is a couch and a hi-fi set, bare hardwood floors and tall windows. He always offered bourbon, my favorite drink at the time, and we would sip it with ice and talk about Harlem, the South, the racial madness, and politics, but mainly we talked about writing. After reading *Notes of a Native Son*, I had quickly devoured Baldwin's two published novels, *Go Tell It on the Mountain*, a powerhouse family drama of growing up black, and *Giovanni's Room*, about a middle-class American boy in Paris who discovers his homosexuality.

I showed Baldwin the pieces I was writing, and he read them and gave me encouragement, not always in an immediate way, with a "That's good" or "I like it," but sometimes in a later conversation on another subject, when his praise would surprise me. I went to him once full of enthusiasm for a book by John Reed I hadn't read before, praising Reed's prose and his compassion for the people he wrote about, and Baldwin turned those great eyes on me and said, "But that's *you*."

Baldwin and I agreed on our literary preferences, and I loved hearing him extol the virtues of Henry James and deflate what he felt was the overblown literary reputation of the beat writers. He was especially disturbed by Kerouac's romantic portrayal of Negro life, and said once of such a passage in a Kerouac novel, raising his eyebrows with disdain, "He had better not read that from the stage of the Apollo Theater." Referring sardonically to their infatuation with Zen Buddhism and the teachings of D. T. Suzuki, Baldwin liked to refer to Ginsberg, Kerouac, and their followers as "the Suzuki Rhythm Boys."

Sometimes he passed on advice he had gotten from someone else and had adopted for himself. Once, he came back from giving a talk at Howard University extremely stirred by a conversation with a venerable Negro professor he admired on the faculty. The professor had told him always to keep in mind that the work of a writer was first of all to write—rather than to speak or picket or campaign for causes—and that his primary goal in life should be to end up with his own "shelf of books." Baldwin was constantly asked to lend his name and presence to civil rights and other causes he deeply believed in, and he was often torn by the question of how much time to devote to those endeavors. The counsel of the old Howard professor had seemed like a validation of his own wish to put writing first. In giving me the advice, he was reinforcing it for himself as he nodded, pointed a finger at my chest, and said, "Remember, baby. A shelf of books—a whole *shelf*."

Around five o'clock on those afternoons of our talks, the buzzer would sound and other friends would arrive. By eight a Village party of talk and music and drinking would be in full swing, and ended only when the host announced it was time for dinner. He would lead us across the street to El Faro, a Spanish restaurant, where he would commandeer a big table. Baldwin usually paid the bill with a personal check, and those who could afford it tossed in some money.

The talk was always good with Baldwin—he'd been a preacher as a teenager in Harlem, and he spoke in the cadence of biblical prose and with the clarity of a musical instrument, which matched the clarity of his writing. There was no more brilliant conversationalist, but the talk was not always intense and literary; it was often just fun. Baldwin had a delightful sense of humor and a joy that seemed to explode when his face cracked open in an enormous smile and hearty laughter. He could express mountainous irony with a slight upward shift of his eyes, as he did the night we were at a party and he excused himself to phone an editor who was trying to sign up his next book. "It seems I'm in a Madison Avenue price war," he explained, making that tilt of his eyes that spoke his disdain for the whole commercial literary machine.

When he told me the name of the editor he was calling, I winced and said I hoped he wouldn't sign with that man. He had done gratuitous harm to a friend of mine, and he didn't like me either. Baldwin beckoned me to the phone as he made the call and said to the editor, "Hello, this is Jimmy. I'm calling from a party in the Village. I'm here with my friend Dan Wakefield." He grinned, and I smiled back and raised my glass. It was a cold winter night and Baldwin was wearing one of those Russian-style fur hats—he had kept it on after we'd come inside—and he looked mischievous and happy, like a kid.

Unhappily, even in the Village Baldwin could not escape the reality of racial paranoia and hatred. One night he went to a bar down the street from the White Horse called the Paddock, where working people hung out, and sat drinking in a booth with Dick Bagley, the cameraman who shot *On the Bowery* and was one of the White Horse regulars, and two girls of their acquaintance. Some of the patrons were enraged at the sight of a white girl sitting next to a Negro, and they attacked Baldwin and Bagley, beating them brutally.

Baldwin later reminisced about that nightmare episode when he met up with Mike Harrington in Paris in 1963. Jimmy remembered squeezing himself into a ball under the bar as one of the men tried to kick him in the genitals. It was at that moment, Baldwin said, that he knew he would never be safe in white America.

Nor was it only blacks who experienced the violence of "neighbors" in the Village who regarded all bohemians as suspicious interlopers. The hostility toward all nonconformists was heightened during the McCarthy fervor of the fifties, when mostly Irish kids from the surrounding area made raids on the Horse, swinging fists and chairs, calling the regulars "Commies and faggots."

The White Horse was patronized by Irish longshoremen as well as bohemian writers and politicos, and one night Old Ernie, the owner, asked Mike Harrington if he couldn't have his friends sing their radical songs in French or German instead of English so the other customers wouldn't be able to understand the words and get upset.

Another night the Horse closed early, so Mike and his pals moved on to a bar around the corner. They were singing their labor songs when the trade union regulars who drank at the place took the sentiments the wrong way—and the White Horse guys were merely expressing their solidarity with the workers! When the union men threatened Mike and his friends, who they thought were Commies, the owner had to call the police, and the guys from the Horse escaped through the back door.

There was also a long history of hostility to the bohemians from the Italian residents, who made up the largest ethnic group of the Village. When Seymour Krim first moved to Cornelia Street with his girlfriend, he confessed that he was "scared of the Italian street-threat that used to psychically de-ball all us violin-souled Jewish boys who had fled downtown."

My Italian superintendent on Jones Street banged on my door one morning to yell at me for throwing a party for "beatniks" the previous night. I angrily shouted back that one of the guests was my minister from East Harlem, the *Reverend* Norman Eddy, and this quieted him down. What the super really hated me for was the doe-eyed girl he saw emerging from my place in the mornings. He had been her pal and protector when she had first moved in down the street, in another of his buildings, but he stopped speaking to her when he saw her coming from my place after spending the night.

In the ongoing war between the bohemians and beatniks and the locals—working class Irish and Italians—sexual mores were often at the root of the hostility. As Mike Harrington observed in *Fragments of the Century*, when the neighborhood kids attacked the White Horse regulars as "faggots," the epithet expressed "their fury that we were always in the company of good-looking and liberated women while they drank in the patriotic virility of all-male groups."

The tension between bohemian beatniks and Italians had roots going back to the twenties, but in the fifties the conflict erupted politically when independent Democratic reformers in the Village battled Carmine De Sapio's Tammany Hall. I described it as a contest between "two different tribes" when I wrote about it for *Commentary*. The *New York Daily Mirror* called De Sapio's opposition "Village Commies, lefties, eggheads and beatniks." In fact, they were the first yuppies—a bunch of young lawyers and other professionals. One of their leaders was a young guy whom Mike Harrington judged at the time as "a diffident, somewhat lovable schlemiel" with a "retiring, modest manner." I also thought the man a nice, harmless nerd. His name was Ed Koch.

—1992

Mary McCarthy

(1912–1989)

McCarthy refused to keep up with the times. She was always herself. To cite but one example, up until her last days, she used an old nonelectric typewriter, as if only by the stint of her physical effort, she could truly appreciate the creative act. A graduate of Vassar, McCarthy belonged to an elite circle of New York intellectuals, known for her candor and her lacerating wit. Married four times, including an ill-fated match-up with literary critic Edmund Wilson, she wrote sixteen novels, several memoirs, and countless articles and essays. Among her many books include The Company She Keeps, The Groves of Academe, Memories of a Catholic Girlhood, *and, most famously,* The Group. *In the late 1960s and early 1970s she devoted much of her time to journalism, filing reports on the Vietnam War and covering the Watergate hearings.* Intellectual Memoirs *recalls her early years in New York and, thus, the beginning of a career in letters, the collapse of her first marriage and her subsequent move to a tiny, cramped Greenwich Village studio.*

from *Intellectual Memoirs: New York, 1936–1938*

The one-room apartment I moved into on Gay Street had eleven sides. I counted one day when I was sick in bed. The normal quota, including floor and ceiling, would have been six. But my little place had many jogs, many irregularities. There was a tiny kitchen and a bath suited to a bird. It had been furnished by the owner of the building, an architect by the name of Edmond Martin whose office was on Christopher Street. I am not sure he ever built anything, but he had a genius for getting the good out of space that was already there. At no extra charge, he made me a thin, teetery bookcase to fit into one of the nine perpendiculars—he loved to be given a problem. One nice feature was that the little bath had a window beside it so that you could look at the sky while you bathed. Another amusing oddity of the apartment was that, small as it was, it had two street entrances: one on Gay Street and one, leading through a passageway, to Christopher Street, where the bells and mailboxes were. Mr. Martin, who was an engaging person, owned another old house, on Charles Street, in which Elizabeth Bishop lived. Her living-room was bigger than mine and had a fireplace, I think. It must have been through her that I found the Gay Street apartment after Porter left. Or else it was the other way around and she found her place through me. All Mr. Martin's rents were reasonable, and he took good care of his properties.

My bed was a narrow studio-couch with a heavy navy-blue cover and side cushions, which made the room into a living-room, and I had a desk with drawers beside a recessed window. I could entertain only one couple at a time for dinner by putting two chairs at a card table and sitting on the studio-bed myself. I invited Farrell and Hortense (Farrell, a true-blue Irishman, always asked for more mashed potatoes), Chris and Maddie Rand, and I cannot remember who else. Probably Martha McGahan and Frani, together or separately. Margaret Marshall.

All this was very different from our life on Beekman Place; it was as though the number of my friends had shrunk to fit the space I now lived in. Not counting Johnsrud, who came around from time to time and made biting remarks, the only men I knew were Mr. Martin and the husbands of friends. The assiduous men who had been after me while I was married, such as Corliss Lamont and the absurd Lazslo Kormendi, had vanished. Nobody took me out to dinner, and when I did not cook something for myself, I ate at a second-floor restaurant called Shima's on Eighth Street, where the food was cheap and fairly good. But it typed you to be a regular at Shima's, because no one, male or female, ever went there with a date. Today it would be called a singles' restaurant, with the difference that there were no pick-ups. Night after night at dinnertime, I faced the choice of hiding my shame at home or exposing it at Shima's. I always took a book to bury myself in, on the ostrich principle.

Sometimes on Sundays, Farrell's kindly publisher, Jim Henle of Vanguard Press, asked me to lunch at the house he and his wife, Marjorie, had in Hartsdale, half an hour or so from New York. But I could not hope to meet any unattached men there, I discovered. It was an office group like a family, headed by Evelyn Schrifte, eventually Henle's successor at Vanguard; the only author present was Farrell. Still, going out there was fun; I liked the Henles. But apart from those Sundays, the only break in the monotony of my first months as a divorcee on Gay Street was when the man in the Brooks Brothers shirt—real name George Black—came from Pittsburgh and took me to the World Series. The Giants were playing the Yankees, and Fat Freddie Fitzsimmons was pitching in the game we went to. When, at his insistence, I brought the "man" home, so that he could see how I lived, he was shocked and begged me to move. He still thought he wanted me to marry him, even though I would no longer let him make love to me. In the story I wrote about it nearly four years later (on the Cape during the fall of France), the heroine sees him several times in New York posthumously to their love-affair on the train, but I remember only the once—the excitement of being at the World Series (and with a National League fan; he had arranged our box-seat tickets through the Pittsburgh Pirates), and having dinner with him afterward—at Longchamps, it must have been. I have a very faint recollection of a duck he had shot that started to smell in my icebox because I did not know how to take off the feathers and cook it. In the story, I changed several things about him, including where he was from, in case his wife might somehow come upon it and recognize him. Really he lived in Sewickley, a fashionable outskirt of Pittsburgh, belonged to the

Duquesne Club, and worked for American Radiator and Standard Sanitary—plumbing. The man in the story was in steel. (When it came out in 1941 in *Partisan Review*, Jay Laughlin of New Directions was telling people that the "man" was Wendell Willkie, who had run for president the year before.) George Black's ardor was an embarrassment to me—a deserved punishment. Hard up as I was for male company, I kept him out of sight. None of my friends knew about him, and until now I have not told his name.

Those must have been the harshest months of my life. My grandfather was sending me an allowance of $25 a week, since the Capital Elevator stocks I had inherited from the McCarthys were not paying dividends any more, or very little. I did some reviews for *The Nation* and I looked for a job. Someone sent me to a man who lived in the St. Moritz Hotel and needed a collaborator for a book he was writing on the influence of sunspots on the stock market. No. At last Mannie Rousuck, now with Ehrich Newhouse and starting on his upward climb, was able to give me half a day's work at the gallery, writing descriptions of paintings for letters he sent to prospects. Some of the addressees were the same ones we had written to at the Carleton Gallery—Ambrose Clark, Mrs. Hartley Dodge—though my subjects were no longer just dogs but English sporting scenes with emphasis on horses, English portraits, conversation pieces, coaching scenes. I think he paid me $15 a week, which, with the allowance from my grandfather, was more than enought to support me. I could even serve drinks.

Nonetheless I was despondent. If I had been given to self-pity, I would surely have fallen into it. I did not much regret breaking up with John,* especially because he was taking a sardonic, mock-courteous tone with me, and I had almost forgotten Porter. It was not that I wanted either of them back. I saw plenty of John as it was, and I would have been horrified if Porter had appeared on my doorstep. There was no room for him in my multi-faceted apartment. My renting it showed that I had not thought of him as being in my life at all.

---

* McCarthy's first husband, Harold Cooper Johnsrud.

In recent years I have read more than once that Edmund Wilson was on the Trotsky Committee. What an opportunity for us to have to got to know each other! But I never saw him at any Committee meeting.

Being on the Committee marked the end of my awful solitude. Some time around Christmas things began to improve. I was meeting people—*men*. Part of that had to do with the Committee. ("Dear Abby" in her column advises her lonely-heart readers to join a group—church group, she recommends), but a lot was coincidence. For instance, Bob Misch of the Wine and Food Society. How had I met him? Maybe through my friends Gene and Florine Katz. Misch was in the advertising business, single, German Jewish, and the very active secretary of the wine and food organization, whose head was André Simon, in London. He fancied himself as a cook and a knowledgeable bon vivant. His short, stocky, dark, well-fed body made me think of a pouter pigeon. Probably someone took me to one of his Wine and Food tastings: on a series of tables various wines were grouped around a theme—Rhine wines, Loire wines, Burgundies—one sampled them, made notes, and compared. On the tables there were also little things to eat, "to clear the palate," and probably water to rinse your mouth out. It was educational, it was intoxicating, and it was free. After the first time, my name was on their list, and I always accepted. Soon he was asking me to the little dinners he gave in his West Side apartment, quite evidently as his partner; his specialty was black bean soup with sherry and slices of hard-boiled egg. The reader will find something like those dinners in the chapter called "The Genial Host" in *The Company She Keeps*. If I may give an opinion, it is the weakest thing in the book. No doubt that is because I was unwilling to face the full reality of the relationship. In real life I slept with him and in the story I don't. I suppose I was ashamed. Misch was eager to make me expensive presents (such as handbags) and to do services for me that I didn't want. Even after I stopped sleeping with him, which was soon, he kept on asking me to those dinners, and I kept on accepting, because of his insistence and because, as the chapter says (though without mentioning sex between us), I was not quite ready to break with him, being still "so poor, so loverless, so lonely."

The guests at those little dinners were mostly Stalinists, which was what smart, successful people in that New York world were. And they were mostly Jewish; as was often pointed out to me, with gentle amusement, I was the only non-Jewish person in the room. It was at Misch's that I first met Lillian Hellman, who had been brought, I guess, by his friend Louis Kronenberger. But I may mix her up with another Stalinist, by the name of Leane Zugsmith. It was with Hellman, just back from Spain, that I had angry words about the Spanish Civil War. Probably, as happens in the chapter, I grew heated about the murdered POUM leader, Andrés Nin.

That same evening (more or less as related), I started on a brief affair with Leo Huberman (*Man's Worldly Goods*), who was a suave sort of Stalinist and married. But I no longer needed Misch's dinners to meet new people, not even new Stalinists. Suddenly the woods were full of them. If I met Huberman there, I was also seeing Bill Mangold (not Jewish; it means a kind of beet in German), a Yale classmate of Alan Barth's whom I first met at Webster Hall a couple of years before. Now he took me to dinner, at a fun place where we danced. He was separated from his wife; he was going to a psychoanalyst (the first analysand in my personal history); he was amusing and worked for medical aid to the Loyalists in Spain, a Stalinist front. We did not discuss politics, which no doubt eased the difficulty of having a quite active and friendly love-affair with a distinctly Trotskyist girl. Of all the men I slept with in my studio-bed on Gay Street (and there were a lot; I stopped counting), I liked Bill Mangold the best. Until I began to see Philip Rahv.

Once I got started, I saw all sorts of men that winter. Often one led to another. Most of them I slept with at least one time. There was Harold ("Hecky") Rome, who wrote the lyrics for the ILGWU musical *Pins and Needles* ("Sing me a song with social significance"); we cooked a steak together one night in his apartment—perfect. There was a little man who made puppets that appeared on the cover of *Esquire* and another little man, very droll and witty, who was married and worked for a publisher—he came to my place from the office in the afternoon and was a bit nervous despite his aplomb. There was a truck driver whose name I have forgotten, if I ever knew it, whom I met in the bar at Chumley's. I did not go to bars alone, so someone must have taken me—probably John—and then left.

It was getting rather alarming. I realized one day that in twenty-four hours I had slept with three different men. And one morning I was in bed with somebody while over his head I talked on the telephone with somebody else. Though slightly scared by what things were coming to, I did not *feel* promiscuous. Maybe no one does. And maybe more girls sleep with more men than you would ever think to look at them.

I was able to compare the sexual equipment of the various men I made love with, and there were amazing differences, in both length and massiveness. One handsome married man, who used to arrive with two Danishes from a very good bakery, had a penis about the size and shape of a lead pencil; he shall remain nameless. In my experience, there was usually a relation to height, as Philip Rahv and Bill Mangold, both tall men, bore out. There may be dwarfish men with monstrously large organs, but I have never known one. It was not till later, after my second divorce, that I met an impotent man or a pervert (two of the latter). Certainly sexual happiness—luxurious contentment—did make quite a difference in my feeling for a lover. Yet it was not always the decisive factor. None of my partners, the reader will be relieved to hear, had a venereal disease.

The best news was that I had found a job in publishing. Before I went to Reno, Eunice Clark, no longer married to Selden, had taken me to the cafeteria in the Central Park Zoo (really a menagerie), where at some outdoor tables near the seal pool a group of young people of the intellectual sort gathered in the late afternoon to drink beer and watch the seals. There I had met Pat Covici, of the firm Covici-Friede, who was aware of my *Nation* articles. I told him I was looking for a job in publishing. One day in the fall, when I was long back from Reno, there was Mr. Covici again, white-haired and benevolent, who claimed to have been looking for me. "You are as evanescent as a cloud," he told me, in his accented voice, and offered me a job in his office.

At Covici, I read manuscripts and looked for new authors in quarterly magazines like the *Southern Review*: when I came on a story I liked, I would write the author and ask for a possible sample of a longer work. One of those I wrote to was Eudora Welty. Besides this scouting and manuscript-reading, I edited, proofread, and farmed out texts in foreign languages to qualified readers to report on. Opposite me, in a medium-sized office, sat a long-nosed Stalinist woman named Miss Broene, who intensely disapproved of my politics, my many telephone calls and long lunch hours, my arrival time at work in the morning. Our boss was Harold Strauss (later at Knopf), who had a lisping disapproval of what he called "photographic realism," meaning specifically my friend Jim Farrell. Strauss was not especially political, but there were several Stalinists in our top management, not including Mr. Covici, thank God. Mr. Covici read literary books and magazines and was a fatherly sort of person. One day he took me to lunch with his star author, John Steinbeck, at the Prince George Hotel. I did not care for Steinbeck's work (as I had said in *The Nation*) and I did not care for him. He reciprocated.

I am eternally grateful for having learned the mechanics of publishing at Covici, how to copy-edit and how to proofread. I learned printer's signs and the marks to make on a manuscript before sending it to the printer. For instance, you lower-cased a capital letter by drawing a slash through it; to upper-case, you drew three lines under a letter and wrote "cap" in the margin; if you wanted to retain a hyphen, you made it into an "equals" sign. In all this, the dour Miss Broene, who had turned Communist after being fired from Consumer Research for union organizing, was instructive and really quite helpful. All the while she was denouncing me to the office chapter of the Book and Magazine Guild for my persistent lateness to work.

Also to enter on the plus side was Philip Rahv. Remembering him from Farrell's parties, I called him one day when we needed a reader for a German text Mr. Covici was considering. Or it may have been the memoirs in Russian of the wonderful Angelica Balabanov, who had been close to Mussolini in his socialist days, then close to Lenin, and was now a left-wing anti-Communist. Rahv, who had been born in the Ukraine of Zionist parents, knew Russian, German, and Hebrew and he was able to read some French. When I called him, he came to the Covici office, and we talked a little in the waiting-room. He had a shy, soft voice (when he was not shouting), big, dark lustrous eyes, which he rolled with great expression, and the look of a bambino in an Italian sacred painting. I liked him. Soon he was taking me out to dinner in the Village, holding my elbow as we walked, and soon we were lovers. I gave up Bill Mangold with a small pang. Politically Rahv and I were more alike—he was breaking at last with the Party and joining the Trotsky Committee—and I was greatly excited by his powerful intellect, but Mangold, with his Yale background, was more my kind of person. Had I not got to know Rahv, I might have married Mangold, if he ever got his divorce. Years later an avatar of him took form in *The Group*, in the figure of Gus Leroy, the publisher, with whom Polly Andrews, poor girl, is in love.

Rahv worked on the Writers' Project—part of President Roosevelt's WPA program—and did occasional reviews for *The Nation*. But he had no other source of income, except odd jobs like the one he was doing for Covici. That did not trouble me. It only meant that we couldn't get married. Somewhere there was a wife named Naomi, whom I never saw. He had lived apart from her for a long time but could not pay for a divorce. But we did not think of marriage anyway. I believed in free unions, and so, I guess, did he. He and William Phillips dreamed of reviving *Partisan Review*, but for that they would have had to have money or an organizational tie, such as the one with the Party that they had lost when they crossed over. When we first became lovers, Philip, as I recall, had not yet met Dwight Macdonald, who in turn would introduce him to his Yale friend George L. K. Morris (of the Gouverneur Morris family; his brother was Newbold), an American abstract painter and our future backer.

I believe I had been instrumental in the de-Stalinization of Dwight. When he left *Fortune,* over their censoring of his U.S. Steel article, I took him downtown to lunch with Margaret Marshall, so that he could have an outlet for his views in *The Nation's* back pages. In the course of one of those lunches I discovered that dear Dwight actually believed in the Moscow trials. Once he was set straight by the two of us, he swiftly rebounded as far as one could go in the opposite direction; characteristically, he did not come to rest at a midpoint, such as entering the Socialist Party. Almost before I knew it, he was an embattled Trotskyite, of the Schachtmanite tendency. Meanwhile, through me or through Fred Dupee, he met Rahv and Phillips, who were already seriously talking to Fred with a view to his leaving *New Masses* to join them in a revived, anti-Stalinist *PR* and take a list of their subscribers with him. Dwight brought George Morris into the project, proposing to make him the art critic, with a monthly column, and the new *PR* was born.

By early summer, while all this was starting to happen, Philip and I had moved in together. The Gay Street apartment was too small for us (Philip, though still slender then, was a big man), but by good luck I had friends, Abbie Bregman and his wife, Kit, a descendant of Julius Rosenwald—Sears, Roebuck—who had a Beekman Place walk-up apartment that was going to be empty all summer. Unless I wanted to use it? Of course I accepted; the problem was how to convey that there would be another occupant, to them a complete stranger. Well, I told them, and they still urged me to use the place and the maid who came with it. Thus Philip and I found ourselves living amid severely elegant modern furnishings, all glass, steel, and chrome on thick beige rugs. I think Philip felt compromised by that apartment (which did not resemble either of us) and by the Sears, Roebuck money behind it, which did not resemble us either. He was embarrassed to receive his friends, such as Lionel Abel, whom I remember there one night as a malicious, watchful presence out of Roman comedy.

—1992

Anatole Broyard

(1920–1990)

Anatole Broyard was a book critic, columnist, and editor for the New York Times *for nearly twenty years. His memoir of Greenwich Village in the late 1940s captures the sounds and scents, the personalities and rich street life of a particular time and place. Evocative and pungent, Broyard uses his remarkable sense of recall to conjure up vivid word pictures. His writing is precise and muscular, a poignant portrait of the way things used to be. This was the time, he writes, "when Kafka was the rage, as were the Abstract Expressionists and revisionism in psychoanalysis.*

from *Kafka Was the Rage: A Greenwich Village Memoir*

Nineteen forty-six was a good time—perhaps the best time—in the twentieth century. The war was over, the Depression had ended, and everyone was rediscovering the simple pleasures. A war is like an illness and when it's over you think you've never felt so well. There's a terrific sense of coming back, of repossessing your life.

New York City had never been so attractive. The postwar years were like a great smile in its sullen history. The Village was as close in 1946 as it would ever come to Paris in the twenties. Rents were cheap, restaurants were cheap, and it seemed to me that happiness itself might be cheaply had. The streets and bars were full of writers and painters and the kind of young men and women who liked to be around them. In Washington Square would-be novelists and poets tossed a football near the fountain and girls just out of Ivy League colleges looked at the landscape with art history in their eyes. People on the benches held books in their hands.

Though much of the Village was shabby, I didn't mind. I thought all character was a form of shabbiness, a wearing away of surfaces. I saw this shabbiness as our version of ruins, the relic of a short history. The sadness of the buildings was literature. I was twenty-six, and sadness was a stimulant, even an aphrodisiac.

Five or six weeks after moving in with Sheri, I opened a bookshop on Cornelia Street. This was something I had decided to do while I was in the army. It started with some money I made on the black market in Tokyo, where a suit of GI long johns brought $120. I was thinking about what I might do with the money.

I was working the night shift in Yokohama harbor and I was lonely, cold, and bored. Yokohama was a sad place that had been flattened by bombs and the inhabitants were living in shacks made of rubble, propped up in fields of rubble. Since they couldn't lock up these shacks, they took all their belongings with them when they went out. They carried their whole lives on their backs, wrapped in an evil-smelling blanket or a sack that made them look like hunchbacks.

My outfit, a stevedore battalion, had arrived right after MacArthur, and my first job as a dock officer was to scrape a solid crust of shit off a dock a quarter of a mile long. I didn't realize at first that it was human shit. As I figured it out later, Japanese stevedores and embarking soldiers had had no time for niceties toward the end and had simply squatted down wherever they stood. The entire dock was covered with a layer that was as hard as clay. The rain and traffic had packed it down.

I had my own company of 220 men to supervise the job and I was given 1,500 Japanese who would actually chop the stuff away. We provided them with axes, shovels, sledgehammers, picks, crowbars—whatever we could find. We had no bulldozers. They chopped and scraped for three days and then the Medical Corps hosed down the dock with chemicals.

It was on this same dock, where you could still smell the chemicals, that I was wondering the night I got the idea of the bookstore. I had two gangs unloading the forward hatches of a ship and I was leaning on the rail, under the yellowish overhead spots. It was about three o'clock in the morning and I felt a million miles from home, from anywhere. For something to do, I was thinking about books, trying to see if I could quote passages or whole poems the way some people can.

Mostly it was only single lines I remembered, perhaps because I was tired. Wallace Stevens was my favorite poet and I murmured a few scraps from his books to myself: "Too many waltzes have ended." "Apostrophes are forbidden on the funicular." "The windy sky cries out a literate despair." "These days of disinheritance we feast on human heads." It was reassuring to think, in the middle of the night in this foreign place, that there were people in the world who would take the trouble to write things like that. This was another, wonderful kind of craziness, at the opposite end from the craziness of the army.

We were unloading boxes of condensed milk and as I watched a pallet swing over the rail, I thought that when I got home I would open a bookshop in the Village. It would be a secondhand bookshop, specializing in twentieth-century literature. I remember that the idea made me feel warm. I took my hands out of my pockets and squeezed them together. To open a bookstore is one of the persistent romances, like living off the land or sailing around the world.

After a couple of months of looking, I bought out an old Italian junk dealer on Cornelia Street. I paid him three hundred dollars and agreed to move his stock to a new location. I hired a truck and we carried out old boilers, radiators, bathtubs, sinks, pipes of all sizes, and miscellaneous bits and pieces of metal.

Nineteen forty-six was a good time for a secondhand bookshop, because everything was out of print and the paperback revolution had not yet arrived. People had missed books during the war, and there was a sense of reunion, like meeting old friends or lovers. Now there was time for everything, and buying books became a popular postwar thing to do. For young people who had just left home to go live in the Village, books were like dolls or teddy bears or family portraits. They populated a room.

When I left Brooklyn to live in the Village, I felt as if I had acquired a new set of relatives, like a surprising number of uncles I had never met before, men who lived in odd places, sometimes abroad, who had shunned family life and been shunned in turn, who were somewhere between black sheep and prodigal sons of a paradoxical kind. An aura of scandal, or at least of ambiguity, hovered over these uncles, as if they had run away with someone's wife or daughter. There was a flaw in their past, some kind of unhealthiness, even a hint of insanity.

These uncles were, of course, my favorite authors, the writers I most admired. I felt them waiting, almost calling out to me. They were more real than anything I had ever known, real as only imagined things can be, real as dreams that seem so unbearably actual because they are cleansed of all irrelevancies. These uncles, these books, moved into the vacuum of my imagination.

They were all the family I had now, all the family I wanted. With them, I could trade in my embarrassingly ordinary history for a choice of fictions. I could lead a hypothetical life, unencumbered by memory, loyalties, or resentments. The first impulse of adolescence is to wish to be an orphan or an amnesiac. Nobody in the Village had a family. We were all sprung from our own brows, spontaneously generated the way flies were once thought to have originated.

I didn't yet see the tragedy of my family: I still thought of them as a farce, my laughable past. In my new incarnation, in books I could be halfway heroic, almost tragic. I could be happy, for the first time, in my tragedy.

I realize that people still read books now and some people actually love them, but in 1946 in the Village our feelings about books—I'm talking about my friends and myself—went beyond love. It was as if we didn't know where we ended and books began. Books were our weather, our environment, our clothing. We didn't simply read books; we became them. We took them into ourselves and made them into our histories. While it would be easy to say that we escaped into books, it might be truer to say that books escaped into us. Books were to us what drugs were to young men in the sixties.

They showed us what was possible. We had been living with whatever was close at hand, whatever was given, and books took us great distances. We had known only domestic emotions and they showed us what happens to emotions when they are homeless. Books give us balance—the young are so unbalanced that anything can make them fall. Books steadied us; it was as if we carried a heavy bag of them in each hand and they kept us level. They gave us gravity.

If it hadn't been for books, we'd have been completely at the mercy of sex. There was hardly anything else powerful enough to distract or deflect us; we'd have been crawling after sex, writhing over it all the time. Books enabled us to see ourselves as characters—yes, we were characters!—and this gave us a bit of control.

Though we read all kinds of books, there were only a handful of writers who were our uncles, our family. For me, it was Kafka, Wallace Stevens, D. H. Lawrence, and Celine. These were the books I liked, the books that I read, and they wouldn't fill more than a few shelves, so I went over to Fourth Avenue, which was lined with bookshops, and bought books by the titles, the subjects, the bindings, or the publishers. I was given a 20 percent dealer's discount and I thought I could charge my customers fifty cents or one dollar more for the pleasure of findings these books in a clean, well-lighted place. Although I had never read Balzac, I bought a fifty-volume uniform edition of his novels in a red binding with gold-edged pages. I got it for only nineteen dollars.

There were people in the Village who had more books than money, and I appealed to them in the literary quarterlies. Like someone buying a dog, I assured them that I'd give their books a good home. But it was an unhappy business, because many of

these people suffered from separation anxiety. Those who were depressed by letting their books go tended to devaluate them, while
others who were more in the hysterical mode asked such enormous
sums that I knew it was their souls they were selling. Pricing an
out-of-print book is one of the most poignant forms of criticism.

Seeing how young I was, everyone gave me advice. Get
Christopher Caudwell, they said. Get Kenneth Burke, William
Empson, F. R. Leavis, Paul Valery. Get Nathanael West, Celine, Un-
amuno, Italo Svevo, Hermann Broch, *The Egyptian Book of the Dead*.
Edward Dahlberg, Baron Corvo, Djuna Barnes—get them too. But
above all, at any cost, I must get Kafka. Kafka was as popular in the
Village at that time as Dickens had been in Victorian London. But
his books were very difficult to find—they must have been printed
in very small editions—and people would rush in wild-eyed, almost foaming at the mouth, willing to pay anything for Kafka.

Literary criticism was enjoying a vogue. As Randall Jarrell said,
some people consulted their favorite critic about the conduct of
their lives as they had once consulted their clergymen. The war had
left a bitter taste, and literary criticism is the art of bitter tastes.

A thin, intense young man with a mustache came into the shop
and instructed me in bibliophilic etiquette. A bookshop, he said,
should have an almost ecclesiastical atmosphere. There should be
an odor, or redolence of snuffed candles, dryness, desuetude—
even contrition. He gazed at the shelves, the floor, the stamped tin
ceiling. It's too clean here, he said, too cheerful.

I had imagined myself like Saint Jerome in his study, bent over
his books, with the tamed lion of his conquered restlessness at his
feet. My customers would come and go in studious silence, pausing, with averted eyes, to leave the money on my desk. But it didn't
turn out like that. What I hadn't realized was that, for many people,
a bookshop is a place of last resort, a kind of moral flophouse. Many
of my customers were the kind of people who go into a bookshop
when all other diversions have failed them. Those who had no
friends, no pleasures, no resources came to me. They came to read
the handwriting on the wall, the bad news. They studied the shelves
like people reading the names on a war memorial.

There was something in the way a particular person would take a book from a shelf, the way it was opened and sniffed, that made me want to snatch it away. Others would seize upon a book that was obviously beyond them. I could tell by their faces, their clothes, by their manners, the way they moved, that they'd misread the book or get nothing out of it. The kind of person who is satirized or attacked in a book is often the very person to buy it and pretend to enjoy it. As Mallarme said, "If a person of average intelligence and insufficient literary preparation opens one of my books and pretends to enjoy it, there has been a mistake. Things must be returned to their places."

It was the talkers who gave me the most trouble. Like the people who had sold me books, the talkers wanted to sell me their lives, their fictions about themselves, their philosophies. Following the example of the authors on the shelves, infected perhaps by them, they told me of their families, their love affairs, their illusions and disillusionments. I was indignant. I wanted to say, Wait a minute! I've already got stories here! Take a look at those shelves!

While I pretended to listen, I asked myself which were more real—theirs, or the stories on the shelves. "The familiar man makes the hero artificial," Wallace Stevens said. In the commonplaceness of their narratives, some of these talkers anticipated the direction that American fiction would eventually take—away from the heroic, the larger than life, toward the ordinary, the smaller than life.

As they talked on, I thought of all the junk I had carried out of the shop—the boilers, bathtubs, and radiators. These people were bringing it all back—all the clutter, the cast-off odds and ends of their lives. It was more than I had bargained for. Literature was tough enough, with its gaudy sadness, but this miscellany—these heartaches off the street—was too much for me. In the contest between life and literature, life wins every time.

—1993

Herbert Gold

(b. 1924)

Raised in Cleveland, Ohio, Herbert Gold, like many a Midwestern boy made his way around the world, before eventually spending some time in Greenwich Village, the queen of America's bohemias. He wrote about the Village, past and present, in Bohemia: Where Art, Angst, Love, and Strong Coffee Meet, *his whirlwind tour of bohemian communities around the world. A longtime resident of San Francisco, Herbert Gold was awarded the Sherwood Anderson Prize for fiction in 1989.*

from *Bohemia: Where Art, Angst, Love, and Strong Coffee Meet*

"Greenwich Village, a Palimpsest"

More than a hundred years before the words *underground* and *counterculture* wafted through the air of the sixties, America's first Bohemians—the first to take the name—gathered in a basement beer hall called Pfaff's in Greenwich Village and plotted to produce the *New York Saturday Press*. Its stars were Edgar Allan Poe and Walt Whitman. Whitman liked to drink his beer underground with an audience of manly compañeros at Pfaff's: Artemus Ward and Mark Twain also blew foam, told lies, and contributed to the *Saturday Press*.

Herbert Gold. From *Bohemia: Where Art, Angst, Love, and Strong Coffee Meet* (1993). Reprinted by permission of the author.

One of the Pfaff's circle, FitzHugh Ludlow, who competed with Poe as a consumer of opium and hashish, was more successful as a drug addict than a writer. He lives on through the library of psychedelic lore, established in San Francisco in the 1960s and then moved hither and yon, called the FitzHugh Ludlow Memorial Library. The daughter of one of its curators, not to be named here, is a contemporary movie star. "As a result of my strict psychedelic discipline, she's no flakier than the rest of them," declares her proud father.

Bohemians have grown rich in names for themselves—beatniks, hippies, counterculturalists, punks, New Wavers, and more, reflecting changes in the species. Techno-shamanists use virtual-reality machinery and smart drugs to time-trip into cyberspace . . . or back to the origins among the volcanic gods in the Promised Land of Maui . . . or at least downtown into a cool club which serves Gatorade fortified with extra vitamins on weekend blissouts. Of the making of movements there is no end; nor to the naming of them—*techno-shamanism?* Trance-dancing, Ecstasy (formerly an animal tranquilizer), ultrasaturated inner-childism were briefly revived as vanguard innovations of the early nineties. Memory is not the strong suit here.

Real estate sorceror's apprentices have responded to the inflation of demand by extending New York's Bohemia into a half dozen neighborhoods; Greenwich Village begat the East Village, Soho, the Upper West Side, the gentrifying Noho now seeping inexorably toward the Bowery, and Loizaida (Hispanic for "Lower East Side"). What I happen to be revisiting these days is Village Classic, not yet totally zoned for tourism or condominiumized into a safe haven for professionals. Specifically where I'm staying for some months is the far western portion of the Village which has earned its own nickname, the Fertile Crescent, because of the prevalence of handsome young families. It's not all just beautiful models, actors, poets, and crazies. It's also architects with long-legged wives pushing baby strollers into Lanciani's on West Fourth Street for their breakfast coffee and a session of "sharing."

Since this is real life, not a movie, some of the lovely long-legged mothers have short legs. One of them uses the insights gained from Eli Siegel's Aesthetic Realism to manage mutual funds while the kid is in day care. Those are mere details.

The first time I found the Village, as a teenage runaway from Lakewood, Ohio—bidding formal good-byes to tearful parents and declaring my intention to explore the world, so it was more wanderjahr than runaway extrachromosome fugue—I stayed at the Mills Hotel on Bleecker Street. Fifty cents a night, and cubicles hosed down with disinfectant every morning, so you had to carry your bundle all day and reapply for admission in the evening. I was kept awake by coughers hacking, spitters spitting, and religious fanatics throwing Bibles at each other, and couldn't afford the fifty cents anyway, not to complain of the germs or all-male sexual harassment offered a seventeen-year-old. I moved into a hot-sheets rooming house, one boy among the whores—it was healthier and more congenial. An older woman of nineteen shared her frozen Mars bars with me.

Now the old Mills Hotel has evolved into some kind of arts center, next door to the Village Gate, which I sometimes visit for its jazz or when Garry Goodrow is performing. For a while just before he took his life, Abbie Hoffman used to broadcast his shrewd, brave, goofy calls to revolution from underground at the Gate. It was pirate radio but listed on your FM dial. Due to plastic surgery while a fugitive, plus the plain passing of time, he had lost his heroic incendiary look.

In that dreamy chaos of my seventeenth year, I worked first as a Mercury messenger and then as a busboy, hurrying back and forth over the Minetta stream without knowing it was buried there. I tramped past artists—berets, capes, beards—and knew they were weird and I liked them. Their real lives were as secret and hidden from me as the Minetta stream.

Years and years later, I suavely took beer or meals at the San Remo with Anatole Broyard the writer, or at the Lion's Head with David Amram the Renaissance musician, or with the actor and poet Garry Goodrow at the Rio Mar on Little West Twelfth Street, or Indian vegetarian food with my actress daughter Nina or with the novelist Jerome Charyn, or muffin and coffee breakfasts at Lanciani's with the theater director Arthur Sherman and whoever happened by until the consensus seemed to quarrel with management (maybe someone tried to escape without paying and was rudely yelled at), or escorted various women companions to various up- or down-scale places in the rituals of courtship and trying to seem *interesting*. The traditional Village has seeped east and west, and south to Soho, Noho, and TriBeCa. Bohemia in Manhattan is a spreading stain. Brooklyn Heights, the Upper West Side, and even distant Hoboken catch the urban overflow.

Recently I sat at Art D'Lugoff's Village Gate with Art D'Lugoff, being treated, and remembered the Mills Hotel next door, where they didn't treat. At that time I fretted about the nickel subway fare, half the cost of pea soup with two slices of rye bread and good sweet butter in a nearby Sheridan Square diner. Now I complained about people asking if I used a word processor. A writer shambled up and asked if he could telephone my publisher to ask for a free copy of one of my books. "Sure, that's the best way," I said.

"Who's your publisher?"

"Souvlaki, Burrito, and Knish."

"Are they good? Would they like to see a road novel that blows Kerouac, Burroughs, and Bukowsky right out of the water?"

"That's just what they're looking for, man. Tell 'em I sent you."

He gazed at me fondly. "You're a terrific dude. . . ." The four dots implied: for a guy who has lived too long, taking up room in the world which rightly belonged to him.

In the late fifties, sex and abstract expressionism came together for me when I was sprung out of Detroit and a dire marriage. First a beautiful heroin-addicted Scandinavian dancer, unspeaking and mysterious, seemed willing to undertake a rescue mission. But Lenka also engaged in secret communications with my wife. She asked one of her jealous lovers to spy under the blinds and report to my wife what he saw. You might say I was restarting sex and love on the bottom rung.

After I left Detroit for the Village, first one and then another abstract expressionism painter taught me that actual companionship could be brought to the play of sex; a weather of goodwill could remain steady rather than as merely an intermittent prayer by one or the other huffing partner. There could be friendship.

The spacey dancer decided the opportunities for jazz and metaphysic were greater on Thompson Street in the Village than on Cass Avenue near Wayne State University in Detroit. She floated back into my scene, her wafting at me seemed unfinished business. I still wanted her. She couldn't be mad, I decided, because she looked into my eyes so hospitably, pitilessly, when we made love. Yet I gradually discovered that she was also the girlfriend of a famous heroin-addicted black jazz drummer, that she used too, that her other lover sent her onto the streets to earn money for smack, that she still wrote pain-giving letters and made pain-giving telephone calls to my former wife . . . that she was mad. She was a would-be who sought destruction. She looked at me coolly as I groaned, wondering what it was like to be alive.

To learn so much about harm from someone whose eyes became the eyes of God when we made love was an instruction in my lack of immortality. I could fail myself and others. I could lose. I'm still learning that lesson with the losses time brings.

Pernicious and premature nostalgia was one of the felonies of the Bohemian life; nameless longing merely a misdemeanor, punishable by being forced to linger at café tables, gazing at representatives of whatever dream of fulfillment passed by. The passersby were probably committing the same error, only with different fulfillments in mind.

Otto, an old-time nostalgist, used to murmur in Julius's and the San Remo, "Too many dances have ended," perhaps misquoting Wallace Stevens or even making it up for himself. I urged him not to surrender. But the generalized torporous grief was real (as real as generalized torpor). If Otto and the other poets weren't heard by America or answered by God, it was because they couldn't murmur louder than the shouting jukeboxes stacked with Jerry Lee Lewis, the Temptations, Fabian, and Frankie Avalon. Whatever Renaissance of the Arts was happening in the Village, the music seemed to express the Renaissance of South Philadelphia and the marriage of Italian and black pop soul music. There were still only a few blacks in the Village—mainly the A-Trainers who came on weekends to pick up the Bronx Bagel Babies—but there seemed to be a thin Harlemesque sultriness in the air. The few blacks that actually lived around Washington or Sheridan Squares were treasured as emissaries and pioneers. We were the Indians greeting them on the beaches. The highest levels of colonizing blacks were the few who attended lectures at the New School on West Twelfth Street. As a Jew, one from the Midwest, I had a minimum cachet for the long-tressed young beauties out of Smith and Bryn Mawr. The black guys had the maximum. Even the ones strolling round and round the fountain in Washington Square, the beatnik naval basin, could pretty much get what they wanted while not giving up that ungiving pout, the inward silence, which later became the fashionable face for Black Panthers and Black Muslims.

Of course, the previous is false and misleading as all true generalizations are false. Ted Joans was a jokey, affable, easygoing charmer, a poet, a survivor, offering unabashed fun for himself, for me, apparently for the women he loved, and even for the many children he sired. Ted Joans had the charm of a man in a role that fit him perfectly, hustling poetry and merriment.

The rest of us were busy being not what we had been, although not quite sure what we would be busy with when we became what we dimly imagined we were supposed to be. We were less snug in our new roles. I had the advantage over some of knowing what I *wanted* to be, a writer. It was an edge I shared, of course, with a working percentage of artists. But my evolving condition of would-be-ness didn't seem different to the world from those whose final resting place was in the ultimate status of would-be. Even those of you who occasionally finished a story, a painting, a song, had to start from zero again after the brief throb of satisfaction. Virginity grew back anew each time the moon was full.

The smoky dusks of the Village, the smells of wine, coffee, cigarettes, and girls—I cite the now-forbidden word because that used to be the name for these bearers of magic—the hope and desire and dreaming, the anguish of time passing without results despite our convictions of immortality. . . . That's what the Village was to a fellow traveler of the Beatnik party of the late fifties.

Just a Boy without a Dog

I've known three Greenwich Villages, and yet I'm still just a boy without a dog. The first was when I came to New York as a teenage midwestern kid, finding my best level running up and down the avenues for Mercury Messenger Service. On my first delivery I knocked at a door on Washington Square, answering the question, Who was I? with: "I'm Mercury."

"Then where are the wings on your feet?" said the artist who received me. It was still the Village of caped poets, red-checked tablecloths in cheap spaghetti restaurants, and pale huge-eyed seekers from elsewhere. When the Minetta stream, flowing beneath, burst into a basement of MacDougal Street, I realized that this had been farm and pasture land, not so long ago, before e. e. cummings came to mope and sing on Patchin Place.

Then, as a young writer in the fifties, I slipped into "the Village scene" of that period, playing softball with painters from the Cedar Tavern, hanging out at the Eighth Street Bookstore, engaging in nonfights with literary pugilists at the White Horse Tavern, where Dylan Thomas topped himself off with fatal alcohol. When I sneered at the man at the next table, or he thought I had sneered, he put up his fists and said, "Come on, fight." Reluctantly I went along with the program, lifted my hands. But then, before the first blow could be struck, he asked, "What's your name?" and when I answered, said, "Hey, I kind of like your stuff."

He told me his name, Seymour Krim, and I kind of liked his stuff, too, so we knocked down a pitcher of beer instead of each other.

During the explosive sixties period of be-ins, storefront psychedelic religions, street poetry readings, adolescents of all ages on the move, *Evergreen Review* published an advertisement for "The 10,000 Franz Kafka Challenge . . . *From Old Bohemia Comes This Amazing Offer!*" Followed a list of 200 hip names, ranging from Gershon Legman to Antonin Artaud, Pauline Réage to Allan Kaprow, and if you could identify all 200 of these Bohemian heroes, "I, Franz Kafka, will send you my personal check for $10,000." You didn't even have to offer proof; a postcard saying, "I did it!" would suffice. The only catch was that it had to be postmarked by June 4, 1924.

In fact, the 200 names were a pretty good collection of the camp icons of the time: Anais Nin, Antoni Gaudi, Alice B. Toklas, Richard Brautigan, Jean Shrimpton, Timothy Leary, with a few ringers thrown in, such as Touissant i'Ouverture and Vikki Dugan, a pinup model famed for roller-skating in her New York apartment. (Pauline Réage is a pseudonym for the author of *The Story of O.*) If the young read novels, they read *Steppenwolf.* If they went to the theater, they preferred the Living Theater's audience participation revolutionary romps. In a late-sixties happening, a team of demolition artists attacked a VW Beetle while a poet read (inaudibly), a rock band played (loudly), and a Master of Revels threw live chicks and mice at the participants. The door was locked so we couldn't escape: squeals, panic, bloody critters underfoot. Mason Hoffenberg whispered to me: "I dreamed I went to a happening in my Maidenform bra."

He was worried about the neighbors calling the police (noise) or the SPCA (trampled mice and chicks). Since he was on probation for sale of a consciousness-raising substance, he wanted to go home early.

Now, when I return to the Village in the early nineties, Sam Kramer, the death's-head jewelry maker of Eighth Street, is still dead, and Anatole Broyard, Mason Hoffenberg, and Seymour Krim have gone to the Great Happening on High, too, but the Minetta stream in its secret channel beneath Sixth Avenue, Fourth Street, MacDougal Street, Minetta Lane, still occasionally invades a basement to signal that nature exists, insists on it, in this determinedly urban place. The Lion's Head and the White Horse Tavern carry on a literary tradition. In the far West Village, newer joints, like Florent, or a coffeehouse like Lanciani, appeal to the upper-scale artists, theater people, gentrified Bohemians who haven't relinquished the palimpsest of America's Oldest Living Bohemia.

Truth to tell, the Bohemian hordes have long overflowed the boundaries of the Village. To the south, Soho, Noho, and Tribeca have attached themselves; for many years the Upper West Side and Brooklyn Heights have been suburban annexes for families needing larger apartments. In beatnik and hippie times, the East Village began to play the old role—cheap eats, cheap digs, youth, stringent causes, galleries, and radical street life. When I stay with my actress/waitress daughter on Avenue B, near Tompkins Square Park, I don't know if I'll be awakened by antilandlord rioting or dope dealers whispering, "Smoke, smoke," outside my window. Sometimes I've even awakened by the wan yellow first sun of the morning which says, There's still time, there's a whole new day out there, you can do anything. Get into the Daffodill Café and start working on a bowl of Ukrainian kasha and an epiphany.

"What time is it?"

"Three-twenty." I was standing in the West Fourth subway station.

The questioner fumbled in his pocket, taking out a piece of paper which might have been a prescription for glasses. He needed to prove a point with me. "I don't want you to think I'm high or anything. See, my eyes are funny like this because they just give me eyedrops, see, and they make my eyes funny—I'm not high."

"I appreciate that. You're not high."

"So you better not fuck with me say I'm high, mister."

Now she might be called the painter, my Significant Other; then she was Alice, my girlfriend, long neck, black black hair and ivory skin, close-bitten fingernails. I met her at the Eighth Street Artists Club, which met in a loft on Fourteenth Street, where I had gone to hear a talk by Philip Johnson. Alice said she liked words and I told her that's what I did, I wrote words. And I told her I liked paintings and she said that's what she did, she painted paintings. I asked her if she would give up smoking for me. She said she could discuss it. But we mostly discussed words, colors, shapes, and each other, and I forgave her the smoking. She forgave me my smug forbearance.

But without my mentioning it, she stopped biting her finger-nails. Her hair was long and glossy, her stride was long and quick, we liked each other. She had come to the Village from Indiana, I from Ohio and Michigan, and we both had metabolisms stirred by the intention to be merry and bright.

During that long-ago sojourn in the fifties, Alice lived in a studio off a courtyard on Commerce Street, with a tree rubbing its filmy leaves on her filmy windows, frost edging the glass, a lot of snow falling during that winter. The new year was exceptional for its sudden night blizzards, leaving the Village clean and silent in the morning, bringing kids out with Christmas sleds and red Christmas hats and mittens. We would wake with that unearthly white light reflected into the room from the snow-edged tree, the snow-filled courtyard; and the silence also pouring in. By silent agreement we didn't put on the usual Nonesuch baroque wake-up music, trumpets, flutes, and a rhythm that worked like coffee or rock and roll: no music this morning. The snow made her think of Turner or Brueghel, it made me think of Henry James on Washington Square, but we were both thinking: clean snow, nice snow, it's good to be together.

She had a job as a photographic stylist. I walked with her to Jim Atkins', the diner on Sheridan Square, for pancakes, eggs, and a wake-up blast of breakfast noise. The *Times*, the *Voice*. Other couples, one dressed for work, one dressed for hanging out. I said good-bye to her at the subway entrance, wrought iron, elegant, Manhattan Belle Epoque, but already smelling of aging snow and pee, and then walked east to my own apartment on Waverly Place, kicking at clots of rapidly graying slush, hoping to write a few good words.

The dope dealer in the doorway at the center of Waverly and Sixth was already at his station for a day's patient waiting for business. He was wearing a long black overcoat, had an umbrella furled at his side, his hands in his pockets, and wished me the top of the morning, as usual. A few good words, I prayed, and once he took my mumbling, trying out the words, for a business inquiry. I wrote a few okay words. I waited for the mail, a letter from an

editor or my daughters in Detroit, or the telephone to ring, or that
metabolic surge which came along with words I really liked.

At night, alone together after the day apart, Alice and I slowed
down, made toasted cheese sandwiches in a pan on her stove
(cooking wasn't what she came from Indiana to the Village to do; it
was too early in history for the man to do any cooking), and confided some of our deepest thoughts to each other. Some of them we
kept in reserve.

If we wanted sociability and a hot meal, we wound long
scarves about our necks and trampled through the snow to the
okay hot meals available on Bedford Street at Chumley's, a dark
cavern down a few steps with hardly any announcement that it
was a public place. A few steps away was the narrowest house
around, the Edna St. Vincent Millay house, barely room for a witty
couplet; the Cherry Lane Theater stood nearby, still does; and another friend—a Catholic philosopher who liked to think about Jews
and borrowed my leather jacket to stimulate his meditations—
lived in the smallest house in the Village, a tiny pile of two rooms
in a courtyard on Barrow Street or maybe it was Jones. Once, in
need of inspiration and a shiver, he asked if I would buy a package
of condoms while he watched from outside the drugstore.

My friend, the Catholic philosopher, still lives in the Village,
has a wife and children, and continues to write about the Jews.
Goes to Zionist meetings, Jewish book fairs, synagogues, and
hangs at the edges, observing. When I moved to San Francisco, he
took the plunge and bought his own leather jacket.

This was a peculiar community, it still is, and people move here
because they want some of both its peculiarities and its community.
The Village mobilizes to fight for libraries, end police harassment
of sexual minorities, prevent prison barges from being moored in
the Hudson River nearby; the Seventh Day Adventists can have
West Eleventh Street closed to traffic for a weekend street fair of
clean living. The Village builds studios fit for sculptors and
painters but at prices suited to pre-October 1987 yuppies. Even the
B. Dalton bookshop on Eighth Street has gotten "sensitive"; stock-

ing poetry and local writers. When I arrived, the manager hastened to beg the computer to deliver up some of my books.

It would only be a few days. Then I could lurk outside, waiting for the thrill of spying someone picking up a book, reading the jacket, glancing here and there, buying the book. Maybe I could ask my old friend, the Catholic philosopher, to repay me for letting him watch the purchase of three Trojans with the red-helmeted warrior on the package.

Passing a spell in Greenwich Village during the late eighties, I used to walk for breakfast to a truck-driver's joint, the West Coast on West Street near the river. The prices were like the East Village, cheap bran muffins, skimpy on the raisins, bargain eggs, although it seemed to me they put more sugar than absolutely required in the muffins. Probably teamsters burn quick energy faster than combustible novelists. Part of the pleasure of my morning stroll from West Eleventh Street was a regular visit to the *Pathfinder* mural in progress on the wall of a building at West and Charles Streets, bringing Lenin to the People, also Marx, Castro, Malcolm X, Mother Jones, icons and leaders of revolution. The building contains the offices of Pathfinder Press, which has outlets in Chicago, San Francisco, and other warmbeds of overthrow.

The artists painted from high scaffolding along the wall. It was a game to figure out who some of the less-familiar faces were— Nelson Mandela (that was easy), John Reed (not looking much like Warren Beatty), César Sandino, Thomas Sankara of Burkina Faso, Maurice Bishop, a whole variety-pak of national and international heroes blending into each other in a rainbow coalition created (this was part of the theory) by artists from many nations. Some of them had trouble getting visas to visit the U.S.

This was America. Occasionally skinheads or Village right-wingers came in the night to splash rival graffiti on the mural or to harass the gay men from the meat-rack piers nearby. Lights and guards were installed. I saw a trio of transvestite male hookers singing "Amazing Grace" under the spotlight in memory of a colleague brought down by AIDS. They said they were demanding that Charles Ludlum of the Theater of the Ridiculous be painted immediately onto the wall. They said they'd also like Joan Baez and Judy Garland, but they could wait for them, and then they sang "Over the Rainbow."

The Pathfinders Project was alive, it was a happening thing. Gradually Trotsky, Zinoviev, Bukharin, and Karl Radek came out of the mists. The sketches were filled in with honest, courageous, proletarian primary colors. Pipes, guns, flags, and parades. The mural was eclectic and ecumenical. Pathfinder Press is an equal opportunity revolutionary press. Pete Seeger helped to raise funds. The heroes and heroines were marching into a wind-furled banner which proclaims A WORLD WITHOUT BORDERS in French, Spanish, and English.

Both the too-sweet West Street muffins and Revolution via Mural Action express something of the old-fashioned values of Greenwich Village. In the East Village, agitprop tends to be more about local issues, such as the La Lucha antigentrification murals. They are all inspired by Diego Rivera, the honored ancestor whose portraits of Lenin and Abraham Lincoln were painted out of Rockefeller Center when Nelson Rockefeller decided it was not the People's but the Rockefellers' wall. Downtown, things are different.

Sitting at the outdoor terrace at the Figaro, waiting for my daughter to come dancing across Bleecker Street with three or four or five of her hungry Loizaida friends, I suddenly started. *Lenka!* I saw her, the graceful, lovely, heroin-addicted dancer with her sunny hair cropped furiously short, and here she was again floating down MacDougal toward me. Whatever else she had done, however she had caused unnecessary hurt, she had pulled me away from a disastrous marriage and suggested the idea of pleasure. It had previously occurred to me as a rumor, some kind of distant ideal, but Lenka brought her downy hair and dreamy eyes to bear on the subject.

I jumped up to greet her and called her name. She paused, she smiled her heart-breaking smile—she smiled so rarely, lost in her internal ballet, fixed and floating there, that it always made me think everything could be done anew and better—she opened her arms to the intensity of my joy, my forgetting that she had gone from me to the drug-dealing jazz drummer, and then from him to me, and then from me to him again, and then at his urging to any paying customer in the club. I forgive, I forgive, I still love you, you saved me!

She smiled and smiled. "I'm not Lenka, but I do look like one, don't I?"

Lenka was dead many years now. But the young woman on the Village street with the smart Village mouth lived, still lives, and I saw her. She gave me that sweetness of smile. She shrugged. She continued on her way.

And then my daughter clattered up with a band of her colleagues, actors and dancers, to be taken to an Indian restaurant for yogurt, spices, vegetables, and brown rice.

—1993

Mary Cantwell

(b. 1922)

Like countless young women before and since, Mary Cantwell arrived in Manhattan in the early 1950s as a stranger, a good Catholic girl from New England trying to make her mark in the world. She wanted to do something with her English major, "but what, besides teach, can one do with Chaucer?" she wondered. Upon arrival, her entire possessions consisted of $80 in cash, a portable typewriter, and a copy of The Poems of Gerard Manley Hopkins. *From the first time she saw the Washington Square Arch, she felt peace. She knew the Village was where she belonged. Eventually Cantwell found a job at* Mademoiselle *and thus began her entry into New York's stressful publishing life.* Manhattan, When I Was Young *recalls her sometimes painful, sometimes exhilarating memories of Manhattan in the 1950s, as a working girl and later as a young wife and working mother. Mary Cantwell is a member of the editorial board of the* New York Times *and is the author of* American Girl.

from *Manhattan, When I Was Young*

I had wanted to come back to Greenwich Village ever since I had left Waverly Place, and since moving to West Eleventh Street. I have never lived anyplace else. I do not want to. That is not because of what the Village is but because of what I have made it, and what I have made it depends on who I am at the time. The Village is amorphous; I can shape it into any place. The rest of Manhattan is rectilinear, its grid an order, a single definition, that I dislike. But the Village is a collection of cowpaths and landfill and subterranean rivers, visible, if you know about them, because they are traced by streets paved to mask them.

If some areas have a certain architectural unity, it is not because an architect had a grand scheme but because rowhouses with common walls were put up hastily for people fleeing a yellow fever epidemic downtown. One of the streets is called Little West Twelfth, which distinguishes it from West Twelfth and is a distinction that makes no sense whatsoever, because the two streets are unconnected. Everything in the Village—the way Waverly Place takes a right turn, for instance, and West Thirteenth Street's sudden transformation into Horatio—seems haphazard, accidental. When we first moved there, the old-timers told us the Village had changed. People still tell me the Village has changed. The Village does not change, not really. The Village—the *real* Village, the one bounded by Fifth Avenue on the east and the Hudson River on the west—remains an accident.

In the years on West Eleventh, it became the Europe I had yet to see. On Saturday nights we would walk along West Fourth Street to a store that sold Scandinavian modern everything and served free glogg. I didn't like Scandinavian modern anything, and I hated glogg, but I loved the store owner's accent. It and the glogg and the Swedish candleholder that was his best seller—six metal angels that revolved around a candle when it was lighted—raised possibilities, unveiled horizons.

When we went to the Peacock to drink espresso, it was because I believed there were a million Peacock Cafés in Italy, and if I sat in this one, on West Third Street, staring at a waitress who looked like a Veronese, I was sitting in all of them. If we had a drink at the San Remo, it was because of its name and not because everybody hung out there. A lot of famous and about-to-be-famous people hung out at the San Remo. I must have seen them all, and cannot remember any of them. They were not the point. Even if they had been, I would have been too timid to strike up a conversation. Working for a fashion magazine, however distinguished its fiction, separated me, in my eyes and doubtless in theirs, from the literati.

I started walking again, alone. In Bristol I had walked all the time, long walks that would take me to solitary picnics on the low stone wall surrounding an estate a few miles from our house, or to the meadow a mile further on where the grass seemed a thin skin between myself and the Indians I imagined lying in layers beneath my feet. Walking in the Village, I would quickly exhaust the import shops and the bars, into which I peered, believing that all of America's young literary life was being lived in them, mostly by fast, fluent talkers like Jerry, and head for the docks.

There was nothing over there then—no gay bars, no young men in leather jackets and button-front Levis—but nineteenth-century warehouses, a few houses, some vacant lots, and beyond them the river. One block I liked especially. It had two trees and ten or so tired old houses, was paved with cobblestones and littered with whatever the sanitation trucks had missed, and led to the garbage pier. The street was wholly desolate and, for someone who was slowly developing a taste for the seedy and the out-of-season, a magnet.

The garbage pier was precisely that, the pier where the tugs that lugged garbage out to sea made their pickups. No one ever went that far west then, not on weekends anyway, but myself and the young Italians from the South Village who would park their cars on the dock and curry them as if they were horses. They never bothered me; I never bothered them. They would curry their cars, I would lean against a piling and watch the boats, and all of us would allow ourselves to be wrapped in silence. Silence was the cure, if only temporarily, silence and geography. But of what was I being cured? I do not know, have never known. I only know the cure. Silence, and no connections except to landscape.

The first time I took Katherine on an outing, on a Sunday afternoon in May when she was six years old, the wheel came off her green plaid baby carriage. A garage mechanic repaired it—"On the house, lady," he said—and set me, grinning, back on West Tenth Street. There could have been no stronger line of demarcation between me and those people up on the Upper East Side, I thought, infatuated with my fecklessness, than the distance between a fabric carriage with dodgy wheels and a Silver Cross pram. Actually, B. [Cantwell's husband] might have preferred a Silver Cross pram, but it would not have gone with the new identity I was coining for myself: Village mother.

That day and many days thereafter I took my daughter to Washington Square, to the southeast corner, where a big sycamore that I came to call the baby tree spread its branches over a large, grubby sandpit. A certain kind of Village mother spent hours there, offering chunks of raw potato to her teething child. The purest example (all struck me as variations on a type) was a sallow, stringy-haired young woman who, talking constantly, made much of her Jewishness and her husband's blackness. She brandished his color, in fact, as if it were a flag. Meanwhile the baby, scrawny and dun-skinned, was treated with the rough affection due a puppy. But then, rough affection—dumping one's offspring in its carriage, carrying it more or less upside down on one's hip—was, like the raw-potato teething tool, a function of Village style.

I would have loved to talk to someone, especially about Beechnut's as compared to Gerber's and whether pacifiers made for buckteeth, but I was too shy to start a conversation, and nobody was inclined to start one with me, probably because my face is stony in repose, and forbidding. Still, it was pleasant under the baby tree—the drunks mostly clustered by the fountain, and the folksingers who preceded the drug dealers hadn't yet arrived—and membership in the club to which I had so desperately wanted to belong was glorious.

About four o'clock, about the time the air began to turn blue, I would rise from the bench and kick up the carriage brake and off we would go, past the stern, beautiful houses that were all that was left of Catherine Sloper's Washington Square to Bleecker Street, where strolled another kind of Village mother. This one pushed an enormous perambulator in which lay, banked in pillows and laces and fleecy wools, a fat little boy who was almost always named Anthony. I know this because a silver tag on a chain, reminiscent of the kind that drapes decanters, invariably swagged his coverlet. There it was, inscribed for all to see: ANTHONY.

Lucky Anthony, to be going home to a crowd. Like a lot of people with small families and without a strong ethnic identity, I thought the spirits were higher and the sentiments warmer in big Italian and Jewish households. Not in B.'s Jewish household—he had never even had a bar mitzvah, and if his parents knew a word of Yiddish, I never heard it—but in the kind I had glimpsed in old photographs of tenement life. Snug as bugs in a rug those families were. I couldn't see the poverty for the coziness.

So when I saw Anthony after Anthony moving like Cleopatra on her barge through the dusk of late afternoon on Bleecker Street, I saw their grandparents and their aunts and uncles and cousins lined up to greet them. I saw first communions and weddings and funerals at Our Lady of Pompeii, and statues of saints dressed in dollar bills, and a network of Philomenas and Angelas and Roses stretched over the whole South Village. I envied Anthony all of them, for Katherine's sake. For my sake, too.

—1995

Ethan Mordden

(b. 1947)

Born in Heavensville, Pennsylvania, Ethan Mordden is a prolific writer and the author of many works of fiction, including Buddies *(1987),* Everybody Loves You: Further Adventures in Gay Manhattan *(1989),* I've a Feeling We're Not in Kansas Anymore: Tales from Gay Manhattan *(1996),* Some Men Are Lookers *(1998), and* The Venice Adriana *(1998). He has also written extensively on the history of the Broadway musical and pop culture, such as* The Hollywood Studios, Opera in the Twentieth Century, *and* Medium Cool: The Movies of the 1960s. How Long Has This Been Going On? *follows the lives of several gay men in the Village from 1949 to the present, from the seedy bars of the post–World War II underground to the era of Gay Pride marches.*

from *How Long Has This Been Going On?*

Frank, so amiable when on the job behind the Hero's bar, goes sad when he trudges home. He can get through the empty hours before work well enough, listening to the radio or taking walks; and tending bar does keep one busy. But once he locks up and heads downtown to West Tenth Street, he starts wondering about what chances he missed.

I blew it, he keeps thinking. Everything just came to me, right? Jobs, friends, sex. I never needed anything, so I didn't work for anything. Now I have nothing.

Ethan Mordden. From *How Long Has This Been Going On?* (New York: Villard Books, 1995).

What am I? I've been a cop, a mover, a movie extra. I acted off-Broadway now and again, when they needed a guy with a build. I had a shot at fashion modeling and I hustled when I had to. I'm a solo kind of guy, I guess, though I had Larken, didn't I? There was a good man. A man who knew what was right—except, mostly, in boy friends. Where did he find all those schmucks? It finally drove me away, fighting with them on the phone all the time. But I never could replace Larken. I've tried to. You meet some guy who seems more special than the others, get him to stay over, and make him breakfast, smiling at him, trying to get to know him. But you can see him fading out on you even before the toast is browned. Everyone wants to get in my bed but nobody wants to *talk* to me.

I *blew it* is a rough thing to face at forty-one, but is Frank the best possible Frank he could have been? Or is he a gorgeous hunk of waste?

Eric is sitting on Frank's stoop, shivering in the cold, as Frank arrives.

"They throw you out again?" asks Frank, coming up the steps. Eric rises, nodding, and as he turns to come inside, Frank puts an arm on the kid's shoulder.

"Wait a minute," says Frank. "You hungry?"

Eric nods again.

"Let's stop at the deli."

A bit later, Frank is cooking bacon and eggs in his kitchenette—half-size fridge, one cabinet, no counter space. Eric is sitting in the armchair, silent and upset. Like all teenagers, he dresses total slob: T-shirt hanging out, holes in the sweatshirt, a jacket he must have found in Mammy Yokum's garbage can. It's one of the many things his parents don't like about him. Every now and then they give him a lecture on what a disgrace he is, and they get so impressed with their grief that they kick him out. A pretty teenager walking Village streets at night can usually find some obliging stranger hoping to trade favors: my bed, your body. But Frank knows that this is not good. Besides, as far as Frank can make out, Eric is straight.

The kid is ravenous, scarfing down everything on his plate plus three apples for dessert. The phone rings, and Eric glances quizzically at the clock on the night table: 3:27. But many a New York phone rings that late, especially when the guy you need to speak to works till 2:30 A.M.

Frank picks up with "Yo," a usefully neutral greeting, fit for everyone from a long-lost boy friend to an anonymous fan who wants to close down his day with a jack-off session.

The caller, Bart Stokes, is something between a colleague and a pardner, an old trick Frank occasionally bumps into along the bar, street, and beach circuit.

"Hey, Bart."

"Frank, this is a business proposition."

"Shoot."

"Okay, this guy I know. He's got a loft and a camera and some lighting equipment. He's a commercial photographer or something, but now he's branching out. He wants to make a sexy movie."

"Stag films, you mean?"

"For *our* kind, yes sir. And *real* sex, he says—not that Athletic Model Guild stuff where they just stand around."

"What for?"

"Seems he's going to show them. In a *theatre*, pal."

"You're kidding."

"This place on Eighth Avenue in the Forties. He's run three of them already. Claims to be cleaning up."

"Bart, I'm nuts even to ask this, but where do I fit in?"

"Looks like it's your big showbiz break, my friend. You ready to turn pro?"

"What do I have to do and how much?"

"It's good bread—three hundred smackers for four or five afternoons' work. Three, maybe, the way you heat up a room. What you do . . . Well, you show up, I show up, Phil Neil shows up—"

"The blond with the . . ."

"That's the one. Guy's shooting silent, so there's no script to worry about. There's a story line, but it's . . . you know, some bunch of excuses to get two guys together and then the next two guys. So on, so forth. Like, I'm the plumber working in Phil's apartment and my clothes get all wet, so . . ." Bart chuckled.

"Who am I?" Frank asked.

"You play a cop."

Silence.

"Frank, you there?"

"Yeah, I'm there."

"So are you in or out? He's shooting this week, so I've got to . . . See, he's kind of unhappy with the quality of the talent he's been using. I promised to assemble a more, uh—"

"What the hell."

"That's yes?"

"Sure. Yeah."

"Great. Keep your afternoons open. I'll get back to you with the details."

"I could be crazy."

"Way I see it is, it's nothing you wouldn't be doing anyway. And think of how you'll brighten the dreary lives of our less distinguished cousins. Seeing us in action will inspire and bless them."

"Phil, you are a gentleman and a slut."

"Too kind of you, too kind. See you, Frank."

As Frank pensively put down the phone, Eric asked, "What was that all about?"

"Bedtime for you, youngster."

A typical New York walk-up, the apartment is cold by now, with the radiators dead till dawn. But Frank has stripped and now he peels Eric to the skin and steers him to the shower.

"I'm already clean," Eric complains. But when Frank holds him, under the running water, the boy leans back into the embrace, whimpering for affection—and later, in bed, he says it's Frank's choice, anything he wants.

"I don't go with straight kids."

"Other guys make me," says Eric, complacently.

"That's why I told you, Always come to me. Kid like you loose on the streets, getting into all kinds of . . . Move your arm. Right. There you go."

Eric shifted a bit, then settled his head on Frank's chest. Stroking Eric's hair, Frank said, "If you were gay, I'd sure take you for a ride. But fair is fair."

"Frank? Do you know about a job that I could get?"

"Sixteen, no experience, and—sorry—not the smartest guy in sight."

"I'm seventeen."

"I'll ask around."

"Frank," Eric went on, taking hold of the big guy, heavy pleading, genuine distress, "please, please help me."

"I will, okay?"

"Frank." Holding on.

"Look, I told you, right? So stop sighing or I'll screw your ass."

"I just wish I could be like you."

"The hell you say."

"Because you're so independent. With your own place, for instance, and if you feel like breakfast, you just dish it up no matter what the clock says."

Eric snuggled up closer to Frank, who growled, "Stop trying to get me hot for you."

"I'm not. Anyway, you are hot now. I can tell."

"Yeah?" Frank took Eric's hand under the blanket and guided it down for a tour. "You ready to take that up your tail?"

"Come on," said Eric with adolescent bravado. "You couldn't get that up the Lincoln Tunnel."

"I'll say one thing for you, you don't scare easy."

"You scare me? Come on, you're this big cream puff."

"Well, three creeps lying unconscious on Eleventh Avenue don't think so."

"What does that mean?"

"That means I went over to my buddy Gordon Niles's place on my break tonight, to pick up his house keys so I can feed his cats while he's in Key West next weekend. Coming back, I turned the corner on Eleventh and saw three guys with a baseball bat jumping two leather boys."

Eric whistled, No kidding!

"Right. Well, I'm not about to walk away from that, so I did a little jumping on my own. Those fuckers were so happy in the act of cornering their victims they didn't hear me coming up behind them. They're shouting away. They're like . . . like vampires. 'We're going to kill you faggots!' Suddenly I've got the bat from them and I'm doling it out. First one in the stomach, second sharp on the knees—boy, does he scream—third on the side. Down they go, a perfect strike."

"Are they dead?"

"I doubt it. But sure as shit those guys have something in them leading them to kill. Tonight it was gays. Tomorrow it's blacks. I say, Kill them first. Then the only guys who die are the ones who deserve to."

"What did the gay guys do?"

"Took off like rabbits."

"You're making this up."

"Sure I am."

After a pause, Eric said, "My brother does that. With his friends. Going after gay guys. They call it 'hunting.'"

"So do we."

"Boy."

"There's this war going on," Frank explained. "But one side doesn't know it. Hunting, right. Hunt them from their jobs and their apartments. Deny them. Jail them. And, for the sportsmen among you, hold a miniature Tet Offensive with baseball bats on Eleventh Avenue."

Frank grunted. "Had a dear friend," he said. "He was murdered in Central Park last year by your brother and his friends. Great guy, he was—smart and funny and generous. A man like that leaves a hole in your being that you never refill. Why's he dead? Defending his country? Battling a fire? He's dead for somebody's *fun!*"

Eric was asleep.

Frank gently moved the kid to the side to give himself some room. Yeah, he'll find the boy a job, and he'll see about getting him a place to stay in, maybe share the rent with some good-humored gay guy with a spare couch. Frank will work on it, though he's got a lot on his mind as it is. He has the Failure of Frank to ponder. He hears the history meter ticking away while he dicks around tending bar and amounting to nothing more than being one of the town's most essential lays. He has middle age to face; once, he had planned to have made Captain by then. Captain Frank the Cop.

What is he instead? He'd say, *Nothing*; but he's wrong. Frank is the Saint of Christopher Street.

How do you forge a long-lasting, meaningful relationship? Easy: You collaborate on a spaghetti carbonara dinner. Henry was the geneticist and Andy the gosling, in Henry's apartment. Henry was teaching life to Andy. Browning the bacon, chopping the cheese, cooking the pasta, readying the egg.

Henry said, "As soon as the pasta is drained, pop it in the pot, beat in the egg, and add the cheese all at once. It happens in a blink, like all the great things in life."

"Yes," said Andy, madly in love with Henry, the first man he'd known who treated him with respect.

"So we have Kingdom Come for the dance," Henry went on, stirring the pasta. "The third Saturday in May. Saturday's the gay night there, anyway." Stirring. "Do you know of an opening somewhere? For a job?"

"Who for?"

"Oh, this kid, one of Frank the Bartender's protectees. Frank's always trying to . . . No, grate the cheese the long way so it . . . That's right. . . . That guy's always got some charity case he . . . I think the pasta's done."

"How does it come about that a dance hall can be gay on a certain night? Who spreads the word?"

"I always wondered. Now, quick, throw it all back in the pot and I'll do the egg. . . . Yes. . . ."

"Is Frank Italian?"

"I have no idea. Why do you ask? See how you thrust it all around till it melts all . . . Looking good, pardner."

"Well, it's sort of Italian to watch out for each other. That's why I thought—"

"Ha! Gays should be like that," said Henry. "Clannish and defensive."

"And do I stir it now?"

"Why can't we . . . Yes, stir it quickly. It's supposed to fall all over itself and melt into—"

"This total mess?"

"Exactly," said Henry, reaching for the plates. "Keep stirring, it'll come."

The phone rang.

"Oh, hell!" said Henry, struggling to get dinner onto the plates. "We'll take control and ignore it."

"I'll get it," said Andy, leaving the stove.

"No, just—"

"It's no trouble."

"*Leave* it," Henry insisted, grabbing Andy's arm with his free hand.

"Well, it might be . . . See, I gave my parents this number, in case of an emergency."

Henry put down the plates and stared at Andy.

"What emergency?" Henry finally said, his voice like nails ready for a crucifixion.

"It's still ringing," said Andy, moving to the phone—but Henry got there first, picked up, and said hello. Two beats. Then he held the receiver against his chest and told Andy, "In this apartment, there are no parents. By which I mean to say, There are no archons of the system that destroys anyone who insists on living his own—"

"Is that my parents?"

Henry said, "I don't let anyone interpose heterosexual biology into my life." Andy could hear a buzzing through the receiver dots; Henry pulled the phone back as Andy tried to grab it. "You really *have* to talk to your parents now?"

"Is it them?"

Into the receiver Henry said, "Your son is a real sweetheart, lady."

Turning the shade of white the monument to Vittorio Emanuele in Rome, Andy tried to grab the phone, but Henry added, "He's so tasty, I can see why you're after him, too," and, with a wry look, gave Andy the phone. Control.

Andy had the devil of a time placating his mother, while Henry saw to the carbonara. He chuckled as Andy tried to pass off Henry's remarks as the joking of an outrageous friend. Setting down the pepper mill, Henry murmured, "You have ten seconds to get off that phone," and Andy quickly promised to call back the next day, and hung up.

Andy told Henry, "I can't believe you did that." He wasn't angry—just a bit hurt—and he made the best of it because he knew that Henry was his hook shot into a happier life, quick and true. Henry was all set to chide Andy for allowing his parents to encroach upon Henry's existence, but Andy's undemanding charm touched Henry. He said, "I really am sorry, but I've got this thing about parents pushing in where they don't belong."

Andy said, "That's because you're not Italian."

"That's because I'm not taking orders from anyone. Anyway, let's eat." It was plates on laps, and Henry said, "Was your mother shocked at what I said? I guess I really went overboard, Andy." Henry got up and moved the plates out of the way and pulled Andy up and held him. That's sweet: their first little quarrel-and-make-up.

"Actually," said Andy, as they broke, "she doesn't know what anything you said means. She thought you were one of my rougher friends from high school—they were always using sex talk that way. Like, it wasn't I'll beat your brains in but I'll ream your ass out."

As they sat down to eat, Andy said, "You know, this pasta is *wonderful*"; and they went on to other things. But I'm worrying, because Henry does not realize how tightly Andy's parents have bound him to them, and Andy does not understand how profoundly Henry mistrusts the motivation of parents. I hope these two will talk it out and work up a game plan before there is another incident. But I also think Andy is old enough not to have to leave a number Where He Can Be Reached every time he leaves a six-block radius surrounding his place of birth, nurture, religious instruction, and high-school graduation. Everyone, at some point in her or his life, has to tell the monitors, *Hold it!*

—1995

Frank O'Hara

(1926–1966)

Born in Baltimore in 1926 but raised in Massachusetts, Frank O'Hara served in the Navy before enrolling at Harvard and the University of Michigan. He then moved to New York City. From 1952 until his death in 1966 he was on staff at the Museum of Modern Art. Active within the city's abstract expressionist circle, he was a poet, playwright, and critic as well as a member of a group of poets later known as the New York School of Poets, which included John Ashbery, Kenneth Koch, and James Schuyler. He was also a regular denizen of the famous but run-down Cedar Tavern. They, in turn, were inspired by the paintings of Jackson Pollock, Franz Kline, and Willem de Kooning and were further influenced by the contemporary visual artists Larry Rivers and Fairfield Porter—all of whom either lived or worked in the Village at some point during their careers. David Lehman has described O'Hara as "Irish-American, a lapsed Catholic," and "possessed of a marvelous bitchy wit. . . ." O'Hara published six volumes of poetry. He died a bizarre death on Fire Island when he was run over by a dune buggy. Barely forty at the time, he lived fast and died young, the proverbial artist in search of a touch of immortality. For a particularly vivid portrait of O'Hara, see Harold Brodkey's essay, "Frank and Harold," when the city, according to Brodkey was "raunchy with words . . . one of the wonders of the world."

FRANK O'HARA

"Night Thoughts in Greenwich Village"

O my coevals! embarrassing
memories! pastiches! jokes!
All your pleasaunces and
the vividness of your ills
are only fertilizer for
the kids. Who knows what
will be funny next year?
The days will not laugh
at what we say is dry, but
wheeling ridicule our
meanings. The too young
find the grave silly and
every excess absurd. I,
at twenty four, already
find the harrowing laugh
of children at my heels—
directed at me! the Dada
baby! How soon must we all
get rid of love to save
our energy, how soon our
laughter becomes defensive!
O my coevals! we cannot die
too soon. Art is sad and
life is vapid. Can we thumb
our nose at the very sea?

"Washington Square"

That arch bestrides me, French
victory! the golden staff of the savior

with blue lids. The soldiers filing
at my feet hiss down their drinks

and one savagely decorated, savagely
turned, their gentle feathers torn to medals

in the air. Gold falls upon them, because
there is no love, and it is not the sun.

Jane and Mark flutter along the plaza
underneath the fainting gingko trees

and are cheered by pearly uniform horses,
still, at parade rest. The guns ejaculate

into clouds abstractly, and the day
is in danger of passing without wickedness.

—1995

Gregory Corso

(1930–2001)

One of the most popular and influential of the Beat poets, Gregory Corso was born in the heart of Greenwich Village at 190 Bleecker Street, the son of Italian immigrants. For this reason he has often been called the only true Villager of the Beat writers. Sent to state prison for robbery at age sixteen, Corso, whose formal education ended in the sixth grade, began to write poetry in prison. He was particularly impressed with the poetry of Marlowe and Shelley. After his release, he met Allen Ginsberg in a Village bar. Ginsberg encouraged Corso to continue writing. His first collection of poetry, The Vestal Lady on Brattle and Other Poems, *was published in 1955, followed, three years later, by* Gasoline. *He wrote or co-wrote some twenty collections of poetry and other works. The character of Yuri Gregorovic in Jack Kerouac's novel* The Subterraneans *is reportedly based on Corso. In 1998 Thunder's Mouth Press published* Mindfield: New & Selected Poems *with an introduction by jazz musician David Amram. Corso died in 2001 at the age of seventy of prostate cancer in Robbinsdale, Minnesota. The following poems all have a Village setting: a human tragedy, a return visit to the poet's place of birth, and a paean to Welsh poet Dylan Thomas who virtually drank himself to death at the White Horse Tavern.*

Gregory Corso. "Birthplace Revisited," "St. Luke's, Service for Thomas," and "Greenwich Village Suicide" from *Mindfield: New & Selected Poems* (New York: Thunder's Mouth Press, 1998).

"Greenwich Village Suicide"

Arms outstretched
hands flat against the windowsides
She looks down
Thinks of Bartok, Van Gogh
And *New Yorker* cartoons
She falls

They take her away with a *Daily News* on her face
And a storekeeper throws hot water on the sidewalk

"Birthplace Revisited"

I stand in the dark light in the dark street
and look up at my window. I was born there.
The lights are on; other people are moving about.
I am with raincoat; cigarette in mouth,
hat over eye,
I cross the street and enter the building.
The garbage cans haven't stopped smelling.
I walk up the first flight; Dirty Ears
aims a knife at me . . .
I pump him full of lost watches.

"St. Luke's, Service for Thomas"

The White Horse innkeeper
Leaned nervously against the stained-glass;
He shifted his feet, and Cummings mourned by.

A sightseer whispered into a sightseeing ear.
And a Swansea woman entered . . .

Two neo-villagers underarmed her;
Sat her down in the first row.
She raised her head, and peered
. . . The body wasn't there.

The service ended in illimitable whispers.

A Ceylonese prince was first to leave.
He waited by the church gate
And little groups gathered, chattered.

Across the street the school children
Were playing tag-ball.
The ball rolled in front of the innkeeper;
He kicked it hard
And strode back to his inn.

—1998

Samuel Menashe

(b. 1925)

Samuel Menashe was born in New York in 1925. During World War II he was an infantryman who fought in France, Belgium (the famous Battle of the Bulge), and Germany. In 1950 he was awarded a doctorate by the Sorbonne. His first book, The Many Named Beloved, *was published in 1961. Menashe, a current and longtime resident of the Village, composes poems that have a stark, concise quality. They are quite beautiful and in their glowing simplicity they capture the timelessness of Village life and, indeed, of life itself. Despite enjoying a long career, Menashe has been largely ignored by the mainstream press. In the preface to* The Niche Narrows, *from which the following poems are taken, poet Dana Gioia, describes him as living "a bohemian life in an age of academic institutionalism." His themes are the common concerns of the poet—purpose, meaning, faith, time—and yet he is no common poet. He is a modern-day mystic and one who is capable of great depth. His other works include* No Jerusalem But This *(1971),* Fringe of Fire *(1973),* To Open *(1974),* Collected Poems *(1986), and* Penguin Modern Poets, Volume 7 *(1996).*

Samuel Menashe. "At Millay's Grave," "Transplant," "Promised Land," "Dusk," "The Dead of Winter," "At a Standstill," and "Improvidence" from *The Niche Narrows: New and Selected Poems* (Jersey City, New Jersey: Talisman House, Publishers, 2000). Reprinted by permission of the author.

SAMUEL MENASHE

from *The Niche Narrows: New and Selected Poems*

At Millay's Grave

Your ashes
In an urn
Buried here
Make me burn
For dear life
My candle
At one end—
Night outlasts
Wick and wax
Foe and friend

Transplant

For Amy and Michael

I would give
My liver, kidneys
Heart itself
For you to live
In perfect health
With me, your clone
Whose grafted cells
Grow marrow, bone

If all else fails
Do not reject
My skin or nails
Whatever's left
Of me for you
By a hair's breadth
Will see us through

Promised Land

At the edge
Of a world
Beyond my eyes
Beautiful
I know Exile
Is always
Green with hope—
The river
We cannot cross
Flows forever

Dusk

night
into
earth
from
rise
Voices

The Dead of Winter

In my coat I sit
At the window sill
Wintering with snow
That did not melt
It fell long ago
At night, by stealth
I was where I am
When the snow began

At a Standstill

That statue, that cast
Of my solitude
Has found its niche
In this kitchen
Where I do not eat
Where the bathtub stands
Upon cat feet—
I did not advance
I cannot retreat

Improvidence

Owe, do not own
What you can borrow
Live on each loan
Forget tomorrow
Why not be in debt
To one who can give
You whatever you need
It is good to abet
Another's good deed

Edward Hoagland

(b. 1932)

Whether writing about rural life among the hippies of Vermont or the vast wilderness of Alaska, Edward Hoagland is a writer's writer. The author of numerous novels, essays, and travel narratives, Hoagland was the editor of The Best American Essays for 1999 *and teaches at Bennington College in Bennington, Vermont. He has written nearly twenty books, including* Walking the Dead Diamond River *(a 1974 National Book Award nominee),* African Calliope *(a 1980 American Book Award nominee), and* The Tugman's Passage *(a 1982 National Book Critics Circle Award nominee). One of our best nature writers—he belongs on the same shelf as Henry David Thoreau, John Muir, John McPhee, and Peter Matthiessen—his travels have taken him to the bayous of Louisiana, to Canada's Pacific coast, as well as to India and Africa. This selection from* Compass Points, *his 2001 memoir, describes the denizens of the Lion's Head, the famous Christopher Street writers' bar, that closed in 1996.*

from *Compass Points: How I Lived*

I was the New Yorker in the family. Born there in 1932, I returned for the key decades of my adulthood, age twenty-five to fifty-five, when you do whatever you're really going to do. The piano lessons at Mrs. Holcombe's house on God's Acre (where three of New Canaan's churches surrounded a traffic triangle), and the ice-skating on Mud Pond, the good English and biology

Edward Hoagland. From *Compass Points: How I Lived* (2001).

classes with Mr. Swallow and Mrs. Morris at New Canaan Country Day School—that's all behind you now, you think; you're on your own. Of course not quite. And in my case in the metropolis, my new friends who weren't Jewish were mostly Irish lapsed Catholics, the other ethnic group that had been looked at queerly in the suburb where I'd lived from eight to eighteen: which cut both ways. There was a certain resentment of me as a WASP, as well as the necessity for me to make my own mental readjustments. I'd recognized and hated hometown anti-Semitism from the age of twelve, but to try to correct parental indoctrination in one's unconscious mind is a complicated process, whereas the New Canaan (ironic name for anti-Semitic town) boys of my generation who hadn't bothered themselves about it at all remained in orbits throughout the nineteen-fifties and even sixties and seventies paralleling their parents', where Jews were not permitted to function, and scarcely afterwards.

Maintaining a Protestant mien of reserve and understatement was okay (under the rubric of eccentricity) in my Irish saloon on Christopher Street, The Lion's Head, because I did love storytelling, although I couldn't do much of it, and laughed immoderately at blarney, knew poverty—even though my novitiate had been voluntary—and understood from the exigencies of my handicap the basic imperatives of the Irish virtue of loyalty. Photographers, sportswriters, carpenters, seamen, firemen, screenwriters, celebrity chasers, a bank branch manager, a Transit Authority bureaucrat, a marijuana dealer, union officials, police-beat reporters, publicity flacks, salesmen, agents, accountants: for Manhattan it was a reasonably polyglot hangout, and there were also chummy women bellying up to the bar—painters, teachers, editors, credit-checkers, secretaries—who were for the most part middle-aged, buxom, and maybe remembered sleeping with Jimmy Dean or Norman Mailer or Marlon Brando, and who drank a bit too much, though not as much as the men, who, they claimed, seldom performed more than limply if you softened to their pleas and brought them on home. Later in the evening the atmosphere turned mildy rancid, as the people with structured lives left and the souls newly alone after a split-up faced the rows of bottles against the mirror across the bar. We had waitresses such as Jessica Lange, who were on their way up, to stare at, and others on the way down, but scarcely less haunting.

Wes Joyce, The Lion's Head co-owner, had been a gloomy cop and flounder-dragger on Cape Cod before he'd invested in this rather theatrical project, moving it from Hudson Street over to Sheridan Square in the center of Greenwich Village. The other owner, Al Koblin, was saturnine more than gloomy, distrustful but merciful, and formerly the manager of the Figaro coffeehouse on Bleecker Street throughout the Beatnik epoch. Tommy Sugar, the night bartender, had quit construction work in the Bronx after an accident and before it got to him. Shaped like a heavy crate, he could block a door, return a punch, pick up the phone and deal with the Mafia jukebox guys when needed. His partner, Mike Reardon, an actor, was matinee-handsome and smooth, a ladies' man. The day bartenders were Don Schlenk, who had cultivated a contemptuosly snappish temper that went with the chip-on-the-shoulder aspects of the place, and Paul Schiffman, a retired ship's captain, who lived with his mother uptown and preferred a persona that was uncommunicative and sulky, though he wrote poetry. Three lawyers, a speechwriter, a bookie, an adman, an ambulance attendant, and an apartment house owner might face Paul, each with an amputated marriage or an undertow of the fatalism of the lapsed Catholic or kicked-out Jew, but demonstrating an elaborate patience with each other that helped keep despair at bay. Virtuoso conversationalists like the Clancy Brothers, Tom and Liam, or Frank and Malachy McCourt were not daily visitors, yet faith in friendship can be almost as brave a leap for some people as conversation or religious belief, with everybody glancing sideways as they gimp along, through a magnetic field that galls them but that they depend on.

At The Lion's Head I needed some schooling because of my fastidious physical offishness, verbal reserve, and ignorance of many customs. For example, when I spilled coins on the floor I'd stoop to pick them up instead of leaving them "for the sweeper."

I thought struggling artists were supposed to be frugal and my tips were mathematical, not flamboyant. Nor did I get drunk and run up a tab, like some of my neighbors who had already skipped through a bankruptcy. And my sense of public gesture was paltry, though I soon grew to appreciate other people's shticks, and saloon talk, if nothing else, improved my teaching. The slightly stinging atmosphere in which the evening peters out in watering holes where people have nowhere else they want to go and hope that they sleep late tomorrow to cut short tomorrow's disappointments, was a small price to pay; and you escaped it entirely if you left early. Soon, however, I was an honorary Irishman; and a long-shoreman blacklisted for being a Communist was bear-hugging me until my bones cracked; a wizened TV documentary cameraman was telling me about the upper Orinoco River; and a tabloid writer trying to transplant himself to Hollywood was arguing the merits of a Philadelphia light-heavyweight whom he thought I'd over-praised. The derailed sea captain behind the bar was praising my tugboat essays; the Clancy Brothers liked the frontier stuff I'd done; and, as a foreign bird of passage, I roused myself, when kidded, to defend American and British WASPs as having introduced free speech and parliamentary democracy to national governance.

These Irish American guys had "cheatin' hearts" like me when their marriages went sour, and I saw with a bit of surprise that in some cases they abandoned or betrayed their male friends, too, just as readily as a Protestant might have, all the blather about Emerald Isle loyalty notwithstanding. The behind-hand snickering at blacks was no better and no worse than what I had grown up with, but I was startled by how cavalierly the bar talk applauded the blood-oath bombings that were rocking Belfast at this time, and the ex-ploits of the silencer-and-trench-coat hit men, though I did sympa-thize politically with the Catholic cause.

Joe Flaherty, whose father had been a longshoresman mur-dered and dumped off a Brooklyn wharf into the harbor for chal-lenging the power of the Mafia (his mother then worked in the lunch line of his grammar school), found crossing the East River to marry, then getting divorced—with the anguish of suffering kids—

and becoming a newspaper columnist in Manhattan plenty jam-packed with risk. But he may have died because, loyal to his roots, he kept using chiropractors, not doctors, for his aches and pains. Around fifty, he discovered that advanced prostate cancer was the cause of the discomfort he had thought was from "throwing out" his back. Lying in his hospital bed, he remarried the night before the operation which castrated him: timing it for the insurance. And because of how authentic his affections were, he was as beloved as any man I've ever known, but both his wives were dumped by his many friends as soon as Joe was off the scene.

There was drama to these Irishers—Pete Hamill caroming between streetwise opining in the *New York Post* or *Daily News* and dashing off movie scripts in Hollywood (an "Irish Ben Hecht," he called himself), while squiring screen stars like Shirley MacLaine and Mary Tyler Moore, and Puerto Rican or Japanese-American wives. He lived a good, generous, voluble, energetic life, though without the literary acclaim that his honest but more astringent friends William Kennedy and Frank McCourt won—just as Pete himself had more success than Joe Flaherty did, who seemed to me still more a prince among men. I haven't found, over the half-century that I've been observing the literati (since, let's say, meeting John Steinbeck in 1950), that "nice guys finish last." They tend to finish in the middle—Steinbeck a nicer guy than Hemingway and not as good a writer, though better than many; Bernard Malamud a nicer guy than Norman Mailer and not as talented, yet more so than many. Frank McCourt suffered a harder-scrabble, back-street misery between his marriages than Hamill. His travels, his interests, his outlets were fewer, his anger more confusedly diffuse, his pen coagulated, and had less energy and money. But Frank's wounds obsessed him in a way that eventually hemorrhaged like a burst blood vessel into brighter colors than most newspapermen can muster; their vociferousness, if not their cynicism, defeats them.

However, bar-drinkers aren't risk takers, as a rule. They fence-sit on a stool, contemplate the options, comment if a parade goes by. I'd hear the banker confess to having fired a man that afternoon for "sexual harassment" who was probably too old to find another job. He was fifty-plus himself; his brandy shook in his hand. And Marty, the real estate man on the other side of me, who called himself Vox Populi and spoke as if his marriage were a wound, responded to my kidding that he must sometimes accept sex in lieu of rent by saying, "No, sir. Rent is a religious experience. Better to take the rent and pay for sex." My friend Joel Oppenheimer had grown up in Yonkers but gone to Black Mountain College in North Carolina to study with Robert Creeley and Robert Duncan, then been a printer's devil, while writing slews of poetry. He was a romantic, a lyricist with a sweet sense of line right out of William Carlos Williams—a thorough night person and downtown habitué, yet loved such tokens of the Old West as the buffalo rifle that an astute girlfriend had given him, and poured his heart into a book about baseball, then ended his life by leaving the city with lung cancer to teach at a little college in Henniker, New Hampshire. Like many of us, his writing lent him a sense of mission and importance that civilians with just a day job never have. Also it provided him with a considerable love life, even though he bathed irregularly, and even after he had lost his teeth. Hirsute, lurching, doggish-headed, Joel cultivated the suffering aura of the quintessential Greenwich Village poet after the death of Maxwell Bodenheim, which indicated that in spite or because of his muddled drinking and querulous indiscipline, it might become important to have known him. Maybe he'd break through! He was endearingly jittery, shaggy, in earnest, and looked the part. I never had that specific sort of confidence in him, but, like my other favorite Village friend, Ross Wetzsteon, who edited twenty of my essays at the *Village Voice* before he died, Joel's picture remains on my wall: along with my dairy-farmer sister, Mary, now fifty-eight, whom I love, of course, and who was adopted at three months old but often appeared beleaguered by a sense that only her mother, or her parents, had truly wanted her. And still another teacher, Alfred Kazin, is on the side of my refrigerator, for his essays and memoirs, like *A Walker in the City*, his comprehensive intellect, and his personal courage. "Edward, my son," he sometimes said, when we stumbled on each other at a literary party. Once, he asked me to edit his journals if he died before he had a chance to. Though I knew him in college, he ended up influencing me most during my forties and fifties—as [Archibald] MacLeish and [Henry Steele] Commager had in my teens and twenties. He was the best of critics and best Americanist.

Our family lived almost next door to Oppenheimer's in a huge so-called Artists' Housing Project, one block square and government-funded, called Westbeth, on the Hudson River near Twelfth Street. It had a lot of actors, painters, jazz and other musicians—Gil Evans, Ornette Coleman, Billy Harper, David Del Tredici—and on the top floor, Merce Cunningham's dance studio, with troupers and students coming and going. His own limber stride and riveting face lent justification to the whole funky place, and it seems to have been a good spot to grow up, because a quarter of a century later my daughter and her actor husband still chose to live there. I thrived, too, and Marion was wryly fond of Westbeth, claiming that she felt comfortably middle-class, ensconced in a thirteen-hundred-square-foot duplex in the midst of so many bohemians, whereas uptown, in a smaller, more expensive apartment in a well-heeled building, she would have felt comparatively poor. The West Village maintained its stamp and character better, was cozier and more livable as the years went on than many fancier neighborhoods. Everyone and practically everything coexisted, the drug deals and leather clubs and prostitution in the blocks beside the river, the bachelor career people getting started, the middle-level couples, hetero- and homosexual, raising children or living quietly, and the Gay Revolution engineered in their spare time mainly by other middle-income people, assisted by frenetic "bridge and tunnel" visitors from the Boroughs—plus the throngs of customers enjoying our savory little food joints, our Indian, Burmese, Ethiopian, Italian, Vietnamese, Thai, or Tunisian restaurants, or oddball, raggedybag, cosmopolitan shops.

Marion was not a walker: in fact by preference was an extraordinarily *slow* walker. Her mind was her speedy vehicle and worked on indoor matters. But she liked the European low-roofed charm and continuity of Greenwich Village, the stable quality of neigh-borliness, of greengrocers and wine-sellers whom you knew, eater-ies with only eight tables, and little triangular parks like Abingdon Square's playground near us, with zigzag vistas of eccentrically colored buildings and a sky that remained close and accessible. The Village had an edge-of-city flavor, and not just because you could walk from these mild climes to Midtown's gridlocked, electric scramble in hardly more than half an hour. It was also because we lived alongside the Hudson, which is so big that it retains its mag-nificent out-of-city majesty, yet feeds raffish New York Harbor, where banana boats were still tying up in downtown Manhattan during our early years, next to miscellaneous barges, lighters, fire-boats, Coast Guard patrol craft, and glamorous Holland-American passenger liners. And because I wrote about this stuff, for me the gritty streets were always juxtaposed to the jumbo flow of Adiron-dack water and Mount Marcy where it came from; or else the tug-boats that I went out on for other stories. For Marion, the nearby area had ben an incubator for experimental theater, zany sculptors, Spinozan loners cogitating in walk-up cubbyholes, or refugee in-tellectuals struggling in the fashion of Pnin to adapt to the strange New World. From Bertolt Brecht's son, who lived across the street, to Thomas Pynchon, hiding incognito on Charles Lane, the neigh-borhood had remained hospitable to strugglers. But the reality for her was a slog and then a subway trip uptown to a nine-to-five commitment of generous but wearying time, editing the work of others, which drained her of the energy that she had hoped to de-vote to writing books of her own. This effort often continued in the evenings and through the weekends because as *Commentary*'s pol-itics shifted from the sort of conventional liberalism that most in-tellectuals and writers continued to adhere to and it became a spearhead for Neoconservatism, it lost its dependably graceful ros-ter of well-known authors and began to publish a new crowd that, however innovative their ideas were, wrote with their thumbs and required exhaustive penciling.

—2001

Paul Colby

(b. 1917)

The Bitter End: Hanging Out at America's Nightclub by Paul Colby and Martin Fitzpatrick is the autobiography of Mr. Colby's life in show business, especially his more than 35 years association with The Bitter End, one of the original Greenwich Village coffeehouses and now considered the longest operating rock and roll club in the world. The Bitter End started in June 1961 and has since been the feeding ground for most of American popular entertainment. Bitter End alumni include Peter, Paul, and Mary; Bob Dylan; Judy Collins; Joni Mitchell; Woody Allen; Bill Cosby; George Carlin; James Taylor; Neil Young; Neil Diamond; Curtis Mayfield; Bette Midler; and thousands more. The following excerpt from The Bitter End *chronicles the beginning of Bob Dylan's career in Greenwich Village, his early coffeehouse performances, his early influences and relationships, and Mr. Colby's friendship with him.*

"Bob Dylan: The King and His Court" from *The Bitter End: Hanging Out at America's Nightclub*

Bob Dylan and Greenwich Village and the Bitter End have been so inextricably connected with one another for such a long time that it is almost impossible to describe one scene without the others.

For Dylan the Village must have seemed like Paris of the 1920s, if you were a budding writer. Around one corner was the White Horse Tavern where Brendan Behan and the Clancy Brothers used to sing and hang out and where Dylan Thomas drank himself to death. Bobby Zimmerman started calling himself Bobby Dylan in honor of Dylan Thomas. Around another corner, on Patchen Street, lived e. e. cummings, who demolished all the rules of punctuation and grammar. If you look at the liner notes on the back of Dylan's early albums, which he himself composed, you get that same iconoclastic style and the influence of cummings is pretty obvious. Greenwich Village was where Pete Seeger lived and where Woody Guthrie used to hang out before he got sick. These were the men whom Dylan adopted as his spiritual fathers. These people weren't vague, historical figures that lived centuries ago. There was no need to search down back alleys for their ghosts or hang out at old haunts trying to divine their spirits. You could run into most of them right on Bleecker Street and introduce yourself or buy them a beer. This was where they lived. For Dylan, coming to the Village from his birthplace in Hibbing, Minnesota, this must have been like coming home.

In the beginning Dylan was managed by a guy named Roy Silver. Roy managed a lot of good people until he would eventually do something awful like steal their wives or their money and then he'd get fired. But Roy was only with Dylan for a short time. Roy initially worked for Albert Grossman. I think he was assigned to Dylan before anybody really understood what was going on. Eventually Albert took over the management. In the early sixties it seemed like everybody either wanted to perform or else manage a performer. If most of these guys hadn't supported each other and gone to each other's shows there would have hardly been anybody in the audience.

I don't know if Grossman had Dylan in the back of his mind when he created Peter, Paul, and Mary, but it worked out great for everybody, especially Bob. They always did refer to Albert as "The Genius." When Peter, Paul, and Mary got their start at the Bitter End and recorded all those early albums that seemed to shoot instantly to number one, it was the first time that the average American got to hear a Bob Dylan song. All those tunes that PP&M covered like "Blowin' in the Wind" and "The Times They Are a Changing'" that became anthems for a lot of people and a lot of causes, were heard long before Bob Dylan became a household name. I believe most people knew Dylan, if they knew him at all, from other artists performing his material.

When Dylan first came to the Village he was really a nobody from nowhere. He fooled everybody because he was so unique and so sure of himself. It was as if he were dropped here from outer space. Bob Dylan, the Dylan that everybody thinks they know, was born in Greenwich Village. The first place he went was Gerde's Folk City, which was run at that time by my old friend Mike Porco. Mike became another kind of a father to Dylan; the kind that gives you money and feeds you. It was Mike who actually signed as next of kin so Dylan could get a cabaret license and perform legally in the clubs. Bob was only about nineteen when he first came to New York.

Jimmy Gavin, who later changed his name to Weston Gavin, was a singer, actor, comedian, and musician. He played the Bitter End once in a while, but everybody worked wherever they could. For a while he was Wavy Gravy's roommate over on Tenth Street. Jimmy was hosting the hootenanny at Gerde's during Dylan's first night in Greenwich Village. Jimmy recounted to me recently, "I remember him wearing a railroad cap. I wasn't particularly impressed with him. At the time he was doing a very derivative Woody Guthrie imitation, but he managed to overcome it."

Tom Paxton also remembered that night: "Dave Van Ronk and I were sitting at Gerde's Folk City on a Monday night hootenanny when Bobby Dylan sang the first three songs that he ever sang in New York. They were three Woody Guthrie songs, and he had on his harmonica rack and a black corduroy cap and you didn't have to be a genius to realize that here was someone special. Bob became, from day one, the hottest topic of gossip. You take an enigmatic personality and a first-rate talent and you have someone people talk about."

It was true. People couldn't get enough of Dylan, but nobody could have foreseen that he would ever make it as big as he did. In the beginning he was just one of a hundred or more unpolished guitarists singing protest songs in the basket houses. But there was a lot to learn playing the basket houses.

One crazy place was called the Fat Black Pussycat. It had a runway and people would toss money on the stage—dimes and nickels. There were poor people who were in the audience for whom a dime was a lot of money. And there were people on stage for whom a dime was a lot of money too. Oscar Brand and Dave Van Ronk went down one night because Bobby Dylan was going to perform. They supported him. Dylan would eat dinner over at Oscar's house and sleep on Van Ronk's sofa. They liked him but neither of them ever thought of the possibility of Dylan being a success.

In the early sixties there were two schools of folk music. One school was interpretive. You sang all the old songs: sea chanteys, wandering rover songs, work songs, chain gang songs, and so on. The other school was more creative and tried to write contemporary songs about hot topics or controversial problems of the day. Most performers were from the first school. Woody Guthrie was from the second. Pete Seeger could do both. Dylan stood firmly in the second school and placed his feet unapologetically into Woody's footprints. He was just like a little boy walking in the snow, following his Dad's longer and deeper strides.

One of the biggest issues at the time was the possibility of nuclear war. There were an awful lot of people who were scared to death. The United States was testing nuclear bombs in the Pacific and in the Nevada desert. People were building fallout shelters back then and kids at school actually had to practice nuclear war drills the way kids today practice fire drills. And then there was the Cuban missile crisis, which intensified the already anxious mood. The uneasiness was palpable.

Dylan used that whole intriguing and frightful tableaux to create and perform all those early masterpieces. For Bob the Village offered support, camaraderie, and escape from hunger. It also afforded him the give and take that artists need. When artists become successful and they rise out of the squalor that often inspires their first compositions, they end up in seclusion on the ritzy side of life, which is great except that they very often cannot maintain their success. Something is missing. Some gutsy fire gets extinguished or they lose their street smarts and start playing from memory. Dylan was somebody who used all the elements that the Village had to offer, especially its spontaneity. And he was smart enough to return to the Village whenever he felt he was losing his edge.

He wrote "A Hard Rain's a Gonna Fall" on Wavy Gravy's typewriter. Wavy, whose name at that time was Hugh Romney, was a leftover poet from the Beat era. He was one of the first artists ever to perform at the Bitter End. Wavy's apartment at the time was right above the Gaslight on MacDougal Street. When Dylan finished typing out "A Hard Rain . . ." he walked right downstairs into the Gaslight and performed it. I think he sang it with Hamilton Camp backing him on guitar. You can't get anymore spontaneous and contemporary than that.

Dylan played "Blowin' in the Wind" for Dave Van Ronk and a couple of friends up at Van Ronk's place. Dave told him, "Bobby, that is the dumbest fucking song I ever heard in my life. What wind? What answer? Let's get a little specific here." You could always say anything to Dylan because he'd never listen anyway. Van Ronk said, "So that was my opinion of the song for about three or four months. Then one day as I was walking across Washington Square Park, I heard a couple of young kids singing:

How much wood
Could a woodchuck chuck
If a woodchuck could chuck wood?
The answer, my friend,
Is blowing out your end
The answer is blowing out your end.

"And I realized that if this song is being parodied after only a couple of months in circulation, and not even recorded, maybe I better go back and listen to the fucking song again. And I did, and I changed my mind."

Now these kids could have heard Dylan doing the song at one of the clubs or they could have read it in publications like *Sing Out!* and *Broadside,* which were contemporary folk song magazines put out by Pete Seeger and Sis Cunningham. These were little, mimeographed sheets that published the first songs of people like Dylan and Phil Ochs. It was another facet of life in the Village that made it so inspiring for young artists.

Dylan also used to hang out at Chip Monck's basement apartment with Richard Alderson. Chip invented concert lighting at the Village Gate in the early sixties. He was the guy on the street that people would go to light their shows. Because of Chip's talent and intuitive theatrical sense, the clubs became little jewel boxes for the artist rather than the artist being part of the wallpaper by the coffee machine. One of Chip's protégés was Jon Gibbs who did the same thing at the Bitter End. Richard Alderson was Chip's counterpart in sound. Wavy Gravy found him making speakers for Leopold Stokowski. He eventually went on to tour with and recorded for Nina Simone. Richard was often at Chip's apartment and did a lot of recording. There are tapes somewhere of Dylan and Fred Neil and Hamilton Camp sitting around on weekends, passing guitars and singing and talking. These are the real "basement" tapes that should be heard, that is if anyone could get their hands on them.

There was always a lot of technical talk among the artists, and consequently Dylan became keenly aware of all the mechanics of putting on a good show. Dylan was very good at taking little bits and pieces of other people's inventions and absorbing them and making them work for him. He took this great energy that was all around him and channeled it and made it his own. That's what genius does.

Dylan, by the way, could be very funny on stage in a Chaplinesque manner. He had all these little bits of hand movements, a very kinetic style that was sort of based on Chaplin. People who saw him at the big arena shows later on, when he was a dot on stage, missed all that because, for awhile in 1971 and 1972, he wasn't trying anymore. It was only when he played the smaller venues, when he used to open for people like John Lee Hooker, that's when the Chaplin character really came out, especially when he did all those crazy songs like "Talking Bear Mountain Picnic Massacre Disaster Blues" and "If I Had To Do It All Over Again, Babe, I'd Do It All Over You," which he wrote on a bet.

A bunch of people were sitting around the Kettle of Fish one afternoon. In between beers somebody started rattling off jokey song titles like, "Take Back Your Heart, I Ordered Liver." According to Dave Van Ronk, "Somebody said, 'Bobby, I bet you couldn't write a song to *that* title, 'If I Had To Do It . . . '." So he came back a few days later with about six verses, which I recorded. I think it was the first Dylan song to make it on to an album. It wasn't a great song, but it was good enough. I still think it's pretty funny.

When folk music looked like it might get popular the record company executives were going crazy trying to sign artists. They were scared. They thought folk music might take off like rock and roll did in the fifties. They didn't understand the music or the artists, but every label seemed to want a stable of folk acts just in case. You didn't have to be brilliant to get a record deal. Still, the promotion people and the executives didn't know what they had. I don't think anybody bought Dylan's first album when it came out except a few enlightened souls like my friend Beverly Bentley. It was through Beverly that I first came to be aware of Dylan and his music.

Around the same time that Dylan's first album was released, I had a great apartment on Fifty-first Street and Second Avenue. It was a bachelor's apartment with a bedroom and a huge terrace. It had an aboveground swimming pool, where we used to hang out. Beverly Bentley lived down the block. She was shooting a movie called *Scent of Mystery*, and she was also on Broadway in a play called *The Heroine*. This was before she married Norman Mailer. She was hanging out with Miles Davis then. That's where I met Miles and got to know him. It was also the first time I was ever offered cocaine.

It was a social scene. She would come to my house. I would go to hers. My house was the main hangout because of the pool. On the weekends all my friends, whom I called Fire Island Rejects, would come over. They couldn't afford the train fare to the beach so they went to my place.

Beverly came over one night with an album, a Bob Dylan album. She said, "You understand music; I want you to hear this guy." And she played Dylan's first album. It had just been released, that day I think, on Columbia. She played it over and over and over. She said, "How do you like it?" I was a good friend. I said, "Give me some time to get into it."

I remember there was a black girl in the room. I can't remember her name or even why she was there, but there was a terrific fight. The black girl said, "Get that fucking piece of shit off the record player. I can't stand it." Beverly and the girl started fighting. Beverly kept saying, "Don't you understand this? You're not hearing something?" It was nuts. The black girl tried to take the album off the turntable and break it. But really most of the people at the party couldn't stand it. Beverly was the only one who liked it. This was sometime in 1962.

And then a week later Beverly said to me, "We've got to go down to the Village." "Why?" I asked. "I've got to meet this Bob Dylan," she replied. So we went down to Folk City that night, but the club was closed or Dylan was off, I don't know. But she was desperately seeking Bob Dylan. She was the first one with ears that were so rarefied that she could listen and say, "This is magic."

I still wasn't convinced until I found out it was John Hammond who signed him, which forced me to look at Dylan in a different light because I respected Hammond. John used to come down to the Bitter End often. I knew him. I liked him. There was an internecine faction that tried to force him out of Columbia but they weren't successful. I don't think that first Dylan album helped his career much. I found out later that a lot of Columbia's sales staff said openly that the album was a piece of shit and wouldn't get behind it.

I don't know where Beverly met Norman Mailer. Probably at some party. She wanted to marry him very badly. She wanted me to meet him but she warned, "Be careful what you say." She invited me out to his house, and it must have been the Fourth of July because we were sitting on the veranda looking at the Statue of Liberty and watching the fireworks. It wasn't particularly pleasant. Mailer was pretty full of himself by that time. He was full of other things too. It was a long time since he had delivered copies of the *Village Voice*, a newspaper he helped found, to newsstands out of the back seat of his car at four in the morning. Sometimes I think Beverly would have been better off with Miles. That was the last time I saw her but she did introduce me to Dylan's music, which I shall never forget.

Dylan was never officially booked at the Bitter End. Bobby was very loyal to Mike Porco and in the beginning, when he was an advertised performer doing a small club, it was almost always at Folk City. Individual acts often became associated with one club or another. John Hammond Jr. always seemed to play the Cafe Au Go Go, The Lovin' Spoonful were usually at Nobody's, somebody else would be married to the Gaslight, and so on. The Bitter End had some great acts that were also pretty loyal. If you wanted to see Woody Allen or Bob Gibson or Theo Bikel you would have to come to the Bitter End. For Dylan, the Bitter End was the place to go to listen and take it all in. It was not where he worked but where he hung out.

Now the other great topic of debate at that time was civil rights. This was before Vietnam really became an issue. The first American casualty in Vietnam was just before Christmas in 1961, and about six months later there was a Greenwich Village Peace Committee formed to sponsor lectures on Vietnam. They eventually brought in guest lecturers like Bob Kerry long before he became a senator, but it was not a burning issue yet. Civil rights, however, was on fire. Theo Bikel and Pete Seeger and others were very involved in the civil rights movement. There were always rallies or benefits going on somewhere in the Village. And folk musicians were always on the bill. When I think of all the black jazzmen who played all over the Village back then like Sonny Rollins, Roland Kirk, Charlie Mingus, James Moody, it was truly astonishing. But those guys lived in their own jazz world. It was a separate community. Every time there was a rally for the civil rights movement, the entertainment would always be a white folk singer. I never could figure that out.

Theo Bikel used to play the club in the early sixties. He even did a live radio show on Sunday nights. Theo was very busy at the time. He was starring in *The Sound of Music* with Mary Martin, where he created the role of Captain Von Trapp and after the performance he would come down to the club to sing or hang out. Dylan would wander in and out, lugging his guitar with him. He was often over at Theo's Greenwich Village apartment getting a bite to eat and playing his songs, which were very evocative. Theo was so involved in the civil rights movement that he used to go down South and get arrested, which was a dangerous pastime. He took Dylan aside one night and said, "Bobby, you shouldn't just write songs about this stuff. You should experience it firsthand. I want you to come down South with me." But Dylan said he couldn't afford the fare. Just to call his bluff, Theo told Albert Grossman to buy Bobby a ticket and not tell him where it came from. He finally went down but not until much later.

Another act that was very big at the time was the Tarriers. The Tarriers were also involved, like most of us were in one way or another, with the civil rights movement. It was hard for the Tarriers not to be because they were one of the first, if not the first, interracial groups. Two white guys, two black guys. One night during Theo's radio show, with Dylan in the audience, the Tarriers's spokesman and bassist, Marshall Brickman, was recounting from the stage a recent trip down South. "The four of us," he said, "were driving through Arkansas, about ten miles south of Little Rock. We were driving fast, very fast. It was a balmy summer evening. The air was thick and heavy with the scent of magnolias and honeysuckle and tar and feathers." Everybody laughed but even with a free bus ticket it was not the kind of trip that everybody wanted to experience.

Curt Flood, the St. Louis Cardinal outfielder, once said that a person could be segregated in the back seat of a limousine. But Dylan wasn't like that. You didn't have to go down South to experience racism. The Village, after all, was not the idyllic neighborhood it sometimes gets credit for being. The Village could be crude and hateful too. There was a lot going on back then—it wasn't all flowers and love beads. There were working-class gangs, and the Mob was always just around the corner.

When Len Chandler, a black folk singer who played all over the Village in the early sixties, almost died from a beating it was Dylan who came to visit him in Bellevue Hospital. Chandler had been instrumental in bringing the Freedom Singers to New York. At the Newport Folk Festival in 1964, the Freedom Singers ended one of the evenings with a sing-a-long when Peter, Paul, and Mary, Pete Seeger, and Bob Dylan joined them. Because of Village regulars like Len Chandler and the Tarriers, Dylan understood the anger and frustration and pain associated with racism. Thanks to people like Richie Pryor he also understood the need for a sense of humor.

One of the original Tarriers, by the way, was Alan Arkin before he became famous as an actor. Years later when Arkin and Theo Bikel starred in the movie *The Russians Are Coming . . . The Russians Are Coming* I heard that in between takes the movie set was very often turned into the stage of the Bitter End, as both actors sang folk songs to pass the time. People like Bikel and Arkin and Leon Bibb were very good actors and whenever they doubled as folk singers their performances were tremendously effective because they could really act out a song. Lou Gossett Jr. did an act for years at the Village Gate with Felix Papalardi on guitar. It was quite an act. Dylan had seen and absorbed them all. And when these acts were impeccably staged by people like Jon Gibbs or Chip Monck or Richard Alderson and his protégés, it took on all the power of a theatrical experience. Of course when Dylan picked an actor to imitate he chose Charlie Chaplin. It was all part of his learning process and something of which Dylan was keenly aware.

Bob Dylan didn't play the little clubs for long. He was soon being booked into places like Town Hall and the big folk festivals. After the Beatles made it big in 1964 and folk music began to get stale, Dylan did his great makeover from protest singer to rock star. When he played his famous electric set at the Newport Folk Festival in 1965—the one that got Pete Seeger so outraged he tried to cut the power cables with an ax—it was Theo Bikel who wisely restrained him. That was when Dylan said, "Folk music is a bunch of fat people." But he kept his apartment in Greenwich Village, and he also remembered the most important lesson folk music had to teach: The words are important.

By the late sixties Dylan was writing rock and roll songs with lyrics of such complexity and intensity that they frankly shocked people. He worked with Village-based bands like Paul Butterfield and the Blues Project, whenever Danny Kalb wasn't busy falling off rooftops that is, as well as musicians like Mike Bloomfield and Al Kooper. Dylan chose rock and roll as his musical medium but wrote lyrics that you would expect to hear only in a folk song. The music spoke to a lot of people, not only fans but other artists as well.

I really got to know Dylan well in the early seventies through Al Aronowitz, a rock critic for the *New York Post*. Al came running up to me on Bleecker Street one day as I was headed for the club.

"Where have you been?" he asked. It was early in the day.

"I didn't know I had an appointment," I said.

"Bob Dylan wants to come to the club."

"So let him come. I'll give him a good table."

Now there was nothing stopping Dylan from dropping in by himself, but that was no longer the way Bob worked. That night Al brought Dylan, and I gave them my table. I believe Bunky and Jake were playing, one of Dylan's favorite acts. We all sat down and before the performance started I decided to make conversation. I knew Dylan had a house in Woodstock so I said, "Bob I just bought a house in Woodstock myself. How do you like it up there?" "Nice," said Dylan. I tried another angle. I started talking about food because I knew he loved our hamburgers. I asked him if the hamburgers were okay. "Nice," he repeated. That was pretty much it. I let them enjoy the show.

About a week later I was outside the club checking on some posters, and Al frantically comes running up. "Paul, where have you been? I've been here since this morning."

"Al, the club doesn't open until six o'clock at night. What can I do for you?"

"Dylan wants to come by the club again."

"So let him come," I said.

"But he wants to make sure you'll be here."

"Why?" I asked incredulously.

"Because he likes you," said Al.

When Kris Kristofferson played for me back in the early seventies he was not yet a big name, but he was gathering quite a reputation. One day Kris said, "Let's go see Bob Dylan." Now I knew Dylan, of course, but you never know how well you knew him. I may have had a drink or two that night. Kris had more than two, which was his way back then.

It was the apartment on MacDougal Street. We knocked and Dylan's wife came to the door. We felt as if we were in a spy movie. "We want to see Bob Dylan," we announced. "Who wants to see Bob Dylan?" she asked. So Kris said, "Kris Kristofferson and Paul Colby." Well, she locked the door and went away. By now Kris and I are not sure what to do. About five minutes later she came back, unlocked the door, and we went inside.

Whenever I hung out with Kris it was always a blast. The guitars would come out and lots of drinks would follow. But not tonight. We talked a little bit about music. Out came the tea set. I felt like we were old people all of a sudden. Here was Dylan, but he was very subdued. It was like intelligent people talking about the stock market. We all kept saying things like, "Oh really?" and "Hmmm, interesting." It was completely nuts. I think Kris felt like screaming. At home with the Dylans. "Do come again. Don't forget to call before you come." That kind of thing. When Kris went on to do his cowboy movie about Billy the Kid [Sam Peckinpah's *Pat Garrett and Billy the Kid*], Dylan would co-star in it. But that night they didn't quite find each other. Dylan was at home with his wife that night.

At the time I didn't know much about Kristofferson. All I knew was that I liked him. Shel Silverstein sent me Kris's first album before the public knew about it. It had not been released worldwide yet. After this many years in the business I know when I hear a song whether or not it is going to fly. Sometimes I'm wrong but it's usually for different reasons. The artist may have political enemies in the business. Maybe the artist is arrogant or a fuck up. Many of them are. But when I heard "Me and Bobby McGee" and "For the

Good Times" and especially "Sunday Morning Coming Down," I knew Kris was the real thing. I remember telling Shel that I would put Kris on if he would stop by and do a song. Shel said no. He procrastinated and said he wasn't prepared. When Shel finally came down I could barely get him off the stage to introduce Kris.

Kris made his formal debut at the Bitter End about six months later and that's when he got the Columbia record deal. He was the hottest thing around. You could not get near the club on that Friday night, that's how popular he was. The *New York Times* ran a spread on him that made Kris seem as enigmatic as Dylan: helicopter pilot, Rhodes scholar, background in law, his father a general. From that day on he was a star, and we became great friends.

Time moved on, and Dylan had gone off and done his country and western album, including that famous duet with Johnny Cash. I remember seeing his first television appearance on the *Johnny Cash Show*. He also toured with the Band. People started talking about how his best stuff was behind him. By 1975, it was time for Dylan to come back to the Village. That's just what he did.

When Patti Smith played the club in the summer of 1975, she had already acquired cult status. A lot of people couldn't, or wouldn't, understand where she was coming from but the club was always packed with fanatics. That's when I remember Dylan coming back. Patti could be arrogant and blasé at the same time. The novelist Jerzy Kosinski came in to see her one night, and he had a copy of her book of poems called *Witt*. Kosinski got her to autograph it, but I don't think she even knew who he was. When Kosinski spelled his first name for her so Patti wouldn't confuse it with the state, she misunderstood and wound up drawing a little map of Jersey anyway. He seemed satisfied or, perhaps, resigned. Then Dylan came in. Patti knew who he was.

I think she was doing a cover version of a Rolling Stones song when he arrived. They locked onto each other immediately. She said something to him from the stage like, "Don't think you can park your car next to my meter." The word was out. Dylan was back.

From that moment on, through all of July and August, Dylan was the hottest topic of conversation. Everybody wanted to know what he was doing back in the Village. What was up? I think he just wanted to hang out. He came to the club practically every night that summer.

Now by this time I had bought the club next door, connected the two clubs together and called the whole operation the Other End because Freddy Weintraub still had control of the Bitter End name. For people hanging around from the beginning it was still the Bitter End except now it was huge. I was able to run a separate restaurant and even keep a pool table. Dylan used to shoot pool with my good friend Billy Fields practically every night.

It was a special time for Bob. That's why he kept coming back. I made sure no one bothered him. When he first came by, I didn't realize it. He had walked in unexpectedly, and one of my bartenders said, "Oh my God, that's Bob Dylan." He had walked out again. I overheard the whole thing and ran after him. "Where are you going?" I said. "What are you doing here?" he said to me. I said, "This is my place," and with that he came back inside.

Now that Dylan was hanging around I decided to turn the July 4th weekend into the First Annual Village Folk Festival, which it certainly was not, but hyperbole was always standard advertising procedure in the Village. After all, I had learned from a master. I knew we had Jake and the Family Jewels on board and also Bunky and Jake, whom Dylan loved. It was a field day for the press. Bobby Neuwirth was hanging out, and so was Ramblin' Jack Elliot. Whenever Bunky and Jake or Ramblin' Jack got on stage, Dylan would join them and play and sing. It felt like Hoot night again. Dylan sat down at the piano and everybody on stage began singing "Will the Circle Be Unbroken." Phil Ochs was hanging around too, getting drunk. Dylan was laughing, talking, and singing. He was so happy and relaxed. Bob looked at me and said, "This is like the old times." And it was. He was comfortable. He saw people he hadn't seen in years.

One night John Prine was playing. Bob got up, stood behind Prine, and played the harmonica. Just little grace notes at first until he picked up the melody and then he started to wail. John turned around when they finished and pointed his finger at Bob and said, "Dylan." That was it. There was a big round of applause. After the song he came back to my table. I stood up to let him in and he sat next to me. Two girls were at the next table and one of them said, "You're not really Bob Dylan are you?" And I said, "No, but I am." With that the one girl turns to the other and says, "See, I told you it wasn't really Bob Dylan." And the two of them walked out. The elusive Bob Dylan.

More and more people began stopping by the club. Cindy Bullins, Ronnie Blakely, Allen Ginsberg, Eric Katz, Logan English. Logan English was one of the first folkies to get on stage in the Village. I think Logan was playing around while Dylan was barely out of diapers. After one night of wine and tequila it seemed everybody wound up on stage. Eric Katz sang "Love Has No Pride," the abstract painter Larry Poons got up and sang a song, and Patti Smith recited some poem about King Faisal's nephew while Ramblin' Jack Elliot yodeled behind her. Dylan would just sit back in that dreamy way he had and smile. As Logan walked by Dylan asked, "Is that you Logan? I thought you were dead." Logan said, "I heard the same thing about you a couple of times." They both giggled. It was an incredible scene.

The only cloud over the space was Dylan's very justifiable fear that someone would tape record him. He had a lot of new songs at the time, like "Joey Gallo" and "Hurricane Carter," and he wanted to break them in. This was another great aspect of the little Village clubs. You could introduce new material, try it out in front of a live audience, and work out any kinks. You could choose the best three verses out of half a dozen, tighten up a line here and there. But no professional would ever want his first drafts recorded. It also proved that Dylan needed something substantial to write about. Vietnam was over, civil rights was no longer the big issue it was in the early sixties. Some artists saw the future as belonging to disco but not Bob Dylan. He was writing a song to try to free a black convict that he thought got railroaded.

On this particular night, it was getting late and the place was closing up but nobody would leave. Dylan told me that he wanted to get on stage so bad he could taste it but he was worried. "These are new songs. I just want to make sure I'm not recorded." I said, "All you have to do is let me know." Now I don't know if Dylan saw something that made him suspicious or not but sure enough there was a girl in one of the back tables with a tape recorder and her pocketbook open.

I went to her and said, "You're involved in a happening here. This is a very special scene you're in. People would give their right arm to be here." I told her to shut the thing off. I grabbed the recorder and told her I would return it when she left. Charlie Rothchild was standing by the bar rail. Charlie was a producer and worked with Allen Ginsberg and Judy Collins. He said, "Paul, they've got another tape recorder." Then I blew my top. I got so angry I pulled the tape out of the machine, and Charlie Rothchild started pulling the tape out of the reel. The girl's boyfriend said, "Hey, I got other stuff on there."

"I don't give a fuck!" I shouted, holding a glass of wine in my hand. He tried to say something else, and I threw the wine in his face. Then I tossed him and his girlfriend out of the club. That's when Bobby Neuwirth came over to me and said, "Paul, Bob Dylan and I want to do a tour." "Great," I replied. "Do you think you could do it?" "Sure," I said. I had no idea how to do a tour but I figured I could get people, organize them. I felt I could do anything. No big deal. That was the beginning of the Rolling Thunder Revue.

As we talked about it a little more I said, "Look, you guys are having such a great time here. Musicians need to get back to their roots, to the small clubs. You're always talking about how sick you are of the concert scene. Let's not do arenas. Let's do the small, intimate two- or three-thousand seat theaters."

Both Dylan and Neuwirth said, "Great idea." Everybody in the room that night was titillated. It was as if they were all somehow involved in the tour. Jack Elliot was having a large tequila when Bob called out, "Hey Jack, you want to go on tour?"

"Sure," Jack answered. A couple of weeks later I saw Jack and asked, "So are you going on tour with Bob?"

"Hell no," he said, "I thought they were all drunk."

In walks Roger McGuinn from the Byrds. "Roger come here." Roger goes over and sits next to Bob and the next thing I know McGuinn is on the tour. Ronnie Blakely was in the room. She was on the tour. Everybody was getting an invite. "We're having a party, come along." I was going to be the tour director. Finally the police came and told everybody to go home. It must have been five in the morning when we finally left.

Then the musicians actually got serious. They started to rehearse at the Bitter End practically every night after the regular shows were over. Ginsberg, McGuinn, Blakely, I think Joan Baez too got involved around this time. Joan was never really of the Village. She was from the upper crust of Massachusetts, but if Dylan was involved she would deign to hang out with the proletarians. I think she was always a little bit miffed that she and Dylan never created some kind of dynastic marriage. Here, the guy is married with five kids, but she always considered herself the queen, and so it was only natural that she should be bonded to the king. Everybody wants to be The One.

Dylan and I went out a couple of times. Bob liked to get laid of course, but he was discreet. One girl came to me and said, "You know I have to talk to you. You seem to know Bob Dylan. Well I had an affair with him a couple of weeks ago. He said he cared about me, but I haven't heard from him." "Did you enjoy yourself?" I asked. She said, "Yes." I said, "Well think of it as a fond memory." They're all the same. She had his body, now she wanted his brain.

The rehearsals went on for weeks. They were always late night affairs. I went home one night to Jersey at about four in the morning. Someone called me an hour later and said the cops are at the door. "What'll we do?"

"Keep the doors locked and pretend you're not there," I said.

The regular shows for the public would end around 2:00 A.M. Then everybody would start drifting in to rehearse. The audience would leave as the cast members and friends would be coming in. One night around 3:00 A.M. I'm listening to them rehearse and the telephone rings. It was Eric Anderson calling from Woodstock.

When he heard the music in the background he asked, "What the hell is going on there?" So I told him Dylan was here with everybody, and they're all rehearsing for a tour.

"Wow," said Eric, "It sounds great. How long will it be going on?"

"What do you mean?" I asked.

"If I drive down right now will it still be going on when I get there?"

"Drive slow," I answered. "They'll be here for two more weeks."

Phil Ochs was around a lot then too. Bob thought I was being cruel to Phil because I was short with him. But he was driving me crazy. He was drinking heavily. Basically, he was a mess, and I told him I would buy him no more booze. I didn't want to encourage him. Dylan told me to buy him a bottle of wine, which I did. I couldn't sit Bob down and explain to him that Phil was going off his rocker. Phil would come around drunk and badmouth Dylan. Then when Bobby would show up they would be best buddies again, and Phil would have his arm around him. I don't think he even remembered half the things he said. This happened a lot.

Many of Dylan's contemporaries had a love-hate relationship with him. They all started in the business around the same time and in the beginning everybody was on an equal footing. I think the feeling was: Sure Bobby's good, but he's no better than I am. Why don't people buy my albums anymore? How come I'm not making a million dollars? Dylan inspired a lot of jealousy but very few people would ever say so to his face. In fact, just the opposite happened. There was always that one big question. Why him and not me? There's an easy answer to that, and everybody knows what it is. Some people accepted it and others, like Phil, became self-destructive.

When the Rolling Thunder Revue finally started, I was pushed out of organizing the tour. It would have been difficult in any event but I think I could have handled it as well as it eventually was done. In the beginning, I saw about four or five shows. I was something of a fixture. I guess they felt indebted to me or guilty, I don't know which. I went up to Plymouth, Massachusetts, to see the first concert, which was done in a church. About a thousand people showed up, just as I had expected. Everyone on the tour was staying at the local inn. I was the only outsider allowed in. Even the press had to stay in Plymouth. Bob invited me up on stage to sing for the finale. I got to watch all the intrigue up there.

The tour was eventually given over to Barry Imhoff. Bob Dylan's best friend Lou Kemp was also around a lot. Barry and Kemp were the leaders of the pack. The Rolling Thunder Revue became the last great tour that Dylan did. It was a great success. They really did try to keep the original feeling. By the end though it had more or less reverted back to the big venues. The tour was going to finish at Madison Square Garden.

I remember running into Kemp just before the Garden show and I told him, "I've seen four or five of these things already. I'm not going to the Garden."

"Yes you are."

"No I'm not. I've seen enough of him."

"I'll bet you."

"What do you want to bet?" I asked.

"A high-priced hooker," he replied.

So we bet a high-priced hooker, and I lost. I did go to the Garden show because Hurricane Carter was going to be there. They had a lot of celebrities, and they made a big deal out of it. The next time Kemp comes to New York I intend to pay him off, except in this day and age, he may want to change the stakes.

That was the last time I saw Dylan. Why he never came around again I don't know. When someone asked me why Dylan was back in the Village and why he kept coming to the club, I said, "Because he likes my hamburgers." But that was another aspect of Dylan. He was serendipitous. He could cut you off as fast as he could embrace you. I don't think it was spite. It was simply time to make a change. Time to go. When Jackson Browne played the club for the first time in 1972 he was still unknown. He was very respectful, and we became friendly. One night Dylan stopped by to see the show, and Jackson begged me to introduce him. I did. He and Dylan talked for a minute and then Jackson confidently went on stage. In the middle of the second song, Dylan got up and left. Poor Jackson stood there singing, thinking, "It's the end of my career." Not so. It was just time for Dylan to go. His disappearances were as quixotic as his appearances. He was a guy you simply enjoyed but could never get close to. Many people think they are close to him and they are . . . until he disappears.

When his new album came out in the late nineties I got the feeling that it was missing that edge. I think Dylan needs to hang out in the Village again and stop by the club. I think it's about time for that. When he got sick a few years ago I got calls from all the newspapers. Why call me? I thought. Then I suddenly realized that Folk City is gone. The Au Go Go is gone. Nobody's is gone. The Gaslight is gone. Art D'Lugoff and Manny Roth and Mike Porco are all gone. I'm the last one left. The Bitter End and me.

I told the newspapers, "I'm sorry he's sick, but I'm eighty years old and I'm down here working. What do you want me to say? He doesn't call me. I hope he feels better."

—2002

Barney Rosset

(b. 1922)

*In the early 1950s Barney Rosset purchased a little known publishing
house in Greenwich Village called* Grove Press *for $3,000. During the
late 1950s and much of the 1960s,* Grove Press *was considered the most
influential and innovative—some would say subversive—publishing
company in the country. Rosset, the Chicago-born son of an Irish Catholic
mother and a Russian Jewish father, published books that interested him,
and damn the consequences. He introduced American readers to the work
of European dramatists of the Absurd, French surrealists, Beat writers
from both coasts, and New York abstract expressionists, including such titles as* Waiting for Godot *by Samuel Beckett,* Last Exit to Brooklyn *by
Hubert Selby, and* Naked Lunch *by William Burroughs, among others.
He also published such controversial books as D. H. Lawrence's* Lady
Chatterley's Lover *and Henry Miller's* Tropic of Cancer—*two modern
classics that had long been banned in the U.S. In 1957, he established the*
Evergreen Review, *which featured articles on civil right issues, new
American poetry, and the growing popularity of jazz. In the increasingly
conservative field of publishing, Rosset remains a true maverick. The following selection from his memoir recalls the early days of* Grove Press—
*when everything seemed possible and the literary world appeared to be at
his beck and call.*

Barney Rosset. From *Misc.: Subject Is Left-Handed* (unpublished). (New York: 2002).
Copyright © 2002 by Barney Rosset.

from
Misc.: Subject Is Left-Handed

May 29, 2001

In the fall of 1949, Joan Mitchell and I moved into our first Green-wich Village living space: 267½ West Eleventh Street, New York City. To us Midwesterners, that was a strange address, not to mention its odd configuration as a place in which to live. How West Eleventh Street joined West Fourth Street, one block to our east then to our west ran into Bleecker, jammed again by Hudson Street a few hundred feet further west after passing Abington Square on its north en route, was a mystery which was never clarified. We did however know that if you made it to Hudson and crossed over you ran more or less smack into the White Horse Tavern. A bit later this bar became famous because of the nightly presence of Dylan Thomas, the great Welsh poet, flaming himself out and turning to ashes a few blocks away at St. Vincent's Hospital, or was it the Chelsea Hotel? Hardly in the Village, on West Twenty-third Street between Seventh and Eighth Avenue, the hotel was already the famous abode for poets, artists, composers, famous types of all kinds. And it was a beautiful building.

Joan and I had gone there that fall, straight from the pier when we arrived back from France. Living there then were such people as Roger Flaherty, the maker of such films as *Men of Aran* and *Nanook of the North;* and Virgil Thompson, a leading American composer who had helped in 1948 to add the musical score to *Strange Victory* (the film which I produced in 1948). He had assembled an ad hoc group of musicians, every one of them a top soloist, and then conducted the recording of David Diamond's score.

Reputedly there were fantastic residential suites on the top floor of the hotel—one of them occupied by Susan LaFolette—an artist and a member of the great liberal political family from Wisconsin.

Years later, Maurice Girodias, a person who became an important integral part in my life and book career, checked in for a lengthy stay. His Olympia Press brought forth such books as *Lolita* and *The Ginger Man*, and the English version of *The Story of O.*

That first Village apartment was a strange little one-room house perfectly in sync with its address. It had been planted down in the middle of a garden behind a brownstone. Maybe it had been meant for a children's playroom, but it was our living space and included Joan's studio. Some agile carpenter-type friends from Chicago helped us put dry walls in its basement, keeping out the dampness a bit. Turning east from our narrow entrance lane took you not only to West Fourth Street but also to Seventh Avenue and the Village Vanguard. Max Gordon was the great proprietor and we got to know him and his wife Lorraine very well. Over a period of time, even when we no longer lived nearby, we spent hours at the Vanguard with the likes of Pete Seeger and his folk group, The Weavers. One night Marion Makeeba came on stage fresh from the shabeens of Soweto and Johannesburg. On stage, Lenny Bruce fingered a cop in a raincoat standing near the exit, who really was a cop; stalking his prey, Lenny. There was Miles Davis playing his horn, facing the wall because the listeners annoyed him; Jack Kerouac delivering his more than slightly drunk monologue; and Hettie Ledbetter, Leadbelly himself, fresh out of a southern prison singing his new song "Good Night Irene." It was nice even when Lenny told Max, from the stage, that the waiters were robbing him. Who cared? Not Max.

One night Max came in to the '55 on Christopher Street, which had become by then our bar of preference, next door to the sort of literary Lion's Head, to tell me that Charlie Mingus had not shown up that night. So Max had closed the place for the night, refunded the money to the customers, and totally calm, strolled over to the '55. Charlie was indisposed, a little bit, might be tomorrow too, so would I walk over with him to another bar, where Sun Ra had a gig?—and there Max signed him up for the next night and spoke to Charlie's wife. It was another uneventful evening for Max, but not for me.

267½ became a bit too much for a painter whose canvases were growing larger by the week. We decided to move. Before leaving, Joan had an acute attack of appendicitis at four o'clock one morning. A doctor who had helped create the first mobile hospital units at the battlefields during the Spanish Civil War rushed over to the Beth Israel Hospital to perform the operation. He looked in on her a few hours later and then went off to jail to begin his sentence for refusing to answer questions before the Un-American Activities Committee.

Grove Press had been almost stillborn right there at 267½ because of carelessness on my part; specifically because of getting a parking ticket placed on my convertible Oldsmobile while I was delivering freshly printed copies of the highly literate political magazine, the *Monthly Review,* to some "workers" in a building near Union Square. I had volunteered for the job, today's style intern you might say, and I paid the parking ticket myself, but the good leftist that he was, Leo Huberman, co-editor with Paul Sweezey, an economist from Harvard, decided that an untrustworthy person like me, who got parking tickets while delivering the goods, was not the person to help the people on the left side of the spectrum.

Many years later, Harry Braverman, a Grove stalwart for years, left us to become the head of *Monthly Review Magazine and Book Publishing.* Times they did a change.

Joan and I moved to a brownstone, a lovely one at 57 West Ninth Street, between Fifth and Sixth Avenues, nearer to Sixth. At the east end of the block, Fifth Avenue was sedate and serene, while at the other corner was the then Jefferson courthouse, the bustling women's prison—a small skyscraper by itself—and, later to arrive, Trudi Heller's great nightclub, the perfect counterpart to its neighbors.

At 57 West Ninth we had the top floor of the original house. Best of all, reached through an inner staircase, the owner had constructed another large room with a vaulted ceiling; a large fireplace, windows and glass doors, with a large terrace overlooking Ninth Street. From it we had a great view of former mayor Jimmy Walker's prison, the Courthouse, and Trudi Heller's club.

By 1950, I was working hard and also enjoying myself at the New School only three blocks away. Among my professors, whom I admired greatly, were Wallace Fowlie, Stanley Kunitz, Meyer Shapiro, and Alfred Kazin, all provided thanks to the G.I. Bill. I was actually awarded a B.A. in 1952, something which Swarthmore, the University of Chicago, and UCLA combined had not let me accomplish.

Further by the time of my graduation, Grove Press had become my reality. That was in 1950.

Joan's painting flourished. She rented another studio in a marvelous clone of a French studio building, also on Twelfth Street. It occupied her attention and presence more and more. Our own relationship slowly dissolved, but in a rather final, beautiful act, Joan brought to me, with the aid of a friend—a fellow student at the Art Institute in Chicago—copies of three titles, *The Confidence Man* by Herman Melville, an inspired reprint, a new collection of the religious love poetry of Richard Crashaw, and a collection of writings of Aphra Behn, who was described as the first feminist author.

I was very receptive to the idea of becoming a publisher. My documentary filmmaking was no longer appealing, and I was ready to segue naturally from studying Proust, Rimbaud, Mallarme, et al., to publishing others like them. Becoming a self-employed entrepreneur seemed to be the next natural step.

Joan also provided the spark leading me to my first publishing decision. She suggested we reprint *The Golden Bowl* by Henry James, recently reviewed in its film version by the *New York Times*, which called it his masterpiece.

Without then having read Ezra Pound's dictum, saying that if you read a good book of Jame's you will get hooked on him and continue on to his other works, I obviously took the same path and published seven or eight additional James novels, all of which had gone out of print. Leon Edel, James' biographer, wrote prefaces for a few.

Being basically a child of the city and the Depression—during a period of much migration some desired and some forced—I was used to moving from one apartment to another in Chicago. Albeit they were all in what would be considered very small apartment buildings today, perhaps having from ten to twenty apartments in each, they were most certainly not the brownstones. One road ran in an almost straight line and the other was circular.

In Chicago we—my mother, father, and I—started from the far North Side near Howard Street, the demarcation point between Evanston and Chicago, in a neighborhood called Rogers Park and ultimately reached Lake Shore Drive. There were a number of pit stops along the way, but this short end marathon always hugged Lake Michigan, and never went further inland from the lake than the nearest street running into it or running alongside of it. We must have gone ten miles in fifteen years, always in the same direction, always near the lake. In Greenwich Village it would take me fifty years to circle around one eight or nine block area, and that inward thrust was certainly voluntary.

Even though the Depression interruped our "Great March," this time a capitalist one (another of my self-created parallels to Edgar Snow's *Red Star Over China*, which I republished at Grove), it resolutely continued.

Despite the Republicans and Herbert Hoover, Roosevelt did finally bring back alcohol and prosperity. I had the best or worst of that passage. My father was a Jewish Republican, my mother an Irish Democrat. People like Joan's family, good Protestant gentiles, were above guiding the puppets below: the Irish, the Jews, and the Mob. Believing the above, as I did, can you understand why I became a communist for a while?

In Greenwich Village it was a little bit the same, but it was also different. People hung around. Where would you go? You were already *there*. The Irish, the Jews, and another element, the Italians, were present. It was a community, a culture of its own making, and there were the artists, the writers, and the theater people. Books, curtains, canvases were in the air. Eugene O'Neill's plays were put on, the Communists, the anti-Communists, gathered in Union Square, the mounted police rode. (See the film *Reds*.) Joan and I had found home. Disparate souls, now joined. Location is so important. In Chicago one chased the Holy Grail from Sheridan Road to

Michigan Avenue, and then perhaps found it on the Gold Coast, as it was called. It could finally become your neighborhood too. Only, the enemy had arrived before you.

My mother, in my hearing, often told my father that he belonged in New York. I listened, and I took her advice. Second City is such a sweet insult when you're not there to live with it.

The ten miles from Evanston to the Lindbergh Beacon, "The Miracle Mile" leading to the river which runs backwards, appropriately guarded by the *Chicago Tribune* home fortress, does not bring up the same memories as Washington Square.

So in the Village, along with my companions at Grove Press, we did change our address from time to time, one block here, a jump across Broadway there, back to University Place, from the old Cedar Bar to the new Cedar Bar. It was never too unfamiliar, it was just that our space demands changed, expanding and contracting. Somebody told me that the description of a Jack Russell dog is that it is an animal which has four legs, one at each corner. But remember that dog also has character, just like University Place and Eleventh Street, which also has four corners plus character. Our offices had occupied three of them, or close to them, at one time or another. We provided some of the character too, enough in fact to provoke leftover losers from the Bay of Pigs to launch a grenade through our second floor glass front at 80 University Place, maybe because Che Guevara adorned that month's cover of the *Evergreen Review.* Nobody was injured. It was the second blast on Eleventh Street. Kathy Boudin had already blown up her stepfather's house on Eleventh Street between Fifth and Sixth Avenues, apparently while constructing some new weaponry for the Weathermen. But the two houses in which I had lived on that block remained unscathed. When Samuel Beckett came to stay with us on Houston Street, where we were in 1964—his one trip here—he saw little else than the Village.

Our biggest and most disastrously expensive office was in a building we were responsible for creating on Mercer and Bleecker. When a short distance along the Broadway Central Hotel collapsed of its own weight, I could only have hoped that it had been our dinosaur going down, leaving people intact and insurance policy in place. Our smallest office site, aside from my brownstone apartment on Ninth Street and the floor in the house adjoining it, was our place near the corner of Broadway and Eleventh, nicely perched over a very good hotdog stand. We should have stayed there, or better still at our own building on Eleventh between Broadway and University, the one that housed our lovely Black Circle Bar and our Evergreen Theater. Our one live production there was Michel McClure's *The Beard*, the story of Jean Harlow and Jesse James, directed by Rip Torn. Valerie Solanis, after her failed attempt to kill Andy Warhol, tried again with me as the intended victim. She got to our theater but then failed again.

We rented out the theater for a while, keeping of course the offices and bar in our own hands, to a wonderful theater company, appropriately named for their own talents and accidentally those of their landlord. It was called The Theater of the Absurd.

Where else could all of this have happened? Paris? The Left Bank? No, there the blade of insight had been dulled and burnished over with dark gold. We, all of us, the denizens of Greenwich Village, were the cutting edge, and we knew it.

—2002

Village Writers, Etc.

A partial list of writers—and other creative types—who either were born in, lived in, or wrote extensively about the Village:

Bernice Abbott
86 Greenwich Avenue

James Agee
38 Perry Street (1932–37)
172 Bleecker Street (1941–1951)
17 King Street (1951–1955)

Edward Albee
238 West Fourth Street (finished his first play *The Zoo Story* here)
50 West Tenth Street (1960s)

David Amram
461 Sixth Avenue (1959–1996)

Sherwood Anderson
12 St. Luke's Place (1923)

W. H. Auden
7 Cornelia Street (1945–1953)

Djuna Barnes
5 Patchin Place (early 1940s–1982)
86 Greenwich Avenue

Saul Bellow
17 Minetta Lane

William Rose Benét
36 West Ninth Street (1926)

Maxwell Bodenheim
34 Washington Square

Randolph Bourne
18 West Eighth Street

Joseph Brodsky
44 Morton Street

Anatole Broyard
23 Jones Street

Louise Bryant
1 Patchin Place

William Cullen Bryant
147 West Fourth Street (former site of Polly Holladay's restaurant)

William Burroughs
69 Bedford Street (lived in a second-floor apartment in 1943 and
    1944)

Lucien Carr
92 Grove Street (frequented by Carr's Beat friends, including Jack
    Kerouac, Peter Orlovsky, Joyce Johnson, and Allen Ginsberg)

James Fenimore Cooper
145 Bleecker Street

Willa Cather
82 Washington Place (1909–1913)
5 Bank Street (wrote *My Antonia* here); seven rooms on the second
    floor of a spacious brick house (1913–1927).

George Cram Cook and Susan Glaspell
Milligan Place

Gregory Corso
190 Bleecker Street (birthplace of Corso)

Malcolm Cowley
86 Greenwich Avenue

Hart Crane
54 West Tenth Street (1917)
25 East Eleventh Street (1917)
45 Grove Street (residence of Crane as well as the house of Eugene
O'Neill [Jack Nicholson] in *Reds*).
69 Charles Street (formerly Van Nest Place; 1910–1913)

e. e. cummings
11 Christopher Street
9 West Fourteenth Street
4 Patchin Place (1923–1962)

Dorothy Day
86 Greenwich Avenue

Floyd Dell
106 West Thirteenth Street
11 Christopher Street

Mabel Dodge
Formerly 23 Fifth Avenue (former building on this spot was the site
of Mabel Dodge's famous salon)

John Dos Passos
14A Washington Mews
11 Bank Street

Theodore Dreiser
Mills House, 160 Bleecker Street
165 West Tenth Street (finished *The "Genius"* here; 1914–1920).
16 St. Luke's Place (1922–1923)
118 West 11th Street (wrote *An American Tragedy* here; 1923–27).

Martin Duberman
70 Charles Street

Bob Dylan

161 West Fourth Street (Dylan lived here in a two-room apartment in the early 1960s while he was performing at Gerde's Folk City; recorded "Positively 4th Street" while living here)

92–94 MacDougal Street

Max Eastman

12 East Eighth Street (lived here in a room on the second floor).

118 Waverly Place (lived here from 1909 to 1911 and again in 1914).

8 West Thirteenth Street (spent the last twenty-five years of his life).

James T. Farrell

Brevoort Hotel, Fifth Avenue and Eighth Street

Lawrence Ferlinghetti

235 W. Thirteenth Street (lived here after World War II when he was attending Columbia University as a graduate student)

William Glackens

3 Washington Square North

Emma Goldman

208 East Thirteenth Street, formerly 210 East Thirteenth Street (lived here from 1903 to 1913. Published *Mother Earth* from this location).

36 Grove Street (last residence in the U.S. before deported to the Soviet Union)

John Guare

105 Bank Street

Woody Guthrie

74 Charles Street (lived here in the 1940s)

Bret Harte
487 Hudson (the writer's former boyhood home and today the St. Luke's Parish Church).
16 Fifth Avenue
713 Broadway

Edward Hopper
3 Washington Square North (lived on the Fourth floor from 1913 until his death in 1967)

William Dean Howells
48 West Ninth Street

Henry James
21 Washington Place (born here in 1843)
1 Washington Place
58 West Fourteenth Street
19 Washington Square North

Ted Joans
4 Barrow Street (the poet lived here in the early 1950s)

Leroi Jones and Hettie Jones
7 Morton Street

Rockwell Kent
3 Washington Square North

Andre Kertesz
2 Fifth Avenue

Galway Kinnell
155 Bank Street

Seymour Krim
224 Sullivan Street

Stanley Kunitz
157 West Twelfth Street

John Lennon and Yoko Ono
105 Bank Street (early 1970s)

Denise Levertov
52 Barrow Street
727 Greenwich Street

Sinclair Lewis
69 Charles Street
37 West Tenth Street (1928–1929)

Anne Charlotte Lynch
116 Waverly Place (teacher and poet; considered America's first literary salon, Edgar Allen Poe gave his first public reading of "The Raven" here)

Mary McCarthy
18 Gay Street (1940s)

Herman Melville
103 Fourth Avenue

Edna St. Vincent Millay
139 Waverly Place (1931)
25 Charlton Street (1918)
75½ Bedford Street (narrowest house in the Village; 1923–1925)

Marianne Moore
14 St. Luke's Place (Moore and her mother lived here from 1918 to 1929)
35 West Ninth Street

Anais Nin
215 West Thirteenth Street (1940–1948)
145 MacDougal Street

Frank Norris
61 Washington Square

Frank O'Hara
90 University Place (1957–1959)

Eugene O'Neill
38 Washington Square
45 Grove Street (movie version of O'Neill's residence in Warren Beatty's 1981 *Reds*)

Thomas Paine
309 Bleecker Street
59 Grove Street (site of a piano bar called Marie's Crisis, named as homage to the old wood farm house, where Thomas Paine once lived and wrote his pamphlet, "The Crisis of 1776;" also commemorates Romany Marie, whose tearoom operated on Washington Square South)

Edgar Allan Poe
85 West Third Street (originally Amity Place)
133½ Carmine Street (wrote *The Narrative of Arthur Gordon Pym* here).

Dawn Powell
46 West Ninth Street
72 Perry Street
106 Perry Street

Thomas Pynchon
Charles Lane (worked on *Gravity's Rainbow* here).

John Reed
42 Washington Square South
147 West Fourth Street (finished writing *Ten Days That Shook the World* here; Polly Holladay's second restaurant opened here in 1918)

Edwin Arlington Robinson
53 Washington Square South (1906–1909, when it was then the Judson Hotel)
121 Washington Place
28 West Eighth Street
1 MacDougal Alley (housed an early Village tearoom, the Jumble Shop)

Lincoln Steffens
42 Washington Square

William Styron
43–45 Greenwich Avenue

Allen Tate
27 Bank Street (1927)

Sara Teasdale
1 Fifth Avenue (1932)

Mark Twain
14 West Tenth Street (1900–1901)

Carl Van Doren
123 West Eleventh Street (1927)

Mark Van Doren
43 Barrow Street (1920)
393 Bleecker (1929–1959)

Edith Wharton
7 Washington Square North (lived here with her mother in 1882)

Edmund Wilson
3 Washington Square North (1921–1923)
1 University Place

Thomas Wolfe
13 E. 8th Street (began work on *Look Homeward, Angel* here)
263 West Eleventh Street (1923)
27 West Fifteenth Street (1928)
263 West Eleventh Street (1927–1928)

Richard Wright
82 Washington Place (1945)
13 Charles Street (1945–1947)

Other Writers Who Lived or Spent Considerable Time in the Village

James Baldwin
Elizabeth Bishop
Harold Brodkey
Kenneth Burke
Hortense Calisher
Stephen Crane
Joan Didion
Joseph Herbst
Patricia Highsmith
Alexander King
Kenneth Koch
Alfred Kreymborg
Norman Mailer
Cynthia Ozick
Grace Paley
Felice Picano
Ned Rorem
Maurice Sendak

Sam Shepard
Charles Simic
Terry Southern
James Thurber
Calvin Trillin
Lionel Trilling
Alexander Trocchi
E. B. White
Walt Whitman
William Carlos Williams

Sources: *New York: Literary Lights* by William Corbett (Greywolf Press, 1998); *Literary New York: A History and Guide* by Susan Edmiston and Linda D. Cirino (Gibbs-Smith, 1991).

Additional List of Works of Fiction Set, or Partially Set, in Greenwich Village

About the Author by John Colapinto
Another Country by James Baldwin
Auntie Mame by Patrick Dennis
The Blowtop by Alvin Schwartz
Cain's Book by Alexander Trocchi
Color Studies by Thomas A. Janvier
Crazy Cock by Henry Miller
The Group by Mary McCarthy
I Thought of Daisy by Edmund Wilson
The Iceman Cometh by Eugene O'Neill
Macdougal Alley by Tatheena Roberts
Manhattan Transfer by John Dos Passos

My Sister Eileen by Ruth McKenney
Of Time and the River by Thomas Wolfe
The Recognition by William Gaddis
The Sign in Sidney Brusteins Window by Lorraine Hansberry
The Web and the Rock by Thomas Wolfe
The Villagers: A Novel of Greenwich Village by Edward Field and Neil Derrick
You Can't Go Home Again by Thomas Wolfe

Partial List of Movies Set or Shot in Greenwich Village

The April Fools
Barefoot in the Park
Cruising Bright Lights, Big City
Desperately Seeking Susan
The Godfather, Part II
The Group
Hannah and Her Sisters
Hester Street
The January Man
Moonstruck
The Next Man
Next Stop, Greenwich Village
The Out of Towners
A Place in the Sun
Raging Bull
Ragtime
Rear Window
Reds
Serpico
Shaft
Wait Until Dark

Select Village Literary Sites

Cafe Bohemia
15 Barrow Street
Kerouac hangout where he went to hear the jazz greats.

Cafe Figaro
186 Bleecker Street
Formerly The Borgia. Originally opened in 1956 at 195 Bleecker Street.

Cafe Reggio
121 MacDougal Street

Cedar Tavern
82 University Place
Originally located at 24 University Place, this later reincarnation doesn't have much in common with the famous original. The artist's bar in New York in the 1950s, regulars included painters Robert Rauschenberg, Willem de Kooning, Jackson Pollack, Mark Rothko; and writers Jack Kerouac, Allen Ginsberg, Gregory Corso, LeRoi Jones, and Frank O'Hara. Torn down on March 30, 1963.

Cherry Lane Theatre
38–42 Commerce Street
The Living Theatre staged many of their plays here.

Chumley's
86 Bedford Street
One of the oldest taverns in the Village. Established in 1928 as a speakeasy, it was frequented by Theodore Dreiser, Edna Ferber, F. Scott Fitzgerald, Mary McCarthy, Edna St. Vincent Millay, Anais Nin, Eugene O'Neill, J. D. Salinger, Upton Sinclair, William Burroughs, and Lawrence Ferlinghetti.

Eighth Street Bookshop
32 W. Eighth Street
Known for its Beat collection. Ted and Eli Wilentz opened it in 1947. Published books under the name of Corinth Books.

The Liberal Club
137 MacDougal Street
Located above Polly's. The Washington Square Players started here.

The Lion's Head
59 Christopher Street
Regulars included Pete Hamill, Jimmy Breslin, and Edward Hoagland. Now defunct.

The Little Review
31 West Fourteenth Street

Marie's Crisis Cafe
59 Grove Street

The Masses
91 Greenwich Avenue
The magazine of the Village in the 1910s.

Minetta Tavern
1 Minetta Lane
A former speakeasy. Associated with Joe Gould. The back room contains a mural of the Village as it looked at the turn of the century. *Reader's Digest* was founded in the basement in 1922.

Phoenix Bookshop
18 Cornelia Street
Founded in the 1950s; considered one of the best bookstores in the city for modern poetry. Now defunct.

Polly's Restaurant/Provincetown Playhouse
139/133 MacDougal Street
Polly's Restaurant was located in the basement next to 139 MacDougal Street. Operated by anarchist Paula Holladay in the 1910s. Village radical Hippolyte Havel cooked and waited tables here.

Provincetown Playhouse
133 MacDougal Street
Originally at 139 MacDougal Street in 1916 before moving to the 133 address in 1918. Founded by novelist Susan Glaspell and her husband George Cram Cook.

San Remo
93 MacDougal Street
Now Carpo's Cafe; a bohemian coffeehouse favorite in the 1940s and 1950s. Opened in 1923. Regulars included James Agee, Judith Malina, and James Merrill.

Stonewall Inn
51-53 Christopher Street
Point of origin for the 1969 Stonewall riots.

White Horse Tavern
567 Hudson
Built in 1880; great literary watering hole: Norman Mailer, William Styron, Lawrence Ferlinghetti, Delmore Schwartz, Jack Kerouac, and most famously, and tragically, Dylan Thomas.

Village Vanguard
178 Seventh Avenue, South
Located in the basement. Founded by Max Gordon in 1934. At this location since 1935. The place for jazz in the Village.

The Village Voice
22 Greenwich Avenue
Founded October 26, 1955, at this location.

Sources: Joyce Gold, *From Trout Stream to Bohemia: Greenwich Village, A Walking Guide through History* (New York: Old Warren Road Press, 1996); Bruce Kayton, *Radical Walking Tours of New York City* (New York: Seven Stories Press, 1999); Bill Morgan, *The Beat Generation in New York: A Walking Tour of Jack Kerouac's City* (San Francisco: City Lights Books, 1997.)

Further Reading

Addickes, Sandra. *To Be Young was Very Heaven: Women in New York Before the First World War*. New York: St. Martin's Griffin, 1997.

Alleman, Richard. *The Movie Lover's Guide to New York*. New York: Harper & Row, 1988.

Amram, David. *Vibrations: A Memoir*. Foreword by Douglas Brinkley. New York: Thunder's Mouth Press, 2001.

Anderson, Margaret, editor. *The Little Review Anthology*. New York: Hermitage House, 1953.

Arens, Egmont. *The Little Book of Greenwich Village: A Handbook of Information Concerning New York's Bohemia*. New York: Washington Square Bookshop, 1919.

Ayers, Bill. *Fugitive Days*. Boston: Beacon Press, 2001.

Beard, Rick and Leslie Cohen Berlowitz, eds. *Greenwich Village: Culture and Counterculture*. New Brunswick, N. J.: Published for the Museum of New York by Rutgers University Press, 1993.

Beer, Thomas. *The Mauve Decade: American Life at the End of the Nineteenth Century*. New York: Carroll and Graf, 1997.

Bradbury, Malcolm, general editor. *The Atlas of Literature*. New York: Stewart, Tabori, & Chang, 1998.

Bradshaw, Steve. *Cafe Society: Bohemian Life from Swift to Bob Dylan*. London: Weidenfeld and Nicolson, 1978.

Brands, H. W. *The Reckless Decade: America in the 1890s*. New York: St. Martin's Press, 1995.

Brevda, William. *Harry Kemp: The Last Bohemian*. Cranbury, N.J.: Associated University Presses, 1986.

Brightman, Carol. *Writing Dangerously: Mary McCarthy and Her World*. New York: Clarkson Potter, 1992.

Brinnin, John Malcolm. *Dylan Thomas in America: An Intimate Journal*. New York: Viking Press, 1957.

Brodkey, Harold. "Frank and Harold in *Sea Battles on Dry Land: Essays*. New York: Metropolitan Books, 1999.

Brooks, David. *Bobos in Paradise: The New Upper Class and How They Got There*. New York: Simon & Schuster, 2000.

714

Brossard, Chandler, ed. *The Scene Before You: A New Approach to American Culture*. New York: Rinehart and Co., 1955.

Campbell, James. *Talking at the Gates: A Life of James Baldwin*. New York: Viking, 1991.

———. *This Is the Beat Generation: New York—San Francisco—Paris*. London: Secker and Warburg, 1999.

Cantor, Mindy, ed. *Around the Square, 1830–1890*. New York: New York University Press, 1982.

Carduff, Christopher. "Fish-eating, whiskey, death & rebirth." *The New Criterion*, November 1992.

Carroll, Kent. "In the Echoing Grave: Fifty years of avant-garde publishing in New York." *TLS*, January 12, 2001.

Carter, David, ed. *Allen Ginsberg: Spontaneous Mind, Selected Interviews, 1958–1996*. Preface by Vaclav Havel. Introduction by Edmund White. New York: HarperCollins, 2001.

Cassady, Carolyn. *Heart Beat: My Life with Jack & Neal*. Berkeley, Calif.: Creative Arts Book Co., 1976.

Charters, Ann, ed. *Beat Down to Your Soul: What Was the Beat Generation?* New York: Penguin Books, 2001.

———. *The Beats: Literary Bohemians in Postwar America*. Vol. 16 of *Dictionary of Literary Biography*. Detroit: Gale, 1984.

———. *Kerouac: A Biography*. San Francisco: Straight Arrow, 1973.

———, ed. *The Portable Beat Reader*. New York: Viking, 1992.

———, ed. *Jack Kerouac: Selected Letters 1957–1969*. New York: Viking, 1999.

Chauncey, George. *Gay New York: Gender, Urban Culture, and the Making of the Gay Male World, 1890–1940*. New York: Basic Books, 1995.

Cheney, Anne. *Millay in Greenwich Village*. Tuscaloosa, Ala.: University of Alabama Press, 1975.

Clark, John. "Telling a Secret: Stanley Tucci, star and director of *Big Night*, takes up the story of a New York literary legend for his new film." *Book*, March–April 2000.

Clayton, Bruce. *Forgotten Prophet: The Life of Randolph Bourne*. Baton Rouge, La.: Louisiana State University Press, 1984.

Clayton, Douglas. *Floyd Dell: The Life and Times of an American Rebel*. Chicago: Ivan R. Dee, 1994.

Colapinto, John. *About the Author*. New York: HarperCollins, 2001.

Cook, Bruce. *The Beat Generation: The Tumultuous '50s Movement and Its Impact on Today*. (1971) New York: Quill, 1994.

Cook, George Cram, and Frank Shay, eds. *The Provincetown Plays*. Cincinnati: Stewart Kidd, 1921.

Corbett, William. *New York: Literary Lights*. Saint Paul, Minn.: Graywolf Press, 1998.

Cowley, Malcolm. *—And I Worked at the Writer's Trade: Chapters of Literary History, 1918–1978*. New York: Penguin Books, 1979.

Crunden, Michael C. *American Salons*. New York: Oxford University Press, 1993.

Curtiss, Thomas Quinn. *The Smart Set: George Jean Nathan and H. L. Mencken*. New York: Applause Theatre Book Publishing, 1997.

Dabney, Lewis M., ed. *The Edmund Wilson Reader*. New York: Da Capo Press, 1997.

Day, Dorothy. *The Long Loneliness: An Autobiography*. New York: Image Books, 1959.

DeCurtis, Anthony. "Greenwich Village in the 60's" in *Bleecker Street: Greenwich Village in the 60's*. Liner notes. (Astor Place Recordings, 1999).

Dell, Floyd. *Intellectual Vagabondage*. Introduction by Douglas Clayton. Chicago: Ivan R. Dee, 1990.

Deutsch, Helen, and Stella Hanau. *The Provincetown: A Story of the Theatre*. New York: Farrar and Rinehart, 1931.

Di Prima Diane. *Recollections of My Life as a Woman: The New York Years*. New York: Viking Press, 2001.

"Disillusioned by 'Bohemia'?" *Literary Digest*. September 16, 1916: 688–93.

Dorman, Joseph. *Arguing the World: The New York Intellectuals in Their Own Words*. New York: Free Press, 2000.

Douglas, Ann. *Terrible Honesty: Mongrel Manhattan in the 1920s*. New York: Farrar, Straus, and Giroux, 1995.

Durant, Will. *Transition: A Sentimental Story of One Mind and One Era*. New York, 1927.

Edel, Leon. *Henry James: A Life*. New York: Harper & Row, 1985.

Edmiston, Susan, and Linda D. Cirino. *Literary New York*. Boston: Houghton Mifflin, 1976.

Edwards, Bobby. "The Story of Greenwich Village." *Quill*, January 14, 1924.

———. "The Village Epic." Quoted in Egmont Arens. *The Little Book of Greenwich Village*. New York: Washington Square Bookshop, 1919.

Elledge, Scott. *E. B. White: A Biography*. New York: W. W. Norton & Company, 1985.

Epstein, Daniel Mark. *What Lips My Lips Have Kissed: The Loves and Love Poems of Edna St. Vincent Millay*. New York: Henry Holt, 2001.

Erenberg, Lewis A. *Steppin' Out: New York Nightlife and the Transformation of American Culture, 1890–1930*. Westport, Conn.: Greenwood Press, 1981.

Falk, Candace. *Love, Anarchy, and Emma Goldman*. New York: Holt, Rinehart, & Winston, 1984.

Fishbein, Leslie. *Rebels in Bohemia*. Chapel Hill, N.C.: University of North Carolina Press, 1982.

Garrison, Dee. *Mary Heaton Vorse: The Life of an American Insurgent*. Philadelphia: Temple University Press, 1989.

Gelb, Arthur, and Barbara Gelb. *O'Neill*. New York: Harper & Row, 1962.

George-Warren, Holly, ed. *The Rolling Stone Book of the Beats: The Beat Generation and American Culture*. New York: Hyperion, 1999.

Gilmer, Walker. *Horace Liveright: Publisher of the Twenties*. New York: David Lewis, 1970.

Glaspell, Susan. *The Road to the Temple*. New York: Frederick A. Stokes, 1927.

Gold, Joyce. *Greenwich Village: From Trout Stream to Bohemia: A Walking Guide through History*. New York: Old Warren Road Press, 1996.

Goodman, Paul. *Growing Up Absurd*. New York: Random House, 1960.

Grauerholz, James, and Ira Silverberg, eds. Introduction by Ann Douglas. *Word Virus: The William S. Burroughs Reader*. New York: Grove Press, 2000.

Gruen, John. *The New Bohemia*. Chicago: a cappella books, 1990.

Hahn, Emily. *Romantic Rebels: An Informal History of Bohemianism in America*. Boston: Houghton Mifflin, 1967.

Hajdu, David. *Positively 4th Street: The Lives and Times of Joan Baez, Bob Dylan, Mimi Baez Fariña, and Richard Fariña*. New York: Farrar, Straus, and Giroux, 2001.

Harrison, Helen A. "Recreating Pollock, Gingerly." *New York Times*, February 16, 2001.

"Harry Kemp Comes Home from the Cape." *Village Voice*, October 13, 1960.

Heide, Robert, and John Gilman. *Greenwich Village: A Primo Guide to Shopping, Eating, and Making Merry in True Bohemia*. New York: St. Martin's Griffin, 1995.

Hentoff, Nat. *The Nat Hentoff Reader*. New York: Da Capo Press, 2001.

———. *Speaking Freely: A Memoir*. New York: Knopf, 1997.

Herbst, Josephine. *The Starched Blue Sky of Spain and Other Memoirs*. Introduction by Elizabeth Francis. Boston: Northeastern University Press, 1999.

Herring, Phillip. *Djuna: The Life and Work of Djuna Barnes*. New York: Penguin Books, 1995.

Hill, Lee. *A Grand Guy: The Art and Life of Terry Southern*. New York: HarperCollins, 2001.

Holden, Stephen. "When All Were Young and So Very Earnest: New York in the 50's." *New York Times*, February 10, 2001.

Holcomb, Grant. "John Sloan and 'McSorley's Wonderful Saloon.'" *American Art Journal*, Spring 1983: 5–20.

Howe, Irving. *A Margin of Hope: An Intellectual Autobiography*. New York: Harcourt Brace, 1984.

Humphrey, Robert E. *Children of Fantasy: The First Rebels of Greenwich Village*. New York: John Wiley & Sons, 1978.

Huncke, Herbert. *The Herbert Huncke Reader*. New York: William Morrow, 1997.

Isserman, Maurice. *The Other American: The Untold Life of Michael Harrington*. New York: Public Affairs, 2000.

Jackson, Kenneth T., ed. *Encyclopedia of New York City*. New Haven, Conn.: Yale University Press, 1995.

Jacoby, Russell. *The Last Intellectuals: American Culture in the Age of Academe*. New York: Noonday Press, 1987.

———. *The End of Utopia: Politics and Culture in an Age of Apathy*. New York: Basic Books, 1999.

Johnson, Paul. *Intellectuals*. New York: HarperCollins, 1990.

Kaiser, Charles. *The Gay Metropolis: 1940–1996*. New York: Harvest Books, 1998.

Kayton, Bruce. *Radical Walking Tours of New York City*. New York: Seven Stories Press, 1999.

Kemp, Harry. *Chanteys and Ballads: Sea-Chanteys, Tramp Ballads, and Other Ballads and Poems*. New York: Brentano's, 1920.

———. *More Miles: An Autobiographical Novel*. New York: Boni and Liveright, 1926.

———. *Tramping on Life: An Autobiographical Narrative*. New York: Boni and Liveright, 1922.

Kerouac, Jack, and Joyce Johnson. *Door Wide Open: A Beat Love Affair in Letters 1957–1958*. New York: Viking Press, 2000.

Kiernan, Frances. *Seeing Mary Plain: A Life of Mary McCarthy*. New York: Norton, 2000.

Kilian, Michael. "Drinking buddies: Unlikely venue endures to become a literary landmark." *Chicago Tribune*, June 8, 2000.

King, Alexander. *Mine Enemy Grows Older*. New York: Simon and Schuster, 1958.

Klonsky, Milton. *Discourse on Hip: Selected Writings of Milton Klonsky*. Edited by Ted Solotaroff. Detroit, Mich.: Wayne State University Press, 1991.

Knight, Arthur, and Kit Knight, eds. *Kerouac and the Beats: A Primary Sourcebook*. New York: Paragon House, 1988.

Knoll, Robert E., ed. *McAlmon and the Lost Generation*. University of Nebraska Press, 1962.

Kramer, Hilton. *The Twilight of the Intellectuals: Culture and Politics in the Era of the Cold War*. Chicago: Ivan R. Dee, 1999.

Kreymborg, Alfred, ed. *Others: An Anthology of the New Verse*. New York: A. A. Knopf, 1917.

Kugelmass, Jack, ed. *Masked Culture: The Greenwich Village Halloween Parade*. New York: Columbia University Press, 1994.

Laskin, David. *Partisans: Marriage, Politics, and Betrayal Among the New York Intellectuals*. New York: Simon & Schuster, 2000.

Lauerman, Connie. "The Broad Reach of the Beats: Generations Later, the Literary Rebels Still Have a Cause." *Chicago Tribune*, October 24, 1999.

———. "Beat poet Diane di Prima reflects on life outside the mainstream." *Chicago Tribune*, April 19, 2000.

Lehman, David. *The Last Avant-Garde: The Making of the New York School of Poets*. New York: Anchor Books, 1999.

———. *The Daily Mirror: A Journal in Poetry*. New York: Scribner, 2000.

Leisner, Marcia. *Literary Neighborhoods of New York*. Washington, D.C.: Starrhill Press, 1989.

Lingeman, Richard. *Theodore Dreiser: At the Gates of the City, 1871–1907*. New York: Putnam, 1986.

Lipton, Lawrence. *The Holy Barbarians*. New York: Julian Messner, 1959.

Lopate, Phillip, ed. *Writing New York: A Literary Anthology*. New York: The Library of America, 1998.

Loughery, John. *John Sloan: Painter and Rebel*. New York: Henry Holt, 1995.

McAuliffe, Kevin Michael. *The Great American Newspaper: The Rise and Fall of the "Village Voice."* New York: Scribner's, 1978.

McDarrah, Fred W., and Patrick J. McDarrah. *The Greenwich Village Guide*. Chicago: Chicago Review Press, 1992.

Macdougall, Allan Ross, ed. *The Letters of Edna St. Vincent Millay*. New York: Harper, 1952.

McFarland, Gerald W. *Inside Greenwich Village: A New York City Neighborhood, 1898–1918*. University of Massachusetts Press, 2001.

McNally, Dennis. *Desolate Angel: Jack Kerouac, the Beats, and America*. New York: Random House, 1976.

McNeill, Don. *Moving Through Here*. New York: Citadel Underground, 1990.

Meyers, Jeffrey. *Edmund Wilson: A Biography*. New York: Houghton Mifflin, 1995.

Miles, Barry. *Ginsberg: A Biography*. New York: Simon & Schuster, 1989.

———. *The Beat Hotel: Ginsberg, Burroughs, & Corso in Paris, 1957–1963*. New York: Grove Press, 2000.

Milford, Nancy. *Savage Beauty: The Life of Edna St. Vincent Millay*. New York: Random House, 2001.

Millay, Edna St. Vincent. *Early Poems*. Edited with an introduction and notes by Holly Peppe. New York: Penguin Books, 1998.

Miller, Richard. *Bohemia: The Protoculture Then and Now*. Chicago: Nelson-Hall, 1977.

Miller, Terry. *Greenwich Village and How It Got That Way*. New York: Crown Publishers, 1990.

Mitchell, Joseph. *Up in the Old Hotel and Other Stories*. New York: Vintage Books, 1993.

———. *McSorley's Wonderful Saloon*. New York: Pantheon, 2001.

Morgan, Bill. *The Beat Generation in New York: A Walking Tour of Jack Kerouac's City*. San Francisco: City Lights Books, 1997.

Mumford, Lewis. *The Story of Utopias*. New York: Viking Press, 1922.

Muschamp, Herbert. "The Village as a Satirist's Milieu and Muse." *New York Times*, December 4, 1998.

Nicosia, Gerald. *Memory Babe: Jack Kerouac*. New York: Grove Press, 1983.

Norris, Kathleen, ed. *Leaving New York: Writers Look Back*. Saint Paul, Minn.: Hungry Mind Press, 1995.

O'Connell, Shaun. *Remarkable, Unspeakable New York: A Literary History*. Boston: Beacon Press, 1995.

O'Neill, William L., ed. *Echoes of Revolt: "The Masses," 1911–1917*. Introduction by Irving Howe. Afterword by Max Eastman. Chicago: Ivan R. Dee, 1989.

———. *The Last Romantic: A Life of Max Eastman*. New York: Oxford University Press, 1978.

———. *My Ears Are Bent*. New York: Pantheon, 2001.

Page, Tim, ed. *The Diaries of Dawn Powell 1931–1965*. South Royalton, Vt.: Steerforth Press, 1995.

———. *Dawn Powell: A Biography*. New York: Henry Holt and Company, 1998.

Parry, Albert. *Garrets and Pretenders: A History of Bohemianism in America*. New York: Covici-Friede, 1933.

Patrick, Robert. *Temple Slave*. New York: Masquerade Books, 1994.

Phillips, Lisa. *Beat Culture and the New America 1950–1965*. New York: Whitney Museum of American Art, 1996.

Picano, Felice. *A House on the Ocean, A House on the Bay: A Memoir*. Boston: Faber and Faber, 1997.

Podhoretz, Norman. *Ex-Friends: Falling Out with Allen Ginsberg, Lionel and Diana Trilling, Lillian Hellman, Hannah Arendt, and Norman Mailer*. New York: Free Press, 1999.

———. *My Love Affair with America: The Cautionary Tale of a Cheerful Conservative*. New York: Free Press, 2000.

"Postscript: Joseph Mitchell: Three Generations of *New Yorker* Writers Remember the City's Incomparable Chronicler." *The New Yorker*, June 10, 1996.

Powers, Ann. *Weird Like Us: My Bohemian America*. New York: Simon and Schuster, 2000.

Ramirez, Jan Seidler. *Within Bohemia's Borders: Greenwich Village 1830–1930*. Interpretive Script Accompanying an Exhibition at the Museum of New York. New York: Museum of the City of New York, n.d.

Rickett, Arthur. *The Vagabond in Literature*. Port Washington, N.Y.: Kennikat Press, 1906.

Rorem, Ned. *Lies: A Diary 1986–1999*. Washington, D.C.: Counterpoint Press, 2000.

Rood, Karen Lane, ed. *Dictionary of Literary Biography. Volume 4. American Writers in Paris, 1920–1939*. Detroit, Mi.: Gale Research Co., 1980.

Rosenstone, Robert A. *A Romantic Revolutionary: A Biography of John Reed*. New York: Knopf, 1975.

Roszak, Theodore. *The Making of a Counter Culture*. New York: Doubleday, 1969.

Rudnick, Lois Palkin. *Mabel Dodge Luhan: New Woman, New Worlds*. Albuquerque, N.M.: University of New Mexico Press, 1984.

Schwartz, Judith. *Radical Feminists of Heterodoxy: Greenwich Village, 1912–1940*. Norwich, Vt.: New Victoria Publishers, 1986.

Sochen, June. *Movers and Shakers: American Women Thinkers and Activists, 1900–1970*. New York: Quadrangle Books, 1972.

Stansell, Christine. *American Moderns: Bohemian New York and the Creation of a New Century*. New York: Holt, 2000.

———. "Whitman at Pfaff's: Commercial Culture, Literary Life, and New York Bohemia at Mid-Century." *Walt Whitman Quarterly Review* 10 (Winter 1993): 107–26.

Stoddard, Charles Warren. "Ada Clare, Queen of Bohemia." *National Magazine*, September 1905: 637–45.

Tytell, John. *Naked Angels: The Lives and Literature of the Beat Generation*. New York: McGraw-Hill, 1976.

Ulin, David. "The Disappearing Bohemian." *Hungry Mind Review*, December 1, 1998.

Veyscy, Laurence. *The Communal Experience*. New York: Harper & Row, 1973.

Vorse, Mary Heaton. *Time and the Town: A Provincetown Chronicle*. New York: Dial Press, 1942.

Watson, Steven. *Strange Bedfellows: The First American Avant-Garde*. New York: Abbeville Press, 1991.

———. *The Birth of the Beat Generation: Visionaries, Rebels, and Hipsters, 1944–1960*. Circles of the Twentieth Century. New York: Pantheon Books, 1995.

Watts, Jerry Gafio. *Amiri Baraka: The Politics and Art of a Black Intellectual*. New York: New York University Press, 2001.

Weegee. *The Village*. New York: Da Capo Press, 1989.

Wertheim, Arthur Frank. *The New York Little Renaissance, 1908–1917*. New York: New York University Press, 1976.

Wetzsteon, Ross. *Greenwich Village: The American Bohemian, 1910–1960*. New York: Simon and Schuster, forthcoming.

Wharton, Edith. *A Backward Glance*. New York: Touchstone Books, 1998.

Wilson, Edmund. *The Bit Between My Teeth: A Literary Chronicle of 1950–1965*. New York: Farrar, Straus and Giroux, 1965.

Wilson, Elizabeth. *Bohemians: The Glamorous Outcasts*. New Brunswick, N.J.: Rutgers University Press, 2000.

Wolf, Daniel, and Edwin Fancher, eds. *The Village Voice Reader: A Mixed Bag from the Greenwich Village Newspaper*. New York: Grove Press, 1963.

Woliver, Robbie. *Hoot! A 25-Year History of the Greenwich Village Music Scene*. New York: St. Martin's, 1994.

Wood, Clement. "The Story of Greenwich Village." *Haldeman-Julius Quarterly*, October 1926.

Wreszin, Michael, ed. *A Moral Temper: The Letters of Dwight Macdonald*. Chicago: Ivan R. Dee, 2001.

Zurier, Rebecca, ed. *Metropolitan Lives: The Ashcan Artists and Their New York*. New York: W. W. Norton & Co., 1996.

Sources & Permissions

Dan Balaban. "The 'Gypsy' Lady Who Fed Bohemia," from *The Village Voice Reader: A Mixed Bag from the Greenwich Village Newspaper* (New York: Grove Press, 1962).

Djuna Barnes. "Greenwich Village As It Is," *Pearson's Magazine*, October 1916. Public Domain.

Madison Smartt Bell. "Johnny B." From *The Washington Square Ensemble.* © 1983, by Madison Bell. Reprinted by permission of the Author and Gelfman Schneider Literary Agents, Inc.

Caroline Bird. "Born 1930: The Unlost Generation," *Harper's Bazaar*, February 1957.

Maxwell Bodenheim. "Gertrude Stein in Macdougal Alley" and "The Waldorf: A Cafeteria a la Einstein" from *My Life and Loves in Greenwich Village* (New York: Bridgehead Books, 1954).

Randolph Bourne. From *History of a Literary Radical and Other Essays* (1920). Public Domain.

Maeve Brennan. "The Farmhouse That Moved Downtown" from *The Long-Winded Lady* by Maeve Brennan. Copyright (c) 1998 by The Estate of Maeve Brennan. Reprinted by permission of Houghton Mifflin Company. All rights reserved.

Chandler Brossard. Excerpted and reprinted by permission of Herodias from *Who Walk in Darkness*, Herodias Classics Edition, 2000, by Chandler Brossard. Copyright © 1952 by Chandler Brossard.

Anatole Broyard. From *Kafka Was the Rage* by Anatole Broyard. Copyright © 1993 by Alexandra Broyard. Reprinted by permission of Carol Southern Books, a division of Random House, Inc.

Guido Bruno. From *Fragments from Greenwich Village* (New York: Published Privately by the Author, 1921). Public Domain.

Herbert Gold. From *Bohemia: Where Art, Angst, Love, and Strong Coffee Meet* (1993). Reprinted by permission of the Author.

Max Gordon. "You Don't Need Any Money" from *Live at the Village Vanguard* (New York: St. Martin's Press, 1980). Reprinted by permission of Lorraine Gordon.

John Gruen. From *The Party's Over Now: Reminiscences of the Fifties* (New York: The Viking Press, 1972). © 1967, 1972 by John Gruen.

Hutchins Hapgood. "The Stream of the World" from *A Victorian in the Modern World* (New York: Harcourt, Brace, 1939).

Michael Harrington. "The Death of Bohemia" from *Fragments of the Century: A Social Autobiography* (New York: Saturday Review Press/E. P. Dutton & Co., 1973).

Hippolyte Havel. "The Spirit of the Village" in *Greenwich Village: A Fortnightly*, January 20, 1915. Public Domain.

O. Henry. "The Last Leaf" (1902). Public Domain.

Edward Hoagland. From *Compass Points: How I Lived* by Edward Hoagland, copyright © 2001 by Edward Hoagland. Used by permission of Pantheon Books, a division of Random House, Inc..

John Clellon Holmes. From *Go* by John Clellon Holmes. Copyright © 1952, 1988, 1997 by John Clellon Holmes. Reprinted by permission of Thunder's Mouth Press.

William Dean Howells. From *The Coast of Bohemia* (New York: Harper & Brothers, 1901). Public Domain.

Herbert Huncke. From *Guilty of Everything: The Autobiography of Herbert Huncke* (New York: Paragon House, 1990).

Jane Jacobs. From *The Death and Life of Great American Cities*. Copyright (c) 1961 by Jane Jacobs. Reprinted by permission of Random House, Inc.

Henry James. From *Washington Square*. First published in 1880. Public Domain.

Joyce Johnson. From *Minor Characters* (1983) by Joyce Johnson. Reprinted by permission of Penguin, a division of Penguin Putnam Inc.

Hettie Jones. From *How I Became Hettie Jones* by Hettie Jones. Copyright © 1990 by Hettie Jones. Used by permission of Grove/Atlantic, Inc.

Harry Kemp. "A Poet's Room: Greenwich Village 1912" and "Street Lamp: Greenwich Village" from *Chanteys and Ballads* (1912) and "Leaves of Burdock" from *The Masses* (May 1914). Public Domain.

Jack Kerouac. From *Desolation Angels*. Copyright © 1965 by Jack Kerouac, renewed © 1993 by Jan Kerouac. Reprinted by permission of Sterling Lord Literistic.

Milton Klonsky. "Greenwich Village: Decline and Fall." Reprinted by permission from *Commentary*, November 1948; all rights reserved.

Alfred Kreymborg. "Greenwich Village" from *Troubadour: An Autobiography* (New York: Boni and Liveright, 1925). Public Domain.

Seymour Krim. "Two Teachers—Nuts, Two Human Beings!" from *Views of a Nearsighted Cannoneer* (New York: E. P. Dutton & Co., 1968).

Sinclair Lewis. "Hobohemia," from *The Saturday Evening Post*, April 1917. Public Domain.

Mabel Dodge Luhan. "The Evenings" from *Movers and Shakers: Intimate Memories*, vol. 3 (New York: Harcourt Brace, 1933–37).

James D. McCabe. "Bleecker Street" from *Lights and Shadows of New York Life: or, the Sights and Sensations of the Great City* (Philadelphia: National Publishing Co., 1872). Public Domain.

Mary McCarthy. Excerpt from *Intellectual Memoirs: New York 1936–1938* by Mary McCarthy. Copyright © 1992 by The Mary McCarthy Literary Trust, reprinted by permission of Harcourt, Inc.

Judith Malina. From *The Diaries of Judith Malina, 1947–1957* (New York: Grove Press, 1984). Reprinted by permission of the Author.

Samuel Menashe. "At Millay's Grave," "Transplant" "Promised Land," "Dusk," "The Dead of Winter," "At a Standstill," and "Improvidence" from *The Niche Narrows: New and Selected Poems* (Jersey City, New Jersey: Talisman House, 2000). Reprinted by permission of the Author.

Edna St. Vincent Millay. "First Fig," "Macdougal Street," and "Weeds" from *A Few Figs from Thistles* (1922). Public Domain.

Joseph Mitchell. "Professor Sea Gull." Originally appeared in the December 12, 1942, issue of *The New Yorker*. Copyright 1942 by Joseph Mitchell. Published in paperback by Vintage Books, a division of Random House in 1999. Originally published in hardcover by Modern Library, a division of Random House, in 1996.

Ethan Mordden. From *How Long Has This Been Going On?* (New York: Villard Books, 1995).

Anais Nin. From *The Diary of Anais Nin, Volume Three, 1939–1944* (New York: Harcourt Brace Jovanovich, Inc., 1969).

Harold Norse. "Greenwich Village" and "Allen Ginsberg" from *Memoirs of a Bastard Angel* (New York: William Morrow and Co., 1989).

Frank O'Hara. "Night Thoughts in Greenwich Village" and "Washington Square" from *The Collected Poems of Frank O'Hara*, copyright © 1971 by Maureen Granville-Smith, Administratrix of the Estate of Frank O'Hara. Reprinted by permission of Alfred A. Knopf, a division of Random House, Inc.

Norman Podhoretz. "The Know-Nothing Bohemians," from *Doings and Undoings: The Fifties and After in American Writing* (New York: Farrar, Straus & Co., 1964). Reprinted by permission of the Author.

Dawn Powell. An excerpt from *The Wicked Pavilion*, by Dawn Powell, published by Steerforth Press of South Royalton, Vermont, 802-763-2808. Copyright © 1954, 1996 by The Estate of Dawn Powell.

John Reed. From *The Day in Bohemia, or Life Among the Artists* (New York: Printed for the Author, January 1913). Public Domain.

Barney Rosset. From *Misc.: Subject Is Left-Handed* (unpublished). (New York: 2002). © 2002 by Barney Rosset.

Howard Smith. "Jack Kerouac: Off the Road, Into the Vanguard, and Out," from *The Village Voice Reader: A Mixed Bag from the Greenwich Village Newspaper* (New York: Grove Press, 1962).

Harold Stearns. "When Greenwich Village Was Youth" from *The Street I Know* (New York: Lee Furman, Inc., 1935).

Ronald Sukenick. "The Remo" from *Down and In: Life in the Underground* (New York: Beech Tree Books/William Morrow, 1987). Reprinted by permission of the Author.

Lionel Trilling. From *A Gathering of Fugitives* (1956). Copyright © 1956 by Lionel Trilling, reprinted by permission of the Lionel Trilling Estate.

John Updike. "Snowing in Greenwich Village." From *The Same Door* (1959) by John Updike. Copyright (c) 1956 by John Updike. Reprinted by permission of Alfred A. Knopf, a division of Random House Inc.

Dan Wakefield. "Home to the Village" from *New York in the Fifties* (New York St. Martin's Press, 1992). Copyright © 1992 by Dan Wakefield. Reprinted by permission of the Author.

Caroline F. Ware. Excerpt from *Greenwich Village 1920–1930*. Copyright, 1935, by Caroline F. Ware. Copyright (c) renewed 1963 by Caroline F. Ware. Reprinted by permission of Houghton Mifflin Company. All rights reserved.

Edith Wharton. From *The Age of Innocence* (1920). Public Domain.

Edmund White. From *The Beautiful Room Is Empty* by Edmund White, copyright © 1988 by Edmund White. Used by permission of Alfred A. Knopf, a division of Random House, Inc.

Edmund Wilson. From *The Twenties: From Notebooks and Diaries of the Period* (1975). Excerpts from "Return to New York" and "New York" copyright © 1975 by Elena Wilson. Reprinted by permission of Farrar, Straus, and Giroux, LLC.

727